W9-BBH-493

ENVIRONMENT AND SOCIAL JUSTICE: AN INTERNATIONAL PERSPECTIVE

RESEARCH IN SOCIAL PROBLEMS AND PUBLIC POLICY

Series Editor: Ted I. K. Youn

RESEARCH IN SOCIAL PROBLEMS AND PUBLIC POLICY
VOLUME 18

ENVIRONMENT AND SOCIAL JUSTICE: AN INTERNATIONAL PERSPECTIVE

EDITED BY

DORCETA E. TAYLOR

*University of Michigan, Ann Arbor,
Michigan, USA*

Emerald

United Kingdom – North America – Japan
India – Malaysia – China

HUMBER LIBRARIES LAKESHORE CAMPUS
3199 Lakeshore Blvd West
TORONTO ON M8V 1K8

DISCARD

Emerald Group Publishing Limited
Howard House, Wagon Lane, Bingley BD16 1WA, UK

First edition 2010

Copyright © 2010 Emerald Group Publishing Limited

Reprints and permission service
Contact: booksandseries@emeraldinsight.com

No part of this book may be reproduced, stored in a retrieval system, transmitted in any
form or by any means electronic, mechanical, photocopying, recording or otherwise
without either the prior written permission of the publisher or a licence permitting
restricted copying issued in the UK by The Copyright Licensing Agency and in the USA
by The Copyright Clearance Center. No responsibility is accepted for the accuracy of
information contained in the text, illustrations or advertisements. The opinions expressed
in these chapters are not necessarily those of the Editor or the publisher.

British Library Cataloguing in Publication Data
A catalogue record for this book is available from the British Library

ISBN: 978-0-85724-183-2
ISSN: 0196-1152 (Series)

Emerald Group Publishing
Limited, Howard House,
Environmental Management
System has been certified by
ISOQAR to ISO 14001:2004
standards

Awarded in recognition of
Emerald's production
department's adherence to
quality systems and processes
when preparing scholarly
journals for print

INVESTOR IN PEOPLE

CONTENTS

LIST OF CONTRIBUTORS

A. Karen Baptiste	Colgate University, Hamilton, New York, USA
Marlene Barken	Ithaca College, Ithaca, New York, USA
Asmita Bhardwaj	Cornell University, Ithaca, New York, USA
Tendai Chitewere	San Francisco State University, San Francisco, California, USA
Sarah Darkwa	University of Cape Coast, Cape Coast, Ghana
Joseph Effiong	Centre for Social Policy Research and Development, Uyo, Nigeria
Stephanie Freeman	Alabama A&M University, Normal, Alabama, USA
June Gin	Fritz Institute, San Francisco, California, USA
Shumaisa Khan	University of Michigan, Ann Arbor, Michigan, USA
Sarah Lashley	Colby College, Waterville, Maine, USA
Brenda J. Nordenstam	State University of New York, College of Environmental Science and Forestry, Syracuse, New York, USA
Beth Pallo	Advion BioSciences, Ithaca, New York, USA

Dorceta E. Taylor   University of Michigan,
                              Ann Arbor, Michigan, USA

Shalini P. Vajjhala   Resources for the Future, Washington,
                              District of Columbia, USA

Jumana Vasi   The Charles Stewart Mott Foundation,
                              Flint, Michigan, USA

PART I
OPEN SPACE, GENTRIFICATION, FOOD SECURITY AND SUSTAINABLE LIVING

INTRODUCTION

Dorceta E. Taylor

Somber pictures of black protestors lying prostrate across a rural road in North Carolina while a large dump truck brimming with polychlorinated biphenyl (PCB)-laced dirt loomed ominously over them captivated readers and shocked the nation. Black congressional delegates were among the hundreds who protested and were arrested at the site in 1982 (New York Times, 1982a, 1982b, 1982c; *Washington Post*, 1982; LaBalme, 1988). Soon stories of resistance and protests of the siting of hazardous facilities or dumping of toxic substances in other poor, minority communities began to filter out. Four years later, when Hatians stopped the crew of the *Khian Sea*, a garbage barge laden with 14,855 tons of incinerated household garbage from Philadelphia from unloading all its contents on a beach,[1] the event was front-page news. Bahamians, Panamanians, and several African nations also barred the *Khian Sea* from depositing its cargo on their shores (Avril, 2002; Burling, 2000). Nigerians made headlines too in 1988 for refusing to keep 2,100 tons of hazardous wastes from Italy that was dumped in the small port town of Koko, Nigeria (Greenhouse, 1988). To some it seemed like almost overnight, American ethnic minorities, low-income people as well as poor people in other countries had agency in environmental disputes and were asserting themselves in environmental affairs. However, a careful analysis of environmental actions in poor communities show that these high-profile events were just a reflection of years of activity that went largely unnoticed and a harbinger of things to come.

The American environmental justice movement (EJM) emerged as an organized social and political force in the 1980s. Since then, it has spread to

Environment and Social Justice: An International Perspective
Research in Social Problems and Public Policy, Volume 18, 3–27
Copyright © 2010 by Emerald Group Publishing Limited
All rights of reproduction in any form reserved
ISSN: 0196-1152/doi:10.1108/S0196-1152(2010)0000018003

other industrialized countries such as Canada and Britain. EJMs can also be found in numerous countries in the developing world. The American EJM arose as a response to conditions prevailing in low-income and minority communities as well as a critique of traditional, mainstream environmentalism. The American environmental movement began about 150 years ago, and since then, there has been great interest in the study of environmental dynamics, policies, and practices. However, by the 1960s, critics noted that environmentalists paid scant attention to the ways in which social factors influenced environmental outcomes. In particular, social justice advocates contended that there was a relationship between social inequality and environmental inequality that needed to be recognized and understood more clearly. They also noted that traditional or mainstream environmentalists were not examining environmental degradation and other environmental problems that pervaded poor or minority communities. In other words, when it came to social justice issues, mainstream environmentalists did not focus on environmental inequalities (especially as it related to racial and ethnic minorities or the poor) to the extent they should have Taylor (1992).

As the environmental movement matured, a number of branches have emerged; however, one of the most dynamic to emerge in recent decades is the EJM. The EJM asserted that minorities and the poor lived in the most degraded environments and that mainstream environmentalists tended to turn a blind eye as such communities were chosen as sites to host hazardous and noxious facilities, bulldozed for freeways or commercial development, deprived of amenities such as parks and open space, and saddled with poor transportation and garbage removal services. Environmental justice activists coined the term "environmental racism" to describe processes that resulted in minority and low-income communities facing disproportionate environmental harms and limited environmental benefits.

It did not take long for the EJM to become a global phenomenon as activists around the world echoed the sentiments expressed by American environmental justice activists vis-à-vis the relationship between environment, race/ethnicity, and social inequality. From its inception, the EJM was studied by scholars, policymakers, and activists worldwide. As a result, an impressive body of scholarship has emerged to describe and analyze the American as well as the global movement. Over time, this body of scholarship has grown in stature and significance. Environmental justice activists and researchers recognized a major gap in traditional environmental thinking, organizing, and policymaking. Once this was articulated through the lens of inequality, discrimination, and justice, it spawned a whole new era of organizing and a new field of research.

THEORETICAL DISCUSSION OF THE EMERGENCE OF THE ENVIRONMENTAL JUSTICE FRAME

The environmental justice perspective represents a significant reframing of the traditional environmental discourse. Although few scholars in the environmental field pay attention to environmental framing, it is extremely important in the field. Environmental activists, policymakers, government, politicians, and business have long perceived, contextualized, and battled over environmental issues by establishing frames of reference. Framing refers to the process by which individuals and groups identify, interpret, and express social and political grievances. It is a scheme of interpretations that guides the way in which ideological meanings and beliefs are packaged by movement activists and presented to would-be supporters. Beliefs are important because they can be defined as ideas that might support or retard action in pursuit of desired values, goals, or outcomes. Social movement collective action frames are injustice frames because they are developed in opposition to already existing, established, widely accepted ideas, values, and beliefs. However, the social movement frames are intended to identify, highlight, and/or define unjust social conditions. Activists trying to develop new frames have to overcome the hurdle that many people (including would-be supporters) might accept the established or hegemonic frame as normal and/or tolerable. Collective action frames deny the immutability of undesirable conditions and promote the possibility of change through group action. Hence, social movement activists become potential social change agents in charge of their own destiny. They feel empowered to alter conditions (Goffman, 1974; Snow & Benford, 1992, 1988; Snow, Rochford, Worden, & Benford, 1986; Turner & Killian, 1987; Piven & Cloward, 1979, p. 12; McAdam, 1982; Gamson, 1992; Gamson & Meyer, 1996).

To gain support, activists must frame an issue in a way that would-be supporters can identify with it. This means either interpreting the issue in a way that is aligned with how their supporters perceive it or helping supporters expand or transform their interpretations or perceptions of an issue to match that of the movements. Social movement scholars such as Snow et al. (1986), McCarthy (1987), and Gamson (1992) believe that this is critical to success. Activists also need to amplify the significance of an issue by (1) focusing on the seriousness of a given grievance or issue, (2) identifying the causes and fixing blame for problems, (3) stereotyping opponents, (4) focusing on the likelihood of change and the efficacy of the movement, and (5) realizing the urgent need to take a stand (Gamson, Fireman, & Rytina, 1982; McAdam, 1982; Turner, 1969; Feree & Miller,

1985). In short, social movements have to frame issues in ways that are salient to their supporters to be effective.

Master Frames and Submerged Frames

The environmental justice frame has emerged as a master frame used to mobilize activists desirous of linking racism, injustice, and environmentalism as one ideological construct. Master frames can be viewed as crucial ideological frameworks akin to paradigms. A master frame provides a language that organizes and connects experiences and events in the world around us with our own lives. They magnify the attribution function of collective action frames, that is, they magnify the ability to identify problems and assign blame or causality (Snow & Benford, 1992; Kelley, 1972; Mills, 1940).

Early American ethnic minority environmental activism was often characterized by the absence of explicit environmental master frames. However, careful analysis of these and other environmental actions by people of color and low-income communities indicate the existence of submerged environmental frames (Taylor, 2000). That is, although activist master frames might have focused on the denial of rights or ending racism, prejudice, and discrimination, as shown in later discussions, there were minor or submerged frames present that were environmental in nature.

Today, the master frames of environmental racism or environmental justice are used to amplify the framing used by minorities and working class activists. These concepts provide a label for the activism occurring in communities of color and low-income communities. It links racism or injustice with environmental actions, experiences, and outcomes. The concepts are also important because they bridged past social justice activism that focused on racial injustice and civil rights with past and present environmental experiences. That bridging elevated the environment from an implicit or submerged frame to a master frame – one that was explicit, public, and potent not only to American minorities but also to poor and nonwhite people around the world.

SUBMERGED ENVIRONMENTAL FRAMES IN PEOPLE OF COLOR ACTIVISM IN THE PRE-ENVIRONMENTAL JUSTICE MOVEMENT ERA

In America, environmental justice scholarship traces its roots back more than two centuries and people of color environmental justice activism even longer. Although the environmental justice label did not exist to describe the early precursors of modern environmental justice thinking, writing, and action, historical analysis indicates that for a long time minority activists and intellectuals sought to frame people of color environmental experiences and behaviors through the lens of race relations and social justice (see Taylor, 2009).

Nonetheless, although researchers had examined environmental behavior and the demographic characteristics of the mainstream environmental movement since the 1960s, they showed a general lack of insight into the relationship between people of color and the environment. Studies in this genre found that the environmental movement was an upper-middle class, predominantly white movement. Such studies tended to look only at participation in traditional environmental activities such as hiking, mountain climbing, bird watching, wilderness and national park visitation, membership in mainstream environmental organizations, and attendance at environmental hearings. Consequently, the studies tended to frame minorities in negative terms, that is, under-participating in environmental affairs and lacking in knowledge of and concern for the environment (see, for example, Devall, 1970; Faich & Gale, 1971; Zinger, Dalsemer, & Magargle, 1972; Milbrath, 1984; Buttel & Flinn, 1974, 1978; Cotgrove & Duff, 1980; Dillman & Christenson, 1972; Harry, 1971; Harry, Gale, & Hendee, 1969; Hendee, Gale, & Harry, 1969; Lowe, Pinhey, & Grimes, 1980; Tognacci, Weigel, Wideen, & Vernon, 1972; Kellert, 1984; Kreger, 1973; Meeker, Woods, & Lucas, 1973; Van Liere & Dunlap, 1980; Morrison, Hornback, & Warner, 1972; Washburne, 1978). In general, the studies did not recognize minority participation in environmental issues because minorities blended environmental activism with social justice activism.

Notwithstanding, at the same time such findings were being published in scholarly outlets, there was ample evidence that people of color were interested in their environment, knowledgeable about and active in environmental affairs. Minority environmental activism could be found in the civil rights movement, red power movement (new Indianism), and the Chicano movement (Chicanismo). That is, throughout the 1950s, 1960s, and 1970s, African Americans, Native Americans, Latinos, and Asians were engaging in environmental battles involving access to open space (fighting to desegregate parks, beaches, etc.); transportation (challenging those expecting them to enter and sit at the rear of busses); arranging car pools (when they boycotted entire city public transportation systems over discriminatory treatment); campaigning to reduce the incidence of lead poisoning in public housing projects, air pollution, the use of pesticides, and the exposure of farm workers to pesticides; taking part in fishing rights, hunting rights, and treaty rights struggles; and fighting to enhance occupational safety (see the following for examples of such actions: Drake & Cayton, 1993; Morris, 1984; Simon, 1968; Robinson, 1991; California Department of Industrial Relations, 1986; Lenarcic, 1982; Nabakov, 1991; Robbins, 1992; Steiner, 1968; Deloria, 1977; Acuna, 1988; Grebler, Moore, & Guzman, 1970; Moore, 1970; Taylor, 1975; Hurley, 1995). I argue that these should not be considered solely as civil rights, Chicanismo, or red power activities; they were also actions with submerged environmental justice frames.

Early Attempts to Bridge the Environment and Social Justice Frames

By the 1970s, it was clear that the environmental ideological divide between mainstream environmentalists and minorities had to be bridged. Furthermore, efforts were needed to raise the profile of environmental issues in minority communities to the extent that they became master frames in and of themselves. In so doing, not only would activists find it easier to mobilize larger numbers of people of color, but they would also find it easier to gain broader support for and understanding of their work in the policy, planning, and regulatory arenas.

To this end, some African-American activists began to articulate a discourse that linked race, environment, and social justice. They used the high-profile organizing for Earth Day among mainstream environmentalists as the vehicle not only to challenge the discourse of white environmentalists but also to raise consciousness among people of color. Hence, in the midst of the Earth Day celebrations, two prominent African Americans penned and voiced themes that are now central to the EJM. In essence, they outlined an embryonic agenda for the EJM. Although they were flatly ignored by white middle-class environmentalists, their ideas resonated in black and other communities of color.

In 1970, Nathan Hare writing in *The Black Scholar* made explicit connections between racial and environmental inequality. He argued that environmental movement had "blatantly omitted" blacks and their environmental interests and that there was little exchange between the two. He continued that blacks and white environmentalists differed on the causes and solutions to environmental problems in both the suburbs and the ghettos and that the reformist approach to solve environmental problems was evasive of the social and political revolutionary environmental changes that blacks demand. Given this reality, the reformist solutions of the environmental movement appear ludicrous to blacks (Hare, 1970).

Richard Hatcher, Mayor of Gary, Indiana, speaking to a group of white middle-class environmentalists from the Community Action to Reverse Pollution in May 1970, echoed similar themes. He argued that blacks did not share their definition of ecology. Like Hare, Hatcher told his audience that for blacks, the relevant environmental issues were poor sanitation, overcrowding and substandard housing, and vermin. Hatcher rejected what he considered to be the false dichotomy between environmental change and social justice. He argued that a nation wealthy enough to send spaceships to the moon could combat poverty and pollution if there was a will to do so (Hurley, 1995).

Hatcher's comments resonated with blacks because African Americans always understood environmental problems in the broader context of social, political, and economic inequalities. Hatcher – the first black to be elected mayor of Gary – used his office as a platform from which to launch an attack on pollution and heighten blacks' environmental awareness. He began to emphasize air quality in his speeches, press conferences, and public appearances, dispelling the myth among blacks that pollution was a concern of whites that was irrelevant to blacks. At the 1972 National Black Political Convention, he urged black activists from across the nation to be wary of their relationship with major corporations that degraded the environment and exploited their workers (Hurley, 1995; *Gary Info*, 1972).

Fishing rights emerged as a prominent issue for Native Americans in the 1960s, particularly those living in the Pacific Northwest and in Wisconsin. Fish constituted a significant part of the diet of the Indians in the Pacific Northwest; for many, life centered around the runs of salmon and steelhead trout that spawn in the waterways of the region. In 1964, the National Indian Youth Council (NIYC) helped organize protests to challenge Washington state's restriction of Native American fishing rights. NIYC organized a "fish-in," challenged the restrictions in the courts, and participated in a number of nonviolent collective actions. Although the battle between Indians and the state of Washington over fishing rights was not resolved till 1974 (in favor of the Native Americans), NIYC, buoyed by its success in challenging a state government, undertook a series of initiatives during the 1960s and 1970s to enhance Indian rights. NIYC collaborated with the National Congress of American Indians on some of these initiatives. Between 1964 and 1974, there were a number of other demonstrations, road blockades, land seizures, and building occupations involving Indians. In 1966, Alaska Natives formed the Alaska Federation of

Natives to protect and preserve native culture, land, and resources (Lenarcic, 1982; Nabakov, 1991; Robbins, 1992; O'Brien, 1989; Steiner, 1968; Berthrong, 1973).

Native Americans also disrupted Earth Day proceedings in 1970 to assert their land rights at one event. When Robert Marshall (founder of the Wilderness Society) was director of forestry for the Bureau of Indian Affairs, he created 16 wilderness areas on Indian reservations from 1933 to 1937. However, within a few decades, Indians asserted themselves to be more in control of preservation efforts on Indian lands. Consequently, during the Earth Day celebrations, Gaylord Nelson, one of the sponsors and key supporters of the event, was greeted by Indian demonstrators who threw garbage on the stage and accused him of sponsoring legislation that would take land away from the Chippewa tribe to facilitate the creation of a national park. Although Senator Nelson assured the crowd that Indian lands would not be appropriate to create a national lakeshore, he had spent a decade working on a plan to incorporate two small reservations (Red Cliff and Bad River) in the proposed Apostle Island National Lakeshore in Michigan. The tribes were resisting attempts by the National Park Service to encroach on Indian lands by converting them to national parks. The impasse was settled later that year when the park was created without the taking of Indian land (Keller & Turek, 1998; Ironwood Daily Globe, 1970; Fox, 1981).

Chicano activists were busy spearheading environmental campaigns also. Since the 1960s, the United Farm Workers (UFW) has been at the forefront of the battle to protect farm workers. As the grape pickers strike and the grape boycott – both launched in 1965 – progressed, farm workers in California began complaining about illnesses they suffered in the fields. The UFW investigated these complaints and discovered high concentration of pesticides on grapes being sold in stores across the country. In the wake of Rachel Carson's (1962) immensely popular book, *Silent Spring*, the public was particularly sensitive to the issue of pesticides. The charge of pesticide residues in food gained immediate national attention and put the plight of the farm workers in the spotlight. The UFW's first contract with Delano-area table-grape growers contained protection for farm workers including a ban on the use of dichloro-diphenyl-trichloroethane (DDT), aldrin, dieldrin, and parathion on unionized ranches. Similarly, the Ohio-based Farm Labor Organizing Committee founded by Baldemar Velasques has made farm worker protection from pesticides a central focus of their contract negotiations with pickle and tomato growers in the state. It was not until 1972 that the EPA banned the agricultural use of DDT and until 1974 before aldrin and dieldrin were banned. In 1985, Ceasar Chavez and UFW again called for ban on parathion, and four other pesticides commonly used on table grapes – phosdrin, dinoseb, captan, and methyl bromide. Fifteen months later, the EPA suspended the registration of dinoseb and finally banned it in 1988. Parathion remained on the market, and in 1990, the UFW again called for its ban. In 1992, the EPA took limited action against the pesticide, canceling authorization for half of its registered uses (Moses, 1993; Taylor, 1975).

THE BIRTH OF THE CONTEMPORARY ENVIRONMENTAL JUSTICE MOVEMENT

Contemporary environmental justice activism is shaped by the early and modern social movements of minorities and low-income people. Although the environmental justice label was not coined till the early 1990s, the modern EJM grew out of the struggles occurring in minority communities beginning in the late 1970s. The struggles of the 1970s to early 1980s that launched the EJM differed from earlier conflicts and organizing campaigns in that both the environment and social justice were master frames. Gone were the submerged frames of earlier eras and in their place emerged framing that placed environment, inequality, and justice at the center of the campaigns.

For instance, in 1978 black residents of Triana, Alabama, began fighting to reduce the exposure to DDT that arose from consuming fish caught in contaminated streams (Maynard, Cooper, & Gale, 1995; Press, 1981; *Washington Post*, 1980). It was first discovered that DDT – leaking from an industrial facility – was contaminating the local waterways in 1948. The chemical was found in samples taken from local streams during the 1950s and 1960s. During this time, research evidence was beginning to mount that DDT was harmful to humans and the environment. By the mid-1950s, researchers and DDT manufacturers were aware that the chemical was very toxic. In fact, Olin (the same company from which the DDT was leaking into the local streams around Triana) began putting warning labels on some of its DDT products between 1957 and 1958 that alerted users that the products should not be used near children, fish, or wild fowl. As early as 1959, the U.S. Fish and Wildlife Service reported that there was a 97 percent drop in the number of double-crested cormorants at the nearby Wheeler National Wildlife Refuge. By 1963, there was also a 90 percent decrease in the number of red-shouldered hawks. Unaware of the dangers to their health, local residents of Triana continue to fish in the streams and consume their catch (*Olin Corporation v. Insurance Company of North America*, 1992, 1991; Press, 1981; Maynard et al., 1995).

Similarly, in 1982, residents of predominantly black Warren County (North Carolina) began protesting the construction of a 19.3 acre hazardous waste landfill near Warrenton where the state planned to bury 400,000 cubic yards of soil contaminated with PCBs. Opposition to the states plan began years earlier, when in 1979, critics of the proposed landfill filed two lawsuits to prevent its construction. The Warren County site was chosen from among 90 sites considered. At the time, the county had the highest percentage of blacks of any county in the state. It was 64 percent black and the unincorporated Shocco Township, site of the landfill, was 75 percent black. Warren County was also one of North Carolina's poorest counties. It ranked 97th out of 100 counties in per capita income out of 100 counties. The demonstrations drew national attention as local police and Army troops from Fort Bragg (that was also contaminated with PCBs) were called in to quell the protests in which 523 people were arrested. Activists from the Warren County protests urged the U.S. General Accounting Office (USGAO) to examine the relationship between the location of landfills in the Southeast and the demographic characteristics of surrounding areas. This led to the publication of the 1983 USGAO study. This study pioneered the use of spatial analysis to try to understand the relationship between race and the siting of hazardous facilities. Four years later, the United Church of Christ (UCC) Commission for Racial Justice (some of whose members had participated in the Warren County protests) published a national study examining the siting of hazardous facilities and waste sites. Both studies linked race and class with the increased likelihood of living close to hazardous facilities and toxic waste sites [Twitty v. North Carolina, 1981; Warren County v. North Carolina, 1981; Twitty v. North Carolina, 1987; *Washington Post*, 1982; LaBalme, 1988; U.S. General Accounting Office (USGAO), 1983; United Church of Christ (UCC), 1987]. The UCC study claimed that race was the most reliable predictor of residence near hazardous waste sites in the United States (UCC, 1987).

The Impact of Toxic Waste and Race

Toxic Wastes and Race had an immediate and profound impact. It did for environmental mobilization in minority and low-income communities what

Rachel Carson's (1962) *Silent Spring* did in middle- and upper-class white communities. The UCC report resonated with segments of the population that mainstream environmental movement activists had spent little or no time recruiting or appealing to. The framing was simple, potent, and effective. Starting with a cover image of a map of the United States showing the location of hazardous sites, the message was clear even before the reader turned the first page. Anyone knowing where minority populations are clustered in the United States had no difficulty sizing up the map and recognizing that there was some overlap between location of the hazards and high concentrations of minority population. The colors chosen for the map – shades of red – foreshadowed the ominous tale the report would tell residents of minority and low-income communities. Unlike a typical environmental report that is often bathed in soothing shades of blue and green, the UCC report signaled right away that it was different. It signified that it was first and foremost and environmental report by the use of a spatial map on its cover, but it signaled its departure from traditional reports in its color scheme and its title. Here was a report on the environment that made race such a central tenet that the word appeared in the title. In so doing, race and environment became intertwined as inseparable parts of a master narrative. The report did a masterful job of reiterating and reinforcing this master frame throughout the document.

As the discussion in the preceding text has shown, *Toxic Wastes and Race* was not the first document to attempt to bridge the race relations, social justice, and environmental discourses. However, unlike earlier documents of this genre, *Toxic Wastes and Race* succeeded as it was widely read and debated. It also set off a wave of environmental mobilizing in minority and low-income communities that was unprecedented. In these respects, the similarities between *Toxic Wastes and Race* and *Silent Spring* are striking. *Silent Spring* was not the first book to discuss the harmful effects of pesticides; however, it did it more effectively than earlier works; so much so that it motivated millions of people to take environmental action. The same is true for *Toxic Wastes and Race*.

Like *Silent Spring*, *Toxic Wastes and Race* had its critics (Anderson, Anderton, & Oakes, 1994; Anderton, et al., 1994c; Anderton, Anderson, Oakes, & Fraser, 1994a; Anderton, Oakes, & Egan, 1994b; Hamilton, 1995a, 1995b; Baden & Coursey, 1997). Industry took note of the report and the intense mobilizing occurring in people of color and low-income communities. One counter-mobilization tactic used by a waste-management conglomerate was the funding of university researchers who produced findings that contradicted the results of *Toxic Wastes and Race*

(Anderson et al., 1994; Anderton et al., 1994a, 1994b, 1994c). This brought heightened attention to the UCC report. It also resulted in new waves of research reinforcing the findings of the UCC report and challenging the methodologies and results of the industry-sponsored studies (Goldman & Fitton, 1994; Mohai, 1996, 1995; Mohai & Saha, 2007; Szasz & Meuser, 2000, 1997; Walsh, Warland, & Smith, 1997). Despite efforts to develop effective counterframes to *Toxic Wastes and Race*, the master frame of race, environmental hazards, and justice is still a very salient one that has not diminished in stature over the past two decades.

Toxic Wastes and Race had important submerged frames embedded in the document too. One of the most important of these was the discussion of the demographic characteristics of the mainstream environmental movement. The report argued that

> the environmental movement ... has historically been white middle and upper-class in its orientation. This does not mean, however, that racial and ethnic communities do not care about the quality of their environment and its effect on their lives. (UCC, 1987)

Although brief, this discussion pointed to the marginality of people of color in the mainstream environmental movement and their alienation from it. The statement also served the purpose of bringing the issue of the demographic characteristics of the environmental movement to the forefront. It implicitly raised the question of whether an upper-middle class predominantly white movement would or could have the best interests of people of color and their communities at heart.

A Letter and a Conference

Although *Toxic Wastes and Race* did not expound on the issue of diversity in the mainstream environmental movement, around the same time it raised the issue scholars were beginning to call attention to the lack of diversity in the mainstream environmental movement and challenging the negative portrayal of minorities in the scholarly writing on environmental participation, attitudes, and perceptions (Taylor, 1989, 1993a). Environmental justice activists paid attention to the demographic composition of the mainstream environmental movement too. They took matters into their own hands when they used the events surrounding Earth Day 1990 to put the issue in the spotlight. In January 1990, several environmental justice activists and organizations sent a letter to the heads of the country's largest environmental NGOs[2] claiming that the organizations hired few minorities and that said organizations were alienated from minority communities – the chief victims of pollution.

Representatives of the targeted organizations responded to the letter by saying that though their organizations had a poor track record of hiring minorities, racism was not a factor in their hiring decisions. The spokespersons also hastened to say that they were trying to rectify the situation. At the time the letter was written, only 14 (1.9 percent) of the 745 workers of the Audubon Society, Friends of the Earth, Natural Resources Defense Council, and Sierra Club were minorities. Leaders of the environmental organizations offered several explanations for the lack of minorities on their staff. They argued that minorities were not applying for jobs in environmental NGOs, the environmental groups did not recruit minorities aggressively, there was a scarcity of minorities among the pool of trained environmental specialists, and that minorities did not want to work for the low salaries being offered by environmental organizations. Furthermore, as Frederic Krupp, executive director of the Environmental Defense Fund, argued, minorities are "cause oriented." They are attracted to issues such as discrimination and poverty rather than environmental issues (Shabecoff, 1990).

The timing of this letter was significant. It was released about three months before Earth Day 1990 (the 20th anniversary of the first Earth Day), and plans were underway for a huge celebration of the achievements of the environmental movement. The letter, which was the first to openly question the hiring practices of the environmental groups, issued an ultimatum for increased hiring of minorities, and framed the demographic characteristics of the environmental workforce in terms of racist hiring practices (rather than lack of interest or inaction on the part of minorities), generated a lot of attention. The letter, the contents of which was published in the *New York Times* on February 1, also coincided with other environmental justice organizing events like the Agency for Toxic Substances and Disease Registry's National Minority Health Conference (Institute of Medicine, 1999) and the University of Michigan's conference on race and the incidence of environmental hazards (Bryant & Mohai, 1992).

The Michigan conference that was also held in January 1990 was significant too. It was the first gathering of its kind to bring together scholars and policymakers to discuss environmental justice research and the discriminatory effects of environmental policies and practices. It also produced a path-breaking book containing research articles presented at the conference, *Race and the Incidence of Environmental Hazards: A Time for Discourse*[3] (Bryant & Mohai, 1992). *Race and the Incidence* as well as other such as *Dumping in Dixie* (Bullard, 1990) and *Confronting Environmental Racism* (Bullard, 1993) were instrumental in movement building and the development of the field of environmental justice research.

Competing Frames

Environmental justice activists had developed alternative frames to that of mainstream leaders. As a result, there were two competing frames of minority environmental participation. Although leaders of mainstream environmental NGOs perceived that minorities were too concerned with social justice and poverty-related issues, minorities saw these as core organizing themes. In contrast, mainstream environmental leaders made a distinction between social issues and environmental issues. Scholars, mainstream environmental activists, and policymakers buttressed this position by explaining what is perceived to be the lack of participation of minorities in environmental affairs by citing minorities' preoccupation with their basic needs and their inability to shift their concerns to focus on the environment. Because the environmental justice frame deliberately aligns environment and social justice concerns, there is no disjuncture between the two.

Environmental justice activists and mainstream environmental leaders had competing frames when the question of the diversity within environmental institutions arose. On the one hand, leaders of mainstream environmental organizations, believing there is a limited talent pool of potential minority workers, portray minorities as unqualified for environmental jobs, unwilling to apply for them, and desirous of salaries too high for the environmental NGOs to afford. These perceptions are bolstered by studies like the ones mentioned earlier that claim that minorities are uninterested in the environment and are lacking in knowledge of and concern for the environment. In assessing whether there are structural barriers in environmental organizations that limit the hiring, retention, and promotion of minorities, some leaders of those organizations perceive none [Environmental Careers Organization (ECO), 1992]. However, environmental justice activists articulated a competing frame. They also argue that racist and exclusionary hiring practices explain the demographic characteristics of the environmental workforce. They also argue that minorities are qualified, willing, and capable of working in environmental organizations and agencies. The environmental justice claims were supported by studies showing that a robust pool of qualified minority applicants exists and that minorities are willing to work in environmental organizations and have salary expectations that fall within the range of the salaries paid by environmental organizations and agencies (ECO, 1992; Taylor, 2008, 2007a, 2007b).

ADDITIONAL ASPECTS OF
ENVIRONMENTAL JUSTICE RESEARCH

As mentioned earlier, the 1983 USGAO and the 1987 UCC reports spawned waves of spatial analyses examining the relationship between demographic factors and the exposure to environmental hazards. Related studies also examined community responses to siting decisions (Walsh et al., 1997; Blumberg & Gottlieb, 1989; Gedicks, 1993) and corporate countermobilization strategies aimed at stymieing environmental justice activities (Gedicks, 1998, 2001). Although much of the early environmental justice research relied heavily on case studies (e.g., see Hofrichter, 1993; Bullard, 1993; Bryant & Mohai, 1992; Gedicks, 1993; LaBalme, 1988), recent work has produced more nuanced case study analyses employing social, economic, and historical methodologies (Pellow, 2000; Szasz & Meuser, 2000; Hurley, 1995; Pulido, 1996).

Other genres of environmental justice research have found that minorities are more likely to have elevated blood lead levels, experience pesticide poisoning, debilitating occupational injuries, and live in communities with polluted air than whites [Goldman, 1993; UCC, 1987; Moses, 1989; Moses et al. 1993; Cory-Slechta, 1990; *Morbidity and Mortality Weekly Report* (MMWR)], 1997; Phoenix, 1993; Bryant & Mohai, 1992]. Moreover, Rabin's (1989) study indicates that zoning laws have been used to encourage the siting of noxious facilities in minority neighborhoods. Research examining corporate behavior and toxic emissions has also been conducted (Simon, 2000; Grant, 1997), so has research on the media and environmental justice issues (Hamilton, 1995b). Research has also been conducted on the racial effects of expulsive zoning (Rabin, 1989), legal theories and environmental justice law (Gerard, 1999), and on land-use managers' attitudes towards environmental justice (Padgett & Imani, 1999).

THE INTERNATIONAL DIMENSIONS OF
ENVIRONMENTAL JUSTICE RESEARCH

International environmental justice research has grown in stature and significance also. From the outset, activists and scholars found the American environmental justice rhetoric compelling and sought to apply it internationally. Even within the United States, activists drew on concepts such as toxic terrorism, internal colonialism, as well as core–periphery relations that could be readily applied in developing countries. The environmental justice analyses of resource extraction and processing in marginal communities (such as Native American reservations) and the South to power the core areas of the country were salient in developing countries (see, e.g., Adeola, 2000; Subramaniam, 2000; LaDuke, 1999; Jaimes, 1992; Kokole, 1995; Hussein, 1995; Goodland, 1995; Agyeman, Bullard, & Evans, 2003). In addition, power dynamics that resulted in strong environmental regulations in northern states and the relaxing or abandonment of environmental policies and regulations in the American South or in low-income and minority communities (Lester, 1994; Lavelle & Coyle, 1992) resonated with the colonial, core–periphery, and North–South discourses already well developed in poor countries (Escobar, 1995; Bello, 1994; Shiva, 1989; Steady, 1982, 1993; Guha, 1989; Gedicks, 2001). The issue of toxic dumping and exposure to pesticides was also readily translatable in the international context where scholars examined the dumping of hazardous wastes from developed countries in developing countries (Mpanya, 1992) and the toxic boomerang effects of pesticides that are banned in the United States reappearing on imported products from Latin American countries because banned pesticides are shipped overseas to be used on farms (Perfecto, 1992; Moyers, 1991).

In industrialized countries, the marginalization of ethnic and racial minorities resulted in environmental dynamics similar to ones articulated by American environmental justice activists. Scholars found minorities articulating lack of access to outdoor recreational opportunities in Britain (Taylor, 1993b; Neal & Agyeman, 2005) and racial inequalities in Canadian cities (Teelucksingh, 2002, 2006).

DESCRIPTION AND ORGANIZATION OF THIS VOLUME

The introduction provided an overview of the history of the EJM and the ways in which movement-building and environmental justice scholarship were intertwined. It provides a broader context in which to understand the research articles contained in this book. The book showcases some of the latest environmental justice research. Although some follow in the classic tradition of environmental justice scholarship (such as spatial analyses, attitudes and behavior, and institutional diversity), chapters examine new dimensions of environmental scholarship such as sustainability, food security, green lifestyles, and consumerism.

The volume, *Environment and Social Justice: An International Perspective*, examines domestic and international environmental issues from an environmental justice perspective. The book is a compilation of original research articles that range in scope from a focus on Michigan and the Great Lakes to national studies, as well as international case studies. Drafts of some of these research articles were presented at the University of Michigan's School of Natural Resources and Environment (SNRE) at an international conference held in June 2007. The conference was made possible by funding from the Ford Foundation and the National Science Foundation.

The volume is divided into six parts. Part I focuses on urban environmental issues and sustainability. It contains a chapter by Dorceta E. Taylor on Central Park's influence on historical and contemporary models of funding public parks. The chapter examines how inequities arise in contemporary funding models. Chapter 2 was authored by June Gin and Dorceta E. Taylor. This chapter examines how the media portrayed and framed efforts by activists in predominantly Hispanic and African-American communities in the San Francisco Bay Area to mobilize their communities to prevent displacement from neighborhoods facing high gentrification pressures. In chapter 3, Shumaisa Khan examines food security in London. She analyzes access to fresh food in impoverished neighborhoods in London and looks at community-based efforts to deliver affordable fresh food to the poor. Tendai Chitewere and Dorceta E. Taylor's chapter analyzes an ecovillage just outside of Ithaca, New York. The chapter examines the relationship between sustainable living, green consumption, and social justice concerns. It also incorporates the theme of food security in the chapter.

Part II of the volume focuses on water resources and the hazards of consuming toxic fish. Toxic food consumption raises the question of access to safe and healthy food – another aspect of food security. Beth Pallo and Marlene Barken's chapter examines toxic fish consumption. It analyzes fish advisories and explores how consumption of toxic fish affects vulnerable populations. The next chapter is also related to toxic fish consumption. In it, Brenda Nordenstam and Sarah Darkwa examine how minority and white anglers on the Great Lakes adjust their fishing and consumption patterns in response to the issuance of toxic fish advisories. Part III of the volume continues the theme of food security in the international context in the chapter authored by Asmita Bhardwaj. It examines both land loss and food security in India. The chapter explores the relationship between crop failure in India, the introduction of genetically modified seeds, and the rise in farmers' suicides. The other chapter in this section analyzes agriculture and loss of land. Stephanie Freeman and Dorceta E. Taylor's chapter examines land loss among African-American farmers in the South. The chapter analyzes the use of heritage tourism as a mechanism for preserving black family farms.

The two chapters in Part IV examine energy – oil and gas exploration in the Caribbean and Africa. They also incorporate the theme of land and resource loss in host communities. April Baptiste and Brenda Nordenstam explore attitudes toward oil and gas drilling in rural Trinidad, whereas Joseph Effiong's chapter analyses the oil and gas industry in Nigeria. Both chapters discuss the poverty that is pervasive in communities hosting extractive oil and gas installations. Part IV also contains two chapters.

Part V contains a chapter that employs spatial analyses techniques to examine siting and toxic releases. Shalini P. Vajjhala's chapter examines whether the Environmental Protection Agency's small grants reached the counties it was intended to reach – those with the highest levels of toxic releases and highest percentages of poverty and minority residents. The final section, Part VI, contains three chapters that examine diversity and environmental attitudes. Dorceta E. Taylor's chapter focuses on diversity. It examines the status of minority faculty in academic environmental programs. It presents the findings of a national study. Sarah Lashley and Dorceta E. Taylor authored the chapter examining environmental conflicts in two Southeastern Michigan communities. They examine why community activists were unable to collaborate with each other although they were fighting against the same corporation. Jumana Vasi examined the attitudes and perceptions of American Muslim women toward the environment. It presents the results of a national study. The volume ends with a concluding chapter that summarizes the general thrust of the volume.

NOTES

1. After 11 countries refused to take the waste, the *Khian Sea* plied the ocean. Most of the ash disappeared from the ship. By the time it arrived in Singapore in 1989 under the name *Pelicano*, the ash was gone. Two Maryland businessmen who operated the *Khian Sea* were imprisoned for illegal dumping. Approximately 2,500 tons of ash that was dumped on the beach in Haiti in 1986 was eventually retrieved 12 years later – because of public pressure – and returned to Pennsylvania to be buried 16 years after leaving the state (Avril, 2002; Burling, 2000).

2. The letter was sent to most of the members of the "Big Ten" environmental groups, namely, Natural Resources Defense Council, Sierra Club, Wilderness Society, National Wildlife Federation, Environmental Defense Fund (now Environmental Defense), Friends of the Earth, the National Parks and Conservation Association, the National Audubon Society, and the Izaak Walton League. This group was later renamed the "Green Group."

3. The original draft of this book was printed in 1990.

REFERENCES

Acuna, R. (1988). *Occupied America: A history of Chicanos* (3rd ed.). New York: Harper and Row.

Adeola, F. O. (2000). Cross-national environmental injustice and human rights issues: A review of evidence in the developing world. *American Behavioral Scientist, 43*(4), 686–706.

Agyeman, J., Bullard, R., & Evans, B. (Eds). (2003). *Just sustainabilities: Development in an unequal world.* Cambridge, MA: The MIT Press.

Anderson, A. B., Anderton, D. L., & Oakes, J. M. (1994). Environmental equity: Evaluating TSDF siting over the past two decades. *Waste Age, July,* 83–84, 86, 88, 90, 92, 94, 96, 98, 100.

Anderton, D., Anderson, A. B., Oakes, J. M., & Fraser, M. R. (1994). Environmental equity: The demographics of dumping. *Demography, 31*(2), 229–248.

Anderton, D., Oakes, J. M., & Egan, K. (1994). Environmental equity in Superfund: Demographics of the discovery and prioritization of abandoned toxic sites. *Evaluation Review, 21*(1), 3–26.

Anderton, D. L., Anderson, A. B., Oakes, J. M., Fraser, M. R., Weber, E. W., & Calabrese, E. J. (1994). Hazardous waste facilities: "Environmental equity," issues in metropolitan areas. *Evaluation Review, 18*(2), 123–140.

Avril, T. (2002). 16-year-old Philadelphia trash finally dumped into PA landfill. *Philadelphia Inquirer,* June 28.

Baden, B., & Coursey, D. (1997). *The locality of waste sites within the city of Chicago: A demographic, social, and economic analysis.* Chicago: University of Chicago, Irving B. Harris Graduate School of Public Policy.

Bello, W. (1994). *Dark victory: The United States, structural adjustment and global poverty.* London: Pluto Press.

Berthrong, D. J. (1973). *The American Indian: From pacifism to activism.* St. Charles, MO: Forum Press.

Blumberg, L., & Gottlieb, R. (1989). *War on waste: Can America win its battle with garbage?* Covelo, CA: Island Press.

Bryant, B., & Mohai, P. (Eds). (1992). *Race and the incidence of environmental hazards: A time for discourse.* Boulder, CO: Westview Press.

Bullard, R. D. (1990). *Dumping in Dixie: Race, class and environmental quality.* Boulder, CO: Westview Press.

Bullard, R. D. (Ed.) (1993). *Confronting environmental racism: Voices from the Grassroots.* Boston: South End Press.

Burling, S. (2000). Unwanted ash in Florida may come to LA. *Times-Picayune,* May 1.

Buttel, F. H., & Flinn, W. L. (1974). The structure and support for the environmental movement, 1968–1970. *Rural Sociology, 39*(1), 56–69.

Buttel, F. H., & Flinn, W. L. (1978). Social class and mass environmental beliefs: A reconsideration. *Environment and Behavior, 10*, 433–450.

California Department of Industrial Relations. (1986). *California work injuries and illnesses*. San Francisco: Division of Labor Statistics and Research.

Carson, R. (1962). *Silent spring*. Boston: Houghton Mifflin Press.

Cory-Slechta, D. A. (1990). Lead exposure during advanced age: Alterations in kinetics and biochemical effects. *Toxicology and Applied Pharmacology, 104*, 67–78.

Cotgrove, S., & Duff, A. (1980). Environmentalism, middle-class radicalism and politics. *Sociological Review, 28*(2), 333–351.

Deloria, V., Jr. (1977). *Indians of the Pacific Northwest: From the coming of the white man to the present day*. Garden City, NY: Doubleday Publishers.

Devall, W. B. (1970). Conservation: An upper-middle class social movement. A replication. *Journal of Leisure Research, 2*(2), 123–126.

Dillman, D. A., & Christenson, J. A. (1972). The public value for pollution control. In: W. Burch, et al. (Eds), *Social behavior, natural resources, and the environment* (pp. 237–256). New York: Harper and Row.

Drake, St. C., & Cayton, H. R. (1993 [1945]). *Black metropolis: A study of Negro life in a northern city*. Chicago: University of Chicago Press.

Environmental Careers Organization. (1992). *Beyond the green: Redefining and diversifying the environmental movement*. Boston: Environmental Careers Organization.

Escobar, A. (1995). *Encountering development: The making and unmaking of the third world*. Princeton, NJ: Princeton University Press.

Faich, R. G., & Gale, R. P. (1971). The environmental movement: From recreation to politics. *Pacific Sociological Review, 14*(2), 270–287.

Feree, M. M., & Miller, F. D. (1985). Mobilization and meaning: Toward an integration of social psychological and resource perspectives on social movements. *Sociological Inquiry, 55*, 36–61.

Fox, S. (1981). *The American conservation movement: John Muir and his legacy*. Madison, WI: University of Wisconsin Press.

Gamson, W. A. (1992). The social psychology of collective action. In: A. D. Morris & C. M. Mueller (Eds), *Frontiers in social movement theory* (pp. 53–76). New Haven, CT: Yale University Press.

Gamson, W. A., Fireman, B., & Rytina, S. (1982). *Encounters with unjust authority*. Homewood, IL: Dorsey Press.

Gamson, W. A., & Meyer, D. A. (1996). Framing political opportunity. In: D. McAdam, J. D. McCarthy & M. Zald (Eds), *Comparative perspectives on social movements: Political opportunities, mobilizing structures, and cultural framings* (p. 285). Cambridge, UK: Cambridge University Press.

Gary Info. (1972). December 28, p. 4.

Gedicks, A. (1993). *The new resource wars: Native and environmental struggles against multinational corporation*. Boston: South End Press.

Gedicks, A. (1998). Corporate strategies for overcoming local resistance to new mining projects. *Race, Gender and Class, 6*(1), 109–123.

Gedicks, A. (2001). *Resource rebels: Native challenges to mining and oil corporations*. Boston: South End Press.

Gerard, M. B. (Ed.) (1999). *The law of environmental justice: Theories and procedures to address disproportionate risks*. Chicago: American Bar Association.

Goffman, E. (1974). *Frame analysis*. Cambridge, MA: Harvard University Press.

Goldman, B. (1993). *Not just prosperity: Achieving sustainability with environmental justice*. Washington, DC: National Wildlife Federation.

Goldman, B., & Fitton, L. (1994). *Toxic waste and race revisited*. Washington, DC: Center for Policy Alternatives.

Goodland, R. J. A. (1995). South Africa: Environmental sustainability needs empowerment of women. In: L. Westra & P. S. Wenz (Eds), *Faces of environmental racism: Confronting issues of global justice* (pp. 207–226). Lanham, MD: Rowman and Littlefield.

Grant, D. S. (1997). Allowing citizen participation in environmental regulation: An empirical analysis of the effects of right-to-sue and right-to-know provisions on industry's toxic emissions. *Social Science Quarterly, 78*(4), 859–874.

Grebler, L., Moore, J. W., & Guzman, R. C. (1970). *The Mexican American people*. New York: Free Press.

Greenhouse, S. (1988). Toxic waste boomerang: Ciao Italy! *New York Times*, September 3.

Guha, R. (1989). *The unquiet woods: Ecological change and peasant resistance in the Himalaya*. Berkeley, CA: University of California Berkeley Press.

Hamilton, J. T. (1995a). Pollution as news. Media and stock market reactions to the toxics release inventory data. *Journal of Environmental Economics and Management, 28*, 98–113.

Hamilton, J. T. (1995b). Testing for environmental racism: Prejudice, profits, political power. *Journal of Policy Analysis and Management, 14*(1), 107–132.

Hare, N. (1970). Black ecology. *The Black Scholar, 1*(April), 2–8.

Harry, J. (1971). Work and leisure: Situational attitudes. *Pacific Sociological Review, 14*(July), 301–309.

Harry, J., Gale, R. P., & Hendee, J. (1969). Conservation: An upper-middle class social movement. *Journal of Leisure Research, 1*(2), 255–261.

Hendee, J. C., Gale, R. P., & Harry, J. (1969). Conservation, politics and democracy. *Journal of Soil and Water Conservation, 24*(November–December), 212–215.

Hofrichter, R. (1993). *Toxic struggles: The theory and practice of environmental justice*. Philadelphia: New Society Press.

Hurley, A. (1995). *Environmental inequalities: Class, race, and industrial pollution in Gary, Indiana, 1945–1980*. Chapel Hill, NC: University of North Carolina Press.

Hussein, A. M. (1995). Somalia: Environmental degradation and environmental racism. In: L. Westra & P. S. Wenz (Eds), *Faces of environmental racism: Confronting issues of global justice* (pp. 181–206). Lanham, MD: Rowman and Littlefield.

Institute of Medicine. (1999). *Toward environmental justice: Research, education, and health policy needs*. Washington, DC: National Academy Press.

Ironwood Daily Globe (1970). New controversy over Apostles. *Ironwood Daily Globe*, August 4, p. 5.

Jaimes, M. A. (Ed.) (1992). *The state of native America: Genocide, colonization, and resistance*. Boston: South End Press.

Keller, R. H., & Turek, M. (1998). *American Indians and national parks*. Tucson, AZ: University of Arizona Press.

Kellert, S. R. (1984). Urban American perceptions of animals and the natural environment. *Urban Ecology, 8*, 220–222.

Kelley, H. H. (1972). *Causal schemata and the attribution process*. Morristown, NJ: General Learning Press.

Kokole, O. H. (1995). The political economy of the African environment. In: L. Westra &
     P. S. Wenz (Eds), *Faces of environmental racism: Confronting issues of global justice*
     (pp. 163–180). Lanham, MD: Rowman and Littlefield.
Kreger, J. (1973). Ecology and black student opinion. *The Journal of Environmental Education*,
     4(3), 30–34.
LaBalme, J. (1988). Dumping on Warren County. In: B. Hall (Ed.), *Environmental
     politics: Lessons from the grassroots* (pp. 25–30). Durham, NC: Institute for Southern
     Studies.
LaDuke, W. (Ed.) (1999). *All our relations: Native struggles for land and life*. Boston: South End
     Press.
Lavelle, M., & Coyle, M. (1992). The racial divide in environmental law: Unequal protection.
     National Law Journal. September issue.
Lenarcic, R. J. (1982). The moon of red cherries: A brief history of Indian activism in the
     United States. In: G. R. Bayado (Ed.), *The evolution of mass culture in America, 1877 to
     the present*. St. Louis, MO: Forum Press.
Lester, J. P. (1994). A new federalism? Environmental policy in the states. In: N. J. Vig &
     M. E. Kraft (Eds), *Environmental policy in the 1990s* (pp. 51–68). Washington, DC: CQ
     Press.
Lowe, G. D., Pinhey, T. K., & Grimes, M. D. (1980). Public support for environmental
     protection: New evidence from national surveys. *Pacific Sociological Review*, *23*(October),
     423–445.
Maynard, Cooper, & Gale, P. C. (1995). Fish-monitoring data for the Huntsville spring Branch-
     Indian Creek system released. *Environmental Compliance Update*, *3*(9).
McAdam, D. (1982). *Political process and the development of black insurgency: 1930–1970*
     (p. 51). Chicago: University of Chicago Press.
McCarthy, J. D. (1987). Pro-life and pro-choice mobilization: Infrastructure deficits and new
     technologies. In: M. Zald & J. McCarthy (Eds), *Social movements in an organizational
     society* (pp. 49–66). New Brunswick, NJ: Transaction.
Meeker, J. W., Woods, W. K., & Lucas, W. (1973). Red, white and black in the national parks.
     North American Review, *258*, 6–10.
Milbrath, L. (1984). *Environmentalists: Vanguard for a new society* (pp. 17, 163). Albany, NY:
     State University of New York Press.
Mills, C. W. (1940). Situated actions and vocabularies of motive. *American Sociological Review*,
     5, 404–413.
Morbidity and Mortality Weekly Report (MMWR). (1997). 46(7), U.S. Department of Health
     and Human Services, Public Health Services, Washington, DC.
Mohai, P. (1995). The demographics of dumping revisited: Examining the impact of alternative
     methodologies in environmental justice research. *Virginia Environmental Law Journal*,
     14, 615–653.
Mohai, P. (1996). Environmental justice or analytic justice? Reexamining historical
     hazardous waste landfill siting patterns in metropolitan Texas. *Social Science Quarterly*,
     77, 500–507.
Mohai, P., & Saha, R. (2007). Racial inequality in the distribution of hazardous waste:
     A national-level reassessment. *Social Problems*, *54*(3), 343–370.
Moore, J. W. (1970). *Mexican Americans*. Englewood Cliffs, NJ: Prentice Hall.
Morris, A. (1984). *The origins of the civil rights movement: Black communities organizing for
     change*. New York: Free Press.

Morrison, D. E., Hornback, K. E., & Warner, W. K. (1972). The environmental movement: Some preliminary observations and predictions. In: W., Burch, Jr., et al. (Eds), *Social behavior and natural resources and the environment* (pp. 259–279). New York: Harper and Row.

Moses, M., et al. (1989). Pesticide related health problems in farm workers. *American Association of Occupational Health Nurses Journal, 37,* 115–130.

Moses, M., et al. (1993). Environmental equity and pesticide exposure. *Toxicology and Industrial Health, 9*(5), 914–959.

Moyers, B. (1991). *Global dumping ground: The international traffic in hazardous wastes.* Cambridge, UK: Lutterworth Press.

Mpanya, M. (1992). The dumping of toxic waste in African countries: A case of poverty and racism. In: B. Bryant & P. Mohai (Eds), *Race and the incidence of environmental hazards: A time for discourse* (pp. 204–215). Boulder, CO: Westview Press.

Nabakov, P. (1991). *Native American testimony.* New York: Penguin.

Neal, S., & Agyeman, J. (2005). *The new countryside? Ethnicity, nation and exclusion in contemporary rural Britain.* Bristol, UK: Policy Press.

New York Times. (1982a). Carolinians angry over PCB landfill. *New York Times,* August 11, Lake City Final Edition, Section D, p. 17.

New York Times. (1982b). Congressman and 120 arrested at PCB protest. *New York Times,* September 28.

New York Times. (1982c). Carolinians see governor in PCB landfill dispute. *New York Times,* October 10, Lake City Final Edition, Section 1, p. 31.

O'Brien, S. (1989). *American Indian tribal governments.* Norman, OK: University of Oklahoma Press.

Olin Corporation v. Insurance Company of North America. (1991). 762 F. Suppl. 548, pp. 565–566.

Olin Corporation v. Insurance Company of North America. (1992). 966 F.2d 718; U.S. App.

Padgett, D. A., & Imani, N. O. (1999). Qualitative and quantitative assessment of land-use managers' attitudes toward environmental justice. *Environmental Management, 24*(4), 509–515.

Pellow, D. (2000). Environmental inequality formation: Toward a theory of environmental injustice. *American Behavioral Scientist, 43*(4), 581–601.

Perfecto, I. (1992). Pesticide exposure of farm workers and the international connection. In: B. Bryant & P. Mohai (Eds), *Race and the incidence of environmental hazards* (pp. 177–203). Boulder, CO: Westview Press.

Phoenix, J. (1993). Getting the lead out of the community. In: R. Bullard (Ed.), *Confronting environmental racism: Voices from the grassroots* (pp. 77–92). Boston: South End Press.

Piven, F. F., & Cloward, R. (1979). *Poor people's movements: Why they succeed, how they fail* (p. 12). New York: Vintage Books.

Press, R. M. (1981). 'Love Canal south': Alabama DDT residue will cost millions to clean up. *Christian Science Monitor,* June 12, p. 11.

Pulido, L. (1996). *Environmentalism and economic justice: Two Chicano struggles in the Southwest.* Tucson, AZ: University of Arizona Press.

Rabin, Y. (1989). Expulsive zoning: The inequitable legacy of Euclid. In: C. M. Haar & J. Kayden (Eds), *Zoning and the American Dream* (pp. 101–121). Chicago: Palmers Press.

Robbins, R. L. (1992). Self-determination and subordination: The past, present, and future of American Indian governance. In: M. A. Jaimes (Ed.), *The state of native America: Genocide, colonization and resistance* (pp. 87–122). Boston: South End Press.

Robinson, J. (1991). *Toil and toxics: Workplace struggles and political strategies for occupational health.* Berkeley, CA: University of California Press.

Shabecoff, P. (1990). Environmental groups told they are racists in hiring. *New York Times,* February 1, p. A20.

Shiva, V. (1989). *Staying alive: Women, ecology and development.* London: Zed Books.

Simon, A. K. (1968). Citizens vs. lead in three communities: Chicago. *Scientist and Citizen, April,* 58–59.

Simon, D. R. (2000). Corporate environmental crimes and social inequality: New directions for environmental justice research. *American Behavioral Scientist, 43*(4), 633–645.

Snow, D., Rochford, B., Jr., Worden, S., & Benford, R. (1986). A frame alignment processes, micromobilization and movement participation. *American Sociological Review, 51,* 464–481.

Snow, D. A., & Benford, R. D. (1988). Ideology, frame resonance, and participant mobilization. *International Social Movement Research, 1,* 197–217.

Snow, D. A., & Benford, R. D. (1992). Master frames and cycles of protest. In: A. Morris & C. M. Mueller (Eds), *Frontiers of social movement theory.* New Haven, CT: Yale University Press.

Steady, F. C. (1982). African women, industrialization and another development: A global perspective. *Development Dialogue, 1–2*(82), 51–64.

Steady, F. C. (1993). *Women and children first: Environment, poverty and sustainable development.* Rochester, NY: Schenkman Books.

Steiner, S. (1968). *The new Indians.* New York: Dell.

Subramaniam, M. (2000). Whose interests? Gender issues and wood-fired cooking stoves. *American Behavioral Scientist, 43*(4), 707–728.

Szasz, A., & Meuser, M. (1997). Environmental inequalities. *Current Sociology, 45,* 99–120.

Szasz, A., & Meuser, M. (2000). Unintended and inexorable: The production of environmental inequalities in Santa Clara county, California. *American Behavioral Scientist, 43*(4), 602–632.

Taylor, D. E. (1989). Blacks and the environment: Towards an explanation of the concern and action gaps between blacks and whites. *Environment and Behavior, 21*(2), 175–205.

Taylor, D. E. (1992). Can the environmental movement attract and maintain the support of minorities? In: B. Bryant & P. Mohai (Eds), *Race and the incidence of environmental hazards* (pp. 28–54). Boulder, CO: Westview Press.

Taylor, D. E. (1993a). Environmentalism and the politics of inclusion. In: R. Bullard (Ed.), *Confronting environmental racism: Voices from the grassroots* (pp. 53–61). Boston: South End Press.

Taylor, D. E. (1993b). Minority environmental activism in Britain: From Brixton to the Lake District. *Qualitative Sociology, 16*(3), 263–295.

Taylor, D. E. (2000). The rise of the environmental justice paradigm: Injustice framing and the social construction of environmental discourses. *American Behavioral Scientist, 43*(4), 508–580.

Taylor, D. E. (2007a). Employment preferences and salary expectations of students in science and engineering. *BioScience, 57*(2), 175–185.

Taylor, D. E. (2007b). Diversity and equity in environmental organizations: The salience of these factors to students. *Journal of Environmental Education, 39*(1), 19–43.

Taylor, D. E. (2008). Diversity and the environment: Myth-making and the status of minorities in the field. *Research in Social Problems and Public Policy, 15,* 89–148.

Taylor, D. E. (2009). *The environment and the people in American Cities: 1600s–1900s. Disorder, inequality and social change*. Durham, NC: Duke University Press.

Taylor, R. B. (1975). *Chavez and the farm workers: A study in the acquisition and use of power*. Boston: Beacon Press.

Teelucksingh, C. (2002). Spatiality and environmental justice in Parkdale (Toronto). *Ethnologies, 24*(1), 119–141.

Teelucksingh, C. (Ed.) (2006). *Claiming space: Racialization in Canadian cities*. Wilfred Waterloo, ON: Laurier University Press.

Tognacci, L. N., Weigel, R. H., Wideen, M. F., & Vernon, D. T. A. (1972). Environmental quality: How universal is public concern? *Environment and Behavior, 4*(March), 73–86.

Turner, R. H. (1969). The theme of contemporary social movements. *British Journal of Sociology, 20*, 390–405.

Turner, R. H., & Killian, L. M. (1987). *Collective behavior* (3rd ed.). Englewood Cliffs, NJ: Prentice-Hall.

Twitty v. State of North Carolina. (1981). 527 F. Suppl. 778; 1981 U.S. Dist., November 25.

Twitty v. State of North Carolina. (1987), 85 N.C. App. 42; 354 S.E.2d 296; 1987 N.C. App., April 7.

United Church of Christ. (1987). *Toxic wastes and race in the United States*. New York: United Church of Christ.

U.S. General Accounting Office. (1983). *Siting of Hazardous waste landfills and their correlation with the racial and socio-economic status of surrounding communities*. Washington, DC: U.S. General Accounting Office.

Van Liere, K. D., & Dunlap, R. (1980). The social bases of environmental concern: A review of hypothesis, explanations, and empirical evidence. *Public Opinion Quarterly, 44*(2), 181–197.

Walsh, E., Warland, R., & Smith, D. C. (1997). *Don't burn it here*. University Park, PA: Penn State Press.

Warren County v. State of North Carolina. (1981). 528 F. Suppl. 276; 1981 U.S. Dist., November 25.

Washburne, R. F. (1978). Black under-participation in wildland recreation: Alternative explanations. *Leisure Sciences, 1*(2), 175–189.

Washington Post. (1980). Town files DDT suit. *Washington Post*, March 17, p. A5.

Washington Post. (1982). Dumping on the poor. *Washington Post*, October 12, p. A12.

Zinger, C. L., Dalsemer, R., & Magargle, H. (1972). *Environmental volunteers in America*. Prepared by the National Center for Voluntary Action for the Environmental Protection Agency, Office of Research and Monitoring, Washington, DC.

Dorceta E. Taylor is an associate professor at the University of Michigan's School of Natural Resources and Environment. She teaches courses in environmental history, environmental justice, tourism and climate change, and social movements. She is the director of the Multicultural Environmental Leadership Development Initiative (http://www.meldi.snre.umich.edu) and author of *The Environment and the People in American Cities, 1600s–1900s: Disorder, Inequality, and Social Change*. She can be reached by email at dorceta@umich.edu or by telephone at 734-763-5327.

EQUITY, INFLUENCE, AND ACCESS: CENTRAL PARK'S ROLE IN HISTORICAL AND CONTEMPORARY URBAN PARK FINANCING

Dorceta E. Taylor

ABSTRACT

Purpose – *This chapter will examine the role of Central Park in setting in motion certain practices related to park development as well as revolutionizing park financing in the mid-nineteenth century and again in modern times. It will examine the shift from public financing of parks to the development of public–private partnerships to design, build, fund, and administer urban parks.*

Design/methodology/approach – *The author takes an historical approach to put contemporary park debates vis-à-vis funding and administration in context. Archival materials are used to examine park financing models all over the country.*

Findings – *Central Park still continues to revolutionize urban park financing. Cities are cutting back on funding for public parks; as a result, there is a greater reliance on private financing options. Not all parks are in a position to rely heavily on private financing, and this raises questions about access to open space in cities.*

Environment and Social Justice: An International Perspective
Research in Social Problems and Public Policy, Volume 18, 29–73
Copyright © 2010 by Emerald Group Publishing Limited
All rights of reproduction in any form reserved
ISSN: 0196-1152/doi:10.1108/S0196-1152(2010)0000018004

Originality/value – *The chapter raises questions about equity in the shift toward the private financing of urban parks. It extends the environmental justice discourse to examine open space issues. It examines long-term historical trends in helping the reader understand the contemporary state of urban park financing.*

INTRODUCTION

Parks and Social Inequality

Researchers in the United States, Britain, and Canada have been interested in the leisure behavior of racial and ethnic minorities for several decades. Much of the research on this topic focused on park visitation and participation in recreational activities. Scholarly journals such as *Journal of Leisure Research, Leisure Sciences,* and *Leisure Studies* are replete with articles on this topic. As mentioned in the introductory chapter, before the emergence of the environmental justice movement, the tendency was to examine participation in traditional recreational activities and paint a portrait of minorities as under-participating, marginal, and lacking in knowledge of or interest in recreational activities. This pattern was evident in the reports of research findings in the United States as well as in other postindustrial countries where this genre of research was in vogue.

The advent of research informed by an environmental justice perspective has added a needed counterbalance to study of parks, recreation, and inequality. Scholars now examine a wider range of recreational activities in comparative studies; they are also more willing to examine how historical, institutional, and social factors influence access to recreation and participation in leisure activities. This chapter illustrates how historical environmental justice analysis can shed light on contemporary policies and practices in park development and management. It also helps us to identify mechanisms by which inequities evident in contemporary settings are tied to deeply embedded institutional norms that replicate themselves over time.

Early Public Parks[1]

The first publicly financed open space was realized in Boston during the seventeenth century. In 1634, when the city wanted to create open space on the outskirts of town, each household was charged six shillings to provide the funds to purchase 45 acres of Reverend Blaxton's (Blackstone) farm to be converted into the "The Commonage." The Common was not conceived of the way we think of parks today. From the mid-nineteenth century on, parks were developed as recreational spaces. However, the Common and other seventeenth- and eighteenth-century open spaces were multipurpose spaces used for recreation, pastures, military grounds, open-air markets, hanging people, the seat of government, burial grounds, and religious services. Despite the range of uses, the establishment of the Boston Common signaled the birth of America's first public park (City of Boston, 1990; Warner, 2001; Macieski, 2005). Although American cities such as New Haven, Philadelphia, and New York reserved small parcels of land for commons or town greens over the next two centuries, it was not till the middle of the nineteenth century that a concerted campaign arose in New York to develop large, landscaped parks and to approach urban park development in a systematic and coherent fashion (Sletcher, 2004; Schiff, 1981; Dunn, 1982; *Journal of Commerce*, 1851a, 1851b; Spann, 1981). From this time on, parks were thought of and designed primarily as spaces of leisure, resort, and recreation.

As the parks campaigns got under way in New York, questions about who should pay for the construction and maintenance of urban parks surfaced. That is, what role should the government, private sector, and citizenry play in urban park financing? Questions also arose about access and equity. Such questions gained currency as cities competed with each other to build expensive, elaborate parks that were hundreds of acres in size. From the mid-nineteenth century on, park promoters, critics, and advocates of the poor battled over where parks should be located and whether the poor should be taxed for park development. Because some of the parks were developed on the outskirts of town (in the case of Central Park – six miles from the city center), activists battled over whether the new parks would be de facto playgrounds for the rich. They argued that most of the people living in cities were poor and would find it too expensive and difficult to travel to the parks. During the nineteenth century, the debate over access and equity was primarily a class debate. The fight was about whether the white working class would be able to use the parks as freely and easily as their white middle and upper class contemporaries. The question of access for blacks, Native Americans, and other minorities was not on the agenda for even the most ardent social justice advocates.

Questions about financing, access, and equity have been with us ever since. These questions are pertinent today as American park administrators deal with crumbling, inadequate and poorly maintained, under-financed park infrastructure and explore ways of managing the more than 1 million acres of urban parkland currently in existence. These issues are even more pressing as it is projected that urban parks will face a $38 billion budget deficit over the next several years (Trust for Public Land [TPL], 2006; National Park and Recreation Association [NRPA], 2006). Using Central Park as a case study, this chapter will examine how urban park advocates dealt with the issue of urban park financing in the nineteenth century. It will examine how the campaign to build Central Park changed the discourse around urban park financing and how the park is still influencing the way in which parks are financed today.

LOOKING TO THE CEMETERIES FOR A PRIVATE FINANCING MODEL

Although some early American cities such as Philadelphia and New Haven were designed to be built around public open space, this was not the norm. So as cities grew, people clamored for open space, which they could use for leisure purposes. Hence, by the nineteenth century, city leaders realized they needed to develop public recreation space. During the early part of that century, wealthy urbanites responded to the shortage of open space by developing private parks on their estates, building their mansions around the few existing public green space and privatizing them, or building shared private parks like Gramercy Park and St. Johns Park (also known as Hudson Square, New York) or Louisburg Square (Boston). The shared private parks were built as part of exclusive developments in which the mansions of the rich surrounded the parks, and only property owners in the subdivisions had keys to these gated parks. In essence, fees assessed against property owners built and maintained these parks; the public had no access to them (Taylor, 2009; Scherzer, 1995; Burrows & Wallace, 1999; Blackmar, 1989; McNulty, 1999; Shand-Tucci, 1999; Wolfe, 1995).

By the mid-nineteenth century, critics of private parks as well as other park advocates launched a concerted campaign to develop more public urban parks (*The Subterranean*, 1845; Child, 1843; Hunt, 1866; Cook, 1854; Schuyler, 1986; Sedgwick, 1841; Bryant, 1844; Downing, 1851a, 1851b, 1848). They also made proposals about how park development could be financed. Andrew Jackson Downing (1848), one of the most prominent landscape architects of the time and a leading park advocate, proposed that parks could be funded the same way cemeteries were. Downing, who also designed cemeteries, was familiar with the funding structure of the new breed of cemeteries[2] that were springing up on the fringes of urban areas. He was also well aware of the urgent need for parks and the fact that urbanites desperate for open space were flocking to the new landscaped rural cemeteries on the weekends to recreate. At the time, the new cemeteries were funded by creating joint stock companies that had shareholders. If the parks adopted this model, only shareholders and non-share holders who paid an entrance fee would be admitted to the parks. Downing felt this model would generate enough funds to pay for park construction and provide surplus funds for cities (Downing, 1848; Schuyler, 1986; Chadwick, 1966; Jackson & Dunbar, 2002).

Downing also suggested that cities acquire parkland by asking rich individuals to donate land; their gifts should be commemorated in the parks with inscribed statues or marble vases. Moreover, the rich could donate money for trees while well-to-do ladies could fund-raise for the parks by holding tea parties and fairs (*Park International*, 1920; Downing, 1848). Downing, who designed country estates for wealthy merchant families, was expressing a sentiment held by them. Many wealthy families believed that public parks should be a space to exhibit and commemorate the achievements of the rich (Rosenzweig & Blackmar, 1992; Beveridge & Rocheleau, 1998). Although the idea of private financing resonated with some and remained a part of the discourse throughout the nineteenth century, Downing's proposal was opposed by other outspoken park advocates. Downing's critics argued that the parks should be publicly funded and remain free to all; a democratic institution so to speak (Cranz, 1982; San Francisco Park Commission, 1897; *San Francisco Bulletin*, 1900).

Recognizing that the private financing schemes espoused by Downing could exacerbate inequalities and limit access to urban parks, Frederick Law Olmsted (who along with Calvert Vaux designed and built Central Park) opposed them. Instead, Olmsted called on municipalities to fund their parks through public spending rather than relying on private donors (Olmsted, 1865; Cranz, 1982). He was a proponent of the idea that parks could be funded by charging passengers extra to ride the street cars. Although he recognized the inequities that could arise from Downing's funding scheme, Olmsted did not discuss the regressive nature of the transportation tax he proposed or whether the poor had as much access to the parks as the wealthy.

PAYING FOR PARKS: BENEFITS ASSESSMENTS VERSUS GENERAL TAXATION

Although activists had been campaigning for a large landscaped park in New York City for years, it was not till 1851 that several events converged that resulted in a group of park activists organizing themselves to finance and build a large landscaped park in the city. The catalyst was an anonymous "gentleman" recently returned from a two-year trip to Europe, who wanted to an elegant park in New York (*Journal of Commerce*, 1851a). The anonymous gentleman was Robert Bowne Minturn, one of the richest men in New York. He was a merchant and co-director of the Bank of Commerce (*Journal of Commerce*, 1851a; Wilson & Fiske, 1887–1889). Soon after his return to New York, Minturn called a dinner meeting of a select group of wealthy and influential gentlemen at his home to discuss the possibility of a park in Manhattan. Like his upper class contemporaries who toured Europe, Minturn thought New York City needed a large landscaped park to compare more favorably with European cities that sported lavish parks and open spaces. Without hesitation, the group – which I will refer to as the Minturn Circle – picked Jones Wood, a site on the East River (close to the estates of some at the meeting), as the site of the proposed park. They also decided that the park should be funded by a general tax to be levied on the residents of New York City (Minturn, 1871; *Journal of Commerce*, 1851a; Rosenzweig & Blackmar, 1992; *The New York Times*, 1853; Spann, 1981; Bridges, 1984; Beveridge & Rocheleau, 1998).

The Minturn Circle was composed of powerful and influential men who were rail and steamship magnates, real estate brokers, bankers, international traders, and large landowners. They were East Side aristocrats and club men. That is, some had multiple memberships in the most exclusive social clubs in the city (Wilson & Fiske, 1887–1889; *Journal of Commerce*, 1851a; Rosenzweig & Blackmar, 1992; Homberger, 2002; Spann, 1981).

Although Boston financed its Common by levying a general tax on the populace more than 200 years earlier, this practice was not commonplace at the time it was proposed in 1851 in New York. A general taxation for funding the Common might have been more acceptable because Boston was still a relatively small and new colony. The Common was also used for various purposes including pasturage, so that each resident could see how they would benefit directly from helping to pay to acquire the land. However, it was much more difficult for New Yorkers, crammed in the deplorable slums of the city, to see how paying taxes on a distant park, nestled amidst the estates of the rich, would be of direct and immediate benefit to them.

As cities grew and became more complex, it became harder to make the case that all infrastructure projects benefited everyone equally. Therefore, at the time of the New York park proposal, it was unusual for the public or city to be solely responsible for the cost of building major public works projects such as large landscaped parks. Those were usually funded by benefits assessment taxes levied against property owners deemed most likely to reap the benefits of the project. For instance, the Battery, City Hall Park, and Washington Square were built with public subsidies and benefits assessments. As no park on the scale of what was being proposed by the Minturn Circle had been built yet in the country, the financing proposal garnered much attention and scrutiny.

The site chosen for the park – Jones Wood – was about 150 acres and it was estimated it would cost about $1.5 million to acquire the land to build the park. At the time, the city's existing 17 squares and private parks totaled about 144 acres. However, about two-thirds of them were still undeveloped lots Uptown. The largest were the 24-acre Hamilton Square and 20-acre Mount Morris Park (renamed Marcus Garvey Park). Not only was the proposed park larger than all of the city's open space combined, the cost dwarfed the price tag for developing each existing open space (Spann, 1981; *Journal of Commerce*, 1851b; Rosenzweig & Blackmar, 1992; Homberger, 2002).[3]

Property owners near Jones Wood took an interest in the park proposal because such a park had the potential to be costly to them because the common practice was to tax adjacent property owners for land improvements such as streets, lights, sewers, and development of squares. In 1837, as the cost of these benefits assessments soared, large landowners began organizing themselves. They argued that instead of charging landowners for improvements, the cost of streets, sewers, and so on should be borne by the general public (Rosenzweig & Blackmar, 1992). For instance, the *Journal of Commerce* (1851a) editorials argued soon after the Minturn Circle proposal became public that "The expense of public parks, and all other public improvements should be paid for by the public, and not assessed on the lands of a few individuals."

Minturn Circle members wanted to reap the benefits of living adjacent to a park without being taxed heavily for its development. Thus, it is not surprising that the Minturn Circle, aware of the growing aversion of the wealthy to benefits assessments tax and wishing to avoid a large tax bill, sought to spread the burden of taxation by proposing a general public tax. Under the general tax, city residents – property owners and nonproperty owners alike – would be taxed. It would also be irrelevant how close one lived to the site of the proposed project when it came to the matter of taxation. This was an important break with tradition that would set a new precedent for financing public works projects. As one might imagine, some objected to funding the park through general taxes. Although some elites declined to support the park because of the controversial tax proposal, several large landowners with property adjacent to Jones Wood supported the Minturn Circle's position (Minturn, 1851; Prime, 1851; Rosenzweig & Blackmar, 1992).

Although the Minturn Circle was able to get quick approval for the park in the Common Council (city council) and state legislature, objections to the proposed general tax and the refusal of powerful landowners to sell their property (on which their country estates were located) for the purposes of developing a park slowed down the process considerably (Rosenzweig & Blackmar, 1992; Homberger, 2002). As the Jones Wood proposal became mired in controversy, a rival group of Upper West Side activists put forward a proposal to build a much larger, centrally located park in Manhattan. The chosen site was closer to the homes of West Side elites than Jones Wood. West Siders proposed the development of a central park that was approximately 778 acres (expanded to 843 acres in 1863) because they thought the Jones Wood site was too small (Beveridge & Schuyler, 1983; Rosenzweig & Blackmar, 1992).

Ergo, in the summer of 1853, a group of leading Upper West Side landowners endorsed and helped to get the Central Park bill passed. The West Siders were interested in pursuing the same development strategies pioneered by the East Siders in the Minturn Circle. They supported Central Park because they believed the park would keep property values high, help gentrify the area and regulate land use, eliminate nuisance industries, and establish the West Side as an elite residential enclave. Park advocates also argued that the park would be a work of art that would improve the civility and culture of the city. It would also improve people's health. Similar arguments were made by park advocates campaigning to increase access to parks in England (Taylor, 1999, 1995).

In 1850, West Side residents tried unsuccessfully to develop a 50-acre private park modeled on London's Regent's Park. A similar fate had befallen the East Side plan for a private park. It should be noted that the existing private villa parks like St. Johns and Gramercy were quite small and activists seeking to finance even a 50-acre park found it quite costly. Thus, by 1853, West Siders were convinced that they would get a landscaped park only with government intervention and public financing. Although wealthy land speculators stood to benefit from the development of Central Park, this time the chosen park site was not inhabited by wealthy residents; the site was inhabited primarily by about 1,600 Irish and German immigrants and blacks living in modest homes park advocates characterized as shanties. Wealthy New Yorkers who owned inholdings on the proposed site tended to lease those properties to poor people, and therefore, the landowners stood to gain from the city's purchase of their land (Tiemann, 1852; Rosenzweig & Blackmar, 1992; Blackmar, 1989).

West Siders got support for Central Park because of its size, location, and the financing model proposed. They proposed that Central Park should be financed, in part, by benefits assessments on property surrounding the park. One-third of the cost of the park would be assessed on adjacent landowners. However, the benefits assessment area was drawn much broader than usual to include a larger group of landowners, thereby making the taxies levied against each landowner's property smaller than usual. The West Siders learned from the mistakes of the Minturn Circle who refused to back away from the general tax proposal. The Jones Wood bill was finally defeated, in part, because neighboring landowners were not assessed any surcharges on their taxes. When the city was authorized to spend $5 million to acquire property for Central Park in 1854, only about 1.7 million of that cost was assessed against adjacent landowners (Rosenzweig & Blackmar, 1992).

The move toward funding parks and other public works through general taxes rather than relying solely on benefits assessment had been gaining momentum for some time, but the Central Park debate brought issues to a head and became a catalyst that set a new pattern for financing of public works projects. Before 1850, awards paid to landowners whose properties were acquired by eminent domain for parks (such as Washington, Union, Tompkins, and Madison Squares) amounted to $444,106. In addition, all but $500 of the cost of building these parks was assessed to landowners whose properties lay adjacent to the new developments. However, the Croton Aqueduct and Central Park project changed all that. Beginning with the Croton Aqueduct, the city began to assume public debt to pay for such immense public works projects. In 1850, the city's debt was $12.2 million; most of that amount was incurred for the purposes of building the Croton Aqueduct. The city issued municipal bonds to build Central Park as well as other parks. As part of the financing for Central Park, the city issued municipal bonds to generate about $5.4 million to acquire parkland initially. Between 1850 and 1863, an additional $11 million in bonds were issued for park construction. Another $6.5 million worth of bonds was also issued for street and boulevard construction. Between 1870 and 1871, $21 million dollars worth of bonds was issued to acquire lands for

Morningside Park and additional street and boulevard construction (Scobey, 2002).

The complete reliance on benefits assessment to develop public works projects began to crumble with the issuance of bonds to construct the Croton Aqueduct (built between 1835 and 1842). By the late 1840s, landowners were becoming increasingly strident in their opposition to benefits assessment. They argued that major projects such as the Croton Aqueduct were public goods that should be paid for by the general public. The anti-assessment advocates used Central Park as a test case to make their point and won a major victory when the financing structure of the park did not levy the entire cost onto adjacent landowners. Although adjacent landowners were assessed a tax in the Central Park case, it amounted to a minor portion of the eventual cost of the park (Scobey, 2002; Rosenzweig & Blackmar, 1992; Cohen & Augustyn, 1997).

Several factors might account for public spending on the Croton Aqueduct rather than a complete reliance on benefits assessment. The project began just months before the Great Fire of 1835 that burned 674 buildings (Cohen & Augustyn, 1997). The fire took a heavy toll on the businesses. Just as the business community was recovering from the fire, they were hit by Panic of 1837. It took until the early 1840s for many businesses to recover from that depression. However, it was not just the financial hardships businesses faced in the latter half of the 1830s that made it politically impractical to levy huge benefits assessment against them; it was also the nature of the Croton Aqueduct project. Unlike small parks or streets where the developed project clearly benefited adjacent property owners more than it did others across town, the Croton Aqueduct was different. The massive undertaking of diverting the Croton River from Westchester County to lower Manhattan meant that the aqueduct traversed a lot of sparsely populated land between Westchester and Upper Manhattan before reaching Lower Manhattan. It would be hard to argue that merely having the aqueduct traverse one's land constituted a development from which one benefited. This was particularly true because the aqueduct was not supplying water to residents in these outlying areas. As an 1842 Endicott map shows, the water pipes and stop cocks were located primarily below 14th Street (Endicott, 1842).

The Croton Aqueduct project also differed from earlier projects in that it was clearly a project that had widespread public benefits. Unlike street paving, lighting, and small parks that might benefit small localized areas, the aqueduct benefited the whole city. Furthermore, it was a project in which the beneficiaries could be taxed directly each time they used the system (i.e., user fees could be charged). Because the water could be metered and users charged according to their usage, it was more pragmatic for the city to pay for the cost of construction then recoup its expenses by collecting user fees in perpetuity, rather than trying to assess the benefits taxes to a relatively small group of landowners (the numbers of which pales in comparison to the number of residents who would eventually be taxed to use metered water).

However, paying for the development of a park was tricky. Unlike water that can be metered and beneficiaries charged, most people objected to the idea of charging park users to use a park. It was clear, therefore, that the Croton financing model could not be applied directly to the financing of parks. The cemetery model was unpalatable for similar reasons – while those with cemetery plots could be charged directly, the idea of applying user fees to park users in the same way did not seem viable to park advocates. Although the Croton model taxed beneficiaries through user fees, the project provided the opening park advocates needed to propose a new tax model. The Croton project involved massive public expenditures; therefore, by the time the Jones Wood proposal became a reality, opponents of benefits assessments had the ammunition they needed to argue that public funding of public works projects was more equitable and appropriate than benefits assessments. By that time also, complete reliance on benefits assessment to fund the project was no longer a practical option. The question really was what was the appropriate balance of public and private funding that was feasible at the time? As the Minturn Circle discovered, completely jettisoning benefits assessment was not a viable proposition in the 1850s.

Early Gentrification and the Dislocation the Poor and Minorities

Although they did not evoke much debate and rancor among activists, there were other issues in Central Park's development that are causes for concern. Central Park was an early form of gentrification on a massive scale. Although the site was inhabited by roughly 1,600 inhabitants, park advocates and designers saw it as a blank canvas on which to engineer landscape art on a scale never before undertaken in the country. Residents of the racially mixed communities that predated the park, subsisted on the natural resources of the area (fish in the streams and materials from the plants), raised their own domestic animals, reused materials salvaged from dumps, and carried on small-scale commercial operations. The black communities were particularly interesting because this section of the city was one of the few in which black were allowed to own property. Hence, black communities such as York Hill, Yorkville, Seneca Village, and Pig Town had the highest rate of black landownership in the city. Blacks built their own churches and schools in the area. Tragically, two weeks before the Central park bill was passed, black residents broke ground on a new church. Ironically, some of the blacks who lived in what would become Central Park were evicted once before when they were forced to move to make way for the building of the Croton Reservoir (Rosenzweig & Blackmar, 1992; Downing, 1851a; Bunce, 1874; Cohen & Augustyn, 1997).

To make matters worse, blacks found out that once evicted from Central Park, even in the midst of one of the worst depressions to hit the city, they could not get a job at Central Park. Central Park was built with an all-white, all-male workforce. At the time blacks made up the majority of the non-white population of the city; most Native Americans were long ago driven from the city and there were relatively few Chinese living there. At a time when the city underwent a depression lasting several years, Central Park provided work for thousands of workers each week. Fearful of labor unrest (from white workers objecting to working alongside blacks), the Commissioners of Central Park did not to hire blacks (Rosenzweig & Blackmar, 1992; Riis, 1890; Burrows & Wallace, 1999).

The Jones Wood–Central Park debate imprinted ideas about public parks on people's consciousness that are still with us today. The debate left us with the idea that parks were valued assets and that cities had an obligation to provide its residents with adequate access to parks and other open spaces. Moreover, parks are public goods that should be financed through public spending. In addition, the debate fostered the idea that park planning, management, and administration should not be the sole domain of the wealthy; input from the populace was important. Central Park's development also framed park building as a form of gentrification that would raise property values. The park opened the possibility to the massive removal of minorities and poor whites to make way for upper class whites to develop exclusive residential enclaves anchored by publicly financed open space. It was an early form of zoning that helped elites to eliminate noxious facilities and control land uses, thereby, making it possible to develop upscale residential communities. Gentrification operates in a similar way today. Quite frequently, low-income and minority communities are cleared and residents displaced to make way for upscale housing and commercial development.

CENTRAL PARK'S INFLUENCE ON CONTEMPORARY URBAN PARK FINANCING

Central Park's Mystique

Central Park has a mystique that still beguiles many today. Thus, in February 2001, many Americans watched closely as the former President Clinton searched for an office with an unobstructed view of Central Park. After the House Appropriations subcommittee (that oversees former presidents' budgets) balked at paying the $800,000-a-year price tag for his preferred office space on the 56th floor of the Carnegie Hall Tower located on West 57th Street, Clinton took his search to Harlem. Determined to have an office with a panoramic view of the park, Clinton set his sights on a cheaper, 7,000 square foot, 14th-floor office space that rented for about $210,000 per year (Lipton, 2001; Getlin, 2001; Bumiller, 2001; Wasserman & Herman, 2001). Clinton settled for a Harlem office with a view of the park rather than take one in Manhattan without the coveted prize because he knew that the view of Central Park – even if it is from Harlem – is more valuable than the actual use of the park itself.

The Central Park Conservancy, the Barlow Circle, *and Modern Day Power Elites*

Clinton's quest for a view of the park illustrates that 150 years after it was conceived, Central Park is still a potent symbol of wealth, power, and prestige in the city. It was exactly that prestige that Elizabeth Barlow Rogers sought to capitalize on when she became the Administrator of Central Park in 1979. At the time the city's Commissioner of Parks, Gordon Davis, described the park as a "disaster zone." Senator Daniel Patrick Moynihan described it as a "national disgrace" and threatened a federal takeover. Some wanted to make Central Park into a state park, whereas Moynihan wanted it to be taken over by the National Park Service. Hence, Rogers, an advocate of public–private funding and management of public parks, created the Central Park Conservancy in 1980 to help enhance the image of the park and transform it into a prestigious institution that wealthy people wanted to associate with and donate time and money to (Rosenzweig & Blackmar, 1992; Rogers, 1987).

With the creation of the Central Park Conservancy, Central Park and the Conservancy revolutionized the way in which urban parks were financed.

Once again, Central Park was at the forefront of changing the way people thought about, funded and administered urban parks. This is the case because up until the 1970s, most of the funding for urban parks came from local government spending. However, as cities began experiencing fiscal hardships, there was a dramatic reduction in park funding as cities slashed their budgets. This provided an opening for the development of public–private partnerships to help finance and administer parks (Harnik, 1998; Project for Public Spaces [PPS], 2003). Therefore, during the early 1970s, when others despaired about the condition of the Central Park, Rogers got a taste of how one could fund-raise successfully for Central Park. As a volunteer leading a youth program for the Parks Council, she wrote an article entitled "33 Ways Your Time and Money Can Help Save Central Park." Within a week of publication, $25,000 in contributions flooded into the Parks Council office (Madden, Myrick, Brower, Secunda, & Schwartz, 2000; Rogers, 2004).

As head of the Central Park Conservancy, Rogers capitalized on people's desire to contribute to the park. That giving is changing the way in which urban parks are being funded. As the twenty-first century unfolds, Central Park is once again at the forefront of the debate over the financing of urban parks. Given the park's place in American urban park history, it is not surprising that Central Park continues to provide a model for urban park development, financing, and management.

During the 1850s, park advocates envisioned Central Park as an elite, landscaped park ringed by the dwellings and businesses of the wealthy. That idea is still so firmly entrenched, that today, a century and a half later, Central Park has on its eastern, western, and southern borders, one of the largest and most densely packed group of rich and powerful people in America. Although the wealthy continued to live adjacent to the park during the twentieth century, they were not as involved with the park as their nineteenth-century counterparts. Consequently, by the 1970s, the park deteriorated, and the cash-starved city seemed unable or unwilling to provide the funds for needed repairs and maintenance. Nonetheless, the park remained popular. More than 25 million people visit the park annually (Central Park Conservancy, 2002, 2005; Harden, 1999; Madden et al., 2000).

From her earlier work raising funds for the Central Park Task Force, Rogers knew that the rich had an affinity to the park that could be tapped to help alleviate Central Park's cash flow problems (Rosenzweig & Blackmar, 1992; Madden et al., 2000). A long-time Olmsted and Central Park scholar, she was fully aware of the role that the city's business elite (the Minturn Circle) played in helping New Yorkers embrace the idea of developing the country's first landscaped park. Thus, she set out to create an organization whose members and board would form what I will call the Barlow Circle, a re-creation of the Minturn Circle on a more gigantic and deliberate scale. The Barlow Circle would be composed primarily of a network of corporate executives and wealthy New Yorkers living close to Central Park who could donate time and money to the park and make it their *cause célèbre*.

The Central Park Taskforce was created to raise funds for Central Park and to help with repairs and maintenance of the park. The Central Park Task Force and the Central Park Community Fund (both founded in 1975) were replaced by the Central Park Conservancy. Since the Central Park Conservancy was created, the organization has raised and spent more than $300 million restoring the park. Rogers harkened back to the 1850s and classic Downing–Olmsted–Vaux ideology as she set out to rehabilitate the park "as the original creators saw it – a scenic retreat, a peaceful space that would be an antidote to urban stress." She claimed that "the park is foremost a work of landscape art" and she was "not prepared to accept that it's anything else." Ergo, Rogers and the Conservancy presented the park as an elite cultural institution in which "The trees and the monuments and the gardens are our collection" (Stewart, 2000; Rogers, 1987; Central Park Conservancy, 2006d).

Framing the park in nineteenth-century Romantic ideology has been very successful. It has helped to transform Central Park into a cultural institution, which is one of the major targets of charitable giving in the city. Philanthropists now put it on a par with the Museum of Modern Art and Carnegie Hall. Understanding how and why the wealthy give was critical to the Central Park Conservancy's success. First, the Conservancy understood that within moneyed circles, there is tremendous social pressure to give, to make donations to each others' pet causes, and to give to elite charities. There is also a kind of herd mentality, that is, once a charity has attracted prominent donors, others are drawn to it for fear of being ostracized or being excluded from the most prestigious networks. Funding also begets more funding. Organizations that are on sound financial footing are more likely to leverage additional funds than struggling institutions teetering on the brink of bankruptcy (Harden, 1999).

Richard Gilder, a stockbroker who grew up playing in Central Park and who lives beside it on Fifth Avenue, gave $17 million to the park. He is typical of the kind of donor the Conservancy courts because the rich also tend to give to what they are familiar with and to what gives them personal satisfaction. Because so many of Central Park's wealthy neighbors grew up in the fashionable dwellings around the park, played in it as children, can view the park from the homes and offices, or jog or stroll in the park, the Conservancy thought they would have tremendous interest and personal stake in reversing the decline of the park and helping to restore it to its former glory. Therefore, it is not surprising that 80 percent of donations to the Conservancy have come from about 20 percent of the donors and that hundreds of the largest donors live within a block of the park (Harden, 1999).

The Central Park Conservancy does not only court and receive donations from donors while they are alive, the Conservancy has an estate planning program that allows supporters to contribute to the park in their wills. Like Gilder, Janet Kramer lived across the street from Central Park and regarded it as her backyard. When she passed away, she left $2.9 million to help with the restoration of the park's Historic Playground Landscape (Central Park Conservancy, 2006a).

Douglas Blonsky, the current president of the Central Park Conservancy, described the affinity Central Park supporters have for the park as he reflected on his personal experiences with the park. He said, "Every morning at 6:30, I walk through Central Park on my way to work and savor the view from the Great Lawn. It's a beautiful sight, and it's different every day" (Central Park Conservancy, 2005). As one wealthy park neighbor commented, "Central Park is our only estate where I didn't have to hire a hundred gardeners." According to Central Park Conservancy board member, Michael R. Bloomberg (a major donor to the park and founder of Bloomberg Financial Markets), "The park is visible, you can touch it, you can partake of it, you can brag about it, you can see the difference your money makes." According to Gilder, giving to the park "is a natural for people who live near the park … There are so few things you can give money to that aren't in desperate shape." Charitable giving can also help to protect and enhance the value of investments. As one park donor noted, "In the real estate field, it is just smart business for us to try and improve the quality of life in the city where we have our major holdings." Ostrower's research supports the pattern of charitable giving to the Central Park Conservancy thus far. She found that the rich gave to universities, symphony orchestras, art museums, and other elite charities that they use and that enhance their social status, business networks, and provide opportunities for them to move in the exclusive circles of charitable benefits and social events (Odendahl, 1990; Harden, 1999; Ostrower, 1995).

Understanding that the rich, in true Veblenian fashion, emulate each other and apply tremendous social pressure to each other – more so than an outsider can apply – the Conservancy sought to involve rich and powerful people like Phyllis Wagner, William S. Beinecke (formerly chief executive officer of Sperry and Hutchinson), and Henry R. Kravis (the billionaire leveraged-buyout specialist) whose phone calls and requests for aid cannot be ignored, in running the organization. According to William Beinecke, who was "shocked" at the park's appearance, he had no trouble recruiting the top executives at corporations like Morgan Stanley and American Express to sit on the board of the Conservancy (they later donated money). Several donors attest to the fact that when Henry R. Kravis, a trustee of the Conservancy, requested money, they could not ignore him. "If he helps your charity, then you must help his" said Howard J. Rubenstein, the multimillionaire head of a public relations firm. Rubenstein continued, "in the upper echelons of millionaire's row, it [charitable giving] is almost a trade." Other philanthropists and long-time park supporters like Lucy Moses and Iphigene Ochs Sulzberger (wife of a former publisher of the *New York Times*), foundations like the DeWitt Wallace-Readers Digest Fund[4] and the Arthur Ross Foundation, and corporations like Time Warner, Tropicana Products, and Trump Organization have given large donations to the park (Veblen, 1899; Harden, 1999; Rosenzweig & Blackmar, 1992; Rogers, 1987; Madden et al., 2000).

Tea Parties, Luncheons, Benches, and Trees

When Downing suggested in 1848 that the wives of wealthy men host tea parties to raise funds for public parks, he could not have imagined the Central Park Conservancy's Women's Committee raising over $30 million for the park and hosting the annual Frederic Law Olmsted Luncheon attended by more than a thousand guests that brought in over $2 million in 2002 (Downing, 1848; Central Park Conservancy, 2003a).

According to Phyllis Cerf Wagner (widow of Robert F. Wagner of Bennett and Cerf, and the cofounder of Random House), the luncheon is a highly anticipated event and timing is everything. "It [the luncheon] is in May ... Everyone has new spring clothes. They have new hats" (see Cunningham, 2001).

The Conservancy's Women's Committee has evoked and re-created the nineteenth-century Romantic history of the park wherein wealthy men and women repair to the park in their latest fashions to socialize, see, and be seen. Wagner and the Women's Committee also realized another of Downing's visions (and one that was rejected by Olmsted); that is, allowing the public to endow park benches and trees (Downing, 1848; Olmsted, 1870;

Schuyler, 1986). Today, the rich can announce their largesse and leave testaments of their wealth and legacy by endowing buildings and other park structures. Opportunities have also been created for the general public to endow the benches, trees, flowers, and other objects in the park. In 1991, the Women's Committee established the Adopt-A-Bench program. The Central Park Tree Trust was also established that year. Almost 2,000 of Central Park's approximately 9,000 benches have been endowed for between $7,500 and $25,00. More than 400 of the park's approximately 26,000 trees have also been endowed for between $5,000 and $100,000. For a $100 annual fee, dog owners can enroll each of their pets as members of the Central Barkers. Park supporters can also commemorate anniversaries or the death of a loved one by planting bulbs (Central Park Conservancy, 2006b, 2003a). Because naming opportunities are now seen as lucrative fund-raising ventures, sprinkled throughout Central Park are benches, trees, groves, nooks, and crannies with names like the Lila Wallace-Reader's Digest Terrace, Doris C. Freedman Plaza, Wagner Cove, Kerbs Boathouse, Robert Bendheim Playground, Rudin Family Playground, Bernard Family Playground, Abraham and Joseph Spector Playground, and the Charles A. Dana Discovery Center (Central Park Conservancy, 2003a).

The Rise of Public–Private Partnerships for Parks

The Central Park Conservancy and its precursors, The Central Park Task Force and the Central Park Community Fund, are among the oldest groups of their kind. They have also been very influential in spreading the public–private partnership model. As a result, other urban parks have created fund-raising opportunities similar to Central Park's. For example, in September 2001, the Young Friends of the Public Garden's annual Swing Into Fall Gala attracted 250 people and raised $26,500 for the parks they supported[5] in Boston (Bisbee, 2001).

My examination of 28 park partnerships groups shows that the Central Park Conservancy has the most elaborate and diversified funding structure (Table 1). The table also shows that memberships, corporate sponsorships, and foundations are the most common fund-raising strategies. Almost all the park partnerships groups relied on memberships (either through payments that run from $5 to thousands of dollars or through the unpaid work that volunteers do on behalf of the park). Sixty-four percent of the groups got corporate donations, whereas 42.9 percent had created foundations to help raise funds. Adopting benches (39.3 percent) and trees (35.7 percent) were also popular; so were planned giving opportunities (35.7 percent), the establishment of endowments (32.1 percent), and tributes or memorials (32.1 percent). Depending on the park, the sponsorships of benches, trees, carousels, flower-beds, paving stones, and so on ranged from $50 to $100,000.

As the above discussion indicates, since the 1970s, there has been growing interest in public–private partnerships as a way of funding and managing parks. Although the Central Park Conservancy is the most successful public–private park management partners, there are several models of public–private ventures being tried all over the country. These partnerships, in which nonprofits and private groups enter into partnerships with cities and counties to help run public parks, fall into five general categories (Table 2).

The first wave of partnerships – those that emerged in the 1970s – was by and large assistance providers; an exception was the Maymont Foundation, a sole manager. The 1980s ushered in the era of conservancies; the Central Park Conservancy led the way. The public–private partnerships were attractive for a number of reasons. While some city parks departments were mired in red tape, bureaucracy, and inaction, the nonprofits could make decisions fast, fund-raise, and save money. Nonprofits could also be strong park advocates and pressure groups. Nonprofits marketed parks effectively and were also more effective fund-raisers than city governments. As was the case in Central Park, wealthy donors reluctant to give money to local governments were much more willing to give money to nonprofits where their money went to the upkeep of a specific park or for specific projects, not to general funds (Madden et al., 2000).

Table 3 summarizes the kinds of fund-raising activities the various types of park partners are engaged in. The comanagers and catalysts are engaged in the widest range of fund-raising activities. The mean number of fund-raising activities was also calculated. Overall, partnerships engaged in a mean of 5.18 fund-raising activities. However, the mean for comanagers was 8.57; it was 6.50 for sole managers, 4.00 for city-wide partners, 3.75 for assistance providers, and 3.73 for catalysts. Park partners in the Northeast had the highest mean at 6.00. The mean was 5.75 in the West, 4.25 in the South, and 3.67 in the Midwest.

Replicating the Central Park Conservancy: A New Model for Managing Public Parks?

Because of the success of the Central Park Conservancy, Central Park is being held out as a model of private–public park management, but can this

Table 1. Fund-Raising Activities Undertaken by Urban Park Supporter Groups.

Park Support Group	City	Capital Campaigns	Naming Opportunities	Endow Park or Structures	Planned Giving	Luncheons or Dinners	Dances, Balls, Banquets, Gala	Commemorations, Memorials, Tributes	Adopt historic buildings	Adopt trees	Adopt benches	Plant flowers	Trails, sidewalks	Paving stones	Adopt site	Adopt wildlife	Adopt horses, carousels	Memberships	Pet memberships	Groom a fixture	Perimeter	Fashion shows	Concession funds	Walkathon, run	Exhibits	Festivals	Foundations	Corporate sponsorship
The Battery Conservancy	New York	•																							•			•
Central Park Conservancy	New York	•	•	•	•	•												•	•	•	•		•		•		•	•
Emerald Necklace Conservancy	Brookline, MA							•										•										•
Fairmount Park Conservancy	Philadelphia								•																			•
Forest Park Forever	St. Louis	•		•	•			•		•	•	•						•									•	•
Forever Park (Balboa Park)	San Diego			•	•					•		•		•				•								•	•	•
Friends of Buttonwood Park	New Bedford, MA							•										•										
Friends of Garfield Park	Indianapolis				•		•											•										
Friends of the Public Garden	Boston			•						•																		•
Garfield Park Con. Alliance	Chicago			•				•			•							•								•	•	•
Golden Gate Parks Conservancy	San Francisco							•		•		•	•					•										•
Great Park Conservancy	Orange County														•			•				•					•	•

Great Plains Trail Network	Lincoln, NE
Greater Newark Conservancy	Newark
Greening of Detroit	Detroit
Hermann Park Conservancy	Houston
Knox Greenway Coalition	Knoxville
Louisville Olmsted Parks Conservancy	Louisville
Maymont Foundation	Richmond, VA
National AIDS Memorial Grove	San Francisco
The Parks Foundation	Cincinnati
ParkWorks	Cleveland
Piedmont Park Conservancy	Atlanta
Prospect Park Alliance	New York
Riverside Park Fund	New York
San Francisco Parks Trust	San Francisco
South Suburban Park Foundation	Littleton, CO
Yakima Greenway Foundation	Yakima, WA

Sources: Battery Conservancy (2007), Central Park Conservancy (2006), Emerald Necklace Conservancy (2007), Fairmount Park Conservancy (2007), Forest Park Forever (2007), Forever Park (2007), Friends of Buttonwood Park (2007), Friends of Garfield Park (2007), Hermann Park Conservancy (2007), Friends of the Public Garden (2006), Garfield Park Conservatory Alliance (2007), Golden Gate National Parks Conservancy (2007a, 2007b), Great Park Conservancy (2005), Great Plains Trail Network (2007), Greater Newark Conservancy (2007), Greening of Detroit (2007), Knox Greenway Coalition (2007), Louisville Olmsted Parks Conservancy (2007), Maymont Foundation (2007), National AIDS Memorial Grove (2007), Parks Foundation (2007), ParkWorks (2007), Piedmont Park Conservancy (2007), Prospect Park Alliance (2007), Riverside Park Fund (2006), San Francisco Parks Trust (2007), South Suburban Park Foundation (2007), and Yakima Greenway Foundation (2007).

Table 2. Characteristics of Five Different Types of Parks
Partnership Models.

Activities	Assistance Providers	Catalysts	Comanagers	Sole Managers	Citywide Partners
Advocates for all city parks					•
Advocates for one/few parks	•	•	•	•	
Fund-raising	•	•	•	•	•
Public education	•	•	•	•	•
Programming	•	•	•	•	
Volunteering	•	•	•	•	
Park design	•	•	•	•	
Envision and create park spaces		•	•	•	
Initiate park projects		•	•	•	
Implement projects			•	•	
Provide staffing for parks			•	•	
Maintain parks			•	•	
Renovate or restore parks			•	•	
Partner with city to manage parks			•		
Has complete control of park management operations				•	
Fund local parks					•
Examples of partnership models					
Forever Park	•				
Friends of the Public Garden	•				
Friends of Buttonwood Park	•				
Knox Greenway Coalition		•			
South Suburban Park Foundation		•			
National AIDS Memorial Grove		•			
Central Park Conservancy			•		
Prospect Park Alliance			•		
Forest Park Forever			•		
Maymont Foundation				•	
Yakima Greenway Foundation				•	
Partnerships for Parks					•
Philadelphia Green					•
The Greening of Detroit					•

Sources: Madden et al. (2000), National AIDS Memorial Grove (2007), Parks Foundation (2007), Forest Park Forever (2007), and Greening of Detroit (2007).

model be replicated across the country the way the Central Park design was propagated in the nineteenth century? To assess whether the Central Park Conservancy can be a viable model for urban parks to copy, an examination of the budget will be helpful. The Central Park Conservancy, working in concert with the Park Commissioner and City Hall, oversees the restoration

Table 3. Types of Fund-raising Activities Conducted by Park Support Partners.

Fund-Raising Activity	Total Sample		Type of Park Support Partners					Region			
	Number of partners (n = 28)	Percent	Assistance providers (n = 4)	Catalysts (n = 11)	Comanagers (n = 7)	Sole managers (n = 2)	City-wide partners (n = 4)	Northeast (n = 10)	South (n = 4)	Midwest (n = 6)	West (n = 8)
Memberships	26	92.9	4	10	7	2	3	9	4	5	8
Corporate sponsorship	18	64.3	1	7	6	2	2	8	1	3	6
Create foundations	12	42.9	1	6	2	1	2	5		1	6
Adopt benches	11	39.3		3	4	1	3	3	2	2	4
Adopt trees	10	35.7	2	2	4	1	1	4	2	2	2
Planned giving	10	35.7	1	2	3	2	2	1	2	3	4
Endow park structures	9	32.1	2	1	5	1		3	1	1	4
Commemorate, memorials	9	32.1		2	5	1	1	2	2	2	3
Capital campaigns	6	21.4		1	4		1	4		1	1
Banquets, balls, gala	5	18.0		1	6			3		1	1
Plant flowers	4	14.3	1	1	1		1	1		1	2
Sponsor trails, sidewalks	3	10.7	2	1				1			2
Paving stones	3	10.7		1	1	1		1	1	1	
Naming opportunities	2	7.1		1	1			2			
Luncheons, dinners	2	7.1			2			2			

Table 3. (Continued)

Fund-Raising Activity	Total Sample		Type of Park Support Partners					Region			
	Number of partners (n = 28)	Percent	Assistance providers (n = 4)	Catalysts (n = 11)	Comanagers (n = 7)	Sole managers (n = 2)	City-wide partners (n = 4)	Northeast (n = 10)	South (n = 4)	Midwest (n = 6)	West (n = 8)
Groom a fixture	2	7.1			2			2			
Fashion shows	2	7.1		1	1			1			1
Exhibits	2	7.1			2			2			
Festivals	2	7.1	1		1			1			1
Walkathon, run	2	7.1		1	1			1	1		
Adopt historic buildings	1	3.6		1				1			
Adopt site	1	3.6			1						1
Adopt wildlife	1	3.6				1			1		
Adopt horses, carousels	1	3.6			1			1			
Pet memberships	1	3.6			1			1			
Perimeter association	1	3.6			1			1			
Concession funds	1	3.6			1			1			

and maintenance of the park, construction of new facilities, and programming. In 2001, the Conservancy had 223 employees and a payroll of $12.1 million. The Conservancy's payroll continues to grow. In 2005, the payroll was $14.54 million. That year, Central Park had a staff of 240, all but four of whom were paid for by the Central Park Conservancy (2005, 2003b, 2002, 2001, 2004).

As Table 4 indicates, the Central Park Conservancy had almost $26 million in revenues in 2000. The Conservancy's budget nose-dived in 2001

Table 4. Central Park Conservancy's Operational Revenues and Expenses (in Thousands of Dollars), 2000–2005.

Revenues and Expenses (in Thousands of Dollars)	2005	2004	2003	2002	2001	2000
Net assets at the beginning of the year	$124,708	$109,541	$98,940	$99,861	$118,362	
Net revenues	45,033	39,682	32,804	21,186	5,933	$25,817
Total expenses	29,172	24,514	22,203	22,107	24,434	24,876
Total net assets at the end of the year	140,569	124,708	109,941	98,940	99,861	
Revenue Stream:						
Contributions	23,883	16,464	16,067	18,659	13,149	13,055
Revenue from the City of New York	3,670	3,650	3,353	2,807	3,702	2,926
Special events	2,965	4,744	3,458	2,336	2,392	2,515
Interest and dividends	757	977	3,343	2,785	3,959	
Net (loss) gain on sale of investments	1,007	11,207	−5,325	−9,452	5,654	
Change in unrealized gain/ loss on investments	4,141	494	10,828	3,085	−23,960	
Change in value of split interest agreements	−13	−28	−26	−4	−9	
Other revenue	8,623	2,174	1,538	970	1,046	2,068
Net assets released from restrictions						2,547
Endowment fund income						1,924
Administrative cost recovery						782
Annual revenues before adjusting for losses	45,033	39,682	38,587	30,639	29,902	25,817
Total Investment Losses	−13	−28	−5,321	−9,456	−23,969	

Source: Compiled from Central Park Conservancy (2005, 2004, pp. 15–20, 2003b, pp. 37–39, 49, 2002, pp. 14–15, 2001, p. 12; *Annual Report*).

when it lost almost $24 million in investments in the stock market crash that followed the bombing of the World Trade Center. Despite the heavy losses, the Conservancy still managed to have almost $6 million in net revenues and ended the year with almost $100 million in endowment. By 2005, the Conservancy's revenues and assets were robust. The Conservancy had more than $45 million in revenues and ended the year with $140.6 million in total net assets. That year contributions constituted 53 percent of the Conservancy's revenue stream – up from 41 percent a year earlier (Table 5). Thanks to Christo and Jeanne-Claude's, "The Gates" project in Central Park that netted the Conservancy $5.9 million. Despite getting $3.67 million from the City in 2005, this accounted for only 8.2 percent of the Conservancy's budget. Under the Management Contract that the Central Park Conservancy has with the City Department of Parks, the Conservancy can get a maximum of $4 million annually from the city to operate the park. More than 100 corporations contribute to the park. In addition, there is a Perimeter Association, composed of 115 residential buildings, hotels, and clubs that surround the park. The Perimeter Association, in collaboration with the Women's Committee, helps to maintain the park's six-mile perimeter (Central Park Conservancy, 2005, 2002, 2001).

Although all agree that the Conservancy has done a magnificent job of restoring Central Park and insulating it from budget cuts, critics are

Table 5.   Percentage Distribution of Revenues in the Central Park Conservancy's Budget, 2000–2005.

Percentage Distribution of Revenues before Adjusting for Losses	2005	2004	2003	2002	2001	2000
Contributions	53.03	41.49	41.43	60.89	43.97	50.57
Revenue from the City of New York	8.15	9.20	8.69	9.16	12.38	11.33
Special events	6.58	11.96	8.96	7.62	8.00	9.74
Interest and dividends	1.68	2.46	8.66	9.09	13.24	
Net (loss) gain on sale of investments	2.24	28.24			18.91	
Change in unrealized gain (loss) on investments	9.20	1.24	28.06	10.07		
Other revenue	19.15	5.45		3.17	3.50	8.01
Net assets released from restrictions			3.99			9.87
Endowment fund income						7.45
Administrative cost recovery						3.03
Total Revenues	100.00	100.00	100.00	100.00	100.00	100.00

Source: Compiled from Central Park Conservancy (2005, 2004, pp. 15–20, 2002, pp. 14–15, 2001, p. 12, 2003b, p. 39).

troubled by some aspects of the Conservancy's role in the management of a public park. They are doubtful that the model can be applied to a wide variety of parks. Although the Conservancy has been brilliant in securing funds for Central Park, it should be noted that Central Park is unique, and that is a big reason it can be a fund-raising success. Many parks will have a difficult time emulating the Conservancy's strategies because not all parks are surrounded by wealthy people or have the cultural and artistic stature of Central Park. For instance, Central Park's paid staff is assisted by more than 3,000 volunteers who do more than 35,000 hours of work annually in the park (Central Park Conservancy, 2005, 2002, 2003a, 2003b).

The Central Park Conservancy also raises funds successfully because of the board of trustees it has assembled. The 62-member board of trustees had 11 life members and four officers. Thirty-eight trustees were executives at major corporations such as Marsh & McLennan, Lehman Brothers, Deloitte & Touche, AOL Time Warner, Ernst & Young, JP Morgan Chase, Goldman Sachs, Estée Lauder, Morgan Stanley, Bank One, Credit Suisse First Boston, Rubenstein Associates, Bloomberg, and American Securities (Central Park Conservancy, 2002). In 2002, approximately 25,000 individuals, foundations, and corporations made donations to Central Park. While some contributed as little as $35 to become members, some Central Park donors contributed millions. By 2003, the number of financial supporters had grown to 30,000 (Central Park Conservancy, 2002, 2003b).

In fact, other New York parks have tried to copy Central Park with much less success. For instance, the Prospect Park Alliance, founded as a public–private comanagement nonprofit in 1987, had a budget of $8,516,255 in 2005 (Table 6). The Alliance has an endowment of around $5 million. The 526-acre Prospect Park lags far behind Central Park despite the fact that it is an Olmsted–Vaux park begun shortly after Central Park. Although Prospect Park has the history and the designers' imprimatur, it lacks the neighbors, location, and social cachet of Central Park. In 2002, Prospect Park had about 7 million visitors. It had a staff of 101, 23 of whom were paid for by the City of New York and the Department of Parks and Recreation. The Prospect Park staff was aided by 6,117 volunteers who contributed 26,399 hours of work to the park (Prospect Park Alliance, 2002; Prospect Park Alliance, 2003a, 2003b).

Prospect Park has several corporate executives on its board of directors. The Prospect Park Alliance gets donations from more than 100 corporations, foundations, and associations. Since 2001, 26 donors have given $125,000 or more to the park. This still lags behind Central Park where

Table 6. Prospect Park Alliance Budget: 2002, 2003, and 2005.

Revenues and Expenditures	2005 Budget		2003 Budget		2002 Budget	
	Amount	%	Amount	%	Amount	%
Total assets	$8,516,255				$6,818,920	
Total revenues	7,221,450		5,414,522		4,937,022	
Total expenses	8,208,224		5,414,522		4,937,022	
Net assets at the start of the year	5,959,492					
Net assets at the end of the year	4,972,718					
Revenue stream						
Foundations	1,873,299	25.9	1,087,531	20.1	1,215,093	24.6
Individuals	833,498	11.5	1,610,141	29.7	1,108,150	22.5
Concessions and revenue			1,226,678	22.7	997,705	20.2
Design and construction	320,362	4.4	595,877	11	887,748	18.0
Corporations	417,311	5.8	660,763	12.2	425,253	8.6
Funds reserved from prior year					137,067	2.8
Government	276,859	3.8	214,272	4	130,205	2.6
Interest, dividends and gains	109,864	1.5	19,256	0.4	35,801	0.7
Investment income	77,434	1.1				
Fund-raising events	415,402	5.8				
Donated goods and services	624,114	8.6				
Visitor services and events	2,223,307	30.8				
Total revenues	7,221,450	99.2	5,414,522	100.1	4,937,022	100.0

Source: Compiled from Prospect Park Alliance (2005, p. 15, 2002, p. 19, 2003c, p. 18).

corporations give large donations. For instance, the Brothers Foundation gave Central Park $10 million in 1998. Whereas 3,519 individuals made contributions to Prospect Park in 2002, only three of those gave $50,000 or more. Nonetheless, the Prospect Park Alliance relies heavily on donations (Central Park Conservancy, 2003a, 2002; Prospect Park Alliance, 2005, 2002, 2003c).

While the Central Park Conservancy has a management contract that allows it to get up to $2 million from concession revenues generated by Central Park back from the City each year since 1988, other urban parks do not have this arrangement. In most cities, revenues generated from park concessions disappear into the city's general funds. It is very difficult for the parks department, much less a single park, to see a return of the revenues from concessions. In 1995, Mayor Guliani signed an agreement with the New York City's parks department to allow parks to keep a portion of the concession revenues they generated. The agreement was in place for only one year, but it increased the parks' budgets dramatically. Prospect Park

Alliance was able to retain concession fees in 2002 and 2003; the effect on their budget is quite noticeable. As Table 6 indicates, the Alliance earned $997,705 and $1,226,678 in concession revenues in those two years (Prospect Park Alliance, 2005; Harnik, 1998).

In an effort to raise funds for New York City's parks (except Central Park), the City Parks Foundation was created. However, the organization has not even come close to matching the success of the Central Park Conservancy. In 2005, the City Parks Foundation spent about $7 million and had an endowment of about $13.3 million (Table 7). In comparison, the Central Park Conservancy had an endowment of $140.57 million in 2005 and expenses of around $29.2 million (Charity Navigator, 2006).

However, some of New York's smaller parks are not relying solely on the City Parks Foundation to generate additional revenues for them. Around 42 park advocacy groups exist in the city; plus another nine groups functioning as city-wide park advocates have been formed (Citizens Budget Commission, 2007). For instance, the Riverside Park Fund works on behalf of Riverside Park and The Battery Conservancy focuses on Battery Park. But the parks that are off the well-beaten track find it challenging to raise the funds needed to facilitate adequate maintenance and administration. In essence, parks like Marcus Garvey Park located at Fifth Avenue between 120 and 124th streets in Harlem languish in the shadows of fund-raising behemoths like Central Park. Although Marcus Garvey Park evokes its Olmsted roots and illustrious history on its website, neighborhood park advocates find it difficult to raise funds for the park. Residents like Helen Murray who live close to Marcus Garvey Park are trying to raise money from local businesses, hospitals, and so on and have recruited volunteers to clean up and maintain the park. But while Marcus Garvey Park's October 1999 fund-raising dinner brought in $7,000, Central Park's Halloween Ball – that was attended by 615 guests – raised $805,000 that same month.[6] A fund-raising event at Prospect Park brought in $15,000 that year (Harden, 1999; Cohen & Augustyn, 1997; Madden et al., 2000).

ENVIRONMENTAL JUSTICE GROUPS AND GREATER ACCESS TO PARKS

Environmental justice groups are getting involved in the parks debates. Groups such as Sustainable South Bronx contend that the amount of open space in low-income minority neighborhoods is inadequate. They also argue

Table 7. A Comparison of the Revenues, Expenses, and Assets of Private Park Partners.

Name	Year Founded	City Located In	Park(s) Supported	Total Revenues ($)	Total Expenses ($)	Excess or Deficit ($)	Net Assets ($)	Fiscal Year
Central Park Conservancy	1975/1980	New York	Central Park	40,954,120	29,220,720	11,733,400	140,569,894	2005
Golden Gate National Parks Conservancy	1981	San Francisco	Golden Gate, Presidio	17,386,163	14,592,813	2,793,350	22,910,820	2005
Maymont Foundation	1975	Richmond, VA	Maymont Estate	3,223,927	4,010,106	−786,179	21,842,029	2004
Houston Parks Board	1975	Houston	City parks	2,261,747	2,832,865	−571,118	15,555,976	2005
Forest Park Forever	1986	St. Louis	Forest Park	7,839,250	3,193,495	4,654,755	14,839,094	2004
City Parks Foundation	1989	New York	City parks	7,575,528	7,013,836	561,692	13,303,286	2005
Friends of the Public Garden	1970	Boston	Boston Common, the Public Garden, Commonwealth Avenue	1,936,466	465,882	1,470,584	6,842,686	2004
San Francisco Parks Trust	1971	San Francisco	City parks	6,754,459	6,171,243	583,216	6,247,090	2005
Prospect Park Alliance	1987	New York	Prospect Park	6,022,128	6,485,641	463,513	5,959,492	2004
Greater Newark Conservancy	1987	Newark	City parks	1,351,188	1,060,621	290,567	5,380,222	2005
Piedmont Park Conservancy	1989	Atlanta	Piedmont Park	3,384,817	3,376,604	8,213	5,276,481	2004
Hermann Park Conservancy	1990	Houston	Hermann Park	1,689,642	1,295,598	394,044	3,828,421	2005
Cincinnati Parks Foundation		Cincinnati	City parks	827,632	596,358	231,274	2,090,627	2004
Riverside Park Fund	1986	New York	Riverside Park	1,896,553	1,135,508	761,045	1,582,701	2004
ParkWorks	1977	Cleveland	City parks	1,466,235	1,436,782	29,453	692,467	2004
The Battery Conservancy	1994	New York	Battery Park	1,946,797	1,289,284	4,189,757	657,513	2004
Garfield Park Conservatory Alliance	1994	Chicago	Garfield Park	1,194,146	1,115,985	78,161	503,140	2005
The Greening of Detroit	1989	Detroit	City parks	992,120	1,062,221	−70,101	306,012	2004

Source: Compiled from Charity Navigator (2006).

that the existing park space is poorly maintained. As a result, Sustainable South Bronx is working on the South Bronx Greenway Project – a plan to expand and develop the green space in the Hunts Point section of the Bronx. The group has completed one park, Barrett Point Park, and is working on the second, Hunts Point Park. In the mean time, Sustainable South Bronx is trying to convince the city that instead of the planned 2,000-bed $375 million jail that is planned for the neighborhood, what residents want is more parks, open space, and recreational amenities. In their Greening for Breathing in Hunts Point campaign, Sustainable South Bronx has already planted 400 trees and plans to plant 375 more (Matthews Neilsen Landscape Architects, PC, 2006; Sustainable South Bronx, 2008).

Another environmental justice group, WE ACT (West Harlem Environmental Action), also contends that low-income minority neighborhoods are saddled with waste transfer stations and other noxious facilities at the same time they lack open space. In response, WE ACT has teamed up with park activists to plan activities in Morningside Park. WE ACT has also collaborated with Manhattan Community Board 9 to develop the Harlem on the River plan for the Harlem Piers that call for a landscaped park on the riverfront as part of the redevelopment plan (WE ACT, 2000, 2002, 2006). Another New York City environmental justice, El Puente, has been active in park building in Brooklyn (El Puente, 2008). The Greater Newark Conservancy has environmental justice as a part of its organizing and planning (Greater Newark Conservancy, 2007).

CITIES EXPLORE PUBLIC–PRIVATE MANAGEMENT OPTIONS

Despite the skepticism about and criticism of the Central Park Conservancy's model, budget cuts are forcing many cities to explore private management and revenue-generating options in their parks. The demise of the Urban Park and Recreation Recovery (UPARR) program has only served to exacerbate matters and push urban parks further down the road of public–private management options. UPARR was a federal matching grants program administered by the National Park Service that ran from 1978 to 2002 (70 percent of the funding was federal and 30 percent local). At its inception, $725 million was authorized over a five-year period to help urban parks. However, over the 25 years the program operated, only about $272 million was spent. Over the life of the program, 1,461 projects in 380 municipalities in 43 states as well as the District of Columbia and Puerto Rico were funded. Of the projects funded, 714 went to rehabilitate facilities, 191 were for innovations, and 556 were planning grants. Funding was erratic under the program. Whereas more than $62 million was awarded in 1980 and again in 1981, nothing was funded from 1985 to 1990 or in 1993. Cities' response to the program gave an indication of the need for funding. In 2002, the last year the program was funded, the National Park Service received 191 proposals totaling $78.1 million in requests for funding. That year, only 71 proposals totaling $8.9 million were funded (National Park Service, 2007; National Parks and Recreation Association, 2003).

Not only was UPARR inadequate to meet the demand, the loss of funding from this program will deal a huge blow to struggling urban parks. UPARR funds were used to rehabilitate heavily used city parks far from the glow of Central Park's fund-raising machine. For instance, the Swaggerty Creek Park in Little Rock, Arkansas, was deemed unsuitable for recreational use. The basketball courts were so dilapidated that they were unusable. The picnic and play area, equally dilapidated, had to be fenced in to prevent entry, and the bleachers were unsafe. It was a $543,400 UPARR grant that was used to repair the park. Similarly, Cambridge Park in Concord, California, that serves a low-income Hispanic community was very run down. It was also the only open space in the area. The soccer fields were in need of repair and the park had no restroom facilities or drinking water fountains. Martin Luther King Jr. Park in East Palo Alto was also over-used and in need of repairs. The structures were so deteriorated that the facilities had to be closed in 2001. UPARR funds were used to help rehabilitate these parks and restore them so that community residents could use them (National Parks and Recreation Association, 2003).

Some cities are in such desperate financial straits that they consider jettisoning some of their parks. Detroit made headlines in 2007 with its "park repositioning" proposal that called for the city to sell off 92 small "vest-pocket" city parks. Detroit has 367 parks. The parks being sold total about 124 acres of the roughly 6,000 acres of park land in the city. The city hopes to reap $8.1 million in revenues and save about $540,000 in maintenance bills for the parks being considered for sale. The city also expected to generate about $5.4 million in tax revenues from new development on the land. To counter opposition and criticism, Detroit City officials are quick to point out that the city renovated 11 parks in 2007. It spent about $16 million to rehabilitate one recreation center. The city also spent about $18.5 million building two new recreation centers and improving 18 city parks in 2006 (Saulny, 2007; Gorchow, 2007).

In their quest for solutions, cities look to New York and Chicago for leadership because these are the two largest fee-generating urban park systems in the country. The New York City has 37,000 acres of parkland. The 2007 operating budget was $315 million; an additional $246 million was earmarked for capital expenditures. The operating budget was projected at $326 million for 2008. About $65 million (or 22.6 percent) of the $288 million city park operating budget in 2006 came from private sources (Citizens Budget Commission, 2007). The city is looking for ways to increase this. City officials have just announced plans to allow major corporations to buy naming rights in the parks; they hope to generate around $3 million annually from corporate naming (Edozien, 2008). The city is still seeking added revenues because it estimates that approximately $394 million are needed to rehabilitate the parks. The amount – $44 million allocated in 2007 – is nowhere near the amount needed to get the parks in good operating condition. The Citizens Budget Commission report the claims of environmental justice activists in the city that parks in poor neighborhoods are poorly maintained (Citizens Budget Commission, 2007).

Chicago's 2008 parks operating budget is approximately $397 million (up from $394 million in 2007) (Chicago Park District, 2007). New York and Chicago also have the two park systems in the country that outsource much of their operations. That is, the cities have contracted out more park operations (like running parking garages, stadiums, marinas, skating rinks, swimming pools, golf courses, and so on) to private companies and concessions than any other urban park systems in the country. City parks departments outsource because it can be profitable. For example, the New York Department of Parks generates around $63 million in concession revenues annually (Harnik, 1998; Citizens Budget Commission, 2007).

Some city parks departments have explored the idea of charging fees and generating revenues from private sources tentatively. For instance, the Baltimore Parks and Recreation Department had a $29 million operating budget in 2006 but generated only about 4 percent of it in special events and activities. However, the parks department has created an Office of Partnerships to promote public–private collaborations. Almost 40 such partnerships have already been created (Baltimore City Department of Recreation and Parks, 2006). Similarly, the Providence Parks Department generates only about 3 percent of its budget in fees. At the other extreme is Wheeling, West Virginia. The Wheeling Parks Commission is one of the most self-supporting city parks departments in the country. Wheeling gets less than 10 percent of its $25 million budget from the city. In fact, G. Randolf Worls, Chief Executive Officer of the Oglebay Foundation in

Wheeling, predicts that private funds will become the dominant form of financing for urban parks. The Oglebay Foundation raises funds to help administer and maintain Wheeling's Oglebay Park and Wheeling Park. Worls' goal is to increase the parks' endowment to $75 million at which point he believes the parks can operate without any outlay of public funds (Oglebay Foundation, 2006; Harnik, 1998).

Increasingly, urban parks are relying on private partnerships to finance them. Across the country, city parks departments are broadening their funding bases to rely on sources of income beyond tax revenues (Harnik, 1998). However, a 2000 study of 16 public–private partnerships nationwide showed that most raised relatively small sums of money and had small operating budgets. Only six – the Central Park Conservancy, Friends of Hermann Park, Marymont Foundation, Partnerships for Parks, Philadelphia Green, and Prospect Park Alliance – had operating budgets over a million dollars (Madden et al., 2000). This is changing. My analysis of the 2004 and 2005 budgets of 17 such partnerships shows all, but one has an operational budget of at least a million dollars (see Table 7). Moreover, all but four also had endowments over a million dollars. Table 7 also reports the huge gap between the Central Park Conservancy's operational budget and endowment compared to other park partners (Charity Navigator, 2006).

Critics of the public–private park management model argue that Central Park's wealth creates a two-tiered park system with well-endowed parks and parks with little or no money. In New York, for instance, the Central Park Conservancy has raised vastly more money than the Prospect Park Alliance or the City Parks Foundation. In other cities and states, nonprofits cherry-pick and promote the best parks while the others are left to languish. In Massachusetts, for instance, a deliberate attempt was made to trade on Olmsted's name in deciding which parks to rehabilitate. A study of the 280 public spaces in the state designed by Olmsted's firm was conducted and 10 parks were chosen to represent Olmsted and his firm's work. Similarly, the Louisville Olmsted Parks Conservancy highlights the Olmsted-designed parks in their work (Madden et al., 2000).

The Central Park Conservancy's presence buffers Central Park against budget shocks – a luxury not afforded by other parks. The Conservancy steps in to pay for maintenance and salaries when there are budget shortfalls. In February 1998, the Conservancy signed a renewable eight-year management agreement with the City of New York and the Department of Parks and Recreation. Under the contract, the Conservancy must raise and spend $5 million annually for maintenance and repairs, public programs, landscaping and rehabilitation, or repair of existing facilities.

If the Conservancy meets these requirements, the Department of Parks and Recreation pays the Conservancy a minimum of $1 million. The amount paid by Parks and Recreation can be increased to a maximum of $2 million, depending on how much the Conservancy exceeds its $5 million threshold in any given year. Under the contract, the Conservancy also gets a portion of net concession revenues earned in Central Park. The Central Park Conservancy gets 50 percent of net concession revenues earned in excess of $6 million. The amount the Conservancy can receive from concession revenues is capped at $2 million per year. The total annual payments Parks and Recreation is obligated to the Conservancy under this agreement is capped at $4 million (Central Park Conservancy, 2005, 2002).

This arrangement buffers the park from budget cuts. Other parks do not have such luxuries; therefore, their budgets are slashed and maintenance falls by the wayside. Some argue that the presence of organizations like the Conservancy allows the city to pare away at parks budgets and allows it to step away from its commitment to provide public recreation to all citizens. Finally, critics also argue that the Central Park Conservancy undertakes projects that it can raise money for, not necessarily projects that are in the best interest of the park or that would benefit the majority of users (Madden et al., 2000; Harden, 1999).

However, as Elizabeth Barlow Rogers sees it, we are moving into an era of contract management for parks (Rogers, 2004), and given the projected budget shortfall for urban parks, many cities may not have much choice but to look at public–private management arrangements. Some city parks departments are not even at the level of funding they were before the financial crises of the 1970s. For instance, although New York's Park and Recreation Department has been innovative in getting funding, it is not back to the level of funding it had in 1978 before the city's financial crisis took a toll on parks budget. In the current economic and political climate, market-based park recreation is gaining legitimacy around the country (Harnik, 1998).

NEW FRONTIERS IN URBAN PARK FINANCING – MEGA PARKS AND PUBLIC–PRIVATE MANAGEMENT

Not only is it exceedingly difficult for cities to generate the amounts needed to adequately administer and maintain their existing parks, it is even more difficult to finance the construction of new ones. One of the most common ways in which cities and suburbs increase the amount of open space they have is through developer exactions. That is, get developers of new housing or commercial enterprises to donate or develop parks and other open space as part of their contract to build on parcels of land. However, despite the cities' best efforts, most of the parks being developed through exactions are being built in the suburbs or counties on the urban fringes (Harnik & Yaffe, 2006; Harnik, 1998; Hopper, 1998). Cities are also exploring the possibility of turning defunct landfills into parks as a means of increasing urban open space. Nationwide between 250 and 1,000 landfills have been converted to parks, golf courses, and so on (Harnik, Taylor, & Welle, 2006).

Despite the growing popularity of developer exactions as a tool to offset the impact of new development and acquire and develop urban parks, a study done by the Trust for Public Land found that even when cities have exaction ordinances, such initiatives do not always result in land acquisition. The study found that the formula to exact fees or land from developers varied widely around the country. For instance, Chicago requires that developers set aside 1.7 acres of land for every 1,000 residents a development will contain. On the contrary, Austin (Texas) mandates 5 acres per 1,000 residents, whereas San Diego seeks about 20 acres per 1,000. In six of the 12 cities studied (Austin, Forth Worth, San Antonio, Long Beach, San Jose, and Portland – Oregon), exactions resulted in the creation of 1,572 acres of new parkland. However, according to the exaction ordinances in these cities, 2,594 acres of new parkland should have been generated. That means that only about 61 percent of the parkland that should have been generated by developer exactions was actually generated. Portland generated about 2.33 times more parkland than their exaction ordinance stipulated because they issued bonds to acquire the land with the hope that the bonds would be paid off by future exaction taxes. Portland expected to generate 39 acres of parkland through exaction but actually acquired 90.86 acres by issuing bonds for land acquisition. Other cities generating a relatively high percent of parkland in relation to the stipulations of their ordinances were Austin (77 percent) and Fort Worth (63 percent). At the other end of the spectrum, San Antonio acquired no parkland while 227 acres should have been generated as per the ordinance. Six of the cities in the study (Albuquerque, Atlanta, Chicago, Los Angeles, San Diego, and Miami) had very poor tracking of whether the ordinances had generated parkland and how much land had been acquired (Harnik & Yaffe, 2006).

Even in cities that did track and generate new parkland from exactions, several factors hindered the generation of new parkland. Parks have to be close to the subdivision that generated the tax for it; it is sometimes impossible to find nearby land that can be converted to parks. Another factor is cost – some cities underestimate the cost of acquiring land, especially in places such as California where the cost of land is skyrocketing. Sometimes new parkland is not generated because cities use the funds obtained from exaction fees to restore existing parks rather than acquiring new ones. Some cities also provide exaction exemptions to developers who construct facilities like dependent care complexes, shelters, or group homes that are deemed beneficial to the community (Harnik & Yaffe, 2006).

Parks being planned for Orange County, California (The Great Park at El Toro); Denver, Colorado (Stapleton); and Fairfax County, Virginia (Laurel Hill Park) will arise through developer exactions (Great Park Conservancy, 2005; Orange County Great Park, 2006; Coangelo, 2005; Denver City Council, 1998; *Denver Post Corporation v. Stapleton Development Corporation*, 2000; EDAW, 2003). A large park being planned for Staten Island, New York (Fresh Kills Park), will result from landfill conversion (Department of City Planning, 2003a, 2003b). Although these locales are developing gigantic urban parks that will dwarf the likes of historic parks like Central Park, Prospect Park, and Franklin Park (Boston), these new parks will not be among the largest urban parks. There are currently in existence 12 city parks that range in size from the 5,554-acre Unstead State Park in Raleigh, North Carolina, to the 495,996-acre Chugach State Park in Anchorage Alaska. In addition, there are 69 urban parks that are between 1,000 and 5,000 acres in size (TPL, 2006; Swope, 2003).

Some of the new parks are made possible because of the closure of military bases, airports, prisons, and landfills. Even in these newer parks, Central Park's design and funding structure is still influencing how they are being built and operated. However, these new urban parks, coaxed from defunct, recycled industrial landscapes, are pushing the boundaries – they are coming up with new variations of public–private comanagement partnership arrangements for funding and managing urban parks. The parks are also redefining the concept of "park" and how space is used within. They are multipurpose spaces that serve recreational functions. However, they reserve space for housing, commercial facilities, educational use, and farming among other things. Typically residential communities, schools, and commercial buildings are tucked away amid green space. In addition to recycling industrial land and structures, these new parks are also at the cutting edge of adopting green technologies into their design and operation.

These parks are also breaking with tradition in that the work of designing, building, managing, and maintaining these parks are being completely outsourced by cities. City parks departments have virtually nothing to do with the design and management of these parks. Instead, corporations and corporate leaders have significant influence over the development of these parks. The financing of these parks rests heavily on property taxes (residential and commercial) and user fees (for activities like golf). This is a kind of benefits assessments that residents of developments to which parks are attached seem comfortable paying – they know before purchasing homes in a subdivision that part of their taxes will go toward developing open space that will benefit them and their neighbors. In these park developments, park advocates focus on minimizing city funding or raising funds from individual donations.

CONCLUSION

During the nineteenth century, wealthy businessmen helped to spearhead the development of Central Park. Today, the development and administration of Central Park is still being driven by wealthy corporate executives. As was the case in the mid-nineteenth century, models of design, development, and management pioneered in Central Park have been replicated around the country. However, in some of the newest urban park, corporate control over park development and management has gone to greater extremes than is evident in Central Park. In places such as Stapleton and Orange County, citizens have already raised concerns about lack of public input and oversight into park affairs.

The question of access remains a major concern. Not only are critics raising questions about access to park planning and management processes that are increasingly controlled by wealthy executives and corporations, they also worry about access to parks in poor and minority communities. The shift to private partnerships has left parks for which corporate campaigns are not viable in the dust. Cities and friends of the parks groups identify and focus on parks for which they can fund-raise effectively while ignoring parks for which fund-raising is most challenging. Already, minority environmental justice activists are campaigning for the development of new parks in their neighborhoods. As they contend, it is not just a matter of maintaining existing parks adequately, some neighborhoods lacked adequate park space to begin with. With the tightening of city government budgets and the general trend of moving away from the commitment to providing public park space for urban dwellers, it will be increasingly difficult for underserved inner-city neighborhoods to see new parks being developed in their section of cities. This means that urban residents have to become involved in park affairs. They have to pay greater attention to park budget and financing issues. If cities follow Detroit's lead, then low-income minority communities will not only have to contend with inadequate park facilities, they might also face the prospects of real decline in open space as they watch parks in their neighborhoods being put up for sale.

Urban parks are still evolving and, as such, it is likely that new models of financing will emerge. The emergence of new parks arising from developer exactions indicate a shift to parks with multiuse spaces serving various recreational, business, educational, cultural, and residential functions. Given the state of city parks budgets, it seems likely that new park developments will involve some level of public–private partnerships in the future. As such, park financing will remain a relevant and controversial issue for some time to come.

NOTES

1. For a detailed account of the rise of urban parks and the financing of them, see Taylor (2009).
2. Unlike the crowded downtown cemeteries that were the norm, during the nineteenth century, developers began building elegant, spacious, park-like land-scaped cemeteries with family plots.
3. See *Journal of Commerce* (1851b) for slightly different estimates of park acreage and value.
4. The Wallace-Reader's Digest Funds have committed $25 million to create and restore urban parks.
5. In the wake of the World Trade Center bombing, one-fourth of the money raised was sent to New York for the police and firefighters fund.
6. In 2006, tickets to the Halloween Ball ranged from $1,000 to $50,000 (Central Park Conservancy, 2006c).

REFERENCES

Baltimore City Department of Recreation and Parks. (2006). *Annual report fiscal year 2006.* Baltimore, MD: Baltimore City Department of Recreation and Parks.

Beveridge, C. E., & Rocheleau, P. (1998). *Frederick law Olmsted: Designing the American landscape.* New York: Universe.

Beveridge, C. E., & Schuyler, D. (1983). *The papers of Frederick law Olmstead (III): Creating central park, 1857–1961.* Baltimore, MD: Johns Hopkins University Press.

Bisbee, D. (2001). Hub benefit swing into fall to aid parks and N.Y. *The Boston Herald*, September 24.

Blackmar, E. (1989). *Manhattan for rent: 1785–1850*. Ithaca, NY: Cornell University Press.

Bridges, A. (1984). *A city in the republic: Antebellum New York and the origins of machine politics*. New York: Cambridge University Press.

Bryant, W. C. (1844). A new park. *New York Evening Post*, July.

Bumiller, E. (2001). Deal allows Clinton to lease space he wants in Harlem. *The New York Times*, February, p. 6.

Bunce, O. B. (1874). New York and Brooklyn. In: W. C. Bryant (Ed.), *Picturesque America; or, the land we live in* (p. 549). New York: D. Appleton and Company.

Burrows, E. G., & Wallace, M. (1999). *Gotham: A history of New York City to 1898*. New York: Oxford University Press.

Central Park Conservancy. (2001). *Annual report*. New York: Central Park Conservancy.

Central Park Conservancy. (2002). *Annual report*. New York: Central Park Conservancy.

Central Park Conservancy. (2003a). *Central Park: Then and now*. New York: Central Park Conservancy.

Central Park Conservancy. (2003b). *Annual report*. New York: Central Park Conservancy.

Central Park Conservancy. (2004). *Annual report*. New York: Central Park Conservancy.

Central Park Conservancy. (2005). *Annual report*. New York: Central Park Conservancy.

Central Park Conservancy. (2006a). *The gift of a lifetime*. New York: Central Park Conservancy.

Central Park Conservancy. (2006b). *Central Park Conservancy: Support CPC*. New York: Central Park Conservancy.

Central Park Conservancy. (2006c). *Halloween ball 2006*. New York: Central Park Conservancy.

Central Park Conservancy. (2006d). *About the Central Park Conservancy*. New York: Central Park Conservancy.

Chadwick, G. F. (1966). *The park and the town: Public landscapes in the nineteenth and 20th century*. New York: Praeger.

Charity Navigator. (2006). *Charity Navigator rating*. Mahwah, NJ: Charity Navigator.

Chicago Park District. (2007). *2008 Chicago Park District appropriations*. Chicago, IL: Chicago Park District.

Child, L. M. (1843). *Letters from New York*. New York: Charles S. Francis & Company.

Citizens Budget Commission. (2007). *Making the most of our parks* (September). New York: Citizens Budget Commission.

City of Boston. (1990). *Boston Common management plan*. Boston, MA: Boston Parks and Recreation Commission.

Coangelo, L. L. (2005). NYC mayor unveils park plan near Staten Island landfill. *Daily News*, August 23.

Cohen, P. E., & Augustyn, R. T. (1997). *Manhattan in maps: 1527–1995*. New York: Rizzoli International Publications, Inc.

Cook, C. C. (1854). New York daguerrotyped. Private residences. *Putman's Monthly*, 3(March), 247–248.

Cranz, G. (1982). *The politics of park design: A history of urban parks in America*. Cambridge, MA: MIT Press.

Cunningham, B. (2001). Abloom in the park. *The New York Times*, May 6, p. 50.

Denver City Council. (1998). *A bill for an ordinance approving a proposed agreement between the City and County of Denver and Stapleton Development Corporation concerning the master lease and disposition agreement* (July 2). Denver, CO: Denver City Council.

Denver Post Corporation v. Stapleton Development Corporation. (2000). 19P.3d 36, & 2000 Colo. App. November 24, 2.

Department of City Planning. (2003a). *Fresh Kills: Landfill to landscape.* New York: Department of City Planning.

Department of City Planning. (2003b). *Mayor Michael R. Bloomberg kicks off the transformation of Fresh Kills in Staten Island* (September). New York: Department of City Planning.

Downing, A. J. (1848). A talk about public parks and gardens. *Rural Essays,* October, pp. 138–146.

Downing, A. J. (1851a). The New York park. *Rural Essays,* August, pp. 147–153.

Downing, A. J. (1851b). The New York park. *Horticulturist,* August 8, pp. 345–349.

Dunn, M. M., & Dunn, R. S. (1982). The founding, 1681–1701. In: R. F. Weigley (Ed.), *Philadelphia: A 300-year history* (pp. 1–32). New York: W. W. Norton & Company.

EDAW. (2003). *Laurel Hill draft park conceptual plan* (July 8). Fairfax, VA: EDAW.

Edozien, F. (2008). Parks may 'name' price for biz labels. *New York Post,* January 28.

El Puente. (2008). History and mission. Available at http://elpuente.us/organization/index.htm. Retrieved on January 28, 2008.

Emerald Necklace Conservancy. (2007). *Join us.* Brookline, MA: Emerald Necklace Conservancy.

Endicott. (1842). *Map of the Croton water pipes with the stop cocks* [Uncolored lithograph]. Endicott, cartographer. New York: New-York Historical Society. 13 3/4 × 10 1/2 inches.

Fairmount Park Conservancy. (2007). *Support your park.* Philadelphia, PA: Fairmount Park Conservancy.

Forest Park Forever. (2007). *Park history.* St. Louis, MO: Forest Park Forever.

Forever Park. (2007). *Support forever park.* San Diego, CA: Forever Park.

Friends of Garfield Park. (2007). *Friends of Garfield Park: Become a friend.* Indianapolis, IN: Friends of Garfield Park.

Friends of the Public Garden. (2006). *Accomplishments.* Boston, MA: Friends of the Public Garden.

Garfield Park Conservatory Alliance. (2007). *Support us.* Chicago, IL: Garfield Park Conservatory Alliance.

Getlin, J. (2001). Deal permits Clinton to get Harlem office space. *Los Angeles Times,* February 17, p. 14.

Golden Gate National Parks Conservancy. (2007a). *Support the parks.* San Francisco, CA: Golden Gate National Parks Conservancy.

Golden Gate National Parks Conservancy. (2007b). *Parks for all forever.* San Francisco, CA: Golden Gate National Parks Conservancy.

Gorchow, Z. (2007). Detroit seeks to sell off 92 parks. *Detroit Free Press,* October 26.

Great Park Conservancy. (2005). *News from the park: The jewel of orange county* (November 4). Irvine, CA: Great Park Conservancy.

Great Plains Trail Network. (2007). *Membership.* Lincoln, NE: Great Plains Trail Network.

Greater Newark Conservancy. (2007). *Support us.* Newark, NJ: Greater Newark Conservancy.

Harden, B. (1999). Neighbors give Central Park a wealthy glow. *The New York Times,* November 22, p. 1.

Harnik, P. (1998). *Local parks, local financing, 2.* San Francisco, CA: Trust for Public Land.

Harnik, P., Taylor, M., & Welle, B. (2006). *From dumps to destination: The conversion of landfills to parks.* San Francisco, CA: Trust for Public Land.

Harnik, P., & Yaffe, L. (2006). *Who is going to pay for this park?* San Francisco, CA: Trust for Public Land.

Hermann Park Conservancy. (2007). *Donate to the conservancy.* Houston, TX: Hermann Park Conservancy.

Homberger, E. (2002). *Mrs. Astor's New York: Money and social power in a gilded age.* New Haven, CT: Yale University Press.

Hopper, K. (1998). *Local parks, local financing, 1.* San Francisco, CA: Trust for Public Land.

Hunt, R. M. (1866). *Designs for the gateways of Southern entrances of the central park.* New York: Commissioners of the Central Park.

Jackson, K. T., & Dunbar, D. S. (2002). *Empire city: New York through the centuries.* New York: Columbia University Press.

Knox Greenway Coalition. (2007). *Greenways 5K run.* Knoxville, TN: Knox Greenway Coalition.

Lipton, E. (2001). City rejects the first two offers for Clinton's Harlem office site. *New York Times,* February 15, p. 8.

Louisville Olmsted Parks Conservancy. (2007). *Get involved.* Louisville, KY: Louisville Olmsted Parks.

Macieski, R. L. (2005). Cities and suburbs. In: B. Feintuch & D. H. Watters (Eds), *The encyclopedia of New England* (p. 188). New Haven, CT: Yale University Press.

Madden, K., Myrick, P., Brower, K., Secunda, S., & Schwartz, A. (2000). *Public parks, private partners: How partnerships are revitalizing urban parks.* New York: Project for Public Spaces.

Matthews Neilsen Landscape Architects, PC. (2006). *South Bronx greenway.* New York: Matthews Neilsen Landscape Architects.

Maymont Foundation. (2007). *Support Maymont.* Richmond, VA: Maymont Foundation.

McNulty, E. (1999). *Boston then & now.* San Diego, CA: Thunder Bay Press.

Minturn, R. (1851). Letter to James W. Beekman. James W. Beekman Papers. New York Historical Society, New York, June 23.

Minturn, R. B. (1871). *Memoir of Robert Bowne Minturn.* New York: A. D. F. Randolph and Company.

National AIDS Memorial Grove. (2007). *Support, ensure and remember.* San Francisco, CA: National AIDS Memorial Grove.

National Park and Recreation Association. (2006). *NRPA advances urban park and recreation agenda* (May 18). Ashburn, VA: NRPA.

National Park Service. (2007). Urban park & recreation recovery: Program in brief. Available at http://www.nps.gov/ncrc/programs/uprr/program_inbrief.html. Retrieved on January 25, 2007.

National Parks and Recreation Association. (2003). The ABCs of UPAAR: The nuts and bolts of the Urban Park and Recreation Recovery Program – history: UPARR at 25. *Parks & Recreation,* January.

Odendahl, T. (1990). *Charity begins at home: Generosity and self interest among the philanthropic elite.* New York: Basic Books.

Oglebay Foundation. (2006). *Park history.* Wheeling, WV: Oglebay Foundation.

Olmsted, F. L. (1865). *Preliminary report upon the Yosemite and big tree grove*. Library of Congress, Papers of Frederic Law Olmsted, Washington, DC.

Olmsted, F. L. (1870). *Public parks and the enlargement of towns*. Cambridge, MA: Riverside Press.

Orange County Great Park. (2006). *News details: Great Park master designer selected*. Irvine, CA: Orange County Great Park.

Ostrower, F. (1995). *Why the wealthy give: The culture of elite philanthropy*. Princeton, NJ: Princeton University Press.

Parks Foundation. (2007). *Cincinnati Parks Foundation*. Cincinnati, OH: City of Cincinnati.

ParkWorks. (2007). *Help us*. Cleveland, OH: ParkWorks.

Piedmont Park Conservancy. (2007). *Support the park*. Atlanta, GA: Piedmont Park Conservancy.

Prime, R. (1851). Letter to James W. Beekman. James W. Beekman Papers. New York Historical Society, New York, June 23.

Project for Public Spaces. (2003). *New York city parks: Thriving in tough times. Making places* (May). New York: Project for Public Spaces.

Prospect Park Alliance. (2002). *Annual report*. Brooklyn, NY: Prospect Park Alliance.

Prospect Park Alliance. (2003a). *Help the park*. Brooklyn, NY: Prospect Park Alliance.

Prospect Park Alliance. (2003b). *About park and alliance: President's message* (Summer). Brooklyn, NY: Prospect Park Alliance.

Prospect Park Alliance. (2003c). *Annual report*. Brooklyn, NY: Prospect Park Alliance.

Prospect Park Alliance. (2005). *Annual report*. Brooklyn, NY: Prospect Park Alliance.

Prospect Park Alliance. (2007). *Get involved*. Brooklyn, NY: Prospect Park Alliance.

Riis, J. A. (1890). *How the other half lives*. New York: Penguin.

Riverside Park Fund. (2006). *Riverside Park*. New York: Riverside Park Fund.

Rogers, E. B. (1987). *Rebuilding Central Park: A management and restoration plan*. Cambridge, MA: The MIT Press.

Rogers, E. B. (2004). *Making partnership work: The Central Park model*. New York: Project for Public Spaces.

Rosenzweig, R., & Blackmar, E. (1992). *The park and the people: A history of Central Park*. Ithaca, NY: Cornell University Press.

San Francisco Bulletin. (1900). November 3.

San Francisco Park Commission. (1897). *Report*. San Francisco Park Commission, San Francisco, CA, pp. 18–19.

San Francisco Parks Trust. (2007). *History and accomplishments*. San Francisco, CA: San Francisco Parks Trust.

Saulny, S. (2007). Detroit considers selling small parks. *The New York Times*, December 29.

Scherzer, K. A. (1995). St. John's park. In: K. T. Jackson (Ed.), *The encyclopedia of New York city* (p. 1035). New Haven: Yale University Press.

Schiff, J. A. (1981). The social history of new haven. In: F. Shumway & R. Hegel (Eds), *New Haven: An illustrated history* (p. 104). Woodland Hills: Windsor Publications, Inc.

Schuyler, D. (1986). *The new urban landscape: The redefinition of city form in nineteenth-century America*. Baltimore, MD: Johns Hopkins University Press.

Scobey, D. M. (2002). *Empire city: The making and meaning of the New York City landscape*. Baltimore, MD: Temple University Press.

Sedgwick, C. M. (1841). *Letters from abroad to kindred at home*. New York: Harper.

Shand-Tucci, D. (1999). *Built in Boston: City and suburb, 1800–2000*. Cambridge, MA: The MIT Press.
Sletcher, M. (2004). *New Haven: From Puritanism to the age of terrorism*. Charleston, SC: Arcadia Publishing.
South Suburban Park Foundation. (2007). *Current events*. Littleton, CO: South Suburban Park Foundation.
Spann, E. K. (1981). *The new metropolis: New York City, 1840–1857*. New York: Columbia University Press.
Stewart, B. (2000). College president to lead Central Park Conservancy. *The New York Times*, December 1, p. 6.
St. John's park. (1845). *The Subterranean*, *3*(July 26), 2.
Sustainable South Bronx. (2008). *South Bronx residents have far less open space and waterfront access than other parts of NYC*. New York: Sustainable South Bronx.
Swope, C. (2003). Green giants: Fortuitous land windfalls have given some cities the opportunity to create huge urban parks – and debate their design. *Governing Magazine*, December.
Taylor, D. E. (1999). Central Park as a model for social control: Urban parks, social class and leisure behavior in nineteenth-century America. *Journal of Leisure Research, 31*(4), 420–477.
Taylor, D. E. (2009). *The environment and the people in American cities: 1600s–1900s. Disorder, inequality and social change*. Durham, NC: Duke University Press.
Taylor, H. A. (1995). Urban public parks, 1840–1900: Design and meaning. *Garden History, 23*(2), 201–221.
The Battery Conservancy. (2007). *About the conservancy*. New York: The Battery Conservancy.
The East River park. (1851b). *Journal of Commerce*, June 5, p. 2.
The Friends of Buttonwood Park. (2007). *The friends of Buttonwood Park*. New Bedford, MA: The Friends of Buttonwood Park.
The Greening of Detroit. (2007). *Get involved*. Detroit, MI: The Greening of Detroit.
The middle park. (1853). *The New York Times*, June 23, p. 4.
The proposed Great Park. (1851a). *Journal of Commerce*, June 24, p. 2.
Tiemann, D. (1852). Letter to James W. Beekman. James W. Beekman Papers. New York Historical Society, New York, February 23.
Trust for Public Land. (2006). *City park facts*. San Francisco, CA: Trust for Public Land.
Veblen, T. (1899). *The theory of the leisure class*. New York: Penguin Books.
Warner, S. B. (2001). A brief history of Boston. In: A. Kreiger & D. Cobb (Eds), *Mapping Boston* (pp. 3–14). Cambridge, MA: The MIT Press.
Wasserman, J., & Herman, E. (2001). Mayor clears the way and Bill's movin' on up. *Daily News*, February 17, p. 4.
WE ACT. (2000). *Harlem on the river planning document* (November 8). New York: WE ACT.
WE ACT. (2002). Earthday 2002 in morningside park. Available at www.weact.org/savethedate/2002/2002_Apr_21.html. Retrieved on January 25, 2007.
WE ACT. (2006). *Official executive summary on Columbia's proposed Manhattanville in West Harlem Zoning and academic mixed-use development environmental impact statement draft scope of work*. New York: WE ACT.
Wilson, J. G., & Fiske, J. (1887–1889). *Appleton's Cyclopedia of American biography*. New York: D. Appleton and Company.

Wolfe, G. R. (1995). Governors Island. In: K. T. Jackson (Ed.), *The encyclopedia of New York city* (p. 493). New York: Yale University Press.

Yakima Greenway Foundation. (2007). *Membership*. Yakima, WA: Yakima Greenway Foundation.

Dorceta E. Taylor is an associate professor at the University of Michigan's School of Natural Resources and Environment. She teaches courses in environmental history, environmental justice, tourism and climate change, and social movements. She is the director of the Multicultural Environmental Leadership Development Initiative (http://www.meldi.snre.umich.edu) and author of *The Environment and the People in American Cities, 1600s–1900s: Disorder, Inequality, and Social Change*. She can be reached by email at dorceta@umich.edu or by telephone at 734-763-5327.

MOVEMENTS, NEIGHBORHOOD CHANGE, AND THE MEDIA – NEWSPAPER COVERAGE OF ANTI-GENTRIFICATION ACTIVITY IN THE SAN FRANCISCO BAY AREA: 1995–2005

June Gin and Dorceta E. Taylor

ABSTRACT

Purpose – *This chapter examines the factors that influence the ability of anti-gentrification movements to get media coverage for their core policy goals. It takes, as a point of departure, the suggestion that the media supports the growth machine and is not inclined to provide favorable coverage to movements trying to limit development.*

Design/methodology/approach – *In comparing six newspapers' coverage of anti-gentrification movements in San Francisco's Mission District and West Oakland, we suggest a more nuanced theoretical understanding of media coverage of urban movements against development. The analysis of newspaper articles published in six Bay Area newspapers from 1995 to 2005 illustrates tremendous variations in favorability of coverage between the two movements.*

Environment and Social Justice: An International Perspective
Research in Social Problems and Public Policy, Volume 18, 75–114
Copyright © 2010 by Emerald Group Publishing Limited
All rights of reproduction in any form reserved
ISSN: 0196-1152/doi:10.1108/S0196-1152(2010)0000018005

Findings – *There are also large variations in the extent to which movements' core policy goals are represented in newspaper articles. Although the Mission District received more coverage than the West Oakland movement, the West Oakland movement was better able in getting its core policy goals into its coverage than the Mission District movement. The West Oakland movement was more effective in generating media attention for its core policy goals through its organized public protests than the Mission District movement.*

Originality/value – *This chapter adds to the genre of research analyzing newspaper coverage of social movements. It demonstrates that the coverage is more nuanced than previously reported. Factors such as phase in the movement and the framing of the issues are related to whether the media covers the story in a negative or positive manner.*

INTRODUCTION

In recent years, environmental justice activists and scholars have begun to examine the detrimental effects of inequality on regional metropolitan sustainability. Policymakers and activists have raised questions about whether residents of disadvantaged communities bear the burdens of growth without receiving its benefits, and researchers have responded with greater attention to possible inequities that might accrue from development (Glickfeld, Levine, & Fulton, 1996; Orfield, 1997). Growing numbers of scholars have argued that the costs and benefits of growth are not shared equitably (Dubin, 1993; Logan & Molotch, 1987; Warner, 2001). High concentrations of low-income minority populations currently living in cities and inner-ring suburbs further increase the likelihood that disparities in the spatial distribution of costs and benefits will arise.

This process is described in Harvey Molotch's (1976) essay, "The City as a Growth Machine," which suggested that land-use intensification in cities is driven by a group of local land-based elites who build upon, and directly benefit from, civic support for urban growth. These elites, including business people, local financial institutions, property owners, and neighborhood associations, typically shape social, economic, and political forces so as to generate a consensus supporting urban growth in the region. This dynamic, known as the "growth machine," provides a framework for understanding some of the mechanisms by which urban growth processes reproduce conditions such as pollution and congestion, whose costs are largely borne by populations that are the least able to absorb them (Gibson, 2004; Logan & Molotch, 1987; Molotch, 1976). Thus, the "growth machine," driven by municipal elites mainly interested in maximizing exchange values or profits associated with land use, enjoys significant political advantages over opponents, namely planners, community groups, and environmental interests who prefer more carefully regulated urban development.

An environmental justice perspective also helps to orient this analysis. This perspective suggests that particular attention be paid to the unequal distribution of the costs and benefits of urban growth. Consequently, activist organizations have emerged around the country to address issues of equitable development, including the First Suburbs Coalition in Cleveland, PolicyLink, and Urban Habitat in the San Francisco Bay Area. In addition, a growing number of neighborhoods such as the residents living around the Staples Center in Los Angeles, the area around the Detroit intermodal freight terminal, the Park East neighborhood of Denver, the Park East neighborhood of Milwaukee, and Inglewood and Lennox in Los Angeles are negotiating community benefits agreements with corporations and developers interested in locating buildings and facilities in their communities (Larsen, 2009; Pellow, 2001).

These trends lead us to ask: how effective are low-income and minority communities and their supporters in advocating greater equity in local land use and development decisions? Low-income and minority community residents typically lack the political resources and are often excluded from decision- and policy-making processes in their communities. The media offers an important venue for these groups to get their perspectives onto the public agenda and is often a critical stepping stone for activists to gain access to and influence these processes (McCarthy, Smith, & Zald, 1996). It is thus important to social movement activists to attract the media's attention and get their issues covered. However, they must do more. Activists must also frame their issues to the media persuasively so that their viewpoints will be represented in a positive light. However, obtaining favorable media coverage remains a challenge for those trying to draw public attention to equity issues within urban development (Gibson, 2004; McCarthy et al., 1996; Molotch, 1979; Gamson, 1992).

This essay examines media coverage of anti-gentrification movements in two different neighborhoods in the San Francisco Bay Area – San Francisco's Mission District and West Oakland. These movements advocate equitable development, affordable housing, and other measures to prevent residential displacement, often opposing high-end development projects in the process. As examples of efforts to counter the growth machine in low-income minority communities, they offer an opportunity to examine the ability of local activists to accomplish the important task of getting their policy message into the public arena through the media.

Despite the importance of media access to activists' success, there has been little focus on the types of movements that will foster their ability to acquire beneficial media coverage. This chapter seeks to rectify this gap by examining the nature of media coverage that these movements received, and how differences in movement conditions and characteristics may have led to different media coverage. Following a short description of the movements, the analysis focuses on the relative effectiveness of these two groups of movement activists in gaining newspaper coverage for their policy goals. It examines the amount of newspaper coverage provided, the favorability of that coverage, and the extent to which core movement policy goals are represented in news articles.

THE MEDIA

Although media coverage has been a significant focus of social movement research (Earl, Martin, McCarthy, & Soule, 2004; Jenkins & Perrow, 1977; Lewis, 2000; McCarthy et al., 1996), little attention has been paid to coverage of urban development controversies. Only recently has the media's coverage of urban growth become a serious subject of scholarly examination. Scholars find that media coverage may not always represent the perspectives of growth opponents. More often than not, media coverage gives the impression that there is little or no opposition to development, that consensus has been reached that development projects will be unequivocally beneficial (Gibson, 2004; Lewis, 2000; Logan & Molotch, 1987; Molotch, 1979). Logan and Molotch (1987) describe the historically critical role the *San Jose Mercury*, the *Los Angeles Times*, and the *New York Times* played in advocating the urbanization of their respective local metropolises in their news coverage and editorials.

In a study of major Seattle newspapers' coverage of a local development controversy, Gibson (2004) found that newspapers take a "consensus" approach to cover development, quoting business sources in 49.3 percent of the 679 articles published; nonprofits in 11.8 percent and citizens/academics in 7.5 percent of the articles (Gibson, 2004). Scholars have also found a similar pattern in international politics. In a study of themes of newspaper articles on sustainable development over 10 years, Lewis (2000) found that U.S. newspapers produce discourses that legitimate mainstream growth-oriented development and marginalize alternative forms of development. She found that these papers tend to promote a U.S. corporate-driven, growth-oriented political ideology that marginalizes grassroots efforts toward non-growth-oriented development in developing countries (Lewis, 2000).

Despite the importance of media coverage in framing urban growth issues and the challenges supporters of equitable development face in obtaining coverage for their viewpoints, we know little about the conditions under which activists are most effective in their quest. This chapter examines the extent to which supporters of equitable development in low income, predominantly minority neighborhoods are able to get media coverage that reflect their perspectives on the issues they are trying to influence.

Harvey Molotch's essay on media and movements offers a heuristic to help us understand the difficulties that social movements face in their efforts to access the media (Molotch, 1979). Although the media is an important resource for movements to convey their messages and engage in agenda setting, they must contend with the media's goals that tend to support status quo institutions. According to Molotch, the media cover social movements for two basic reasons: (1) the movement generates enough publicity through its tactics to be perceived as a viable challenge to the status quo that the media must provide information about so that the authorities can deal with them accordingly; (2) the media is able to successfully make the case that the movement's critique highlights very real threats to existing institutional legitimacy. Hence, the media, which thrive on reporting on spectacles and other potential threats to the status quo, is less likely to cover more complex aspects of a movement's issue positions than radical confrontational protest tactics (Molotch, 1979).

Social movement scholars argue that the media does not always cover social protest accurately, reproducing social perspectives that represent the same status quo that social movements often seek to change (Earl et al., 2004; Gamson, 1992). The news industry, as a whole, makes it difficult for movements whose core message may be more complex than meets the eye to get those messages accurately reported in media coverage. Moreover, news reports tend to be fragmented, so that issues and events that are related are not presented as being connected to one another (Gamson, Croteau, Hoynes, & Sasson, 1992).

Media critics cite the "political economy" of news, wherein the increased routinization of news production is transforming the process into one where profit motives have gained influence in driving news content (Gamson, 1992). Movements promoting equitable development and opposing gentrification are trying to protect neighborhoods for residents who use urban spaces to carry out basic life functions such as home, work, and leisure. These movements face another obstacle – the media's vested interest in supporting growth, particularly in locations where profits from land use or exchange values have yet to be fully realized. In such neighborhoods, the notion of the "highest and best use" of land tends to favor the growth of institutions catering to the business and consumption interests of more affluent users. Thus, groups supporting equitable development face an uphill battle in getting their perspectives favorably covered in the media (Smith, 1996; Smith & Williams, 1986; Logan & Molotch, 1987).

As the preceding discussion implies, the media tends to favor the promotion of development and increased intensification of land use while opposing barriers to growth. Indeed, the media is considered a key player within the growth machine. This is particularly true of newspaper owners, editors, and reporters, who have a stake in promoting growth and increasing investment in the metropolitan region so as to increase their own readership and local relevance. The media often engages in civic boosterism, that is, portraying the city as an attractive place for investment. Despite claims of impartiality, the media is not generally considered an honest broker when it comes to mediating growth controversies. Although the media can evoke neutrality to enhance the credibility, observations and analyses of media coverage often find that news reporting is not always neutral (Logan & Molotch, 1987; Molotch, 1976).

Poor and minority communities are at a resource disadvantage, and they find it very difficult to argue for preserving their neighborhood institutions – including housing projects, corner markets, and other cultural establishments that often depress property values and discourage outside investment (Logan & Molotch, 1987). This makes it difficult for poor and minority communities to master the media game. The media's "consensus" frame around development erases discussion of dissent over growth, opting instead to cover these issues from the perspective of business interests. This practice marginalizes the arguments of growth opponents who focus on the impacts of development (such as traffic, noise, infrastructure costs, air quality) and express concerns about equity, affordable housing, environmental quality, social diversity, and democratic participation (Gibson, 2004) in the media's coverage.

This bias exists because the political and business elite, including developers, major retailers, and other financial entities have greater "symbolic capital" in the eyes of the media than the community activists and non-profit organizations that often make up the movements advocating alternative urban visions. Local activists are hard pressed to match the level of prestige and legitimacy accorded to growth proponents when the media perceives business groups as "experts" on urban development and revitalization issues. It is difficult for community groups to compete for media attention with the considerable power and political advantages that business interests enjoy (Gibson, 2004, p. 299; Logan & Molotch, 1987).

The literature suggests that movements against urban development, particularly in disinvested urban neighborhoods, face a considerable task in getting their perspectives into the media. The challenge involves framing their political grievances in a way that identifies the problem and creates a compelling call for reform to ameliorate the problem (Benford & Snow, 2000; Croteau & Hicks, 2003; Gamson, 1992; Snow & Benford, 1992). Framing is critical to the environmental justice movement, as themes of injustice, civil rights, and shared identity became the lens through which environmental issues were viewed (Jones & Carter, 1994; Taylor, 2000). Thus, a major task of the environmental justice movement is to reframe these problems by calling into question established assumptions about the fairness of established systems.

Framing is the process of presenting claims in such a way as to highlight certain facts while rendering other facts invisible or irrelevant (Ryan & Gamson, 2006). Because social movement frames are "challenger frames" that seek to counter the "dominant frame" on issues, they face special difficulties in gaining access to favorable media coverage (Ryan, 1991). Because "challenger frames," unlike "dominant frames," articulate perspectives that take issue with the ideologies of the media and other established institutions, they have less access to the media than do their opponents. Unlike dominant frames, challenger frames must present information that the media is not familiar with, organized around political assumptions that are foreign to the media.

For movements able to get their frames – specifically their concerns about the impacts of development – into news stories, increased media's attention toward the issue helps confer a sense of legitimacy toward their goals of influencing policy. Movement success in media framing can parlay the opening of the media's "political windows" (Kingdon, 1984) to shift the public debate and make the case for change.

Although the case for business-driven development is one frame favored in the media, growth opponents must articulate an alternative frame to counter that dominant frame. The process of movement framing in the media is contentious, as the issue of whose interpretation and perception of reality matters, and therefore is covered and represented, is at stake

(Ryan, 1991). Hence, the challenge for such movements is to reframe the core issues within land use policy debates as issues of affordable housing, social diversity, democratic decision-making, and environmental justice.

Examining the media coverage of movements is an important way to evaluate activists' effectiveness at infusing their ideas into the public consciousness and integrating their frames into the public agenda. Media discourse is thus an outcome, wherein the media becomes a "site of struggle over the definition of social reality" (Gamson et al., 1992). However, there has been less work on the factors that make some movements more effective in getting their frames into the media. If movements opposing development do, in fact, face power disadvantages in their efforts to access media agendas, then under what conditions, if any, can such movements achieve success?

NEIGHBORHOOD RESPONSE TO GENTRIFICATION

This chapter examines two Bay Area communities to see how activists used the media to disseminate their political message and to evaluate their effectiveness in doing so. The story begins during the "dot-com" boom of the late 1990s to early 2000s, when the region experienced a tremendous period of economic growth and investment associated with the information technology and computer industry. During this period, $7.5 billion of venture capital – 37.5 percent of the $20 billion in venture capital investments invested globally – was invested in Bay Area businesses, according to major investment indices (Cavenaugh, Taylor, & Wood, 2001; Guynn, December 12, 2006).

Despite the boom, the region's low-income communities of color did not receive many of the benefits of the increased investment. Rather, this period of economic prosperity exacerbated the pre-existing housing shortage in the area. This trend created concerns about residential displacement in disadvantaged urban neighborhoods that suddenly became attractive to developers as demand for commercial and upscale residential development skyrocketed. Consequently, when Urban Habitat, a Bay Area environmental justice organization, held its first Leadership Institute in 1999, the 16 community leaders participating identified "gentrification," the displacement of low-income residents as neighborhoods are renovated for higher-income residents, as the most pressing issue within their communities (Yee & Quiroz-Martinez, 1999).

The term "gentrification" was first coined in 1964 by British sociologist Ruth Glass to describe patterns of residential turnover in working-class neighborhoods in London where professionals had moved in, renovated homes, and created a shortage of affordable housing (Glass, 1964; Smith & Williams, 1986). In the San Francisco Bay Area, urban communities that historically housed people who would otherwise have difficulty finding a foothold elsewhere because of their income, race, or ethnicity were suddenly, after decades of disinvestment, rediscovered for their amenities that were previously overlooked. Such neighborhoods were close to business centers, had views of the Bay, access to transit hubs, and cultural diversity (Yee & Quiroz-Martinez, 1999).

Gentrification issues are intimately connected to environmental justice, as community stability and access to neighborhoods are at stake. They are also the quintessential case of the growth machine in action. Since disinvested urban areas are the places where rehabilitation is most profitable, they are particularly vulnerable to development pressures. Therefore, the low-income and minority residents of these places are likely to be concerned about displacement and the effects of development on their quality of life.

Leaders in San Francisco's Mission District and West Oakland (Map 1), both historically low-income neighborhoods that serve as centers of ethnic culture, have mobilized residents in efforts to prevent gentrification and displacement in their communities. The Mission District has been the heart of the Latino community in San Francisco since the 1950s. It is a neighborhood where working class immigrants and artists live adjacent to downtown San Francisco. Many nonprofit organizations are also located in this neighborhood. As concerns about gentrification and displacement grew, five community organizations in the Mission District joined forces to form the Mission Anti-Displacement Coalition (MAC) in May 2000, a collaborative that emerged out of their noontime lunch meetings on the issue.

Concerns about gentrification and displacement also surfaced in similar neighborhoods across the Bay. West Oakland is a historically African-American neighborhood that suffered from urban decline from the 1960s through the 1980s, when the region lost much of its manufacturing jobs. Now, the neighborhood is experiencing a renaissance driven by new residents seeking housing, a resurgence of investment capital for transit-oriented and infill development, the opening of the new Mandela commercial corridor in the footprint of the earthquake-damaged Cypress Freeway, and the subsidence of the wave of crime associated with the crack-cocaine epidemic of the 1980s. As with the Mission District, housing costs have risen dramatically there, spurring concerns about displacement.

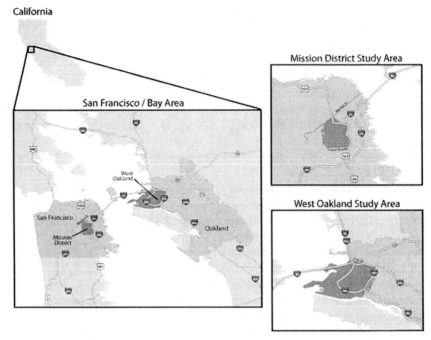

Map 1.   Mission District and West Oakland Neighborhoods in California.

To deal with these issues, six local organizations initiated a set of loosely affiliated efforts in 1998 to organize efforts to prevent the displacement of low-income residents due to gentrification.

RESEARCH DESIGN AND METHODOLOGY

This chapter takes a comparative approach in examining the two case studies. It focuses on each movement's respective ability to get its frames into the media. The Mission District and West Oakland are both located in the San Francisco Bay Area and thus experience similar development and housing pressures. However, they mobilized in different contexts, with little contact or collaboration between them. For the purposes of this study, they are treated as two different community movements. By examining them in a comparative framework, one can begin to analyze their coverage in the media. Are there differences in the media's coverage of these movements, and how can these differences be understood or explained? To answer these questions, three key aspects of media coverage will be examined: the amount of coverage the media provides of each movement, whether the coverage was favorable or unfavorable in its portrayal of the movement, and the extent to which the movements' core frames got into the media coverage.

A multi-method approach that employed both qualitative and quantitative techniques was used to explore these questions. Participant observation fieldwork was conducted from 2002 to 2003 in community organizations in both the Mission District and West Oakland. Documents were also collected up until 2007 to keep abreast of movement developments. Formal structured interviews as well as unstructured interviews were conducted with activists in both movements from 2002 to 2004. The information collected from participant observation and preliminary background interviews was used to identify the core activists for formal interviews and to develop a structured interview schedule. Using this schedule, interviews ranging from 45 minutes to an hour-and-a-half long were conducted with 16 core activists in the Mission District and 14 in West Oakland. Activists were asked about their understanding of gentrification and neighborhood change. They were also asked to explain the strategies they used to get other people to participate, get media coverage, influence the political debate, and get progress on their desired policy outcomes. Data on the activists' frames were collected from the structured interviews. The interview data were analyzed using NVIVO textual analysis software.

Newspaper articles were also examined in this study to see how the movements were covered in the press. These articles were collected using Lexis-Nexis. A total of 215 newspaper articles published in six regional newspapers located in the San Francisco Bay Area from 1995 to 2005 were collected and analyzed. Because this project explores the role of local media in weighing in on local development issues, it focused primarily on Bay Area newspapers. However, articles from national newspapers were collected to provide background and perspective on the issues.

These newspapers analyzed three mainstream daily papers – the *San Francisco Chronicle, San Francisco Examiner*, and the *Oakland Tribune*, two weekly alternative newspapers – the *San Francisco Bay Guardian* and *East Bay Express*, and a weekly trade publication – the *San Francisco Business Times*. The articles were read and coded according to the variables being analyzed, such as their portrayal of the movement and their mention of key movement frames, including affordable housing and equitable development. The data were analyzed using SPSS/PASW 18.0 software. In addition to cross-tabulations, chi-square tests were conducted to identify statistically significant relationships.

NEIGHBORHOOD SIMILARITIES AND DIFFERENCES

There are a number of core similarities between these two neighborhoods being studied worth highlighting here. Both of these communities have historically experienced disinvestment, yet in locations that increase, to varying degrees, their attractiveness to development and hence their gentrification pressures. Both of these communities are strategically located on the Bay Area Rapid Transit (BART) high-speed rail lines placing them just minutes from downtown San Francisco's financial center. Both neighborhoods face similar conditions of vulnerability to gentrification due to their proximity to the urban core, their high percent of low-income renters, relatively inexpensive housing stock, desirable type of housing stock (roomy, old Victorian houses) residents' lack of control over the built environment in their communities, and the influx of global capital into the region.

However, there are also variations in the degree to which the respective geographic and political economies of the Mission District and West Oakland fostered gentrification pressures. The Mission District experienced the gentrification phenomenon to a greater extent than West Oakland, largely due to these differences. Although the two neighborhoods are in the same metropolitan area and roughly similar distances to downtown San Francisco, the Mission District lies directly adjacent to downtown San Francisco, whereas West Oakland lies across the Bay from downtown – accessible mainly via the Bay Bridge, BART, and ferries. The South of Market (SOMA) neighborhood adjacent to the Mission was the original site of live-work loft development and the dot-com technology boom beginning in the late 1990s. West Oakland began experiencing the ripple effects of this economic pressure in 2000, when the town of Emeryville, on West Oakland's north border, became an alternative to SOMA, which was becoming more crowded and expensive (Ducker, January 1, 2003).[1] Hence, West Oakland experienced a wave of gentrification somewhat less dramatic, but nonetheless paralleling, that in the Mission District.

These communities share more than economic context. Both neighborhoods have strong histories of political activism around land-use issues dating back to the 1960s. In the Mission District, the Mission Coalition

Organization successfully lobbied for local control over federal Model Cities Project funds in 1968 (Hartman & Carnochan, 2002). That same year, residents of West Oakland's Oak Center neighborhood organized a successful effort to gain control over urban renewal funds and stopped bulldozers from leveling their neighborhood (Rhomberg, 2004). Given this history, and the indigenous institutions and activists still remaining from that era, it was not entirely unexpected for both neighborhoods to organize collective responses to the perceived threat of displacement. Community groups in both locations mobilized against gentrification by advocating affordable housing and community benefits from development.

CORE MOVEMENT FRAMES

An analysis of the ethnographic fieldwork, interviews, documents, and newspaper articles revealed three core movement frames that activists in both communities expressed in their political claims. The first is that of affordable housing. This focused on activists' concerns about the growing shortage of affordable housing, which they linked to gentrification pressures in the neighborhood, increased land prices, and the focus on high-end development. Low-income residents' struggles, including the impacts of overcrowding, paying too much of their income for housing and the threat of evictions are expressed within this frame. The NVIVO analysis revealed that the majority of activists – 64.3 percent of those interviewed in the Mission District and 68.8 percent in West Oakland – invoked the affordable housing frame during their interviews.

The second core movement frame is a community identity frame. This refers to activists and residents' arguments about the uniqueness of the neighborhood they live in. They contend that not only are their homes located in these neighborhoods, but also the neighborhoods as a whole are a part of their ethnic place-based identities. They also attach symbolic cultural attachments to place – the local establishments that house their daily routines and "inherited folkways" – in other words, they articulate the "use values" of place and the neighborhoods in which they live as an alternative to the growth machine's "exchange value" lens. As gentrification pressures rose in these neighborhoods, movement activists expressed concerns about what they perceived as a loss of community, as more affluent newcomers replaced long-time residents (see Logan & Molotch, 1987 for a more detailed discussion of use values). This frame was, once again, pervasive in activist interviews. In West Oakland, 78.3 percent of activists invoked community identity during their interviews, whereas 73.6 percent of activists in the Mission District employed a community frame. However, some Mission activists sought to downplay this frame in their discourse as the MAC movement matured and broadened its sphere of activism.

The third frame is equity (or the equitable development frame). It argues that new development should provide benefits to meet the needs of pre-existing low-income residents in a neighborhood. This frame also asserts democratic participation in land-use planning and an adherence to environmental justice principles as values to govern development decisions. Of the three frames, equitable development comes closest to being a cohesive "master frame." A master frame can be described as the assemblage of concepts and ideas organized in innovative and compelling ways to propose a coherent ideological worldview that supplant pre-existing frames (Snow & Benford, 1992; Taylor, 2000; Oliver & Johnston, 2000).

Although all three of these frames are translatable across different movements, the equitable development frame provides a broad set of principles to reinterpret the gentrification issue, providing a basis of entitlement for claims-making, rather than having to articulate a case based simply on narrow self-interest or dire human suffering. Such claims could be easily dismissed. The equitable development master frame inserts a dimension of justice and moral propriety into urban growth debates that facilitated the movements' efforts to counter the arguments of the growth machine.

There were substantial differences between activists in the Mission District versus West Oakland in their usage of the equitable development frame. Although 85.7 percent of Mission activists articulated the equitable development frame in their interviews, this frame was present in only 56.3 percent of interviews with West Oakland activists. However, the frame's lessened prominence in West Oakland may be due to the interview timing. The final interviews were conducted from 2003 to 2004, when the Central Station issue first catalyzed the amplification of the equity frame. Since the frame was only just beginning to emerge as a core organizing frame for the movement, activists may have been getting adjusted to this new frame and might not have evoked it quite as readily. Mission District activists, on the other hand, had been calling for equity to be a guiding principle for city planning since 2000. When interviews were conducted in 2002 and 2003, they had already had more than two years to develop the frame in their discourse.

Despite the similarities between the movements identified earlier, the comparative case study approach also allows the researcher to examine differences between the movements and consider how such differences might have influenced their media coverage.

MOVEMENT DIFFERENCES

Analysis of the data yielded several important differences between the Mission District and West Oakland movements. Mission District groups formed MAC, a coalition group that launched a radical campaign against gentrification calling for the transformation of the city planning process to provide more affordable housing for low-income residents. In contrast, organizations in West Oakland worked within established policy processes and employed market-based channels to develop initiatives to address ongoing concerns about displacement, inequality, and poverty in their economically disinvested neighborhood.

Given these contrasting approaches in their efforts to prevent gentrification in their neighborhoods, MAC activists and West Oakland activists articulated different versions of the three master frames identified earlier. In their community identity frame, MAC articulated a discourse of militant class struggle that drew on communitarian themes to emphasize the solidarity of neighborhood residents and their allies in opposition to the influx of high-end development that attracted affluent outsiders. MAC's version of this frame evoked communitarianism and explicitly condemned the market systems of land use that were driving up prices due to development pressures in the Mission District. It targeted the larger social structure in its attribution of blame and called for systemic reform of land use at the citywide level. MAC's reliance on communitarianism linked the gentrification debate in their community to broader movements opposed to globalization and neo-liberalism.

In contrast, the West Oakland movement's core frames evoked individual rights in their desire to prevent gentrification from displacing pre-existing low-income residents in their neighborhood. They carefully avoided ascribing blame toward white middle-class newcomers who moved into the neighborhood. Instead, they emphasized the idea that everyone has "the right" to buy property and live in the community. Emphasizing homeownership and other market mechanisms as solutions to the problem, West Oakland activists articulated a more mainstream position in their framing of community identity and equitable development. As such, they emphasized helping individuals generate wealth and assets to become home owners by investing in efforts to enhance residents' job skills through workforce training, working with land trusts, increasing social services, and making low-interest loans for home renovation available to residents. These programs implicitly situate the locus of control over outcomes in the domain of individual activity within the market structure. Their logic was that if individuals owned homes and had access to capital, they would not be at risk of displacement.

Notably, these differences in the movements were also apparent in their approach to policy. Although MAC called for wholesale reform of citywide planning processes to provide redistributive benefits to low-income groups, West Oakland activists focused on redress of conditions of inequality and alleviating poverty, seeking to use existing institutional mechanisms to effect neighborhood improvements. These differences may have arisen, in part, from the different ethnic histories of activist groups.

For instance, African-Americans began settling in West Oakland during the expansion of the railroads in the West in the 1900s and during World War II, when factories and shipyards hired numerous workers from the South. Because Oakland was racially segregated, this was one of the few neighborhoods in the East Bay where blacks were able to own homes, consequently, West Oakland had a thriving middle-class black community by the 1950s. Successive waves of urban renewal, in the 1940s, the 1950s, and the 1970s, replaced the Victorian homes with somber housing projects and new highways that sliced through the heart of the neighborhood. From the 1960s through the 1980s, much of West Oakland's black population lost their homes, and the area continued to experience urban decline. In the meantime, the Bay Area in general flourished (Bagwell, 1996; Kahn, April 26, 1985; Rhomberg, 2004; Walker, 2004).

The role of private homeownership in the historic development of West Oakland as a flourishing middle-class black community helps to explain its importance. To African-Americans, whose ancestors immigrated to West Oakland from the South from 1900 to the 1940s to start a new life, private homeownership represents a hard-fought struggle for the right to build community and enjoy a measure of economic self-determination. Access to capital, property, and other wealth has always separated the status of blacks and whites. This contentious issue dates back to the nation's founding, when slaves were denied the right to own property. Blacks in West Oakland have a specific story wherein their access to the American dream has been systematically compromised. This occurred historically through force during urban renewal and is now being replicated in a de facto manner through the market. Its salience as an issue to West Oakland activists is connected to these historic narratives (Gin, 2007).

Local ethnic history also lends insight into activists' emphasis on collective-community values in the Mission District. The Mission District has housed a politically active immigrant Latino population dating back to the 1950s. In the 1970s and 1980s, thousands of immigrants fleeing the civil wars in Central America joined the predominantly Mexican/Chicano immigrant population in the area (Alejandrino, 2000; Feldman, October 18, 2000; Hartman & Carnochan, 2002). The Mission District became the base for groups such as the Committee for Solidarity with the People of El Salvador (CISPES), forming a growing leftist solidarity movement connected with economic populist and human rights campaigns in Latin America. These newcomers, many of whom had been involved with agricultural reform movements, Latin American groups such as the El Salvador socialist party Farabundo Martí National Liberation Front (FMLN), the Nicaraguan Sandinistas, and other ideologically complementary efforts, brought new energy and perspectives to the neighborhood's political life (Gin, 2007).

Hence, the Mission District activist identity is shaped by its decidedly Latin American immigrant orientation. Having experienced social life in countries where populist politics and Catholic liberation theology enjoy greater prominence than in the United States, these activists have access to a "cultural stock" (Swidler, 1986), thematic elements that lend themselves to use in popular discourse, different from that of mainstream America. These cultural elements, which promote collective-community values, are widely disseminated throughout the Mission District's activist community (Gin, 2007).

In particular, Mission activists with experience with the aforementioned leftist groups have developed a broader narrative of antagonism toward U.S. foreign and economic policies, particularly the pursuit of structural adjustment, that is, trade liberalization, privatization, and de-regulation in Latin American countries often linked to the U.S. military support of pro-American governments in these countries. Moreover, they view private property and "capitalism," broadly interpreted, in inherently pejorative terms, instead favoring more communitarian systems for the allocation of goods such as housing. Hence, their approach to addressing gentrification concerns is intensely shaped through this collective-communitarian lens (Gin, 2007).

Given these differences, it is not surprising that the two movements exhibited stark differences in the tactics they employed to work toward their political goals. MAC engaged in mass rallies and marches, protests, sit-ins, and other direct action or civil disobedience tactics that targeted and blamed city planning commissioners for their failure to proactively regulate development, developers, and "dot-com" companies that had carried out illegal building conversions to create offices.[2] On the contrary, West Oakland activists accepted the system of market-driven land uses and sought instead to employ established channels – the city's redevelopment process, the real estate market, and foundation grants – to develop programs to protect local residents from displacement.

Hence, despite their shared opposition to gentrification, these were actually very different sorts of movements. Their differences illustrate that there is a wide range of local community-based responses to urban development. Some of those call for an alternative urban agenda that takes residents' land-use needs into consideration, while others work within the pre-existing structure. The following section examines the media coverage of these two movements.

MEDIA COVERAGE

Duration and Volume of Coverage

There was noticeable variation in the media coverage of the two movements. The media coverage also varied widely, depending on movement dynamics at different time periods and stages of the movements. As indicated in Fig. 1, the MAC movement in the Mission District was able to generate a much greater volume of media coverage of gentrification issues in the neighborhood – 156 newspaper articles in a 10-year period – than the West Oakland movement, which only had 59 newspaper articles during the same time period.

Fig. 1 also illustrates that volume of coverage varied over time, particularly in the Mission District. Although Mission District activists and community organizations were engaged in advocacy at the Planning Commission/Department and holding protests against high-end development well before MAC's official formation in March 2000, both the controversy and movement activity peaked in that year. This is represented in a spike in the media coverage of the anti-gentrification issue during that year. The decline in media coverage of gentrification in the Mission District began in 2001, when the "dot-com" bubble collapsed and activists began working on systemic policy reforms, and tapered off by 2005.

Although the West Oakland movement received less coverage in general, coverage of gentrification issues in the area remained somewhat steady throughout the entire 10-year period. Gentrification concerns remained a consistent topic of media coverage throughout the neighborhood irrespective of the actual shifts in the larger regional economy (such as the dot-com bubble) or other movement-related events. In examining volume of coverage, the media does not appear to be as responsive to the West Oakland movement as it did for MAC.

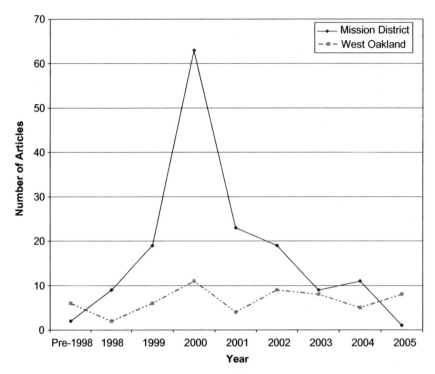

Fig. 1. Extent of Newspaper Coverage in the Mission District and West Oakland.

Portrayal of the Movements

In examining the actual content of the media coverage, particularly in answering the question of whether the movement was portrayed favorably, unfavorably, neutrally, or not mentioned, the analysis yields similar, but slightly more complex, results. Table 1 indicates that a significant proportion of the articles either portray the movement unfavorably or do not mention the movement at all. The analysis found that 46.8 percent of the articles written about the Mission fell into this combined category, whereas 62.7 percent of the articles written about West Oakland either did not mention the movement or mentioned it unfavorably.

However, there were also some differences in the coverage that each movement received. Although only 37.3 percent of the articles published about the West Oakland movement portrayed it positively/neutrally, a greater proportion – 53.2 percent – of articles about the MAC movement

Table 1. Newspaper Portrayal of the Movements in the Mission District and West Oakland.

Newspapers	Mission District					West Oakland				
	Total number of articles	Unfavorable/no mention		Neutral or favorable portrayal		Total number of articles	Unfavorable/no mention		Neutral or favorable portrayal	
		Number of articles	Percent	Number of articles	Percent		Number of articles	Percent	Number of articles	Percent
San Francisco Chronicle	60	28	46.7	32	53.3	19	14	73.7	5	26.3
San Francisco Bay Guardian	63	31	49.2	32	50.8	2	2	100.0	0	0.0
San Francisco Business Times	11	7	63.6	4	36.4	3	3	100.0	0	0.0
San Francisco Examiner	22	7	31.8	15	68.2	5	3	60.0	2	40.0
East Bay Express		Did not cover				11	6	54.5	5	45.5
Oakland Tribune		Did not cover				19	9	47.4	10	52.6
Total newspaper articles	156	73	46.8	83	53.2	59	37	62.7	22	37.3

accorded it such beneficial coverage. A chi-square test confirmed that these differences were marginally statistically significant ($\chi^2 = 7.8$, df $= 2$, $p = .051$).

The coverage was analyzed in greater detail by newspaper to more clearly demonstrate how different papers portrayed the two movements. In the Mission District case, both the *San Francisco Chronicle* and *San Francisco Bay Guardian* portrayed the movement favorably or neutrally in 53.3 and 50.8 percent, respectively. Although the *Bay Guardian* often ran stories about gentrification that did not pertain to the Mission District, the *Chronicle* focused more heavily on the controversy in that area. The *San Francisco Examiner*, the city's other mainstream daily newspaper,[3] provided the highest proportion of favorable or neutral articles about MAC – 68.2 percent. The *San Francisco Business Times* was much less likely to provide favorable coverage of the MAC than all the other newspapers; only 36.4 percent of the articles in the *Business Times* were favorable or neutral.

The four San Francisco-based newspapers did not provide as beneficial coverage to the West Oakland movement. Overall, 62.7 percent of the coverage of West Oakland was either unfavorable or made no mention of the movement. However, much of this may be due to the low amount of resources that San Francisco-based newspapers allocated to West Oakland coverage. The *Chronicle, Oakland Tribune*, and *East Bay Express* provided the most coverage to gentrification issues in West Oakland. Of the articles published in Oakland papers, half either did not mention the movement or mentioned it only unfavorably. Although 73.7 percent of the articles in the *San Francisco Chronicle* and 60 percent of those in the *San Francisco Examiner* either made no mention of the West Oakland or covered the issues unfavorably, all the articles by the *San Francisco Bay Guardian* and the *San Francisco Business Times* did the same. In addition to the differences in the media coverage of the two movements identified earlier, it is useful to examine whether the activists' core frames were included in newspaper articles.

Movement Frames and the Media

Affordable Housing
Table 2 shows the frame's prevalence in the media coverage. Overall, 96 or 61.5 percent of the articles on the Mission District mentioned affordable housing. In comparison, 31 or 52.5 percent of those on West Oakland mentioned this frame. A closer look at the pattern of coverage of this issue

Table 2. Mention of the Core Frames during the Phases of the Movements in the Mission District and West Oakland.

Core Frames Mentioned	Mission District							West Oakland				
	Total number of articles	Before movement peak, 1995–1999		During movement peak, 2000		After movement peak, 2001–2005		Total number of articles	Before movement peak, 1995–2003[a]		During/after movement peak, 2003–2005	
		Number of articles	Percent	Number of articles	Percent	Number of articles	Percent		Number of articles	Percent	Number of articles	Percent
Affordable housing												
Yes	96	25	75.5	29	49.2	42	65.6	31	18	42.9	13	76.5
No	60	8	24.2	30	50.8	22	34.4	28	24	57.1	4	23.5
Community identity												
Yes	63	20	60.0	24	40.7	19	29.7	46	31	73.8	15	88.2
No	93	13	39.4	35	59.3	45	70.3	13	11	26.2	2	11.8
Equitable development												
Yes	43	13	39.4	14	23.7	16	25.0	26	19	45.2	11	64.7
No	113	20	60.6	45	76.3	48	75.0	29	23	54.8	6	35.3
Total newspaper articles	156	33	21.2	59	37.8	64	41.0	59	42	71.2	17	28.8

[a]The "movement peak" in West Oakland occurred in December 2003.

over time reveals two different trends in coverage in the two communities. For analysis of the coverage of the MAC, the newspaper articles were divided into three time periods – before, during, and after the peak of MAC protest activity. Articles were divided into two time periods – before and during/after the peak of protests for coverage of West Oakland. These time periods were identified to correspond to recognizable phases of community organizing and other movement activities in the two communities. The logic was that as movements mobilized, they would engage in efforts to get their frames into the political agenda. They would seek to incorporate movement frames into the media and public discourse.

But this was not necessarily the case. In the Mission District, the affordable housing frame, present in 75.5 percent of the articles written before MAC's founding in 2000, was mentioned in only 49.2 percent of the articles written during the peak of the MAC movement, when "gentrification" was the hottest issue in the Mission District. This was a period during which activists staged weekly, if not daily, public events to draw attention to the topic. After the "dot-com" wave subsided in mid-2001, MAC shifted its focus toward working on the systematic reform of citywide planning policy, and the media's focus on the affordable housing frame rebounded, once again, to be mentioned in 65.6 percent of the articles. Yet, it was never as prevalent in the media's discourse as it was before the movement. A chi-square test indicated that this pattern is statistically significant ($\chi^2 = 7.10$, df $= 2$, $p = .029$), suggesting that during the movement in 2000, as the MAC movement began its most visible period of action, there was a noticeable decline in media focus on affordable housing. This occurred despite increased organizing around the issue by activists. In other words, MAC's organizing and focus on the topic did not translate into additional media coverage of the issue.

In contrast, West Oakland's protest activities around affordable housing coincided with increased coverage in newspaper articles. As the West Oakland movement stepped up its protests, activists focused on a controversial development project and called for community benefits including affordable housing. They organized protests around the Train Station Project at Wood Street, a proposed development to construct 1,500 units of market-rate housing that would not be within residents' affordability range; this time period is labeled "During/After Movement." As West Oakland activists evoked the affordable housing frame, the media stepped up its coverage of the issue accordingly. Although the affordable housing frame was present in only 42.9 percent of the articles published before the movement's protests, it was mentioned in 76.5 percent of the articles published during and after the movement began its visible public protests. A chi-square test indicates that this pattern is statistically significant ($\chi^2 = 5.48$, df $= 1$, $p = .019$). This suggests that the increase in media mention of affordable housing dramatically increased with the onset of public protest over the Train Station Project. The data indicate that the media responded differently to the use of the affordable housing frame by activists in West Oakland and Mission District.

Community Identity

Table 2 also indicates the extent to which this frame was represented in the media coverage. On the whole, 63 or 40.4 percent of the articles on the Mission District mentioned community identity while 46 or 78 percent of those on West Oakland mentioned this frame. The community identity frame was mentioned less often over time in the Mission District. That is, it was mentioned in 60 percent of the articles before the movement activity began, in 40.7 percent of the articles published during the movement activities, and in only 29.7 percent of the articles written in the period after the movement peak. This difference is statistically significant ($\chi^2 = 7.11$, df $= 2$, $p = .008$). Again, the media seemed to lose interest in the community identity frame as a core movement frame, just as it had with the affordable housing frame, when movement activities peaked. The decline in interest in the frame carried over into the period after the movement's peak. Over the movement's course, MAC activists sought to broaden its relevance by expanding their appeals and domain of change sought from one focused on neighborhood land-use conflicts to one focused on citywide policies and procedures. In so doing, they shifted gears and began calling for wholesale changes to the city's land use and housing development policies. In the meetings and interviews, activists stressed the importance of not being perceived as a Mission District–specific movement. As one activist put it, "I'd like to think we're fighting for others as well as fighting for ourselves." Hence, the decline in the media coverage of the community identity frame could be a reflection of the activists' attempts to reduce the prominence of this frame as they shifted focus and energy to concentrate on citywide affairs.

In West Oakland, media coverage of the community identity frame showed the opposite trend. Although this frame appeared in 73.8 percent of the articles published before the movement, it appeared in 88.2 percent of the articles printed during or after movement. Despite the increase in percentage, this difference is not significant ($\chi^2 = 1.46$, df $= 1$, $p = .226$).

The community identity frame grew more prominent in the West Oakland movement during the train station project protests. Indeed, the train station's historical significance to the African-American community was marked not only by its role in the Pullman Porters movement[4] but also as a port of migration for later generations of African-Americans migrating from the South to work during the two World Wars. In drawing upon these themes, West Oakland activists framed the train station issue in ways that compelled their constituents to mobilize in response to the project. Hence it is possible that the media's increase in focus on community identity themes may have been driven by the activists' framing.

Equitable Development
The equitable development frame was present in less than half of the newspaper articles published on both communities (Table 2). Forty-three or 27.6 percent of the articles on the Mission District mentioned the equitable development frame. In comparison, 26 or 44.1 percent of the articles on West Oakland mentioned this frame. In the Mission District, coverage of the equitable development frame was highest before the movement; it was mentioned in 39.4 percent of the articles published in the era before the movement. Mention of this frame receded to the point that only 23.7 percent of the newspaper articles on the Mission District mentioned this frame during the movement and 25 percent mentioned it after the movement peak. In West Oakland, the equitable development frame became more prominent in news coverage as time went on. That is, 45.2 percent of the articles published before the movement's peak mentioned this frame. This percentage increased such that 64.7 percent of the articles published during and after the movement's peak mentioned this frame. The difference in coverage was not significant ($\chi^2 = 3.00$, df $= 2$, $p = .223$).

In West Oakland, the activists' launching of protests around the train station project seemed to introduce the equitable development frame into media coverage. The media coverage of the equitable development frame in West Oakland mentioned it in 45.2 percent of articles published before the movement peak, but in 64.7 percent of those published during or after movement peak. West Oakland activists used the train station controversy to transform and amplify the equitable development frame into a focused master frame that resulted in increased media coverage. However, the difference in coverage was not significant ($\chi^2 = 1.84$, df $= 1$, $p = .176$).

The Changing Nature of Media Coverage

This section of the chapter analyzes whether the core movement frames were portrayed in a neutral/favorable light or whether the portrayal was unfavorable or the frame not mentioned at all.

Affordable Housing

Overall, only 74 or 47.4 percent of articles on the Mission District mentioned affordable housing positively or neutrally. In comparison, 23 or 39.0 percent of those on West Oakland featured either positive or neutral coverage of the frame (Table 3). The affordable housing frame was neutrally or positively mentioned in 60.6 percent of articles before MAC was founded; this declined sharply to only 35.0 percent of articles written during MAC's peak, and only rebounded to 52.4 percent of articles after MAC shifted its focus to promote affordable housing through citywide institutional reforms. This is significant ($\chi^2 = 7.939$, df = 2, $p = .019$). An examination of the content of newspaper articles also indicated that as the movement became institutionalized within city policy circles, its frame became increasingly vulnerable to negative criticism. Articles portrayed their affordable housing policy demands as overly bureaucratic, inflexible, and unrealistic in relation to the market. They suggested that activists pursuing affordable housing would hamper the building of more housing units that would ultimately lower the cost of middle-class housing by increasing supply.

In West Oakland, the activist protests amplified the affordable housing frame, both in their own discourse and in the media. Although the majority of the articles (52.9 percent) published after the train station project mobilization began were either positive or neutral, only 33.3 percent before the movement were positive/neutral. This increase is not statistically significant. Many of the articles expressed the pro-development view either first or at the start of the article, whereas activists' views were presented second or at the end of the article. Reporters frequently used phrases such as "however, activists complain..." before describing the movement's position.

Community Identity

In the Mission District, only 52 or 33.3 percent of all the articles published mentioned community identity neutrally or positively. In West Oakland, 32 articles or 54.2 percent of all articles mentioned the frame neutrally or positively (Table 3). It was mentioned positively or neutrally in 51.5 percent of articles before the movement, in 31.7 percent of articles during the

Table 3. Portrayal of the Core Frames during Movement Phases in the Mission District and West Oakland.

Core Frames Portrayed	Mission District							West Oakland				
	Total number of articles	Before movement peak, 1995–1999		During Movement Peak, 2000		After Movement Peak, 2001–2005		Total number of articles	Before movement peak, 1995–2003		During/after movement peak, 2003–2005	
		Number of articles	Percent	Number of articles	Percent	Number of articles	Percent		Number of articles	Percent	Number of articles	Percent
Affordable housing												
Neutral/favorable	74	20	60.6	21	35.0	33	52.4	23	14	33.3	9	52.9
Unfavorable/no mention	82	13	39.4	39	65.0	30	47.6	36	28	66.7	8	47.1
Community identity												
Neutral/favorable	52	17	51.5	19	31.7	16	25.4	32	24	57.1	8	47.1
Unfavorable/no mention	104	16	48.5	41	68.3	47	30.8	27	18	42.9	9	52.9
Equitable development												
Neutral/favorable	36	12	36.4	11	18.3	13	23.1	20	13	31.0	7	41.2
Unfavorable/no mention	120	21	63.6	49	81.7	50	76.9	39	29	69.9	10	58.8
Total newspaper articles	156	33	21.2	59	37.8	64	41.0	59	42	71.2	17	28.8

movement peak, and only 25.4 percent of articles after the movement. This decline was statistically significant ($\chi^2 = 8.345$, df $= 2$, $p = .015$).

In West Oakland, percentage of articles portraying this frame neutrally/ favorably declined from 57.1 percent to 47.1 percent over time. This difference was not statistically significant ($\chi^2 = .496$, df $= 1$, $p = .481$). This analysis along with the media's unfavorable treatment of this frame in the Mission District suggests that the media may not necessarily be sympathetic to activists' claims of cultural significance as a basis for policy. The claim of neighborhood use value to community residents as a basis for preservation remains a politically challenging frame for movements opposing gentrification.

Equitable Development
Table 3 shows that 36 or 23.1 percent of the articles on the Mission District portrayed the equitable development frame positively or neutrally. In comparison, 20 or 33.9 percent of the articles on West Oakland mentioned it positively or neutrally. In the Mission District, 7 or 16.3 percent of the articles that mentioned this frame mentioned it negatively; many of the articles simply did not mention the frame at all. In contrast, 10 or 38.5 percent of the West Oakland articles that mentioned the frame portrayed it negatively.

In the Mission District, the equitable development frame was covered in a neutral or favorable manner in 36.4 percent of articles that appeared before the movement. This period had the most positive coverage that the frame would ever receive. During the movement peak, coverage of this frame in either a positive or a neutral lens declined to only 18.3 percent of the newspaper articles on the Mission District and rebounded to only 23.1 percent after the peak period. This trend was not statistically significant ($\chi^2 = 4.254$, df $= 2$, $p = .119$). In West Oakland, 31 percent of articles published before the movement peak offered a neutral or positive lens on the equitable development frame, whereas 41.2 percent of articles published during and after the movement offered such beneficial coverage. This increase was small and not statistically significant ($\chi^2 = 1.835$, df $= 1$, $p = .176$).

Changing Coverage in Individual Newspapers Over Time

Movement Coverage
To analyze more fully whether the media were indeed resistant to the movements as they became more publicly visible and evolved over time,

the each newspaper's portrayal of the movements was analyzed for each time periods. Table 4 shows the newspapers' portrayal of the movements over time in the different newspapers that covered them.

First, the alternative weekly *Bay Guardian*'s coverage was not more favorable toward MAC than the mainstream *San Francisco Chronicle*. The *San Francisco Chronicle* featured unfavorable/no mention articles of the Mission District 4 or 80 percent of articles published before the movement, 51.9 percent of articles published during the movement, and 35.7 percent of articles published after the movement. The *Bay Guardian* made unfavorable portrayal or no mention in 80 percent of the articles published before the movement, in 36 percent of articles during the movement peak, and in 50 percent of articles published after the movement. The *Examiner*, also considered a mainstream newspaper before closing in 2000, mentioned the movement in unfavorable terms or not at all in 33.3 percent of the articles before the movement and in 25 percent of articles during the movement peak. The *Examiner*'s more favorable coverage than the *Bay Guardian*'s coverage was consistent with what MAC activists reported during interviews. It seemed ironic that the movement appeared to have won over the mainstream papers more than the alternative paper. But upon closer inspection of the articles in the *Bay Guardian*, it appeared that while the *Bay Guardian* sided with activists' stance on land use more often than in other papers, many articles did not mention the MAC activists at all.

In West Oakland, the weekly *East Bay Express* mentioned the West Oakland movement unfavorably or made no mention at all in 44.4 percent of articles before the movement, and in both articles published during/after movement peak. The mainstream daily *Oakland Tribune* mentioned the movement unfavorably or not at all in 16.7 percent of articles before the movement and 61.5 percent during/after movement peak. The *Oakland Tribune*, the only newspaper to cover the train station protests, shifted from positive to negative portrayal of the activists when they began the public protests over the train station. In examining the articles, it seemed as though the activist groups were treated as important civic leaders in West Oakland until they formed a coalition to oppose development.

Coverage of the Core Frames

Table 4 also shows how the newspapers covered the core frames in each time period. In the Mission District, the *San Francisco Bay Chronicle* was the only paper in which the negative coverage of the affordable housing frame declined steadily over time. In contrast, the percentage of unfavorable/no mention articles in the *San Francisco Bay Guardian*'s articles went from

Table 4. Number and Percent of Unfavorable/No Mention Articles in Each Newspaper Over Time for the Movements and for Core Movement Frames in the Mission District and West Oakland.

Newspapers	Mission District							West Oakland				
	Total number of unfavorable articles	Before movement peak, 1995–1999		During movement peak, 2000		After movement peak, 2001–2005		Total number of unfavorable articles	Before movement peak, 1995–2003		During/After Movement Peak, 2003–2005	
		Number of articles	Percent	Number of articles	Percent	Number of articles	Percent		Number of articles	Percent	Number of articles	Percent
Movement mentioned in articles												
San Francisco Chronicle	28	4	80.0	14	51.9	10	35.7	14	13	76.5	1	50.0
San Francisco Bay Guardian	31	8	80.0	9	36.0	14	50.0	2	2	100.0		
San Francisco Business Times	7	0	0	3	75.0	4	57.1	3	3	100.0		
San Francisco Examiner	7	6	33.3	1	25.0	Closed down		3	3	60.0	Closed down	
East Bay Express				Did not cover				6	4	44.4	2	100
Oakland Tribune				Did not cover								
Affordable housing frame												
San Francisco Chronicle	36	4	80.0	19	70.4	13	48.1	14	13	74.5	1	50.0
San Francisco Bay Guardian	26	1	10.0	14	56.0	11	39.3					
San Francisco Business Times	9	3	75.0	6	85.7	9	81.8					
San Francisco Examiner	11	8	44.4	3	75.0	Closed down		3	3	60.0	Closed down	
East Bay Express				Did not cover				8	6	66.7	2	100
Oakland Tribune				Did not cover				8	3	50.0	5	38.5

	N	n	%	n	%	n	%	n	%	n	%
Community identity frame											
San Francisco Chronicle	44	3	60.0	22	81.5	19	67.8	10	58.8	0	0
San Francisco Bay Guardian	37	3	30.0	13	52.0	21	75.0	3	100.0	0	0
San Francisco Business Times	10	0	0	3	75.0	7	100.0	4	80.0		
San Francisco Examiner	13	10	55.6	3	75.0	Closed down					
East Bay Express		Did not cover						1	11.1	2	100
Oakland Tribune		Did not cover						0	0	7	53.8
Equitable development frame											
San Francisco Chronicle	46	5	100.0	25	92.6	22	78.6	14	82.3	1	50.0
San Francisco Bay Guardian	43	3	30.0	19	76.0	21	75.0	1	50.0	0	0
San Francisco Business Times	9	0	0	2	50.0	7	100.0	3	60.0		
San Francisco Examiner	16	13	72.2	3	75.0	Closed down					
East Bay Express		Did not cover						5	55.6	2	100
Oakland Tribune		Did not cover						3	50.0	7	53.8

10 percent before the movement to 56 percent during movement peak and back down again to 39.3 percent after the movement's peak. The *San Francisco Business Times'* unfavorable/no mention articles was lower before the movement than in the two later periods. The *San Francisco Chronicle*'s negative coverage of the affordable housing frame also declined over time West Oakland – going from 74.5 percent before movement peak to 50 percent of the articles written during/after movement peak. The percentage of unfavorable articles or those not mentioning the frame at all also declined in the *Oakland Tribune*.

The community identity frame in the Mission District received more negative coverage in all the newspapers as time went on. However, this was not the case in West Oakland. The percentage of articles that were unfavorable/no mention declined in the *San Francisco Chronicle, San Francisco Business Times*, and the *Oakland Tribune,* whereas they increased in the *East Bay Express.*

The use of the community identity frame as a political claims-making tool is indicative of the type of thorny framing dilemmas that these anti-gentrification movements were forced to navigate in their message to the media. We see coverage that is sympathetic to the frame before the movement. Such framing of community identity often takes on a quasi-romantic flavor not beneficial to the movement. The media are sympathetic, but only because it assumes that nothing can be done about such "inevitable" neighborhood changes. These articles are more human interest stories in both the Mission District and West Oakland. Once the movement begins to illustrate the power of invoking community identity for mobilization and public agenda-setting, the media starts to recognize the conflict between the community identity perspective and their own ideological support for market-driven growth. Because of the overtones of authenticity and the elevation of previously subaltern identities, the media may also be inclined to express hostility toward the political implications of the frame, as in: why is this neighborhood and this group given "special treatment" to preserve their community when other communities and residents do not have access to this political capital?

The *San Francisco Chronicle*'s coverage of the equitable development frame in the Mission District was less negative as time went on. This was in contrast to the *San Francisco Bay Guardian*'s coverage that was markedly more unfavorable before the movement peaked than afterwards. The unfavorable coverage in the *San Francisco Business Times* also increased over time. In West Oakland, the *San Francisco Chronicle*'s negative coverage of the equitable development frame declined over time. So did the negative coverage in the *San Francisco Bay Guardian*. However, coverage in the East Bay Express was more negative during/after movement peak period than it was during the before movement peak period.

DISCUSSION AND IMPLICATIONS

These data present a more complicated picture of the media's role in covering movements that challenge development interests than that has been reported elsewhere. Now that we know that not all media is hostile to all movements all the time, what lessons can we distill from these cases about what factors might lead the media to be more favorably inclined toward opposition movements toward local development?

First, the media's devotion of greater resources toward covering the Mission District movement than West Oakland tells us something about which movement was viewed as more "newsworthy." Indeed the peak in news coverage in 2000 upon MAC's founding coincided with the height of protest and controversy in the Mission District, mirroring the classic media issue–attention cycle. The criteria for newsworthiness, as defined by Molotch (1979), is a movement's ability to draw in the media's attention in a contest: the movement's struggle is to challenge the legitimacy of the status quo, whereas the media seek to reinforce the status quo by covering the deviant aspects of the movement, shifting the focus from the frames/issues important to the movement to a view of the movement as a threat to social norms. In other words, the legitimacy of a movement's political claims must be thrown into question to preserve the legitimacy of the status quo that is under challenge. Although Mission District activists were able to get the media to cover their activities, they were not always successful in getting their core frames into the coverage. Moreover, even the *Bay Guardian*, which would have been expected to sympathize with the activists, was often unfocused in its coverage and did not support the core frames.

West Oakland, in contrast, was treated as a "human interest story" in the media (McCarthy et al., 1996). There was rarely more than one story about West Oakland focusing on any given policy issue within the gentrification debate. Rather, the coverage followed a sort of "scattershot" pattern; with one story about one policy issue followed by another story a few weeks later about a completely separate policy issue. This pattern is consistent with the fragmentation of meaning in the media, wherein the focus is on "the immediacy of surface meaning and the absence of depth" that hinders the transmission of any organizing frame in media coverage

(Gamson et al., 1992). The fragmented coverage both reflected and transmitted the perception that West Oakland was a disadvantaged community whose residents were deserving of sympathy.[5]

As a result, many of the articles published on the activist groups in West Oakland did not actually mention activism. Most focused instead on pre-existing problems of blight and crime facing the neighborhood. They portrayed the area as being desperately in need of revitalization and development. Activists opposing this agenda were often ignored, particularly in the period before the movement peak. This pattern is particularly evident in the San Francisco-based newspapers' coverage of West Oakland. The *San Francisco Chronicle*, which published 19 articles about West Oakland, failed to mention the movement at all in 73.7 percent of them. The Oakland-based newspapers mentioned the activists in a greater proportion of their articles, but still excluded them in 40 percent of their articles.

When West Oakland activists were mentioned, stories mainly depicted them working for positive neighborhood improvements to benefit local residents, even though the effort was often viewed as an uphill battle amid the urban chaos. The Oakland-based newspapers that did mention the activists portrayed them most positively before the movement, as 71.4 percent of the Oakland articles mentioning them were neutral or positive. Once they began mobilizing, the Oakland newspapers' positive portrayals declined. This chapter suggests that while the "human interest" nature of the West Oakland movement made it less "newsworthy" – leading to overall lower levels of media attention – it also provided an opening to get sympathetic coverage that activists would not have gotten otherwise. Unfortunately, as time went on and activists shifted their tactics to mobilize for community benefits from the train station proposal, the media did not seem so positively inclined to continue covering their stories. The media's treatment of the community identity and equitable development frames also mirrors this temporal trend.

The earlier discussion of the literature also mentioned that the nature of the media news cycle tends to discourage coverage of the more complex nature of movement issue positions in favor of more radical confrontational protest tactics (Molotch, 1979). This is particularly likely in the case of issues in inner-city neighborhoods, which tend to foster media expectations of urban pathologies, so that any alternative vision that the neighborhood has value without redevelopment tends to run counter to the narrative the media is comfortable portraying (Dreier, 2005; Gibson, 2004). Both of these dynamics may have hurt the movements, particularly in the latter stages of mobilizing, when they emphasized equitable development and the need to ensure that pre-existing disadvantaged residents receive community benefits.

It could also be the case that news coverage evolves over time. Activists and communities might start out with favorable coverage early on in the news cycle of a particular issue or controversy. This is particularly true if the reporters covering an issue do so because they sympathize with the activists' viewpoints. However, as time goes on, reporters can begin probing deeper into activists' claims, grow skeptical, develop fatigue with an issue, or cycle off a story. In the West Oakland case, community residents were split on support versus opposition to the train station proposal, and the project supporters' efforts to influence the media benefited from their ability to point out the need for physical improvements in this disinvested neighborhood. In the case of the Mission District's MAC movement, some of the *Bay Guardian*'s reporters actually became more interested in gentrification and housing issues as a result, but found that neither the movement nor the city's planning officials had the innovative solutions they wanted to support. Hence, they began to look elsewhere for interesting stories on these issues, resulting in activists and their frames being excluded in what would have otherwise been sympathetic coverage. These dynamics can change the extent to which an issue is covered and the nature of that coverage.

The most significant consequence of this difference in these two movements' media coverage can be found in the coverage of core frames. As mentioned earlier, movements benefit from coverage if the media conveys the activists' framing of the issue to the public in news stories. When the West Oakland movement flexed its growth-control muscle, the media did increase its focus on activists' message that housing affordability should be a major factor in the city's consideration of development. The media also increased coverage of its equitable development master frame, but its coverage was not favorable. However, MAC's efforts to control development in the Mission District coincided with a decrease in the media's focus on its core policy frames, and some of that coverage became less favorable.

Given the importance of these three core frames to the movements, why did the media coverage of them increase as one movement initiated public protests, whereas the other movement's protests seemed associated with a decline in coverage of this frame? The differences in both these movements' strategies and their treatment within the media coverage suggest a possible explanation, with deep implications for our thinking about media coverage of urban development issues in low-income communities.

The MAC movement in the Mission called for wholesale reform of the citywide planning process, suggesting that proposed development, particularly in transitioning industrial land areas, be more stringently regulated by city planning authorities. MAC positioned itself as a watchdog of the city's development activities, directly challenging the practices that promote profit-driven land use policies, a role it still played as late as 2007. Specifically, MAC asked government to prioritize housing policies to benefit the poorest citizens and increase democratic participation in land use. As such, these activists represented a challenge to the economic interests and politics of the city and its growth machine.

West Oakland, on the contrary, was portrayed as a neighborhood desperate for economic growth. As such, its activists were somewhat more benign to the growth machine, particularly since their neighborhood improvement efforts embraced market-friendly strategies such as home-ownership, wealth/asset accumulation, vehicles, social services, and land trusts. Undoubtedly, their careful assertion that "everyone has the right to buy property and live in West Oakland" helped the movement retain media support. These frames are compelling, not necessarily because the media consciously seek to uphold "growth machine" values, but because many news reporters are socialized within a particular ideological framework in the United States to be pre-disposed to value market-based systems of land distribution. Thus, it was easier for these activists' policy messages to resonate with their pre-existing values and beliefs.

As movement activists entered their respective peak protest periods, they amplified their core frames, particularly affordable housing and equitable development. This represented a critical moment to get their frames into the media. MAC was able to increase slightly the number of stories that featured affordable housing and equity frames into the newspapers. However, much of the increased media attention they received appears to have been diverted into other aspects of the controversy.

Despite the challenge of getting their core frames into the media at the peak of their organizing, MAC activists were able to get seven anti-gentrification candidates elected to the nine-seat city Board of Supervisors and a growth moratorium onto the citywide ballot in 2000. West Oakland activists appeared to be more successful in getting the affordable housing frame into the media when they launched their Train Station campaign, also a significant achievement. Yet the media tended to emphasize low-income residents' dire economic conditions rather than the broader policy debate around growth and the distributive policy implications of development.

There are a number of implications. First, these findings broadly reinforce Logan and Molotch's (1987) assertion that movements make real challenges to the growth machine will find it difficult to get sympathetic media coverage. However, the analysis suggests that researchers go beyond such generalized assertions and examine how the media coverage vary depending on the stage of development the movement is in, phase of the issue–attention cycle a controversy is in, claims-making, framing, and organizing strategies, to name a few. Data presented earlier suggest that activists who advocate for affordable housing and equitable development and are willing to accept the terms and concessions offered by the growth machine and developers are likely to receive more favorable coverage. However, activists who push for more systemic reforms and redistributive policies may gain more publicity for their strategies but run the risk of antagonizing the media.

The implications for environmental justice scholars and advocates cannot be overlooked. This research suggests that low-income communities seeking to address concerns about the inequitable consequences of proposed growth should not simply assume that that they will be denied coverage or get unsympathetic coverage. Rather they must decide whether they are willing to accept the trade-off of articulating frames that are resonant with mainstream ideological perspectives and forgo challenging the status quo ideology in exchange for beneficial media coverage and possible political support.

NOTES

1. Ask Jeeves and Pixar were among the many multimedia companies that sited their headquarters in Emeryville. Ask Jeeves signed its Emeryville lease in mid-1998, whereas Pixar moved there in 2000.

2. Because San Francisco's Proposition M (passed in 1986) limits the amount of office space that can be created each year, the boom created incentives for companies to illegally convert lofts into offices.

3. The *San Francisco Examiner* was run through a joint operating agreement with the *San Francisco Chronicle* until the Hearst Family purchased the *Chronicle* in 2000 and had to divest from the *Examiner* due to federal anti-trust laws governing newspaper ownership. At this point, the *Examiner* was shut down and sold to the Fang family, who completely revamped its format.

4. The Pullman Porters, or the Brotherhood of Sleeping Car Porters, was the first African-American labor union in the nation. The Porters, who were all African-American, worked as service employees on passenger railroad cars traveling across the country from the late 1800s to early 1900s. West Oakland was the last stop on the West-bound route. Thus, it gained prominence as both a community for the Porters and as a center for their organizing efforts (Bagwell, 1996; Rhomberg, 2004).

5. The media highlighted the dire nature of conditions in West Oakland, contributing to the association of minority neighborhoods, particularly black neighborhoods, with crime and poverty. Scholars have critiqued this media portrayal for its perpetuation of stereotypes (Domke, 1997), asserting that it compounds urban

problems, creating the perception that problems in urban areas are fundamentally intractable (Dreier, 2005; Gibson, 2004) and bolstering political support for gentrifying these areas by implying that the neighborhood cannot improve unless current residents are replaced.

ACKNOWLEDGMENT

Funding for this research was provided by the Rackham School of Graduate Studies and the School of Natural Resources and Environment at the University of Michigan. Thanks to Ken Anderson for assistance with formatting maps.

REFERENCES

Alejandrino, S. V. (2000). *Gentrification in San Francisco's mission district: Indicators and policy recommendations*. San Francisco: Mission Economic Development Association.

Bagwell, B. (1996). *Oakland: The story of a city*. Oakland, CA: Oakland Heritage Alliance.

Benford, R. D., & Snow, D. A. (2000). Framing processes and social movements: An overview and assessment. *Annual Review of Sociology, 26*, 611–639.

Cavenaugh, F., Taylor, J., & Wood, M. (2001). *Boom: The sound of eviction (video recording)*. San Francisco: Whispered Media.

Croteau, D., & Hicks, L. (2003). Coalition framing and the challenge of a consonant frame pyramid: The case of a collborative response to homelessness. *Social Problems, 50*(2), 251–272.

Domke, D. (1997). Journalists, framing and discourse about race relations. *Journalism and Mass Communication Monographs* (December), 164–204.

Dreier, P. (2005). How the media compound urban problems. *Journal of Urban Affairs, 27*(2), 193–201.

Dubin, J. C. (1993). From junkyards to gentrification: Explicating a right to protective zoning in low-income communities of color. *Minnesota Law Review, 77*(4), 739–801.

Ducker, J. (2003). Overdeveloped town is an object lesson. *Cupertino Courier*, January 1.

Earl, J., Martin, A., McCarthy, J. D., & Soule, S. (2004). The use of newspaper data in the study of collective action. *Annual Review of Sociology, 30*, 65–80.

Feldman, C. (2000). Defending the barrio: Will working-class activists save the Mission? *San Francisco Bay Guardian*, (October 18), p. 35.

Gamson, W. (1992). *Talking politics*. Cambridge: Cambridge University Press.

Gamson, W. A., Croteau, D., Hoynes, W., & Sasson, T. (1992a). Media images and the Social construction of reality. *Annual Review of Sociology, 18*, 373–393.

Gibson, T. A. (2004). Covering the world-class downtown: Seattle's local media and the politics of urban development. *Critical Studies in Media Communication, 21*(4), 283–304.

Gin, J. (2007). *"We're here and we're not leaving": Framing, political history, and community response to gentrification in the San Francisco bay area*. Dissertation, School of Natural Resources and Environment, University of Michigan, Ann Arbor, MI.

Glass, R. (1964). *London: Aspects of change.* Centre for Urban Studies, Ed. London: MacGibbon & Kee.

Glickfeld, M., Levine, N., & Fulton, W. (1996). Home rule: Local growth ... regional consequences, Part II. Paper for Metropolitan Governance Research Project, Claremont, CA.

Guynn, J. (2006). Venture capital funding may top $32 billion: Recovery from dot-com bust continues with more money. *San Francisco Chronicle,* December 12.

Hartman, C., & Carnochan, S. (2002). *City for sale: The transformation of San Francisco.* Berkeley, CA: University of California Press.

Jenkins, C., & Perrow, C. (1977). Insurgency of the powerless: Farm worker movements, 1946–1972. *American Sociological Review, 42,* 249–268.

Jones, R. E., & Carter, L. F. (1994). Concern for the environment among black Americans: An assessment of common assumptions. *Social Science Quarterly, 75*(3), 560–579.

Kahn, B. (1985). On the street where we live: Fighting gentrification in West Oakland. *East Bay Express,* April 26.

Kingdon, J. W. (1984). *Agendas, alternatives, and public policies.* Boston: Little, Brown.

Larsen, L. S. (2009). *The pursuit of responsible development: Addressing anticipated benefits and unwanted burdens through community benefit agreements.* Working Papers Series No. 9. Center for Local, State, and Urban Policy, University of Michigan, Ann Arbor, MI.

Lewis, T. L. (2000). Media representations of "sustainable development". *Science Communication, 21*(3), 244–273.

Logan, J. R., & Molotch, H. L. (1987). *Urban fortunes: The political economy of place.* Berkeley, CA: University of California Press.

McCarthy, J. D., Smith, J., & Zald, M. N. (1996). Accessing public, media, electoral, and governmental Agendas. In: D. McAdam, J. D. McCarthy & M. N. Zald (Eds), *Comparative perspectives on social movements* (pp. 291–311). Cambridge: Cambridge University Press.

Molotch, H. L. (1976). The city as a growth machine: Toward a political economy of place. *American Journal of Sociology, 82*(2), 309–332.

Molotch, H. L. (1979). Media and movements. In: M. N. Zald & J. D. McCarthy (Eds), *The dynamics of social movements: Resource mobilization, social control, and tactics* (pp. 71–93). Cambridge, MA: Winthrop Publishers.

Oliver, P. E., & Johnston, H. (2000). What a good idea! Ideology and frames in social movement research. *Mobilization, 5*(1), 37–54.

Orfield, M. (1997). *Metropolitics: A regional agenda for community and stability.* Washington, DC: Brookings Institution Press.

Pellow, D. N. (2001). Environmental justice and the political process: Movements, corporations, and the state. *Sociological Quarterly, 42*(1), 47–67.

Rhomberg, C. (2004). *No there there: Race, class, and political community in Oakland.* Berkeley, CA: University of California Press.

Ryan, C. (1991). *Prime time activism.* Boston, MA: South End Press.

Ryan, C., & Gamson, W. A. (2006). The art of reframing political debates. *Contexts, 5*(1), 13–18.

Smith, N. (1996). *The new urban frontier.* London: Routledge.

Smith, N., & Williams, P. (1986). *Gentrification of the city.* London: Allen and Unwin.

Snow, D. A., & Benford, R. D. (1992). Master frames and cycles of protest. In: A. D. Morris & C. M. Mueller (Eds), *Frontiers in social movement theory* (pp. 133–155). New Haven, CT: Yale University Press.

Swidler, A. (1986). Culture in action: Symbols and strategies. *American Sociological Review*, *51*, 273–286.

Taylor, D. E. (2000). The rise of the environmental justice paradigm: Injustice framing and the social construction of environmental discourses. *American Behavioral Scientist*, *43*(4), 508–580.

Walker, R. A. (2004). Industry builds out the city: The suburbanization of manufacturing in the San Francisco Bay area, 1850–1940. In: R. Lewis (Ed.), *The manufactured metropolis*. Philadelphia: Temple University Press.

Warner, K. (2001). Managing to grow with environmental justice. *Public Works Management and Policy*, *6*(2), 126–138.

Yee, C. Y., & Quiroz-Martinez, J. (1999). *There goes the neighborhood: A regional analysis of gentrification and community stability in the San Francisco Bay Area*. Report by Urban Habitat, San Francisco.

June Gin received her Ph.D. in Environmental Resource Policy and Behavior (Environmental Justice) from the University of Michigan School of Natural Resources and Environment. She is a researcher at the Fritz Institute in San Francisco, CA. She can be reached by email at june.gin8@gmail.com or by telephone at 415-279-2784.

Dorceta E. Taylor is an associate professor at the University of Michigan's School of Natural Resources and Environment. She teaches courses in environmental history, environmental justice, tourism and climate change, and social movements. She is the director of the Multicultural Environ-mental Leadership Development Initiative (http://www.meldi.snre.umich. edu) and author of *The Environment and the People in American Cities, 1600s–1900s: Disorder, Inequality, and Social Change*. She can be reached by email at dorceta@umich.edu or by telephone at 734-763-5327.

FOOD SECURITY AND SUSTAINABILITY: COMMUNITY FOOD INITIATIVES IN LONDON

Shumaisa Khan

ABSTRACT

Purpose – *European studies of alternative food networks have covered primarily rural or periurban initiatives that connect producers and consumers directly. For the most part, those studies overlook nonprofit urban community initiatives. This chapter begins to address the gap by presenting preliminary findings from a study that examines the development of community food initiatives that sell green produce in London.*

Design/methodology/approach – *The first part of the chapter draws on content analysis of literature produced by 15 initiatives and presents a brief overview. The second part presents case study analysis of the organizational, physical, and social context of two of the initiatives.*

Findings – *The findings indicate that many urban green produce initiatives have an explicit emphasis on the demand side of the producer–consumer connection. Those that emphasize sustainably produced food and fair trade may have difficulty drawing low-income customers, even if located in areas with high levels of deprivation. Initiatives oriented toward basic food access rather than sustainability are expanding their scope to include more "local" food.*

Environment and Social Justice: An International Perspective
Research in Social Problems and Public Policy, Volume 18, 115–139
Copyright © 2010 by Emerald Group Publishing Limited
All rights of reproduction in any form reserved
ISSN: 0196-1152/doi:10.1108/S0196-1152(2010)0000018006

Originality/value – *Although this study does not represent urban green produce initiatives throughout England or beyond, it provides some examples of how such initiatives can develop and the extent to which they claim social justice and environmental considerations in their efforts. This study is a step toward empirical examination of nonprofit urban green produce initiatives, and contributes to a broader, more inclusive conceptualization of alternative food networks.*

INTRODUCTION

In the past, food security was considered mostly an issue of concern in less industrialized nations. However, volatility in food commodity prices, climate change, and the recession have all contributed in making domestic and global food security an important issue for industrialized nations as well (Sustainable Development Commission, 2009). Food security is defined as a condition in which "all people, at all times, have physical, social and economic access to sufficient, safe and nutritious food that meets their dietary needs and food preferences for an active and healthy life" (Food and Agriculture Organization, 2002).

Food security has emerged as a major issue of concern in poor urban areas. Addressing lack of access to fresh food has become more urgent as the global recession and climate change dynamics (such as floods, droughts, and other weather phenomenon that have devastated crops) have resulted in an increase in food prices (Brown, 2009). This means the poor are less able to purchase food or afford a healthy diet. One of the ways that communities in industrialized nations are coping with this is to develop green produce initiatives to ensure that the poorest people have access to fresh food. In the United Kingdom, these initiatives – that are heavily reliant on volunteers – acquire produce in bulk from wholesalers or direct from producers and sell them in venues such as outdoor stalls, community centers, schools, nonprofits, or social enterprises. These local initiatives serve several important functions. In addition to providing fresh food to the poor, they provide an alternative to conventional means of food distribution. Some provide sustainably produced food where it is beyond the capacity of the community gardens to meet local demand. Though these initiatives tend to serve only a small portion of the population when compared to that served by commercial food retailers, they often emerge through the efforts of local residents or community organizations.

More and more cities are grappling with the social and ecological implications of their food systems. They are becoming more aware of and proactive about food-related problems such as obesity, "food miles," and food-related waste. As urban policy makers recognize the need to create a more sustainable and equitable food system, it is important to find out more about a range of existing efforts working toward this goal, not just those that directly connect consumers and producers. This essay is a step in that direction. It presents findings from a study examining nonprofit green produce initiatives in London. Like many cities, London has areas with poor access to healthy food retailing, areas of high concentrations of poverty and ethnic minorities, and a large food-related environmental footprint. Understanding how such initiatives emerge and the kinds of models that are successful can be of value for other major urban settings. This chapter examines alternative food networks (AFNs) in London. It analyzes two case studies of initiatives that provide fresh food in low-income areas.

ALTERNATIVE FOOD NETWORKS

Conventional food systems comprise a critical nexus of sustainability issues due to the economic, health, environmental, and social impacts associated with the journey of food from its source to its fate as consumption or waste. Food options are diminishing for those living in many urban areas. A 2003 study by the New Economics Foundation has shown that between 1997 and 2002 a few major supermarket outlets continued to take over more of the food retail market, small stores such as butchers, bakers, fishmongers, greengrocers and newsagents selling confectionery, tobacco, and newspapers closed at a rate of 50 per week in the United Kingdom (Oram, Consibee, & Simms, 2003). In addition, wholesale suppliers in the food industry have closed at a rate of six per week during 2001–2003, whereas the five largest supermarkets continue to use a limited number of suppliers (Oram et al., 2003).

The food system can also contribute to poor health and environmental outcomes. Inadequate access to a variety of quality food can lead to greater consumption of high calorie food with little nutritional value. Energy and resources used in production, packaging, and transport of food as well as chemical inputs and genetic modification used in intensive agriculture all take a toll on the soil, air, and water, and contribute up to 18 percent of UK carbon emissions (The Strategy Unit, 2008). Finally, the dominant food system and increasing privatization of space can isolate people from each other and from their food, and in the increased exploitation of workers (Gottlieb & Fisher, 1996). In contrast, engagement in small, food-based projects such as community gardens or kitchens can provide valuable experiences in community building, collective decision-making, civic values, interacting with people of different backgrounds, as well as a deeper understanding of the food system (Levkoe, 2006).

It is in response to the adverse effects of the global food system that a set of oppositional food system ideas and practices have emerged, largely organized around relocalizing production and consumption of food (Watts, Ilbery, & Maye, 2005). Although no precise definition of an AFN exists, the term describes alternatives to conventional, industrial means of food supply and distribution. In practice, those involved in projects described as AFNs typically do not use the term themselves (Venn et al., 2006). Moreover, some of what was considered "alternative," such as organic food has become part of the global food system. However, Born and Purcell (2006) warn that food system localization may not always result in positive sum gains to society, the economy or the environment. They assert that localization serves as a scalar strategy that can result in different outcomes depending on the agenda of those advancing the strategy.

Thus far, much of the scholarship on AFNs has focused on food production or spaces of exchange in the global North; they examine cases of shortened food chains (Renting, Marsden, & Banks, 2003; Watts et al., 2005), alternative agro-food systems (Goodman, 2003; Watts et al., 2005), and local food systems (Born & Purcell, 2006; Feagan, 2007; Feenstra, 1997). In contrast, Venn et al. (2006) examined AFNs at a broader level. In their study of European AFNs, they analyzed how empirical studies have operationalized the concept and identified key criteria for identifying them. According to them, AFNs:

- place emphasis on reducing distances between consumers and producers of food,
- have nonconventional supply and distribution channels,
- encourage the principles of trust and community building, and
- focus on "quality" food while attempting to preserve cultural traditions or heritage.

Using this framework, Venn et al. (2006) identified projects that met at least one of these criteria to create a database of AFNs. They found that many projects considered things such as nutrition education, independent living skills, and social cohesion activities as important dimensions of their work. In several cases, the provision of food served as a mechanism to achieve broader aims, and some groups used food procurement and delivery as a means of tackling social inequalities. The researchers also identified four categories of AFNs:

1. Producers as consumers – community gardens with food production.
2. Specialist retailers – retail outlets selling "high value-added, quality foods" – a more direct route for producers than supermarkets.
3. Producer–consumer partnerships such as community supported agriculture.
4. Direct sell initiatives such as farmers markets and box initiatives (Venn et al., 2006).

Although the authors rightly assert that AFN as a term can obscure the diversity of food initiatives, their categorization of AFNs excluded many community food initiatives, such as the types examined in this chapter.

In a similar vein, Abrahams' (2006) study of AFNs in Johannesburg, South Africa revealed that the urban poor use AFNs for basic food access and ethnic foods rather than for ethical consumption. Such findings demonstrate a contrast to the northern-dominated conceptualization of AFNs, which are seen as largely catering to white, middle class consumers in search of ethical consumption. She argues that broadening understanding of AFNs to include those centered around issues of cultural diversity, survival, and food security is relevant not only for the global South, but also for the urban poor and multicultural communities in the North.

Scholars have also critiqued the exclusionary nature of many American-based organizations related to AFNs or community food security. Slocum (2006) and Guthman (2003) have shown that farmers markets and community food security efforts can have discriminatory outcomes. Farmers markets tend to serve predominantly white, middle class consumers (Guthman, 2003). The leadership of community food security organizations also tends to be white and middle class (Slocum, 2006). In addition, an examination of "buy local" campaigns in the United States has revealed a general failure to deal with inequalities in agri-food policy (Hinrichs & Allen, 2008). For instance, Slow Food USA, while mentioning the value of fair compensation for workers and universal access to "good" food on its website, only engages in activities pertaining to the consumption of "good" food (Allen & Wilson, 2008).

FOOD ACCESS

Researchers have also looked at food from the perspective of the right to healthy food. In the United Kingdom, the Lower Income Project Team developed the term "food deserts" in a 1995 report to refer to areas of cities with few or no sources of cheap, nutritious food (Wrigley, 2002). However, studies of this topic have yielded conflicting results. Most of the British studies have examined either parts of a city or an entire city. Some studies reveal an association between poor neighborhoods and the presence of food deserts (Donkin, Dowler, Stevenson, & Turner, 1999; East London and the City Health Authority [ELCHA], 1999; Wrigley, Warm, & Margetts, 2003), whereas other studies do not show such an association (Cummins & Macintyre, 2002; Guy, 2004; White et al., 2001). One study showed the many "food deserts" in East London. The 1999 study of four boroughs in East London revealed that in 29 of 66 wards, 50 percent of people lived more than 500 m from the nearest food retailer. In 13 of those wards, 70 percent lived more than 500 m from the nearest food retailer (ELCHA, 1999). Five hundred meters continues to serve as what is considered a reasonable walking distance to obtain food in food access studies. In the United States, where large-scale, cross-sectional studies have been conducted, evidence suggests low income and predominantly African–American neighborhoods may have very poor access to healthy foods (Morland, Wing, Roux, & Poole, 2002; Zenk et al., 2005).

Research on the noncommercial provision of food is limited; however, in 2006 a study was conducted to evaluate the impacts of one organization's green produce initiatives in London. Researchers at King's College in London conducted a six-month study of users and nonusers of green produce initiatives run by an East London community food organization (Nelson, Suleiman, & Gu, 2008). This organization has received support from several programs, including the New Deal for Communities (NDC) program, a national fund intended to help facilitate the regeneration of the deprived communities in the United Kingdom. Contrary to expectation, reported levels of consumption did not vary between users and nonusers, but users reported spending half the amount of money on fruits and vegetables than nonusers. This suggests the possibility of lower consumption among users in the absence of the initiative, which provides affordable produce. In terms of longevity of use, the study found that of the 141 users, those that had used the initiative for 12 or more weeks were more likely to eat vegetables on more days of the week, or eat more portions per day relative to those who had used the initiative for less than 12 weeks. Among men, this difference was significant. However, only one significant difference between users and nonusers was seen; male users reported significantly more portions of fruit consumption per day compared to nonusers (Nelson et al., 2008).

Although the study also looked at change in blood pressure and body size, it did not find a clear difference between baseline and subsequent measurements, and where a change existed, it occurred in the opposite direction than expected. The authors speculated that this could be due to the higher level of smoking and drinking, and lower levels of reported physical activity – all known risk factors for blood pressure – among the users compared to nonusers (Nelson et al., 2008). Nonetheless, the findings indicate that green produce initiatives can reach residents less likely to engage in healthy lifestyles, not just those who are already health-conscious.

GREEN PRODUCE INITIATIVES IN LONDON: AN OVERVIEW

This chapter reports on a study of green produce initiatives in London that I undertook from 2008 to 2009. I identified initiatives to include in this study by using the website of Sustain, a national food and farming organization that lists farmers markets, coops, and other initiatives selling green produce, and from Internet searches (Sustainweb, 2008). I focused on initiatives that operate as social enterprises or on a nonprofit basis, which meant that farmers markets were excluded from the study. This resulted in the identification of 14 nonprofit green produce initiatives that currently sell fruits and vegetables at approximately 80 venues across London, and one initiative that operates a home delivery service only. Six additional initiatives were identified, but they were not operating at the time of the study.

Most of the initiatives started as projects of community organizations such as housing associations, community centers, and in one case, a church. Four initiatives began with support from the National Health Service (NHS): two began solely through the local Primary Care Trust (PCT), one began solely through a regional branch of the NHS, and one began as a partnership between the PCT and cooperative development agency (CDA). Some of these initiatives had conducted formal needs assessments before starting up an initiative, but none of the organic food initiatives had done so. Only four had origins in local residents' initiatives – two were affordable food initiatives and the other two organic food initiatives. One initiative developed after a new resident to an area lacking food retailers began making weekly trips to the market to bring back produce to sell in the neighborhood. This has evolved into a vast enterprise, which includes delivery of a national training program for community food workers. It also supplies produce for another network of coops, and has recently received a grant to develop a hub for the distribution of local and sustain ably produced food in coordination with a regional food organization in the east of England.

I am interested in the question of how green food initiatives that have as their goal the provision of affordable food differ from those that have a stated goal of providing organic produce differ. To this end, I sorted the initiatives being studied into two groups – those providing affordable produce and those focused on providing organic produce. Five initiatives fit in the first category and 10 in the second. It should be noted that some organic initiatives also stressed reasonable prices.

I studied the initiatives' promotional or programmatic literature, websites, and reports to assess what they claimed as benefits of buying produce through them, and then performed a content analysis on these. Eight themes emerged from this exercise: affordability, health, community, quality, environment, justice, economy, and awareness. Table 1 presents the themes and claims associated with them. The table shows that these food initiatives think of food security in a way that is much more than access to green produce. They link access to food to environment and human health, social justice and the political economy of food production.

Though fewer in number, the content analysis also indicates that organic initiatives communicate significantly more about their ideology than affordable initiatives do ($p = .002$). One long-standing organic initiative has produced a lengthy document outlining 12 principles that informs its work; a newer organic initiative has added these principles to its own promotional literature. Environment featured prominently as a theme among the organic initiatives – 38 percent of the theme references involved environment (Table 2). As expected, affordability was the theme most frequently mentioned by affordable initiatives; affordable initiatives were more than twice as likely as organic initiatives to mention affordability. Health and quality were also themes that were more likely to be mentioned by affordable initiatives than organic ones. This may be the case because organic food is already associated with high quality and people drawn to outlets selling organic food tend to be health-conscious. Although five percent of the organic initiative literature themes involved awareness, this theme did not occur in the literature of affordable initiatives.

Among organic initiatives, justice generally referred to fair deals for producers from the global South, whereas it referred to accessibility of basic, healthy food for local consumers in affordable initiatives. In only one

Table 1. Themes, Claims, and Strategies Related to the Benefits of
Green Produce Initiatives.

Theme	Rationale	Claims and Strategies
Affordability	Reasonably priced food	Sold with little markup on prices Volunteer-run Produce bought in bulk Savings passed on to customers
Health	Encourage healthy eating	Fresher food retains more nutrients Fruits and vegetables contribute to better health outcomes Demonstrations/recipes for healthy cooking
Community building	Encourage greater interaction between community residents	Private gardeners or community food growing projects can share produce Meet people at the stalls Community residents can help run coop
Quality	Fresh, seasonal, traceable food	Direct from wholesaler Direct from farm or community garden
Environment	Reduce pollution	No use of greenhouse-produced food Local sourcing cuts down on food miles Less food transport and consumer transport to commercial retailers No use of plastic packaging Less intensive agricultural practices Less chemical inputs into soil and water
Justice	Eliminate barriers to "right food" Alleviate food poverty Fair trade	Making healthy food more accessible physically and economically Fair prices for producers in the global South
Economy	Help local economies	Small-scale operations more labor-intensive, employing more people rather than using machinery Linking community enterprises with each other
Awareness	Increased knowledge of food chain	People learn what is in season and how to prepare seasonal foods

organic initiative did justice refer to a similar concept, but its definition of healthy entailed organically produced food.

CASE STUDIES

Information on the two case studies presented below is based on data collected from May–September 2009. I used participant and nonparticipant

Table 2. Comparison of Themes Referenced in the Literature
of Two Types of Initiatives.

Theme	Percentage of Total References	
	Organic initiatives ($n = 81$)	Affordable initiatives ($n = 36$)
Environment	38	11
Community	15	8
Economy	11	8
Affordability	10	22
Justice	9	13
Health	6	19
Quality	6	19
Awareness	5	0

observation of coops; in-depth, semistructured interviews with coop staff;
semistructured interviews with customers and residents of the area; and
programmatic and promotional literature. Spatial analysis was also
employed to map the food retailing outlets located within 500 m of each
coop. In the discussion of the case studies I use pseudonyms for individuals,
organizations directly involved in the initiatives, and housing estates.

Greenham Coop-Part of the South London Food Coop Group

Background
The Greenham Housing Estate is located in 1 of the 10 most deprived lower
layer super output areas (LSOAs) in England (LSOA is a census unit that
contains approximately 1,500 people). Seventy-five percent of the residents
in the LSOA live in rented social housing. Fig. 1 shows deprivation levels
according to the Index of Multiple Deprivation (IMD) which combines
37 indicators covering income, employment, health and disability, education, skills and training, barriers to housing and services, and living
environment and crime. As the estate had been planned to undergo
regeneration following "decant," or removal of existing residents, the few
small businesses on the estate shut down years ago. The local council has
been removing residents since 2004, and as of February 2009, approximately
1,100 empty homes existed on the estate. Greenham is surrounded by much
green space, but no food retailers, except for one store that sells liquor, other
drinks, and snacks (see Fig. 1). The estate has had a coop stall running

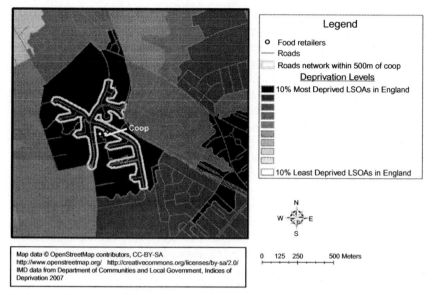

Map data © OpenStreetMap contributors, CC-BY-SA
http://www.openstreetmap.org/ http://creativecommons.org/licenses/by-sa/2.0/
IMD data from Department of Communities and Local Government, Indices of
Deprivation 2007

Fig. 1. Index of Multiple Deprivation Levels and Commercial Food Retail
Presence around Greenham Coop.

weekly since 2002, and today constitutes one coop in a network of coops
delivered by South London Food Coop Group (SLFCG).

SLFCG has its origins in a food project delivered by the local PCT from
1999 to 2002. The project focused on increasing consumption of fruits and
vegetables and was funded by the Single Regeneration Budget, a national
fund that existed at the time. After community researchers conducted
a needs assessment on Greenham Estate, the Greenham Food Project
group, comprised of residents and community food workers, was established
in 2001 to consider options for a community food project. The needs assessment also recruited three directors for the project, who continue to serve as
the management committee. The PCT approached the local Cooperative
Development Agency (CDA) for technical assistance in starting a social
enterprise, launching an enduring partnership.[1]

Consultations with the community revealed a preference for a market
stall, rather than a membership coop or box delivery initiative, and the
group piloted one in February 2002. The stall on a square in Greenham
Estate continues to this day, and serves as a case study for this research.
At that point, the project was called Greenham Food Coop. The success of
the first stall triggered interest in other areas of South London, leading the

local CDA and PCT to seek and receive funding from the Healthy South London Network to set up the South London Food Initiative (SLFI). The Healthy South London Network is a Healthy Living Centre (HLC), a project originally funded by the National Lottery and other national funds, to cultivate partnerships between private and public sector organizations on activities that improve health.[2] SLFI was created with the mandate to work in areas of the borough characterized by high levels of health inequalities to establish initiatives aimed at improving access to healthy, affordable food.[3]

Additional funding supported the employment of a part-time coordinator and the establishment of another stall in 2003. Around the same time, SLFG was established as an umbrella organization for all coops established under the SLFI, replacing Greenham Food Coop. Originally, SLFI planned to create separate businesses throughout the area. However, after the first annual review, the directors felt that this would entail the logistics of separate accounts, committees, and require more volunteers to handle the acquisition, pricing, and stocking of produce. The organization believed an umbrella approach would also provide the advantages of greater consistency in price, service, and quality across all coops, financial benefits of joint purchasing, and less waste as produce leftover at one stall could be used at another stall.

Over the years, several other coops have started, each of which began after a community needs assessment that gauged demand and the prevalence of green produce suppliers. A large publicity campaign occurred in 2005, with the establishment of four new coops; it involved the circulation of postcards to residences in postcodes around the coops and the circulation of posters and leaflets to doctors' surgeries, community centers, libraries, and housing offices. In addition, the delivery van has the logo and information, serving as another means of publicity. Currently SLFG delivers to 11 stalls, which are set up outside schools, community centers, and one church; in addition to these coops, it delivers produce to over 25 other points such as schools and workplaces. The project is approximately 65–70 percent self-financing, but receives £40,000 a year in funding from the local branch of the NHS to support the stalls.

Organizational Structure
SLFCG is a company limited by guarantee, a British legal structure used by many nonprofit organizations that require corporate status, and is registered as a cooperative with Cooperatives UK, a national organization that provides training and other support to cooperatives. Three people have served as the directors/management committee since the inception of the

project, and are responsible for all financial, legal, and human resource issues. The remaining employed staff includes four part-time positions: two drivers – one who also stocks produce; a coordinator; and an administrator. The drivers also set up and take down each stall, and usually two volunteers run each stall. The operation has a centralized structure; no local organizations are involved in setting up or running the coops. The project also has a constitution and a comprehensive volunteer handbook, which includes a "good practice agreement" each volunteer must sign. The agreement covers reimbursement procedures; attendance policies; and mentions types of support provided by SLFCG such as training. The handbook also covers:

- recruitment procedures,
- health and safety policies,
- supervision details (this includes on-the-job and formal supervision every 4–6 weeks),
- volunteer communication,
- complaints policy and procedure,
- disciplinary rules and grievance procedure,
- equal opportunities policy, and
- a confidentiality policy.

Volunteers
This coop is unusual in that all three of the volunteers at the Greenham stall are retired men, although one of them also works part-time as a driver, delivering produce and setting up other stalls for SLFG. In SLFG, the role of volunteers involves assessing the produce delivered to the coop, removing and documenting spoiled or damaged produce, weighing produce that customers select, and handling cash transactions. Elias is African and has worked there since the beginning. The driver/volunteer, Sam, is white and has worked at the coop for 5 years. John is also white and has worked at the coop for a few months. Elias and John live outside of the estate and travel to the coop by public transport, one traveling 20 min, the other 30–45 min. Elias learned about the coop through and advertisement in its early days, and John had passed a coop in his neighborhood and learned about the project then. After reading more about it in one of the local newspapers, he talked to the women volunteering at the stall near him, and then decided to volunteer.

Elias, who has had the most experience with the stall, cited customer relations as the biggest challenge in running the stall. He noted the importance of understanding cultural differences and knowledge of the produce:

> Some customers do come who are very, very selective, you see-they might say "Oh no I don't want anything from Australia. Oh! I don't want anything from America". So they try to ask you [about the origins of the produce], so you must know your products.

He continued, "People won't buy products when it comes from a certain part of the world. Ethical reasons ... you see, it's a cultural thing ... [pointing to produce] Certain people wouldn't buy them if they come from Israel."

Elias's statement suggests ethical consumerism occurs even at coops oriented toward basic food access.

Food
Food is obtained from New Spitalfields Market, which is located on 31 acres in East London. A driver collects the produce from the market and delivers it to a storage area provided by the council at Greenham Estate; deliveries to the various stalls are arranged from here. SLFCG attempts to obtain seasonal, regional produce that is reasonably priced. They also get foreign produce to meet the needs of ethnically diverse communities. The group is currently working on increasing the proportion of seasonal, "low-impact" produce. They are applying for a local food grant to expand office delivery service as a way of generating more profit. Occasionally, small amounts of produce from some staff members' allotments or from community food growing projects is donated and sold for a token amount; these are referred to as organic by volunteers at the stall. The range of food reflects the diversity of people it serves; on a typical day the stall has yams, plantains, cassava, garden eggs (a type of eggplant), okra, as well as standard fruits and vegetables. One of the drivers had previously worked as a quality manager at a major supermarket, and sometimes gets produce from small farmers in the region who he knows from his past work. The amount of markup on the food price varies, but is 33 percent on average. No comparison could be made with prices at other retailers in the area as no other retailers exist within 500 m that sell green produce.

Customers
The Greenham stall runs from 8 a.m. to 2 p.m. on Tuesdays and 8 a.m. to 12 noon on Wednesdays, though the staff members have the discretion to close earlier if usage is low. I conducted interviews with nine customers after they had purchased produce from Greenham Coop. I also interviewed three residents while they were waiting at a nearby bus stop. All of the customers

learned about the coop by walking past it on the estate and have used the coop since its launch. All but two of the respondents were women, and all but two were ethnic minorities. The two white women were the only nonresidents of the estate, and used it because they worked at the health clinic on the estate.

The customers expressed much enthusiasm for the coop and for the volunteers running it. One East Asian woman interviewed at the coop stall stated, "I use because I can pick something I want; in the store sometime the food is in a pack." A retired African man who was also interviewed at the stall said, "It's cheaper than Lewisham, and over here I come and buy, I don't need transport to go ... and the people are friendly." According to a retired African woman, "They have fresh vegetables, and the people are very friendly. The staff, you know it's easy to communicate with them, they give good advice when you ask anything about the foods here, they know about it." Three other customers shopping with their young children made similar statements.

One of the residents interviewed when the coop was not operating works as a security guard at a Tesco supermarket. Despite the fact that Tesco is a national chain and he works there, he prefers to buy his produce at the coop. He stated, "I use it- very nice, very, very nice ... every week and I use it because it's very cheap. And not only that, because it's fresh, direct from the, you know direct from the wholesalers."

One woman sitting at the bus stop with her young children said she used the coop occasionally, because her husband likes a particular national chain, but she noted that if the coop was open more often, she would use it more. This woman was content with her local food environment except for transport; she wanted to see more frequent buses. Another woman at the bus stop had mobility problems, so her son, who has a car and lives nearby helps her with shopping; she uses the coop occasionally.

Among regular coop users, when asked if there is any way the coop could improve, six felt it was ideal; one man commented on the hours, saying that it would be better if one of the times could be after work-hours. The man who works at Tesco wanted more varieties of produce and in greater quantities stating, "The quantity is not enough. By the time you get there, most of the foods are gone, like yams, African food ... [they should] increase the quantity of African, Afro-Caribbean food."

These comments show the unique niche food initiatives like this occupy. They strive to meet the need to provide green produce in areas underserved by traditional food outlets. However, the clients also want ethnic foods and foods from the global South. Such foods are unlikely to be found at a typical farmers market. Because of the paucity of food stores in the area, many residents of the estate do use the coop at least sometimes, and many use it regularly. The customers are primarily women. According to a volunteer, approximately 40 people use the coop in the 10 h it is open each week, spending an average of £6. Given that several hundred people still live on the estate, the amount of customers seems small. As the stall only sells fruits and vegetables, most residents make trips to supermarkets and other markets to buy food. The value of the coop is that it is the only place to buy food locally.

South London Coop

Background

The South London Coop differs from the SLFG model in terms of its operations, range of food sold, venue, and organizational structure. However, there is some overlap in ethos. As its leaflet states, "It was set up in 1988 by local people to provide good food for the community at affordable prices in the belief that decent food is a basic necessity for health, regardless of means." The concept of good food, however, encompasses broader social justice and ethical concerns. The leaflet continues, "For need not greed- [South London Coop] supports patterns of consumption that promote social justice and sustainable agriculture and fosters an awareness of the political and ecological effects of consumer actions."

The space the coop operates from was originally seized by squatters who used it to create a radical social center. Around 2004, the center obtained a formal lease from the local council. At the time the coop started, much of the estate on the street had been squatted, however, many of the squatters later gained formal tenancy. Although the neighborhood is undergoing gentrification, the area immediately surrounding the coop is among the 12 percent most deprived LSOAs in England. Seventy-seven percent of the residents live in rented social housing. I conducted a census of the food outlets in the area and found that 34 food retailers lie within walking distance of the coop, including several that sell fresh green produce. These outlets are mapped in Fig. 2 and contained in the list presented in Table 3. As Fig. 2 also illustrates, a major shopping center with additional food retailers lies just beyond the 500 m road distance from the coop.

The coop has received funding only once; its organic green produce supplier gave it a small grant to fund the refurbishment of the floors several years ago. The coop's leaflet, as well as a sign on its premises, asks for

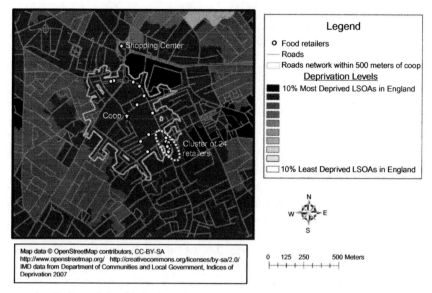

Fig. 2. Index of Multiple Deprivation Levels and Commercial Food Retail Presence around South London Coop.

Table 3. Number of Commercial Food Outlets near the South London Coop.

Store Type	Examples	Quantity
Independent stores selling green produce	Ethnic grocery stores, convenience stores	5
National supermarket chains	Tesco, Morrisons, Marks and Spencer	1
Independent specialty stores that do not sell green produce	Health food stores, bakeries	3
Eat-in and takeaway	Cafes, restaurants, pubs, fast-food outlets	23
Liquor stores	Food and wine, off-license	2

donations to help cover rent and bills. When asked about measures to make the food accessible to lower income customers, a volunteer stated:

> What we did try doing was having the donations box system, and the idea of that was so that we could keep our prices on the shelf as low as possible and people would donate money every time they shopped if they felt they weren't lowest income customers. And those donations that we got in at least cover our utility bills, like the electricity, water, and things like that we have to pay for, the rent and whatever, then we could actually bring the

shelf prices lower, but I think a lot of customers haven't really understood that, and a lot of people really don't think of themselves as well-off even if actually in terms of benefits they are-so it's something-we're still working on it, I think we'd like it to be better.

Organizational Structure

The food coop occupies one part of a collectively managed space that includes a one-room library containing literature on things "radical," as well as a do-it-yourself bicycle repair workshop. Thus, it differs from many coops in that it operates out of a more permanent space. Nonetheless, it does not operate daily. The entire collective has a strong ethos of autonomy, and prides itself on being run entirely by volunteers and without funding from sources that many coops rely upon. The food coop runs on a do-it-yourself basis as well. Customers bring their own bags or pick up used bags stored on site, and use scales, papers, pens, and calculators provided to weigh items and tally their bill before paying.

The collective meets weekly to discuss matters related to all aspects of the center. The meetings are open to anyone who wants to get involved; the collective uses consensus-based decision making. Compared to others, this coop has a more informal structure. It does not have a legal structure, a business strategy or other documents, and only began formal volunteer training in 2009. It manages to run without ongoing funding, having benefited from many years of rent-free existence while it was establishing itself in the community.

Volunteers

Volunteers run all aspects of the coop, however, unlike at other coops, they do not weigh the produce or tally the bills for customers. Usually two volunteers are present when the store is open: Thursday 2 p.m. to 8 p.m., Friday 3 p.m. to 7 p.m., and Saturday 3 p.m. to 5 p.m. Most of the volunteers are white females who travel from other parts of London to volunteer in the coop. The volunteers typically found out about the coop by word-of-mouth, though one, an Australian immigrant, found it through a search on the Internet. The volunteers vary to a greater extent than at stall-based food coops, where one finds the same volunteers each session. Many of the volunteers running shifts at the South London Coop have only worked there for a year or less. However, Sandra, a volunteer who has been very active in the collective has been involved in running the coop for 10 years. She learned of it when squatting and visiting social centers in Brixton. She used using it for about 4 years as a customer before becoming an active volunteer.

According to Sandra, the biggest challenge the coop has to overcome has to do with "functioning well as a collective." She identified an additional challenge that arose in 2009 – the coop might face a rate increase from the council:

Rates is like the local tax that you pay, it's what businesses pay instead of council tax, basically. For the last two years, we've been locked into a dispute with the council about whether we should pay 25 percent of the rates or 50 percent of the rates. Cuz they have this thing called rates which is discretionary, they normally award to charities and nonprofit groups where you only pay a small share of what a commercial business would pay. We've paid this 25 percent rate in the past, and then for the last 2 years, we've kind of been arguing about it because they haven't run our application through properly, they've never given us an answer about it, they haven't got back to us one way or the other, but we're assuming they actually want to stop us from getting this. So yeah, that's the biggest struggle this year definitely.

To help bolster its case, the coop has put out a comment book for customers to write down the value of the coop to them, and has started a bulletin board with pictures of volunteers and customers and index cards of their comments.

Food and Other Items
People from the area set up the South London Coop to provide affordable whole foods, and in its early days a volunteer went to Borough Market in London to obtain fresh green produce to sell at the coop. It continues to stock dried foods obtained in bulk to sell cheaply, and uses a regional organic supplier, Hughes Organics, to obtain fresh green produce. This limits the green produce to what is in season. Moreover, the coop does not have the range of produce sought by the ethnically diverse residents in the area. It only sells food that is animal, sugar, and GMO-free, and gets its whole foods from other workers cooperatives and collectives with similar aims. Customers can, however, order items from these suppliers through the coop if the coop does not sell them. The markup on food varies; fresh green produce and fresh bread have a markup of 15 percent but most of the other food items are marked up 10 percent. Palestinian fair trade products constitute the only food items not marked up. Sandra said this is the case because, "The Palestinian olive oil we just sell at the price we get for it because it's a solidarity thing, and we want as much money for the Palestinians as possible, we don't need to make a profit on that."

The coop itself does not do price comparisons with other stores noting that as a nonprofit, volunteer-run initiative, its products are cheaper than those of commercial stores that pay for staff and other costs associated with running daily. No stores within the 500 m distance sell organic green produce, but a health food store within this distance does sell other organic products.

Customers

I interviewed nine customers during or after their shopping activities at the coop. Of these, only two were from the vicinity, and both had just discovered the coop recently. The rest lived 20–45 min away and came by train, bus, or bike. Four were of African-Caribbean descent, while the rest were white. All of the customers interviewed learned of the coop by word-of-mouth. An exception was a Canadian couple that has lived in the neighborhood for 2 years as students and only recently discovered the coop when looking up the history of the estate on the street that the coop is located near. This led them to the radical social center that the coop is housed in. The location of the coop at the end of a residential street, combined with the limited open hours, may contribute to the large number of people coming from other parts of London. Sandra noted:

> I know a lot of people find it really hard to find this place first time they come here. I remember when I first came, the first couple of times I came here, I remember like never quite-always taking ages to find it ... Once you know it you're fine ... and I know that people quite often come here and say yeah it's taken me ages to find this place, and I can still empathize with them.

She continued:

> I'd say people that live on the actual, who have lived on the P- estate for a while or on this estate here for a while, will know that we exist. A lot of them come in because it's convenient and done it for years, so that's one definite group of people. But then there's other people that live just as geographically close, like that new block of flats down the road, and a lot of them don't even know, probably don't know that we exist because they come out of their flat and they all go out to, they don't come this way, and they never walk past. And there's people I know that have lived around here that walked past the shop and it's taken them years to make it inside. So it's not that everyone who lives right around here comes here, but I think the ones who do come back pretty regularly, like every week at least. There's lots of people that have lived around this area and moved a bit further away and still live in London and come back here to shop.

Customers gave several reasons why they shopped at the coop. Their reasons ranged from the unique shopping experience to the affordability of organic produce. A white female who has shopped at the coop for 3 years stated, "It's really fairly priced, it makes a contribution to the local economy rather than to supermarkets, it's organic, and the shopping experience is quite interesting." An African woman who has been shopping at the coop for 20 years said she shopped there because "It is friendly, easy to use, you can choose how much you want, it's relaxed." A retired white man who had been shopping at the coop for a few months said he shopped at the coop because it was unique and had low prices. According to him, there was "Nothing like this-there's Holland & Barrett [a national health food chain] but that's expensive. Nothing with good quality organic, and reasonable prices."

The South London Coop tends to draw people who are highly conscious about health and ecological issues. Three of the customers interviewed work in professions that entail awareness of health or environmental issues: aromatherapy, environmental education, and community food-skills education. Another customer became interested in the link between food and health after experiencing a major health problem 5 years ago, and one customer who is retired himself, had a partner who was studying herbal therapy. In an area with a large African-Caribbean population, the limited range of produce may deter neighborhood residents from using the coop, especially since there are three African-Caribbean markets in the vicinity.

The average amount of spending per customer and average number of customers per week was difficult to ascertain, as customers often purchase some items, linger and chat, then purchase some more items, and the same customers may come on more than a day during the week. Customers who want to buy fresh green produce tend to shop on Thursday, the first day the coop runs and the day with the longest running hours. Because of the longer hours and the freshness of the green produce, sales are several times greater on Thursday and Friday than on Saturday.

Informal interviews with two women at a local church indicated that many people in the neighborhood shop at a supermarket a little more than 500 m from the coop and do not know of the coop. One woman from an estate adjoining the coop said she might pop in to get something if she had run out and the coop happened to be open, but generally people from her estate do not use it and go to other stores with regular hours. My own observations of people walking around in a nearby park with carrier bags of the supermarket supported her claim.

CONCLUSION

The two case studies have had unique paths of development, but they also illustrate characteristics shared by other initiatives with similar foci. Like other sustainable food-oriented initiatives, South London Coop has never received any resources from the NHS or PCT, but has benefited from the local council-initially by existing for many years on council property without paying rent, and then by entering into a lease at a subsidized rate for nonprofits. In contrast, like nearly every other affordable food initiative in London, SLFCG has received support from the PCT and other organizations. SLFCG also conducts needs assessments before setting up coops and sets up coops in areas lacking adequate fresh green produce provision. Several, but not all, of the affordable food initiatives have taken this approach, whereas none of the sustainable food initiatives have done so. In the United Kingdom, which has a national health care system, local health authorities are increasingly turning toward community projects to encourage healthy eating as a means of preventing chronic disease. Thus, PCTs have set up coops on or near housing estates in deprived areas, even if adequate numbers of retailers selling green produce exist in the vicinity. In cases where retailers do exist, the initiatives provide either higher quality produce at comparable prices, or produce of comparable quality at lower prices.

In contrast to much of the published research on AFNs, this study finds that AFNs exist in urban settings beyond the spaces of farmers markets and includes initiatives attempting to mitigate the impacts of environmental injustice and social inequality. In London, most of the schemes emerged to provide affordable, fresh green produce in areas with high levels of multiple deprivation. Some food initiatives operate with a very nuanced articulation of food security, linking their activities with justice and human rights, and seeing access to high-quality food as a human right. Many initiatives work in partnership with other community organizations, and some have become quite sophisticated enterprises, providing services to tens of thousands of residents in addition to schools and workplaces.

This study shows that the poor will buy healthy food if it is available to them at reasonable prices. It also suggests that coops can survive in impoverished communities for lengthy periods of time. Moreover, it indicates that food deserts still exist in cities such as London, and that without the presence of local initiatives of the sort discussed earlier, the poorest people would live without a source of fresh produce that is easily accessible.

Although many of the food initiatives do not involve direct interaction between producer and consumers, they often involve linkages with other community food projects. Several of these schemes incorporate environmental concerns by attempting to acquire some of their produce from nearby counties, whereas also meeting their objective of selling at affordable prices. In fact, affordable community food initiatives, because of their network of coops and stalls, are well-positioned to develop as hubs of local food distribution.

The study indicates the need for coops to be sensitive to the food preferences of the ethnic and racial groups they serve, a challenge for those focused on sustainable food. This might mean striking a compromise between trying to stock locally grown or seasonal food and the importation of foods from other countries – which can have a large carbon footprint – that serve important cultural functions among the populations served. In addition, it found that ethical consumerism occurs at both types of community food initiatives, not just at organic ones.

This chapter draws on schemes operating in London, which are influenced by the existence of a healthcare system unique to this country and its support of community health projects. However, not all initiatives receive health authority funding, and of those that do, some receive only small amounts of funding. Nearly all benefit from subsidized or free venue or food growing space from the local council. The lack of funding constrains the operation of these food initiatives – to be more effective in reaching the poor, greater funding should made available to these coops.

The above findings are based on examination of operating coops, but it is possible that coops that have shut down may yield different insights. Further research by this author will explore a wider range of green produce schemes in London including initiatives that are no longer running. London's food initiatives operate under a variety of models; they are of much relevance to how projects such as these could be established in other nations. The initiatives have operated for years and serve important neighborhood functions as well as national goals related to having a healthier population. In the future, not only should more initiatives such as these be funded to operate in poor neighborhoods in the United Kingdom, activists in other countries should examine the various models with an eye toward finding one that works best in the communities in which they operate.

NOTES

1–2. This is based on information in the South London Food Coop group's business plan.

3. This is based on information in the South London Food group's volunteer handbook.

ACKNOWLEDGMENTS

The Center for Education of Women at the University of Michigan provided a research grant for this study. I am grateful for the assistance of Danielle Gwinn with network analysis for the maps. Thanks also to Dorceta Taylor and Larissa Larsen for guidance on this project, and to Larissa Larsen and Ashley Fuller for feedback on earlier drafts.

REFERENCES

Abrahams, C. (2006). Globally useful conceptions of alternative food networks in the developing south: The case of Johannesburg's urban food supply system. Institute of Geography. School of Geosciences, University of Edinburgh, Available at http://www.era.lib.ed.ac.uk/handle/842/1465. Retrieved on May 10, 2009.

Allen, P., & Wilson, A. B. (2008). Agrifood inequalities: Globalization and localization. *Development*, *51*(4), 534–540.

Born, B., & Purcell, M. (2006). Avoiding the local trap: Scale and food systems in planning research. *Journal of Planning Education and Research*, *26*, 195–207.

Brown, L. R. (2009). *Plan B 3.0: Mobilizing to save civilization*. Washington, DC: Earth Policy Institute.

Cummins, S., & Macintyre, S. (2002). A systematic study of an urban foodscape: The price and availability of food in Greater Glasgow. *Urban Studies*, *39*(11), 2115–2130.

Donkin, A. J. M., Dowler, E., Stevenson, S., & Turner, S. (1999). Mapping access to food at a local level. *British Food Journal*, *101*(1), 554–564.

East London and the City Health Authority (ELCHA). (1999). *Food access in East London: East London Health Action Zone*. London: ELCHA.

Feagan, R. (2007). The place of food: Mapping out the 'local' in local food systems. *Progress in Human Geography*, *31*, 23–42.

Feenstra, G. (1997). Local food systems and sustainable communities. *Journal of Alternative Agriculture*, *12*, 28–36.

Food and Agriculture Organization (2002). The State of Food Insecurity in the World 2001, Rome. Available at http://www.fao.org/docrep/003/Y1500E/Y1500E00.htm. Retrieved on June 23, 2009.

Goodman, D. (2003). The quality 'turn' and alternative food practices: Reflections and agenda. *Journal of Rural Studies*, *19*, 1–7.

Gottlieb, R., & Fisher, A. (1996). Community food security and environmental justice: searching for a common discourse. *Agriculture and Human Values*, *3*(3), 23–32.

Guthman, J. (2003). Fat food/organic food: Reflexive tastes and the making of 'yuppie chow'. *Social and Cultural Geography*, *4*(1), 45–58.

Guy, C. (2004). Neighbourhood retailing and food poverty: a case study in Cardiff. *International Journal of Retail & Distribution Management*, *32*(12), 577–581.

Hinrichs, C., & Allen, P. (2008). Selective patronage and social justice: Local food consumer campaigns in historical context. *Journal of Agricultural and Environmental Ethics*, *21*(4), 329–352.

Levkoe, C. (2006). Learning democracy through food justice movements. *Agriculture and Human Values, 23*, 89–98.

Morland, K., Wing, S., Roux, A. D., & Poole, C. (2002). Neighborhood characteristics associated with the location of food stores and food service places. *American Journal of Preventive Medicine, 22*(1), 23–29.

Nelson, M., Suleiman, S., & Gu, F. (2008). *Better health through better food: The impact of community food initiatives on health outcomes in the London borough of Newham.* London: Department of Nutrition and Dietetics, King's College.

Oram, J., Consibee, M., & Simms, A. (2003). Ghost town II: Death on the high street-How Britain's local economies are losing ground and fighting back. New Economics Foundation. Available at http://www.neweconomics.org/gen/z_sys_publicationdetail. aspx?pid = 168. Retrieved on January 5, 2009.

Renting, H., Marsden, T. K., & Banks, J. (2003). Understanding alternative food networks: Exploring the role of short food supply chains in rural development. *Environment and Planning A, 35*, 393–411.

Slocum, R. (2006). Anti-racist practice and the work of community food organizations. *Antipode, 38*(2), 327–349.

Sustainable Development Commission. (2009). Food security and sustainability: The perfect fit, London. Available at http://www.sd-commission.org.uk/file_download.php?target = / publications/downloads/SDCFoodSecurityPositionPaper.pdf. Retrieved on June 18.

Sustainweb. (2008). Food Coops. Accessed at http://www.sustainweb.org/foodcoops/. Retrieved on March 20.

The Strategy Unit. (2008). Food matters-towards a strategy for the 21st century. Cabinet Office, London. Available at http://www.cabinetoffice.gov.uk/strategy/work_areas/food_policy. aspx. Retrieved on August 20, 2009.

Venn, L., Kneafsey, M., Holloway, L., Cox, R., Dowler, E., & Tuomainen, H. (2006). Researching European 'alternative' networks: some methodological considerations. *Area, 38*(3), 248–258.

Watts, D. C. H., Ilbery, B., & Maye, D. (2005). Making reconnections in agro-food geography: Alternative systems of food provision. *Progress in Human Geography, 29*, 22–40.

White, M., Bunting, J., Raybauld, S., Adamson, A., Williams, I., & Mathers, J. (2001). Do food deserts exist? A multi-level geographical analysis of the relationship between retail food access, socio-economic position and dietary intake. Food Standards Agency, London. Available at http://www.food.gov.uk/science/research/researchinfo/nutritionresearch/ foodacceptability/n09programme/n09projectlist/n09010/. Retrieved on June 10, 2009.

Wrigley, N. (2002). Food deserts' in British cities: policy context and research priorities. *Urban Studies, 39*(11), 2029–2040.

Wrigley, N., Warm, D. L., & Margetts, B. M. (2003). Deprivation, diet and food retail access: Findings from the Leeds 'food deserts' study. *Environment and Planning A, 35*(1), 151–188.

Zenk, S. N., Schulz, A. J., Hollis-Neely, T., Campbell, R. T., Holmes, N., Watkins, G., Nwankwo, R., & Odoms-Young, A. (2005). Neighborhood racial composition, neighborhood poverty, and the spatial accessibility of supermarkets in metropolitan Detroit. *American Journal of Public Health, 95*(1), 660–667.

Shumaisa Khan is a doctoral candidate at the University of Michigan's School of Natural Resources and Environment. She can be reached by email at shumaisa@umich.edu

SUSTAINABLE LIVING AND COMMUNITY BUILDING IN ECOVILLAGE AT ITHACA: THE CHALLENGES OF INCORPORATING SOCIAL JUSTICE CONCERNS INTO THE PRACTICES OF AN ECOLOGICAL COHOUSING COMMUNITY

Tendai Chitewere and Dorceta E. Taylor

ABSTRACT

Purpose – *Ecological cohousing communities, or ecovillages, are emerging as contemporary housing models that attempt to recreate a sense of community and encourage an environmentally sustainable lifestyle. This chapter analyzes a rural ecovillage (Ecovillage at Ithaca – EVI) to find out how the community conceptualizes and practices sustainability. The chapter also examines whether and how the community incorporates issues of equity and social justice into its activities.*

Environment and Social Justice: An International Perspective
Research in Social Problems and Public Policy, Volume 18, 141–176
Copyright © 2010 by Emerald Group Publishing Limited
All rights of reproduction in any form reserved
ISSN: 0196-1152/doi:10.1108/S0196-1152(2010)0000018007

Design/methodology/approach – *The chapter uses a multi-method approach. It is a case study; however, participant observation was conducted at the site. In addition, interviews with residents were conducted and archival materials from the community's newsletters as well city government documents were also used.*

Findings – *As practiced at EVI, the green lifestyle emphasizes comfortable living that is both esthetically appealing and good for the environment. In making the decision to focus on building a community for the middle class, residents have limited their engagement with social justice issues and have struggled with incorporating minorities and the poor into their community.*

Originality/value – *This is one of the first papers to analyze the ecovillages from an environmental justice perspective. It shows where there are overlaps between the ecovillage and environmental justice movements. The chapter also fits into a growing body of scholarship that examines the concept of sustainability from a social justice perspective also.*

INTRODUCTION

Indigenous peoples in the America, Asia, and Africa have constructed settlements with closely built clusters of housing, communal buildings, and shared space for centuries. In the Middle East, the ancient Turkish city of Çatal Hüyük was constructed around 7500 B.C. with homes joined together, common buildings, terraced roof for communal activities, and shared open space (Mellaart, 1967). This model of community design grew scarce in post-industrial countries as most people dwell in detached single family homes, apartment buildings, etc. In the United States, the growth in suburbia in the 1960s and 1970s meant that middle class families moved even further away from each other in single family homes on separate parcels of land (Fishman, 1987; Jackson, 1985). By the 1990s, sprawl begun to engulf exurban spaces. This trend has alarmed many. Consequently, over the past four decades, growing numbers of people have rejected this way of living and have returned to developing settlements with homes joined together, communal buildings, and common open space.

The environmental crisis, made evident and urgent through images and reports of melting glaciers, rising oceans, and extreme weather patterns around the world, has motivated some Americans to re-examine the way they live and how they relate to the environment. One movement that exemplifies this re-evaluation is the ecological cohousing community movement (ecovillage). In these communities activists try to create neighborhoods that attempt to blend living close to nature with an enhanced sense community. These new developments are advocating the adoption of a green lifestyle that balances comfortable living with positive environmental change (Chitewere, 2006). Thus far cohousing and ecovillage projects have been organized and developed primarily by white and middle class activists (Meltzer, 2000; Kirby, 2003; Schaub, 2000). Meltzer (2000) conducted a study of cohousing residents and found that 95 percent of them were white, 80 percent had a college degree, and 50 percent had a graduate degree. As a result, some are taking a closer look at diversity in these settlements. Social observers and scholars are also starting to examine the extent to which ecovillages incorporate equity and social justice concerns into their development and day to day operations.

Equity and social justice are two of the core organizing principles of the environmental justice movement. Although the cohousing/ecovillage movement emerged around same time as the contemporary environmental justice movement, there are stark differences between the two. By and large, environmental justice activists tend to focus on the persistence of environmental hazards in neighborhoods that are poor and often where people of color live, closing or regulating noxious facilities, and remediating hazardous sites in these communities. When it comes to community vitality, environmental justice advocates focus on affordable housing, retrofitting existing houses, neighborhood revitalization, the reduction of sprawl, and increased access to open space (Taylor, 2000). Environmental justice activists have not advocated for the construction of new green villages in the urban fringes or in the countryside as a mechanism for experiencing an enhanced quality of life or a green lifestyle. The two perspectives – ecovillages and environmental justice – provide examples of how different communities are confronting environmental problems. There is common ground; both movements are seeking ways of creating a more sustainable way of life for people in the United States as well as in other countries.

Although there is a plethora of scholarly writing on green living and ecovillages, analyses of the movement from a social justice perspective is still in its infancy. To this end, this chapter examines the extent to which residents of an ecovillage in Upstate New York incorporated social justice concerns into their activities. This is important because such an exploration may shed light on the ways Americans think about and respond to environmental crises. More specifically, it can help us understand the tensions inherent in creating idyllic green villages, the conceptualization of sustainability that underpin such developments, and the consumption of the green commodities that make such communities possible. It can also shed some light on the nature of the activism in green enclaves and the extent to which equity and social justice are incorporated into them.

METHODOLOGICAL APPROACH

The study of EcoVillage at Ithaca (EVI) focuses on the experience of residents as they developed the settlement. Through this case study, we examine the challenges of developing a sustainable community that is responsive to the needs and desires of its members as well as those of the world around them. This chapter analyzes data collected from residents in the first and second neighborhoods as well as former participants in the planning and design stages, neighbors, and former residents. The ethnographic fieldwork was carried out over 15 months in 2001 and 2002; the data come from extensive participant observation and archival research. Semi-structured interviews were conducted with 50 households from the first two neighborhoods. Six former participants of the project were also interviewed; two residents provided access to archival materials on the project. A content analysis of EVI's newsletters published between 1999 and 2007 was also conducted. Archival data from Ithaca's Town Planning Board meetings were also used.

ECOVILLAGES

Architects, Kathryn McCamant and Charles Durrett, are credited with bringing the Danish concept of boffællesskabers or "living communities" to life in the United States during the 1980s. They coined the term "cohousing" to describe the practice of clustering 4–30 houses around a shared common house. In general, residents (families who own the shares of their home, as opposed to families who rent from a shareholder) in cohousing participate in the creation, governance, and daily maintenance of the neighborhood. Residents typically own the inside of their home, whereas the external components such as the roof, siding, and yard are owned cooperatively by all shareholders. Although monthly maintenance fees are charged for each home, individual households control their own financial resources.

A key component of cohousing is that vehicles are purposefully located away from the houses to allow children to play safely around the homes and encourage greater interaction between neighbors. Consequently, homes are designed around pedestrian-only walkways with windows facing into the common spaces. It is therefore easy to see who is home (McCamant & Durrett, 1994).

Cohousing communities reflect the culture and desires of the families who come together to build the neighborhood. Some such as the Berkeley Cohousing in California and Pioneer Valley in Greenfield, Massachusetts, are urban, whereas others such as Dancing Rabbit Ecovillage in Missouri are rural. Most cohousing communities do not have an explicit ecological focus. However, they are implicitly organized on ecological principles of resource conservation, alternative energy use, recycling, and organic food consumption. Ecovillages are a subset of cohousing communities that are explicit about their attempt to incorporate environmental sustainability into their everyday activities (Global Ecovillage Network, 2009; Intentional Communities, 2009).

The Global Ecovillage Network (2009) identifies 445 ecovillages world-wide. Of those, 49 (11 percent) are urban. One hundred and two or 22.9 percent of those ecovillages are located in the United States. The American ecovillages follow the global pattern – only 16.8 percent (17) are urban. Table 1 shows the domestic and international distribution of these communities (Global Ecovillage Network, 2009). Many ecovillage identify strongly with being located outside the city. They are located in places where residents feel physically and psychologically connected to nature. For many ecovillage residents, the proximity to nature is one aspect of what the "eco" in ecovillage means. The adoption of the cohousing model helps them to define the "village" portion of the concept.

Green Lifestyle and Consumerism

EVI is an innovative and growing ecological cohousing community in Upstate New York. Designed and built in the 1990s, the community's mission includes an attempt to redesign the human habitat. But communities such as EVI are not occurring in isolation of the larger political and ecological debates in the United States. Despite having a goal of sustainable living, EVI and other ecovillages find this challenging because they are deeply embedded in a culture of consumption. Over-consumption is often identified as one of the leading causes of the environmental crisis

Table 1.   Ecovillage Developments in the U.S. and Other Countries.

American Ecovillages		International Ecovillages			
State	Number of ecovillages	Country	Number of ecovillages	Country	Number of ecovillages
Arkansas	1	Argentina	5	Liberia	1
Arizona	8	Australia	31	Lithuania	2
California	11	Austria	4	Malaysia	1
Colorado	5	Bangladesh	1	Mexico	13
Connecticut	1	Belgium	2	Morocco	1
Florida	1	Belize	2	Nepal	1
Georgia	2	Bolivia	1	The Netherlands	3
Hawaii	2	Brazil	8	New Zealand	10
Idaho	1	Bulgaria	1	Nicaragua	1
Iowa	1	Canada	27	Northern Ireland	2
Kentucky	1	Columbia	13	Norway	5
Massachusetts	5	Costa Rica	13	Peru	3
Maryland	2	Croatia	1	Poland	2
Michigan	4	Cyprus	1	Portugal	3
Minnesota	1	Denmark	8	Romania	5
Missouri	4	Ecuador	4	Russia	10
Montana	2	Egypt	1	Scotland	4
New Hampshire	1	El Salvador	1	Senegal	4
New Mexico	4	England	11	Slovakian	2
New York	3	Estonia	1	Slovenia	1
North Carolina	3	Ethiopia	1	South Africa	8
Ohio	3	Finland	8	Spain	16
Oklahoma	1	France	6	Sri Lanka	2
Oregon	7	Germany	22	Sweden	2
Pennsylvania	1	Ghana	1	Switzerland	6
South Carolina	1	Greece	2	Thailand	5
Tennessee	7	Guatemala	1	Turkey	6
Texas	4	Haiti	1	Uruguay	2
Virginia	5	Hungary	5	Venezuela	4
Washington	7	Iceland	2	Wales	2
Wisconsin	2	India	4	Zimbabwe	1
Other	1	Ireland	2		
		Israel	3		
Total	102	Italy	15	Total	343
		Kenya	4		
		Latvia	1		
		Lebanon	1		

Source: Compiled from Global Ecovillage Network (2009).

(Smith, 1998; Guha, 2000; Guha, 2006; O'Connor, 1994). Green lifestyle is broadly defined as living a way of life that seeks to reduce one's negative impact on the environment in a proactive manner. Unfortunately, this lifestyle can be driven by an impulse to consume commodities marketed as good for the planet. In effect, those attempting to adopt a green lifestyle can find themselves reducing consumption in some areas only to replace them with the consumption of green products. Popular magazines such as *E-Magazine* and *Plenty* proclaim that "it's easy being green." By purchasing commodities marketed as "green," consumers feel they are improving the environment and creating a distinct green identity aimed at protecting resources for future generations. If one believes the marketing pitch of the green consumer magazines, these lofty goals are achieved through personal consumerism (Smith, 1998). In effect the green magazines occupy the border between educating the public about environmental choices and being a marketing tool for the businesses that profit from the growing interest in green consumerism.

Irvine (1989) describes green consumerism as the adoption of an "individual consumer preference to promote less environmentally-damaging products." Green consumerism is growing, in part, because consuming green has become a straightforward, convenient, and easy way to respond to environmental degradation. Green lifestyles are practiced by consumers whose attitudes and values center around the environment and who are predominantly middle class and thus can afford the choice of greener products. Although Campbell (1995) argues that consumers are not able to easily "adopt a new lifestyle" by altering their consumption patterns, ethnographic field observations at EVI indicates some residents were able to make dramatic changes in the way they lived. For example one of the families studied moved out of a sprawling home set apart from neighbors into a compact house at EVI where neighbors could look into every window of their new home.

Consumption can be seen as a signifier of identity, status, and lifestyle (Veblen, 1931; Bourdieu, 1984). The green lifestyle is attractive to many because it offers an opportunity to live comfortably while seeking to protect the environment at the same time. Although the green products are aimed at enhancing environmental conservation, in places such as ecovillages, one can see how green consumption is integrated with green living. The question arises: to what extent does green consumption and green living carry with it a concern for environmental equity and social justice?

When being green is defined as consuming green, one is provided a simple and convenient way to view the environmental crisis and its possible solutions. That is, if the current crisis is fueled by the over-consumption of limited resources such as oil, then the consumption of more ecologically friendly alternatives will postpone any negative environmental consequence. Thus, the solutions to environmental problems are framed in a personal consumerist paradigm – buy alternative products to reduce your impact on the environment. This problem identification and prescription stands in contrast to the efforts of environmental justice activists who try to hold corporations and government agencies responsible for their outputs, environmental degradation, flawed policies, and negative impacts on communities.

Bringing these two perspectives together can be daunting. This is the case because environmental justice is focused on ameliorating threatening conditions in poor neighborhoods, while ecovillages are enhancing the lifestyles of the more privileged living in relatively pristine spaces and consuming the latest new green products. Yet, both perspectives are aimed at creating the same outcome – a sustainable way to live in harmony with each other and nature. There could be more overlap in the activities of both groups by expanding the awareness of environmental justice issues among ecovillagers, conducting critical analyses of green lifestyles, and creating more opportunities for environmental justice communities explore green living alternatives and become more sustainable.

The Quest for New Models of Living

Disasters such as Hurricane Katrina have left little doubt in the public's mind that significant changes in the way people live will be necessary in the coming years. The location and design of our neighborhoods as well as the way we live together as a community will have to be altered if we are to find solutions to the root causes of environmental and social injustice. Pellow and Brulle (2005) point out that there is a need to expand environmental justice discourses to make them more relevant to those who are living outside of nonwhite or poor communities. The environmental justice movement has demonstrated the value of using community as a mechanism for change. Environmental justice groups advocate for a sustainable lifestyle that brings people together to work on addressing social injustice and actively advocate for healthy communities by demanding that those who harm communities be held accountable. The environmental justice movement has been engaged in these efforts for a long time. Yet, because class is an important factor in how one perceives and experiences the environment, it is important that environmental justice scholars examine how middle and upper class communities either engage in environmental justice actions or fail to include environmental justice in their efforts to find solutions to environmental problems.

The number of environmental justice organizations increased dramatically during the1980s and 1990s (Taylor, 2000, 1999). Around the same time the ecological cohousing communities emerged as a new form of intentional community that articulated a very different model for confronting environmental and social ills. As a response to the perceived threat to the environment and the anomie evident in urban living, many ecovillagers focused on creating utopian villages that could be models for sustainable living. The emergence of these forms of environmentally focused communities indirectly reflects a struggle in the United States that revolves around race, class, and place. They highlight the ability of some groups to create and move to pristine or idyllic spaces, whereas others remain trapped in toxic environments.

Despite the heightened awareness of the disproportionate environmental hazards that exist in communities of color, these are not usually the sites for reform for activists attracted to the ecovillage movement who want to practice sustainable lifestyles. As was the case with early nineteenth century preservationists like Ralph Waldo Emerson and Henry David Thoreau who fled the cities and took up residence in bucolic hamlets (Taylor, 2009, forthcoming), more often than not, developers of ecovillages create them in suburban, exurban and rural green enclaves. Ecovillages are framed as the antithesis of the city and set apart from them. Despite the rural location of many, they are also set apart from impoverished rural communities too.

Ecovillages have emerged in response to real and perceived social dislocation and environmental degradation. Although both ecovillages and environmental justice are responses that emphasize the central role of community building in addressing environmental problems, ecovillages tend to stress the consumption of green commodities such as solar panels and wind turbines as a means of facilitating desired environmental change. Ecovillages also strive to create a "sense of community" among residents by encouraging the sharing of resources. This reduces individual resident's need to acquire unnecessary commodities such as their own personal washing machines. Many ecovillages are comprised of like-minded individuals who share a similar vision of the village and the future. In contrast, environmental justice activists typically work in various neighborhoods and communities that they do not build from scratch. Quite often they have to work with people of diverse backgrounds and perspectives and the act of bringing such people together to work for common causes is an important element of community building. It is not typical for them to select out and work only with those committed to their views and visions.

Ethnographic fieldwork at EVI revealed that some residents wanted to develop a community that took equity and environmental justice issues into consideration. However, all desired to build a community in which they were financially secure and that reflected their cultural norms. As it turned out, concerns over equity and social justice were often lost at EVI because of the tremendous focus on developing the settlement. Much energy and time was expended on identifying products to purchase to build and run homes, common buildings, the sauna, bus shelter, walkways, etc. In the decision to buy products, little attention is paid to issues such as who actually makes the products. What are the working conditions in the factories? What wages are workers paid? How do factories dispose of their wastes and where are such wastes disposed? What are the demographic characteristics of the workforce? And, what kinds of occupational health issues do workers face? The focus on buying locally is heavily focused on food – and even then – during long, cold winters, this goal is not easily met.

For a long time, the discourse around nature was framed narrowly. It was a discourse that did not make the connection between race, class, and environmental inequalities explicit. It was also a discourse that tended to exclude or limit discussion of the human condition as part of the formulation (Escobar, 1996; Shiva, 1993; Guha, 2006; Taylor, 2000). It is not surprising, therefore, that some environmental activists still do not understand how their actions and decisions fit into larger social, political, and economic contexts. Therefore, the trend toward creating green communities in response to environmental problems and promoting them as models of sustainable living has to be assessed in broader terms. This is the case because ecovillages run the risk of providing a desirable lifestyle primarily for those who can afford it. Moreover, the abandonment of the cities by movement adherents could contribute to the decades-long process of white flight. This could contribute to the decline of urban neighborhoods already faced with shrinking tax bases (Gregory, 1998; Self, 2003).

That is, as ecovillages are being constructed in the United States, we need to ask, who is included and who is excluded? An even more pressing question arises: can we develop a sustainable society if only some racial groups and social classes can afford the cost of sustainable living? Moreover, how can sustainable living be framed and practiced to allow all people in a given society to participate if they so desire? As the number of ecovillages increase we have to evaluate whether they contribute to sprawl? Do they siphon off city resources and services? And, do they contribute to the tax bases of the cities they are close to?

ECOVILLAGE AT ITHACA

EVI was formed in early 1991 after a group of about 150 friends and families walked across the United States with the mission of bringing attention to the unsustainable ways in which Americans lived. Led by Joan Bokaer, the "Global Walk for Peace" was a grassroots event involving artists, teachers, college students, and professionals. As the group of participants walked through various cities, they held workshops and spontaneous meetings in churches and people's homes in 200 communities to discuss the state of the environment. New walkers joined the group as others left along the way (Walker, 2005). When one person who participated in the walk was interviewed he said the walk was a very transformative experience for him. One recurrent theme emerged during the walk – participants were told on numerous occasions that people felt disconnected from their neighbors. Walkers came away with the feeling that there was a tremendous need to create a sense of community by redesigning the way homes and neighborhoods were planned and built. As a result, the two leaders of the Global Walk, Joan Bokaer and Liz Walker, formed the first interest group for the EVI project. They planned to begin building the community once the walkers had traversed Europe and Asia. Several of the members from the walk wanted to participate in the ecovillage project. They saw the project as a way of building a grassroots movement that could solve the problems they observed all over the country. About 100 adults attended the first visioning meeting in 1991 (Walker, 2005; EVI, 2009).

EVI is a cohousing community development situated on 176 acres of former farmland two miles outside of the city of Ithaca, New York. The property was acquired for $380,000 in 1992 – residents paid off the mortgage on the land in 2003. EVI falls under the jurisdiction of the City of Ithaca and pays taxes to that entity (Walker, 2005, 2004a; Town of Ithaca Planning Board, 2001a). This cohousing community is unique because the project's plan includes the creation of a green village that incorporates more than one cohousing neighborhood. Two neighborhoods – First Neighborhood Group (FRoG) and Second Neighborhood Group (SoNG) – are complete, and the development of a third – the Third Residential Ecovillage Experience (TREE) – is underway. The TREE is expected to be completed in 2011. The long-term vision of the project is to construct a total of five cohousing neighborhoods with a maximum of 150 units that will constitute a village of about 500 full-time and temporary residents. Ninety percent of the land will be left as open space (EVI, 2009; TREE, 2008; Town of Ithaca Planning Board, 2001c).

In 2004 EVI sold the city of Ithaca an acre of their land on which to construct a water tower. Although EVI residents were reluctant to do this, the move benefited EVI in that residents got the city to pave their access road. It also allowed them have a reliable source of water for emergency purposes without having to pay for the cost of constructing their own water tower. During the application for permits to build SoNG town, Planning Board members raised concerns about the lack of water for emergency purposes at EVI so the construction of the tower resolved a problem the subdivision would have had to deal with at some point (Walker, 2004b; Town of Ithaca Planning Board, 2001b). The following year when a 35-acre parcel that abuts EVI came on the market, EVI residents contributed more than half the $66,000 needed to acquire the property. EVI residents were familiar with the property as they had obtained an easement in earlier years that allowed them to use the trails on the property. In addition to the approximately 15 homes that will be built on the parcel by another entity, EVI residents hope to build a park on the property (Bokaer-Smith, 2005).

EVI is governed by several interrelated but separate entities. It is a nonprofit corporation that is charged with the mission of being an educational institution on sustainable living. A board of directors advises the nonprofit. Under the aegis of the nonprofit – EVI, Inc. – the first group of residents created the EcoVillage Cooperative Cooperation an independent entity sometimes referred to as the First Resident Group. Residents of the FRoG hired a cohousing architect and design team to construct all the homes in the neighborhood. The Ecovillage Cooperative Cooperation bought land from EVI, Inc. The neighborhood was completed in 1996 and is a semi-private cooperative owned collectively by residents (Walker, 2005; Chitewere, 2006).

The SoNG was constructed five years later with residents hiring their own architect and builder. The residents of the SoNG leased the land that their homes are built on from EVI, Inc. The two neighborhoods created a third entity called the Village Association that functions to coordinate the resources shared between the two neighborhoods such as the roads, sauna, and the pond. As the subdivision evolves, new legal entities have been created to support the growing needs of the community.

Neighborhood Design, Community, and Consumption

As is typical of cohousing developments, both FRoG and SoNG have homes that encircle a pedestrian-only walkway and the cars are located away from the homes. The one- to five-bedroom homes in the FRoG range from 950 to 1,650 square feet (Walker, 2005; Town of Ithaca Planning Board, 2001c). They are designed to be open, giving the residents a continuous view from the kitchen, through the dining and living room, and into the outside garden. Although the minutes of Ithaca's town planning board indicate that the homes in the SoNG were intended to range in size from 600 to 1,500 square feet and designed to be more affordable than those in the FRoG (Town of Ithaca Planning Board, 2001c), the SoNG homes tend to be larger than those in the FRoG and include more innovative green designs such as strawbale insulation. Homes in the TREE will range in size from 650 to 1,450 square feet (EVI, 2009; TREE, 2008).

A common house in each neighborhood contains a large community kitchen, dining space, laundry facilities, a guestroom, a children's playroom, and a few offices for residents who work from home. The common house provides resources that an individual household may not use on a regular basis, but benefit from if shared; this design is key to support the creation of a sustainable community.

Residents of EVI work hard to create a unique place and a sense of community that they value highly. Christine Somerfeldt (2002) describes EVI as follows:

> The houses were amiably drawn together like a bunch of kids looking at a cool bug in the grass. The gracious space in the center was filled not with driveways, roads and lawns, but curving pathways, play areas and dense, vibrant gardens.

The sense of community is a powerful reason why people want to live at EVI. A 2006 survey of 58 EVI residents found that 83 percent of the respondents indicated that the sense of community was very or quite important to them. Eighty-five percent also indicated that sustainable living was a very/quite important reason for living at EVI (Jacob, 2007). The development attracts people from all over the United States who make a decision to settle in EVI. Kirby (2003) found that many residents of EVI were environmental and social activists before moving to EVI and they moved to live there because EVI "held out the promise of a fulfilling a way of life that would serve to confirm self-identity as a socially or environmentally concerned individual. ..." Jacob (2007) also found that 62 percent of the respondents in his survey indicated that they had demonstrated against corporate and government policies in the past and 38 percent indicated that they committed acts of civil disobedience opposing such policies in the past. Hence, moving to an intentional community such as EVI allowed residents to reconcile their identity with their convictions and behaviors.

EVI's model has demonstrated how creating a sense of community can overcome the challenge of getting people to practice and support sustainability efforts. EVI has capitalized on residents' willingness to support community goals, share, and support each other in the effort to achieve the larger goal of sustainable living. However, the cooperative approach has some implications we should be aware of. Living cooperatively allowed families to collaborate on purchasing greener technology that would otherwise be too expensive for one family to afford on their own. But this was an important part of what residents considered sustainability to be. When asked what made the community ecologically sustainable, one interviewee responded by listing consumables the family owned or used such as a hybrid cars, organic food, and sustainably harvested bamboo flooring. However, Jacob (2007) found that residents engaged in a number of sustainable practices. Ninety-two percent of the respondents in his survey reported using fluorescent light bulbs, 91 percent purchased local foods and 88 percent purchased organic foods often or always. When asked to indicate the things that were very or quite important to them, 87 percent of the respondents said reducing personal energy consumption, 71 percent thought growing one's own food, and 59 percent thought that living communally was very or quite important.

Not surprisingly, residents of EVI are interested in knowing whether they consume fewer resources than others in the region. To this end, in 1999 Jay Jacobson reported that his analysis of water consumption indicated that EVI residents consumed about 20 percent of the amount of water used by the average northeastern household. He also reported that EVI residents consumed only about 39 percent of the electricity and 49 percent of the natural gas consumed by the average northeastern household. EVI's director, Liz Walker, also reported in 2007 that the 160 residents of the community used 40 percent fewer resources than "a comparable group of Americans" (Jacobson, 1999; Walker, 2007, 2005).

Living a green lifestyle has the effect of creating an expansion of the green identity. It is no longer enough to say one is green by joining an environmental organization, donating to one, or participate in environmental activities. To be considered green now-a-days, one has to consume green products. Green consumption has become a public signifier of status and environmental identity. Many residents of ecovillages struggle to "do something" about the environmental crisis and the consumption of green commodities has been one way of responding.

The consumption of green commodities was an important way in which residents defined their green lifestyle. This led one resident of the SoNG to point out that she felt privileged to be able to identify herself as living a green lifestyle because she could afford to buy a home in a "green" community. Still, some were more ambivalent about the lifestyle. Noting that more environmentally harmful practices could have been adopted at EVI but was rejected, one resident commented that she felt better about the choices she made. She hastened to add that the she was aware that substituting one commodity for another was still not enough to reach sustainability goals. However, the commodity substitution mindset was evident in the way some of the residents articulated the choices they made. Rather than using public transportation, they emphasized the improved gas mileage of their hybrid cars. Similarly, rather than being critical of locating EVI two miles outside the city, residents celebrated the short driving commute into town.

Generally speaking, EVI residents do not see themselves as being embedded in a green culture of consumption. To the contrary, they see ecovillages as places where they can live intentionally, reduce their consumption, and work towards their goal of sustainable living (Somerfeldt, 2002; Walker, 2000). As Irma Rodriquez sees it, "I like EcoVillage because of the philosophy of trying to live without consuming so much and also the sense of community" (Walker, 2000). Bill Goodman, an attorney from Buffalo who moved to live in the SoNG, stated that he was attracted to EVI because he was "excited about joining the SONG. I was impressed with First Residence Group. What I wanted to do was very sympathetic with the goals and visions that they had at EcoVillage" (Town of Ithaca Planning Board, 2001b). Although residents are critical of the general consumerism in society and moved to EVI as a way of rejecting that culture (see Fischetti, 2008), they consume green commodities with ease and offered little or no critique of that practice.

Affordability

From the outset, making the homes at EVI affordable has been a major challenge. The cost of housing in EVI is higher than that of the nearby city

Table 2.   A Comparison of the Demographic Characteristics of EVI:
The City, County, State, and the United States.

Demographic Characteristics	2002		2000 Census			
	FRoG	SoNG	Ithaca	Tompkins county	New York state	United States
Population size	78	78	29,287	96,501	18,976,457	281,421,906
Children under 18 years (%)	37.2	39.7	9.2	19.0	24.7	25.7
Race						
White (%)	81	93	70.4	85.5	67.9	69.1
Black (%)	2	1.5	6.7	3.6	15.9	12.3
Hispanic (%)	4		6.3	3.1	15.1	12.5
Asian (%)	4	5.5	13.7	7.2	5.5	3.6
Native American (%)			0.4	0.3	0.4	0.9
Mixed race (%)	9		3.4	2.3	3.1	2.4
Other race (%)			2.0	1.1	7.1	5.6
Gender						
Male (%)	46	49	50.6	49.4	48.2	49.1
Female (%)	54	51	49.4	50.6	51.8	50.9
Home ownership						
Own (%)	93	95	26.0	53.7	53.0	66.2
Rent (%)	7	5	74.0	46.3	47.0	33.8
Median value of owner-occupied homes			$96,200	$101,600	$148,700	$119,000
Employment status						
Employed full time (%)	48	37	56.1	63.6	61.1	63.9
Employed part time (%)	18	26				
Retired (%)	20	5				
Other (%)	14	32				
Income						
Earning $25,000–$50,000 (%)	47	63				
Earning $51,000–$70,000 (%)	34	10				
Earning $71,000–$100,000 (%)	19	21				
Earning $101,000 or more (%)		6				
Median family income			$42,304	$53,041	$51,691	$50,046
Families below the poverty level (%)			13.5	6.8	11.5	9.2

Source: The EcoVillage at Ithaca Newsletter (2002a), U. S. Bureau of the Census (2000).

and in the county in which it is located. Homes in the FRoG ranged
in price from $90,000 to $170,000 (TechPractices, 2008; Walker, 2005).
Despite efforts to make the homes in the SoNG affordable, homes in the
development ranged in price from $120,000 to $300,000. Homes in the
TREE will range from $130,000 to $200,000 (Walker, 2005; EVI, 2009;

TREE, 2008). As Table 2 shows, the median value of an owner-occupied home in Ithaca was $96,200 and $101,600 in Tompkins County. The median value of such a home was $148,700 in the state of New York and $119,000 in the United States as a whole (U.S. Bureau of the Census, 2000).

A stated goal of the SoNG was to be more affordable than the FRoG. To this end, EVI worked with a local affordable housing agency that planned to use tax credits to fund the building of homes in the subdivision. However, after months of planning and negotiations, the collaboration fell apart and the initiative was not funded. EVI also included design elements into SoNG to make it more affordable such as simple floor plans, stacked units, one-bedrooms and studios, and allowing residents to build their homes with "sweat equity." However, as Walker (2000) acknowledges, "For many of those attracted to living at EcoVillage, even these measures have left homeownership as a distant dream."

EVI was able to obtain a $112,000 affordable housing grant from the Home Loan Bank of New York in 2002 to subsidize the construction of six homes. Each of the chosen homes received a grant of between $17,000 and $20,000.The goal was to make 20 percent of the homes in the SoNG affordable (Walker, 2002). With the subsidy the home prices were expected to range from $78,000 to $120,000. The families chosen to inhabit the subsidized homes were selected from among 24 applicants using the following criteria. They should (1) have income of 80 percent or less of the median income for Tompkins County – the lending institution required that three of the households be no higher than 50 percent below the median income, two be between 51 and 65 percent of the median income and one be between 66 and 80 percent of the median income of the county, (2) be able to afford mortgage and fees at EVI, (3) have prior involvement with EVI, (4) be given priority if they could not otherwise live at EVI without the subsidy, (5) be given priority depending on their household characteristics – size, age, ethnicity, and (6) be given low priority if they have low incomes and high assets. The FRoG kept 10 percent of its units affordable by building several smaller units. Nonetheless, one EVI newsletter admits that "the dream of offering affordable housing at EcoVillage has been an illusive one" (Walker, 2002).

Affordability, diversity and a focus on non-material things has become a more explicit goal for the TREE. As the neighborhood's website proclaims,

We aspire to live simply, reducing costs while making ecologically responsible and non-toxic choices. We hope to cultivate a sense of enoughness that allows us to focus on non-material assets. We envision having time for the work that matters to each of us while enjoying our homes and each other. We will work to include people with diverse needs, abilities, backgrounds, and finances. (TREE, 2008)

It remains to be seen whether EVI will be able to create a more racially and economically diverse neighborhood at the TREE than it has done in the FRoG and the SoNG. The challenge EVI faced in their quest to build affordable housing is not unique to this ecovillage. As Riddell (2004) writes, ecovillages "are, for their inhabitants, safe, pleasant and interesting places in which to live – but they do not come cheap. In other words new urbanist settlements are not likely to provide any 'affordable housing' for low-income households, although moving in the direction of such a household balance is an objective."

Focus on the Middle Class
The location of EVI increased the cost of land and the overall project, thereby, preventing many of the participants in the Global Walk or other modest- or low-income families from being able to afford it. Thus, the debate over the type of community EVI would become split the group into two camps – those who saw the project as an alternative model of housing for well-to-do families who would otherwise build sprawling homes on large lots in rural or semi-rural areas and those who envisioned a new model housing that took equity and environmental justice concerns into consideration. The view that prevailed was one that eventually made the community unaffordable to some of the activists who had a strong social justice orientation. Consequently, many of those pushing for the social justice perspective angrily withdrew from the project as it made the decision to appeal to middle class households (Walker, 2005). The director of EVI contemplates the outcome of the decision when she states that "I wonder if we have created a beautiful haven that will eventually be affordable only to upper middle class and wealthy people" (Walker, 2005).

Despite the decision to move away from addressing social justice issues at EVI, some residents still think about them. One resident expressed her disappointment in the lack of racial and class diversity in the community during an interview.

> The neighborhood is not diverse enough; there are virtually no minorities here, except people's adopted children. You have to be pretty well off to move in and everybody here would agree that they would like it to be more diverse, and they would like to be more equitable but nothing ever happens to make it possible for anybody to live here – a handicapped person or a poor person or you know, let alone a welfare mother.

Other residents agree with EVI's approach. They argue that by creating a comfortable community that appealed to the middle class was in and of itself a worthy social and ecological achievement. As EVI's director saw it, the decision to limit the attention paid to social justice issues was a difficult one. According to her, "we made a key decision. We were aiming to reach middle-class Americans" (Walker, 2005). EVI's planners and early residents did this because they believed that it was the wealthy – with their enormous homes and multiple gas-guzzling cars – who were most responsible for overconsumption and environmental degradation. Thus, EVI provided an opportunity for such people to reduce their consumption without having to abandon comfortable living. Hence, for some a green lifestyle was achieved by being able to purchase one's way into an intentional ecological community. So, while some scholars argue that an ecovillage such as EVI is "the unit of resistance to capitalism and the ills of consumer culture" (Fischetti, 2008), this conclusion may be overstating the case. It is worth examining whether the consumption of green commodities in ecovillages is an emergent form of a new green culture of consumption that might replace the more generalized culture of consumption that environmental activists and others are rejecting.

The Demographics Characteristics of EVI

Ecovillages tend to be homogenous – consisting of middle class, college-educated families (Kirby, 2003; Schaub, 2000; Meltzer, 2000). Despite have a stated goal of increasing diversity in the subdivision, EVI has struggled with this. In 2002 EVI conducted a demographic analysis of the FRoG and SoNG and found that 81 percent of the residents in the former were white and so were 93 percent of those in the latter neighborhood. The 2000 Census indicates that EVI had a higher percentage of whites living in the subdivision than is residing in Ithaca, the county, the state of New York, and the United States as a whole (Table 2). In 2000, whites comprised 70.4 percent of the population of Ithaca and 85.5 percent of Tompkins County. They comprised 67.9 percent of the New York's population and 69.1 percent of the nation's population. In particular, blacks and Hispanics are under-represented in the subdivision. Although blacks constitute 15.9 percent of the residents of New York and 12.3 percent of the population nationwide, they comprised two percent of the population of the FRoG and 1.5 percent of the SoNG. The same goes for Hispanics. Although Hispanics constituted 4 percent of the population in the FRoG, there were none in the SoNG. In 2000, Hispanics made up 12.5 percent of U.S. population and 15.1 percent of the population of the state.

EVI is a community that attracts families with children. The percentage of children in the FRoG (37.2) and SoNG (39.2) exceeds that found in the county, state, and the U.S. by far. Only 19 percent of the population of Tompkins County is under the age 18. In comparison, 24.7 percent of New York's population and 25.7 percent of the population of the United States is under the age of 18.

EVI is a community organized around home ownership. Consequently, the rate of home ownership is much higher in the subdivision than in any of the other units to which it is being compared. Although 93 percent of the FRoG and 95 percent of the SoNG residents owned their homes, only 26 percent of the residents of Ithaca were home owners (it should be noted that Ithaca is a college town with many students who rent). However, only 53.7 percent of the families in Tompkins County and 53 percent of New York's families own their homes. In the United States 66.2 percent of families own their home.

Instead of becoming more diverse EVI seem to be trending in the opposite direction. The SoNG that was intended to attract more a more diverse pool of residents has fewer minorities living in it than the FRoG. The village still has very few renters. In fact, there are fewer renters in 2009 than there were in 2002. In 2009 EVI has 165 residents; 155 of the residents live in homes they own, whereas the remaining 10 are renters. That is renters constitute only 6.1 percent of the community (EVI, 2009).

The Potential to Contribute to Sprawl

The siting of the development was contentious. EVI's planning group considered several locations including an old gun factory in the heart of Ithaca and property located about 10 miles away from the city before settling on the current site (Walker, 2005). There was an irreconcilable ideological split that surfaced during the debate over where EVI should be sited. Two groups – the urbanists and the ruralists – emerged. Some of the early participants (the urbanists) in the project believed that the "eco" in ecovillage was best modeled by being physically located in the city where goods and services would be easily accessible and where residents could rely on public transportation, biking or walking. On the contrary, others (the ruralists) believed that it was more appropriate that a village centered on environmental themes and practices be situated in the countryside.

Some EVI planners and local area residents were concerned that the project would contribute to sprawl (Chitewere, 2006). This was ironic since sprawl was one of the environmental ills ecovillages were intended to combat. This is a legitimate concern since during the first phase of development 30 families or about 80 people lived on 176 acres of land. Although the actual homes did not occupy more than four acres in any of the neighborhoods, the reality is that the residents controlled all 176 acres (EVI is also part owner of an additional 35 acres that will not be used in these calculations). This means that EVI had a population density of about one person per 2.2 acres for the first phase of the development. When the second neighborhood was completed – 12 years after the property was acquired – the density increased to about one person per 1.1 acres. Assuming that roughly the same number of people occupy the homes, upon completion of the third neighborhood the density will be about one person per 0.73 acres. If the current rate of occupancy of the units hold, then when all five neighborhoods are completed EVI will have roughly 400 residents. That will mean a density of one person per 0.44 acres. Although EVI has projected that the subdivision could reach 500 people upon completion this is unlikely – to reach this target, EVI would have to dramatically increase either the number of units or the number of people inhabiting the units in the last two neighborhoods developed. However, if the village does get to 500 people the density would be about one person per 0.35 acres.

If each group wanting to develop alternative communities seek or acquire this large amount of land, then the result could be sprawl and significant pressure being placed on farm lands and undeveloped parcels. Land prices could also skyrocket. Walker (2005) describes how this happened when EVI purchased their property. The parcel they purchased was offered to them at roughly four times its market value. They eventually paid almost twice what the land was actually worth to acquire it. Not only is the desire for large amounts of land to build ecovillages unsustainable, the effect of increasing land values would also be unsustainable in the long run.

Reliance on Cars

Reliance on the car is an issue that residents have struggled with. Locating an entirely residential community outside of a city forces tradeoffs because residents are forced to commute by private vehicles to work, do errands, etc. After years of trying, EVI eventually got the city to adjust the bus route, so that it stopped by the subdivision. Still, the closest bus stop is a mile from the development. This being the case, EVI residents are concerned with the use of cars and are interested in reducing their reliance on it. To this end they have been tracking the number of cars in the development and the use of those cars.

In 2002 EVI's newsletter reported that the FRoG had 30 households. Of those, 26 households had 39 cars. At the time SoNG had 27 households. Of those, 21 households owned 34 cars. A total of 156 people (78 in each development) lived in the community at the time (EVI Newsletter, 2002a). This means there were a total of 73 cars in the village. This amounts to roughly one car per 2.1 people.

A 2005 study of vehicle use at EVI found that the 90 adult residents studied had 73 cars. Approximately 160 people lived in the subdivision at the time. This translates to roughly one car per 2.2 people. Collectively residents took 550 trips in and around Ithaca each week; each car made approximately 1.1 trips per day. Together residents logged around 4, 400 miles per week in their cars. On a typical day, 18 percent of the trips taken were for work-related purposes (Fishman et al., 2005). Hence the car is still an important part of the lives of EVI residents. So much so that Miles (2008) was moved to comment on the frequency with which cars pulled in and out of the EVI complex during the time he did field work there.

As a means of helping residents go car free or otherwise reduce their dependence on cars, EVI has developed a carshare program. They collaborated with the city of Ithaca on this. Despite being a community on the outskirts of town, EVI was the first to take advantage of Ithaca's carshare program. Ithaca Carshare got a $177,000 grant to begin operating a carshare program in December 2006. EVI got the first cars from this program – ahead of poor inner-city residents and students. One of EVI's residents worked with the city on getting the program started (Carson, 2007). EVI introduced its carshare program in 2006 (two cars were operated for this purpose). As an anecdote reported by Sara Pines (2002) suggest, EVI also has informal car-sharing arrangements too wherein neighbors lend each other their cars.

Although jettisoning the car is a goal of some EVI residents, being located atop a steep hill two miles from town makes it difficult to achieve this goal. EVI resident, Ellie, noted that since the two cars in village's carshare program were usually checked out, she found it challenging to get around. To travel outside of EVI she had to walk a mile each way up and down the steep hill to the closest bus stop with her children (Walker, 2006).

The bus stop serving EVI is located on the edge of the subdivision's property, and EVI has erected a moveable, green 144-square-feet bus shelter there. Aware that the bus stop is quite a distance from FRoG, EVI residents have been campaigning for a bus stop inside the complex. If this occurs,

EVI plans to move its current shelter to the location inside the subdivision. However, during planning board hearings to grant permission to build the shelter, a board member – Eva Hoffman – directed this question to Francis Varnek of EVI after it was revealed that EVI wanted to move the bus shelter further into the complex if the bus route was altered: "So it [the bus shelter] would mainly serve the EcoVillage residents rather than other people along Mecklenburg?" Varnek replied, "as far as I know, almost all if not all the passengers who catch the bus at that point are in fact from EcoVillage" (Town of Ithaca Planning Board, 2005).

This exchange provides an example of how – after 14 years of operation – EVI's focus and activism was still inward looking. The group focuses heavily on actions that benefit its residents and fail to consider or pass up opportunities to do projects that benefit those outside of the subdivision. In considering whether to move the bus shelter inside their complex, they had no alternative plan that would allow town residents to continue to enjoy the benefits of a green bus shelter and even after the issue was raised by someone concerned about the benefits reaching a broader group that EVI had considered, the response did not indicate a willingness to think about service to those not living at EVI.

Green Living at EVI: Time Consuming and Inwardly Focused

As practiced at EVI, the green lifestyle is time consuming. This is the case because residents are still constructing and developing the community. It is also time consuming because of the focus on the use and consumption of green commodities. Time spent deciding what green products to consume and how to consume them has been a major part of residents' lives. Residents often spend long hours at meetings deciding what resources to share and how to share them, or whether paving a dirt road would make it feel less "natural." Consequently, residents had little time or energy to address ecological issues occurring outside the community. Consensus decision making, shared governance, chores, and random gathering with neighbors occupied much of residents time. To reside in the community, residents have to commit to a minimum of two to four hours of community work per week; there are two to five communal meals per week (EVI, 2009).

Other researchers studying EVI have found this to be case also. Miles (2008) commented on this in his case study and Jacob's (2007) research also confirms this. According to Jacobs, 66 percent of the respondents in his survey indicated that they attended neighborhood meetings at least once per month and 58 percent attend at least one community meal per week. Furthermore, 69 percent of the respondents reported being very or quite involved in neighborhood work teams, 56 percent reported being quite or very much involved in neighborhood committee work and 53 percent quite/very much involved in neighborhood decision making. Thompson (2009) also made the observation that residents spent long hours in meetings as they planned the TREE. The net effect of this is that such intensive involvement by residents about the issues that affected their lives directly left little time to address environmental and social problems occurring elsewhere.

A content analysis of EVI newsletters shows the vast majority of the topics covered related to life inside the subdivision (Table 3). With the exception of coverage of visitors from other ecovillages, speakers, and technological exchanges (such as those with the Institute of Japanese Permaculture) very little related to the outside world is covered in the newsletters. The most frequently covered topics were issues related to green building design, features, and materials used. Site development and construction as well as several aspects of sustainability also received plentiful coverage. There was also ample coverage of commodities such as solar panels, wind turbines, fuel cells, cars, and appliances.

Even coverage of EVI's sister ecovillage located in Yoff, Senegal is sparse. Collaborations between the two have included a delegation of EVI residents visiting EcoYoff and the cohosting of a 1996 EcoCity conference, consulting on the design of composting toilets and greywater recycling system, and a fundraising dinner to help Senegalese women that netted $400. The one article appearing in the newsletters on EcoYoff was written by resident of that ecovillage (Thiaw, 2003); there were no articles on EcoYoff written by anyone from EVI.

The newsletters also indicate the extent to which EVI's residents work on equity and social justice issues. This is limited. Affordable housing, aging in place, and increased accessibility are the only social justice topics covered – and these are covered from the standpoint of how they affect life at EVI. The affordable housing discussion focus on attempts to build such units at EVI while the aging in place and accessibility articles focus on how to make the subdivision more user-friendly for the elderly as current EVI residents age in place.

This inward-focus of ecovillagers has been facilitated by how narrowly environment is defined (Dobson, 1992; Cronon, 1996; Taylor, 2000). Defining environment as wild, natural places in need of protection is rooted in nineteenth century Romantic conservation ideology (Cronon, 1996;

Table 3. Issues Covered in EVI's Newsletters, 1999–2007.

Topics Covered	Number of Articles Mentioning Topic	Topics Covered	Number of Articles Mentioning Topic
Green building design, features, materials	16	Building, construction grants	2
Student research projects, participation in EVI	11	New families	2
Site development and construction	8	Organizational development and structure	2
Media coverage of EVI	7	Health care and support	2
Home stays – hosting visitors	7	Communal land use	2
Organic farming – agriculture	7	Sustainable land use	2
Village design and visioning	7	Energy STAR appliances	2
Birth and death announcements, in memoriam	6	Biodiversity management at EVI	2
Community spirit	6	Gaia education	2
General finances, budget	6	Recognition, awards	2
Building world-wide ecovillage community	6	Land acquisition , preservation	2
Environmental education	5	Aging in place at EVI, accessibility	2
Financing homes, land	5	Energy use	2
Carshare, carpooling	5	Gardening	2
Community building – constructing community	4	Global warming	2
Affordable or subsidized housing at EVI	4	History	2
Root cellar	4	Mini-grants to residents	1
Solar panel, power	4	Community – mutual support of each other	1
Sustainability – general	4	Selecting new residents	1
Courses	4	Demographic analysis of EVI	1
Healthy living, lifestyle	4	Nature feature	1
Research grants	3	Care-free at EVI	1
Birds	3	Cost of cars	1
International ecovillage partnerships	3	Fuel cells	1
Ecovillage life	3	Education/visitor center	1
Book, research published on EVI	3	LEED certification	1
Sustainability education	3	Sustainable landscaping	1
Kids page in EVI newsletter	3	Work teams	1
Permaculture	3	Water tower	1
Wind turbine	3	Bike tour	1
Ecological footprint	3	Homeschooling	1

Sources: The EcoVillage at Ithaca Newsletter (1999, 2000, 2002b, 2003, 2003–2004, 2005a, 2005b, 2006, 2007).

Taylor, 2000, forthcoming) and has provided a framework in which residents place their collective energy. As a result there is a reduced focus on the urban condition or the plight of the poor.

EVI: THE RURALIST IMPULSE AND
THE ROMANTIC INFLUENCE

Although many aspects of EVI appear to be influenced by Romanticism, the community has developed a unique model that draws deeply from the Romantic tradition, but also displays some fundamental differences with it. EVI's development also bears resemblance to transcendental collectives; other influences seem to be the countryside movement and notions of the picturesque.

Emerson was an early critic of the industrialization; he saw degrading Boston where he lived; consequently, he urged people to go and live in the countryside. He moved to *Bush*, his estate in Concord, Massachusetts (that was located about 20 miles west of Boston) in 1835. He considered Concord a refuge from "the compliances and imitations of city society." He also liked the "lukewarm milky dog-days of common village life" (quote copied from Richardson, 1995; see also Taylor, 2009). Thoreau, whose family had lived briefly in Boston, lived in Concord; he was an impressionable young man and a student at Harvard who quickly became a disciple of Emerson. Emerson and Thoreau were Romantics (those professing a love for wild, remote natural places) who also became leading figures in the transcendental movement (that preached closeness and respect for nature and wrote damning critiques of industrialism and environmental degradation). Other movement adherents moved to Concord or spent long periods of time there; Bronson Alcott (Louisa May Alcott's father) and Nathaniel Hawthorne and his wife Sophia Peabody were among those who moved there (Taylor, 2009, forthcoming). Margaret Fuller also spent long periods in Concord.

Andrew Jackson Downing grew up in Newburgh, New York. He was also a leading proponent of country life. He advocated rural living because he thought the rural lifestyle would combat what he saw as the "too great bustle and excitement of our commercial cities." By the 1840s he was designing and building lavish country estates for wealthy urbanites taking up his call to flee the city and experience genteel country living. He was also a gentleman farmer whose nursery business supplied plants to the East Coast gentry seeking to stock the farms on their estate with orchards and beatify the mansions on the estates with flowers (Downing, 1960[1841]; Taylor, 2009). Frederick Law Olmsted, co-designer of Central Park (along with Calvert Vaux), grew up in Hartford, Connecticut. The two are credited with introducing picturesque landscapes in America in the 1850s – beginning with their design of Central Park (Roper, 1973; Rybczynski, 1999; Taylor, 2009).

EVI residents adopted a version of Romanticism that was rooted in the love of nature, a respect for it, an impulse to protect it, and a critique of industrialism. They showed a preference for a gentler form of Romanticism favored by Emerson that called for living in the countryside with easy access to a town or big city. They shunned the more extreme form of Romanticism practiced by Thoreau when he moved to Walden Pond (on another of Emerson's properties) or by John Muir who lived in Yosemite and other parts of the Sierra Mountains for several years. Of the three, John Muir – a Scottish immigrant and Transcendentalist who grew up on a pioneer farm in Wisconsin and who was an admirer of Emerson and Thoreau – pushed the envelope the furthest in his quest to experience Romanticism (Taylor, 2009).

In choosing country living, EVI residents chose to live a comfortable lifestyle *a la* the urban elites of the nineteenth century who fled the city or who had second homes in the countryside. Several prominent environmental advocates were among those living this way. Theodore Roosevelt (president and co-founder of the Boone and Crockett Club), William Cullen Bryant (preservationist and park advocate), and George Bird Grinnell (founder of the original Audubon Society as well as the Boone and Crockett Club) are among them. However, instead of building sprawling mansions on expansive acreage in the East or ranches in the West, EVI residents acquired a lot of rural acreage for their community but built compact attached homes on a small portion of it.

Like Thoreau they wanted to live deliberately. The notion of deliberate living is expressed most clearly in the concept of intentional living that drives EVI and other ecovillages. As Thoreau wrote as he planned to move to Walden Pond, "I went to the woods because I wished to live deliberately, to confront only the essential facts of life, and see if I could not learn what it had to teach" (Thoreau, 1971). This theme is apparent in quotes from residents of EVI that's written earlier. EVI residents also take from Thoreau and Muir the concepts of living simply and self-sufficiency. When Thoreau went to Walden Pond and on his travels to the Mount Khatadin wilderness, he led a spartan existence. Muir also lived an austere lifestyle during his wilderness travels (Muir lived as a member of the West Coast elite on his father-in-law estate and orchard later in life in Martinez, California, whereas Thoreau lived a genteel lifestyle at the Emerson's when not at Walden). The concept of living on the bare essentials appears repeatedly in Muir's writings (Wolfe, 1938; Taylor, 2009, forthcoming). EVI residents embrace the notion of self-sufficiency and simple living, but they do not necessarily aspire to live on the bare essentials. EVI residents also rejected the kind of rugged individualism espoused by the nineteenth century environmental activists named earlier. Many, such as Thoreau, Muir, Roosevelt, Grinnell, went to the woods alone and sought a solitary experience (Taylor, 2009, forthcoming). This is in direct opposition to the way EVI and other ecovillages function. A core organizing principle is communitarianism – capitalizing on collective efforts to foster strong communities.

In many ways, EVI resembled the short-lived transcendental intentional utopian farming communities established in the 1840s at Brook Farm and Fruitlands in Massachusetts. Transcendentalists were criticized for not having a practical agenda for executing the theoretical ideas and critiques of industry they wrote and lectured about. With the exception of their stand against slavery, they had a very limited social justice agenda also. In response to this, some transcendentalist began the aforementioned projects. Although Thoreau and Emerson were invited to join these collective efforts, they both declined. Hawthorne was a member of Brook Farm for a short time while Alcott was a co-founder of Fruitlands. These initiatives were characterized by communal housing, common buildings, sharing of resources, long hours farming, and crude living conditions overall. However, their goal was to create communities in which wealth was evenly distributed and in which workers had a decent quality of life (Taylor, 2009).

Conservation as articulated and practiced in the nineteenth century had limited social justice component – especially when it came to issues related to the urban poor. In addition to the transcendentalists, Muir was weak on social justice too, so was Olmsted and Grinnell, as well as Gifford Pinchot (first director of the U.S. Forest Service). Roosevelt is something of an anomaly – he lived in New York City and as someone who was quite involved in city and state politics – had to deal with urban poverty throughout his career (Taylor, 2009). The role issues related to the urban poor play on the agenda of EVI is reminiscent of role such issues played in nineteenth century conservation politics.

EVI's development evokes a feeling of the picturesque. Olmsted and Vaux designed picturesque landscapes that had broad stretches of gently rolling greensward (lawns), interrupted by a sparse arrangement of trees, and limpid reflecting ponds. This pastoral landscape was juxtaposed to a more sublime one characterized by rugged rock outcrops, ravines, and thick arrangement of trees and shrubs. Pictures of EVI show homes clustered in open fields, a calm pond, and trees framing the scenery (Olmsted & Vaux, 1958; Taylor, 2009). Although the manicured lawns are rejected, other elements of the picturesque are visible at EVI.

THE POTENTIAL TO INCORPORATE SOCIAL JUSTICE INTO EVI'S PRACTICES

Residents who move into ecovillages are not necessarily indifferent to environmental justice. In fact during field work at EVI residents revealed that they were concerned about that state of poor urban neighborhoods, the lack of viable economic opportunities for young adults, and the destruction of open space to make way for suburban sprawl. But these residents were also torn between working within already established neighborhoods to improve the living conditions of residents and leaving those spaces to create a new home outside the city. A resident of SoNG reconciled this dilemma by arguing that the community was at least a step in the right direction, and she was making significant changes in her life simply by living in the EVI community.

There are ways in which residents of EVI can broaden the scope of their activism to include more social justice work without detracting from their own mission. They have experience and expertise that is in demand. Many environmental justice organizations and low-income community institutions lack the expertise that many at EVI have; hence, there is ample room for collaboration on this front. For example, when the attempt to get a local agency to fund the building of affordable homes at EVI fell through, the partnership could have continued if EVI was able to shift focus. That is, EVI could have continued working with the agency or partnered with a low-income community to help get affordable green homes built elsewhere. Such a change in focus would have resulted in an overall increase in the number of affordable green homes constructed in the area – even if that increase did not occur at EVI.

On a broader scale, some environmental justice organizations such as We Stay Nos Quedamos in the Bronx have been retrofitting buildings in their community. Others such as Sustainable South Bronx have been working green buildings and community green space (Nos Quedamos, 2009; Sustainable South Bronx, 2009). There are ample opportunities for ecovillages such as EVI to partner with groups such as these to further sustainability goals.

Another area of collaboration could come from the growing number of inner city neighborhoods that are developing community gardens. Food security has become a pressing concern for many inner city residents. Such residents see access to a secure food supply as a vital part of sustainability. The issue is urgent as some large cities such as Detroit have become virtual urban food deserts as supermarkets and other institutions have closed and moved to the suburbs. Residents of such areas have difficulty finding fresh food to purchase; hence, community gardens have become one way of responding to this problem (Zenk et al., 2005; Gottlieb & Fisher, 1996; Morland, Wing, Roux, & Poole, 2002; Smith & Hurst, 2007; Hargreaves, 2009). EVI's expertise in organic farming could be invaluable to urban communities facing such a crisis. EVI's West Haven Farm currently feeds about 1,000 people per week. Sixty percent of the produce from the 10-acre farm goes to EVI residents, 40 percent goes to the local farmers' market and a small amount goes to Greenstar – a local cooperative store (Walker, 2005). In the future, the farm could provide more of its produce to food banks and other institutions that serve the poor.

EVI faces a significant challenge in making housing in the subdivision affordable to a wider range of people. As mentioned earlier, the residents espouse a philosophy of developing a community based on homeownership. Although this creates a community with greater stability (and by extension residents with a long-term commitment to the goals and vision of the community), it also makes it difficult for those with limited income to participate. To lower the barriers to participation, EVI should examine other models of residency than are currently in place. For instance, could the number of rental units be increased without undermining the sense of community and the spirit of collaboration that is so vital to the functioning of the village?

EVI has been very strategic with its collaborations – EVI residents tend to benefit directly from them. Although this keeps the group focused on its core mission, residents should consider undertaking more activities where the direct benefits go to others and not necessarily to EVI residents.

CONCLUSION

There is little disputing that American lifestyles are consumer driven. We consume more than our share of the worlds resources and show little sign of slowing down (Schor, 1999; Guha, 2006; Erickson, 1987). As a country deeply entrenched in a capitalist mindset, we are accustomed to being bombarded with reasons to shop. Therefore, it is not surprising that being green has become a lucrative marketing niche (Smith, 1998). But creating a sustainable lifestyle is more complicated than simply purchasing green commodities. Some organic food or natural products like Burt's Bees are owned by the same large corporations that have contributed to environmental degradation; they should be scrutinized rather than celebrated uncritically as evidence that corporations are becoming socially responsible (Athanasiou, 1996; Pollan, 2004).

Mulder, Constanza, and Erickson (2005) argue that the transition from high consumer culture to a low one will be possible if it is achieved without compromising people's quality of life. It is here that green consumerism finds its niche in U.S. environmental struggles. Green consumerism offers a mechanism for negotiating environmental change and conserving the environment without needing to sacrifice "quality of life." Specifically, the danger arises when green consumerism focuses on maintaining a comfortable quality of life for wealthy households without any attention being paid to what makes the consumption possible and the effects of that consumption.

Ecovillages have demonstrated that there is interest in creating a sense of community as a way to reduce our negative environmental impact. However, ecovillages do not have to be tucked away in the woods to achieve this end. Urban ecovillages are demonstrating that sustainable urban living is also possible. For example, the Los Angeles Eco-Village makes affordable housing, diversity and sustainable urban living keep components of their practice. Instead of occupying hundreds of acres rural land, this ecovillage is built around a two-block multi-ethnic, working class neighborhood of about 500 people – most of whom were fearful of each other when the project began in 1993. They plan to convert 48 units to permanently affordable housing (Arkin, 2005; Los Angeles Eco-Village, 2009). The Los Angeles Eco-Village also demonstrates that it is possible to build community and work cooperatively when people of different backgrounds and ideologies come together. While EVI capitalizes on sameness, the Los Angeles Eco-Village uses diversity as strength.

The ecovillage model is a good starting point for demonstrating the value of empowering residents to make personal and communal commitments to reducing their consumption. But as they are currently conceptualized and operated, many ecovillages do little to address the pressing long term needs of communities outside their borders. The ecovillage effort must carefully consider choices like where to locate to avoid some of the devastating problems created by sprawl. A more concerted effort should be made to broaden the scope of their ideological thinking and activism to include a wider array of concerns and people. Urban ecovillages are striving to do just this, by creating neighborhoods in existing communities, working with current homeowners and renters. As we consider the potential for environmental justice groups and ecovillagers to work together, the urban ecovillages have greater potential to develop that synergy.

Environmental activism in America should not be bifurcated along racial or class lines. In the future both the ecovillage and environmental justice movements should explore their commonalities and develop mutual partnerships. The challenge for environmental justice and ecovillage activists is to recognize their commonalities and harness the strengths of both perspectives to help address problems related to environmental and social sustainability. Together they can make greater progress than they do apart.

REFERENCES

Arkin, L. (2005). An urban ecovillage of the near future. *Communications Magazine*, Winter (129), pp. 1–5.
Athanasiou, T. (1996). The age of greenwashing. *Capitalism, Nature, Socialism*, 7, 1–37.
Bokaer-Smith, J. (2005). WHALT: Neighbors coming together. *The EcoVillage at Ithaca Newsletter*, Winter (1), pp. 12–13.
Bourdieu, P. (1984). *Distinctions: A social critique of the judgment of taste*. Cambridge, MA: Harvard University Press.
Campbell, C. (1995). The sociology of consumption. In: D. Miller (Ed.), *Acknowledging consumption: A review of new studies*. New York: Routledge.
Carson, G. (2007). Ithaca carshare pilot at EVI nearly ready. *The EcoVillage at Ithaca Newsletter*, Spring, p. 10.
Chitewere, T. (2006). *Constructing a green lifestyle: Consumption and environmentalism in an ecovillage*. Binghamton, NY: Department of Anthropology, State University of New York.
Cronon, W. (1996). *Uncommon ground: Towards reinventing nature*. New York, NY: W.W. Norton.
Dobson, A. (1992). *Green political thought*. London, UK: Routledge.
Downing, A. J. (1960[1841]). *A treatise in the theory and practice of landscape gardening adapted to north America with a view to the improvement of country residences*. New York: C. M. Saxton.
Erickson, R. J. (1987). *"Paper or plastic?": Energy, environment, and consumerism in Sweden and America*. Westport, CT: Praeger.
Escobar, A. (1996). Constructing nature: Elements for a post-structural political ecology. In: R. Peet & P. Watts (Eds), *Liberation ecologies*. London: Routledge.

EVI (2009). EcoVillage at Ithaca. Available at http://directory.ic.org/1722/EcoVillage_at_ Ithaca. Retrieved on October 18, 2009.

Fischetti, D. M. (2008). *Building resistance from home: Ecovillage at Ithaca as a model of sustainable living*. Eugene, OR: Department of Geography, University of Oregon.

Fishman, J., Khanna, U., Robinson, R., Santoro, R., Smith, D., & Story, D. (2005). *Ecovillage carshare project*. Ithaca, NY: Cornell University.

Fishman, R. (1987). *Bourgeois utopias: The rise and fall of suburbia*. New York: Basic Books, Inc.

Global Ecovillage Network. (2009). Directories. Available at http://gen.ecovillage.org/iservices/ index.html. Retrieved on October 16, 2009.

Gottlieb, R., & Fisher, A. (1996). Community food security and environmental justice: Searching for a common discourse. *Agriculture and Human Values, 3*(3), 23–32.

Gregory, S. (1998). *Black corona: Race and the politics of place in an urban community*. Princeton, NJ: Princeton University Press.

Guha, R. (2000). *Environmentalism: A global history*. New York: Longman Press.

Guha, R. (2006). *How much should a person consume? Environmentalism in India and the United States*. Berkeley, CA: University of California Press.

Hargreaves, S. (2009). Hunger hits Detroit's middle class. *CNNMoney.com*, August 13. Available at http://money.cnn.com/2009/08/06/news/economy/detroit_food/index.htm. Retrieved on October 22, 2009.

Intentional Communities. (2009). Available at http://www.ic.org/. Retrieved on October 20, 2009.

Irvine, S. (1989). *Beyond green consumerism*. London: Friends of the Earth.

Jackson, K. T. (1985). *Crabgrass frontier: The suburbanization of the United States*. New York: Oxford University Press.

Jacob, J. (2007). *The EcoVillagers at Ithaca: A community profile*. Calgary, Alta: Department of Education, University of Calgary.

Jacobson, J. (1999). How "eco" is EcoVillage at Ithaca? *The EcoVillage at Ithaca Newsletter*, Winter (9, 1), p. 4.

Kirby, A. (2003). Redefining social and environmental relations at Ecovillage at Ithaca. *Journal of Environmental Psychology, 23*(3), 323–332.

Los Angeles Eco-Village (2009). Los Angeles Eco-Village and sampling of goals for 2007–2008. Available at http://www.laecovillage.org/. Retrieved on October 21, 2009.

McCamant, K. A., & Durrett, C. (1994). *Cohousing: A contemporary approach to housing ourselves*. Berkeley, CA: Ten Speed Press.

Mellaart, J. (1967). *Catal Huyuk: A Neolithic town in Anatolia*. New York: McGraw-Hill.

Meltzer, G. (2000). *Cohousing: Toward social and environmental sustainability architecture*. Queensland, Australia: University of Queensland.

Miles, M. (2008). *Urban Utopias: The built and social architectures of alternative settlements* (pp. 214–219). New York: Routledge.

Morland, K., Wing, S., Roux, AD., & Poole, C. (2002). Neighborhood characteristics associated with the location of food stores and food service places. *American Journal of Preventive Medicine, 22*(1), 23–29.

Mulder, K., Constanza, R., & Erickson, J. (2005). The contribution of built, human, social and natural capital to quality of life in intentional and unintentional communities. *Ecological Economics, 59*, 13–23.

Nos Quedamos (2009). Nos Quedamos. Avaialble at http://www.nosquedamos.org/. Retrieved on October 22, 2009.

Olmsted, F. L., & Vaux, C. (1958). *The greensward plan.* Submitted to the Central Park design competition. Frederick Law Olmsted Papers, Washington, DC, Library of Congress.

O'Connor, M. (1994). *Is capitalism sustainable? Political economy and the politics of ecology.* New York: The Guilford Press.

Pellow, D. N., & Brulle, R. J. (2005). *Power, justice, and the environment: A critical appraisal of the environment.* Cambridge, MA: MIT Press.

Pines, S. (2002). Car share. *The EcoVillage at Ithaca Newsletter,* Spring-Summer (11, 1), p. 12.

Pollan, M. (2004). *The Omnivore's Dilemma: A natural history of four meals.* New York: Penguin Group.

Richardson, R. D., Jr. (1995). *Emerson: The mind on fire.* Berkeley, CA: University of California Press.

Riddell, R. (2004). *Sustainable urban planning* (p. 225). Malden, MA: Blackwell Publishing.

Roper, L. W. (1973). *FLO: A biography of Frederick law Olmsted.* Baltimore: John Hopkins University Press.

Rybczynski, W. (1999). *A clearing in the distance: Frederick Law Olmsted and America in the 19th century.* New York: Touchstone.

Schaub, J. (2000). State of the communities movement: Good things come in threes. In: *Communities Directory: A Guide to Intentional Communities and Cooperative Living.* New York: Routledge.

Schor, J. (1999). *The overspent American: Why we want what we don't need.* New York: HarperCollins.

Self, R. O. (2003). *American Babylon: Race and the struggle for postwar Oakland.* Princeton, NJ: Princeton University Press.

Shiva, V. (1993). *Staying alive: Women, ecology, and development.* London: Zed Books.

Smith, J. J., & Hurst, N. (2007). Grocery closings hit Detroit hard: City shoppers' choices dwindle as last big chain leaves. *The Detroit News,* July 5.

Smith, T. (1998). *The myth of green marketing: Tending our goats at the edge of apocalypse.* Toronto, Ont: University of Toronto Press.

Somerfeldt, C. (2002). Dreams of community in song. *The EcoVillage at Ithaca Newsletter,* Spring-Summer (11, 1), p. 1.

Sustainable South Bronx. (2009). Sustainable South Bronx. Available at http://www.ssbx.org/. Retrieved on October 22, 2009.

Taylor, D. E. (1999). Mobilizing for environmental justice in communities of color: An emerging profile of people of color environmental groups. In: J. Aley, W. Burch, B. Canover & D. Field (Eds), *Ecosystem management: Adaptive strategies for natural resource organizations in the 21st century* (pp. 33–67). Washington, DC: Taylor & Francis.

Taylor, D. E. (2000). The rise of the environmental justice paradigm: Injustice framing and the social construction of environmental discourses. *American Behavioral Scientist, 43*(4), 508–580.

Taylor, D. E. (2009). *The environment and the people in American Cities: 1600s–1900s. Disorder, inequality and social change.* Durham, NC: Duke University Press.

Taylor, D. E. (Forthcoming). Outward bound: Manliness, wealth, race and the rise of the environmental movement, 1830s–1930s.

TechPractices. (2008). TechPractices: EcoVillage at Ithaca, Ithaca, NY. Available at http://www.toolbase.org/Home-Building-Topics/Indoor-Air-Quality/EcoVillage-at-Ithaca. Retrieved on October 19, 2009.

The EcoVillage at Ithaca Newsletter. (1999). *The EcoVillage at Ithaca Newsletter*, Winter (9, 1).
The EcoVillage at Ithaca Newsletter. (2000). *The EcoVillage at Ithaca Newsletter*, Winter (10, II).
The EcoVillage at Ithaca Newsletter. (2002a). At a glance comparison. *The EcoVillage at Ithaca Newsletter*, Spring-Summer (11, 1), p. 11.
The EcoVillage at Ithaca Newsletter. (2002b). *The EcoVillage at Ithaca Newsletter*, Spring-Summer (11, 1).
The EcoVillage at Ithaca Newsletter. (2003). *The EcoVillage at Ithaca Newsletter*, Winter-Spring.
The EcoVillage at Ithaca Newsletter. (2003–2004). *The EcoVillage at Ithaca Newsletter*, Winter.
The EcoVillage at Ithaca Newsletter. (2005a). *The EcoVillage at Ithaca Newsletter*, Fall.
The EcoVillage at Ithaca Newsletter. (2005b). *The EcoVillage at Ithaca Newsletter*, Winter.
The EcoVillage at Ithaca Newsletter. (2006). *The EcoVillage at Ithaca Newsletter*, Winter.
The EcoVillage at Ithaca Newsletter. (2007). *The EcoVillage at Ithaca Newsletter*, Spring.
Thiaw, A. A. (2003). Sister EcoVillage in Senegal. *The EcoVillage at Ithaca Newsletter*, Winter-Spring, pp. 7–8.
Thompson, J. (2009). As more search for community, Ithaca's EcoVillage gets ready to expand. *The Post Standard*, January 25.
Thoreau, H. D. (1971). *Walden*. Shanley Lyndon, Ed. Princeton, NJ: Princeton University Press.
Town of Ithaca Planning Board. (2001a). *Minutes of the Planning Board Meeting*, Planning Board, Ithaca, NY, May 15.
Town of Ithaca Planning Board. (2001b). *Minutes of the Planning Board Meeting*, Planning Board, Ithaca, NY, June 5.
Town of Ithaca Planning Board. (2001c). *Minutes of the Planning Board Meeting*, Planning Board, Ithaca, NY, April 17.
Town of Ithaca Planning Board. (2005). *Minutes of the Planning Board Meeting*, Planning Board, Ithaca, NY, May 17.
TREE (2008). TREE: EcoVillage at Ithaca's third neighborhood. Available at http://www.tree.ecovillageithaca.org/index.php?option=com_content&task=view&id=55&Itemid=71. Retrieved on October 17, 2009.
U. S. Bureau of the Census. (2000). *Census of population and housing*. Washington, DC: Department of Commerce.
Veblen, T. (1931). *Theory of the leisure class*. New York: Viking Press.
Walker, L. (2000). A long winding road towards affordable housing. *The EcoVillage at Ithaca Newsletter*, Spring (10, 1), pp. 1, 7.
Walker, L. (2002). EVI receives affordable housing grant. *The EcoVillage at Ithaca Newsletter*, Spring-Summer (11, 1), pp. 1, 10.
Walker, L. (2004a). Debt-free in 2003. *The EcoVillage at Ithaca Newsletter*, Winter, p. 3.
Walker, L. (2004b). Town builds water tank. *The EcoVillage at Ithaca Newsletter*, Winter, p. 9.
Walker, L. (2005). *EcoVillage at Ithaca: Pioneering a sustainable culture*. Gabriola Island, BC: New Society Publishers.
Walker, L. (2006). Car-free at Ecovillage: An interview with Elisabeth Harrod. *The EcoVillage at Ithaca Newsletter*, Winter, p. 10.
Walker, L. (2007). When the ice melts. *The EcoVillage at Ithaca Newsletter*, Spring, p. 2.
Wolfe, L. M. (Ed.) (1938). *John of the mountains: Unpublished journals of John Muir*. Boston: Houghton Mifflin Company.

Zenk, S. N., Schulz, A. J., Hollis-Neely, T., Campbell, R. T., Holmes, N., Watkins, G., Nwankwo, R., & Odoms-Young, A. (2005). Neighborhood racial composition, neighborhood poverty, and the spatial accessibility of supermarkets in metropolitan Detroit. *American Journal of Public Health*, *95*(1), 660–667.

Tendai Chitewere is an assistant professor in the Liberal Studies Program at San Francisco State University. She teaches interdisciplinary social science courses and is an associated faculty member in the Environmental Studies Program where she is teaching the course Nature, Culture, Technology. She can be reached by email at tendai@sfsu.edu or by telephone at 415-405-2676.

Dorceta E. Taylor is an associate professor at the University of Michigan's School of Natural Resources and Environment. She teaches courses in environmental history, environmental justice, tourism and climate change, and social movements. She is the director of the Multicultural Environmental Leadership Development Initiative (http://www.meldi.snre. umich.edu) and the author of *The Environment and the People in American Cities, 1600s–1900s: Disorder, Inequality, and Social Change*. She can be reached by email at dorceta@umich.edu or by telephone at 734-763-5327.

PART II
WATER RESOURCES AND TOXIC FOOD CONSUMPTION

THE DOMESTIC AND INTERNATIONAL DIMENSIONS OF METHYLMERCURY CONTAMINATION IN TUNA: AN ANALYSIS OF THE EFFICACY OF THE FISH ADVISORY STANDARDS OF TWO FEDERAL AGENCIES

Beth Pallo and Marlene Barken

ABSTRACT

Purpose – This chapter examines the literature on the dangers of methylmercury exposure and the 2004 Food and Drug Administration/ Environmental Protection Agency (FDA/EPA) Advisory on fish consumption. It analyzes the extent to which particular groups of people living in the United States are vulnerable to toxic food consumption and the extent to which the advisories put them at risk.

Design/methodology/approach – The authors conducted a review of the literature related to methylmercury. In addition, they used archival information from government documents. They also analyzed the fish

Environment and Social Justice: An International Perspective
Research in Social Problems and Public Policy, Volume 18, 179–210
Copyright © 2010 by Emerald Group Publishing Limited
All rights of reproduction in any form reserved
ISSN: 0196-1152/doi:10.1108/S0196-1152(2010)0000018008

advisories and educational information posted on websites of each state's Women, Infants, and Children (WIC) program.

Findings – *Methylmercury is a potent neurotoxin that can seriously affect fetal brain growth and development. Although the federal government promotes canned tuna as an inexpensive, beneficial protein source, recent reports indicate that a large proportion of America's favorite fish contains unsafe levels of methylmercury. Populations at risk for overconsumption include minorities and low-income groups, particularly recipients of federal subsidies such as WIC.*

Practical implications – *The FDA uses a "nuanced" message to offer consumers information about both the risks and benefits of eating fish. However, the advisory is not widely distributed and information on mercury levels in fish is not available at the point of sale. Minority populations are less likely to be aware of fish advisories and to change consumption habits. Thus, the target population remains largely uninformed and possibly misled about the risks and benefits of eating canned tuna.*

Social implications – *Based on new data, the federal government should recognize mercury as a hazard, update its consumption guidelines, and better monitor the mercury content in canned tuna. Outreach and educational programs should target minority and at-risk groups. The authors recommend an alternative precautionary approach in dealing with the health threats posed by methylmercury in tuna fish.*

INTRODUCTION

Methylmercury is a known chemical contaminant in fish, particularly large predatory ocean fish such as tuna, swordfish, and shark. Mercury has contaminated the majority of waterways in the United States, and high concentrations are found in many freshwater fish, including bottom feeders and predatory species. The Environmental Protection Agency's (EPA) fact sheet for 2008 National Listing of Fish Advisories states that 3,361 fish consumption advisories are due to mercury. Twenty-seven states have issued freshwater mercury advisories and 13 states have issued advisories for coastal waters (Environmental Protection Agency [EPA], 2008).

Of all fish and shellfish advisories issued in the United States, 80 percent are due partly to mercury contamination, and mercury is also responsible for the issuance of the first national fish consumption advisory (EPA, 2008). After years of working on their own, the Food and Drug Administration (FDA), which has jurisdiction over commercial fisheries, issued a joint advisory with the EPA, which oversees noncommercial fisheries. The joint advisory, issued in 2004, was intended to respond to widespread consumer concern that methylmercury can seriously impair fetal and early child brain development.

Understanding the impacts of the fish advisories has important implications for environmental justice advocates. The EPA has recognized that communities of color, low income communities, tribes and indigenous peoples are among the most exposed to environmental contaminants (Environmental Protection Agency [EPA], 2002). The environmental justice literature has well documented the heavy burden such contaminants place on subsistence fishing communities (International Indian Treaty Council, 2004; LaDuke, 1999; Madsen, DeWeese, Kmiecik, Foran, & Chiriboga, 2007; Silver et al., 2007; West, 1992; West, Fly, Larkin, & Marans, 1992). Fish and other seafood products are the main source of methylmercury in the diet, and surveys have documented that Asians, Pacific Islanders, and Native Americans eat more fish than the general public (Environmental Protection Agency [EPA], 2001a). The EPA's environmental justice report found that low-income individuals, people of color, those with limited proficiency in English, and those with little formal education are less likely to be aware of advisories and may be unwilling to change their fish consumption habits due to both cultural preferences and the lack of adequate nutritious alternatives (EPA, 2002). For instance, in one study that focused on fish consumption and advisory awareness of low-income women in California's Sacramento – San Joaquin Delta, it was concluded that consumption rates were highest among African Americans ($41.2 \, \text{g day}^{-1}$) and Asians ($35.6 \, \text{g day}^{-1}$), particularly Vietnamese and Cambodians. Furthermore, the study concluded that 56 percent of white participants had specific awareness of advisories, whereas only 10 percent of Hmong and 17 percent of Vietnamese participants displayed general awareness of advisories (Silver et al., 2007). Though little has been written on how these groups perceive consumption advisories related to imported and canned fish, we need a greater understanding of the impacts of seafood advisories on different groups in the population.

The analysis of the consumption of fish and the government advisories and policies related to them has important implications for equity. Low-income and minority groups comprise the largest segment of eligible recipients under government-funded subsidies such as the Women, Infants and Children (WIC) program. In a 2006 study that collected demographic data for WIC, 44 percent of participants identified themselves as Hispanic, 33 percent as white, 21 percent as African American/black, and 5 percent as other (WIC, 2006). The federal government promotes canned tuna in these programs, and until 2006, it was the only animal protein source offered. The program has since approved the purchase of canned salmon, sardines, and mackerel with vouchers, whereas discontinuing the purchase of albacore tuna, which tends to be higher in mercury than chunk light canned tuna (Federal Register, 2006).

The current FDA/EPA Advisory's guidelines on fish consumption for pregnant women, mothers who are nursing, and young children allow canned tuna in limited quantities. Yet, a 2006 report published jointly by the Defenders of Wildlife and the Center for Science in the Public Interest, in conjunction with the Mercury Policy Project, concluded that due to varying levels of methylmercury in canned tuna, even consuming small amounts poses a danger to this sensitive subgroup (Defenders of Wildlife, Center for Science in the Public Interest, & Mercury Policy Project, 2006).

The FDA has deliberately chosen to use a "nuanced" message to offer consumers information about both the risks and benefits of eating fish. However, the Advisory is not widely distributed, information on mercury levels in fish is not available at the point of sale, and the WIC program does not adequately counsel recipients about the pros and cons of eating canned tuna. Thus, the target population remains largely uneducated about substitutes for canned tuna and possibly misled about its nutritional value. This chapter examines the literature on the dangers of methylmercury exposure as well as the history and shortcomings of the FDA/EPA Advisory. The authors recommend a revision of the guidelines based on new data, outreach action to inform and counsel sensitive subpopulations, and adoption of an alternative precautionary approach in dealing with the health threats posed by methylmercury in tuna fish.

METHYLMERCURY CONTAMINATION

Sources of Exposure

Mercury occurs naturally in the environment, deep within the earth's crust in three different forms: elemental, inorganic, or organic (Schober et al., 2003). It is released into the atmosphere through anthropogenic forces, with industrial emissions accounting for 70 percent of mercury pollution globally

(Defenders of Wildlife et al., 2006). Naturally occurring mercury accounts for 30 percent of atmospheric emissions (Schober et al., 2003). Coal burning power plants, waste incinerators, and chlori-alkali plants emit inorganic mercury into the atmosphere, where it remains suspended until it returns to earth via deposition. Mercury then contaminates the oceans, lakes, groundwater, and other waterways. In an aquatic environment mercury reacts with sulfating bacterial algae, undergoes a methylation process and takes on an even more toxic form: methylmercury. Fish that eat the algae become tainted with this toxic compound, which bioaccumulates as it passes through each trophic level of the food chain (Defenders of Wildlife et al., 2006). In North America, the development of huge hydro-electric projects has exacerbated the problem by flooding mercury-contaminated soils. In northern Quebec, the Cree, Inuit and Innu have been exposed to six times "safe" levels of methylmercury, as high as those found in the Minimata, Japan disaster discussed later, and they have been advised not to eat fish from affected dam complexes (Laduke, 1999). The EPA employs a fish consumption rate of 17.5 g/day for the general population and recreational fishers, and 142.2 g/day for subsistence fishers. Yet some members of the Squamish Tribe of British Columbia consume as much as 1,453.6 g/day, Laotian communities in West Contra County, California 182.3 g/day, Squaxin Island of Oregon and Tulalip Tribes of Washington 391.4 g/ day, and the Four Columbia River Tribes of Oregon 972 g/day. These groups are under protected by the EPA's standards and consume more fish than the general population (EPA, 2001a).

When humans, who are at the top of the food chain, consume large predatory fish, such as king mackerel, shark, tilefish, swordfish, and tuna, they are exposed to methylmercury at high levels of toxicity (Trasande, Landrigan, & Schecter, 2005). See Fig. 1 for the FDA's listing of high mercury fish. Methylmercury can be debilitating to the developing brain, even low levels of exposure can result in permanent damage (McCaffrey, 2004). Exposure to excessive amounts of methylmercury not only harms infants and young children, but can also lead to nervous system dysfunction, memory loss, and organ failure in adults (Defenders of Wildlife et al., 2006).

Research on the Effects of Methylmercury

Several animal studies have examined the toxicological effects of meythl-mercury. Methylmercury is known to cause neurological damage; symptoms of mercury poisoning include sensory impairment in vision, hearing, and

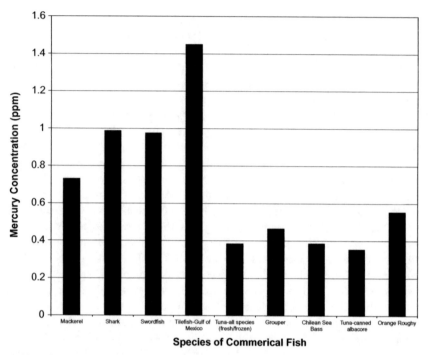

Species of Commerical Fish

Fig. 1. Mercury Levels in Commercial Fish as Reported by the FDA. *Source:* Federal Register, Department of Agriculture, Food, and Nutrition Service (2006).

speech. In humans and rodents, targets of methylmercury toxicity most notably include the cerebellum and cortex. A study in the *Brazlilian Journal of Medical and Biological Research* used chick embryos to demonstrate the mechanisms of neurotoxicity in retinal cells. The study evaluated the effect of methylmercury on nitric oxide synthase, a neurotransmitter that becomes a neurotoxin when overproduced. The results showed that methylmercury promoted a concentration and time-dependent decrease in cell viability. Retinal cell cultures were more sensitive than cortical culture cells to methylmercury exposure (Herculano, Crespo-Lopez, Lima, Picanco-Diniz, & DO Nascimento, 2006). Another body of research worth noting is that of the FRIENDs Children's Environmental Health Center, which is involved in an ongoing study of the neurobehavorial effects of polychlorinated biphenyls (PCBs) and methylmercury on rats. The EPA has funded the University of Illinois to investigate the health effects of exposure to PCBs and methylmercury in Hmong and Laotian refugees who consume contaminated fish from the Fox River in Wisconsin. The objectives are to characterize the cognitive, motor, and sensory effects of perinatal exposure to PCBs, methylmercury, and PCBs and methylmercury combined. The results from these animal experiments will guide the selection of behavioral tests used for children who are exposed to PCBs and methylmercury through maternal consumption of contaminated fish (Environmental Protection Agency [EPA], 2001b). This information could be very useful in setting a standard for the types of children's behavioral tests used when determining methylmercury effects. As noted earlier, several studies have evaluated the effects of methylmercury in children through maternal fish consumption, but the varying types of cognitive tests used may have resulted in different conclusions.

In 1977, a study was conducted to assess methylmercury exposure in a group of aboriginal Quebec Cree adults aged 18–82 claiming ill health from local fish consumption. More than 20 years later, scientists re-analyzed this data to determine the existence of a dose-response relationship between long-term mercury exposure and neurological abnormalities in this group. Hair mercury concentrations ranged from 0.5 to 46.0 ppm (parts per million). The study concluded that dose-dependent effects of methylmercury on tremor may occur below the commonly accepted threshold of 50.0 ppm, particularly in young adults. It is noted that the results should be interpreted with caution, since alcohol use was most likely under reported and multiple outcomes were studied (Auger, Kofman, Kosastsky, & Armstrong, 2005).

Since the late 1980s, several large, long-term epidemiological studies have examined the exposure of children to methylmercury. Neurological examinations, developmental rating scales, and psychological tests were used to evaluate postnatal neurological effects in children exposed in utero to methylmercury. These studies were conducted in the Faroe Islands, The Republic of Seychelles, and New Zealand. Postnatal follow up data is still being collected from the Faroe Islands (Trasande et al., 2005; Spurgeon, 2006; Grandjean, Debes, Weihe, & White, 2006).

The Faroe Islands, nestled between Norway, Shetland, and Iceland in the North Atlantic, was of interest to researchers because of the population's seafood-rich diet. The average Faroese eats about three meals of marine fish per week, along with the occasional meal of pilot whale, which is particularly high in methylmercury. The study monitored 1,022 children born during the period 1986–1987 to mothers who ate a diet containing fish and whale meat during pregnancy (Steingraber, 2001). Exposure to methylmercury was determined from mercury concentrations in umbilical cord blood and maternal hair samples.

Comparison of prenatal exposures within the cohort group demonstrated that cord blood is the most sensitive measurement of in utero exposure, because it consistently predicted nervous system deficits determined during post-natal follow-up (Grandjean et al., 1997). Postnatal follow-up evaluated the neurobehavioral performance of 7-year-olds. Researchers found deficiencies in the children's memory, learning, and attention. These results demonstrate a dose-dependent relationship between delays in mental development and prenatal exposure to methylmercury. Cognitive problems were found to develop at very low exposure levels (Steingraber, 2001). The Faroe Island study found that children with higher prenatal exposures also had higher blood pressure than other children (Steingraber, 2001).

The association between exposure to high levels of methylmercury and high blood pressure came from the assessment of 878 of the children when they were 14 years old. During this assessment, researchers also found that the toxic effects of prenatal mercury exposure may have permanent effects on cognitive function. Impaired neurological regulation of heartbeat was observed in some of the teenagers; this is a sign of mercury toxicity in the brainstem. In addition, the findings obtained when the children were 7 persisted in 14-year-olds (Grandjean et al., 2006; McCaffrey, 2004).

Researchers clearly observed a dose-dependent relationship between prenatal mercury exposure measured in cord blood and delays in nerve transmission in the 14-year-olds. Methylmercury exposure was significantly associated with deficits in motor, attention, and verbal tests. Along with performing the basic tests for cognitive and motor skills, the study went a step further and measured hearing-related electrode activity in the brainstem. The electrode analysis showed that nerve signal speed was lower in the children who experienced prenatal exposure to higher levels of mercury (Grandjean et al., 2006; McCaffrey, 2004).

The Faroe Island's data has been controversial. Some scientists and the tuna industry have challenged its validity. Those discrediting the study argue that confounding factors, such as dichlorodiphenyltrichloroethane (DDT) and PCBs found in whale blubber, make its validity questionable. It is also argued that there was no control group in this study, because the entire Faroese population had been exposed to methylmercury through whale meat before the experiment. Nonetheless, a New Zealand study of methylmercury produced similar results.

The New Zealand study likewise was conducted in the mid-1980s. It evaluated 237 children at ages 6 and 7 using scholastic and psychological tests. Maternal hair was used as the primary biomarker. The main exposure to methylmercury was from the consumption of shark meat used in fish and chips. Using generalized developmental testing such as the Wechsler intelligence scale and the McCarthy perceptual performance and motor test, the New Zealand researchers found adverse mental development in children exposed to levels of mercury in utero similar to that of the Faroe Islands. Both the Faroe and New Zealand studies support the conclusion that adverse developmental effects are evident at extremely low exposure levels (Trasande et al., 2005). The New Zealand study is less controversial as shark meat has undetectable levels of PCBs.

Researchers from the University of Rochester led a third major epidemiological study on methylmercury. The subjects were 779 children born from 1989 to 1990 on the Seychelles Islands in the Indian Ocean. This location was chosen because of the island nation's small population of approximately 65,000 people and its diet rich in seafood. More importantly, their consumption of seafood is relatively steady (mothers typically eat 12 meals of fish per week), the fish they eat has undetectable levels of PCB's, and there are no direct sources of mercury pollution in the area. A series of developmental and neurological tests specially designed to detect the effects of mercury exposure were performed when the children were 6, 19, 29, and 66 months old. The researchers used maternal hair samples as the biomarker to measure mercury levels. These samples allow tracking of mercury exposure during gestation. Since it takes about 2 years for mercury to be expelled from the body after consumption, the mercury present in the hair at the time of collection was also present during pregnancy. The conclusions of this research found no significant association between mercury levels and neurobehavioral performance in the children (Myers et al., 2003). The question of whether or not the Seychelles children will experience developmental problems as they mature still remains unanswered.

These results suggest that different levels of mercury exposure account for differences in the study findings, however the average value of mercury in maternal hair samples in the studies did not differ significantly. The Faroe Island study reported values ranging from .04 to 26.0 ppm with the average mercury exposure at 4.0 ppm in maternal hair samples. The New Zealand study reported an average of 6.0 ppm in maternal hair, and noted a decreased level in test performance in children whose mothers' average hair mercury levels were 13–15.0 ppm, a level similar to the Faroe Island Study. Lastly, the Seychelles Island study reported maternal hair samples ranging from 0.5 to 26.7 ppm, with average levels between 5.9 and 8.2 ppm. The similarity of the mercury levels in maternal hair samples for all three studies makes it difficult to justify the varying results (Davidson et al., 2008; Moore, 2003). Although the Faroe Islands and New Zealand study suggest limiting the intake of some fish, other studies point to the importance of consuming fish particularly when pregnant. A study published in *Lancet* in 2007 highlighted the importance of omega-3 fatty acids and their contribution to neural development. In monitoring the daily intake of fish by 11,875 pregnant women at 32 weeks gestation, researchers found that maternal intake of seafood during pregnancy of less than 340 g/week was associated with the increased likelihood of the child being in the lowest Intelligence Quotient (IQ) quartile. They suggest that limiting seafood intake too severely during pregnancy could be detrimental to a child's development (Hibbeln et al., 2007). Alternatively, a 2004 study in the United States found a significant correlation between the amount of environmentally released mercury and an increased need for special education services as well as an increase in the rate of autism (Palmer, Blanchard, Stein, Mandell, & Miller, 2006). Given the serious implications for health and education policy planning indicated by this ecological study, more research is warranted.

Health and Fish Consumption in American Minorities and Women

A summary of blood mercury levels in women aged 16–49 from the National Health and Nutrition Examination Survey (NHANES) showed a small decline in the geometric mean of blood mercury levels from 1999–2000 to 2001–2002 for three ethnic groups. When these results are stratified across the groups, black, non-Hispanic women had the highest levels in both the 1999–2000 and 2001–2002 surveys (1.4 and 1.1 µg/L, respectively), followed by white non-Hispanics (0.9 and 0.8 µg/L, respectively), and Mexican Americans (0.8 and 0.7 µg/L, respectively) (National Health and Nutrition Examination Survey, 2008). Blood mercury reports based on NHANES data from 2001 to 2002 did not report mercury levels for the "other" subgroup, which includes Asians, Pacific Islanders, Native Americans, and multiracial respondents. However, using NHANES data from 1999 to 2000, a 2006 study showed that these ethnic minorities had statistically significant elevated blood mercury levels. The study concluded that 5.66 percent of the U.S. population as a whole had over 5.8 µg/L mercury in their blood, whereas 16.59 percent of those classified as "other" (Asians, Pacific Islanders, and Native Americans) had blood mercury levels over 5.8 µg/L. These findings are consistent with those of smaller studies that showed a correlation of high mercury levels in those who identified themselves as belonging to the "other" category of NHANES participants (Hightower, O'Hare, & Hernandez, 2006).

Although canned tuna has been implicated as one of the main foods contributing to total mercury intake, there is little data specifically on canned tuna consumption by minority groups. Some studies such as the one mentioned earlier in the Sacramento – San Joaquin Delta region are calling attention to advisory awareness and fish consumption patterns of ethnically diverse low-income women (Silver et al., 2007). A recent study of women with low to moderate exposure to methylmercury during the first 6 months of pregnancy found a significantly increased risk of preterm delivery. The women ate primarily canned fish, with 25 percent of women eating 12 or more meals in the span of 6 months. This study urged further research to determine if women who consume higher quantities of fish were at greater risk of preterm delivery complications (Xue, Holzman, Mohammad Hossein, Trosko, & Fischer, 2007).

Setting Exposure Limits in the United States

There have been widely publicized incidences of methylmercury poisoning arising from the consumption of mercury-contaminated fish in Japan and from the consumption of grains treated with a mercury-based fungicide to control mold in Iraq (Center for Food Safety and Applied Nutrition– [CFSAN] and the Food and Drug Administration [FDA], 2001). The Japanese disaster dates back to the 1930s when the Chisso Company began manufacturing acetaldehyde and vinyl chloride ingredients in plastics. The factory used metallic mercury as a catalyst, which was then dumped into the wastewater that entered Minamata Bay. The elemental mercury was converted into methylmercury and moved up the food chain, and eventually pregnant women who ate fish from the bay passed the toxin on to their developing fetuses. By the late 1950s, thousands of babies were diagnosed with congenital "Minamata disease," another name for the methylmercury poisoning that damaged their brains and nervous systems. Despite evidence showing that Chisso's practices were linked to methylmercury poisoning, the factory continued dumping its wastes into the bay until 1968, and the Japanese government allowed people to fish there until 1976 (Nestle, 2006; Steingraber, 2001). The second food-related scandal linked to methylmercury occurred in Iraq in the early 1970s. As many as 10,000 deaths were attributed to the consumption of bread made from grain tainted with methylmercury. Fish and migratory birds also were affected because they ate the discarded grains (Corrosion Doctors, 2007).

Based on the Minamata tragedy and two additional cases of methylmer-cury poisoning that occurred in Niigata, Japan in 1965, the FDA established an action level of 0.5 ppm for methylmercury in fish as the level at which the agency might take legal action to remove a product from the market. In contrast, the EPA relied on the data from Iraq and established a reference dose for methylmercury in fish of 0.1 µg/kg/day (CFSAN and the FDA, 2001). A reference dose is defined as "an estimate of daily exposure to the human population that is likely to be without appreciable risk of deleterious effects during a lifetime" (Rice, 2004). When establishing a reference dose, scientific bodies include uncertainty factors to account for human population variability and unknown effects due to lack of data (University of Minnesota, undated). The EPA's reference dose is expressed in micrograms of mercury per unit of body weight per day, so the more a person weighs, the higher the reference dose. By increasing proportionally based on an individual's body weight, the reference dose has a stricter standard built in for smaller children who are the most sensitive to the damaging effects of mercury (Defenders of Wildlife et al., 2006). In comparison to the FDA's action level, the EPA's original reference dose was equivalent to approximately 0.3 ppm for the average adult (Defenders of Wildlife et al., 2006). The EPA's reference dose has remained unchanged, though as discussed later, the EPA later updated the basis for that number as per the recommendation of the National Academy of Sciences.

The FDA's action level was challenged in 1978 in the *US v. Anderson Seafood* case, when the FDA took enforcement action against Anderson Seafood for allegedly distributing swordfish adulterated with mercury up to levels of 2.0 ppm. The District Court agreed with the FDA's interpretation of "adulterated" to include substances that are "added" and "may render" the fish injurious. Determining that some unquantified portion of the mercury in swordfish is attributable to human acts such as environmental and industrial pollution, the court upheld the FDA's enforcement power. In reviewing the laboratory evidence, however, the court found that the swordfish distributed by Anderson contained mercury levels ranging from 0.53 to 1.0 ppm. Since the court concluded that a preponderance of the evidence supported an acceptable human intake level for methylmercury, the key question for FDA enforcement became the relevant action level. Experts testified regarding the disputed lowest level of methylmercury in the blood at which a harmful effect on human health can be detected, and the FDA asserted that there may be subclinical effects not yet subject to detection by neurological examination. Rejecting such conjecture as too speculative, the court held that the scientific and empirical data supported an action level of 1.0 ppm (*US v. Anderson Seafood*, 1978).

The FDA's current action level of 1.0 ppm has been in place since 1978. This level reflects an acceptable or tolerable daily intake of approximately 0.4 μg/kg/day, depending on the body weight. Their calculation of acceptable or tolerable daily intake includes a 10-fold margin of safety from levels where adverse effects such as parathesia have been observed in adults (CFSAN and the FDA, 2001). It should be noted that the FDA's figure differs from the EPA's more cautious reference dose, which has remained at 0.1 μg/kg/day. Although the differing threshold standards may be due in part to the different regulatory missions of the two agencies, the resulting inconsistency is troubling. Moreover, the FDA's standard is much higher than the action levels established by several other countries and world health policymaking bodies (Fig. 2). Note that the EPA is at the other end of the spectrum along with the United Kingdom and Japan at 0.3 ppm. The FDA's standard is puzzling in light of findings in recent studies on the health effects of methylmercury and new evidence indicating that the amount of methylmercury in light tuna is higher than previously thought. Although the FDA provides consumption guidelines for high-mercury fish such as king mackerel, tilefish, shark, and swordfish, the agency's action level is among the least protective among several developed and developing nations (Defenders of Wildlife et al., 2006).

THE EVOLUTION OF THE FDA'S AND EPA'S FISH ADVISORY STANDARDS

Discrepancies in the Standards of Two Federal Agencies

As discussed earlier, the FDA and the EPA relied on different studies (the Japan and Iraq data, respectively) to develop their recommended threshold levels for exposure to methylmercury. Since the *Anderson Seafood* litigation in 1978, the FDA has not re-examined its 1.0 ppm action level for removing tuna from grocery stores. It is problematic that agencies charged with protecting public health and regulating the same commodity continue to rely on vastly different standards to determine the level at which exposure to methylmercury is unsafe. Disparities between the FDA and EPA recommendations are still unresolved, despite the fact that the agencies came together in 2004 to form the most recent consumption advisory on fish

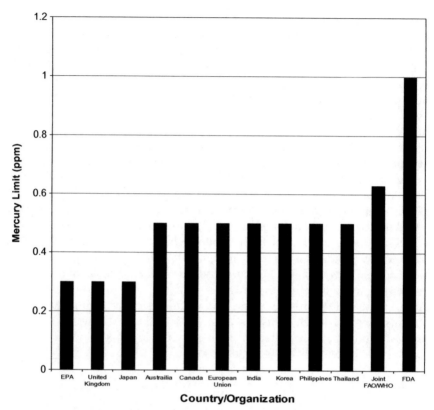

Fig. 2. Maximum Allowed/Recommended Mercury Levels in Fish (ppm) in Selected Countries and International Organizations. *Source:* Defenders of Wildlife, Center for Science in the Public Interest, Mercury Policy Project (2006).

and shellfish. In order to better understand the current advisory, it is helpful to first look at the regulatory and political context in which it evolved.

The 1994 Advisory

The FDA is charged with monitoring all commercial fish sold in the marketplace, both domestic and imported, and its regulatory mission is to balance health risks against cost considerations, including costs to industry (Nestle, 2006). By the early 1990s, public pressure was mounting for formal agency action to notify the public regarding the risks of consuming commercial seafood. Beginning in 1991, the Institute of Medicine, a private nonprofit group that works with the National Academy of Sciences, started advising women who might become pregnant to avoid swordfish altogether (Steingraber, 2001). Due in part to the concerns raised by the results of the Faroe Islands study, in 1992 the Center for Science in the Public Interest petitioned the FDA to adopt a stricter methylmercury standard. The FDA responded that it was waiting to review the then pending results of the Seychelles data, and it delayed issuing its first seafood advisory until September 1994 (CFSAN and the FDA, 2001).

Published in the *FDA Consumer*, that advisory assured the public that given the general pattern of fish consumption in the United States, most people were in no danger of methylmercury poisoning. However, the agency specifically advised pregnant women and women of childbearing age who may become pregnant to limit consumption of shark and swordfish to no more than once a month. The general population (including nursing mothers) could consume no more than one serving (about 7 ounces) of these high mercury level fish, and those fish species with levels averaging between 0.5 and 1.0 ppm should be limited to about 14 ounces/week. The FDA offered no consumption advice for the top 10 most consumed seafood species in America – canned tuna, shrimp, pollack, salmon, cod, catfish, clams, flatfish, crabs, and scallops. These were considered fish with low mercury content (presumed to contain less than 0.2 ppm) and though they represented 80 percent of the market, the FDA believed that few people ate more than the 2.2 pounds suggested limit of these fish (CFSAN and the FDA, 2001).

The fact that the 1994 advisory said nothing about albacore tuna, the most-often consumed predatory fish in America, was at best, an "odd oversight" (Nestle, 2006). Though albacore tuna has less methylmercury than shark or swordfish, at the time the advisory was being drafted, it was believed to have three times the amount of methylmercury found in the smaller and cheaper varieties of canned "chunk light" tuna. Industry lobbyists were concerned that advice to restrict consumption of albacore tuna would be interpreted as advice to avoid all tuna, and they convinced the FDA to keep tuna off of the restricted list (Nestle, 2006).

The 1999–2000 National Academy of Sciences Study

In contrast to the FDA's focus on commercial fish, the EPA and the states are charged with monitoring mercury levels in domestic fish caught for sport and private use (Steingraber, 2001). Since the EPA is responsible for protecting the health of the public against toxic contaminants that are discharged or deposited in the waterways, the EPA also issues advisories about which fish are safe to eat. Unlike the FDA, when the EPA sets its standards, it focuses on the health risks to the people who eat the fish under its jurisdiction, not the impact on industry (Nestle, 2006). In 1999, Congress appropriated funds to the EPA to contract with the National Academy of Sciences to review the validity of the EPA's reference dose. The report was released in July 2000, and it concluded that the EPA's reference dose of 0.1 µg/kg/day was a scientifically justifiable level for the protection of public health, but it recommended basing the reference dose on recent data than the Iraqi study (CFSAN and the FDA, 2001). The National Academy of Sciences committee found the Faroe Islands study to be the most reliable for deriving the reference dose and excluded the Seychelles study because its failure to observe neurodevelopmental effects associated with methylmer- cury exposure conflicted with the dominant body of scientific evidence (CFSAN and the FDA, 2001). Moreover, the National Academy of Sciences report warned that "available consumption data and current population and fertility rates indicate that over 60,000 newborns annually might be at risk for adverse neurodevelopmental effects from *in utero* exposure to methylmercury" (National Academy of Sciences, 2000).

After the National Academy of Sciences report was released, the FDA received numerous requests from industry lobbyists and their congressional allies to delay any decisions on a new consumer advisory until scientific consensus could be reached regarding the validity of the Seychelles study and expected follow-up data. They also argued that the Faroe Islands study was unreliable because of the population's exposure to PCBs and other persistent organic pollutants and that the population's consumption patterns were unlike those of American consumers. However, Senators Leahy and Harkin had been pressuring the FDA to re-examine its action level since 1999. Based on the National Academy of Sciences report, they now called for the FDA to adopt the EPA's stricter standard in the interest of protecting public health and to resume its suspended tests for methylmercury contamination in domestically caught fish (CFSAN and the FDA, 2001).

The FDA 2001 Advisory

In response to the National Academy of Sciences report, the FDA attempted to reconcile the several conflicting studies of methylmercury exposure in human populations, data regarding fish consumption and mercury concentrations, the health benefits of a balanced diet that includes fish, and feedback from eight focus groups asked to react to different types of consumer messages. The FDA's Director of the Center for Food Safety and Applied Nutrition also met with numerous stakeholders, including representatives of the National Food Processors and the canned tuna industry, who argued strenuously that canned tuna was safe at the FDA's action level of 1.0 ppm (the industry based its assertion on estimates of methylmercury levels in canned tuna at approximately 0.17 ppm). The industry also expressed concern that seafood is a good source of protein and that the health benefits of seafood products needed to be considered in any regulatory decision. Finally, industry lobbyists cautioned that reliance solely on the National Academy of Sciences study could do "irreparable" harm to the canned tuna industry (CFSAN and the FDA, 2001).

As a result, the 2001 advisory recommended that pregnant women and women of childbearing age who may become pregnant should avoid eating four kinds of fish with the highest average amounts of methylmercury – shark, swordfish, king mackerel, and tilefish. Largely based on information provided by the National Food Processors, the FDA concluded that canned tuna consumption was not as great as "anecdotal" observations would indicate, and therefore no specific advice for canned tuna was necessary. In fact, all recommendations for tuna, including fresh and frozen tuna which generally use larger fish than those in canned tuna, were subsumed in the general advice to limit all fish consumption to twice a week, not to exceed 12 ounces in total (CFSAN and the FDA, 2001).

Although the tuna industry was delighted by the weakened advisory, public interest watchdog organizations such as the Environmental Working Group were not. Documents obtained by the Environmental Working Group through the Freedom of Information Act revealed that the FDA had originally planned to include warnings about tuna steaks and canned tuna in the advisory, but that it dropped those warnings after three meetings with the tuna industry. Also, the Environmental Working Group charged that the FDA's claim that focus groups misinterpreted advice to limit intake of fish as a directive to abstain altogether was erroneous. When the FDA's advisory was greeted with strong criticism, the agency turned to its Food Advisory Committee for help. In 2002, the Food Advisory Committee recommended that the FDA and the EPA formulate a joint advisory to resolve the inconsistencies in their respective standards for safe levels of mercury consumption and that specific advice should be issued for tuna since it was so widely consumed (Nestle, 2006).

The FDA and EPA 2004 Advisory

Following a process similar to that which generated the 2001 advisory, the FDA and EPA convened focus groups and held four meetings with interested parties between July 2002 and July 2003. Stakeholders included industry, consumer groups and health professionals, the states, and tribes. These briefings and presentations were designed both to elicit commentary on conflicting data and agency approaches and to discuss practical issues concerning the best venues and means of disseminating the ultimate message. For example, consumer groups pointed out that the goal was for consumers to make smart choices. They commented that it would be helpful to adopt the EPA approach of distinguishing between child and adult servings (2 versus 6 ounces), and noted that California required grocers to display advisories targeted at specific audiences. They also emphasized the importance of federal and state consistency because states helped to coordinate health professionals and the implementation of the WIC program. State advisories generally follow a species-specific approach instead of a mixed-fish diet scenario, and representatives urged a comprehensive advisory that considered all contaminants such as mercury, PCBs, banned pesticides, etc. Participants noted that the state of Maine had a stringent advisory in place and urged that any federal advisory should not override state advisories (Food and Drug Administration [FDA] and Environmental Protection Agency [EPA], 2003).

The resulting 2004 advisory was slightly more restrictive than earlier advisories and did directly address the tuna controversy. Women who might become pregnant, pregnant and nursing women and young children were advised to avoid shark, swordfish, king mackerel and tilefish altogether, but they could eat up to two meals (12 ounces total) of low-mercury seafood such as canned tuna. Children should eat proportionally less. Since albacore tuna has more mercury than canned light tuna, only one of the two meals could be albacore tuna. The joint advisory also recommended only eating fish caught for sport once a week, and to abstain from eating fish thereafter. Children should avoid eating sports fish. The Environmental Working Group objected that albacore tuna should have been included in the "do not eat" category for pregnant women, along with the long list of commercial and sports fish that exceed standards for methylmercury. In contrast, the tuna industry was relieved and used the joint federal advisory to extol the nutritional benefits of the omega-3 fatty acids found in canned tuna. Tuna Foundation advertisements highlighted the FDA/EPA's recommendation that pregnant women could consume both canned light and albacore tuna and called both of them low-mercury fish (Nestle, 2006).

Despite the attempt to simplify its advice, the 2004 joint advisory still failed to reconcile the FDA's action level with the EPA's more restrictive reference dose. Eating fish is a personal choice, the decision on what type and how often one eats fish may be based on several social, cultural, and economic factors such as price and availability (Burger, Stern, & Gochfeld, 2005). Under the advisory, it is still up to women in the at-risk group to check sport fish advisories and to abstain or monitor the amount of their fish intake. Likewise, caregivers need to keep track of the type and amount of fish consumed by children. Although tuna canners promote the health benefits of fish on each can of tuna, the cautions laid out in the advisory are only available on the Web and in pamphlets distributed in doctors' offices. Even then, it is only available on the FDA's website in English and Spanish. The EPA's website makes the advisory available in English, Spanish, Cambodian, Chinese, Hmong, Korean, Portuguese, and Vietnamese. As documented in the Defenders of Wildlife study discussed later, these failings are exacerbated by the lack of routine sampling of canned tuna and new data that indicates significantly higher levels of methylmercury in imported canned light tuna.

Pre-emptive Power of the 2004 Advisory

In yet another twist, the FDA has asserted that the joint advisory preempts state attempts to provide consumers with more comprehensive warnings. Pursuant to its Safe Drinking and Toxic Enforcement Act known as Proposition 65, California attempted to require point of sale warnings on canned tuna to better disseminate the FDA's message and the state's own findings regarding the toxicity of methylmercury in tuna and its teratogenic risks. The tuna industry sued, and Lester Crawford, the former Commissioner of the FDA, argued in support of the tuna canners that such warnings would frustrate the FDA's "nuanced" regulatory approach. The trial court found the FDA's position dispositive on this point, and it further ruled in favor of the industry on the issue of the calculation of the maximum allowable dosage level for methylmercury in canned tuna. The trial court also concluded that methylmercury in tuna is "naturally occurring" and hence exempt from application of Proposition 65 (*People of the State of California v. Tri-Union Seafoods* et al., 2006). This last finding seems to be in direct contradiction to the holding in the *Anderson Seafood* case discussed earlier, as well as with the explicit language of the advisory which recognizes that mercury can be released through industrial pollution and once it undergoes the methylation process can cause harm to the unborn (Food and Drug Administration [FDA] and Environmental Protection Agency and [EPA], 2004).

California appealed the case. The San Francisco Medical Society and the San Francisco Bay Area Physicians for Social Responsibility joined with the Natural Resource Defense Council and the Mercury Policy Project in filing a strong *amici curia* brief in support of the state's authority to protect the food supply and to warn citizens of food hazards (Barken & Pallo, 2009). Nonetheless, the appellate court ruled against the state in March of 2009 on the narrow ground that substantial evidence adduced at trial supported the lower court's finding that methylmercury was naturally occurring and hence the tuna companies were exempt from the warning requirements of Proposition 65. Significantly, the court acknowledged the limitations of resolving the controversy through competing expert witnesses at trial, and it left open the possibility that California's Office of Environmental Health Hazard Assessment (OEHHA), the lead agency to implement Proposition 65, could amend its regulations to remove methylmercury from the naturally occurring exception (*People of Ca. v. Tri-Union Seafoods*, 2009). To date, no further action on canned tuna has been taken by the California attorney general's office or the OEHHA, though the state is engaged in ongoing litigation against certain grocers regarding warnings on fresh and frozen fish. One of the state's contentions is that, as discussed later, there is already new scientific evidence that not all methylmercury is naturally occurring (Pollack, 2009).

It is also noteworthy that the California appellate court confined its decision to the naturally occurring ground and did not address the trial court's rulings on preemption and dosage levels. Since it did not affirm the trial court's alternate rulings, those grounds are not conclusively established and could be challenged again. Recent rulings from other courts have rejected the FDA's preemption argument. In *Fellner v. Tri-Union Seafoods*, the plaintiff is suing under New Jersey's Products Liability Act for harm she alleges she sustained as a result of consuming methylmercury contained in the defendant's canned tuna. The tuna industry moved to dismiss the suit on the grounds that Fellner's complaint was preempted by the FDA's "regulatory approach" to warning about the risks posed by mercury compounds found in fish. The District Court dismissed the complaint, but in 2008 the Third Circuit Court of Appeals reversed (*Fellner v. Tri-Union Seafoods*, 2008). The defendants sought Supreme Court review, but in April of 2009, the Court declined to review the case without comment, thus allowing it to proceed to trial (*Tri-Union Seafoods v. Fellner,* 2009). Also in 2009, the U.S. Supreme Court denied a claim of implied FDA preemption in a drug labeling case (*Wyeth v. Levine,* 2009). Moreover, the Obama administration has ordered that in recognition of the valuable role state laws play in protecting health, safety and the environment, federal preemption will not be presumed unless Congress specifically dictates that intent (Mundy & Kendall, 2009).

Though recent developments indicate a positive shift to empower state regulators, to date, litigation with the tuna industry has stymied California's (and perhaps other states) efforts to reach a larger audience concerning the risk to benefit ratio of eating canned tuna. Currently, the FDA largely controls both the message and the means by which it is delivered, and the burden is on the consumer to obtain this information. It is imperative that the federal government reexamines its position.

MONITORING MERCURY LEVELS IN CANNED TUNA

The Defenders of Wildlife released a study in 2006 that tested 164 cans of tuna purchased at large chain stores and small grocery stores across the country. The purpose was to compare the mercury content in chunk light and albacore tuna. The test results showed that there were high mercury levels in both, with chunk light tuna containing levels similar to those in albacore. Nearly 60 percent of the chunk light canned tuna was well above the FDA cutoff for low-mercury fish, which it identifies as having less than 0.12 ppm per 6 ounce can (Defenders of Wildlife et al., 2006). Of the 144 cans of chunk light tested, 31 percent had levels between 0.12–0.3 ppm, 13 percent had levels between 0.3 and 0.5 ppm, 9 percent had levels between 0.5–0.9 ppm, and 7 percent had levels greater than 0.9 ppm. The FDA classifies fish containing 0.3 ppm or more as high-mercury fish. The findings of this study suggest that, contrary to the information contained in the 2004 FDA and EPA Advisory, chunk light tuna is not necessarily a low-mercury fish.

The Defenders of Wildlife report also found a significant relationship between the origin of the tuna fish and its mercury content. This connection can be attributed to the fishing practices of some tuna companies, which aim to catch older, larger fish that have accumulated more methylmercury over time. Tuna from Ecuadorian fishing fleets generally had very high levels of methylmercury. At an average of 0.754 ppm, Ecuadorian canned tuna actually exceeds the average mercury concentrations for king mackerel, a fish the FDA/EPA classify as a high-mercury fish. Tuna originating from Mexico and Costa Rica also had higher than average mercury levels, whereas tuna caught in Asian waters was considerably lower and presumably safe (Defenders of Wildlife et al., 2006). These findings, however, may need to be re-examined. New studies have determined mercury enriched waters are transported by large ocean circulation currents. Much of the methylmercury found in the North Pacific Ocean is transmitted there from Asian factories that emit mercury-tainted coal particulates and waste into the atmosphere (United Press International, 2009). Scientists have predicted that by 2050, methylmercury levels in the Pacific will increase by as much as 50 percent if emissions continue at the projected rate. Furthermore, water sampling from the study concluded that 2006 ocean mercury levels were approximately 30 percent higher than those measured in the mid-1990s (Environment News Service, 2009). In the future it is questionable if the benefits of eating fish will outweigh the risks, especially if our oceans can no longer provide a habitat that produces fish with safe mercury levels. The bottom line is that levels of methylmercury in our fish and bodies of water are proving evermore difficult to contain, posing a threat to not only Americans but people all around the world.

A major concern is that consumers have no way of knowing the exact mercury content in the tuna fish that they eat. In addition, though country-of-origin labeling requirements apply to fresh fish, canned fish is exempt, and consumers cannot differentiate the tuna that they purchase based on its source (Nestle, 2006). Arguing that the 2004 Joint Advisory failed to achieve its goals, the Defenders of Wildlife report urged the government to immediately take the following steps to protect consumers:

1. Conduct more thorough assessments of the mercury content in canned tuna, especially imported brands from Latin America.
2. Issue warnings for canned light tuna equivalent to those for albacore tuna (maximum of 6 ounces/week), with children's consumption limited to 3 ounces or less per week (half a can).
3. Effectively enforce the FDA's 1.0 ppm action level and extend the FDA's Hazard Analysis and Critical Control Point guidelines to include mercury as a likely hazard so that the seafood industry would be required to monitor for high mercury content in fish.
4. Reassess the role of canned tuna in government supported food programs such as WIC.

The report's recommendations also called for a comprehensive scientific review of both the FDA's action level and the EPA's reference dose, with a corresponding revision of the advisory.

Shortly after the Defenders of Wildlife report was published, the July 2006 issue of Consumer Reports echoed a similar message warning consumers of high methylmercury levels in canned tuna. After scrutinizing FDA data, they also found that some light tuna contained mercury levels as high as, and sometimes higher than albacore tuna. The chief medical officer at the FDA's Center for Food Safety and Applied Nutrition, Dr. David Acheson, responded that the agency does not believe these levels pose any significant threat, and he went on to say that a single exposure to high mercury levels will not cause any acute harm to a developing fetus (Consumer Reports, 2006). However, it has been argued elsewhere that even one episode of high mercury exposure may be enough to harm a developing fetus, particularly during the critical period of brain cell migration that occurs during months four and six of pregnancy (Steingraber, 2001). Environmental toxicologist Deborah Rice concurs that derivation of a reference dose for methylmercury may be inappropriate, given that there does not appear to be any threshold for adverse neuropsychological effects based on available data (Rice, 2004).

Taking a much more cautious approach than the FDA, Consumer Reports' fish safety experts advise pregnant women to avoid eating canned tuna altogether due to the uncertain and variable levels of methylmercury within each can. Instead, they recommend women obtain the benefits of omega-3 fatty acids through fish oil supplements, which were found to be an equivalent source and free of heavy metal contamination when tested in 2003. There are many other omega-3 rich foods that can provide the same benefits as tuna fish such as leafy greens, walnuts, and flaxseed, and alternative sources of low-fat protein such as chicken, tofu, and legumes (Consumer Reports, 2006; Schroeder, 2007).

WIC AND TUNA CONSUMPTION

The WIC program is critical in assisting low-income American women and children to meet their nutritional needs, as well as improving their overall knowledge of nutrition. Food packages in the program vary by state, and each state determines which items their specific food packages will include. Breastfeeding mothers receive an enhanced food package. WIC encourages mothers to exclusively breastfeed their infants and promotes breastfeeding as the optimal choice, as it provides many health, nutritional, economical, and emotional benefits. Every state provides canned fish to breastfeeding mothers. Canned tuna fish was the only option in this package until 2006, when the new WIC food packages were approved. Now breastfeeding mothers can also purchase canned salmon, mackerel, and sardines in some states (Federal Register, 2006). Table 1 provides a list of the types of canned fish offered by each state. Under some circumstances in certain states, mothers who are not breastfeeding are also eligible to receive canned fish. Florida and Maine provide canned fish to women pregnant with multiples and under special circumstances. The South Dakota WIC program states on its website that canned fish is assigned per individual needs.

Under the new WIC food package guidelines, states no longer offer canned albacore or white tuna. The majority of state WIC sites include a link to a clear and concise WIC approved foods brochure, emphasizing which foods participants can and cannot purchase. Of the states that offer canned tuna, all except Illinois specify that women receiving canned tuna must purchase the chunk light variety. The typical allotted amount of canned fish is 30 ounces/month, which is consistent with the FDA/EPA advisory, since the tuna in question is light tuna, and the advisory states that one can consume as much as 12 ounces/week of light canned tuna. Whether or not the WIC participant follows the advisory becomes a personal choice. If a participant ate all the canned tuna for the month within a week, she would most likely exceed her reference dose for the month (Defenders of Wildlife et al., 2006). The fish consumption advice in each state varies considerably. Regarding tuna, the majority of states reference the FDA/EPA Advisory; some had distinctive brochures whose recommendations were similar but not identical to the advisory, whereas others had no information available at all. Certain states advised eating 12 ounces of fish per week but did not specify the species. The review of consumption advice for tuna in each state appears in the last column of Table 1 (WIC, 2009). Since many WIC participants consume fish on a regular basis, every state WIC agency should be required to provide the link to the FDA/EPA fish consumption guidelines on their website. In states where the Department of Public Health issues its own guidelines, a link to its brochure should also be included. The information on fish advisories and consumption guidelines should be readily available without searching through multiple documents. Consumption advice also should be provided directly to participants in print form, as many recipients of WIC may not have access to the Internet.

Table 1. State Fish Consumption Guidelines for Women, Infants, and Children.

State	Type of Fish				Fish Consumption Guidelines for At-Risk Women
	Tuna	Salmon	Sardines	Mackerel	
Alabama	✔	✔			12 ounces/week light tuna; AVOID albacore and tuna steaks
Alaska	✔	✔			Consume fish 1–2 × /week
Arizona	✔	✔	✔		FDA/EPA advisory
Arkansas	✔				No information
California	✔	✔	✔		12 ounces/week
Colorado	✔	✔	✔		FDA/EPA advisory
Connecticut	✔				2 × /week light tuna; 1 × /week albacore or tuna steak
Delaware	✔	✔			No information
District of Columbia	✔				No information
Florida	✔	✔			12 ounces/week
Georgia	✔	✔			FDA/EPA advisory
Hawaii	✔	✔	✔	✔	No information
Idaho	✔	✔			No information
Illinois	✔				No information
Indiana	✔	✔	✔		FDA/EPA advisory
Iowa	✔	✔			FDA/EPA advisory
Kansas	✔	✔	✔		FDA/EPA advisory
Kentucky	✔	✔			No information
Louisiana	✔				FDA/EPA advisory
Maine	✔				FDA/EPA advisory
Maryland	✔	✔	✔		12 ounces/week
Massachusetts	✔				12 ounces/week, no tuna steak
Michigan	✔				1 × /week light tuna; 2 × /month albacore, fresh, or frozen tuna
Minnesota	✔				1 × /week light tuna; 1 × /month albacore or tuna steak
Mississippi	✔				FDA/EPA advisory
Missouri	✔				FDA/EPA advisory
Montana	✔				FDA/EPA advisory
Nebraska	✔				No information
Nevada	✔		✔		FDA/EPA advisory
New Hampshire	✔	✔	✔		2 × /week light tuna; 1 × /week albacore or tuna steak
New Jersey	✔				12 ounces/week
New Mexico	✔				FDA/EPA advisory
New York	✔	✔	✔		FDA/EPA advisory
North Carolina	✔	✔			2 × /week light tuna; AVOID albacore, fresh, and frozen tuna

Table 1. (*Continued*)

State	Type of Fish				Fish Consumption Guidelines for At-Risk Women
	Tuna	Salmon	Sardines	Mackerel	
North Dakota	✔	✔			1 × /week light tuna, 1 × /month fresh tuna
Ohio	✔				FDA/EPA advisory
Oklahoma	✔	✔	✔		No information
Oregon	✔	✔			2 × /week light tuna; 1 × /week albacore, 1 × /month tuna steak
Pennsylvania	✔				FDA/EPA advisory
Rhode Island	✔				FDA/EPA advisory
South Carolina	✔	✔	✔		FDA/EPA advisory
South Dakota	✔	✔	✔		FDA/EPA advisory
Tennessee	✔	✔	✔		FDA/EPA advisory
Texas	✔				FDA/EPA advisory
Utah	✔	✔			FDA/EPA advisory
Vermont	✔				12 ounces/week; canned light tuna has less mercury than albacore
Virginia	✔				12 ounces/week
Washington	✔	✔			2–3 × /week light tuna; 1 × /week albacore; AVOID tuna steak
West Virginia	✔				No information
Wisconsin	✔	✔			1 × /week light tuna; 1 × /month albacore or tuna steak
Wyoming	✔				No information

Source: Compiled from Women, Infants, and Children (2009).

CONCLUSION AND RECOMMENDATIONS

Though there does not exist a scientifically accepted value for the level at which methylmercury impedes neurological development, it is undoubtedly a powerful neurotoxin that can cause serious harm to a fetus, infant, or young child. Results from the Faroe Islands and New Zealand studies support the conclusion that mercury causes adverse effects in utero even at very low levels of exposure. These, as well as other studies noted earlier, should provide the basis on which the FDA and the EPA evaluate and establish their fish consumption guidelines. In January 2009, the FDA released two reports reviewing a large number of methylmercury studies for comments. The first is entitled "Report of Quantitative Risk and Benefit Assessment of Commercial Fish Consumption, Focusing on Fetal Neurodevelopmental Effects (Measured by Verbal Development in

Children) and on Coronary Heart Disease and Stroke in the General Population." The report focuses on the effects of the former through methylmercury exposure from fish consumption, and effects of the latter from fish consumption and omega-3 fatty acids found in fish. The second document, "Summary of Published Research on the Beneficial Effects of Fish Consumption and Omega-3 Fatty Acids for Certain Neurodevelopmental and Cardiovascular Endpoints" consists of published FDA research that was used to develop its quantitative risk and benefit assessment. The FDA is seeking public comment on both, but it remains unclear if these reports will be used as a basis to review its current exposure standards and advisory (Federal Register, 2009).

Tuna is the best-selling fish in America, it is also the third most popular item bought in grocery stores after coffee and sugar (Defenders of Wildlife et al., 2006). The volume of canned tuna consumed by Americans and its popularity in this country are key reasons why the mercury levels in this fish pose a serious health threat to large segments of the population. The earlier discussion points to the fact that the public has not been adequately informed about the potential hazard of this particular food source. This is even more problematic in light of the fact that canned tuna is distributed by the United States government to the very people who are most sensitive to methylmercury exposure: women, infants, and children. Women, especially those who are on governmentally funded programs such as WIC, must be warned about methylmercury in the canned tuna they receive. They should know that along with being a good source of omega-3 fatty acids, tuna also contains methylmercury in levels that could potentially harm the fetus and young children. Over 8.7 million American women and children were recipients of the WIC program in 2008 (WIC, 2008). A large percentage of the people enrolled in these programs are poor, minority women (Defenders of Wildlife et al., 2006). The only package that offers tuna through WIC is intended for women who are breastfeeding (Women, Infants, and Children [WIC], 2003). However, mercury is excreted from the body through breast milk (EPA, 2001a). By promoting the consumption of tuna while breastfeeding, the program could actually be inadvertently placing the unborn at risk for exposure to mercury. The information contained in the 2004 Advisory is not widely available to WIC recipients and other vulnerable populations.

In order to fully protect and ensure the health of American women and children, the federal government needs to reconsider the food it is providing to participants in the WIC program and to update its consumer information. The nuanced message that the FDA is presenting to consumers does not equally address the risks and benefits of eating canned tuna. The health claims on a can of tuna can be misleading: a label usually calls attention to the heart healthy omega-3's, but fails to point out that there is also methylmercury in the fish. This misleading labeling information is due, in part, to the aggressive litigation and lobbying efforts of the tuna industry to emphasize the health benefits of tuna and to keep it from being classified as a high-mercury fish. As Consumer Report's recommends, the FDA should require information about mercury risks on canned tuna labels and in stores and restaurants where fish is sold (Consumer Reports, 2006).

Based on the data from the studies discussed earlier, a complete re-evaluation of the 2004 FDA/EPA Fish Advisory is warranted. In addition to adopting the recommendations outlined earlier, the government should adopt a precautionary approach to deal with the health threats posed by methylmercury in tuna fish. Until the science proves otherwise, the FDA should not assume that a fetus can safely be exposed to any level of methylmercury. Another important step the government can take to insure that women gain the health benefits of omega-3 fatty acids is to begin an educational campaign that informs them of alternative food sources high in these important nutrients. The FDA certainly should allow states to proceed with their own advisories and educational campaigns. Lastly, consumers need to know where their food comes from, and country-of-origin labeling should apply to all commercial fish, including canned varieties.

The health of children, the environment, and future generations should be of greatest concern to the federal government. Instead of insisting on more epidemiological studies, the federal government must act on the information available, rather than wait for further evidence of methylmercury's harmful effects. Data from the most recent studies show that the cohorts are experiencing the negative impacts of methylmercury in fish and seafood; its destructive impact on the human fetus and developing brain is irreversible and must be prevented. An outreach program specifically designed to target minority populations should be implemented to address the concerns raised by the EPA's environmental justice report that such groups are less likely to be aware of advisories and to change consumption habits. At the same time, the United States and the international community should develop long term strategies to ensure that people can safely consume tuna and other staple fish. Reducing mercury emissions and adopting sustainable fishing practices are measures that should be taken to improve the economic vigor of the seafood industry and the quality of the fish we eat, providing benefits to both producers and consumers.

ACKNOWLEDGMENTS

The authors wish to thank Paige T. Davis of Ithaca College's Environmental Studies program for her invaluable assistance with this chapter.

REFERENCES

Auger, N., Kofman, O., Kosastsky, T., & Armstrong, B. (2005). Low level methylmercury exposure as a risk factor for neurologic abnormalities. *Neurotoxicology, 26*(2), 149–157.

Barken, M., & Pallo, B. (2009). *People of the State of California v. Tri-Union Seafoods, LLC et al.:* The necessity of local law to protect citizens from harmful tuna sales. *North East Journal of Legal Studies, 22,* 20–44.

Burger, J., Stern, A. H., & Gochfeld, M. (2005). Mercury in commercial fish optimizing individual choices to reduce risk. *Environmental Health Perspectives, 113*(3), 266–270.

Center for Food Safety and Applied Nutrition. (CFSAN) and the Food and Drug Administration (FDA), (2001). *Consumer Advisory on Methylmercury in Commercial Seafood, Office of the Commissioner Meeting Executive Summary.* [Online] Available at http://www.fda.gov/OHRMS/DOCKETS/ac/02/briefing/3872b1.htm

Consumer Reports. (2006). *Mercury in Tuna: New Safety Concern.* [Online] Available at http://www.consumerreports.org/cro/food/tuna-safety/overview/0607_tuna_ov.htm

Corrosion Doctors. (2007). Iraq mercury poisoning. [Online] Available at http://www.corrosion-doctors.org/Elements-Toxic/Mercury-Iraq-1.htm

Davidson, P., Strain, J. J., Meyers, G. J., Thurston, S. W., Bonham, M. P., Shamlaye, C. F., Stokes-Riner, A., Wallace, J. M. W., Robson, P. J., Duffy, E. M., Georger, L. A., Sloane-Reeves, J., Cernichiari, E., Canfield, R. L., Cox, C., Huang, L. S., Janciuras, J., & Clarkson, T. W. (2008). Neurodevelopmental effects of maternal nutritional status and exposure to methylmercury from eating fish during pregnancy. *Neurotoxicology, 29*(5), 767–775.

Defenders of Wildlife, Center for Science in the Public Interest, Mercury Policy Project. (2006). *Is Your Tuna Family Safe? Mercury in America's Favorite Fish.* [Online] Available at http://www.defenders.org/programs_and_policy/habitat_conservation/marine/mercury-tuna/index.php

Environment News Service. (2009). Ocean origin of seafood contaminant methylmercury identified. [Online] Available at http://www.ens-newswire.com/ens/may2009/2009-05-04-02.asp

Environmental Protection Agency. (2001a). *Mercury update: Impact on fish advisories.* Washington, DC: Environmental Protection Agency.

Environmental Protection Agency. (2001b). Neurobehavorial effects of PCBs and methylmercury in rats. National Center for Environmental Research. Available at http://cfpub.epa.gov/ncer_abstracts/index.cfm/fuseaction/display.abstractDetail/abstract/6047/report/0.

Environmental Protection Agency. (2002). *Fish consumption and environmental justice.* Washington, DC: Environmental Protection Agency.

Environmental Protection Agency. (2008). *Fact sheet for national listing of fish advisories.* Washington, DC: Environment Protection Agency.

Federal Register, Department of Agriculture, Food, and Nutrition Service. (2006). Special supplemental nutrition program for women, infants, and children (WIC): Revisions in the WIC food packages, proposed rules. Vol. 71, pp. 151. [Online] Available at http://www.fnsusda.gov/wic/regspublished/foodpackagesrevisions-proposedrulepdf.pdf

Federal Register, Department of Health and Human Services. (2009). Report of quantitative risk and benefit assessment of commercial fish consumption, focusing on fetal neurodevelopmental effects (measured by verbal development in children) and on coronary heart disease and stroke in the general population, and summary of published research on the beneficial effects of fish consumption and omega-3 fatty acids for certain neurodevelopmental and cardiovascular endpoints. Vol. 74, p. 12. [Online] Available at http://www.fda.gov/Food/FoodSafety/Product-SpecificInformation/Seafood/FoodbornePathogensContaminants/Methylmercury/ucm088765.htm

Fellner v. Tri-Union Seafoods. (2008). 539F.3d 237.

Food and Drug Administration and Environmental Protection Agency. (2003) Development of a joint advisory for methylmercury containing fish consumption for women of childbearing age and children. [Online] Available at www.fda.gov/ohrms/dockets/ac/03/minutes/4010m1_Summary%20minutes.pdf

Food and Drug Administration and Environmental Protection Agency. (2004) Fish Advisory. (2004). What you need to know about mercury in fish and shellfish. [Online] Available at http://www.cfsan.fda.gov/~dms/admehg3.html

Grandjean, P., Debes, F., Weihe, P., & White, R. (2006). Impact of prenatal methylmercury exposure on neurobehavioral function at age 14 years. *Neurotoxicology and Teratology, 28*(3), 363–375.

Grandjean, P., Weihe, P., White, R., Debes, F., Arak, S., Yokoyama, K., Murata, K., Sorenson, N., Dahl, R., & Jorgensen, P. (1997). Cognitive deficit in 7-year-old children with prenatal exposure to methylmercury. *Neurotoxicology and Teratology, 19*(6), 417–428.

Herculano, A. M., Crespo-Lopez, M. E., Lima, S. M. A., Picanco-Diniz, D. L. W., & DO Nascimento, J. L. M. (2006). Methylmercury intoxication activates nitric oxide synthase in chick retinal cell culture. *Brazilian Journal of Medical Research, 39*(3), 415–418.

Hibbeln, J. R., Davis, J. M., Steer, C., Emmett, P., Rogers, I., Williams, C., & Golding, J. (2007). Maternal seafood consumption in pregnancy and neurodevelopmental outcomes in childhood: An observational study. *The Lancet, 369*(9561), 578–585.

Hightower, J. M., O'Hare, A., & Hernandez, G. T. (2006). Blood mercury reporting in national health and nutrition survey: Identifying Asian, Pacific Islander, native American, and multiracial groups. *Environmental Health Perspectives, 114*(2), 173–175.

International Indian Treaty Council. (2004). Mercury contamination and community health in northern California. [Online] Available at www.treatycouncil.org/MercuryReportLoRez1.pdf

LaDuke, W. (1999). *All our relations: Native struggles for land and life* (pp. 61–62). Cambridge, MA: South End Press.

Madsen, E. R., DeWeese, A. D., Kmiecik, N. E., Foran, J. A., & Chiriboga, E. D. (2007). Methods to develop consumption advice for methylmercury-contaminated walleye harvested by Ojibwe tribes in the 1837 and 1842 ceded territories of Michigan, Minnesota, and Wisconsin, USA. *Integrated Environmental Assessment Management, 4*(1), 118–124.

McCaffrey, P. (2004). Lasting brain damage found from prenatal mercury exposure. Harvard Environmental Health. [Online] Available at http://focus.hms.harvard.edu/2004/Feb20_2004/environmental_health.html

Moore, C. F. (2003). *Silent Scourge: Children, pollution, and why scientists disagree* (pp. 49–79). New York: Oxford University Press, Inc.

Mundy, A., & Kendall, B. (2009). U.S. News: Shift toward state rules on product liability. *Wall Street Journal*, New York, p. A3.

Myers, G. J., Davidson, P. W., Cox, C., Shamlaye, C. F., Palumbo, D., Cernichiari, E., Sloane-Reeves, J., Wilding, G. E., Kost, J., Huang, L. S., & Clarkson, T. W. (2003). Prenatal methylmercury exposure from ocean fish consumption in the Seychelles child development study. *The Lancet, 361*(9370), 1686–1692.

National Academy of Sciences. (2000). Office of the commissioner meeting executive summary. [Online] Available at http://www.cfsan.fda.gov/~acrobat/hgcomm9.pdf

National Health and Nutrition Examination Survey 1999–2002. (2008). Blood mercury level, report on the environment database, EPA. [Online] Available at http://cfpub.epa.gov/eroe/index.cfm?fuseaction = detail.viewInd%26showQu

Nestle, M. (2006). *What to eat* (pp. 181–202, p. 220). New York: North Point Press.

Palmer, R., Blanchard, S., Stein, Z., Mandell, D., & Miller, C. (2006). Environmental mercury release, special education, and autism disorder: An ecological study of Texas. *Health and Place, 12*(2), 203–209.

People of the State of California v. Tri-Union Seafoods, LLC. et al. (2006). Consolidated Case Nos. CGS-01-402975 and CGC-04-432394, Statement of Decision.

People of the State of California v. Tri-Union Seafoods, LLC. et al. (2009) 171Cal. App. 4th 1549.

Pollack, H. (2009). California Deputy Attorney General (personal communication, 21 July 2009).

Rice, D. C. (2004). The U.S. EPA reference dose for methylmercury: Sources of uncertainty. *Environmental Research, 95*(3), 406–413.

Schober, S. E., Sinks, T. H., Jones, R. L., Bolger, P. M., McDowell, M., Ostcrloh, J., Garrett, E. S., Canady, R. A., Dillon, C. F., Sun, Y., Joseph, C. B., & Mahaffey, K. R. (2003). Blood mercury levels in US children and women of childbearing age, 1999–2000. *Journal of the American Medical Association, 289*(13), 1667–1674.

Schroeder, K. (2007). Good food sources of omega-3 fatty acids. [Online] Available at http://healthlibrary.epnet.com/GetContent.aspx?token = 8482e079-8512-47c2-960c-a40 3c77a5e4c&chunkiid = 10989.

Silver, E., Kaslow, J., Lee, D., Lee, S., Tan, M. L., Weis, E., & Ujihara, A. (2007). Fish consumption and advisory awareness among low income women in California's Sacramento-San Joaquin delta. *Environmental Research, 104*(3), 410–419.

Spurgeon, A. (2006). Prenatal methylmercury exposure and developmental outcomes: Review of the evidence and discussion of further directions. *Environmental Health Perspectives, 114*(2), 307–312.

Steingraber, S. (2001). *Having faith: An ecologist's journey to motherhood* (pp. 44–50, 120–129). New York: Perseus Publishing pp.

Trasande, L., Landrigan, P. J., & Schecter, C. (2005). Public health and economic consequences of methylmercury toxicity to the developing brain. *Environmental Health Perspectives, 113*(5), 590–596.

Tri-Union Seafoods v. Fellner. (2009). U.S. Lexis 3099U.S. Supreme Court cert. denied.

United Press International. (2009). Methylmercury contamination increasing. [Online] Available at http://www.upi.com/Science_News/2009/05/06/Methylmercury-contamination-increasing/UPI-56311241640787/?feature = global_water

United States v. Anderson Seafoods. (1978). 447F.Supp.1151.

University of Minnesota. (Undated). Mercury: risk assessment. [Online] Last accessed on July 24, 2007. Available at http://enhs.umn.edu/hazards/hazardssite/mercury/mercriskassess.html

West, P. C. (1992). Invitation to poison? Detroit minorities and toxic fish consumption from the Detroit River. In: B. Bryant & P. Mohai (Eds), *Race and the incidence of environmental hazard: A time for discourse* (pp. 96–99). Boulder, CO: Westview Press, Inc.

West, P. C., Fly, J. M., Larkin, F., & Marans, R. W. (1992). Minority anglers and toxic fish consumption: Evidence from a statewide survey of Michigan. In: B. Bryant & P. Mohai (Eds), *Race and the incidence of environmental hazard: A time for discourse* (pp. 100–113). Boulder, CO: Westview Press, Inc.

Women, Infants, and Children. (2003). *WIC reauthorization: Opportunities for improving the nutritional status of women, infants, and children.* National health policy forum (NHPF background paper). Washington, DC: The George Washington University.

Women, Infants, and Children. (2006). *WIC Participant and Program Characteristics 2006: Summary.* [Online] Available at http://www.fns.usda.gov/ora/menu/Published/WIC/FILES/PC2006Summary.pdf

Women, Infants, and Children. (2008). *WIC Program Annual Summary.* [Online] Available at http://www.fns.usda.gov/pd/26wifypart.htm

Women, Infants, and Children. (2009). WIC State Agencies- alphabetica. [Online] Available at http://www.fns.usda.gov/wic/Contacts/statealpha.HTM

Wyeth v. Levine. (2009) 129 SCt 1187.

Xue, F., Holzman, C., Mohammad Hossein, R., Trosko, K., & Fischer, L. (2007). Maternal fish consumption, mercury levels, and risk of preterm delivery. *Environmental Health Perspectives, 115*(1), 42–47.

Beth Pallo is a discovery scientist at Advion BioSciences. She can be reached by email at bpallo1@gmail.com or by telephone at 607-266-0665 extension 200.

Marlene E. Barken is an associate professor of legal studies at Ithaca College. She can be reached by email at mbarken@ithaca.edu or by telephone at 607-274-3946.

FISH CONSUMPTION AND ENVIRONMENTAL JUSTICE IN THE GREAT LAKES: THE INFLUENCE OF FISH ADVISORIES ON RISK PERCEPTION, KNOWLEDGE, AND BEHAVIOR OF WHITE AND MINORITY ANGLERS

Brenda J. Nordenstam and Sarah Darkwa

ABSTRACT

Purpose – *This study explores the relationship between fish consumption advisories and risk perception, knowledge, and behavior of anglers in the Great Lakes. The Great Lakes contain elevated levels of critical pollutants and chemicals. Fish consumption advisories have been employed by health and environmental agencies to increase public awareness and lower exposure to contaminated fish caught in the Great Lakes. However, awareness and response to these advisories is not universal and may vary on the basis of sociocultural factors. Poor and minority anglers may be less aware of health advisories and more likely to exceed the recommended fish consumption limits than white anglers. Relying on health advisories as the*

Environment and Social Justice: An International Perspective
Research in Social Problems and Public Policy, Volume 18, 211–238
Copyright © 2010 by Emerald Group Publishing Limited
All rights of reproduction in any form reserved
ISSN: 0196-1152/doi:10.1108/S0196-1152(2010)0000018009

primary mechanism for limiting exposure may not adequately meet environmental justice goals to protect the health and safety of all people.

Design/methodology/approach – *One hundred and twenty Lake Ontario boating anglers were surveyed. Factors examined include awareness and source of health advisories; level of concern about health risks; and fish consumption rate and risk reduction behaviors.*

Findings – *Results indicate that ethnicity, age, and education influence awareness and response to health advisories. We conclude with suggestions to better address environmental injustices by strengthening the inclusion of local knowledge and participation in the decision-making and risk management process.*

Practical implication – *Findings have implications for the impact and future content of Great Lakes fish advisories.*

Originality/value – *There have been few comparative studies using socioeconomic factors, such as race and education, when addressing awareness of fish advisories and relative risk of toxicity from Great Lakes recreational boat anglers.*

INTRODUCTION

Chemical contamination of our nation's waters has been a cause for concern for the environmental justice movement for a long time. Since the 1970s, research has shown that high levels of pollution exist in minority communities. The persistence of pollution in such communities often results from lack of resources and political clout (Council on Environmental Quality [CEQ], 1971; Bullard & Wright, 1986; Lee, 1987; Calderon, et al., 1993; Bullard, 1994; Perlin, Wong, & Sexton, 2001). Water pollution and toxic food consumption threatens minority and low-income communities. Elevated concentrations of chemicals accumulate in the flesh of fish and humans dependent on local streams, rivers, and lakes contaminated with industrial pollution (Tremblay & Gilman, 1995; Kreiss, 1985). The case of Triana, Alabama, known as the "unhealthiest town in America," is emblematic of the close link between fish contamination and adverse human exposure (Reynolds, 1980). For years, the residents of this poor rural hamlet caught fish downstream from a closed manufacturing facility. In 1978, contaminated fish in a local creek were found to contain 40 times the level of dichlorodiphenyltrichloroethane (DDT) considered safe by the federal government. Consequently, the fish-eating population of this community exhibited serum DDT and polychlorinated biphenyl (PCB) measurements several times the national average (Kreiss, 1985). This discovery spurred the residents of Triana to mount a grassroots campaign and lawsuit, providing one of the first examples of environmental activism by a minority community (Bullard, 1994). Triana, and the grassroots mobilization of other marginalized communities throughout the United States, signified the emergence of a new form of environmentalism, eventually growing into a national movement for environmental justice focused on the need for new, more inclusive approaches to better protect our environment and the health of all members of society.

Historically, environmental justice advocates have taken a keen interest in the development and efficacy of health advisories issued by state and federal agencies to control public exposure to toxic chemicals. One underlying problem addressed by environmental justice advocates focused on the utilization of chemical exposure risk assessments to determine allowable levels of water contamination (Calderon et al., 1993; National Environmental Justice Advisory Council [NEJAC], 2002). Under the Clean Water Act, the Environmental Protection Agency (EPA) uses a standard fish consumption rate (currently 17.5 g/person/day) to help set water quality criteria guidance values. The criteria are intended to protect people when consuming fish from state and tribal waters (Environmental Protection Agency [EPA], 2007). The U.S. EPA and other government agencies underestimated fish consumption rates and toxic exposure for many minorities by using data based on the general population. These risk assessments included assumptions about typical exposure and behavior patterns (such as the amount of fish consumed) that failed to accurately describe the exposure and response patterns of poor and minority communities (Calderon et al., 1993). Criticism by scholars and environmental justice activists eventually nudged the EPA and other agencies to begin considering variations in cultural and social characteristics and practices that influence consumption rates for ethnically diverse groups (NEJAC, 2002). EPA's Environmental Justice Strategy for 1995 specifically addressed this issue by stating their intention to "collect, analyze, and maintain information on fish and/or wildlife subsistence consumption patterns" and to "communicate the risks of those consumption patterns" (United States Environmental Protection Agency [USEPA], 1995). New standards for risk assessments were created to better take into account differences in fish consumption based on cultural and economic status. However, improved risk assessments do not necessarily yield corresponding improvements in water quality standards or lowered exposure rates for high-risk groups (Gauna, O'Neill, & Rechtschaffen, 2005; NEJAC, 2002).

A closely related environmental justice concern involves the government's increasing reliance on risk avoidance measures (requiring the public to avoid the risk) as opposed to risk reduction measures (requiring industry to reduce or prevent the risk). The government's expanding embrace of risk avoidance strategies may disproportionately burden poor and minority groups (Gauna, et al., 2005). The use of health advisories and other risk communication methods to manage exposure to chemical contamination requires those most dependent on fishing – subsistence groups that regularly consume large amounts of fish – to monitor and limit their consumption of fish caught in our nation's waters (NEJAC, 2002). Numerous studies provide evidence indicating that ethnically diverse communities are less likely to be reached by advisory information, less likely to reduce their fish consumption, and less likely to alter their fish preparation practices in response to these warnings (Connelly, Knuth, & Vena, 1993; Burger et al., 2001; NEJAC, 2002; Imm, Knobeloch, Anderson, & The Great Lakes Sport Fish Consortium, 2005). This chapter will examine how minority and white anglers recreating on the Great Lakes perceive and respond to fish advisories.

THE CONTEXT

Lake Ontario is generally regarded as the most contaminated Great Lake (USEPA, 1987). The persistent toxic substances that pollute the lake include organochlorine compounds, heavy metals, polycyclic aromatic hydrocarbons, and naturally occurring toxins such as those produced by the *Clostridium botulinum* bacteria. Despite significant government cleanup efforts over the past two decades, there is evidence that the environment of the Great Lakes is put at risk by the long-term accumulation of toxic chemicals. These chemical compounds undergo a biomagnification process as they are consumed by marine life and move up the food chain. Depending on the size and position of the affected species in the food chain, the concentration of these contaminants may be magnified hundreds of thousands of times in the flesh of Great Lakes fish.

HEALTH ADVISORIES

Consumption of Great Lakes fish may be associated with chronic adverse health, developmental, and reproductive effects. To discourage over-consumption of contaminated fish that may pose a risk to human health, the Canadian province of Ontario and the eight American states bordering the Great Lakes (Michigan, New York, Wisconsin, Pennsylvania, Minnesota, Ohio, Indiana, and Illinois) issue advisories to those fishing the waters (Colborn, Davidson, Green, Hodge, & Jackson, 1990). Great Lakes sport fish consumption advisories were first issued during the 1970s after testing detected chemical contaminants in fish tissue (Tilden et al., 1997). From the mid-1970s to the early 1990s, there was a great deal of variability in the information provided to anglers because each state independently developed their fish consumption advisories. States sometimes issued conflicting advisories for the same body of water, confusing anglers and reducing their confidence in the information. The Great Lakes Sport Fish Consumption Advisory Taskforce was formed in 1986 to address this problem. This taskforce, composed of public health and environmental or natural resource agencies from each state, was charged with developing a uniform sport fish consumption advisory protocol for all eight states (Imm et al., 2005).

Fish consumption advisories issued for the Great Lakes warn the public about potential health risks related to the consumption of sport caught fish, educate consumers as to how to minimize their exposure to chemical contaminants, and present advisory information in a manner intended to maximize voluntary compliance (Anderson & Wiener, 1995). States issue both general and specific fish consumption advisories. The general health advisory recommends that people eat no more than one meal (one-half pound) of fish per week. Specific state health advisories may recommend restricted or no consumption of some types of sport fish, whereas other advisories may provide preparation and cooking methods to reduce risk. An advisory may also be targeted to high-risk groups such as pregnant women or children. Advisories are often limited to certain fish species or to a particular water body. Although there are specific state advisories for close to 40 chemical contaminants, most advisories issued for the Great Lakes involve six primary contaminants: mercury, dioxin, PCB, toxaphene, chlordane, and mirex. Table 1 summarizes the six primary contaminants of concern covered by health advisories issued by the eight states bordering the Great Lakes.

The State of New York has issued health contamination fish advisories for Lake Ontario and other freshwaters for nearly 40 years and has developed one of the most comprehensive fish advisory programs in the nation. New York's health advisories are derived from information that the New York Department of Environmental Conservation (DEC) gathers on contaminant levels in fish and game. The DEC collects fish samples each

Table 1. Fish Consumption Health Advisories Issued by Great Lakes States for the Six Primary Contaminants of Concern.

States	Advisories Issued for Contaminants Found in the Great Lakes					
	PCB	Mercury	Toxaphene	Dioxin	Chlordane	Mirex
New York	✔	✔	✔	✔		✔
Michigan	✔	✔		✔	✔	
Wisconsin	✔	✔		✔	✔	
Pennsylvania	✔	✔		✔		
Minnesota	✔	✔	✔	✔	✔	
Ohio	✔	✔		✔		
Indiana	✔	✔		✔	✔	
Illinois	✔	✔		✔	✔	

year from different water bodies. In a typical year, DEC collects approximately 2,000 fish from more than 50 sampling locations and analyzes them for various contaminants. Testing focuses on those species that are most likely to be caught and eaten by sport anglers. The New York Department of Health (DOH) annually reviews the DEC findings to determine whether an advisory should be issued or revised for a given water body or fish species. In deciding how to respond, the DOH considers factors such as potential human exposures and health risks. The yearly health advisories are published in the New York State Freshwater Fishing Regulations Guide issued by DEC for distribution to anglers when they buy or renew their fishing license each year. DOH also makes their updated advisories available online (New York State Department of Health [NYSDOH], 2009–2010).

The health advisories issued by DOH provide anglers with information on which fish to avoid depending on the species, the age and size of the fish, and the water body where the fish was caught. These advisories are issued only for fish caught recreationally and are not issued for fish sold commercially. The NYSDOH for 2009–2010 provides specific fish consumption health advisories that still apply to over 130 of New York State's water bodies. The updates maintain New York's long-standing statewide advisory to recreational fishers that they eat no more than one meal (one-half pound) of fish per week taken from the state's freshwaters (NYSDOH, 2009–2010).

In addition to information about which fish species to avoid, health advisories typically include suggestions for anglers on how to limit fish consumption or change behaviors (e.g., fish cleaning, cooking, or storage) to reduce the level of exposure to contaminants in the fish that they do consume. This information is intended to help consumers to "make their own informed decision" about fish consumption. The reliance on health advisories assumes that potential fish consumers have all the information and skills they need to enable them to make an informed decision (Knuth & Connelly, 1991, 1994). However, research indicates that not all anglers are equally aware, knowledgeable, or informed about health advisories. For example, Beehler, McGuinness, and Vena (2003), in a study to evaluate the efficacy of current risk communication strategies, found that most of the anglers who participated in their study were unlicensed; thus, the state's primary route for communicating advisories was not effective. Of those who were licensed and were aware of the health advisories, only a few were familiar with all the information they contained. An earlier study by MacDonald and Boyle (1997) conducted to examine the effect of a statewide sport fish consumption advisory on open-water fishing in Maine reported that only 33 percent of nonresidents knew about the health advisory. Imm et al. (2005), in a telephone survey of adults residing in all Great Lakes states, found that 30 percent of those who consumed sport-caught fish from the Great Lakes twice a month or more were not aware of consumption health advisories for Great Lakes fish.

Research indicates that poor, minority, and ethnically diverse communities are more likely to exceed fish consumption limits recommended by state health advisories. For example, West, Fly, Larkin, and Marans (1992) conducted a statewide survey of Michigan anglers and their families. Their findings revealed that Native Americans consumed more fish (23.3 g/person/day) than African Americans (20.3 g/person/day) and both groups consumed more fish more than white anglers (17.9 g/person/day). In a comprehensive report on fish consumption and environmental justice conducted by the NEJAC (2002), a number of studies examining various ethnic groups and fish consumption behavior were reviewed. The report found that subsistence anglers consumed up to 213.9 g/person/day. Sechena et al. (2003) reported that consumption rates varied significantly between ethnic groups, with highest levels indicated for Vietnamese and Japanese communities. Judd, O'Neil, and Kalman (2003) reported that certain ethnic groups in Washington's Puget Sound area eat significantly more seafood than the general population. Their findings revealed that Asian and Pacific Islanders consumed the greatest amount of fish per day, with a mean rate of 117.2 g/person/day, and Tulalip and Squaxin Island Tribes also consumed fish at levels much higher than the general population. The consumption rates reported are considerably higher than the national fish consumption rate of 17.5 g/person/day currently used by the EPA for the recommended Clean Water Act Section 304(a) Water Quality Criteria guidance values (EPA, 2007).

Both awareness of health advisories and behavioral changes in response to consumption recommendations may vary significantly across ethnically diverse groups. The NEJAC report on fish consumption and environmental justice concluded that minorities, lower income, less educated, and those with limited English skills are the least likely to be aware of, or to alter, their behavior in response to fish advisories (NEJAC, 2002). In a study by Burger, Pflugh, Lurig, Von Hagen, and Von Hagen (1999), Latinos showed lower levels of knowledge in comparison to whites but indicated a higher willingness to comply with advisories when provided with potential risks. Tilden et al. (1997), in an effort to find out whether the message of health advisories for consumers of Great Lakes Sport fish was being received, found that existing advisory communication programs are less effectively reaching women, nonwhites, and persons with lower levels of educational attainment. Steenport (2000) found that Hmong and Laotians were least likely to have heard about the health risk of fish consumption, but most likely to eat the fish they caught. A study of African-American anglers in western New York revealed that these anglers were either unaware of or did not pay attention to fish advisory information; rather, they utilized traditional knowledge derived from past experience while fishing or consuming the catch (Beehler, McGuinness, & Vena, 2001). West (1992), studying fishing along the Detroit River, found that minority anglers were more likely to eat species with higher contaminant levels, such as white bass and sheephead.

In addition to variations in level of awareness regarding health advisories, levels of perceived risk in response to these warnings may differ significantly. Research suggests that minority and low-income communities may not perceive health and environmental risks in a manner analogous to whites (Vaughan & Nordenstam, 1991). For example, Beehler et al. (2001) determined that although African-American anglers perceived the water they were fishing from to be polluted, it was not viewed as highly contaminated, and thus, their perception of risk from eating contaminated fish was low. Burger et al. (1999) surveyed fishermen in urban New Jersey to assess whether ethnicity affected perception of risk, knowledge about fish advisories, and behavior. Their findings indicated that, in comparison to white anglers, Latino anglers perceived contaminated fish as safer to eat and less of a potential health risk. Beehler et al. (2003) characterized the perceptions of risk and fish advisory awareness of Latino anglers in Western New York. Their research revealed that older Latino anglers differed from younger ones in their risk perceptions of contaminated fish. Specifically, older Latino anglers perceived that the risk of eating fish from the Great Lakes was low and were more likely to consume fish taken from these waters. In contrast, younger Latino anglers were more likely to view the Great Lakes as very polluted and considered it a higher risk to consume fish caught in these waters.

Our study focuses on the risk information presented in the fish consumption health advisories issued by the State of New York. Burger et al. (2003) report that relatively little research has examined the role of organized recreational fishing, such as that done from charter boats, in relation to fish consumption awareness and behavior. Our review of the literature indicated that comparative studies of white and minority fishermen who choose this mode of fishing are lacking. In this research, we specifically focus on white and minority boating anglers. We are particularly interested in examining to what degree minorities are aware of these advisories, how they respond to these advisories, and whether perceived risks are lower in comparison to white anglers.

METHODOLOGICAL APPROACH

A comprehensive review of the literature on angler's risk perception, fish consumption, and health advisory awareness was conducted. Consulted sources included reports and peer reviewed journal articles on toxic fish consumption and health advisories for the Great Lakes (e.g., Beehler et al., 2001, 2003; Burger et al., 1999, 2001, 2003; Imm et al., 2005; Knuth & Connelly, 1991, 1994; West et al., 1992). Following this review, we designed a research study using a multimethod approach (Brewer & Hunter, 2006) in which we administered open-ended interviews and surveys to anglers boating on Lake Ontario.

As the first stage of this multimethod approach, an open-ended interview was developed containing indices to help assess the following: knowledge of exposure processes and effects; general risk behavior and management; general risk comparisons; and perceived risk. Four different Lake Ontario locations (Port Oswego, Lighthouse Marina, Mexico Point, and Pine Grove) were chosen for the open-ended interviews to sample from a sizeable area along the lake and to determine whether the boating anglers' perceptions and fishing behavior varied by site location (Fig. 1). Twenty boating anglers – five from each of these sites – were randomly selected to participate in this phase of the study. The selection criteria were based on adults who

Fig. 1. Lake Ontario Study Sites. Preliminary Interviews Were Conducted at Port Oswego, Mexico Point, Lighthouse Marina, and Pine Grove. The Final Questionnaire Was Administered at Port Oswego and Mexico Point.

fish from these sites and eat their catch. Out of 25 people selected, 20 agreed to be interviewed. The open-ended interviews indicated that anglers from the four sites expressed similar levels of knowledge and concerns about fishing. Therefore, in the second phase of the study, the sites for questionnaire administration were narrowed to two Lake Ontario locations: Mexico Point and Oswego Main Port.

The information gleaned from the open-ended interviews was employed to develop the questionnaire used in the second phase of the study. The questionnaire used in phase two consisted primarily of closed-ended questions designed to ascertain how often respondents fished in the lake, how often they and their family ate fish caught from the lake, their perceptions, beliefs, and knowledge about the risk of eating contaminated fish, their risk reduction behaviors, and awareness and knowledge about the state health advisories. Information on the demographic characteristics of the anglers was also collected. Several open-ended questions allowed participants to express their opinions about New York State health advisories, personal beliefs about fish and lake contamination, and attitudes and concerns about the risks of eating fish caught in Lake Ontario.

The survey was conducted from July 2006 to September 2006. Anglers at Mexico Point and Oswego Main Port were asked to participate in the study. A total of 120 boating anglers completed the survey out of 128 anglers selected. A face-to-face questionnaire was administered. As most boating anglers had limited time to participate in the study, the questions were read to participants while navigation equipment was set up and preparations to sail were being made. The time required to complete each questionnaire ranged from 25 to 45 minutes. Survey responses were compiled and analyzed using the Statistical Package for Social Scientists.

RESULTS

The demographic characteristics of the sample are summarized in Table 2. Anglers in this sample tended to be older than the general population for New York State. Seventy-three (60.8 percent) of the total number of respondents were between the ages of 27 and 49 years, and the remaining 47 respondents (39.2 percent) were between the ages of 50 and 68 years. The mean age for the respondents in this study was 48 years. According to the U.S. 2000 Census, over 43 percent of the general population of New York State is in the age range of 25 through 54 years and over 15 percent are in the age range of 55 through 74 years. These results are consistent with the

Table 2. Demographic Characteristics of the Sample.

Sample Characteristics	Total Sample		White		Minority	
	Number	Percent	Number	Percent	Number	Percent
Number of respondents	120	100	86	71.7	34	28.3
Educational attainment						
High school, trade school, or less	66	55	41	47.7	25	73.5
College or graduate school	54	45	45	52.3	9	26.5
Age						
27–49 years	73	60.8	50	68.5	23	31.5
50–68 years	47	39.2	36	76.6	11	23.4

findings of other Great Lakes anglers' studies. For example, Imm et al. (2005) in a study of fish consumption and advisory awareness in the Great Lakes reported that the sample they worked with consisted of 58 percent of anglers older than 45 years. Tilden et al. (1997), in their study on Great Lakes health consumption advisories, reported that the sample consisted of 49.2 percent of anglers who were above the age of 45.

All the black anglers were African American and they constituted two percent of the total sample. Other minority groups represented by the respondents were Asians/Pacific Islanders (3 percent) and Hispanic/Latino (23 percent). Because of the small sample size, all nonwhite respondents were combined into one category labeled "minority." Minorities constituted 28.3 percent of the sample. How does the racial composition of the study sample compare to the general U.S. population and to that of the state of New York? In 2000, whites comprised 69.1 percent, Hispanic or Latinos 12.5 percent, blacks 12.3 percent, Asians 3.6 percent, American Indians and Alaska Natives 0.9 percent, and Pacific Islanders 0.1 percent of the population. In New York State, whites comprise 70 percent, blacks 15.9 percent, Hispanic/Latinos 15.1 percent, and Asians 5.5 percent of the population in 2000 (United States Census Bureau, 2000). These data indicate that the percentage of minority anglers in this study's sample is similar to that found nationally and in the state of New York.

When race and age was analyzed, white anglers comprised 68.5 percent of the 27–49 age bracket, whereas minorities comprised 31.5 percent of this age group. White anglers constituted a larger proportion of the 50–68 age group. Whites made up 76.6 percent of this age category, whereas minorities comprised 23.4 percent of it. More white anglers had college or graduate school education (52.3 percent) in contrast to 26.5 percent of minority anglers. On the contrary, 73.5 percent of minority and 47.7 percent of white anglers had a high school or less education. Overall, 45 percent of the sample had a college or graduate school education. This percentage is slightly higher than that reported by the 2000 Census. The Census reports that 44.2 percent of the U.S. population has a college or graduate school education.

All participants in this study were men, meaning that women were underrepresented in the sample. However, this is not unusual. According to the American Sport Fishing Association (ASFA, 2007), men comprise 85 percent of Great Lakes anglers. Data on income were not analyzed in this study. This is the case because the preliminary interviews conducted in the first phase of our study indicated that face-to-face questions about income were quite sensitive to anglers and participants did not respond well to them.

Table 3. Anglers' Perceptions of Health Risks Arising from Eating Sport-Caught Contaminated Fish.

Statements	Total Sample		White		Minority		X^2	df	p
	Number agreeing	Percent agreeing	Number agreeing	Percent agreeing	Number agreeing	Percent agreeing			
Health benefits are greater than health risks	106	88.3	77	89.5	29	85.3	0.475	4	0.5143
Health risks are less than other foods	74	61.7	53	61.6	21	61.8	0.000	4	0.172
Health benefits are greater for children than health risks	107	89.2	78	90.7	29	85.3	0.737	3	0.615

Notwithstanding, other studies have found that sport anglers were drawn from an above-average income group (ASFA, 2007).

Table 3 reports on anglers' perception of risk from eating contaminated fish. Both white and minority anglers indicated a strong level of agreement with three statements concerning the health risks associated with eating sport-caught fish. The differences in the percentages reported for each racial group were not statistically significant. Respondents were first asked whether the individual benefits derived from eating contaminated sport-caught fish were greater than the health risks; 89.5 percent of white respondents and 85.3 percent of minority respondents agreed with this statement. When asked whether the risk of eating contaminated sport-caught fish was less than the risk of eating other similar foods, 61.6 percent of white respondents and 61.8 percent of minorities agreed with the statement. Respondents were also asked whether the health benefits for children were greater than the health risks that might arise from eating contaminated sport-caught fish; 90.7 percent of white respondents and 85.3 percent of minority anglers agreed with this statement.

We also examined the interaction effects of these dependent variables with race and additional independent variables (education or age) to see how these interactions influenced patterns described above and the significance levels. There was relatively little variation in responses to the health risks when race, age, and educational attainment were evaluated. There were also no significant differences when the health risks of eating the fish were analyzed. Eighty-three percent of white anglers with college or graduate education agreed that the benefits of eating contaminated fish were more than the risk for both adults and children as compared to 62 percent of white anglers with high school, trade school, or less education (Table 4). We examined the interaction effects of race and education as well as race and age on perception of health risks arising from eating sport-caught fish. None of the interactions examined in Table 4 were significant.

Table 4.   Interaction Effects between Education, Age, Race, and Percent of Anglers Agreeing with Risk Perception Statements.

Statements and Race	Level of Education						X^2	df	p-Value
	Total Sample		High school/trade school/less college/ graduate school		College or graduate school				
	Number agreeing	Percent agreeing	Number agreeing	Percent agreeing	Number agreeing	Percent agreeing			
Education × race × percent of anglers									
Health benefits are greater than health risks									
White	77	89.6	37	90.3	40	88.9	0.986	3	.805
Minority	29	85.3	21	84.0	8	88.9	0.788	3	.852
Health risks are less than other foods									
White	53	61.6	28	68.3	25	55.6	2.121	4	.714
Minority	21	61.7	15	60.0	6	66.7	5.289	4	.259
Health benefits are greater for children than health risks									
White	78	90.7	37	90.2	41	91.1	0.039	2	.981
Minority	29	85.3	21	84.0	8	88.9	0.788	3	.852

Statements and Race	Age (Years)						X^2	df	p-Value
	Total Sample		27–49		50–68				
	Number agreeing	Percent agreeing	Number agreeing	Percent agreeing	Number agreeing	Percent agreeing			
Age × race × percent of anglers									
Health benefits are greater than health risks									
White	77	89.6	45	90.0	32	88.9	1.489	3	.685
Minority	29	85.3	21	91.3	8	72.7	3.321	3	.345
Health risks are less than other foods									
White	53	61.6	29	58.0	24	66.7	1.465	4	.833
Minority	21	61.7	15	65.3	6	54.6	2.032	4	.730
Health benefits are greater for children than health risks									
White	78	90.7	45	90.0	33	91.7	0.857	2	.652
Minority	29	85.3	21	91.3	8	72.7	3.321	3	.345

The study also examined anglers' knowledge of fish consumption health advisories as well as the influence of this health advisory information on their perceptions and behavior. Anglers were asked whether they were aware of the fish consumption advisory. Most (87.4 percent) indicated that they were aware of the fish consumption advisory (Table 5). More specifically, 87.2 percent of white respondents and 85.3 percent of minority respondents were aware of the advisory. The second statement asked respondents whether this health advisory information had influenced their behavior – only 29 (26.9 percent) of respondents reported that advisory information influenced how they catch and eat fish. When race was examined, it was found that 25.6 percent of whites and 30 percent of minorities reported that their behavior was influenced by this information. The third statement asked respondents whether they agreed that there were ways to make fish safe to eat; 73 (60.8 percent) of all respondents agreed with this statement. More specifically, 62.8 percent of whites shared this perception in comparison to 55.9 percent of minority respondents. The fourth statement asked respondents whether the fish from Lake Ontario were safe to eat; 90.7 percent of white respondents and 91.2 percent of minority respondents

Table 5. Knowledge of Health Advisory, Influence of Information on Behavior, and Perceived Safety of Fish Consumption.

Statements	Yes/No	Total Sample		White		Minority		X^2	df	p
		Number	Percent	Number	Percent	Number	Percent			
Are you aware of the fish consumption advisory?	Yes	104	87.4	75	87.2	29	85.3	0.59	2	.744
	No	15	12.6	11	12.8	5	14.7			
Has this information influenced how you catch or eat fish?	Yes	29	26.9	20	25.6	9	30.0	3.076	6	.799
	No	79	73.1	58	74.4	21	70.0			
Are there ways one can make fish safe to eat?	Yes	73	60.8	54	62.8	19	55.9	0.488	1	.485
	No	47	39.2	32	37.2	15	44.1			
Are the fish from Lake Ontario safe to eat?	Yes	109	90.8	78	90.7	31	91.2	0.410	2	.815
	No	11	9.2	8	9.3	3	8.8			

agreed with this statement. No statistically significant racial differences were found for any of the four statements.

When the interaction effects, race, and education on the four statements were examined, a significant difference between white college-educated anglers and those with less than a college education was observed. Whereas 95.6 percent of college-educated whites were aware of the fish consumption advisories, only 80 percent of whites who did not have a college education were aware of them (Table 6). None of the other interactions in the table were significant. There was also one significant relationship observed when the interaction effects of race, age, and knowledge related to health advisories were examined. Whereas 20 percent of minority anglers who were 27–49 years of age said the information in the fish advisories influenced how they caught or ate fish, 44.4 percent of older minority anglers said they were influenced by the fish advisories (Table 7). None of the other interactions examined in this table were significant.

Table 8 presents the level of fish consumption reported by respondents. Almost 70.9 percent of the respondents indicated that they ate more fish from the lake than the New York state fish advisory consumption recommends (not more than one meal of 1/2 pound of fish per week). Out of this total, 69.4 percent of whites and 74.2 percent of minorities indicated that they ate more than the recommended amount. Although minorities were more likely to report exceeding the recommended fish consumption limits, these findings were not significant. Age was significant though as younger anglers were much more likely than older ones to report exceeding the recommended limits; 76.6 percent of younger respondents and 61.5 percent of older respondents reported that they ate more than the recommended amount of fish per week. This finding was statistically significance ($X^2 = 3.325$, df = 4, $p = .097$). Table 9 indicates that one interaction effect was significant. It reports that 90.5 percent of the minority anglers who were under the age of 50 reported eating more sport-caught fish than recommended. In contrast, only 40 percent of minority anglers who were 50 years and older ate more sport-caught fish than recommended ($X^2 = 10.259$, df = 4, $p = 016$).

Table 10 summarizes the number and percent of anglers reporting that they received fish contamination information when they purchased their fishing license. All 120 boating anglers surveyed reported having a valid fishing license. However, only 32.5 percent of them indicated that they received fish contamination information when they bought their license. Whites were more likely to indicate that they were provided with information on fish contamination at the point of purchase than minorities;

Table 6. Education × Race × Anglers' Perceptions of Health Risks Arising from Eating Sport-Caught Fish.

Statements	Race	Yes/No	Total Sample		Level of Education				X^2	df	p-Value
					High/trade school/less		College/graduate school				
			Number	Percent	Number	Percent	Number	Percent			
Are you aware of the fish consumption advisory?	White	Yes	75	88.2	32	80.0	43	95.6	6.040	2	.049*
		No	10	11.8	8	20.0	2	4.4			
	Minority	Yes	29	85.3	21	84.0	8	88.9	0.126	1	.723
		No	5	14.7	4	16.0	1	11.1			
Has this information influenced how you catch or eat fish?	White	Yes	17	22.7	9	27.3	8	19.0	7.651	6	.265
		No	58	77.3	24	72.7	34	81.0			
	Minority	Yes	8	27.6	5	23.8	3	37.5	1.144	4	.887
		No	21	72.4	16	76.2	5	62.5			
Are there ways one can make fish safe to eat?	White	Yes	54	62.8	23	56.1	31	68.9	1.502	1	.220
		No	32	37.2	18	43.9	14	31.1			
	Minority	Yes	19	55.9	13	52.0	6	66.7	0.577	1	.447
		No	15	44.1	12	48.0	3	33.3			
Are the fish from Lake Ontario safe to eat?	White	Yes	78	91.8	38	92.7	40	90.9	1.010	2	.603
		No	7	8.2	3	7.3	4	9.1			
	Minority	Yes	31	91.2	23	92.0	8	88.9	0.080	1	.778
		No	3	8.8	2	8.0	1	11.1			

*$p = 0.05$.
**$p = 0.01$.

Table 7. Age × Race × Anglers' Perceptions of Health Risks Arising from Eating Sport-Caught Fish.

Statements	Race	Yes/No	Total Sample		Age (Years) 27–49		50–68		X^2	df	p-Value
			Number	Percent	Number	Percent	Number	Percent			
Are you aware of the fish consumption advisory?	White	Yes	75	88.2	42	84.0	33	94.2	3.494	2	.174
		No	10	11.8	8	16.0	2	5.7			
	Minority	Yes	29	85.3	19	82.6	10	90.9	0.409	1	.523
		No	5	14.7	4	17.4	1	9.1			
Has this information influenced how you catch or eat fish?	White	Yes	17	22.7	11	26.2	6	18.2	3.997	6	.677
		No	58	77.3	31	73.8	27	81.8			
	Minority	Yes	8	27.6	4	20.0	4	44.4	9.857	4	.045*
		No	21	72.4	16	80.0	5	55.6			
Are there ways one can make fish safe to eat?	White	Yes	54	62.8	30	60.0	24	66.7	0.398	1	.528
		No	32	37.2	20	40.0	12	33.3			
	Minority	Yes	19	55.9	14	60.9	5	45.5	0.717	1	.397
		No	15	44.1	9	39.1	6	54.5			
Are the fish from Lake Ontario safe to eat?	White	Yes	78	91.8	46	92.0	32	91.4	1.414	2	.493
		No	7	8.2	4	8.0	3	8.3			
	Minority	Yes	31	91.2	21	91.3	10	90.9	0.001	1	.970
		No	3	8.8	2	8.7	1	9.1			

*p = 0.05.
**p = 0.01.

Table 8. Percent of Anglers Eating More Fish per Week than Recommended.

Demographic Characteristics	Ate More Fish than Recommended				X^2	df	p
	Yes		No				
	Number	Percent	Number	Percent			
Total Sample	73	70.9	30	29.1	3.558	4	.469
Race							
White	50	69.4	22	30.6	3.558	4	.469
Minority	23	74.2	8	25.8			
Age							
27–49 years	49	76.6	15	23.4	3.325	4	.097*
50–68 years	24	61.5	15	38.5			
Education							
High school or trade school or less	43	72.9	16	27.1	4.738	4	.315
College or graduate school	30	68.2	14	31.8			

*$p = 0.05$.
**$p = 0.01$.

37.2 percent of whites and 20.6 percent of minorities reported getting the information. This difference is statistically significant ($X^2 = 3.069$, df $= 1$, $p = .080$). Age was significant too. Whereas 42.5 percent of younger anglers were provided with fish contamination information, just 17 percent of older anglers got such information ($X^2 = 8.438$, df $= 1$, $p = .004$). Interaction effects are reported in Table 11; none of the interactions reported in the table were significant.

DISCUSSION

In response to pressure from the environmental justice movement, the EPA and other federal and state agencies have invested considerable time and money into the development of environmental justice programs and policies; yet, many environmental justice advocates remain dissatisfied with state and federal progress in this area. Although there has been a dramatic growth in the number of fish consumption advisories issued by Great Lakes States, research indicates that awareness and response has not increased to the

Table 9. The Relationship between Age, Education, Race, and the Percent of Anglers Eating More Fish per Week than Recommended.

Race	Yes/No	Age (Years)						X^2	df	p-Value
		Total Sample		27–49		50–68				
		Number	Percent	Number	Percent	Number	Percent			
Age × race × percent of anglers										
White	Yes	50	69.4	30	69.7	20	69.0	1.035	4	.904
	No	22	30.6	13	30.3	9	31.0			
Minority	Yes	23	74.2	19	90.5	4	40.0	10.259	3	.016*
	No	8	25.8	2	9.5	6	60.0			

Race	Yes/No	Educational Attainment						X^2	df	p-Value
		Total Sample		High school, trade school, or less		College or graduate school				
		Number	Percent	Number	Percent	Number	Percent			
Education × race × percent of anglers										
White	Yes	50	69.4	25	69.4	25	69.4	2.953	4	.566
	No	22	30.6	11	30.6	11	30.6			
Minority	Yes	23	74.2	18	78.3	5	62.5	1.432	3	.698
	No	8	25.8	5	21.7	3	37.5			

*$p = 0.05$.
**$p = 0.01$.

desired level anticipated by responsible state and federal agencies and is lower for poor and minority groups.

One would expect that focused educational efforts would result in significant reduction in exposure to hazards. However, this has not been the case for health advisories in the Great Lakes. The fish advisory compliance rate has been low in the United States (Burger et al., 2003). One factor for this low level of compliance may be due to the sometimes conflicting information provided by various agencies (Burger et al., 2001). Additional reasons for low compliance include controversies over health risks versus health benefits and the unwillingness to adhere to these advisories because of personal beliefs. Burger et al. (2003) suggest the importance of addressing the diverse needs of ethnic groups as critical for changing consumption patterns. Jardine (2003) identified social trust in the agency issuing the advisory as a factor contributing to compliance. Several

Table 10.   Percent of Anglers Given Fish Advisory Information
When They Purchased Their Fishing License.

Demographic Characteristics	Given Fish Advisory				x^2	df	p
	Yes		No				
	Number	Percent	Number	Percent			
Total sample	39	32.5	81	67.5	3.069	1	.080*
Race							
White	32	37.2	54	62.8	3.069	1	.080*
Minority	7	20.6	27	79.4			
Age							
27–49 years	31	42.5	42	57.5	8.438	1	.004**
50–68 years	8	17.0	39	83			
Education							
High school or trade school or less	23	34.8	43	65.2	.369	1	.544
College or graduate school	16	29.6	38	70.4			

*$p = 0.05$.
**$p = 0.01$.

researchers have shown evidence of variation in judgments of particular environmental risks based on differences in ethnicity, gender, socioeconomic status, or educational level (Fessenden-Raden, Fitchen, & Health, 1987; Louis Harris and Associates, 1980; Pilisuk & Acredolo, 1998; Wandersman, Berman, & Hallman, 1989). Vaughan and Nordenstam (1991) examined risk perception among ethnically diverse groups and concluded that variability in perception of health and environmental risks could result from factors such as level of risk exposure or dissimilar prior experience as well as the influence of culturally shared values and beliefs.

Our findings from this study indicate that awareness of advisory information for this sample of Lake Ontario boating anglers was high. Over 85 percent of all respondents reported that they were aware of fish consumption advisories. Yet, less than 30 percent of all anglers reported that this information influenced them to change their behavior. Thus, although most respondents state that they are aware of health advisories (87.4 percent), less than a third (26.9 percent) credits this information with influencing their risk reduction behaviors. Awareness of fish advisories did not vary significantly by race (87.2 percent for whites and 85.3 percent for minorities). The high level of fish advisory awareness and lower level

Table 11.   The Relationship between Age, Education, Race, and the Percent of Anglers Given Fish Advisory Information.

Race	Yes/No			Age (Years)				X^2	df	p-Value
		Total Sample		27–49		50–68				
		Number	Percent	Number	Percent	Number	Percent			
Age × race × percent of anglers										
White	Yes	39	41.1	24	48.0	15	33.3	0.607	1	.436
	No	56	58.9	26	52.0	30	66.7			
Minority	Yes	7	22.6	6	27.3	1	11.1	0.672	1	.412
	No	24	77.4	16	72.7	8	88.9			

Race	Yes/No			Educational Attainment				X^2	df	p-Value
		Total Sample		High school, trade school, or less		College or graduate school				
		Number	Percent	Number	Percent	Number	Percent			
Education × race × percent of anglers										
White	Yes	32	37.2	17	41.5	15	33.3	0.607	1	.436
	No	54	62.8	24	58.5	30	66.7			
Minority	Yes	7	20.6	6	24.0	1	11.1	0.672	1	.412
	No	27	79.4	19	76.0	8	88.9			

of compliance found in our study is similar to that reported by Knuth, Connelly, Sheeshka, and Patterson (2003). They found in a telephone survey of Lake Ontario licensed anglers that 83 percent of the respondents were aware of the health advisory, and 26 percent consumed more fish than recommended in the advisory. Imm et al. (2005) report a somewhat lower level of awareness of fish advisories. They surveyed residents in eight Great Lakes states who consumed sport fish caught in the Great Lakes more than twice a month and found that 70 percent of them were aware of the advisories. Interestingly enough, although only 60.8 percent of the respondents in our study agreed that there were ways to make fish safe to eat, when asked specifically about Lake Ontario fish, more than 90 percent of the anglers in our sample said that these fish were safe to eat. One factor that may confound efforts to encourage anglers to reduce their consumption is the belief that the fish they catch are healthy and that they can somehow identify contaminated fish (Beehler et al., 2003).

More than 70 percent of our sample reported eating more sport-caught fish per week than recommended by the general health advisory (that recommends no more than 1/2 pound per week). Race did not have a significant association with consumption rate, but age did. These differences are similar to the findings of West et al. (1992). They conducted a statewide survey of 2,600 Michigan anglers and found that minority anglers consumed approximately 4 g/person/day more than white anglers. In our sample, education did not have a significant effect on the amount of fish consumed per week by respondents.

Only 32.5 percent of the anglers in our sample indicated that they received health advisory information when they purchased their fishing licenses. This is noteworthy, as all 120 boating anglers surveyed reported having a valid fishing license and therefore should have received the DEC Freshwater Fishing Regulations Guide when they purchased their license. The DOH utilizes the Freshwater Fishing Regulations Guide to publish and distribute these warnings to anglers. This approach presupposes that every angler is provided a copy of the regulations guide when they buy or renew their fishing license. The relationship between age and the likelihood of receiving fish advisory information when purchasing a fishing license was significant. Race was also a significant factor in who got fish contamination information when anglers purchased their fishing licenses. Whites were much more likely to be provided with this information than minorities. Our findings are similar to studies reported by Connelly et al. (1993), Tilden et al. (1997), and Burger et al. (1999). Tilden et al. (1997) reported that fish advisory communication programs are less effective in reaching minorities and persons with lower levels of education. Connelly et al. (1993) reported similar findings. A comparative study of Latino and white anglers found that Latino anglers were less likely to know about fish consumption advisories (Burger et al., 1999). The difference in the distribution of fish advisory information to minority and white anglers points to a continued need to address inequities in communicating critical risk information to all anglers. Our findings suggest that state and federal risk communication strategies be developed to encourage the participation of a wider range of communities and better integrate local knowledge into policies and practices. The disparity observed in the distribution of fish advisory information to older and younger anglers in our sample could probably be explained by the fact that state personnel often assume that older anglers have been fishing for longer periods and thus may have received the fish advisory information earlier and are more knowledgeable about the issues of fish contamination. Therefore, older anglers do not need the fish advisory information and do not distribute it to them.

It is disquieting to note that minority anglers may not be receiving notification of health risks at the same rate as white anglers through this "first line of defense" in health advisory disclosure. These results indicate that further research should be conducted using a large, randomly selected sample of licensed anglers to determine whether these findings will be replicated. Furthermore, even if minority anglers are receiving the DEC Fishing Guide at the same rate as white anglers, their lower level of awareness regarding advisory information suggests that the method of presentation of health advisories in the Fishing Guide may not be effective in communicating to them (Nordenstam & DiMento, 1990).

CONCLUSION

Our study examined a specific subgroup of anglers – Lake Ontario boating anglers. Anglers differ in social and demographic characteristics and by their style of fishing – from boats, piers, along shorelines or river banks, and so on (Aiken, 2004). The results of this study support earlier research indicating that fish consumption patterns, perceptions of risk and benefits, and access to health information vary by race, age, and education. Studies in risk communication suggest that strategies to disseminate information consider these factors during the development of fish contamination advisories. Additionally, this study provides evidence that fish advisory information has not been as effective in changing behavior as government agencies would like to believe. The study also found that behavioral change in fish consumption does not always correspond with increased awareness. Fuller participation by all stakeholders and increased utilization of community-based outreach programs are critical in incorporating their concerns into the policymaking process (Jardine, 2003). Corburn (2004) recommends changes in the risk assessment process used by the EPA and other agencies that would encourage the inclusion of local and traditional knowledge in the decision-making process. Moreover, utilization of nonprofit or community stakeholder groups can enhance the effectiveness of this process (Burger et al., 2001). Chess, Burger, and McDermott (2005) suggest that, in addition to the challenge of developing more effective risk communication approaches, there may be other organizational problems such as prioritization of issues within government that hinder effective communication and perpetuate environmental inequalities.

In a similar vein, Nordenstam (1995) notes the difficulties that arise when agencies charged with addressing the scientific and technical components of health and environmental exposure broaden their mission to incorporate cultural, social, and risk communication dimensions in their mission. Health advisories present a challenge because they rely on individuals to regulate their own activities to reduce exposure. The effectiveness of health advisories also hinge on the way diverse users perceive problems and respond to information provided. Our findings point to the need for regulatory agencies to devise ways of communicating with recreational anglers and ensuring risk information is disseminated in an equitable manner.

REFERENCES

Aiken, R. (2004). *The extent of boating information available in the 2001 survey of fishing, hunting, and wildlife-associated recreation: Monograph 2001-1.* Washington, DC: U.S. Fish & Wildlife Service.

American Sport Fishing Association. (2007). Data and statistics consumer demographics. Available at http://www.asafishing.org. Retrieved on 15 November 2007.

Anderson, P. D., & Wiener, J. B. (1995). Eating fish. In: J. D. Graham & J. B. Wiener (Eds), *Risk versus risk: Tradeoffs in protecting health and the environment* (pp. 104–135). Cambridge, MA: Harvard University Press.

Beehler, G. P., McGuinness, B. M., & Vena, J. E. (2001). Polluted fish, sources of knowledge, and the perception of risk: African American anglers' sport fishing practices. *Human Organization: Journal of the Society for Applied Anthropology, 60*(3), 288–297.

Beehler, G. P., McGuinness, B. M., & Vena, J. E. (2003). Characterizing Latino anglers' environmental risk perceptions, sport fish consumption, and advisory awareness. *Medical Anthropology Quarterly, 17*(1), 99–116.

Brewer, J., & Hunter, A. (2006). *Foundations of multi-method research: Synthesizing styles.* Thousand Oaks, CA: Sage.

Bullard, R. (1994). *Unequal protection: Environmental justice and communities of color.* San Francisco, CA: Sierra Club Books.

Bullard, R., & Wright, B. H. (1986). The politics of pollution. *Phylon, 47*(1), 77–78.

Burger, J., Gochfeld, M., Powers, C. W., Waishwell, L., Warren, C., & Goldstein, B. (2001). Science, policy, stakeholders and fish consumption advisories: Developing a fish fact sheet for the Savannah River. *Environmental Management, 27*, 501–514.

Burger, J., McDermott, M. H., Chess, C., Bochenet, E., Perez-Lugo, M., & Pflugh, K. K. (2003). Evaluating risk communication about fish consumption advisories: Efficacy of a brochure versus a classroom lesson in Spanish and English. *Risk Analysis, 23*, 461–471.

Burger, J., Pflugh, K. K., Lurig, L., Von Hagen, L., & Von Hagen, S. (1999). Fishing in urban New Jersey: Ethnicity affects information sources, perception, and compliance. *Risk Analysis, 19*(2), 217–229.

Calderon, R. L., Johnson, C. C., Jr., Craun, G. F., Dufour, A. P., Karlin, R. J., Sinks, T., & Valentine, J. L. (1993). Health risks from contaminated water: Do class and race matter? *Toxicology and Industrial Health, 9*(5), 879–900.

Chess, C., Burger, J., & McDermott, M. H. (2005). Speaking like a state: Environmental justice and fish consumption advisories. *Society and Natural Resources, 18*(3), 267–278.

Colborn, T. E., Davidson, A., Green, S. N., Hodge, R. A., & Jackson, C. L. (1990). *Great Lakes legacy*. Washington, DC: The Conservation Foundation.

Connelly, N. A., Knuth, B. A., & Vena, J. E. (1993). New York State angler cohort study: Health advisory knowledge and related attitudes and behavior, with a focus on Lake Ontario. In: *Human dimensions research unit series no. 93-9*. Ithaca, NY: Department of Natural Resources, Cornell University.

Corburn, J. (2004). Environmental justice, local knowledge, and risk: The discourse of a community-based cumulative exposure assessment. *Environmental Management, 29*(4), 451–466.

Council on Environmental Quality (CEQ). (1971). *The second annual report of the council on environment quality* (p. 190). Washington, DC: U.S. Government Printing Office.

Environmental Protection Agency. (2007). Environmental justice – information resources. Available at http://www.epa.gov/compliance/environmentaljustice/. Retrieved on 22 May 2007.

Fessenden-Raden, J., Fitchen, J. M., & Health, J. S. (1987). Providing information in communities: Factors affecting what is heard and accepted. *Science, Technology, and Human Values, 12*, 94–101.

Gauna, E., O'Neil, C., & Rechschaffen, C. (2005). *Environmental justice*. CPR White Paper no. 505. Washington, DC: Carolina Academic Press.

Imm, P., Knobeloch, L., Anderson, H. A., & The Great Lakes Sport Fish Consortium. (2005). Fish consumption and advisory awareness in the Great Lakes Basin. *Environmental Health Perspectives, 113*(10), 1273–1277.

Jardine, C. G. (2003). Development of a public participation and communication protocol for establishing fish consumption advisories. *Risk Analysis, 23*, 461–471.

Judd, N., O'Neil, S., & Kalman, D. A. (2003). Are seafood PCB data sufficient to assess health risk for high seafood consumption groups? *Human and Ecological Risk Assessment, 9*(3), 691–708.

Knuth, B. A., & Connelly, N. A. (1991). Objectives and evaluation criteria for Great Lakes health advisories: Perspectives from fishery, health and environmental quality agencies. In: *Human dimensions research unit series no. 91-111*. New York: Department of Natural Resources, Cornell University.

Knuth, B. A., & Connelly, N. A. (1994). Policy implications of communicating risks from fish consumption. In: C. J. Watras & J. W. Huckabee (Eds), *Mercury pollution: Integration and synthesis*. Florida: Lewis Publishers.

Knuth, B. A., Connelly, N. A., Sheeshka, J., & Patterson, J. (2003). Weighing health benefit and health risk information when consuming sport-caught fish. *Risk Analysis, 23*(6), 1185–1197.

Kreiss, K. (1985). Studies on populations exposed to polychlorinated biphenyls. *Environmental Health Perspectives, 60*, 193–199.

Lee, C. (1987). *Toxic waste and race in the United States: A national report on the racial and socio-economic characteristics of communities with hazardous waste sites*. New York: United Church of Christ Commission for Racial Justice.

Louis Harris and Associates. (1980). *Risk in a complex society*. New York: Marsh and McLennan.

MacDonald, H. F., & Boyle, K. J. (1997). Effect of a statewide sport fish consumption advisory on open-water fishing in Maine. *North American Journal of Fisheries Management, 17*, 687–695.

National Environmental Justice Advisory Council (NEJAC). (2002). Fish consumption and environmental justice: A report developed from the NEJAC meeting of December 3–6, 10–11. Available at http://www.epa.gov/compliance/resource/publications/ej/fish_consumption_report_1102. Retrieved on October 17, 2007.

New York State Department of Health. (2009–2010). *Health advisory: Chemicals in sport fish and game.* New York: New York State Department of Health.

Nordenstam, B. J. (1995). *Transformation of grassroots environmental justice into federal agency environmental policy. AAAS/ EPA Environmental Science and Engineering Fellowship Reports.* American Association for the Advancement of Science and the United States Environmental Protection Agency, Washington, DC, pp. 51–66.

Nordenstam, B. J., & DiMento, J. F. (1990). Right-to-know: Implications of risk communication research for regulatory policy. *U.C. Davis Law Review, 23*(2), 333–374.

Perlin, S. A., Wong, D., & Sexton, K. (2001). Residential proximity to industrial sources of air pollution: Interrelationships among race, poverty, and age. *Journal of the Air & Waste Management Association, 51*, 406–421.

Pilisuk, M., & Acredolo, C. (1998). Fear of technology hazards: One concern or many? *Social Science Journal, 24*, 403–413.

Reynolds, B. (1980). Triana, Alabama: The unhealthiest town in America? *National Wildlife, 18*, 33.

Sechena, R. L., Shiquan, L., Nakano, R., Polissar, C., Nayak, & Fenske, R. (2003). Asian American and Pacific Islander seafood consumption, a community-based study in King County, Washington. *Journal of Exposure Science & Environmental Epidemiology, 13*, 256–266.

Steenport, D. M. (2000). Fish consumption habits and advisory awareness among Fox River anglers. *Wisconsin Medical Journal.* Available at http://www.ismed.org/wmj/nov2000/fish.html. Retrieved on 17 October 2007.

Tilden, J., Hanrahan, L. P., Anderson, H. P., Palit, C., Olson, J., Mac-Kenzie, W., & The Great Lakes Sport Fish Consortium. (1997). Health advisories for consumers of Great Lakes sport fish: Is the message being received? *Environmental Health Perspectives, 105*(12), 1360–1365.

Tremblay, N. W., & Gilman, A. P. (1995). Human health, the Great Lakes, and environmental pollution: A 1994 perspective. *Environmental Health Perspectives, 103*(Suppl. 9), 3–5.

United States Census Bureau. (2000). Population Estimates for the US and States by Single Year of Age and Sex Population Estimates Program Division, U.S. Census Bureau, Washington, DC. Available at http://www.census.gov/pop. Retrieved on October 15, 2007.

United States Environmental Protection Agency. (1987). *Reports on Lake Ontario Toxic Management Plan.* Washington, DC: Toxic Release Inventory 798–1990.

United States Environmental Protection Agency. (1995). *Environmental justice strategy.* Washington, DC: United States Environmental Protection Agency.

Vaughan, E., & Nordenstam, B. J. (1991). The perception of environmental risks among ethnically diverse groups. *Journal of Cross-Cultural Psychology, 22*(1), 29–59.

Wandersman, A., Berman, S. H., & Hallman, W. (1989). How residents cope with living near a hazardous waste landfill: An example of substantive theorizing. *American Journal of Community Psychology, 17*(5), 575–583.

West, P. C. (1992). "Invitation to poison?" Detroit minorities and toxic fish consumption from the Detroit River. In: B. Bunyan & P. Mohai (Eds), *Race and the incidence of environmental hazards: A time for discourse.* Boulder, CO: Westview Press.

238 BRENDA J. NORDENSTAM AND SARAH DARKWA

West, P. C., Fly, M. J., Larkin, F., & Marans, R. W. (1992). Minority anglers and toxic fish consumption: Evidence from a statewide survey of Michigan. In: B. Bunyan & P. Mohai (Eds), *Race and the incidence of environmental hazards: A time for discourse* (pp. 100–113). Boulder, CO: Westview Press.

Brenda J. Nordenstam is an associate professor at the State University of New York, College of Environmental Science and Forestry. Her goal as a professor and environmentalist has been to engage in community-based scholarship. As a researcher, she believes that we should support the integration of knowledge through community-based research, teaching, and service. Her research interests involve risk perception and communication, environmental justice, and environmental policy. Her work with individuals and groups struggling to comprehend and respond to environmental hazards in their communities has broadened her own understanding of these risks and deepened her commitment to the view that only through full community partnerships will we begin to address these complex interrelated health and environmental problems. She can be reached by email at bjnorden@esf.edu or by telephone at 315-470-6573.

Sarah Darkwa is on Faculty of Education at the University of Cape Coast, Ghana. She can be reached by email at sardarks@yahoo.com.uk.

PART III
AGRICULTURE, LAND LOSS AND
GENETICALLY MODIFIED CROPS

FROM THE GREEN REVOLUTION TO THE GENE REVOLUTION IN INDIA: UNDERSTANDING THE RISKS AND BENEFITS OF GENETICALLY MODIFIED CROPS

Asmita Bhardwaj

ABSTRACT

Purpose – *The globally controversial genetically modified (GM) cotton has been adopted widely by Indian farmers. Claiming the adoption to be a success of the GM technology, the GM proponents call for a large-scale introduction of GM crops in Indian agriculture. Opposition to GM crops is largely constructed in terms of the environmental risks that GM technologies pose to crop and forest biodiversity. This chapter examines the economic and political context in which these seeds were adopted to see if adequate support mechanisms were available to farmers to facilitate adoption of the new technology.*

Design/methodology/approach – *A field study was conducted in Vidharbha, Eastern Maharashtra. In addition, government reports and newspaper articles were reviewed and interviews were conducted in Maharashtra and Delhi.*

Environment and Social Justice: An International Perspective
Research in Social Problems and Public Policy, Volume 18, 241–259
Copyright © 2010 by Emerald Group Publishing Limited
All rights of reproduction in any form reserved
ISSN: 0196-1152/doi:10.1108/S0196-1152(2010)0000018010

Findings – *This chapetr finds that the problems faced by farmers are much deeper than what technology can solve or which have been addressed in the GM debate. Cotton farmers face persistent problems in the agricultural production process that increase their production costs. A spate of farmer's suicides in Vidharbha and other rain-fed regions of India epitomizes the dire conditions farmers are in. This chapter asserts that state-supported policies transformed India from a food importing to a food surplus country in the 1960s during the green revolution. However, GM cotton has been introduced without a supportive infrastructure for technology transfer in Maharashtra and most cotton-growing states. The lack of support makes the gain of cotton farmers in Vidharbha from the new technology highly uncertain.*

Originality/value – *This analysis shows the need to examine the role of government programs in helping farmers implement technological advances in agriculture.*

INTRODUCTION

The controversial genetically modified (GM) cotton or Bt-cotton (*Bacillus thuringiensis*), produced by the multinational agricultural giant Monsanto, has been widely adopted in India's cotton belt. Even before their official release, "illegal"[1] GM seeds were found growing in the central-western state of Gujarat in 1998. As farmers in Gujarat reaped good returns off the illegal seeds, spurious Bt seeds were smuggled in a number of cotton producing states that had long been seeking a solution to declining cotton yields. Monsanto's varieties were officially approved in 2002, and since then the increasing acreage under Bt cotton has made India the seventh largest adopter of Bt cotton in the world (ISAAA, 2006). According to GM proponents, the popularity of GM crops necessitates its introduction on a greater scale in Indian agriculture. This would call for faster biosafety trials and GM product labeling regimes.[2] Bt technology and GM crops are crucial to increasing agricultural growth and productivity and will usher in a "second green revolution" or a gene revolution (Sibal, 2005; Rai, 2005; Planning Commission, 2006; World Bank Country Report, 2006).

Although GM crops promise a bounty, the condition of cotton and small and marginal farmers in many parts of India is precarious. Table 1 shows the average monthly income and expenditure of farmers of various farm size classes in India in 2003. The table shows that farmers with less than 4 ha of

Table 1. Farm Income and Expenditures Across Farm Sizes
in India in 2003.

Land Size Class (Hectare)	Average Monthly Income (Rs)	Average Monthly Expenditure (Rs)	Income-Expenditure Differential (Rs)
Less than 0.01	1380	2297	−917
0.01–0.40	1633	2390	−757
0.41–1.00	1809	2672	−863
1.00–2.00	2493	3148	−655
2–4	3549	3685	−136
4–10	5681	4626	+1055
Greater than 10	9667	6418	+3249

Source: Compiled from the *National Sample Survey Report 497: Income Expenditure and Productive Assets of Farmers Households. Situational Assessment Survey of Farmers* (2005), Ministry of Statistics and Programme Evaluation, Government of India, December.

Table 2. Area under Bt Cotton Cultivation in Hectares
in Various Indian States in 2006.

States	2002	2003	2004	2005	2006
Maharashtra	12,424	21,854	61,475	508,692	1,840,000
Gujarat	9,137	41,684	125,925	149,258	470,000
Andhra Pradesh	3,906	5,463	71,227	90,419	830,000
Karnataka	2,186	3,035	34,304	29,345	85,000
Tamil Nadu	374	7,685	1,995	17,017	45,000
Other Zones	0	0	0	0	5,000
Total	30,029	81,724	296,930	796,736	3,277,006

Source: Compiled from Gruere, Mehta Bhatt, & Sengupta (2008).

land (small and marginal farmers) have average monthly expenditures that exceed their average monthly income. Moreover, the farmers with the smallest amount of land had the largest deficits in 2003.

Bt cotton has been introduced in all six cotton-growing states since 2002. Table 2 shows the acreage under Bt cotton in various states between 2002 and 2006. Despite the introduction of GM crops farmer's condition is continuing to deteriorate. If GM crops are beneficial, what explains the continuing farmers' distress in cotton areas? Given the farmers precarious condition, do and can cotton farmers gain from these new technologies? Or, do the risks of GM cotton far outweigh their benefits?

This chapter relies on qualitative research methods such as field interviews and analysis of secondary documents to answer the earlier questions.

A field study was conducted in Vidharbha, Maharashtra, a western cotton-growing state of India, which has been epicenter of the farmer's suicides. Farmer's suicides were first reported in Vidharbha, Maharashtra and later in other parts of the country (Suri, 2006; SETHI, 2006; NCF, 2006; Planning Commission Report, 2006; Mishra, 2006). There is a consensus that there is widespread agrarian crisis.[3]

During 4 fieldtrips lasting 10–15 days each from 2006 to 2007, I interviewed leaders of farmers' groups, activist networks, academics, and journalists regarding the farm crisis and the adoption of Bt cotton. I have also analyzed secondary data such as policy documents and news reports to construct the case. To understand the macro-policy context of introduction of GM crops such as the national economic policies and trade-related measures, I have analyzed newspapers, books, and journal articles.

The chapter argues that the pro-GM discourse focuses on the role that new seed technology can play in increasing productivity (Herring, 2005a; Lipton, 2007; Monsanto website, 2007; ISAAA, 2005). The anti-GM discourse largely focuses on the environmental risks that seeds pose to forests and crop biodiversity (Shiva & Jafri, 2006; Shiva, 2000; Shiva, 2006; Sahai & Rehman, 2004). Both these perspectives are limited in understanding the risks and benefits of GM crops.

This chapter asserts the need to understand the impact of these technologies in a wider perspective. It compares the experience of the green revolution, a similar plant breeding technology of the 1960s that raised agricultural productivity in Asia, to provide a conceptual framework to understand the risks and benefits of the GM crops. Briefly, green revolution (GR)[4] literature suggests that the productivity and income gains of 1960s were not simply due to the high-yielding technology but also due to the agrarian condition of farmers and the policy and institutional "package" that allowed the widespread diffusion of green revolution gains (see Pearse, 1980; Griffin, 1974; Frankel, 1971; Herring, 1977). The institutions that the state put in place for GR technology transfer shared the risk that is associated with the adoption of new technologies.[5] This was a critical condition that allowed some farmers to make gains. The chapter examines whether similar support structures were put in place when GM crops were introduced.

THE GM "PACKAGE"

In the past decade, GM crops have received much publicity worldwide. The crops have been widely adopted in developing countries, and in some instances, have increased farm profitability and led to income gains (Brookes & Barfoot, 2006; Qaim & Zilberman, 2003). In India, these crops have been the focus of large conferences and fairs funded by private and international donors as well as the Indian government. In addition, GM testing workshops have been conducted, newsletters circulated, biotech magazines launched, biotech industry bodies formed and reams of analyses undertaken in India that exhort the benefits of GM crops for Indian farmers.[6] "Genes are gems" asserts one publication (ICRISAT-ISAAA, 2006). The "search for new genes is essential to revitalize Indian agriculture," notes the title of the speech of the Director General of the Indian Council of Agricultural Research (Rai, 2005).

Bt cotton is seen as the epitome of success among GM crops. Farmers' gains are expected to increase as more users adopt Bt cotton. According to the proponents, Bt cotton has not only raised yields but also allowed farmers to get better prices. The increase in productivity is solely attributable to superior Bt technology; any failures, or even high seed prices, can be accounted for by failure of public sector regulation, uncertainty of weather, improper planting, or poor germplasm. However, not everyone is enthusiastic about Bt cotton. Some oppose GM crops on the grounds that this technology poses risks to biodiversity, human health, and the economic well being of farmers (Qaim, Subramanian, Naik, & Zilberman, 2006; Bennet, Yousouf, & Morse, 2006; Herring, 2006; Shiva & Jafri, 2006; Shiva, 2000).

Thus, the GM debate is narrowly focused on the role that the seed technology can play in improving or adversely affecting the economic condition of agricultural producers. It fails to look at the "package"[7] that the GM crops are part of and its impacts on the incomes of small and marginal farmers.[8] However, GM crops are not a stand-alone policy. Just like the green revolution that consisted of a package of high yielding seeds, pesticides, fertilizers, mechanical equipment, supportive price measures, procurement options, government-regulated marketing, and farmer-friendly credit policies,[9] the new seeds are also a part of the wider package that comprise the gene revolution.

Unlike the extensive support structure that accompanied the green revolution crops, GM crops are part of a larger neoliberal project of agricultural modernization where there is considerable retrenchment of the state from its welfare functions in rural development. Public–private partnerships with greater involvement of corporate sector actors through measures such as contract farming, agro-business promotion and agro-value chains that are expected to link Indian agriculture to fast changing urban and export markets are part of this project. This "new deal" will

allow Indian agriculture to participate in the larger national project
of 10 percent economic growth and usher in a "second green revolution"
(FICCI-ICAR, 2005)

ECONOMIC AND ECOLOGICAL
CONDITION OF COTTON FARMERS

In order to understand the impacts of the gene revolution technologies on
Indian farmers, it is important, to understand the economic and ecological
condition of cotton farmers.[10] Four million farmers in six Indian states –
Gujarat, Maharashtra, Punjab, Kerela, Andhra Pradesh, and Karnataka –
engage in farming. Farmers' suicides have been reported in many parts of the
country, especially among cotton growers (TISS, 2006; IGIDR, 2006; CSE,
2006; NCF, 2006; Planning Commission, 2006). Table 3 shows the number
of farmers' suicides has been on the rise in several major Indian states. As
Table 3 shows, the number of suicides are more than doubled between 1997
and 2000. By 2006, there were almost three times as many suicides as there
were 9 years earlier. Maharashtra is the state with highest number of suicides.
In contrast, Gujarat, a major cotton-growing state has a much lower rate of
suicides. Suicides have accounted for two percent of the total deaths in the
Maharashtra. In India, suicides have accounted for 1.3 percent of the total
deaths. Suicides have been on the increase for some time in Maharashtra.
They have risen from 1,083 in 1995 to 4,147 in 2004. This is a largely
male phenomenon. Suicides among male farmers have increased from 978 to
3,799 during this period (Mishra, 2006). This raises the question, what is the
economic and ecological condition of farmers in Maharashtra?

Table 3.   Farmers Suicides in Indian States, 1997–2006.

States	1997	2000	2003	2006
Maharashtra	1,917	3,022	3,836	4,453
Andhra Pradesh	1,097	1,525	1,800	2,607
Karnataka	1,832	2,379	2,505	1,720
Gujarat	565	661	594	487
Other States	582	6,105	6,892	6,418
Total	5,993	13,692	15,627	15,685

Source: Compiled from Gruere et al. (2008).

Farmers in Vidharbha have traditionally practiced cotton cultivation mostly without irrigation. Cotton farming is an activity practiced not only by large landholders but by small, marginal and landless farmers as well (TISS, 2006). Cotton yield has been low and inconsistent in the region. Fig. 1 shows the fluctuating yield of cotton in Vidharbha. To exacerbate matters, there have been a series of crop failures since the 1990s. This has led to declining incomes and growing indebtedness among farmers (TISS, 2006). Although data is not available at the level of the region of Vidharbha, data regarding farm indebtedness is available at the level of the state of Maharashtra. Table 4 shows that indebtedness among farm households in select Indian states. As Table 4 shows, the rates of indebtedness in rural Maharashtra are quite high at 54.8 percent.

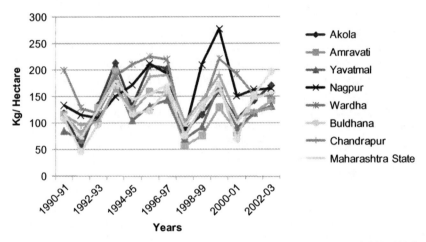

Fig. 1. Fluctuating Cotton Yields in Vidharbha and Maharashtra (1990–2003). *Source:* Data obtained from IGIDR (2006).

Table 4. Indebtedness of Farmers in Various Indian States.

Indebtedness	Maharashtra	Andhra Pradesh	Kerala	Punjab	All India
Percent indebted among rural household	54.8	82.0	64.4	65.4	48.6
Percent indebted among rural households with cultivation as main income	62.6	54.6	14.4	52.7	56.7

Source: Compiled from Gruere et al. (2008).

The crop failures have certain ecological dimensions such as the uncertainty of water availability that are typical of semi-arid regions. In addition, about a third of the state is vulnerable to crop failure because of the vagaries of the monsoons (Brahme, 1983). Water scarcity has both political and geological reasons. The scope of irrigation development is limited in the Deccan plateau and farmers have limited success in finding water by digging wells. As one farmer puts it, "I dug a well to water my cotton field but no water appeared even after second year of digging. I lost all my investments in my cotton field and had to give up farming" (Chowkidar, 2006).

Crop failures have other economic dimensions as well. With the advent of hybrids in the 1980s, cotton became a very input-intensive crop. Although productivity and profits rose in the 1980s, the susceptibility of cotton to pests has also increased (Jaywandhia, 2006). Increasing pest attacks of the American bollworm and the lack of proper extension services to help farmers cope have resulted in increased application of pesticides for instance (Wagadhe, 2006). As things stand, farmers largely depend on the dealers selling the products to provide them with information. Farmers are usually ignorant of how to use the products and solve the problems that arise with their usage. In Vidharbha, there is only one quality inspector who is charged with regulating pesticide use in the entire region. Increased spraying of pesticides has affected farmers' and workers' health as well as the soil quality in the region (Sainath, 2006a, 2006b; IGIDR, 2006; CSE, 2006). In the absence of an appropriate extension system, farmers rely on gossip and myths and often apply increasing amounts of pesticides in an effort to gain a competitive edge (Mahajan, 2006). The cost of increased pesticide use, the low efficacy of pesticides, and general lack of information about pest control has been borne by the cotton cultivators. As a result, the overall cost of cultivation has become very high (IGIDR, 2006; TISS, 2006).[11] Despite the increased costs, the irrigation and power subsidies that were available to wheat farmers during the green revolution are not available to dryland cotton farmers (Jaywandhia, 2006). The skyrocketing cost of producing cotton is one of the reasons for crop failures.

The problems are not confined only to production. Even when farmers are able to produce good cotton crops, they are unable to get good prices for their produce. This is the case because the Indian govern has set a minimum support price (MSP) that is well below the cost of production for the past few years (TISS, 2006; IGIDR, 2006). To make matters worse, farmers are not even able to get the MSP[12] because they go through middlemen who siphon off their income. Farmers are indebted to these middlemen and the middlemen get paid first. In contrast, the Monopoly Cotton Procurement Scheme instituted by Maharashtra state in the 1970s, allowed farmers to get secure prices for their crops. However, the scheme is now dysfunctional because of corruption, recurrent losses, and roll back of the state's role in price stabilization (CSE, 2006). Consequently, farmers are left to negotiate prices on their own and, more often than not, they do not secure good prices from traders (Sandeep, 2006; Talatule, 2006).

Thus farmers are unable to generate sufficient income to cover household expenses or cash to keep operating (Sandeep, 2006). Arid and semi-arid farm areas never had the credit resources and other institutional support that were available to parts of the country that participated in the green revolution. Moreover, what support existed have dwindled since the 1990s (Jaywandhia, 2006; IGIDR, 2006). This makes it more difficult for cotton farmers to obtain credit.[13] Because of the lack of government-backed or approved credit, funding is obtained from private moneylenders at very high interest rates (Hardikar, 2006). However, a recent government crackdown on moneylenders backfired as farmers had nowhere to get credit; this led to increased suicides (interview with Hardikar, 2006).

Because cotton production is affected by climate and pests, crop insurance would be an important safety net for farmers. However, the cost of insurance is too high and the procedures of obtaining it too cumbersome for the small and marginal cotton farmers of Vidharbha and the rest of Maharashtra to navigate (Sandeep, 2006; 11th Five Year Plan, 2007). Such is the context in which GM crops have been introduced. It is imperative to examine how these have been diffused in cotton regions and examine the policy and institutional package conditions under which cotton crops have been adopted.[14]

BT COTTON AND SUPPORT FOR FARMERS

When the GM crops were first introduced in the country, India was undergoing a balance-of-payment crisis. Though India has experienced balance-of-payment crises most years since independence, 1991 was a particularly bad year. That year, India adopted an International Monetary Fund/World Bank directed structural adjustment program that promoted an export-led model of growth as well as liberalization in trade, industrial and foreign exchange policies. The liberalization program strongly favored sectors such as Information Technology, telecommunications, and services that had the potential of increasing India's gross domestic product.

This signified a shift from agriculture as a key sector of the gross domestic product.[15] Liberal policy trends that have been in operation since the late 1980s have led to a significant reduction in public sector expenditure on agriculture. This is accompanied by a consistent reduction in governmental support for a number of rural development programs that create rural employment or provided subsidies to agriculture. Many of these schemes were instituted in the heyday of the welfare state and were part of the green revolution policies (Patnaik, 2003; Budget Track, 2004; Frankel, 2005).

The adoption of GM crops is thus part of this process wherein the state is restricting its welfare functions; the private sector is expected to fill the void. Contract farming and technological advances are expected to be the drivers of agricultural growth. Hence the state no longer provided help in the form of seeds, extension services, stable prices, etc. to farmers. This is significant since the research, development, and dissemination of GM seeds are in the domain of the private sector. As a result, Bt cotton have been available to farmers at rates three times higher than the hybrid seeds and several times more expensive than straight line varieties.[16] Legal action taken by the western state of Andhra Pradesh, has resulted in reduced prices but by the time this came about many farmers were already in trouble.[17] Despite the government's own agencies recommending the introduction of the Bt gene in affordable straight-line varieties, these varieties are yet to materialize in the market (Swaminathan, 2006). This delay has been costly for farmers. As I observed in 2006 during my field work, the market is already flooded by the private sector varieties and the government varieties were nonexistent in the marketplace.

Though the state has developed a biosafety regulatory mechanism to test the environmental effects of GM crops, an extension service was not put in place when the crops were introduced in regions such as Maharashtra.[18] As a result, the precision that was needed to plant Bt seeds was not known by farmers or communicated to them. It was only later that two government commissions declared the initial varieties planted in the region to be inappropriate for growing in areas such as Vidharbha (NCF, 2006; Planning Commission, 2006). Despite this error, no compensation was provided to farmers for the crop failure by the company that introduced the seeds or the Indian government.[19]

These conditions have forced farmers to participate in a flourishing "illegal" market in Bt seeds that exists in Gujarat and a number of other states. The illegal seeds were first discovered in mid-October 2001 when reports of actually existing fields in thousands of hectares of illicit Bt cotton growing in the state of Gujarat came to notice (Herring, 2005b). A local seed company, Navbharat, developed this so-called illegal variety, through a strain selected from an indigenous germplasm collection (Sethi, 2006). This variety produced such good results in the field that during a pest attack in 2001, this was the only variety that survived and produced good yields (Sethi, 2006). Not only was the productivity good (1,200–1,500 kg/ha), which was better than imported varieties, the price at which Navbharat 151 was available was over Rs. 500 (about $11 US) per packet (Sethi, 2006). This was equivalent to the price of normal hybrid seeds such as Ankur in Vidharbha but much lower than the branded Mahyco-Monsanto seeds of Rs. 1,800 ($40 US).

The underground Bt seed market is hard to regulate. Private sector seed agencies, such as Mahyco in Maharashtra, undertook some extension efforts (30 percent extension coverage in 2006) but without much success as their services did not cover the whole cotton-growing region. Although some farmers in Gujarat and other areas might be wealthy enough to experiment when new seeds come on the market, the adoption of seeds adds a new risk for small and marginal farmers given their impoverishment and indebtedness (Herring, 2006). Whether farmers' returns are certain or not, Monsanto charges royalties to ensure a profitable return on their investments.

The conditions of introduction of the GM seeds are very different from that of the green revolution, when the government provided the farmers subsidies and safety nets that helped them bear the risks associated with the adoption of new seeds. The farmers were already bearing a number of risks and the manner of introduction of GM crops increased those risks. Although the welfare functions of the state recede, the state expanded its support to facilitate the entry of capital-intensive agriculture. This was done through biosafety and labeling mechanisms, and the provision of incentives to manufacturing companies. Though India's gross domestic product has grown by 10 percent since 1992 it has not been translated in significantly reduced unemployment. The transformation of the agricultural sector means that it can no longer support a large number of people. This is reflected in the growing indebtedness in the farm sector. Farmers find it difficult to transition out of the sector as the employment opportunities that are being produced require a different set of skills than farmers currently possess.

RISKS IN THE COTTON COMMODITY CHAIN

The removal of the global MultiFibre Agreement in 1995 has expanded the possibilities of textiles exports of developing countries that were hitherto restricted by quotas in developed countries. To strengthen their position in the export marketplace, the Indian government provided numerous incentives to the textile industry as part of the 1991 economic restructuring program. This included de-licensing of the cotton textile industry, de-reservation of the textile sector, removal of export barriers, and slashed import duties for raw cotton for textile exporters. Thus India intervenes in all aspects of the cotton market from raw material production to the export of yarn and textiles. The share of exports and imports of raw cotton is currently small but as time passes, the domestic textile industry could become more vulnerable to global price fluctuations and other trends (CSE, 2006).

In the global cotton market, large subsidies provided by countries such as China and United States, leads to low and fluctuating cotton prices. Farmers in countries that subsidize production overproduce; however, these subsidies remain in place despite the call for their removal by many developing countries in the world trade negotiations. India has tried to respond to the oscillating cotton prices. In 1994, cotton exports and imports that were regulated by the government's Cotton Corporation of India, were placed under the open general license scheme that had no import duty. In 1997, the downturn in global cotton prices hit domestic producers hard as cheaper American cotton flooded the Indian market (CSE, 2006).

Other market conditions make it challenging for farmers to make a living from cotton. Production for the export market differs from production for the domestic market in ways that mean farmers may still get low prices even if they get high yields and adopt GM crops. The export market requires cotton that is clean, uncontaminated and of consistent quality. There is also an increasing demand of extra long staple cotton. The new and evolving structure of cotton textile industry demands finer quality of raw cotton and at a fast speed (USDA, 2006). These factors influence the price that farmers obtain for the cotton they produce.[20]

As is the case with cotton, the prices of agricultural commodities in the global marketplace are depressed because of subsidies and the protectionist measures by many developed countries. There is an impasse over the removal of agricultural subsidies in the international trade negotiations under the General Agreement on Tariffs and Trade. The agricultural subsidies of developed countries make the products of poorer countries uncompetitive thereby reducing their access to the largest markets (Oxfam, 2002, 2006a, 2006b; Klapper, 2007). The Indian government could try to protect their agricultural sector by increasing import duties to protect cotton farmers, however, this has not happened (NCF, 2006).

GOVERNMENT RESPONSE
TO THE AGRARIAN CRISIS

The government is fully aware of the crisis (see 11th Five Year Plan, 2007). To compensate the farmers in distressed districts of Maharashtra, the central government has developed a program worth Rs. 3,7500,000,000 for 6 districts in 2006. This program pardons the interest on all loans taken by farmers, provides increased credit flow to rural banks, investment in 82 major and 442 minor irrigation projects, the development of irrigation schemes, and the development of horticulture and seed replacement programs. High-yielding cows were also given to many families. Another Rs. 5,000,000 were placed at the disposal of the administrative authority in the 6 districts to be used for the relief of families (Hindu Business Line, 2006). This relief effort has been criticized for its failure to cater to the immediate needs of farmers (Hardikar, 2006; Tiwari, 2006). Critics claim that the program makes provisions such as cows that poor families cannot afford to maintain and largely caters to farmers who already have the benefit of irrigation (Sainath, 2006a, 2006b).[21]

The 11th Five Year Plan did not increase the rural budget much over what was allocated in earlier Five Year Plans (Singh, 2008). The 11th Five Year Plan called for a number of pro-farmer measures such as remunerative prices, crop insurance, increased irrigation, development of greater rural infrastructure, improved terms of trade for agriculture and increased focus on rain-fed areas. However, the plan also envisaged significant involvement of the corporate sector through measures such as contract farming and greater focus on biotechnologies. Thus the increase in budget might not be entirely for the benefit of the farmers, especially if monitoring and accountability mechanisms are not put in place to track the flow of money.

CONCLUSION

Both the proponents and the opponents cast the debate over GM crops in very narrow terms of seed technology. However, there is a need to understand the seeds and their impacts in the broader terms of market liberalization that accompanied their introduction. A focus on the policies and institutions allows us to examine the impacts that GM seeds have on ecological conditions and the economic status of farmers in a more complete way. The new seeds were adopted in a context where there is a considerable withdrawal of the welfare functions of the state. That void has not been filled by the private sector. The adoption of seeds without supportive policies or institutional structures to facilitate their adoption exacerbates the risks faced by cotton farmers.

The government, recognizing many of these problems, has provided some relief for rural farm areas in recent years. It is important for scholars, policy makers and advocates of the poor to track the progress and implementation of the new technologies such as the one described above and assess the adequacy of such programs to help the most marginal people. Some factions of the farmer's movement and environmental movement are at odds with each other, particularly over the issue of GM seeds. There is a need to develop a closer collaboration between these groups if the farmers situation is to improve.

NOTES

1. Seeds that were not sanctioned by the Indian government under the biosafety laws.

2. See Conference proceedings of: "National Workshop on Management of field trials of GM crops held in Hotel Nikko in August 2005 by Indian Council of Medical Research, "International Conference on Agricultural for Food, Nutritional Security and Rural Growth" (held by The Energy and Resources Institute, September, 2006), "Policy Dialogue on Economic consideration of Biosafety and Biotechnology Regulation in India" held in September 2006 and various newsletters of South Asian Biosafety Program. Retrieved on July 10, 2007 (http://www.agbios.com/sabp_main. php?action = NewsPage).

3. The term agrarian crisis was largely used by the left (Patnaik, 2003) till the media publicity highlighted the case of farmers suicides. After several Supreme Court public litigations, government studies, debates, and workshops there is a consensus that the agricultural sector is in a state of crisis. This has led Prime Minister Manmohan Singh to claim that there is widespread agrarian crisis. PM's speech retrieved on July 10, 2007 (http://www.ficci.com/news/viewnews1.asp?news_id = 664).

4. Green Revolution was a technology of the 1960s consisting of high-yielding rice and wheat variety and policies such as a fertilizers, pesticides and irrigation subsidies and credit policies. Through a combination of measures this allowed India to become a food sufficient country.

5. The purpose of the green revolution policies was to make the production process safe and remunerative for farmers so that they could produce more food (Subramanium, cited in Frankel, 2005).

6. These include a Confederation of Indian Industries workshop titled "Technology in agriculture – Growing farmer's wealth" held in December 2006, a National Workshop on Management of field trials of GM crops held in Hotel Nikko in August 2005 and a new journal such as Biospectrum, that focuses solely on developments in the biotechnology among others.

7. I have borrowed this concept from green revolution literature as it appropriately reflects the inter-related nature of gene revolution policies.

8. Some mention is made of the manner of diffusion and accompanying institutions that allow GM crops to make an impact on farm productivity and income.

9. This chapter acknowledges the harmful environmental impacts of green revolution but focuses more on the role of institutions or the state which was prominent during the green revolution and is missing during the gene revolution. For instance, the use of chemicals has led to a decline in soil fertility and the expansion of irrigation leading to a decline in the overall water table and problems of waterlogging, salination and desertification in other areas. Mono-cropping promoted by the green revolution system has led to the creation of new pests due to the destruction of ecological diversity which was built into the indigenous cropping system. Intensive fertilization resulted in nitration, in turn causing eutrophication and pollution of freshwater lakes and streams. Excessive amounts of pesticide use applied over large areas were creating health hazards for rural residents (Singh, 2001; Shiva, 1992; Tilman, 2006).

10. The green revolution literature shows that the key elements in farmers gaining from the green revolution technology were: (a) progressive farmers, who were able to access the green revolution technology incentives and (b) institutional package that reduced the risk of the production process for farmers.

11. Owing to some of the physiological factors such as adverse soil conditions, and variable rainfall, the costs of inputs in Maharashtra are higher than other parts of the country.

12. MSP is declared for two varieties by the government in the case of cotton and procurement is done by the Central Cotton Commission for approximately 10 percent of the cotton crop. Maharashtra is an exception over most states as the state used to procure 100 percent cotton till the late 1990s. In the rest of the states, private trade dominates.

13. The 1990s financial sector reforms have been highly unfavorable for the rural credit system, which coupled with shrinking resources for the agricultural sector has siphoned credit and resources away from the rural economy (IGIDR, 2006).

14. A critical condition of the green revolution gains was the state's policy support provided to agriculture, not only in terms of discourse, but also policies and institutional structures for disbursement of subsidized inputs and remunerative prices. During the green revolution, the state adopted the package under conditions of a food crisis (Ford Foundation, 1959; LBS, 1964; Ministry of Food and Agriculture, 1966) and heavy pressure to increase production both internally and externally, from donor governments. Farmers were thus treated as an integral part in meeting this national imperative (LBS, 1964).

15. Agriculture was the key sector for development between 1965 and 1978.

16. The cost of a 450 g seed packet was Rs. 1,600 for the first 3 years, 3 times the cost of the hybrid seeds and many times the cost of open varieties. Unlike the green revolution seeds, which were created and modified in partnership with international public and national agricultural research institutions, the gene revolution seeds were entirely a private sector affair.

17. The Andhra Pradesh state government, in 2006, filed a case on Monsanto in the Monopoly Restriction Trade Petition Commission (MRTPC) and the Supreme Court.

This has led to a price reduction from Rs. 1,800 to 750 of the initial Bt varieties. See News Report: AP government moves MRTPC against Monsanto on Bt cotton royalties. http://www.nwrage.org/index.php?name = News&file = article&sid = 974

18. The initial varieties that were released after a trial period of 7 years were released without an appropriate extension program to train the farmers in their appropriate use. The extension service was so limited that the labeling on the seed packets that contained very important information regarding water application and the applicability of seeds in rainfed areas was incomprehensible to most farmers, many of whom were illiterate. Consequently, farmers had to rely on informal and often incorrect sources for their information. At the same time, Monsanto took out advertisement to promote their product as a "be all" in killing the American bollworm.

19. In fact, there has been a move to attribute the failure to reasons other than the failure of the new seeds. In some areas, the government has classified the failure as physiological wilt or the failure of the crop due to natural and uncertain factors. Some of the academic discourse (Herring, 2006), also supports this position, thus leaving the costs of failed seeds to be borne by cotton farmers who are already in a risky position.

20. There is a recognition regarding this risk in the agricultural community but not much action to regulate it.

21. Sainath (July 2006). Politics of Packages, Packaging of the Politics. See http://www.indiatogether.org/2006/jul/psa-package.htm

ACKNOWLEDGMENTS

I acknowledge the help and support provided by Professors Barbara Lynch, David Lewis, Stephen Hilgartner, and John Forester of Cornell University and Professors Abhijit Dasgupta and Mahesh Rangarajan of Delhi University. I am also thankful to Vijai Jaywandhia, Manika Lal of the TACET Center, Vinayak Deshpande, Pankaj Shiras, Kioko Munyao, Abdurazzack Karriem, and many others for information and support.

REFERENCES

Bennet, R., Yousouf, I., & Morse, S. (2006). Comparing the performance of official and unofficial Bt Cotton in India. *AgBioForum, 8*(1).

Brahme, S. (1983). *Droughts and famines in Maharashtra.* Pune, India: Gokhale Institute of Politics and Economics.

Brookes, G., & Barfoot, P. (2006). *GM crops: The first ten years. Global socio-economic and environmental impacts* (pp. 1–116. Available at http://www.isaaa.org/resources/publications/briefs/36/download/isaaa-brief-36-2006.pdf. Retrieved on July 10, 2007). PG Economics UK Ltd.

Budget Track. (2004). *Response to Union Budget, 2003–04: Marginalised matters.* Delhi, India: Center for Budget and Governance Accountability.

Chowkidar, A. (2006). Interview, Chowkidar Atmaram, YWCA Hostel, Nagpur, Maharashtra.

CSE. (2006). Background paper for Roundtable on the Fabric of cotton: seeds, farmers and textiles: What should be India's cotton agenda? Jointly organized by the National Academy of Agricultural Sciences, the National Commission of Farmers and the Center for Science and Environment, July 3, 2006.

FICCI-ICAR. (2005). Agricultural summit 2005: Reforms for raising farm income. Available at http://agricoop.nic.in/AgriSummit/AgriSummit05.PDF. Retreived on July 10, 2007.

11th Five Year Plan. (2007). *Planning commission, Government of India.* Available at http:// www.ifpri.org/sites/default/files/publications/ifpridp00808.pdf. Delhi, India: Oxford University Press.

Ford Foundation. (1959). *Report on India's food crisis and steps to meet it.* New Delhi, India: Ministry of Food, Agriculture and Community Development.

Frankel, F. (1971). *India's green revolution: Economic gains and political costs.* Princeton, NJ: Princeton University Press.

Frankel, F. (2005). *India's political economy 1947–2004: The gradual revolution.* New Delhi, India: Oxford University Press.

Griffin, K. (1974). *Political economy of agrarian change: An essay on the green revolution.* Cambridge, MA: Harvard University Press.

Gruere, G., Mehta Bhatt, P., & Sengupta, D. (2008). Bt Cotton-farmers suicides in India. IFPRI: Washington DC. Available at http://www.ifpri.org/publication/bt-cotton-and-farmer-suicides-india

Hardikar, J. (2006). Loan after loan devastates farmers in Vidharbha. Available at http:// www.indiatogether.org/2006/jan/agr-landloans.htm. Retreived on July 10, 2007.

Herring, R. (1977). Land tenure and credit-capital tenure in contemporary India. In: R. E. Frykenberg (Ed.), *Land Tenure and Peasant in South Asia.* Delhi, India: Orient Longman.

Herring, R. (2005a). Miracle seeds, suicide seeds and the poor, GMOs, NGOs, Farmers and the State. In: R. Ray & M. Katzenstein (Eds), *Social movements in India-poverty, power and politics.* Lanham, MD: Rowman and Littlefield Publishers.

Herring, R. (2005b). *Miracle seeds, suicide seeds and the poor.* Unpublished.

Herring, R. (2006). "Understanding the BT cotton maze", Interview on India together. Available at http://www.indiatogether.org/2006/jun/ivw-herring.htm. Retrieved on July 10, 2007.

Hindu Business Line. (2006). Rs 3750 core relief for six Vidharbha Districts. Available at http:// www.thehindubusinessline.com/2006/07/02/stories/2006070202980300.htm. Retrieved on June 29, 2007.

ICRISAT-ISAAA. (2006). Genes are gems. Available at http://www.icrisat.org/Publications/ Genes_Gems.htm. Retrieved on July 10, 2007.

Indira Gandhi Institute of Development Research. (IGIDR). (2006). *Background papers: Suicide of farmers in Maharashtra.* Mumbai, India: Indira Ghandi Institute of Development Research.

ISAAA. (2005). Three years of BT cotton. *Outlook on Agriculture, 34*(4)Available at http://www.biospectrumindia.com/content/BioBusiness/10503092.asp. Retrieved on July 10, 2007.

ISAAA. (2006). India shows threefold increase in acreage of BT cotton. Available at http://www. biospectrumindia.com/content/BioBusiness/10602091.asp. Retrieved on July 10, 2007.

Jaywandhia, V. (2006). Interview, Vijai Jaywandhia, Shetkari Sangathana, Wardha, Maharashtra.

Klapper, B. (2007). US, Brazil wrangle about farm subsidies. Available at http://www.
   globalpolicy.org/socecon/trade/subsidies/2007/0619usbrazil.htm. Retrieved on July 11.
LBS. (1964). *Increased production-only solution.* Selected Speeches of Lal Bahadur Shastri, June
   11, 1961–Jan 10, 1986. Publications Division, Information and Broadcasting Ministry,
   New Delhi, India.
Lipton, M. (2007). Plant breeding and poverty: Can transgenic seeds replicate the Green
   Revolution as a source of gains for the poor? *Journal of Development Studies, 43*(1), 31–62.
Mahajan, P. (2006). Interview, Pramod Mahajan, Organic Farmer, Wardha, Maharashtra.
Ministry of Food and Agriculture. (1966). *Report of the Foodgrain policy committee.*
   Delhi, India: Ministry of Food and Agriculture.
Mishra, S. (2006). Farmers suicides in Maharashtra. *Economic and Political Weekly, XLI*(16),
   1538–1545.
Monsanto website. (2007). Available at http://www.monsantoindia.com/monsanto/layout/
   default.asp. Retrieved on July 10.
NCF. (2006). *Series of reports.* Available at http://krishakayog.gov.in/. Delhi, India: National
   Commission of Farmers.
Oxfam. (2002). Stop the dumping. How EU subsidies are damaging livelihoods in the
   developing world. Available at http://www.globalpolicy.org/socecon/trade/subsidies/
   2002/10stopdumping.pdf. Retrieved on July 10, 2007.
Oxfam. (2006a). US must reform agricultural subsidy program. Available at http://www.oxfam.
   org/en/news/pressreleases2006/pr060901_wto_cotton_subsidies. Retrieved on July 10, 2007.
Oxfam. (2006b). Cultivating poverty: The impact of US cotton subsidies on Africa. Avail-
   able at http://www.oxfam.org.uk/what_we_do/issues/trade/downloads/bp30_cotton.pdf.
   Retrieved on August 29, 2006.
Patnaik, U. (2003). Global capitalism, deflation and agrarian crisis in developing countries.
   Journal of Agrarian Change, 3(1–2), 33–66.
Pearse, A. (1980). *Seeds of plenty, seeds of want: Social implications of the green revolution.*
   Oxford, UK: Clarendon Press and Oxford University Press.
Planning Commission. (2006). *Report of the fact finding team in Vidharbha. Regional disparieties
   and rural distress in Vidharbha with particular reference to Vidharbha* (Available at:
   http://planningcommission.nic.in/reports/genrep/rep_vidarbha.pdf). Delhi: Planning
   Commission.
Qaim, M., & Zilberman, D. (2003). Yield effects of genetically modified crops in developing
   countries. *Science, 299,* 5608.
Qaim, M., Subramanian, A., Naik, G., & Zilberman, D. (2006). Adoption of Bt cotton and
   impact variability: Insights from India. *Review of Agricultural Economics, 28*(1), 48–58.
   Available at http://www.botanischergarten.ch/Cotton/Quaim-Economic-Cotton-India-
   2006.pdf. Retrieved on July 10, 2007.
Rai, M. (2005). *Search for new genes essential to revitalize Indian agriculture.* Speech at the BP Pal
   lecture. Available at http://www.icar.org.in/pr/300505.htm. Retrieved on July 10, 2007.
Sahai, S., & Rehman, S. (2004). Fields swamped with Bt variants. *EPW Commentary,* July, 2004.
Sandeep, L. (2006). Interview, Sandeep, Reporter, Lokmat, Vidharbha, Maharashtra, July, 2006.
Sainath, P. (2006a). Creative solutions – sarkari style. Available at http://www.indiatogether.
   org/2006/feb/psa-sarkari.htm. Retrieved on July 10, 2007.
Sainath, S. (2006b). Politics of packages, packaging of the politics. Available at http://
   www.indiatogether.org/2006/jul/psa-package.htm

Sethi, N. (2006). Vidharba cotton farmers hit by state failure. *Down to Earth*, *14*(20060001). Available at http://www.indiaenvironmentportal.org.in/content/long-yarn. Retrieved on November 4, 2009.

Shiva, V. (1992). *The violence of the green revolution: Third world agriculture, ecology and politics*. London, UK: Zed Books.

Shiva, V. (2000). *Seeds of suicide: The ecological and human costs of globalization of agriculture*. Delhi, India: RFSTE.

Shiva, V. (2006). The Indian seed act and the patent act. Available at http://www.zmag.org/content/showarticle.cfm?ItemID = 7249. Retrieved on July 10, 2007.

Shiva, V., & Jafri, A. (2006). GMOs have failed. Available at http://www.mindfully.org/GE/2003/India-GMO-Failure-Shiva31may03.htm. Retrieved on July 10, 2007.

Sibal, K. (2005). Speech by Kapil Sibal, Minister of Science and Technology, India. April 9, 2005, Chicago. Available at http://www.financialexpress.com/fe_full_story.php?content_id=123248. Retrieved on July 10, 2007.

Singh, H. (2001). *Green revolution reconsidered: The rural world of contemporary Punjab*. New Delhi, India: Oxford University Press.

Singh, R. B. (2008). Interview, National Commission of Farmers, Delhi, India, July.

Suri, K. C. (2006). Political economy of agrarian distress. *Economic and Political Weekly*, *41*(16), Sameeksha Trust, Mumbai, India.

Swaminathan, M. S. (2006). Center for Science and Environment – National Commission of Farmers. The Fabric of Cotton: Seeds, Farmers and Textiles: What should be India's Cotton Agenda? Background Paper, Conference jointly organized by the National Academy of Agricultural Sciences, the National Commission of Farmers and the Center for Science and Environment, Delhi: National Academy of Agricultural Sciences.

Talatule, S. (2006). Interview, Sunil Talatule, Ginner, Wardha, Maharashtra.

Tilman. (2006). The greening of the green revolution. *Nature*, *396*, 211–212.

TISS. (2006). *Causes of farmer's suicides in Maharashtra: An enquiry*. Available at http://www.tiss.edu/Causes%20of%20Farmer%20Suicides%20in%20Maharashtra.pdf. Retrieved on July 10, 2007. March 15, 2005. Mumbai: Tata Institute of Social Sciences.

Tiwari, K. (2006). Vidharba Crisis. Available at http://vidarbhacrisis.blogspot.com/2007/12/vidarbha-farm-relief-package-2007.html. Retrieved on August 25, 2008.

USDA. (2006). Growth prospects for India's cotton and textile industry. Available at http://www.ers.usda.gov/publications/cws/jun05/cws05d01/cws05d01.pdf

Wagadhe, S. (2006). Interview, Shyam Wagadhe, Farmer, Wardha, Maharashtra, 2006.

World Bank Country Report. (2006). Available at http://www.worldbank.org.in/WBSITE/EXTERNAL/COUNTRIES/SOUTHASIAEXT/INDIAEXTN/0.contentMDK:20770935~pagePK:141137~piPK:141127~theSitePK:295584,00.html

Asmita Bhardwaj recently completed her doctorate at Cornell University. She can be reached by email at ab345@cornell.edu

HERITAGE TOURISM: A MECHANISM TO FACILITATE THE PRESERVATION OF BLACK FAMILY FARMS

Stephanie Freeman and Dorceta E. Taylor

ABSTRACT

Purpose – *The purpose of this chapter is to explore the viability of heritage tourism as an alternative and/or supplementary economic mechanism to help black farmers retain their lands.*

Design/methodology/approach – *In this case study, a family-owned farm in Virginia was examined to determine why and how people used this black-owned farm to share heritage tourism activities, experiences, and recreational activities. Visitors to the black-owned farm were asked to complete a survey designed to measure various tourism constructs. A total of a 119 surveys were collected from three user groups: a motorcycle recreational group, a correctional officers family day, and horse riders in a Pony Express.*

Findings – *The results demonstrated there was a significant interest in black heritage tourism (BHT) among survey participants. Furthermore, the results suggest that BHT may be a viable supplement to agricultural production for some black farmers.*

Environment and Social Justice: An International Perspective
Research in Social Problems and Public Policy, Volume 18, 261–285
Copyright © 2010 by Emerald Group Publishing Limited
All rights of reproduction in any form reserved
ISSN: 0196-1152/doi:10.1108/S0196-1152(2010)0000018011

Originality/value – This is one of the first chapters to examine the role heritage tourism can play in helping to prevent land loss among black farmers. It will help to stimulate more examination of the possibilities of expanding this genre of tourism in rural areas.

INTRODUCTION

This chapter explores whether black heritage tourism (BHT) is a viable mechanism to help black farmers retain land. This is important because black family farms are disappearing at a rapid rate. The reasons for this are many – discrimination, indebtedness, unfair laws and policies, and migration patterns. In addition, young people have moved away from farms in pursuit of more exciting careers elsewhere (Daniel, 1972; Litwack, 1998; Mcgee & Boone, 1979). As the number of black farmers decrease nationwide, that decline is accompanied by the loss of culture, heritage, legacy, education, and agricultural practices. This being the case, it is urgent that we gain a better understanding of the status of black farmers. We posit that BHT is one option that could help black farmers preserve and retain their ties to their land, culture, and farming heritage. This study examines whether heritage tourism can be an alternative or supplementary income stream that could help to preserve black family farms.

Historically blacks have had difficulty acquiring and holding on to land. Owning arable land was significantly more challenging. Even when blacks owned land, the land was not always suitable for agricultural production (Beauford, 1986; Daniel, 1972; Litwack, 1998; Mcgee & Boone, 1979; Oshinsky, 1996). Immediately after emancipation, blacks managed to obtain some land. Estimates are that non-white farmers owned an estimated three million acres in 1875, eight million in 1890, and 12 million by 1900. Blacks constituted 13 percent of the farmers nationwide that year. Black rural land ownership reached approximately 15.8 million acres in 1920 (Aphteker, 1970; Gilbert, Sharp, & Felin, 2001, 2002a). The number of black farmers and acreage farmed peaked in 1920 when there were 925,708 blacks farming 41,432,182 acres of land. At the time blacks constituted 14.3 percent of the farmers nationwide. The number of black farmers declined throughout the twentieth century hitting an all-time low in 1997 when there were 18,451 black farmers farming 2,384,686 million acres. Black farmers constituted only 1 percent of the farmers nationwide. Since then, there has been an increase in the number of black farmers and acreage farmed. In 2007 there were 30,599 black farmers farming a total of 3,182,313 acres. Blacks comprised 1.4 percent of the farmers in 2007 (Taylor, forthcoming; U.S. Department of Agriculture, 1999, 2009; U.S. Census Bureau, 1922).

The Great Northern Migration

Internal migration patterns played a role in the decline of black farming. Most notably, the Great Northern Migration resulted in a dramatic shift in the black population from the South to the North. Several factors motivated Southern blacks to move to the North triggering in one of the largest internal migrations in the U.S. history. Segregationist Jim Crow laws and the rise in lynching, the devastating effects of the boll weevil on cotton crops, the mechanization of cotton growing, increased demand for industrial labor in the North during World War I, the opportunity to own land, improved quality of life, and greater access to education were factors that contributed to the migration. Most southern blacks were sharecroppers. Sharecropping – a system of tenant farming put in place shortly after the Civil War – became increasingly difficult as plantation owners devised schemes wherein most or all of what sharecroppers produced ended up going to the landowners, not the people working the land. This led to growing indebtedness among blacks. To make matters worse, some planters forced the sharecroppers off the land during the Great Depression (Frey, 1998; Lemann, 1991; Taylor, forthcoming).

The migration actually began in the 1870s. Between 1870 and 1910, approximately 535,000 blacks left the South for the North. In 1910 approximately 91 percent of the nation's 9.8 million blacks still lived in the South – roughly 27 percent of them lived in cities. After 1910, the migration accelerated and over the next four decades approximately 3.5 million blacks left the South. By 1966 the black population of the South had declined by 55 percent and approximately 69 percent of blacks (14.8 million) lived in metropolitan areas in northern and western states. Estimates are that between 1916 and 1970, approximately 7 million blacks left the South (McGee & Boone, 1979; Brown, 1998; Collins, 1997; Grossman, 1989, 2005; Taylor, forthcoming).

The Reverse Migration
Since the 1970s, blacks have reversed the migration trends. Northern blacks are returning to the South in what has been termed a reverse or second

migration. Many of the migrants, a majority of whom are college educated, seek economic opportunities in the Southern economy. Some want to escape deteriorating conditions in Northern cities. Others return to retire, care for aging relatives, reclaim family property, or to seek out a better quality of life than can be found in the North (Phillips, 1986; McGee & Boone, 1979). This trend is evident in the Census. In the 1970s the black population in the South increased by 1.9 million, it increased by 1.7 million in the 1980s and by 3.1 million during the 1990s (U.S. Census Bureau, 1980, 1990, 2000; Harrison, 2001).

Other Factors Contributing to Black Land Loss

Despite the return of blacks to the South, black farmers and landowners continued to face difficulties in trying to retain their land. Demographic factors play a role. As a group black farmers are aging and they are not being replaced by younger blacks. In 1997 the average age of the black farmer was 58.5 years. A decade later the average age has crept up to 60.3 years. Only 0.5 percent of the black farmers in 2007 were younger than 25 years old (U.S. Department of Agriculture, 1999, 2009; Taylor, forthcoming).

Today blacks continue to lose farmland because of inflation, the inability to receive credit, bankruptcy, foreclosures, and rising operational costs (Beauford, 1986). Blacks frequently lose land through tax sales. Tax sales occur when tax delinquent property are seized and auctioned off by municipalities. The land titles are transferred to a third party who pays off the tax debt. Usually blacks cannot afford to participate in this process and lose land as a result (Browne, 1973).

Blacks also lose land because of title disputes and partition sales involving heirs' property. Heirs' property refers to property that is passed on to multiple family members because the landowner dies without leaving a will. Under such conditions, state intestacy laws come into effect, and a broad class of people can be considered heirs to the property. Heirs' property is often divided up and many of the disputes end up in court. If the land is put up for sale, developers can easily outbid family members who might want to retain the land. If the land is partitioned, individual portions are often too small to maintain viable farms (Mitchell, 2001, 2005; Taylor, forthcoming).

Discrimination in Federal Farm Programs
By the early 1990s, black farmers were in a precarious position as they faced systematic discrimination in programs run by the U.S. Department of

Agriculture (USDA). For years black farmers were routinely denied loans, disaster relief, and other forms of aid. It also took longer to process loan applications for black farmers than it did for white farmers. Although farmers who are discriminated against can file a complaint with the USDA's Office of Civil Rights – the office was closed in 1983. A 1997 investigation into the agency's handling of black farmers' complaints showed that though black farmers continued to file complaints with the agency, these were discarded or held at the agency and not processed. Initially 401 black farmers filed a class action lawsuit against the USDA in 1997; thousands more black farmers were allowed to join the suit later. A consent decree was signed between the parties in 1999. By then a total of 22,721 black farmers were a part of the class action. Roughly 69 percent of the claims filed have been approved. The typical award to farmers has been $50,000 in cash payments, plus debt relief from taxes. As of 2009 just over $1 billion has been paid out in awards and tax relief under the settlement agreement. There is still some controversy over this case as there are still 73,820 people who filed claims late and have not been included in the class action (*Pigford, et al. v. Glickman*, 1998; *Pigford v. Glickman* and *Brewington v. Glickman*, 1999; Office of the Monitor, 2009; Taylor, forthcoming).

BLACK HERITAGE TOURISM AND THE POTENTIAL TO HELP PRESERVE BLACK FAMILY FARMS

Gilbert, Wood, and Sharp (2002b) found that most black farmers today depend principally on off-farm income. As a result, it is not farfetched to consider tourism as a feasible income stream. Smith Park, a black family-owned farm in Virginia, was used as a case study to examine what role, if any, BHT could play in preserving such farms. The study examined the beliefs, attitudes, and behaviors of visitors to the farm in an effort to understand how users perceived and related to BHT. Another goal was to assess the visitors' interest in black history, heritage, and the protection of black farmers and land owners' interests.

Historically tourists have been a select group who can afford the cost and time of traveling and sightseeing. Indeed tourism has become commonplace, and it now takes many forms that include rural, agricultural, nature, adventure, and heritage tourism, to name a few. Rural places have traditionally been associated with remoteness, agriculture, and sparsely populated and dispersed settlements (Page & Getz, 1997). According to Keane, Briassoulis, and van der Straaten (1992), there are various terms used to describe tourism activity in rural areas that include agriculture, farming, rural, and "soft" tourism. Keane cautions against using blanket labels such as "rural tourism" to refer to all tourism activities that occur in rural areas (Keane et al., 1992; Page & Getz, 1997).

Agriculture or farm tourism is an activity that can contribute to agricultural sustainability through diversification of its economic base, provision of educational opportunities for tourists, and engendering of greater community cohesion (Colton & Bissix, 2005). Another variant of rural tourism that is relevant is nature-based tourism. Norris (1994) defines nature-based tourism as the non-consumptive enjoyment of natural habitats, whereas Whitlock, Van Romer, and Becker (1991) define it as any tourism that pertains to and relies on the outdoors. This chapter is concerned with a special subset of tourism, cultural heritage tourism. Cultural tourism is a special-interest item or holiday vacation essentially motivated by interests and activities such as trips and visits to historical sites, monuments, museums, galleries, artistic performances, and festivals, as well as to communities with distinctive lifestyles.

According to *The Network Journal of Black Professionals and Small Business Magazine* (2009), African-American travelers generate over $45 billion annually in tourism revenues, and they have a spending power of $798 billion annually; this is projected to grow to $1.1 trillion by 2011. The number of black travelers increased by 4 percent between 2000 and 2002, and heritage tourism is a big driver of this increase. Nationwide travel increased by 2 percent. Heritage tourism is second only to nature-based tourism in revenues generated Walker (2006).

There are many examples of successful BHT projects for example the Farish Street Historic District in Jackson, Mississippi, and the Kentucky African American Heritage Center in Louisville, Kentucky. In the case of the Farish Street Historic District, the community showcased their musical heritage (blues, gospel, and jazz) by focusing on churches, funeral homes, and examples of vernacular architecture to highlight unique cultural aspects of Jackson. In contrast, the Kentucky African American Heritage Center grew out of a public–private partnership that included $1.5 million in State funds and a Congressional grant of nearly $1 billion (Garfield, 1999).

Other models of black heritage sites exist. In the U.S. Virgin Islands preservation districts featuring historic architecture, churches, cemeteries, market places, sites of slave revolts, forts, and homes have been developed successfully, and local preservationists are seeking to expand them. The districts located in Charlotte Amalie (St. Thomas) and Christiansted and Frederiksted (St. Croix) attract millions of visitors annually (United States Virgin Islands Tourist Board, 2009). The Penn School National Historic Landmark District also known as Penn Center is located on St. Helena Island, South Carolina, offers an example of a rural site that uses black heritage as the cornerstone of its farm-based preservation efforts. The Penn Center preserves its land, waterfront, trails, the Gullah language spoken by slaves, crops planted by them, the culture of the Gullah people, its historic school house built by freed slaves, museum, art, as well as its famed conference center and dorms that served as the meeting place for civil rights activists. The Penn Center caters to visitors from all over the country (Penn School National Historic Landmark District, 2009). The 40-acre Freewoods Farm, located in Burgess (Myrtle Beach) South Carolina, replicates life on a nineteenth-century animal-powered African-American farm. Freewoods has a museum, wetlands preserve, and a main street (Freewoods Farm, 2009). There are many more rural black heritage sites that can also be found among the vast network of Underground Railroad sites being developed by the National Park Service. Some such as the Selma-Montgomery Trail commemorating the historic civil rights march are historic trails rather than a single fixed site (National Park Service, 2009).

SMITH FAMILY PARK

The Smith Family Farm Park is located in Dinwiddie County, Virginia. The site is 20 minutes from Petersburg, Virginia, and 45 minutes from Richmond, Virginia, in a heavily traveled and active tourism region. The Smith family has owned their 500-acre farm for three generations. The farm is above-average size for the county – the average farm in the county is 211 acres. The farm boasts forests, ponds, a swamp, farmland, and pasture. The five Smith brothers grow grain, raise cattle, and fish in aquaculture ponds, while utilizing a 41-acre recreational park site for tourism. The brothers share responsibility for operating the park and the farm. According to the *2007 Census of Agriculture*, this is one of only 51 black-owned farms in Dinwiddie County. Black-owned farms make up approximately 13.6 percent of all farms in the county. Five years earlier, the 52 black-operated farms in the county constituted 14.4 percent of the total (U.S. Department of Agriculture, 2004, 2009; Freeman, 2007).

Smith Park is the only black-owned park in the county; the majority of its users are black. The land for the park was acquired in the early 1970s and the construction of the park officially began in 1975. The family regularly hosts weekend events – primarily between May and October – that require advance planning and reservations. The park contains a 14-acre catfish pond, covered pavilions, all terrain vehicle trails, horse trails, a basketball court, a volleyball court, recreational vehicle hookups, restroom facilities, vending machines, and horses (Freeman, 2007).

METHODOLOGY

The study examined the ways in which the farm was being used and what factors influenced its use. Three user groups (bikers, horseback riders, and correctional officers) completed surveys in summer 2006. The survey was designed to measure users' perceptions and attitudes toward the farm and BHT. The questions used in this study were adopted from the Regional Resources Development Institute on Travel and Nature (1991). A combination of close-ended questions using a five-point Likert scale and open-ended questions were used on the survey. In the case of couples or families, only one member of each was asked to complete the survey. Some participants requested that the survey be read aloud to them, whereas others preferred to complete it on their own.

RESULTS

The recreational motorcyclists consisted of bikers from several southeastern clubs and their families. These visitors ranged in age from 23 to 65 years. They organized competitions for cash prizes and hired a disc jockey for entertainment. There were approximately 150 people participating in the gathering at which the survey was administered; 39 surveys were completed. A group of correctional officers who worked at a Virginia prison also used Smith Park for a family celebration. The correctional officers ranged in age from 19 to 65 years old. Food was provided and prizes were awarded to adults and children for various competitions. There were approximately 75 people in attendance at this gathering; 40 surveys were returned (one per family). The horse riders participated in a Pony Express relay around the horse trail where prizes were awarded. They ranged in age from 19 to 65 years old. There were approximately 100 people in attendance; 40 surveys were completed. Other groups use the park for events such as annual church picnics, gospel events and revivals, family reunions, school outings, and camping trips.

Demographic Characteristics

In all a total of 119 surveys were collected and analyzed. As Table 1 shows, 52.9 percent of the respondents were female and 41.2 percent were male. Seven respondents (5.9 percent of the sample) did not identify their gender. Because of the small sample size, these respondents were retained in the sample and classified as "gender unknown." A similar procedure was used for the five respondents who did not identify their age and the nine who did not indicate their family size.

There were 39 motorcyclists – 38.5 percent of them were male, 46.2 percent were female, and 15.4 did not specify their gender. Of the 40 correctional officers, 35 percent were male and 65 percent female. Half of the

Table 1. Demographic Characteristics of User Groups.

Demographic Characteristics	Total (n = 119)	Total Sample Percent	Percent of User Groups					
			Motorcyclists (n = 39)		Correctional officers (n = 40)		Horseback riders (n = 40)	
			Number	Percent	Number	Percent	Number	Percent
Gender								
Male	49	41.2	15	38.5	14	35.0	20	50.0
Female	63	52.9	18	46.2	26	65.0	19	47.5
Gender unknown	7	5.9	6	15.4	0	0	1	2.5
Age group								
23–34 years	27	22.7	7	17.9	14	35.0	6	15.0
35–54 years	65	54.6	23	59.0	22	55.0	20	50.0
55 years and over	22	18.5	6	15.4	4	10.0	12	30.0
Age unknown	5	4.2	3	7.7	0	0	2	5.0
Educational attainment								
High school or less	56	47.1	18	46.2	19	47.5	19	47.5
College or grad school	63	52.9	21	53.8	21	52.5	21	52.5
Family type								
Single	19	16.0	6	15.4	7	17.5	6	15.0
Couple	36	30.3	12	30.8	11	27.5	13	32.5
Family of 3–7 members	55	46.2	15	38.5	21	52.5	19	47.5
Family size unknown	9	7.6	6	15.4	1	2.5	2	5.0

40 horseback riders were male, another 47.5 percent were female and 21.5 percent did not indicate their gender. More than half of the respondents (54.6 percent) were between the ages of 35 and 54 years; more than half of all three user groups were in this age range. Although 47.1 percent of the respondents had less than a college education, 52.9 percent did. The educational attainment of each user group was very similar. Singles comprised 16 percent of the users, couples accounted for 30.3 percent of the visitors, whereas families of 3 or more people constituted 46.2 percent of the park visitors. The majority of the visitors to Smith Park stay for one day or less. Most also travel to the park in a day or less.

Frequency of Participation in Environmental Activities

Respondents were asked to say how frequently they participated in six environmental activities related to wildlife, bird watching, fishing, viewing nature, camping, and hiking. Respondents rated the frequency with which they participated in these activities on a five-point Likert scale with one being very infrequent and five being very frequent. A means comparison analysis was conducted. Table 2 shows the total sample mean as well as the means for each of the demographic variables. Overall, respondents reported participating in all the activities at an above-average (greater than a mean of 3.0) rate. Viewing nature had the highest mean score of 4.14, whereas hiking had the lowest mean of 3.22. Horseback riders were much more likely to report interactions with wildlife than the other two user groups, whereas motorcyclists were much more likely to report participating in fishing and camping than other visitors. Males were much more likely to report interacting with wildlife and participating in fishing and camping than females.

Farm Programming Desired

Respondents were asked to indicate what kinds of programming they would like to see undertaken at the farm. Table 3 provides the number and percent of respondents indicating they would like to see 12 types of activities. By far the most popular type of activity desired is hunting; 48.7% of the visitors would like to hunt. There were significant variations in the sample vis-à-vis hunting. Although a third of motorcyclists and 40 percent

Table 2. The Frequency with Which Respondents Participate in Environmental Activities.

Demographic Characteristics	Number of Participants and Means											
	Wildlife		Birdwatching		Fishing		View nature		Camping		Hiking	
	Number	Mean	Number	Mean	Number	Mean	Number	Mean	Number	Mean	Number	Mean
Total sample	86	3.59	90	3.38	92	3.72	100	4.14	71	3.61	98	3.22
User groups												
Motorcyclists	33	3.39	33	3.18	32	3.47	36	4.17	27	3.81	31	3.13
Correctional officers	32	3.59	34	3.47	37	3.95	34	4.24	24	3.42	37	3.70
Horseback riders	21	3.90	23	3.52	23	3.70	30	4.00	20	3.55	30	2.73
Gender												
Male	36	4.00	36	3.36	35	3.80	41	4.15	29	3.76	40	3.18
Female	45	3.20	49	3.33	52	3.65	54	4.15	37	3.43	54	3.31
Gender unknown	5	4.20	5	4.00	5	3.80	5	4.00	5	4.00	4	2.50
Age group												
19–34 years	24	3.88	23	3.96	23	4.00	25	4.20	21	3.81	24	3.54
35–4 years	48	3.33	52	3.10	52	3.60	58	4.14	39	3.36	59	3.19
55 years and over	11	3.73	12	3.25	14	3.50	14	3.86	8	3.75	13	3.15
Age unknown	3	5.00	3	4.33	3	4.67	3	5.00	3	5.00	2	1.00
Educational attainment												
High school or less	38	3.76	37	3.59	39	3.85	44	4.25	30	3.53	44	3.07
College or grad school	48	3.46	53	3.23	53	3.62	56	4.05	41	3.66	54	3.35
Family type												
Single	15	3.60	16	3.56	17	3.94	16	4.06	13	3.54	17	3.65
Couple	23	3.78	24	3.54	27	4.00	30	4.23	18	4.06	28	2.96
Family of 3–7 members	43	3.44	45	3.20	44	3.55	47	4.15	35	3.34	49	3.31
Family size unknown	5	4.00	5	3.60	4	2.75	7	3.86	5	4.00	4	2.25

Table 3. Number and Percent of Respondents Wishing to See Farm Programming.

Demographic Characteristics	Hunting		Historical Buildings		Hay Rides		Pick Your Own Produce		Farm Vacation		Farm Tours		Retail Market		Farmer's Market		On-site Food Service		Agricultural Fair		Horseback Trips		Hands-On Demonstrations	
	Number	Percent	Number	Percent	Number	Percent	Number	Percent	Number	Percent	Number	Percent	Number	Percent	Number	Percent	Number	Percent	Number	Percent	Number	Percent	Number	Percent
Total sample	58	48.7	39	32.8	25	21.0	20	16.8	19	16.0	17	14.3	14	11.8	14	11.8	13	10.9	10	8.4	10	8.4	10	8.4
User groups																								
Motorcyclists	13	33.3	5	12.8	7	17.9	8	20.5	3	7.7	6	15.4	5	12.8	2	5.1	3	7.7	4	10.3	4	10.3	2	5.1
Correctional officers	16	40.0	13	32.5	6	15.0	5	12.5	8	20.0	6	15.0	4	10.0	4	10.0	3	7.5	1	2.5	3	7.5	4	10.0
Horseback riders	29	72.5	21	52.5	12	30.0	7	17.5	8	20.0	5	12.5	5	12.5	8	20.0	7	17.5	5	12.5	3	7.5	4	10.0
Gender																								
Male	31	63.3	16	32.7	14	28.6	6	12.2	9	18.4	8	16.3	5	10.2	6	12.2	6	12.2	3	6.1	6	12.2	2	4.1
Female	25	39.7	23	36.5	10	15.9	14	22.2	10	15.9	9	14.3	8	12.7	8	12.7	7	11.1	6	9.5	4	6.3	8	12.7
Gender unknown	2	28.6			1	14.3							1	14.3					1	14.3				
Age group																								
19–34 years	16	59.3	8	29.6	2	7.4	4	14.8	6	22.2	4	14.8	3	11.1	5	18.5	3	11.1	3	11.1	2	7.4	3	11.1
35–54 years	31	47.7	24	36.9	14	21.5	11	16.9	10	15.4	10	15.4	7	10.8	6	9.2	5	7.7	7	10.8	6	9.2	5	7.7
55 years and over	10	45.5	6	27.3	8	36.4	4	18.2	3	13.6	3	13.6	3	13.6	3	13.6	5	22.7			2	9.1	2	9.1
Age unknown	1	20.0	1	20.0	1	20.0	1	20.0					1	20.0										
Educational attainment																								
High school or less	25	44.6	17	30.4	15	28.8	11	19.6	7	12.5	3	5.4	5	10.7	6	10.7	6	10.7	4	7.1	2	3.6	3	5.4
College or grad school	33	52.4	22	34.9	10	15.9	9	14.3	12	19.0	14	22.2	8	12.7	8	12.7	7	11.1	6	9.5	8	12.7	7	11.1
Family type																								
Single	9	47.4	5	26.3	6	31.6	3	15.8	6	31.6	4	14.8	2	10.5	3	15.8	2	10.5			2	10.5	2	10.5
Couple	18	50.0	13	36.1	11	30.6	7	19.4	6	16.7	10	15.4	6	16.7	4	11.1	5	13.9	5	13.9	5	13.9	3	8.3
Family of 3–7 members	31	56.4	21	38.2	7	12.7	9	16.4	7	12.7	3	13.6	6	10.9	6	10.9	6	10.9	5	9.1	3	5.5	5	9.1
Family size unknown					1	11.1	1	11.1							1	11.1								

of the correctional officers desired hunting opportunities, 72.5 percent of the horseback riders wanted to hunt. Gender and age were also significantly related to hunting. Males were far more likely to indicate hunting than females; 63.3 percent of males and 39.7 percent of females wished to see hunting. There was an inverse relationship with age, that is, the younger the respondents the more likely they were to indicate they would like to see hunting.

Almost a third of the participants (32.8 percent) wished to see historical buildings incorporated into the site. The differences between the three user groups were significant – 52.5 percent of horseback riders and 32.5 percent of the correctional officers indicated they were interested in historical buildings. In comparison, only 12.8 percent of the motorcyclists indicated such interest.

Twenty-one percent of the sample wished for hay rides. The horseback riders were about twice as likely as the other two user groups to desire hay rides. Males (28.6 percent) were also much more likely than females (15.9 percent) to want hay rides. Respondents who were under the age of 35 were also far less likely than older respondents to desire hay rides. Although 12.7 percent of families of three or more desired hay rides, more than 30 percent of singles and couples wished to see it.

Picking produce at the farm was much more popular among women than men; 22.2 percent of women and 12.2 percent of males indicated they wished to see this activity. Having a farm vacation was least popular among motorcyclists. Although 20 percent of the correctional officers and horseback riders wished to see farm vacations, only 7.7 percent of the motorcyclists desired this activity. Overall, 14.3 percent of the sample wished to see farm tours. Educational attainment was significant. College-educated respondents were much more likely to wish to see this activity – 22.2 percent of college-educated visitors and 5.4 percent of the respondents with less than a college education wished for farm tours.

Respondents also wished to see a retail market (11.8 percent), farmers market (11.8 percent), on-site food service (10.9 percent), agricultural fair (8.4 percent), horseback trips (8.4 percent), and hands-on demonstrations (8.4 percent). In addition to the 12 activities covered in Table 3, study participants also indicated they would like to see a petting zoo (7.6 percent), pumpkin patch (5.9 percent), winery (5.9 percent), corn maze (5.1 percent), and a Christmas tree farm (5.1 percent).

Attitudes toward Black Heritage Tourism

For the purposes of this study, five scales were developed to examine how respondents felt about BHT. The scales examined visitors' attitudes toward education, black heritage, collective memories, land loss, and ethnic identity. These were seen as critical components of BHT. Study participants were asked to say the extent to which they agreed with statements related to the various components BHT.

Attitudes toward education:

1. Elementary and secondary school students should be taught the history of black Americans in the United States.
2. Black farming techniques should be incorporated into heritage, agriculture, and nature tourism sites.

Attitudes toward BHT:

1. It is interesting to visit agriculture, heritage, or nature tourism sites where black Americans live.
2. For too long blacks have overlooked the richness of their heritage.
3. There is a need for black heritage sites.
4. I am interested in learning more about nature, heritage, and agriculture tourism.
5. I would prefer to visit black heritage, nature, or agriculture tourist sites rather than simply read about them.

Attitudes toward collective memories:

1. I don't like the feeling of being around things that reminds me of the hardships imposed on blacks in the past.
2. The history of slavery in the South is best left forgotten.
3. Slave history should be incorporated into heritage tourism sites.
4. Heritage, agriculture tourism, and nature tourism should be used to preserve black history although they may stand in the way of progress.

Attitudes toward land loss:

1. Spending money to preserve black landowners is a luxury we can afford.
2. We need more laws to protect black landowners.
3. The loss of black historical landmarks is a necessary result of progress.

Table 4. Means for Black Heritage Tourism Factors.

Demographic Characteristics	Students Should Be Taught about Black History	Black Farming Techniques Should Be Incorporated in Heritage Sites	Interested in Visiting Heritage Sites Where Black Americans Live	Blacks Have Overlooked the Richness of Their Heritage for Too Long	There Is a Need for Black Heritage Sites	Interested in Learning More about Nature, Heritage, Agriculture Tourism	Prefer to Visit Black Heritage Sites Than Read about Them	I Don't Want to Be Reminded of the Hardships Blacks Faced	The History of Slavery in the South is Best Left Forgotten	History of Slavery Should Be Incorporated in Heritage Tourism	Heritage, Agriculture, & Nature Tourism Should Be Used to Preserve Black History	Spending Money to Protect Black Land Owners Is a Luxury We Can Afford	We Need More Laws to Protect Black Landowners	Loss of Black Historical Landmarks Is a Necessary Result of Progress	Learning More About Black Heritage Fosters Stronger Ethnic Identity
Total sample	4.39	4.37	4.48	4.34	4.75	2.70	2.25	3.85	2.60	2.16	2.37	4.70	4.38	2.73	4.58
User groups															
Motorcyclists	4.57	4.65	4.56	4.47	4.86	2.74	2.00	3.97	1.85	1.77	1.86	4.74	4.29	1.72	4.57
Correctional officers	4.13	4.23	4.29	4.05	4.58	2.34	2.00	3.82	1.95	2.05	2.08	4.69	4.31	1.78	4.55
Horseback riders	4.51	4.27	4.61	4.51	4.84	3.03	2.73	3.78	3.95	2.67	3.19	4.68	4.54	4.65	4.61
Gender															
Male	4.36	4.26	4.48	4.04	4.70	2.85	2.15	3.65	2.63	2.07	2.20	4.68	4.40	2.83	4.47
Female	4.44	4.44	4.46	4.53	4.77	2.56	2.27	3.98	2.57	2.25	2.51	4.71	4.41	2.72	4.67
Gender unknown	4.60	4.60	4.80	4.80	5.00	2.80	2.80	4.20	2.60	2.00	2.40	4.80	3.80	2.00	4.60
Age group															
19–34 years	4.04	4.30	4.23	4.22	4.52	2.54	2.26	3.78	2.37	2.27	2.59	4.52	4.04	2.77	4.30
35–54 years	4.51	4.32	4.54	4.30	4.81	2.74	2.05	3.98	2.63	2.11	2.24	4.82	4.53	2.52	4.69
55 years and over	4.42	4.53	4.60	4.53	4.84	2.61	2.68	3.50	2.55	1.95	2.33	4.53	4.32	3.22	4.56
Age unknown	5.00	5.00	4.67	5.00	5.00	3.67	3.33	4.00	5.00	3.67	3.33	5.00	4.67	4.00	5.00

Table 4. (*Continued*)

Demographic Characteristics	Students Should Be Taught about Black History	Black Farming Techniques Should Be Incorporated in Heritage Sites	Interested in Visiting Heritage Sites Where Black Americans Live	Blacks Have Overlooked the Richness of Their Heritage for Too Long	There Is a Need for Black Heritage Sites	Interested in Learning More about Nature, Heritage, Agriculture Tourism	Prefer to Visit Black Heritage Sites Than Read about Them	I Don't Want to Be Reminded of the Hardships Blacks Faced	The History of Slavery in the South is Best Left Forgotten	History of Slavery Should Be Incorporated in Heritage Tourism	Heritage, Agriculture, & Nature Tourism Should Be Used to Preserve Black History	Spending Money to Protect Black Land Owners Is a Luxury We Can Afford	We Need More Laws to Protect Black Landowners	Loss of Black Historical Landmarks Is a Necessary Result of Progress	Learning More About Black Heritage Fosters Stronger Ethnic Identity
Educational attainment															
High school or less	4.29	4.45	4.55	4.29	4.73	2.98	2.32	3.80	2.52	2.24	2.48	4.78	4.39	2.78	4.67
College or grad school	4.48	4.30	4.43	4.37	4.77	2.45	2.18	3.90	2.67	2.10	2.28	4.63	4.37	2.69	4.51
Family type															
Single	4.32	4.42	4.42	4.16	4.58	2.50	2.05	3.84	2.53	2.28	2.26	4.74	4.21	2.53	4.63
Couple	4.49	4.37	4.63	4.33	4.80	2.59	2.06	3.82	2.53	1.89	2.00	4.76	4.47	2.79	4.66
Family of 3–7 members	4.40	4.38	4.45	4.44	4.85	2.75	2.35	3.88	2.63	2.27	2.60	4.69	4.42	2.71	4.60
Family size unknown	4.00	4.00	4.14	4.00	4.17	3.50	3.00	3.83	3.00	2.50	2.83	4.33	4.00	3.40	3.83

Attitudes toward ethnic identity:

1. By learning more about their heritage, black Americans develop a stronger ethnic identity.

The responses were arrayed on a five-point Likert scale with 1 being strongly disagree and 5 being strongly agree. The means of the demographic factors were compared. These are displayed in Table 4. Respondents were in strong agreement with eight of the fifteen statements. These statements had a mean of 4.34–4.75. As the table shows, there was strong support for the two education variables. The statement, "Elementary and secondary school students should be taught the history of black Americans in the U.S." had a mean score of 4.39. However, motorcyclists (mean = 4.57) and horseback riders (mean = 4.51) were much more likely to agree with this statement than the correctional officers (mean = 4.13). The gender differences were slight; however, the youngest respondents were much less likely to agree with this statement than respondents 35 and older.

Respondents also showed strong support for the statement, "Black farming techniques should be incorporated into heritage, agriculture and nature tourism sites." The sample mean was 4.37. Motorcyclists had a much higher mean than the other two user groups – while the mean for motorcyclists was 4.65, it was 4.23 for correctional officers and 4.27 for horseback riders. Respondents who were 55 and older were also much more likely than younger respondents to agree with this statement.

There was strong agreement with the first three variables that comprised the BHT index, whereas respondents tended to disagree with or remain neutral on the remaining two. The sample mean for the statement "It is interesting to visit agriculture, heritage or nature tourism sites where black Americans live" was 4.48. Correctional officers were less likely to agree with this statement than the other two user groups. The gender means were virtually identical (4.48 for males and 4.46 for females), but 19- to 34-year olds had much lower means than older respondents. Couples had higher means than other family types. The mean for the statement, "For too long blacks have overlooked the richness of their heritage," was 4.34. Correctional officers were much less likely to agree with this statement than other user groups. Males (mean = 4.04) were also much less likely to agree with this statement than females (mean = 4.53). There is a linear relationship with age – that is, the older the respondent the more likely they were to agree with the statement. There is a similar relationship with family type – the larger the group the more likely they were to agree with the statement.

The statement that got the strongest support with a mean of 4.75 was "There is a need for black heritage sites." Agreement with the statement was strongest among the motorcyclists and horseback riders (4.86 and 4.84, respectively). Although women were only slightly more likely to agree with this statement than men, the older the respondent the more likely they were to agree with it. Respondents over 35 years of age were much more likely to agree with it than younger respondents. Singles were also far less likely to agree with this statement than couples or other family groups. Educational differences were slight.

Respondents were neutral in relation to the statement, "I am interested in learning more about nature, heritage and agriculture tourism." The statement had a mean of 2.70. Fewer respondents might have agreed with this statement because it was phrased as learning about these forms of tourism in general rather than learning specifically about BHT. Respondents tended to disagree with the statement, "I would prefer to visit black heritage, nature or agriculture tourist sites rather than simply read about them." The mean was 2.25.

All four factors on the collective memory index had a mean score of less than 4.0; the mean scores ranged from 2.16 to 3.85. The statement, "I don't like the feeling of being around things that reminds me of the hardships imposed on blacks in the past" had a mean of 3.85. However, females (mean = 3.98) were much more likely to agree with this statement than males (mean = 3.65). Respondents who were 35–54 years old were also much more likely than older or younger respondents to agree with the statement. The statement, "The history of slavery in the South is best left forgotten" had a mean of 2.60. However, horseback riders stand out for their much higher level of agreement with this statement than the other two user groups. Although horseback riders had a mean of 3.95 for this statement, the mean for motorcyclists was 1.85 and 1.95 for correctional officers. Horseback riders were also much more likely to agree with the statement, "Slave history should be incorporated into heritage tourism sites." The sample mean was 2.16; however, the mean for horseback riders was 2.67. In contrast the means for correctional officers was 2.05 and 1.77 for motorcyclists. Females were more likely to agree with this statement than males. There was an inverse relationship with age – the younger the respondent the more likely they were to agree with the statement. The mean for the statement, "Heritage, agriculture tourism and nature tourism should be used to preserve black history although they may stand in the way of progress" was 2.37. Women were more likely to agree with the statement than men; the mean for females was 2.51 while it was 2.20 for males. The youngest respondents were more likely to agree with this statement than older respondents.

There was also very strong agreement with the first two land loss indicators. The statement, "Spending money to preserve black landowners is a luxury we can afford" had a mean of 4.70. The gender differences and the differences between the three user groups were insignificant; however, there were significant age differences. Respondents who were 35–54 were much more likely to agree with this statement (mean = 4.82) than those who were younger (mean = 4.52) or older (mean = 4.53). Those with less than a college education was also more likely to agree with the statement (mean = 4.78) than college-educated respondents (mean = 4.63).

Respondents also agreed with the statement, "We need more laws to protect black landowners." It had a mean of 4.38. As was the case with the previous land loss variable, the differences between the user groups as well as gender were slight. Age, however, was significant. The youngest respondents were much less likely than the others to agree with the statement. Respondents were generally neutral when it came to the statement, "The loss of black historical landmarks is a necessary result of progress." This statement had a mean of 2.73. Although motorcyclists (mean = 1.72) and correctional officers (mean = 1.78) tended to disagree with the statement, horseback riders (mean = 4.65) were in strong agreement with it.

Respondents were in strong agreement with the statement, "By learning more about their heritage black Americans develop a stronger ethnic identity." It had a mean of 4.58. Women were much more likely to feel this way than men. Females had a mean of 4.67, whereas males had a mean of 4.47. The youngest respondents were the least likely to agree with the statement. Respondents 19–34 had a mean of 4.30, those 55 and older had a mean of 4.56, whereas those 35–54 had a mean of 4.69. Respondents with less than a college education were also more likely to agree with the statement than college-educated participants.

Composite Indices
Four composite scores were created to see how respondents varied on the aforementioned attitude indices. The scores of the variables in each of the

Table 5. Means Comparison of Composite Attitude Scores.

Demographic Characteristics	Number of Participants and Means							
	Educational attitude		Black heritage tourism		Collective memory		Land loss	
	Number	Mean	Number	Mean	Number	Mean	Number	Mean
Total sample	111	8.76	105	18.49	107	11.06	108	11.81
User groups								
Motorcyclists	34	9.21	32	18.62	34	9.50	32	10.75
Correctional officers	40	8.35	37	17.22	38	9.89	39	10.74
Horseback riders	37	8.78	36	19.67	35	13.83	37	13.86
Gender								
Male	47	8.62	46	18.22	43	10.79	46	11.89
Female	59	8.83	54	18.56	59	11.24	57	11.86
Gender unknown	5	9.20	5	20.20	5	11.20	5	10.60
Age group								
19–34 years	27	8.33	26	17.65	26	11.04	26	11.27
35–54 years	62	8.82	59	18.47	62	10.94	61	11.85
55 years and over	19	8.95	17	19.24	17	10.65	18	12.17
Age unknown	3	10.00	3	21.67	2	18.50	3	13.67
Educational attainment								
High school or less	51	8.75	49	18.82	50	11.08	50	11.94
College or grad school	60	8.77	56	18.20	57	11.04	58	11.71
Family type								
Single	19	8.74	18	17.72	18	10.94	19	11.47
Couple	35	8.86	31	18.39	32	10.31	33	12.00
Family of 3–7 members	52	8.79	50	18.76	51	11.43	51	11.80
Family size unknown	5	7.80	6	19.00	6	12.17	5	12.00

four attitude scales were summed as follows (the fifth – ethnic identity was not summed since it had only one factor):

a.	Attitude toward education,	range of score 1–10
b.	Attitude toward BHT,	range of score 1–25
c.	Attitude toward collective memory,	range of score 1–20
d.	Attitude toward land loss,	range of score 1–15.

The means of each composite score were compared. As Table 5 shows, the most striking differences in the sample were evident in the comparison of user groups. Horseback riders were much more likely to support the idea of BHT; they were also more committed to collective memory and protection of black landowners than the other two user groups.

CONCLUSION

A study of this nature is instructive both for owners of black-owned farms and others interested in developing BHT sites. The study showed that there was a strong basis for developing BHT sites centered around environmental activities. Not only was there strong support for BHT and the protection of black landowners among respondents, users of Smith Park participated frequently in environmental activities such as interacting with wildlife, bird watching, fishing, and camping. Study participants also indicated a range of naturalistic activities that they would like to see developed at a farm such as Smith Park in addition to what was already there. The activity most desired – by young males in particular – was hunting. However, the preservation of historic buildings, hay rides, picking one's own produce, farm vacations, and farm tours was desired by more than 14 percent of the respondents. The study also pointed to ways in which the activities of enterprises such as Smith Park could be targeted to different user groups.

By educating black farmers about ways in which agricultural, nature, and heritage tourism could be developed could help them develop viable heritage tourism components to their operations. This could also enhance their economic outlook as heritage tourism is a strong and growing sector. The Smiths could provide more educational experiences without detracting from the recreational appeal of the park. For instance, visitors could be provided information to help them understand the history of the land and park itself.

Resources should also be invested in trust-building. There is deep distrust among black landowners and local community residents of outsiders. If heritage tourism is to thrive, then there has to be more openness and welcoming of outsiders. Although the mistrust of outsiders is understandable, an essential feature of tourism is interaction with outsiders. The groups now using Smith Park, for instance, have established a relationship with the park over time. However, it is in the nature of tourism that as it develops, the likelihood increases that people – unfamiliar to the operators of a venue – will seek to participate in the activities at a particular site. Over the course of the research, visits were made to a number of farms, and it took a great deal of time and effort to build trust among farmers before being granted permission to conduct the research or to visit the parks and farms. However, once trust was established, farmers and local residents were remarkably helpful.

This study points to areas of additional research in this genre that needs to be conducted as we seek to understand the role heritage tourism can play in black communities. The sample studied was a limited one: it was comprised of southern black recreationist. More research should be conducted on broader samples that include blacks from the North as well as from other countries. If BHT is to expand and serve audiences that are not black, then more information needs to be gathered from white, Hispanic, Asian, Native Americans, and other ethnic groups. Since BHT can be adapted to develop tourism in other communities that are not black, then more effort should be put into studies like this one.

ACKNOWLEDGMENTS

Stepanie Freeman thanks Drs. Sarah Warren, Gene Brothers, Stacy Nelson, and Larry Nielsen and Dean Jose Picart of North Carolina State University for their support and guidance.

REFERENCES

Aphteker, H. (1970). *The Negro in the South: William Levi Bull lectures 1907 by Booker T. Washington and W.E. B. Du Bois.* New York: Carol Publishing Group.
Beauford, Y. (1986). *Dilemmas facing minority farm operators in an agricultural crisis.* Boulder, CO: Westview Press, Inc.
Brown, C. (1998). Racial conflict and split labor markets. *Social Science History, 23*(3), 322.

Browne, R. S. (1973). *Only six million acres: The decline of black owned land in the rural south.* New York: Black Economic Research Center.

Collins, W. J. (1997). When the tide turned: Immigration and the delay of the great black migration. *The Journal of Economic History, 57*(3), 607–608.

Colton, J. W., & Bissix, G. (2005). Developing Agri-tourism in Nova Scotia: Issues and challenges. Available at http://lin.ca/Uploads/cclr10/CCLR10-17.pdf. Retrieved on May 17, 2005.

Daniel, P. (1972). *The shadow of slavery: Peonage in the south, 1901–1969.* Urbana, IL: University of Illinois Press.

Freeman, S. (2007). *A case study of black heritage tourism.* Master's of Science thesis, North Carolina State University, Raleigh, NC.

Freewoods Farm (2009). Freewoods farm. Available at http://www.freewoodsfarm.com/index.html. Retrieved on September 25, 2009.

Frey, W. (1998). Press release from population reference council. *Population Today, 26*(2), 1–3.

Garfield, D. (1999). *African American heritage tourism and community development: A report to the economic development administration.* Based upon the proceedings of the African American Heritage Forum, Kansas City, MO, October 25–26, 1999.

Gilbert, J., Sharp, G., & Felin, M. S. (2001). *The decline (and revival?) of black farmers and rural landowners: A review of the research literature.* Working Paper no. 44. University of Wisconsin-Madison Land Tenure Center, Madison, WI.

Gilbert, J., Sharp, G., & Felin, S. (2002a). The loss and persistence of black-owned farms and farmland: A review of the research literature and its implications. *Southern Rural Sociology, 18*(2), 1–30.

Gilbert, J., Wood, S. D., & Sharp, G. (2002b). Who owns the land?: Agricultural land ownership by race/ethnicity. *Rural America, 17*(4), 56–62.

Grossman, J. R. (1989). *Land of hope: Chicago, black southerners, and the great migration.* Chicago: University of Chicago Press.

Grossman, J. R. (2005). The great northern migration. In: *The Encyclopedia of Chicago.* Chicago: Chicago Historical Society.

Harrison, R. J. (2001). The great migration, south. *The New Crisis,* (July/August).

Keane, M., Briassoulis, H., & van der Straaten, J. (1992). Rural tourism and rural development. In: H. Briassoulis & J. van der Straaten (Eds), *Tourism and the environment: Regional, economic and policy issues, environment and assessment* (Vol. 3). Dordrecht: Kluwer Academic Publishers.

Lemann, N. (1991). *The promised land: The great black migration and how it changed America.* New York: Alfred A Knopf, Inc.

Litwack, L. (1998). *Trouble in mind: Black southerners in the age of Jim Crow.* New York: Alfred A. Knopf.

McGee, L., & Boone, R. (1979). A study of rural landownership, control problems, and attitudes of blacks toward rural land. In: L. McGee & R. Boone (Eds), *The black rural landowner – endangered species: Social, political, and economic implications* (pp. 55–65). Westport, CT: Greenwood Press.

Mitchell, T. W. (2001). From reconstruction to deconstruction: Undermining black land-ownership, political independence, and community through partition sales of tenancies in common. *Northwestern University Law Review* (Winter), 505–511.

Mitchell, T. W. (2005). Destabilizing the normalization of rural black land loss: A critical role for legal empiricism. *Wisconsin Law Review, 2005*(2), 557–615.

National Park Service. (2009). Underground railroad. Available at http://www.nps.gov/history/ ugrr/index.htm. Retrieved on May 28, 2008.

Norris, S. (1994). Discovered country: Tourism and survival in the American west. Albuquerque, NM: Stone Ladder Press.

Office of the Monitor. (2009). National statistics regarding Pigford v. Vilsack track a implementation as of September 22, 2009. St. Paul, MN: Office of the Monitor.

Oshinsky, D. M. (1996). Worse than slavery: Parchman farm and the ordeal of Jim crow justice. New York: Free Press.

Page, S. J., & Getz, D. (1997). Conclusions and implications for rural business development. In: S. J. Page & D. Getz (Eds), The business of rural tourism: International perspectives (pp. 191–205). London: International Thomson Business Press.

Penn School National Historic Landmark District. (2009). The Penn Center. Available at http://www.penncenter.com/resources.html. Retrieved on March 1, 2009.

Phillips, C. (1986). Social structure and social control: Modeling the discriminatory execution of blacks in Georgia and North Carolina, 1925–35. Social Forces, 65(2), 458–475.

Pigford, et al. v. Glickman. (1998). Civil Action No. 97-1978, 182 F.R.D. 341.

Pigford v. Glickman and Brewington v. Glickman. (1999). 185 F.R.D. 82.

Regional Resources Development Institute. (1991). Travel and nature (Survey). Boone, NC: Regional Resources Development Institute.

Taylor, D. E. (Forthcoming). African Americans and the environment: 1619 to the present.

U.S. Census Bureau. (1922). Fourteenth census of the United States taken in the year 1920: Agriculture (pp. 293–313). Washington, DC: Government Printing Office.

U.S. Census Bureau. (1980). Census of population and housing. Washington, DC: Government Printing Office.

U.S. Census Bureau. (1990). Census of population and housing. Washington, DC: Government Printing Office.

U.S. Census Bureau. (2000). Census of population and housing. Washington, DC: Government Printing Office.

U.S. Department of Agriculture. (1999). 1997 census of agriculture (pp. 25–26). Washington, DC: National Agricultural Statistics Service.

U.S. Department of Agriculture. (2004). 2002 census of agriculture. Washington, DC: National Agricultural Statistics Service.

U.S. Department of Agriculture. (2009). 2007 census of Agriculture (pp. 58–64). Washington, DC: National Agricultural Statistics Service.

United States Virgin Islands Tourist Board. (2009). St. Croix. Available at http://www. usvitourism.vi/. Retrieved on January 21, 2009.

Walker, D. (2006). Southern heritage tourism luring a growing market of black Americans. USA Today, Available at http://www.usatoday.com/travel/destinations/2005-07-25- black-tourism_x.htm. Retrieved on September 29, 2009.

Whitlock, W., Van Romer, K., & Becker, R. H. (1991). Nature-based tourism: An annotated bibliography. Clemson, SC: Strom Thurmond Institute of Government and Public Affairs, Clemson University.

Dorceta E. Taylor is an associate professor at the University of Michigan's School of Natural Resources and Environment. She teaches courses in environmental history, environmental justice, tourism and climate change, and social movements. She is the director of the Multicultural

Environmental Leadership Development Initiative (http://www.meldi. snre.umich.edu) and the author of *The Environment and the People in American Cities, 1600s-1900s: Disorder, Inequality, and Social Change*. She can be reached by email at dorceta@umich.edu or by telephone at 734-763-5327.

Stephanie Freeman is a doctoral student at Alabama A&M University. She can be reached by email at sfreeman27@gmail.com

PART IV
ENERGY – OIL AND GAS
EXPLORATION

ENVIRONMENTAL PERCEPTIONS AND ACTION: VILLAGERS' RESPONSE TO OIL AND GAS DRILLING IN THE WETLANDS OF RURAL TRINIDAD

A. Karen Baptiste and Brenda J. Nordenstam

ABSTRACT

Purpose – *Although research has shown that people in developing countries perceive environmental problems and have high levels of concern for the environment, their actions might not always reflect that concern. This study examines how villagers in rural wetland communities in Trinidad and Tobago perceive environmental issues related to oil and gas development that might impact their communities.*

Methodology – *One hundred and thirty villagers in three communities in and around the Nariva Swamp were interviewed to find out about perceptions of, support for oil and gas drilling policies, or opposition to the development of this resource.*

Findings – *The study found that respondents living closest to the swamp and those whose livelihoods depended on the wetlands were more likely than other respondents to perceive oil and gas drilling as dangerous and*

Environment and Social Justice: An International Perspective
Research in Social Problems and Public Policy, Volume 18, 289–321
Copyright © 2010 by Emerald Group Publishing Limited
All rights of reproduction in any form reserved
ISSN: 0196-1152/doi:10.1108/S0196-1152(2010)0000018012

expressed greater opposition to it. Given that direct actions such as protests were not seen among the villagers, an analysis revealed that there are a number of indirect environmental actions that contribute to the protection of the Nariva Swamp. Villagers were seen as having pro-environmental actions such as sustainable farming and fishing practices, carpooling and nongovernmental activity.

Originality/value of paper – *This study adds to the body of environmental research in the Caribbean particularly providing an understanding about rural people's perceptions of environmental issues.*

INTRODUCTION

Traditionally, environmental concern was considered to be most pronounced among those individuals that are highly educated or wealthy, and by extension, within the most affluent countries (Bullard, 1990; Dunlap, Gallup, & Gallup, 1993; Inglehart, 1990; Taylor, 2000). This view which arose among American scholars initially stated that minorities and the poor were less concerned about environment and conservation issues and were, therefore, less involved in the environmental movement (Buttel & Flinn, 1974[1]; Morrison, Hornback, & Warner, 1972). This line of research has been extended to the international realm. For instance, Inglehart's[2] work on the World Values Survey has adopted a similar line of argument regarding less developed or poorer nations of the world. Inglehart argues that environmental concerns are luxury endeavors undertaken by those espousing postmaterialist values. According to this perspective, developed nations having reached the pinnacle of industrialization, are able to invest in the environment. By extension, activists in such countries have the wherewithal to focus on environmental concerns. This is not the case for poor nations – most still struggle to meet their basic needs of their citizens (Inglehart, 1995,[3] 2000; Kidd & Aie-Rie, 1997; Kemmelmeier, Grzegorz, & Young Hun, 2002).

A substantial body of empirical research has challenged these traditional views of environmentalism. They contend that minorities and other marginalized groups in the United States perceive environmental problems, are aware of them and exhibit high levels of environmental concerns. Moreover, minorities are very active in environmental affairs. This is evident in the hundreds of environmental justice groups – most founded and led by minorities and low-income activists – that have been formed in the United States over the past three decades (Bullard, 1990; Mohai & Bryant, 1998;

Taylor, 2000; Uyeki & Holland, 2000; Vaughan & Nordenstam, 1991). Scholars have also found that people residing in less developed countries also have high levels of perception of environmental problems and express concern for the environment. Dunlap and Mertig (1995, 1997) have demonstrated this using data from the Gallup Poll (Dunlap et al., 1993; Dunlap & Mertig 1995, 1997). Likewise, Brechin and Kempton (1992) have used the Gallup Poll data to challenge the postmaterialist thesis.

Environmental sociologists and psychologists have also become interested in examining the factors that influence environmental attitudes, perceptions, and concerns in marginalized communities in developing countries (Rauwald & Moore, 2002; Taylor, 1988; Tuna, 2004). One such study conducted in the Caribbean by Taylor (1988) examined environmental attitudes among secondary school teachers. Rauwald and Moore (2002) also examined the environmental concerns and support for environmental policies among university students within the region. Although these studies provide some information on environmental perceptions in the region, there is still a need for more extensive research in this area. This study will help to add to the body of environmental research in the Caribbean. The essay will help us understand more about rural people's perceptions of environmental issues.

Environmental Perceptions

Within the developing world a number of environmental problems have resulted in increased environmental awareness and concern among the public. These threats have been widely documented and include pesticide contamination, increased incidences of cancers from carcinogens, lack of access to clean water, toxic wastes, and unsustainable extraction of resources (Rossignol & Neumann, 1998). The aforementioned problems have resulted in significant environmental degradation in developing countries. The question arises: What are the attitudes and perceptions of the citizens of these countries toward the environment? More specifically, what are the environmental attitudes and concerns of people living in the Caribbean?

Gender is one variable that is commonly investigated in this genre of research and the results are mixed. Several studies have reported that females tend to be more concerned about the environment than males, but the association is weak (Blocker & Eckberg, 1989, 1997; Bord & O'Conner, 1997; Davidson & Freudenburg, 1996; Stern, Dietz, & Kalof, 1993). This finding has been attributed to the "motherly and nurturing instinct" of a woman, whereas men focus more on the economic concerns of the family (Davidson & Freudenburg, 1996; Dietz, Stern, & Guagnano, 1998; Freudenburg & Davidson, 2007; Stern et al., 1993; Zelenzy, Chua, & Aldrich, 2000). Some studies show either no gender influences or showed increased levels of environmental concerns among males when compared to females (Zelenzy et al., 2000).[4]

Many of the gender studies have been conducted in the United States and may not be representative of the differences one might find in other countries, particularly poor countries (Rauwald & Moore, 2002). Zelenzy et al. (2000) conducted a cross-national analysis of environmental attitudes among university students in the United States and 11 other countries. The results indicated that women generally expressed higher levels of environmental concerns than men in most countries. Hunter, Hatch, and Johnson (2004) examined the relationship between gender and environmental behaviors in 22 countries and had similar findings. Rauwald and Moore's (2002) study of the Caribbean also found that female students expressed higher levels of concern about the environment than their male counterparts. However, one of the limitations of this study is that the sample was drawn only from university students and hence was not as representative of the general population.

Proximity has also been studied extensively in this body of literature. Studies tend to examine rural-urban differences, region, or place of residence (Lowe & Pinhey, 1982). Generally studies find that place of residence has significant influence on the levels of public concern expressed by participants (Buttel & Flinn, 1978). The studies have also found that rural residents tend to express lower levels of concern for the environment than urban dwellers (Buttel & Flinn, 1974; Dietz et al., 1998; Freudenburg, 1991; Hendee, 1969; Tremblay & Dunlap, 1978). Research also showed that those who lived in regions of the United States that were more prone to environmental pollution tended to have higher levels of environmental concern than those of other areas (Lowe, Pinhey, & Grimes, 1980).

Researchers have also examined the link between proximity and the perception of risk associated with environmental hazards. Studies generally find that concern increases with proximity to the facility – those living closer to environmental hazards express greater concern about them (Hallman, 1989; Nordenstam, 1994). Freudenburg and Davidson (2007) also found that women who had children who lived close to a proposed waste repository in the Nehama County, Nebraska were more opposed to the siting of the facility than similar women who lived further away from the proposed repository.

Environmental Action

Researchers have begun to investigate the environmental actions[5] that people undertake in response to environmental dangers in the developed and developing world. Already an extensive body of scholarly literature exists on environmental activism among minorities and the poor in the United States (Mohai & Bryant, 1998; Taylor, 1989, 2000; Vaughan & Nordenstam, 1991). Similar research can be found in on Latin America (Dominguez, 1994), Asia (Gadgil & Guha, 1994, 1995; Guha, 1988; Shiva & Bandyopadhyay, 1986; Shiva, 1994), and Africa (Steady, 1993).

Efficacy and Resource Mobilization

Efficacy is important in whether an individual or group take action on an issue. Two kinds of efficacy are of relevance here: personal and political. Personal efficacy refers to the individual's ability to perceive that they are able to bring about a change in a system by their actions. Political efficacy can be seen as two-dimensional and is described as having a "sense of being capable of acting effectively in the political realm" (Craig, 1979; Finkel, 1985). Political efficacy has two components. Internal political efficacy deals with an individual's perception of being able to influence government and politics while external political efficacy deals with the belief that authorities or a regime is responsive to changes. Studies have shown that both internal and external political efficacy influences participation in political action (Craig, 1979; Finkel, 1985). Additionally, some research has shown that efficacy can be increased when individuals become involved in different organizations and activities (Diani, 2003; McAdam & Paulsen, 1993). Efficacy, however, is not always present among groups that are experiencing poverty and other forms of grievances. Renner (1996) suggests that marginalized and disenfranchised groups have a low capacity to resist and as such their ability to defend their interests are weak. The reason suggested is due to the political, social, and economic vulnerability of these groups, which places them in a position of powerlessness and thus reduces their ability to mobilize and translate their concerns into actions (Adeola, 2000; Renner, 1996).

A group's ability to access needed resources influences their ability to take action. Resource mobilization theorists posit there is always underlying grievances in groups in society, but these do not necessarily trigger mobilization. To mobilize effectively a group must mobilize resources such as time, money, institutional infrastructure, expertise, political support, and human capital (McAdam & Paulsen, 1993; McCarthy & Zald, 1977a, 1977b; Wood & Jackson, 1982). Mohai (1985) argues that the main predictor of environmental participation was personal efficacy and availability of resources. He contended that poor people often lacked personal efficacy; neither did they have the resources to effect change (see also Geschwender, 1968 for more on efficacy and social change). Lundy's (1999) work bears this out. Her research on the growth of the environmental movement in Jamaica found that most of the activists were drawn from the middle class and were among the most educated in the society. She contends that the availability of external funding and expertise facilitated the growth of the movement. The remainder of this essay will examine the environmental perceptions of poor rural villagers in Trinidad. It will examine how they perceive environmental threats and their responses to them.

AN HISTORICAL ACCOUNT OF OIL AND GAS DEVELOPMENT IN TRINIDAD

The State of Oil and Gas Development

Trinidad and Tobago is considered the most prosperous country in the Caribbean. The twin island republic has developed a dynamic economy, which is based on its oil and gas production (LatinFinance, 2005a). Several attempts were made around the mid-19th century to develop oil fields in the southern part of Trinidad. It was in 1902 that the first successful oil well was drilled in the southeast forests of the island (*The History of Trinidad's Oil*, 2009; Khan, Lalla, Roopchand, Dyal, & Ramnath, 2005). Commercial oil production, however, began in the southwest regions of the island between 1908 and 1912 and continues today with both land and marine drilling in the southern part of the island (*The History of Trinidad's Oil*, 2009; *Historical Facts on the Petroleum Industry of Trinidad and Tobago*, n.d.; Khan et al., 2005). The country is the world's largest exporter of two gas derivatives – ammonia and methanol. It is also the fifth largest producer and exporter of liquefied natural gas (LNG) and it has the world's largest LNG train which produces a total of 0.8 billion cubic feet per day of LNG (Petroleum Economist, 2006). Trinidad and Tobago's oil and gas sector is the country's largest revenue earner accounting for 57 percent of the gross domestic product. In 2006 the economy sustained a growth of 12.6 percent, mainly because of the increasing oil and gas prices on the global market (CIA, 2007; LatinFinance, 2005b).

The country has experienced consecutive years of growth in the global petroleum market over the past 12 years. Since 2000 the gas industry has grown at an annual rate of 27 percent per year. In an attempt to assert itself as a leader among petroleum producing and exporting countries, Trinidad and Tobago has outlined plans to expand its energy sector, not only in terms of immediate oil and gas exploration and production activities but also in terms of its by-product and downstream industries. These include the construction of two ammonia and urea plants, an additional methanol to polypropylene plant, a steel plant and two aluminum smelters – both of which have been the focus of protests in recent years (LatinFinance, 2005a; Petroleum Economist, 2006).

Problems Arising from Oil and Gas Production

It has been noted that for the majority of the 20th century, very little attention has been given particularly to the adverse environmental effects of the oil and gas industry in Trinidad and Tobago (Khan et al., 2005). Research has shown that the coastline of Trinidad is highly sensitive to oil spills (Lord, n.d.), particularly in mangrove ecosystems where biodiversity is reduced (Nansingh & Jurawan, 1999; Siung-Chang, 1997). Evidence of oil spills exist and gas explosions are not uncommon to villages on the island (Caribbean Update, 2003; Rights Action Group, 2007). For example, 12 families had to be evacuated from the southern village of Penal in 2006 because of an oil spill having a radius of a quarter mile (Gumbs-Sandiford, 2006). Similar stories were recorded in villages of Vessigny and Preysal, where oil and gas explosions have affected the daily routines of villagers (Kowlessar, 2009; Sookraj, 2005). Khan et al. (2005) indicated that 20–45 percent of the villagers surveyed within fence-line communities in Trinidad, stated that they have been adversely impacted by petroleum-based activities. Additionally, there is no formalized Emergency Response Oil Spill Plan for the petroleum industry (Lord, n.d.), even after 100 years of oil exploration, which increases the vulnerability and risk to both marine and terrestrial environments in the event of oil spills.

One of the main complaints of villagers has been the lack of participation in the decision-making process related to oil and gas activity within their communities. Proper advisories are not provided and there have even been cases where oil companies have made little attempt to relocate or provide redress to communities that are negatively impacted by oil and gas production (Sookraj, 2005). Coupled with this, there is growing sentiment that there is a lack of transparency (Alexander's Oil and Gas Connection, 2004) and mis-management of public funds in the energy sector (Sookraj, 2009). Revenues from the petroleum industry, has been recorded as $8 million US per day/150,000 barrels per day, however, these revenues do not filter out to the wider population, as there is still a lack of proper health care, food prices are high, so are housing costs (No Smelters in T&T, 2009). Finally, the lack of long-term employment of villagers in fenceline communities continues to be a major problem (Khan et al., 2005; Sookraj, 2009; The Trinidad Guardian, 2008). Unemployment rates have been recorded as high as 34 percent in host communities. In some, only six percent of the workforce is employed in the industry (Khan et al., 2005, p. 5). Moreover, villagers believe that foreign nationals are employed before locals. Villagers also allege that they are discriminated against in the hiring process (Bagoo, 2009; Sookraj, 2004). The lack of employment is seen as a contributing factor to social problems such as rime, particularly among youths (Khan et al., 2005).

Local Opposition

Local opposition to oil and gas drilling has been evident in Trinidad and Tobago. Within the past 3 years, this opposition has increased because of growing industrialization of the southwestern peninsula (Greaves & Gour, 2009; Mangrove Action Project, 2008). One of the most common forms of opposition has been seen in complaints to company officials and the media about the effects of oil and gas production (Gumbs-Sandiford, 2006). Some villagers have even sought relief from the local Environmental Management Authority, however they perceive the institution as "not caring" about their plight (Kowlessar, 2009). In some cases, compensation has been sought for damaged property resulting from oil spills and gas explosions (Caribbean Update, 2003; Kowlessar, 2009). Protest actions are on the rise as casual and temporary workers of oil companies, such as the state-owned Petrotrin, seek permanent employment. Villagers have also engaged in protest activities against the expansion of additional oil-and-gas-based industries such as aluminum smelters. However, these actions have been met by police brutality and complacency on the part governmental officials (Gour, 2009; Greaves & Gour, 2009).

Expansion of Oil and Gas Development in the Eastern Block

The current research examines the impacts of resource extraction in impoverished host communities in southeastern Trinidad. It examines the attitudes of residents living in three wetland communities in the path of future oil and gas development. Trinidad is approximately 4,842 km^2 and has 362km of coastline (CIA, 2007). The main cities are located on the western coast of the island. The three isolated, rural villages studied, are located approximately 2 h drive from San Fernando (the second largest city on the island) and 3 h drive from Port of Spain (the capital). In 2002, Talisman Petroleum Trinidad Incorporated (Talisman) was granted permission by the country's Environmental Management Authority to conduct seismic surveying in the Eastern Block of Trinidad (Carbonell, Browne, Alleng, & Massey, 2007; Walsh Environmental Scientists and Engineers, 2002). The Eastern Block is known for its numerous off-shore oil and gas fields; a small amount of the reserves are on-shore. The Nariva Swamp, a Ramsar Protected wetland, is located in this area (Fig. 1). It is the largest freshwater swamp in Trinidad and Tobago, covering an area of 6,000 ha and the first site to be listed on the country's Ramsar list (Nathai-Gyan, 1996). Following the seismic surveying, oil and gas exploration began in 2005 in the block. Residents of communities that are dependent on the swamp are concerned about the exploration. Locals use the swamp for fishing and farming as well as domestic purposes such as washing and bathing. They also use it for recreational activities (Kacal, 1999).

DEMOGRAPHIC CHARACTERISTICS AND LITERACY RATES IN TRINIDAD

Trinidad and Tobago has a population of around 1.2 million. The country is currently experiencing a population growth rate of 0.83 percent per annum. There is a large workforce; 71.6 percent of the population is in the 15–64 year age group. In contrast, the dependent age group is comprised of 0–14-year-olds who constitute 19.5 percent of the population and those 65 years and older comprise 8.9 percent of the population. Indians of South Asian ancestry comprise 40 percent of the population while people of African ancestry constitute 37.5 percent. Roughly 20.5 percent of the population is of mixed ancestry. Another 1.2 percent is classified as "other"

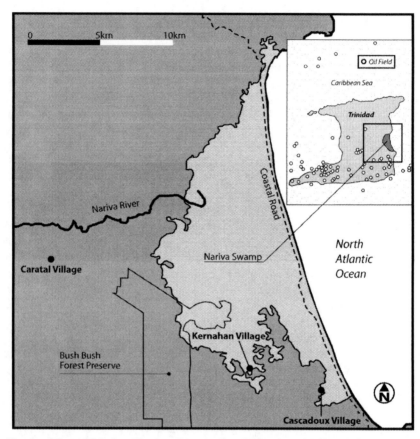

Fig. 1. Map of Nariva Swamp, Surrounding Villages and Oil and Gas Fields in Southeastern Trinidad. *Source:* Reprinted with permission from Cambridge Publishers, Original in Environmental Conservation, March 2009, *36*(1), 14–21.

while the ancestry of 0.8 percent was unspecified (CIA, 2007; Central Statistical Office [CSO], 2002).

Most Trinidadians – 98.6 percent of the population – is literate. The literacy rate among males is slightly higher than among females – 99.1 percent and 98 percent, respectively (CIA, 2007). Illiteracy in Trinidad is largely a rural phenomenon. Of the 1.4 percent illiterate, 65.1 percent live in the countryside or rural areas (ALTA, 1994; UNESCO, 2003). The high literacy rate is due to an excellent school system, however, it must be noted that most of the "prestigious schools" are located within the urban city centers of the country. Additionally, tertiary education while improving significantly on the island is still primarily located in urban areas; this makes it difficult for rural residents to gain access to these institutions. For example the University of the West Indies has one of its campuses in St. Augustine in the northwestern portion of the island. The development of the education system represents an example of classic center-periphery phenomenon that plagues developing countries. The core or power centers are built up and provided with resources – schools, hospitals, good roads, etc., whereas the rural hinterlands are ignored (Adeola, 2000).

Illiteracy arises primarily from the lack of access to educational facilities at primary, secondary, and tertiary levels. Rural children do not attend school because of distance and high transportation costs (Kacal, 1999). In 2003, 11.9 percent of the population resided in urban areas, indicating that a significant portion of the population resides in suburban and rural areas. Seventeen percent of the population lives below the national poverty line (CIA, 2007; UNDP, 2006). This is even more problematic when one considers that the economic driver of the country – the energy sector – extracts its resources in and around the poorest communities in the country. This is another classic center-periphery phenomenon – the periphery provides the raw materials that drive the economy that feeds the wealth of prosperous urbanites living and working in the core. The pollution, environmental degradation, and hazards associated with extraction are not seen as a big a problem in the core, while the periphery suffers the adverse consequences (Adeola, 2000).

METHODOLOGY

Residents of three villages were included in the study. Because of the researchers' interest in examining the relationship between proximity and environmental concern, the villages that were included were located at different distances to the wetlands. The first village, Kernahan is located in the Narvia Swamp, Cascadoux is adjacent to the swamp and the third village Caratal, is located approximately 3km west of the swamp (Fig. 1). The three villages are small, agricultural squatter communities. There are 90 households in Kernahan, Cascadoux has 44, and Caratal has 75.

The study was conducted in two stages and two methodological approaches (interviewing and surveying) were employed. In the first phase a site visit was conducted in December 2005. Local members of the community were interviewed informally and their responses used to develop the semi-structured interview schedule and questions for the survey instrument. In addition, key informants were identified to participate in the full study.

In the second stage (full study), formal interviews and surveys were conducted among the villagers. In July 2006, one key informant from each village was interviewed. The interviewees included the president of a local nonprofit and community leader from Kernahan, a former village council president of Cascadoux, and a former game warden of the Nariva Swamp from Caratal. A semi-structured interview schedule was used to guide the interviews with the key informants. They were asked to describe the uses of the swamp, the values placed on the swamp and how communities perceived oil and gas development, and how they were responding to the development. Each interview ranged from 15 min to an hour. The interviews were taped after obtaining permission from interviewees and were conducted at locations chosen by the interviewees.

A survey instrument was developed using some of the interview responses. The questionnaire was pre-tested in nine households from Kernahan (eight) and Cascadoux (one) in early July 2006. Information gleaned from the pre-test and the interviews were used to modify and develop the final survey instrument. Between mid-July and August 2006, a 30-min face-to-face survey consisting of close-ended questions was administered to householders in the three villages. The household was used as the unit from which the sample was drawn. Only one respondent was selected from a household. Enumeration District maps were used to identify households.[6] Houses on the maps were each given a number, included in the sample, and visited. Within each village there were houses that were unoccupied, nonexistent due to the date of the map (1999) or unreachable because of security reasons.[7] A total of 51 houses were excluded from the sample for these reasons. Sixteen houses were excluded in Kernahan, 9 in Cascadoux and 26 in Caratal. As a result, the sample consisted of 149 households – 66 in Kernahan, 34 in Cascadoux, and 49 in Caratal. This means that 74.5 percent of the census of households was asked to participate in the study. The head of the household was interviewed where possible alternating between adult males and females over the age of 18 (there were few cases where the females who were interviewed were wives of the head and were younger than 18). Only 13 respondents refused to participate in the study (11 in Kernahan, 6 in Cascadoux, and 2 from Caratal. This meant that a total of 130 respondents participated in the study – 55 in Kernahan, 28 in Cascadoux, and 47 in Caratal. This yielded a response rate of 87.2 percent.

The survey asked questions about proximity to the swamp, gender, occupation, age, length of time living in village, ethnicity, land ownership, number of and ages of children. This questionnaire also contained specific questions regarding environmental concern and about perceptions of danger of oil and gas drilling, support for oil and gas drilling policies, and opposition to oil and gas drilling. As the villages are known for its high level of illiteracy (Kacal, 1999), a pictorial Likert scale was developed, with bar height representing the range of possible responses from 1 = high levels of disagreement to 7 = high levels of agreement.

The environmental concern index used in this study was adapted from Schultz (2001) and was used to determine the perceptions of danger related to oil and gas drilling. Villagers were asked to indicate how dangerous they thought oil and gas drilling was on 12 dimensions. Adopting Schultz's (2001) methodology, a score averaging the 12 factors was computed to provide an overall score for perception of danger of oil and gas drilling. Additionally, each of these components was evaluated separately. The index was also evaluated on three components (egoistic – perception of danger for self, altruistic – perception of danger to others and biospheric – perception of danger to the environment). Three questions were used to form a policy index to determine the level of support for oil and gas drilling. Respondents indicated their level of agreement or disagreement using a pictorial Likert scale ranging from 1 = strongly disagree to 7 = strongly agree. These questions were analyzed separately; however an average score was calculated to determine their overall level of support for government policies. Furthermore, to determine the level of opposition to oil and gas drilling within the Nariva Swamp, respondents were asked "To what degree do you support oil and gas drilling to be located in the Nariva Swamp?" Levels of support were indicated on a scale ranging from 1 = strongly opposed to 7 = strongly support.

Data Analysis

Statistical Package for Social Scientists Version 16.0 was used for data analysis. Several independent variables (gender, age, ethnicity, length of time living in the region, number and age of children, occupation, and land tenure) were analyzed. Three dependent variables were examined: perceptions of danger arising from oil and gas drilling, support for oil and gas drilling policies and opposition to oil and gas drilling in the Nariva Swamp. One-way ANOVA was used to compare means between the independent and dependent variables. Reliability analyses using Cronbach's alpha

(Cronhbach, 1951) were conducted to determine the internal consistency of the indices used.

RESULTS

Demographic Characteristics of the Sample

Fifty-five percent of the sample was male and 45 percent was female. Respondents ranged from 16 to 83 years of age; the mean age was 43 years. Indo-Trinidadian comprised 77 percent of the sample, Dougla constituted 14 percent and made up 7 percent of the sample. The remaining 2 percent of the sample described themselves as Spanish Creole. When compared to the national population, this study had an overrepresentation of Indo-Trinidadians and an underrepresentation of Afro-Trinidadians. For analytical purposes, the sample was collapsed into two ethnic categories – Indo-Trinidadians and other.

Most of the villagers lived in the region for more than 20 years. Indeed, 24 percent of the respondents have resided in the region for 31–40 years whereas another 25 percent lived there for over 40 years. Forty-seven percent of respondents had between 1 and 3 children, with the majority (43 percent) of the children ranging between 0 and 14 years. The main occupation groups consisted of farmers (Table 1). As aforementioned, the land around the swamp is government owned, however when asked, 56 percent of respondents stated that they owned the land on which they lived. In Trinidad, ownership of land is not necessarily perceived to be linked to formal deeds, but rather based on the length of residence in a particular location. Of those who responded "yes" to land ownership, 25 percent resided in the village for 21–30 years and another 25 percent resided in the villages for more than 40 years. Of those who responded "no" to ownership, 31 percent classified themselves as squatters and 13 percent as renters.

Perceptions of Danger Arising from Oil and Gas Drilling

When asked about possible dangers of oil and gas drilling, one of the informants responded that the "knowledge of the villagers is poor" with respect to dangers and threats, but

> we (our) main concern is we (our) wildlife and the natural habitat in the community ... it must not be threatened or damaged in no circumstances, so long as this oil and gas going to drill. (Former village council president 2006, personal communication, 17 July)

Table 1. Demographic Characteristics of the Sample and Villages.

Occupation	Total Sample	Gender				Villages					
		Male		Female		Kernahan		Cascadoux		Caratal	
		Number	Percent	Number	Percent	Number	Percent	Number	Percent	Number	Percent
Farmer	52	36	69.0	16	31.0	35	67.0	11	21.0	6	12.0
Government employee	31	20	64.5	11	35.5	7	24.0	6	19.0	18	58.0
Homemaker	26	0	0.0	26	100.0	7	27.0	6	23.0	13	50.0
Other	21	15	71.0	6	29.0	6	29.0	5	24.0	10	48.0

Despite the above comment of "lack of knowledge" of dangers, results from the survey indicated that there was a high level of perceived danger arising from oil and gas drilling amongst villagers with respect to danger to self ($F = 16.02$, $p = .000$), others ($F = 11.56$, $p = .001$), and to the environment ($F = 7.30$, $p = .008$). In general, it was found that those villagers who lived closest to the swamp were most likely to perceive oil and gas drilling to be dangerous. Villagers in Kernahan (closest to the swamp) had the highest scores for the dangers associated with the environment, while dangers to others were the lowest (Table 2). In Cascadoux, the highest scores were for the dangers to others while dangers to the environment had the lowest scores. Caratal, located furthest from the swamp, had the highest scores for dangers to the environment and the lowest scores were for dangers to self. The index used to evaluate perceptions of danger had a Cronbach's alpha of .90. In all cases, Caratal had the lowest scores of the dangers to oil and gas drilling when compared to the two other villages. All the variables with the exception of "plants" and "children" were statistically significant at the .05, .01, and .001 levels indicating that proximity to the swamp and drilling activities was a reliable predictor of perceptions of danger.

Table 2. Assessing the Relationship between Proximity and to Wetlands and Villagers' Perception of Danger in Oil and Gas Drilling.

How Dangerous is Oil and Gas Drilling to	Mean Score			
	Total Sample	Kernahan	Cascadoux	Caratal
Personal danger (egoistic)	5.55***	5.91	5.89	4.91
Me	5.42*	5.69	5.86	4.83
My lifestyle	5.68***	5.95	6.54	4.85
My future	5.37*	5.82	5.11	5.00
My health	5.74***	6.22	6.07	4.98
Danger to others (altruistic)	5.62**	5.89	6.01	5.04
People in community	5.41**	5.65	6.04	4.47
All people	5.23**	5.47	5.96	4.51
My children	5.91	6.20	6.07	5.47
All children	5.93*	6.22	6.18	5.45
Danger to the environment (biospheric)	5.61*	5.95	5.63	5.19
Plants	5.86	6.09	5.82	5.62
Birds	5.01*	5.56	4.79	4.49
Other terrestrial animals	5.57*	6.02	5.43	5.13
Marine life	5.99*	6.13	6.50	5.53

Notes: Two-tailed tests. *$p < .05$; **$p < .01$; ***$p < .001$.

The results in Table 3 indicate that females were more likely to perceive oil and gas drilling as being dangerous to themselves and others than males. However, females were less likely to perceive oil and gas drilling as being dangerous to the environment than males. As one can see from the F values, the gender differences were not significant on any of the three scales – egoistic perceptions ($F = 0.91$, $p = .341$), altruistic ($F = 0.44$, $p = .508$) or biospheric ($F = 2.12$, $p = .149$). Indo-Trinidadians were more likely to perceive oil and gas drilling as dangerous than other ethnic groups for themselves, others, and the environment. Of the 12 factors examined in the index, Indo-Trinidadians scored highest on 8 of them. As was the case with gender, the ethnic differences were not significant. The relationship between the perception of danger and land tenure was also examined. Villagers identified themselves as squatters were more likely to perceive dangers to others and the environment than those who identified themselves as renters

Table 3. Gender, Ethnicity, Land Tenure, and Villagers' Perception of the Dangers of Oil and Gas Drilling.

How Dangerous is Oil and Gas Drilling to	Mean Score							
	Total Sample	Gender		Ethnicity		Land Tenure		
		Male	Female	Indo-Trinidadian	Other	Owner	Renter	Squatter
Personal danger (egoistic)	5.55	5.44	5.68	5.72	5.54	5.36	5.80	5.79
Me	5.42	5.21	5.66	6.25	5.36	5.23	5.53	5.70
My lifestyle	5.68	5.48	5.92	6.62	5.61	5.29	5.94	6.28*
My future	5.37	5.39	5.34	4.50	5.43	5.34	5.65	5.30
My health	5.74	5.68	5.81	5.50	5.75	5.58	6.12	5.88
Danger to others (altruistic)	5.62	5.54	5.72	5.84	5.60	5.48	5.79	5.81
People in community	5.41	5.28	5.56	6.12	5.36	5.25	5.29	5.75
All people	5.23	5.10	5.39	5.50	5.21	5.03	5.12	5.65
My children	5.91	5.86	5.97	5.75	5.92	5.79	6.29	5.95
All children	5.93	5.92	5.95	6.00	5.93	5.84	6.47	5.88
Danger to the environment (biospheric)	5.61	5.76	5.42	5.84	5.59	5.60	4.97	5.89
Plants	5.86	5.99	5.71	6.12	5.84	5.90	5.53	5.92
Birds	5.01	5.27	4.69	5.88	4.95	5.03	4.18	5.32
Other terrestrial animals	5.57	5.75	4.36	5.00	5.61	5.48	5.18	5.90
Marine life	5.99	6.06	5.92	6.38	5.97	6.00	5.00	6.40*

Notes: Two-tailed tests. *$p < .05$.

or landowners. With the exception of "my lifestyle" ($F = 4.16$, $p = .018$) and "birds" ($F = 5.39$, $p = .006$), there were no significant differences related among the three land tenure groups.

Occupation was collapsed into four categories (farmer, government employee, homemakers and other) for analytic purposes. Table 4 indicates that farmers had the highest mean score for perceiving the dangers of oil and gas drilling to themselves, to others and the environment. Government Employees were the least likely to perceive dangers to the environment. Homemakers had the second highest mean scores in perceiving oil and gas drilling as dangerous on the egoistic, altruistic, and biospheric scales.

Table 4. Occupation and Family Type and Villagers' Perception of the Dangers of Oil and Gas Drilling.

How Dangerous is Oil and Gas Drilling to	Mean Score							
	Total Sample	Occupation				Family Type		
		Farmers	Government employee	Homemaker	Other	No children	1–3 children	4 or more children
Personal danger (egoistic)	5.55	5.76	5.17	5.77	5.32	5.57	5.41	5.76
Me	5.42	5.62	5.10	5.65	5.10	5.66	5.11	5.70
My lifestyle	5.68	5.90*	5.03	6.27	5.33	5.59	5.57	5.92
My future	5.37	5.58	5.23	5.31	5.14	5.06	5.31	5.73
My health	5.74	5.94	5.32	5.85	5.71	5.97	5.66	5.68
Danger to others (altruistic)	5.62	5.80	5.31	5.65	5.57	5.32	5.62	5.87
People in community	5.41	5.62	4.97	5.65	5.24	4.91	5.48	5.73
All people	5.23	5.46	4.71	5.46	5.14	4.56	5.34	5.62*
My children	5.91	6.00	5.81	5.81	5.95	5.84	5.85	6.05
All children	5.93	6.13	5.77	5.69	5.95	5.97	5.82	6.08
Danger to the environment (biospheric)	5.61	5.96	5.35	5.44	5.33	5.45	5.61	5.73
Plants	5.86	6.10	5.58	6.00	5.52	5.72	5.85	6.00
Birds	5.01	5.40	5.00	4.46	4.71	4.69	5.07	5.19
Other terrestrial animals	5.57	6.10*	5.00	5.23	5.52	5.34	5.62	5.68
Marine life	5.99	6.23	5.81	6.08	5.57	6.03	5.92	6.08

Notes: Two-tailed test. *$p < .05$

Those villagers in the "Other" category had the lowest scores with regards to dangers to others (5.00) and themselves (4.96). Among the occupational groups there were statistically significant differences with respect to "my lifestyle" ($F = 2.82$, $p = .042$) and "other terrestrial animals" ($F = 2.80$, $p = .043$). Villages who had four or more children were more likely to see oil and gas drilling as dangerous to all people than other respondents ($F = 2.96$, $p = .05$).

The results for homemakers were interesting in that it revealed that they had the second highest means with regards to oil and gas drilling being perceived as dangerous. This differs from the gender results where females had the higher mean scores on perceiving danger to themselves and others. As such a new gender variable was created to look at homemakers as a subgroup of gender. Even though the results were not statistically significant, it was found that homemakers had higher mean scores on perceiving personal dangers (5.69) and dangers to environment (5.62). Males had the highest means on perceiving dangers to the environment (5.76), whereas other females had the highest scores on perceiving dangers to others (5.77).

Support of Oil and Gas Policies and Opposition to Oil and Gas Drilling

During the key informant interviews, respondents expressed strong opposition to the potential expansion of oil and gas drilling in Nariva Swamp. This may be the case because the swamp is heavily used by local people for subsistence activities. They were concerned about how the swamp was developed. One interviewee said,

> as to the question yuh [you] now ask about the use of it (the swamp), is we livelihoods, yuh [you] know how someone does get up on a morning and go to work and come back to earn his income, dat [this] is we work here, so actually we doh [do not] travel outside to earn an income, most times we do gardening or fishing. (Former village council president 2006, personal communication, 17 July)

Villagers were also asked whether or not they supported oil and gas drilling in the Nariva Swamp. As Table 5 shows, villagers living further away from the swamp were more supportive of government policies to limit and regulate oil and gas drilling activities generally ($F = 1.61$, $p = .204$) and in the swamp ($F = 6.02$, $p = .003$). On the contrary, respondents living close to the swamp were more supportive of policies that would protect the

Table 5. Proximity and Villagers' Support for Oil and Gas Drilling
Policies and Opposition for Oil and Gas Drilling.

I Will Support the Following Policies	Mean Score			
	Total sample	Kernahan	Cascadoux	Caratal
Government to closely monitor oil development in swamp areas	5.98*	5.31	6.61	6.38
Regulate and limit oil and gas development	5.67	5.36	6.14	5.74
Protect swamps from oil and gas development	6.33	6.51	6.43	6.06
Oil and gas drilling in the Nariva Swamp	5.58	5.75	5.21	5.62

Notes: Two-tailed tests. $^*p < .05$

marshlands ($F = 1.82$, $p = .167$). They also expressed the highest levels of opposition to oil and gas drilling in Nariva Swamp ($F = 0.65$, $p = .525$).

Males were more supportive of government action that would monitor, limit and regulate oil development than females. Females however, had greater support for policies that protects swamps from oil and gas drilling (Table 6). They also had the greatest opposition to oil and gas development in the Nariva Swamp. When the new gender variable was used, which looks at female homemakers as separate subgroup, the results were only slightly different. The biggest difference was seen where female homemakers had the greatest support for policies that monitor oil and gas drilling in general (mean = 6.33), compared to males (mean = 6.08). Additionally female homemakers had the greatest support for policies that protect all swamps from oil and gas development (mean = 6.46) compared to other females (nonhomemakers) (mean = 6.42). Female homemakers also had the greatest opposition to oil and gas drilling within the Nariva Swamp (mean = 5.96) compared to other females (nonhomemakers) (mean = 5.49) and males (mean = 5.51).

Indo-Trinidadians were more supportive of general mandates for government regulation (mean = 5.88) and monitoring (mean = 7.00) whereas the other groups had higher levels of support for policies specific to swamps (mean = 6.34) and were more strongly opposed to drilling in the swamp (mean = 5.61). The results for land tenure indicated a similar pattern. Renters had the greatest support for policies to limit oil and gas drilling in general (mean = 5.82) and those that protect swamps from oil and gas drilling (mean = 6.65). Additionally, owners had the highest levels

Table 6. Gender, Ethnicity, Land Tenure, and Villagers' Support for Government Policies and Opposition to Oil and Gas Drilling.

I Will Support the Following Policies	Mean Score								
	Total Sample	Gender			Ethnicity		Land tenure		
		Male	Female – nonhomemaker	Female-homemaker	Indo-Trinidadian	Other	Owner	Renter	Squatter
Government to closely monitor oil development in swamp areas	5.98	6.08	5.51	6.33	7.00	5.91	6.00	5.76	6.02
Regulate and limit oil and gas development	5.67	5.75	5.49	5.71	5.88	5.66	5.60	5.82	5.72
Protect swamps from oil and gas development	6.33	6.24	6.46	6.42	6.25	6.34	6.27	6.65	6.30
Oil and gas drilling in the Nariva Swamp	5.58	5.51	5.49	5.96	5.25	5.61	5.70	5.35	5.48

of opposition to oil and gas drilling within the Nariva Swamp (mean = 5.70), whereas squatters had the highest support for policies that limit oil and gas drilling in swamp areas (mean = 6.03).

Surprisingly, farmers had the lowest level of support for policies that require government to monitor oil and gas drilling in swamp areas ($F = 2.331$, $p = .077$) (Table 7). One of the reasons for these results maybe attributed to the expectation of jobs from the oil and gas drilling companies. Even though there is research that shows a lack of long-term employment for villagers from oil and gas companies (Khan et al., 2005; Sookraj, 2009; The Trinidad Guardian, 2008), villagers still seemed optimistic. Additionally there have even been reports of foreign nationals being employed before locals and locals being discriminated against when they seek employment (Bagoo, 2009; Sookraj, 2004). These concerns have not been taken into consideration by villagers as they evaluate the proposed oil and gas drilling within the Nariva Swamp. The net result will be the disenchantment of villagers as they do not benefit from the oil and gas activities, whether it be in terms of employment or basic social amenities such as schools and hospitals.

Those villagers who were grouped in the "other" category had the highest support for policies that protect swamps from oil and gas drilling ($F = 0.762$, $p = .517$). Homemakers had the highest level of opposition to oil and gas drilling ($F = 0.242$, $p = .867$), which was similar to that reported earlier when this group was considered separately. Those families with four or more children had the highest level of support for policies that protect swamps and they had the highest levels of opposition to oil and gas drilling taking place in the Nariva Swamp (Table 7). Those with no children had the highest level of support for those policies that regulate and limit oil and gas development in general. Those with one to three children had the highest levels of support for those policies that require the government to monitor oil and gas development in swamp areas.

When asked what had been done thus far to address the issue, respondents indicated there were no visible action at present, however, it was implied that the potential exists to seek redress either through legal mechanism, retaliation against oil and gas instillations, protests or other methods of civil disobedience. However, this has not yet materialize.

DISCUSSION

The results indicate that the levels of perceptions among the villagers were high as well as there was great support for policies that seek to protect the

Nariva Swamp from oil and gas drilling. Additionally, there was support for policies that monitor exploration development in general. These results are similar to that of other studies which have indicated that there are high levels of environmental concerns among developing countries and furthermore among marginalized groups (Brechin & Kempton, 1992; Dunlap & Mertig, 1995; Taylor, 1988). Further, it can be juxtaposed to the findings of Inglehart (1990) who stated that environmental concerns and perceptions can be considered a postmaterialistic value and hence more prominent among the wealthy and wealthier nations.

The results of gender and occupation revealed that homemakers as a group, considered separate from other women who were not homemakers, had the highest scores with respect to personal dangers and dangers to the environment. Additionally this group of women also had the greatest opposition to oil and gas drilling when compared to other groups. This finding is interesting in that it has not been explored by other gender studies – i.e., women who are homemakers, may need to be studied separately from women in other occupational groups as they may have different value sets that are not always captured in an aggregate gender variable. Further research on this is encouraged.

Moreover, the results indicated that there are high levels of opposition among all groups with respect to oil and gas drilling being located within the Nariva Swamp. The high levels of opposition within the Nariva Swamp indicates that villagers might resist oil and gas activity that cause environmental and social damages (O'Rourke & Connolly, 2003). Oil spills (Godoy, 1985; Siung-Chang, 1997), gas explosions, health concerns for both children and adults, and lack of long-term employment are usually typical of oil drilling operations within rural villagers (Knapp & Pigott, 1997; Von Kemedi, 2003; Watts, 1983). In taking a socio-historical look at the oil and gas industry within Trinidad and Tobago, the ill treatment of host communities is no different from that seen on the global scale. There is evidence of environmental, social, and economic hardships that are faced by these communities that most times go unaddressed by either the industry or government (Bagoo, 2009; Kowlessar, 2009; Sookraj, 2004, 2005, 2009). Khan et al. (2005) provided an analysis of the socio-economic impacts of Petrotrin (largest locally own petroleum organization) on fence-line communities in Trinidad. This study showed that most communities were concerned about the lack of investment into the communities once the level of exploration and production activities had decreased. Forty-five percent of responses from one community indicated that petroleum activities have created "excessive noise, dust and cracking of buildings" (Khan et al., 2005).

Additionally, even though the level of education is high in the country, only four percent of people have attained tertiary level education (Khan et al., 2005, p. 5). These are some of the negative effects that are being resisted by the community members of the Nariva Swamp.

Even though there is little indication of physical direct actions such as protests, petition signing, etc. that shows the opposition to the drilling activity within the swamp, there are other environmental actions that must be explored. It must be noted that local actions against oil and gas drilling as an environmental stressor, will take place within the wider context of existing social and environmental stressors. There is a lack of sufficient resources within the villages that were examined in this study. They are isolated, rural, and agricultural (Kacal, 1999). In addition there is no piped water supply in any of the villages, neither do they have access to government subsidized public transport. Most villages depend on either their own transportation or on their neighbor's vehicles for transportation. In some cases, villagers will utilize their personal vehicles to provide taxi services to other villagers. This is a form of carpooling even though villagers sometimes charge for the rides sometimes. This is similar to the carpooling or ridesharing initiatives found in the United States and other industrialized countries. Just as there are both environmental and social benefits to carpooling within the developed context (they can ride in the high occupancy vehicle lanes, social capital is built among children, tax benefits are accrued, or they engage in an environmental action and derive efficacy from it) the same principles applies in the developing world context. The carpooling villagers do reduce the overall carbon footprint of the region by alleviating the need for all villagers to get a car. This is particularly important as CO_2 emissions of Trinidad and Tobago is currently above that of the global average (GRID-Arendal & Secretariat of Environment and Natural Resources and UNEP's Regional Office for Latin America and the Caribbean (ROLAC), 2005). This also helps to alleviate the traffic congestion that plagues Trinidad's larger cities. This can also be seen as a form of everyday resistance and certainly an effective response to government neglect of public transportation within the villages.

There are no public schools within any of the villages and buildings such as churches are not readily available. For example, in Kernahan there are two church buildings of which only one is operational and there is a Hindi temple. In the other two villages there were no churches or other religious buildings. Additionally, there are no community centers within the villages. Only recently, Kernahan was provided with a community center that is being used as an early education center (Baboolal, 2009). In Kernahan, there is a government owned field station, however this is not open to the villagers for use. Tough access to resources makes it difficult for mobilization (Renner, 1996), it presents an opportunity for villagers to become innovative in seeking avenues to educate other members about the environmental and social problems facing their communities.

The use of farming and fishing techniques that result in minimal damage to the Nariva Swamp also indicates pro-environmental actions on the part of villagers in protecting the resource for future use. Historically villagers have engaged in small-scale farming and methods that were low-impact to the ecosystem of the swamp, i.e., mostly without machinery or use of agrochemicals (Carbonell et al., 2007). Additionally the use of traditional sustainable methods by villagers allow for harvesting of the local cascadura, which is used as a local protein source (Carbonell et al., 2007). These pro-environmental actions of the villagers create a symbiotic relationship with the swamp ecosystem, which would be altered negatively with the onset of oil and gas drilling activities.

Although, the phenomenon of environmental advocacy and activism is relatively new in Trinidad and Tobago (Brown, 2000), there has been at the local level the formation of a few nongovernmental organizations that seek to protect the resources of the Nariva Swamp. The most notable of these is the Manatee Conservation Trust, which has been responsible for the protection of the endangered West Indian Manatee (Manatee Conservation Trust, 2009) with an overarching mission to protect the resources of the Nariva Swamp. The Nariva Environmental Trust, which consists of local community members have also been created in response to a need from within the community to preserve and protect the swamp resources (Carbonell et al., 2007). Together with locally employed government workers, these nongovernmental organizations have the potential to help mobilize the wider public in not only continued protection of the Nariva Swamp but also in increasing efficacy, gaining support and momentum against the proposed oil and gas drilling activities. This will be further enhanced through the support of the media which have been very sympathetic toward the plight of host communities to oil and gas drilling within Trinidad and Tobago.

The results clearly establish that both high salience for the issue and strong oppositional potential are present within the communities, however, there is a lack of visible response in the form of environmental action. Given that immediate direct action against the oil and gas drilling activities in the Nariva Swamp has not been evident to date, an examination of the environmental actions of the villagers, indicate that they are taking actions, not measured on the survey, to protect the resources. Furthermore, there cannot be an analysis of environmental actions/activism without looking at the current social conditions of the deprived. Thus given the context in which villagers of the Nariva Swamp live, there is greater urgency in seeking access to basic social amenities such as public transportation, health care, and schools, which further exacerbates their plight with proposed oil and gas drilling. Further research needs to be conducted to fully explore the underlying factors associated with environmental action in situations such as these. Additionally, further work is needed on environmental activism in Trinidad and Tobago to understand the role that nonprofits in environmental affairs. Greater effort should be made to enhance the quality of life in fenceline communities and to fair and just policies for communities impacted by inequitable resource development.

NOTES

1. Buttel and Flinn (1978) provide a summary of different studies that have concluded this thesis.

2. There have been studies dating back to the 1970s that have alluded to developing countries having lower levels of concerns than developed countries; however it was Inglehart's work with the World Value Survey in the early 1990s that formalized this scholarly view with empirical data (Inglehart, 1995, onwards). This is an ongoing project of Inglehart and is found at http://www.worldvaluessurvey.com

3. There are a number of different books and publications on the issues of postmaterialism and environmental values and perceptions as understood by this school to literature for which Inglehart is considered the classic author.

4. Zelenzy, Chua, and Aldrich have provided a concise review article of all the gendered studies on environmental attitudes and concern since the first review of this kind published by Hines et al. in 1987.

5. Environmental action can be distinguished here from environmental activism, in that I am defining this concept as the stage before environmental activism. Environmental action is seen as those simple steps that are reflected in everyday behaviors toward the environment, for example, recycling, petition signing, attending meeting, etc. Environmental activism, however, is seen as the next step which involves more political action and widespread involvement of the mass to influence change.

6. The definition for household is based on that used by the Central Statistical Office of Trinidad and Tobago i.e., a household is described as one of more persons living in the same house and sharing one or more meals together.

7. Based on the advice of the key informants as well as other villagers, there were some households that were considered to be too dangerous for a young researcher to visit. In some cases this included alcoholic households or parts of the village that were lonely and considered unsafe by the villagers, hence these houses were excluded from the sample.

ACKNOWLEDGMENTS

We like to thank the Program on Latin America and Caribbean Studies, Syracuse University for sponsoring this research. Additionally, we are grateful to the number of reviewers both formal and informal who have helped to shape this manuscript.

REFERENCES

Adeola, F. (2000). Cross-national environmental injustice and human rights issues. *American Behavioral Scientist, 43*(4), 686–706.

Adult Literacy Tutors Association, Trinidad and Tobago (ALTA) (1994). Literacy in Trinidad and Tobago: ALTA national literacy survey, Trinidad and Tobago. viewed April 11, 2007. Available at http://www.alta-tt.org/

Alexander's Gas and Oil Connection. (2004). Oil windfall and the Trinidad stabilisation fund. *New and Trends in Latin America, 9*(12). Available at www.gasandoil.com/goc/news/ntl42456.htm

Baboolal, Y. (2009). Kernahan kids get chance at school. *The Trinidad Guardian,* 29 March, viewed 22 September. Available at http://guardian.co.tt/features/life/2009/03/29/kernahan-kids-get-chance-school

Bagoo, A. (2009). Ramnath alleges discrimination at Petrotrin. *Trinidad and Tobago Newsday,* 24 July, viewed 8 September. Available at http://www.newsday.co.tt/politics/0,104317.html

Blocker, J. T., & Eckberg, D. L. (1989). Environmental issues as women's issues: General concerns and local hazards. *Social Science Quarterly, 70,* 586–593.

Blocker, J. T., & Eckberg, D. L. (1997). Gender and environmentalism: Results from the 1993 General Social Survey. *Social Science Quarterly, 78,* 841–858.

Bord, R. J., & O'Conner, R. E. (1997). The gender gap in environmental attitudes: The case of perceived vulnerability to risk. *Social Science Quarterly, 78,* 830–840.

Brechin, S., & Kempton, W. (1992). Global environmentalism: A challenge to the postmaterialism thesis? *Social Science Quarterly, 75,* 245–269.

Brown, N. A. (2000). Environmental advocacy in the Caribbean: the case of the Nariva Swamp, Trinidad. CANARI Technical Report, No. 268, viewed October 23, 2007. Available at http://www.canari.org/nariva.pdf

Bullard, R. D. (1990). *Dumping in dixie: Race, class and environmental quality.* Boulder, CO: Westview Press.

Buttel, F. H., & Flinn, W. L. (1974). The structure and support for the environmental movement, 1968–70. *Rural Sociology, 39,* 56–69.

Buttel, F. H., & Flinn, W. L. (1978). Social class and mass environmental beliefs: A reconsideration. *Environment and Behavior, 10*(3), 433–450.

Carbonell, M., Browne, D., Alleng, G., & Massey, B. (2007). *Nariva Swamp restoration initiative: Trinidad and Tobago.* Ducks Unlimited Inc, Memphis, TN, viewed October 28, 2008. Available at http://www.ducks.org/media/Conservation/Conservation_Documents/_documents/Nariva%20Swamp%20Restoration%20Initiative%20Final%20Report.pdf

Caribbean Update. (2003). Oil Spill (appeared off Chaguaramas in Trinidad). Viewed September 11, 2009. Available at http://findarticles.com/p/articles/mi_hb6634/is_200301/ai_ n26111006/?tag = content;col1

CIA. (2007). *The World Factbook: Trinidad and Tobago.* Central Intelligence Agency, Washington DC. Available at https://www.cia.gov/library/publications/the-world-fact-book/geos/td.html. Retrieved on September 12.

Craig, S. C. (1979). Efficacy, trust and political behavior: An attempt to resolve a lingering conceptual dilemma. *American Politics Quarterly, 7*(2), 225–239.

Cronhbach, L. J. (1951). Coefficient alpha and the internal structure of tests. *Psychometrika, 16*, 297–333.

Central Statistical Office. (2002). *2000 Population and housing census: Community register.* Port of Spain, Trinidad: Ministry of Planning and Development, Central Statistical Office.

Davidson, D. J., & Freudenburg, W. R. (1996). Gender and environmental risk concerns: A review and analysis of available research. *Environment and Behavior, 28*(3), 302–309.

Diani, M. (2003). Introduction: Social movements, collectives, actions and social networks: 'From metaphor to substance'? In: M. Diani & D. McAdam (Eds), *Social movements and networks: Relational approaches to collective action.* New York: Oxford University Press.

Dietz, T., Stern, P., & Guagnano, G. (1998). Social structure and social psychological bases of environmental concern. *Environment and Behavior, 30*(4), 450–472.

Dominguez, J. (1994). *Social movements in Latin America: The experiences of peasants, workers, women, the urban poor, and the middle sectors.* New York: Garland Publishing Inc.

Dunlap, R., Gallup, G., & Gallup, A. (1993). Of global concern: Results of a health of the planet survey. *Environment, 35*, 7–39.

Dunlap, R., & Mertig, A. (1995). Global concern for the environment: Is affluence a prerequisite? *Journal of Social Issues, 51*(4), 121–137.

Dunlap, R., & Mertig, A. (1997). Global environmental concern: An anomaly for postmaterialism. *Social Science Quarterly, 78*(1), 24–30.

Finkel, S. E. (1985). Reciprocal effects of participation and political efficacy: A panel analysis. *American Journal of Political Science, 29*(4), 891–913.

Freudenburg, W. R. (1991). Rural-urban differences in environmental concern: A closer look. *Sociological Inquiry, 61*(2), 35–45.

Freudenburg, W. R., & Davidson, D. J. (2007). Nuclear families and nuclear risks: The effects of gender, geography, and progeny on attitudes toward a nuclear waste facility. *Rural Sociology, 72*(2), 215–243.

Gadgil, M., & Guha, R. (1994). Ecological conflicts and the environmental movement in India. *Development and Change, 25*(1), 101–136.

Gadgil, M., & Guha, R. (1995). *Ecology and equity: The use and abuse of nature in contemporary India.* New York: Routledge.

Geschwender, J. A. (1968). Explorations in the theory of social movements and revolutions. *Social Forces, 47*(2), 127–135.

Godoy, R. (1985). Mining: Anthropological perspectives. *Annual Reviews of Anthropology, 14*, 199–217.

Gour, E. (2009). Response to Guardian Frontpage Story. *Rights Action Group blog,* weblog post, 11 June. Available at http://rightsactiongroup.blogspot.com/. Retrieved on September 8.

Greaves, M., & Gour, E. (2009). Mr. Manning, Smelter not welcome. *Rights Action Group blog,* weblog post, 9 June. Available at http://rightsactiongroup.blogspot.com/. Retrieved on September 8.

GRID-Arendal, Secretariat of Environment and Natural Resources and UNEP's Regional Office for Latin America and the Caribbean (ROLAC). (2005). *Vital Climate Graphics Latin America and the Caribbean.* Available at http://www.grida.no/publications/vg/lac/page/2766.aspx. Retrieved on September 22, 2009.

Guha, R. (1988). Ideological trends in Indian environmentalism. *Economic and Political Weekly, 23*(49), 2578–2581.

Gumbs-Sandiford, A. (2006). Penal village evacuated. *Trinidad and Tobago's Newsday,* 9 November, viewed 8 September 2009. Available at http://www.newsday.co.tt/news/0,47303.html

Hallman, W.K. (1989). *Coping with an environmental stressor: Perception of risk, attribution of responsibility, and psychological distress in a community living near a hazardous waste facility.* Ph.D. dissertation, University of South Carolina, Columbia, SC.

Hendee, J. C. (1969). Rural-urban differences reflected in outdoor recreation participation. *Journal of Leisure Research, 1,* 337–341.

Historical Facts on the Petroleum Industry of Trinidad and Tobago. (n.d.). Geological Society of Trinidad and Tobago (GSTT), Trinidad, viewed 8 September 2009. Available at http://www.gstt.org/history/chronology.htm

Hunter, L. M., Hatch, A., & Johnson, A. (2004). Cross-national gender variation in environmental behaviors. *Social Science Quarterly, 85*(3), 677–694.

Inglehart, R. (1990). *Culture shift in advanced industrial society.* Princeton, NJ: Princeton University Press.

Inglehart, R. (1995). Public support for environmental protection: Objective problems and subjective values in 43 countries. *Political Science and Politics, 28*(1), 57–72.

Inglehart, R. (2000). Globalization and postmodern values. *The Washington Quarterly, 23*(1), 215–228.

Kacal, S.A. (1999). *Social Assessment and Community Action Plan of Nariva Managed Resource Area.* Ministry of Agriculture, Land and Marine Resources, Port of Spain, Trinidad and Tobago.

Kemmelmeier, M., Grzegorz, K., & Young Hun, K. (2002). Values, economics and proenvironmental attitudes in 22 societies. *Cross-Cultural Research, 36*(3), 256–285.

Khan, F., Lalla, F., Roopchand, J., Dyal, S., & Ramnath, K. (2005). Assessing the socio-economic impacts of petroleum exploration and production operations on rural communities in Southern Trinidad. Paper presented at 2005 SPE/EPA/DOE Exploration and Production Environmental Conference, Galveston, Texas, March 7–9.

Kidd, Q., & Aie-Rie, L. (1997). Postmaterialistic values and the environment: A critique and reappraisal. *Social Science Quarterly, 78*(1), 1–15.

Knapp, B. A., & Pigott, V. (1997). The archaeology and anthropology of mining: Social approaches to an industrial past. *Current Anthropology, 38*(2), 300–304.

Kowlessar, G. (2009). Underground explosions rock Preysal. *The Trinidad Guardian,* 17 July, viewed 8 September. Available at http://guardian.co.tt/news/crime/2009/07/17/underground-explosions-rock-preysal

LatinFinance. (2005a). At the forefront. March, p. 79, viewed 24 August 2007, EBSCOhost, Business Source Premier, item: 16716977.

LatinFinance (2005b). Heading downstream. September, pp. 87–89, 1, viewed 24 August 2007, EBSCOhost, Business Source Premier, item: 18347738.

Lord, D. (n.d.). Oil spill response. Environmental and Remedial Treatment for Hydrocarbons, Trinidad and Tobago, viewed 8 September 2009. Available at http://www.earthtt.com/oil_spill_contingency_.html

Lowe, G. D., & Pinhey, T. K. (1982). Rural-urban differences in support for environmental protection. *Rural Sociology*, *47*(1), 114–128.

Lowe, G. D., Pinhey, T. K., & Grimes, M. D. (1980). Public support for environmental protection: new evidence from national surveys. *Pacific Sociological Review*, *23*(4), 423–445.

Lundy, P. (1999). Fragmented community action or new social movement? A study of environmentalism in Jamaica. *International Sociology*, *14*(1), 83–102.

Manatee Conservation Trust. (2009). About us. Available at http://www.manateetrust.org.tt/aboutus.htm

Mangrove Action Project. (2008). Emergency action: Protect mangrove and fishermen/Trinidad. December 4. Available at http://www.mangroveactionproject.org/news/action-alerts/emergency-action-protect-mangroves-and-fishermen-trinidad/. Retrieved on September 25, 2009.

McAdam, D., & Paulsen, R. (1993). Specifying the relationship between social ties and activism. *American Journal of Sociology*, *99*(3), 640–647.

McCarthy, J. D., & Zald, M. N. (1977a). Resource mobilization and social movements: A partial theory. *American Journal of Sociology*, *82*(6), 1212–1241.

McCarthy, J. D., & Zald, M. N. (1977b). *The dynamics of social movements: Resource mobilization, social control, and tactics*. Cambridge, MA: Winthrop Publishers Inc.

Mohai, P. (1985). Public concern and elite involvement in environmental conservation issues. *Social Science Quarterly*, *66*, 820–838.

Mohai, P., & Bryant, B. (1998). Is there a 'race' effect on concern for environmental quality? *Public Opinion Quarterly*, *62*, 475–505.

Morrison, D. E., Hornback, K. E., & Warner, K. W. (1972). The environmental movement: Some preliminary observations and predictions. In: W. Burch, Jr., N. Check, Jr. & L. Taylor (Eds), *Social behavior, natural resources and the environment*. New York: Harper and Row Publishers.

Nansingh, P., & Jurawan, S. (1999). Environmental sensitivity of a tropical coastline (Trinidad, West Indies) to oil spills. *Spill Science & Technology Bulletin*, *5*(2), 161–172.

Nathai-Gyan, N. (1996). Conservation status of the Nariva Swamp. In: Caribbean Forest Conservation Association (Ed.), *Nariva swamp seminar report*. St. Augustine, Trinidad: Wildlife Section, Ministry of Agriculture and Forestry.

No Smelters in T&T. (2009). Available at www.nosmeltertnt.com/trinidad_wealth.html. Retrieved on October 28.

Nordenstam, B. J. (1994). When communities say NIMBY to their LULU: Factors influencing environmental and social impact perception. Paper presented at the 14th Annual Meeting of the International Association For Impact Assessment, Quebec, Canada, June 14–18.

O'Rourke, D., & Connolly, S. (2003). Just oil? The distribution of consumption. *Annual Review Environment and Resources*, *28*(1), 587–617.

Petroleum Economist. (2006). Reserves scare. May, viewed August 24, 2007, ABI/INFORM.

Rauwald, K. S., & Moore, C. F. (2002). Environmental attitudes as predictors of policy support across three countries. *Environment and Behavior*, *34*(6), 709–739.

Renner, M. (1996). *Fighting for survival: Environmental decline, social conflict and the new age of insecurity*. New York: Norton Press.

Rights Action Group. (2007). Fishermen report largest recorded oil spill off east coast Trinidad. Rights Action Group, September 26, viewed 8 September 2009. Available at http://rightsactiongroup.blogspot.com/

Rossignol, A. M., & Neumann, C. (1998). International environmental health: Priorities from Huairou. *Journal of Public Health Policy, 19*(3), 319–330.

Schultz, P. W. (2001). Assessing the structure of environmental concern: Concern for the self, other people, and the biosphere. *Journal of Environmental Psychology, 21*, 327–339.

Shiva, V. (1994). Women, ecology and health: Rebuilding connections. In: V. Shiva (Ed.), *Close to home: Women reconnect to ecology, health and development*. Philadelphia, PA: New Society Publishers.

Shiva, V., & Bandyopadhyay, J. (1986). The evolution, structure and impact of the Chipko movement. *Mountain Research and Development, 6*(2), 133–142.

Siung-Chang, A. (1997). A review of marine pollution issues in the Caribbean. *Environmental Geochemistry and Health, 19*(2), 45–55.

Sookraj, R. (2004). Shutdown at petrotrin. The Trinidad Guardian, 4 November, viewed September 8, 2009. Available at http://legacy.guardian.co.tt/archives/2004-11-04/news1.html

Sookraj, R. (2005). Petrotrin gas line blows up. *The Trinidad Guardian*, September 5, viewed September 8, 2009. Available at http://legacy.guardian.co.tt/archives/2005-09-05/news5.html

Sookraj, R. (2009). Petrotrin casual workers protest for full-time jobs. *The Trinidad Guardian*. June 9, viewed September 8. Available at http://guardian.co.tt/business/business/2009/06/09/petrotrin-casual-workers-protest-full-time-jobs

Steady, F. (1993). *Women and children first: Environment, poverty and sustainable development*. Rochester, VT: Schenkman Books.

Stern, P., Dietz, T., & Kalof, L. (1993). Value orientations, gender and environmental concern. *Environment and Behavior, 25*(3), 322–348.

Taylor, D. E. (1988). Environmental education in Jamaica: The gap between policymakers and teachers. *Journal of Environmental Education, 20*(1), 22–28.

Taylor, D. E. (1989). Blacks and the environment: Towards an explanation of the concern and action gap between blacks and whites. *Environment and Behavior, 20*(2), 175–205.

Taylor, D. E. (2000). The rise of the environmental justice paradigm: Injustice framing and social construction of environmental discourses. *American Behavioral Scientist, 43*(4), 508–580.

The History of Trinidad's Oil. (2009). Feature address at 1960 annual dinner, Geological Society of Trinidad and Tobago (GSTT), Trinidad, viewed September 8, 2009. Available at http://www.gstt.org/history/history%20of%20oil.htm

The Trinidad Guardian. (2008). OWTU protest yuletide cutback. November 18. Available at http://guardian.co.tt/business/business/2008/11/18/owtu-protests-yuletide-cutback-petrotrin

Tremblay, K. R., & Dunlap, R. E. (1978). Rural-urban residence and concern with environmental quality: A replication and extension. *Rural Sociology, 43*(3), 474–491.

Tuna, M. (2004). Public environmental attitudes in Turkey. Unpublished manuscript.

UNDP. (2006). Human Development Report 2006: Beyond Scarcity, Power, Poverty and the Global Water Crisis, viewed September 25, 2007. Available at http://hdr.undp.org/en/reports/global/hdr2006/

UNESCO. (2003). *Trinidad and Tobago: Adult Illiteracy.* UN Common Database (UNESCO estimates), viewed April 11, 2007. Available at http://globalis.gvu.unu.edu/indicator_detail.cfm?IndicatorID = 27&Country = TT

Uyeki, E. S., & Holland, L. J. (2000). Diffusion of pro-environment attitudes? *American Behavioral Scientist, 43*(4), 646–662.

Vaughan, E., & Nordenstam, B. J. (1991). The perception of environmental risks among ethnically diverse groups. *Journal of Cross-Cultural Psychology, 22*(1), 29–60.

Von Kemedi, V. (2003). *Community conflicts in the Niger Delta: Petro-weapon or policy failure.* Working paper (WP 03-12), Berkeley Workshop on Environmental Politics, Berkeley University, CA, viewed April 11, 2007. Available at http://globetrotter.berkeley.edu/EnvirPol/pubs.html

Walsh Environmental Scientists and Engineers. (2002). Environmental impact assessment: 3-D seismic survey for the Eastern Block Republic of Trinidad and Tobago, Talisman (Trinidad) Petroleum Ltd. Environmental Management Authority Library, Trinidad.

Watts, M. (1983). *Silent violence: Food, famine, & peasantry in northern Nigeria.* Berkeley, CA: University of California Press.

Wood, J. L., & Jackson, M. (1982). *Social movements: Development, participation, and dynamics.* Belmont, CA: Wadsworth Publishing Company.

Zelenzy, L. C., Chua, P., & Aldrich, C. (2000). Elaborating on gender differences in environmentalism. *Journal of Social Issues, 56*(3), 443–457.

A. Karen Baptiste is an assistant professor at Colgate University. Her major interests are environmental justice, environmental psychology, rural development, and the intersection of resource use and policy decision-making. Her research is interdisciplinary and looks at attitudes and concerns to environmental issues among Caribbean communities. Her most recent work examines environmental attitudes and concerns among university students in Chile. She can be reached by email at abaptiste@colgate.edu or by telephone at 315-223-6740.

Brenda J. Nordenstam is an associate professor at the State University of New York, College of Environmental Science and Forestry. Her goal as a professor and environmentalist has been to engage in community-based scholarship. As researchers, she believes that we should support the integration of knowledge through community-based research, teaching, and service. Her research interests involve risk perception and communication, environmental justice, and environmental policy. Her work with individuals and groups struggling to comprehend and respond to environmental hazards in their communities has broadened her own understanding of these risks, and deepened her commitment to the view that only through full community partnerships will we begin to address these complex interrelated health and environmental problems. She can be reached by email at bjnorden@esf.edu or by telephone at 315-470-6573.

OIL AND GAS INDUSTRY IN NIGERIA: THE PARADOX OF THE BLACK GOLD

Joseph Effiong

ABSTRACT

Purpose – *This chapter examines the socio-economic and political challenges facing Nigeria's oil-producing sector. The Niger Delta's main environmental and social problems arise from oil spills, gas flaring and degradation of the land.*

Design/methodology/approach – *This analysis is based on a review of government documents as well as materials produced by international development agencies.*

Findings – *In spite of the large profits made by oil companies operating in the Niger Delta, the people of the region live in squalor without basic amenities. This has resulted in an upsurge of violent activities orchestrated by community-based organizations wishing to draw international attention to the plight of the people in the area. In recent years, both national and international nongovernmental organizations have launched campaigns to address the issues, but little have been achieved because the oil companies are reluctant to be responsible corporate neighbors and the Nigerian government seem unwilling to devise solutions to address the problem.*

Environment and Social Justice: An International Perspective
Research in Social Problems and Public Policy, Volume 18, 323–349
Copyright © 2010 by Emerald Group Publishing Limited
All rights of reproduction in any form reserved
ISSN: 0196-1152/doi:10.1108/S0196-1152(2010)0000018013

Originality/value – *This chapter suggests ways of developing an effective oil policy framework that will include all the stakeholders in the management of oil resources.*

AN OVERVIEW OF SOCIAL AND ECONOMIC CONDITIONS

The Niger Delta's main environmental and social challenges result from oil spills, gas flaring, deforestation, decreasing productivity of the land, and pollution. The seeming insensitivity of the government and the oil companies to these problems, has resulted in a wave of restiveness and agitation by the host communities, which are demanding adequate compensation and a fair share of the profits gleaned from the extraction of the natural resources found in their communities. However, these demands are increasingly politicized and the politics is becoming more and more radicalized. Violent actions such as hostage taking and militancy among youths have assumed criminal proportions. This has far-reaching ramifications in a nation state that is heavily dependent on oil for its revenues.

In 2006, Nigeria had a population of about 144.7 million (Energy Information Administration [EIA], 2006). According to the Federal Office of Statistics (1999), between 1980 and 1996, poverty rate in Nigeria rose from 28 to 66 percent. The gross domestic product (GDP) in 1982 was $860 billion; it stood at $280 billion in 1996 and is currently at $290 billion. Although 17.7 million people lived in poverty in 1980, the number living on less than $1.40 per day rose to 67.1 million by 1996. That number is increasing. An estimated 49 percent of the country's urban population currently lives in poverty. Nigeria is ranked among the 30 poorest countries in the world. Many of the population are either underemployed or unemployed with no source of livelihood. The Nigeria government conservatively estimates unemployment to be 10.8 percent, but the World Bank estimates that 40–50 percent of those living in major urban centers and new graduates are unemployed (World Bank, 2001).

The United Nation Development Program (United Nations Development Program [UNDP], 2006) analyzes social and economic indicators in 177 United Nations member countries and calculates a Human Development Index (HDI) from it. The HDI is also a comparative measure of well being, life expectancy, educational attainment and standard of living. A score of 1 is the highest development and a score below 0.5 is considered to represent low development. The 2006 HDI painted a dismal picture of Nigeria; the country had a low value of 0.448.

A comparison of Nigeria's HDI scores with those of other oil-producing countries of the world shows that Nigeria is falling behind. The HDI for Saudi Arabia in 2000 stood at 0.800, whereas in 2003 the United Arab Emirates had 0.849, Kuwait 0.844, Libya, 0.799, Venezuela 0.772, and Indonesia 0.697 (UNDP, 2006; Table 1).

Life expectancy in Nigeria has dropped from 57 years in 2000 to 43 years in 2006. Infant mortality is 100 per 1,000 live births and 29 percent of the children under the age of 5 are malnourished. Only 48 percent of the population has access to clean water and the literacy rate for the population older than 15 years is 69 percent (World Bank, 2007).

Gender inequality is also a cause for concern in Nigeria. The gender gap in adult literacy has an important effect on growth potential because maternal education is strongly related to children's health, education, and nutrition. In Nigeria, the male literacy rate of 74.4 percent is much higher than the female rate of 59.4 percent. The gender difference reflects the disparities in other social and economic indicators. The labor force participation rate for men is 97 percent whereas women's labor force participation is only 54 percent (U.S. Agency for International Development [USAID], 2006). Nigeria's Gender Development Index (GDI) value is 0.443. Of the 136 countries with both HDI and GDI values, 81 countries have a better ratio than Nigeria's (UNDP, 2006). See Table 2 for additional social and economic indicators of Nigeria.

Conditions are worse in the oil-producing Delta. Health care services remain poor, schools are dilapidated and there is a lack of passable roads in most parts of the region. The UNDP human development report describes conditions in the Niger Delta as such,

The Niger Delta is a region suffering from administrative neglect, crumbling social infrastructure and services, high unemployment, social deprivation, abject poverty, filth and squalor, and endemic conflict. Social and economic deterioration, ignored by policy makers, undercuts enormous possibilities for development. (UNDP, 2006)

As Nigeria's Senator Falorin noted while on a tour of an oil spill site in Ikot Ada Udo Village, an oil-producing community in Akwa Ibom state, "We saw people drinking water from the same place where they are bathing, where they are defecating and where they are doing all sorts of domestic chores. This is totally unacceptable in 2007" (*Punch Newspapers*, 2007).

Nigeria has 35.2 billion barrels of proven oil and 160 trillion cubic meters of gas reserves. This represents 3 percent of the world oil reserves.

Table 1. A Comparative Human Development Index Profile of Nigeria and Five Other Countries.

Human Development Index			Life Expectancy			Education Enrollment Ratio			Gross Domestic Product per Capita (in U.S. Dollars)		
Rank	Country	Value	Rank	Country	Value	Rank	Country	Value	Rank	Country	Value
1	Norway	0.965	1	Japan	82.2	1	Australia	113.2	1	Luxemburg	69,961
158	Rwanda	0.450	165	DR Congo	43.5	139	Yemen	55.4	153	B/Faso	1,169
159	Nigeria	0.448	166	Nigeria	43.4	140	Nigeria	55.0	154	Nigeria	1,154
160	Guinea	0.445	167	E Guinea	42.8	141	Togo	55.0	155	Kenya	1,140
161	Angola	0.439	168	Mozambique	44.1	143	Zambia	54.3	156	CAR	1,094
177	Niger	0.311	177	Swaziland	31.3	177	Niger	21.5	177	Sierra Leone	561

Source: Compiled from UNDP (2006).

Table 2. Indicators of Sustainability.

System Intervention	Well-Being	Organizational Capacity	Empowerment
Economic	• Nigeria ranks 159th of 177 countries • Nigeria's HDI of 0.448 is an indication of the poor investment in policies to improve the quality of life of the citizenry • 60 percent of Nigerians live under the poverty line	• Nigeria ranks 140th on research and development as a percentage of GDP • 30 percent of the industries in the Niger Delta region have closed because of economic losses stemming from violence and conflicts	• The lack of access to information • Lack of infrastructure like telephone and electricity hinders institutional capacity building • Memory loss • Factory closings
Social	• Life expectancy dropped from 53 years in 2002 to 43 years in 2006 • Disease/infection from pollution increased resulting in Nigerians having to pay more for health care	• Disintegration of the social structure • Frustrated expectations • Deep-rooted mistrust	• 30 percent increase in hostage taking, militancy conflict and restiveness since 2005
Ecology	• 50 percent increase in gas flaring and green house gas emissions in the past 5 years • There has also been an increase in respiratory diseases	• High levels of air pollution in oil-producing communities • Presence of ozone-depleting substances	• 20 percent reduction in vegetation cover

Source: Compiled from UN Department of Economic & Social Affairs (2001). Commission on Sustainable Development, New York.

Most of the oil reserves are found along the country's Niger River Delta, off the shore of the Bight of Benin, in the Gulf of Guinea, and along the Bight of Bonny (Fig. 1). In addition, the Nigerian government plans to expand its reserves to 40 billion barrels by 2010 (EIA, 2006). The Niger Delta, that extends over $70,000 \, km^2$ and makes up 7.5 percent of Nigeria's landmass of $923,768 \, km^2$, plays a vital role in the country's economy. Some 20 million people, comprising more than 40 ethnic groups speaking over 250 dialects live in the Niger Delta. The Ijaws, the largest ethnic group, account for approximately 50 percent of the population of the region. Their livelihoods are primarily based on fishing and farming (Adejuwon, 2006). Despite the fact that Nigeria is the eighth largest oil exporter in the world, with

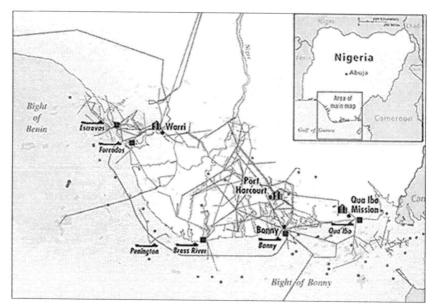

Fig. 1.   Map of the Niger Delta's Oil Infrastructure. *Source:* EIA (2006).

significant oil and gas reserves and daily output of 2.5 million barrels, most of its people live in abject poverty (EIA, 2006).

OIL AND GAS EXPLORATION AND PRODUCTION

Shell BP, a sole concessionaire, discovered oil in Nigeria in 1956 and began the practice of gas flaring during its production of crude oil. Before independence in 1960, agriculture was the mainstay of Nigeria's economy and a major source of foreign exchange. However, with the discovery of oil, emphasis shifted from agriculture to oil production. Agriculture is still declining in significance. In 1986 it accounted for 38.7 percent of the country's GDP, a decade later it accounted for only 30.7 percent (Aigbokhan, 2001). The overall contribution of the oil sector to the national economy grew from 0.1 percent in 1959 to 87 percent in 1976. By 1981, oil revenue had increased to approximately 90 percent of Nigeria's export earnings and approximately 80 percent of government revenues. Approximately 42 percent of Nigeria's oil exports go to the United States, 13 percent to India, 6 percent to Brazil, 6 percent to France, 5 percent to Spain,

4 percent to Italy, and 3 percent to Canada. The remaining exports go to an assortment of African, Asian, and European countries (EIA, 2006).

At the time the oil industry was developing, environmental protection and impacts on host communities were not given full consideration. Because Nigeria was a former colony of Britain, concessions such as monopoly of exploration rights was given to Shell BP in 1938 without competitive bidding or full evaluation of the long-term consequences of oil extraction on the environment. Since there were inadequate government policies to regulate the exploration and exploitation of oil resources, environmental degradation and the impoverishment of host communities became a major problem. Nigeria is not alone. The way the oil industry operates in many developing countries indicates that the interest of host communities and multinational oil companies are often at odds. In short, the host communities bear the brunt of the environmental degradation and other costs, whereas they derive few benefits from the revenues generated (Idemudia & Ite, 2006). Multinational companies do not typically keep the interests of oil-producing communities at the forefront of business decisions; because they are generally driven by profit motives and the desire to maximize returns on their investments (International Crises Group, 2006).

Though it is their obligation under international law to respect and protect human rights, the Nigerian government has often failed to do so. Instead, the government seems willing to collaborate with multinational oil companies to exploit the resources without providing adequate safeguards for host communities (Omeje, 2006). The Nigerian oil industry is operated under a Joint Operating Agreement (JOA) and within the legal and fiscal framework of a Memorandum of Understanding (MoU). The MoU governs how the oil income is allocated among the partners. This includes payment of taxes, royalties and industry margin under Split of the Barrel as a Joint Venture Agreement (JVA) between the government-owned Nigerian National Petroleum Corporation (NNPC) and oil companies such as Shell, Exxon Mobil, Chevron-Texaco, and TotalFinaElf. The NNPC holds majority shares while the oil companies hold minority interests in the oil development (Nigerian National Petroleum Corporation [NNPC], 2006).

The partners fund the joint ventures according to their equity share. Shell, the largest operator, produces more than one million barrels of oil per day (bpd); Exxon Mobil produces approximately 750,000 and Chevron accounts for 520,000 bpd (EIA, 2006). The country has a total production capacity of 2.5 million bpd, a million of which is produced offshore (Fig. 2). In spite of the volume of oil production, local refining capacity is currently insufficient to meet domestic demand so the country has to import petroleum products.

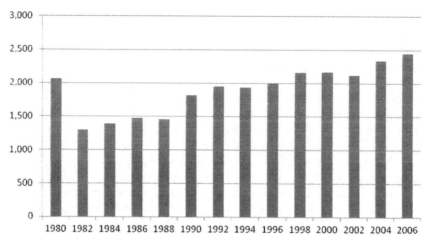

Fig. 2. Nigeria Crude Oil Productions, 1980–2006 (Includes Lease Condensate in Million Barrels per Day (bpd). *Source:* EIA (2006).

Nigeria's state-owned refineries, Port Harcourt I and II, Warri, and Kaduna have a total capacity of 438,750 bpd. But problems including sabotage, fire, poor management, and a lack of regular maintenance contribute to the current operating capacity of approximately 214,000 bpd. To meet local demand, the Nigerian government recently granted licenses to 18 private investors to build independently owned refineries. The private refineries when completed could save Nigeria as much as $2 billion in operational costs for refined petroleum imports (EIA, 2006).

SOCIAL AND ENVIRONMENTAL PROBLEMS

Oil Spills

Oil spills in Nigeria has been a regular occurrence, and the resulting pollution of the environment has caused significant problems for ecosystems and local communities. However, the Nigerian government and the oil companies operating in the region have not taken adequate measures to address the problems. This has resulted in tensions between the people living in the region, the government of Nigeria, and the multinational oil companies that operate in the Delta. The oil sector provides 20 percent of Nigeria's GDP, 95 percent of foreign exchange earnings, and approximately

65 percent of its budgetary revenues (UNDP, 2006). This makes the oil companies a formidable force to be reckoned with when it comes to issues of environmental protection and the social concerns of host communities. As aforementioned, pollution and environmental degradation are major concerns in the oil-producing regions of the country. Research conducted by the Nigerian Environmental Society in 1985 found that between 1970 and 1983, off- and on-shore oil spills amounted to approximately 1,711,354 barrels (Daniel-Kalio & Braide, 2002). In 2006 alone, Shell recorded 241 oil spills in its Nigerian operations; this figure may not include minor spills of less than 25 barrels in inland water and those in their operational areas. During this period too, Shell produced 3,726,000 tons of hydrocarbons, 11,695,000 tons of carbon dioxide, and 53,000,500 tons of methane (Shell Sustainability Report, 2006).

Pollution is not a trivial matter in the Delta region. The World Wildlife Foundation UK, working in conjunction with the World Conservation Union and the Nigeria Conservation Foundation, identified the Niger Delta as one of the five most polluted spots in the world. (Nigerian Conservation Foundation Report, 2005). The report highlighted the threat to rare species including primates, fish, turtles, and birds, and noted that pollution was destroying the livelihoods of many of the people living in the region. The report also indicated that pollution was damaging crops and overall conditions were fueling an upsurge in violence. The report accused the oil companies of "double standards." That is, they were not using technologies that were more in line with advanced practices carried out elsewhere in the world.

The environmental impacts of oil spills have been the subject of research over the past couple of years and much has been established in terms of the impacts. Physical and chemical alteration of the natural habitats results in the stunting of flora and fauna, lethal and sub-lethal toxic effects, and mortality of organisms. Many studies show that the harm done to fish and fish eggs as a result of spillage is very high. Moreover, oil pollution seriously damages the terrestrial and aquatic environment and even small spills can wreak tremendous havoc on aquatic and terrestrial ecosystems. Moreover, damaged ecosystems may take years to recover or may never recover at all (Environmental Protection Agency [EPA], 2007).

In Nigeria, oil spills and accidents are often followed by accusations and counter-accusations levied by oil companies and host communities. Typically, oil companies accuse host communities of sabotage – even when the eruption of oil pipelines cause oil to leak into communities and farmland. Amnesty International reports that the oil companies' use this tactic to avoid paying compensation for damages caused by the spills (Amnesty International, 2005). Attempts by oil companies to avoid owning up to oil spills or cleaning up pollution translates into disputes about compensation to host communities. International oil producers, adopted the Civil Liability Convention as a mechanism to ensure that adequate compensation is available to persons who suffer damages from oil pollution resulting from maritime casualties involving oil-carrying ships. The Convention places the liability for such damage on the owner of the ship from which the polluting oil escaped or was discharged. However, compensation in Nigeria is not up to these international standards (Dicks, 1998).

Gas Flaring

Gas flaring in Nigeria has been a source of concern too. Nigeria's emission of greenhouse gases is equal to all countries in sub-Sahara Africa combined. The World Bank estimates that Nigeria accounts for 12.5 percent of the world's total gas flaring (Nigerian National Petroleum Corporation [NNPC], 2009). Not only are the flares not used as fuel, they contain toxins such as benzene and methane that pollute the air and contribute to acid rain. The frequent complaints by host communities of acid rain corroding the roofs of buildings are routinely ignored. The particles from the flares fill the air, covering everything with a fine layer of soot. Flaring continues despite the fact that it was made illegal by environmental regulations that went into effect in 1984. According to the Associated Gas Re-Injection Act 1979 No.99, it is obligatory for every company producing oil in Nigeria to submit detailed plans for gas utilization. The Act also stipulates that no company engaged in the production of oil shall after January 1, 1984 flare gas produced in association with oil without written permission from the Minister of Petroleum Resources. Flaring was to be allowed only in specific circumstances on a field-by-field basis pursuant to a ministerial issued certificate (Nwokeji, 2007).

However, no sooner had the Act taken effect, it was amended to allow continued flaring. In 1984, the Act was amended under the Associated Gas Re-Injection regulation otherwise known as the Continued Flaring of Gas Regulations 1984. The government defended its action by arguing that the amendment became necessary in view of the limited domestic market for gas and because of the high cost associated with gas development prevented the oil companies from embarking on immediate gas development program. The government also argued that because of its dependence on oil revenues;

it had to review the 1979 Gas Re-injection Decree to enable the oil companies to produce oil under favorable conditions. The Regulation spelled out the conditions for the issuing of certificates by the Minister under Section 3(2) of the Associated Gas Re-Injection Act 1979 for the continued flaring of gas in a particular field or fields by companies engaged in the production of oil and gas (Nwokeji, 2007).

Though at a first glance, it seems like the Act sought to put an end to gas flaring, it did not because companies were still allowed to flare gas with the permission of the minister of Petroleum. More so, the Associated Gas Re-Injection Amendment Degree of 1985 introduced a charge of 2 K per MCF of gas flared at the fields where authority to flare associated gas was not granted. The penalty was later increased to N10 in 1998. With such a minor penalty, the operators chose to pay the penalty than stop gas flaring.

A Nigeria's High Court confirmed the illegality of flaring when it ruled that the burning of gas by oil companies violate the human rights of local people and must be stopped. The case, supported by Environmental Rights Action (ERA), Friends of the Earth, Nigeria and Climate Justice Program, was brought by the Iwherekan Community. In a judgment delivered on November 14, 2005 in Suite No. FHC/B/C/53/05, filed at the Federal High Court of Nigeria in Benin City, the court declared:

That the actions of the companies by continuing to flare gas in the course of their oil exploration and production activities in the Iwherekan community is a violation of their fundamental right to life (including healthy environment) and dignity of human person guaranteed by section 33(1) and 34(1) of the constitution of the Federal Republic of Nigeria, 1999 and reinforced by Act 4, 16 and 24 of the African Charter on Human Procedure Rules (Ratification and Enforcement) Act Cap A9 Vol.1 Laws of the Federation of Nigeria. That the provisions of Section 3(2) (a),(b) of the Associated Gas Re-injection Act Cap A25 Vol. 1 Laws of the Federation of Nigeria, 2004 and section 1 of the Associated Gas Re-injection (continuing flaring of gas) Regulation section 1.43 of 1984, under which the continued flaring of gas in Nigeria may be allowed are inconsistent with the right to life and or dignity of human person enshrine in section 33(1) and 34(1) of the constitution of the Federal Republic of Nigeria, 1999 and reinforced by Act 4, 16 and 24 of the African Charter on Human Procedure Rules (Ratification and Enforcement) Act Cap A9 Vol.1 Laws of the Federation of Nigeria and are therefore unconstitutional, null and void by virtue of section 1(3) of the same constitution. (Environmental Rights Action/Friends of the Earth Nigeria [ERA/FOE], 2005)

Despite the court decision, Nigeria pushed forward the initial 2004 "flares-out" deadline to 2008.

The lack of political will by the government to implement previous laws on gas flaring deadlines calls to question the latest attempt by the national assemble to enact a new law to stop gas flaring by December 2010.

A cursory look at the Gas Flaring Prohibition and Punishment Bill 2009 recently passed by the Senate, stipulates that "Natural gas shall not be flared in any Oil and Gas production operation, block or field onshore or offshore or gas facility, processing, treatment plant, etc. after 31st December 2010." Subsection 3 of the bill says "Any person who flares gas after 31st December 2010 shall be liable to pay a fine which shall not be less than the cost of gas at the international market." The extent to which this bill will be implemented is left to conjecture.

Although the people of the oil-producing communities are left to bear the brunt of gas flaring and live in abject poverty, the oil companies are reaping enormous profits. Exxon Mobil earned the largest annual profit by a US company in 2006. The $39.5 billion in earnings is equivalent to $4.5 million every hour. Likewise, Shell made a profit of $22.94 billion in 2006. This exceeded its previous record profits of $17.59 billion made in 2005 (Nigeria supplies 10 percent of Shell's total output). An assessment of yearly revenues collected by the Nigerian government from oil is very meager when compared with the quantum of profit earned by these companies. In 2004, all the oil companies combined paid the Nigerian government royalties and taxes totaling $27 billion (NNPC, 2006).

OIL PRODUCTION, CONFLICTS, AND VIOLENCE

Much scholarly research has been done on the conflicts arising from oil production in Nigeria. Most of the analyses have focused on the causes, dynamics, and ramifications of oil conflicts. In the context of this essay, conflict is being framed as the "uneasy" "relationship between two or more parties who have, or think they have, incompatible goals." The incompatible goals may include, desire, interest, and aspiration (Omeje, 2006). In the case of Nigeria, oil is at the heart of the conflict. "Black gold" (oil) is the "driving force" of the economy of most countries that are endowed with it. As Watts (2004) puts it, "Oil is of course a biophysical resource; it is also a commodity that enters the market with its price tag, and as such it is the bearer of particular relations of production and quite specific fetishistic qualities." Black gold carries with it influence, hopes, and expectations of unimaginable power. As a result, oil is an important reference point in Nigerian popular culture such as films, soap operas, and popular theater (Watts, 2004).

According to Omeje (2006), four major schools of thought explain the sources of strain and factors contributing to the Nigerian oil conflict.

First, the historical legacy of colonial rule that consolidated communities and ethnic groups with different languages and cultural practices into political and economic entities that satisfied the needs of the colonialists but paid little attention to pre-colonial relationships. This artificial agglomeration gave rise to conflicts that persist today. Omeje also argues that another source of conflict is the federal system of governance in place since the country gained independence in 1960. From the outset, this system was at odds with the expectations of many minorities in the country. Many have argued that the post-independence federal constitution suffered from two fundamental shortcomings or defects. The first is the classification of the country into three unequal regions, and second, the political and demographic domination and marginalization of the minority ethnic groups by the majority ethnic groups. This gave rise to many years of political and power imbalance in the country resulting in the promulgation of laws relating to oil exploration and land ownership that has not benefited the Niger Delta region. Furthermore, the long history of marginalization of the region has resulted in a lack of basic infrastructure such as schools, hospitals, potable water, electricity, and roads (UNDP, 2006).

Another major factor is the lack of a domestic legal framework to deal with the legislative and policy issues arising from oil extraction. One significant issue that has legal ramifications is the payment of compensation by oil companies for oil spills and other forms of environmental degradation. As outlined at the International Civil Liability and Fund Convention 1992, the principle of compensation is meant to ensure that claimants are left in the same financial position as they would have been had oil spills not occurred (Dicks, 1998). This poses a potential problem when it comes to damage to natural resources that are not commercially exploited. In practice, it is difficult to get compensation for the destruction of the ecosystem and the environment in oil-producing regions. In reality, most of the Nigeria's domestic laws and decrees relating to oil production are not in accordance with international agreements. This is particularly true of those related to human rights. Local and international nongovernmental organizations working in oil-producing areas report the occurrence of human rights violations. The UN Committee on the Elimination of Racial Discrimination (CERD) against indigenous people reported various human rights violation against host communities in its 67th session (United Nations Commission for Human Rights [UNCHR], 2005).

CERD noted with concern that the main principles of the 1992 Convention have not been incorporated in the domestic law. This is necessary before it can be invoked directly in the Nigerian courts. The Committee was deeply concerned about the adverse effects on the environment of ethnic communities through large-scale exploitation of natural resources in the Delta region. The failure of the government to engage in meaningful consultation with the communities, about the dangerous effects of the oil production activities on the local infrastructure, economy, health, and education was also a source of concern. In this regard, the Committee noted that the Land Use Act of 1978 and the Petroleum Decree of 1969 are contrary to the provisions of the UN convention (UNCHR, 2005). The Petroleum Act of 1969 placed all minerals in the domain of the federal government. This act provides in Section 1 that "the entire ownership and control of all petroleum under or upon any land to which this section applies (i.e., land in Nigeria, under the territorial waters of Nigeria or forming part of the continental shelf) shall be vested in the state." The spirit and intent of the Petroleum Act was further consolidated in 1978 when the government enacted the Land Use Decree, removing land from the control of local communities to be held in trust for the central government by the state governors. The decree was extended in 2003 to include deep-water offshore oil reserves (Khan, 1994).

Third, the economic approach of win–win can pose problems. It assumes that if people are prosperous and profit is maximized, prosperity will result in better natural resources management and different incentives. However, this market-driven approach has not adequately provided for a balance between natural capital and human capital growth and relied instead on economic growth models (Rodriguez-Pose & Vilalta-Buf, 2005).

Finally, a perspective that shows indifference to or disregard for the ecosystems on which life depends has posed huge problems. The solutions to the problems lie in developing an understanding of and a respect for natural systems, and providing people with mechanisms to express that understanding in their daily choices. The implied governmental role would be to support ecologically based education and values, as well as to promote "green" production and stricter environmental policies (Parker & Blodgett, 2007).

Other factors have fueled resentment and conflicts in the region. For example, rampant corruption in the oil industry has had a negative impact on the economic development of the region. Despite oil production in the region, unemployment remains high among youth; even those graduating from university have difficulty finding employment. A great number of the people in the region remain uneducated. A UNDP report on the Niger Delta argues that

> Declining economic performance leading to rising unemployment or underemployment; the lack of access to basic necessities of life like water, shelter, food and clothing; discriminatory policies that deny access to positions of authority and prevent people from participating in shaping the rules that govern their lives are all indications that

governance over time has fallen short ... and corruption aggravates feelings of being cheated, especially when the rulers live like kings amid extreme want. In spite of the substantial flow of oil money to state and local governments, many communities see no sign of government presence in terms of development projects. This intensifies a sense of hopelessness and mistrust for the most aggrieved people that lead to a call to arms. (UNDP, 2006)

These factors combine to incite restiveness and militant actions by youths. Vandalism of oil installations and kidnapping of oil workers to draw international attention to the plight of the area is increasing. Unfortunately, the government and the oil companies are not doing enough to stem the tide of these activities; few negotiations have succeeded in this regard. Though the government did take some steps toward reducing underdevelopment of the region when it established the Niger Delta Development Commission and the Ministry of Niger Delta Affairs to address the developmental needs of the area more effectively. However, these organs of government have been plagued by political infighting and have not been given a free reign to perform its duties by the government. In addition, the commission and the ministry are not funded sufficiently. The non-release of approved budgetary allocations to these branches is always a source of contention.

One aspect of the recommendations that has received urgent attention is the granting of amnesty to militants who have been subverting oil production in an attempt to make the region ungovernable. This is implemented through disarming process and establishment of Decommissioning Disarmament Rehabilitation (DDR) and post amnesty reintegration programs through leadership and skill acquisition training to give the ex-militants a sense of self-worth. However, the sincerity of government in ensuring the full implementation of these recommendations is yet to be realized. The Nigerian National Petroleum Corporation in July 2009 also signed an agreement with a Russian security and maintenance firm – Ruscorp Integrated Services – which specializes in protecting and maintaining oil and gas infrastructures to provide security and rehabilitation of 6,000 km of oil pipelines in the country. The agreement paves the way for Ruscorp to protect and upgrade ageing oil pipeline networks as well as build new distribution lines. However, there are other major issues that need to be addressed by the government to ensure lasting peace in the region (NNPC, 2009).

The revenue sharing formula of the oil wealth, demand for increased local control of oil property, and lack of transparency of government in handling the oil wealth are other sources of on-going conflicts (Ibeanu, 2005). The control over oil royalty by the oil-producing region has always been a sour point in the relationship between the three large regions. This

Table 3. Revenue Sharing Formula in Nigeria 1958–2001.

Year	Percentage Allocated				Derivation Formula (Percent)
	Federal	State	Local	Special Projects	
1958	40	60	0	0	50
1968	80	20	0	0	10
1977	75	22	3	0	10
1982	55	32.5	10	2.5	10
1989	50	24	15	11	10
1995	48.5	24	20	7.5	13
2001	48.5	24	20	7.5	13

Source: Adapted from World Bank (2001).

resulted in the outbreak of the Nigerian civil war in the 60s leading to the creation of more states out of the regional blocks to reduce the dominance of the major ethnic groups (Omeje, 2006).

Oil revenue allocation has been the subject of much contention well before Nigeria gained its independence. State allocations have varied from as much as 50 percent (when production first began) to as low as 10 percent during the military dictatorships. State allocations are based on five criteria: equal allocation per state, population, social development, landmass, and revenue generation. The derivation formula refers to the percentage of the revenue an oil producing state retain from taxes on oil and other natural resources produced in that state. The sharing formula from 1958 when oil was discovered to 2001 is presented in Table 3.

The people of the Delta region are demanding an increase in the revenue allocation to the oil-producing states. They want to see their share increased from 13 to 25 percent. This demand was turned down during the last political reform conference. Delegates from the region walked out of the conference after they were offered 17 percent of revenues during the negotiations. The oil companies have not been helping residents either. They have not provided the amenities that local communities often demand of them (Idemudia & Ite, 2006).

CONFLICTS, REGIONAL IDENTITY FORMATION, AND COLLECTIVE ACTION

In the analyses of the causes of Nigeria's oil conflicts, little attention was paid to the issue of resource management and its implications on rural livelihoods (Peet & Watts, 1993). In recent years, however, pollution has received international attention because of its effects on humans and the ecosystem. Bryant and Brant (2003) postulate that resource degradation could best be understood by analyzing "the role of various actors in relation to a politicized environment." What is of interest here, is the way in which, multilateralism has been linked to the promotion of economic 'development' in the 'third word' and how, in so doing, it has been associated with economic activities that have frequently produced widespread social hardship and environmental degradation (Peet & Watts, 1993).

Nigeria's post-colonial history is characterized by structural dualism. That is, there is a coexistence of traditional and modern elements in the society vis-à-vis the cultural, social, economic, political, and legal frameworks that govern the society. This structure is characterized by the unfinished nature of state making as well as the institutional and instrumental constraints of the central authorities' attempts to unify the disparate ethnic nationalities into a "modern" nation state (Omeje, 2006).

Since independence, the country has been trying to function effectively as an oil-producing country. The taxes and royalties paid by transnational oil companies are placed into a government account and shared among the federating units. Revenue sharing is based on a formula that is strongly influenced by the population distribution. Under the current revenue-sharing model, oil-producing communities are largely excluded from decision-making relating to revenue sharing or the type of community development projects that are to be undertaken in their locales. The result of this is that, the national government has overwhelming power to make decisions on behalf of host communities. This has lead to resentment and conflicts that manifest themselves in militant action in host communities. A variety of opposition tactics and repertoires have been deployed against oil companies operating in aggrieved communities. These take the form of demonstrations and blockades against oil facilities, occupations of flow stations and platforms, sabotage of pipelines, oil "bunkering," or theft from breaking and hot-tapping fuel lines, large-scale appropriation of crude from flow stations (this oil is then sold illegally), litigation against the companies, hostage taking, and strikes (Watts, 2004).

The dynamics of the oil industrial complex has a profound influence on the character and dynamics of Nigerian development. Civil society has faced the challenges and popular struggles for state and democratic reforms. Though these may relate to the articulation of substantive ethnic, regional and communal demands, few studies have addressed the dynamics and ramifications of their engagement in the struggle other than democratization

(Watts, 2004). As the conflicts with oil companies remain unresolved, groups and organizations in civil society have emerged, taken over and escalated the struggle. Such groups have aligned themselves into a regional resistance. Civil society groups have consolidated local resistance and reconstructed them into a broad, participatory, highly mobilized and coordinated regional struggle. They have also reframed the resistance as a struggle for self-determination, equity, civil and environmental rights (Ikelegbe, 2001).

By early 1980s, the beginning of popular resistance (and the call for "resource control") was already evident. However, it was the 1990 Ogoni Bill of Rights, promoted by the Movement for the Survival of the Ogoni People (MOSOP) under the leadership of Ken Saro-Wiwa that marked a watershed moment in the popular agitation against the consequences of oil development in the Niger Delta. Saro-Wiwa and eight other MOSOP leaders (Baribor Bera, Saturday Doobee, Nordu Eawo, Daniel Gbokoo, Barinem Kiobel, John Kpuinen, Paul Levura, and Felix Nuate) were executed by the military in 1995. Saro-Wiwa and others were opposed to the oil companies turning their communities into a "wasteland." More than a decade after the executions, the skies are still blackened by gas flares, the waters are polluted and the people subsist on less than US$1 per day. However, instead of snuffing out resistance, the murder of the MOSOP leaders outraged locals and emboldened many in oil-producing communities to join the resistance (Obi, 2004). It resulted in growing demands for compensation across the nine oil-producing delta states and the development of wide-ranging pan-ethnic political movements calling for "true federalism" (Okonta & Douglas, 2001).

The growing participation of citizens and grassroots groups in the mid-1980s permitted oil-related grievances to be articulated in the context of what Ikelegbe (2001) calls "participatory, highly mobilized, and coordinated platforms of civil groups in a struggle for self-determination, equity and civil rights." However, recent activities of Delta region social movements such as the Movement for the Emancipation of the Niger Delta (MEND), Niger Delta People Volunteer Force (NDPVF), and Coalition for Militant Action in the Niger Delta (COMA) are such that they threaten the very peace, stability and lives of the people of the host communities they claim to be fighting for (Jerome, 2005).

There is an urgent need for the government to play a greater role in protecting its citizens against the harmful practices and policies of the transnational corporations and promulgating legislation and policies that will give the oil-producing communities greater control and management of the resources found in their area. In fact, many communities in the Niger Delta perceive little difference between the oil companies and the Nigerian state. This perception is not entirely without justification. On countless occasions, oil companies have deployed police, army and security forces to quell disturbances on their installations without seeking help from the government. They see the pipelines traversing their communities as pipelines of operation rather than instruments of wealth. These multinational companies are very often accused of neglecting their corporate social responsibility and do not honor most MoUs with host communities that call for the provision of social amenities and employment (Ikelegbe, 2001).

The current rate of violence in the region confirms Homer-Dixon's (1999) argument that global environmental scarcities will have profound social consequences that can contribute to insurrections, ethnic clashes, urban unrest, and other forms of civil violence especially in the developing world. He concluded that rapid growth in the global economy would spur ever-increasing demands for natural resources. The world will consequently face growing scarcities of such vital renewable resources as cropland, fresh water, and forests.

Reports of pipeline vandalism, kidnappings, and militant takeover of oil facilities in the Niger Delta have been on the increase since December 2005. Although Nigeria earns billions of dollars every year from exporting crude oil, its domestic refineries have been laid waste by corruption and mismanagement and the country thus relies on expensive imports of refined fuels (EIA, 2006). Transparency International 2004 ranked the country as the third most corrupt country in the world (Jerome, 2005). If the latest report on corruption index is anything to go by, it may take many years for Nigeria to eliminate corruption from its system. The specter of corruption, violence, and sabotage is, in a large measure, fed by the organized theft of oil, as distinct from oil revenues, by various sorts of "syndicates." Although low-level operatives take their share along the creeks, so-called oil bunkering (large-scale theft) involves the military, businessmen, and reaches to the highest levels of government. The latest confession of a former executive of Wilbros International, on trial in the United States for bribery, who admitted bribing Nigerian government officials as part of a scheme to win a natural gas pipeline contract is evidence that corruption exists in the Nigerian oil industry (*Punch Newspaper*, 2007). Sensing the larger amounts of money to be made from bunkering, Ijaw militants are fighting to get into the bunkering trade. Some estimates suggest that this innovative form of oil theft siphons off roughly 15 percent of production (*Human Rights Watch*, 2006).

Because of the conflicts and the fear of sabotage, between December 2005 and April 2007, an estimated 587,000 bpd of crude production was shut-in by companies operating in the Niger Delta region. Most of the shut-in production is located offshore. It has been estimated that Nigeria has lost around $16 billion in revenues due to shut-in oil production during this period. Shell has the biggest losses – they have lost approximately 477,000 bpd. Other companies such as Chevron have lost approximately 70,000 bpd and Agip approximately 40,000 bpd (EIA, 2006). In February 2006, attacks in the Delta region forced the Warri refinery (125,000 bpd) and Kaduna refinery (110,000 bpd) to close because of a shortage of feedstock. Niger Delta community-based organizations seeking monetary compensation and/or political leverage claim they are responsible for the attacks. The conflicts have affected how the oil companies have structured their workforce. Oil companies have had to respond because thousands of foreign workers and their families have left the Niger Delta because of the rising hostilities. For instance, Shell has increased the number of Nigerians in its employ to 4,800 of 5,000 employees. Other companies have also adopted a similar strategy. Total has 900 Nigerian employees in a workforce of 1,200 (Business in Africa Online, 2007).

Despite hiring Nigerians, the demographic composition of the oil companies' workforce is still a source of conflict. When Nigerians are hired into these companies, there is ethnic sorting that contributes to continued conflicts and simmering resentment. Typically, the Nigerians who occupy executive positions in the oil companies are from the dominant tribes and ethnic groups that wield political power. If they are lucky enough to get employment, the people of the Niger Delta are hired as unskilled laborers to do menial jobs (Amnesty International, 2005). Militant attacks on the oil infrastructure are usually accompanied by violent responses from the government or the oil companies. Organized protest and activism by affected communities are brutally repressed, sometimes ending in the loss of lives. Oil companies hire security forces and vigilante groups to protect their investments in the region (Osaghae, 1995; Amnesty International, 2006). According to an Amnesty International (2006) report, soldiers fired on protestors at Chevron's Escravos oil terminal killing one person and injuring about 30 others. Though Chevron Nigeria claims that the protestors were armed, video footage of the incident did not show any armed protestors. The protestors were villagers from Ugborodo and Itkesiri communities in the shadows of the Chevron facility. Community leaders claim that they were protesting Chevron's refusal to fulfill an agreement to provide jobs and development projects to the community. At the time of the protests, villagers got only 2 h of electricity that came from a generator they purchased and installed at their own expense. Chevron provided the village with water twice a day 3 h at a time. Despite living in plain sight of the oil terminal, large numbers of youths from the village are unemployed; they complain that they are discriminated against when they seek work at the facility. Chevron denies that Ugborodo villagers are discriminated against in the hiring process. In response to the Escravos incident, Chevron said it had no control over its security forces. As Eghare W.O. Ojhogar, chief of the Ugborodo community in Delta State puts it,

> It is like paradise and hell. They have everything. We have nothing ... If we protest, they send soldiers. They sign agreements with us and then ignore us. We have graduates going hungry, without jobs. And they bring people from Lagos to work here. (Amnesty International, 2006)

Villagers are sometimes caught in the crossfire between the military and the paramilitary groups working on behalf of the oil companies. About two weeks after the Escravos incident, soldiers raided the Ijaw community of Odioma in Bayelsa state. Seventeen people were reported killed and two women were raped. The soldiers were trying to capture members of an armed vigilante group accused of killing 12 people (including four local councilors). A sub-contractor of Shell was said to have recruited the vigilante group. Though the suspects were not captured, in the days that the soldiers occupied the village, they destroyed approximately 80 percent of the homes in Odioma. Reports of the Judicial Commission of Inquiry established in the aftermath of these incidents are not made public. Members of the security forces reportedly are not held accountable for their human right abuses including killing, torture and rape (Amnesty International, 2006). The conflicts have caused some companies to close their operations and pull out of Nigeria altogether. At least three companies, including a private drilling company and pipeline laying company have also left the country because of the crisis (Zachary, 2006).

OIL AGREEMENTS AND POLICY IMPLEMENTATION

Despite the security challenges posed by militant activities in the oil-rich Niger Delta, more and more agreements are being entered into by the Nigerian state for the exploitation of the natural resources without addressing major policy issues that lead to the militancy in the first place. Most of these agreements do not incorporate inputs from all stakeholders neither are provisions made for externalities that will produce adverse impacts on the oil-bearing communities. Rather, the agreements are tailored to pave the way for the state-run NNPC to continue with the current policies of environmental degradation that disregard the interests of host communities. The Russian energy giant Gazprom signed a $2.5 billion joint venture agreement with NNPC to explore and develop oil and gas sector in Nigeria (Nigerian National Petroleum Corporation [NNPC], 2008).

Nigeria has also signed a development agreement with the United Arab Emirate to explore natural resources in the country. Under the cooperative agreement, Dubai Natural Resources World would manage the potential development and production of crude oil and gas reserves through the acceleration of upstream oil and gas asset and the development of gas utilization projects. Before now, there had been many laws guiding the petroleum industry to an extent that it has become cumbersome and technically lopsided for the operators vis-à-vis the oil communities to understand its implementation. The Federal government has considered the need to put in place proper framework that will be used for the running of the system as the best way to sustain the oil and gas sector. Therefore, the government has proposed a Petroleum Industry Bill to help set out clear rules, procedures, institutions, and regulatory authorities for the administration of the petroleum industry in Nigeria (NNPC, 2008).

However, many technical issues have not been addressed in the proposed bill. One of such areas is the right of ownership of oil resources by the central government without fair compensation to the people of the oil-bearing communities. The bill neither addresses the fundamental issues of environmental degradation caused by oil drilling activities nor the equitable participation of the people in the joint venture operation. The people, therefore, will continue to resent the oil industry and oppose oil pipelines traversing their land.

CONCLUSION

A major challenge facing Nigeria is for the country to figure out a way to develop a holistic approach that will foster a just and sustainable development in oil-producing communities. Such a plan needs to consider ways of reducing environmental degradation and social problems that the current system fosters. Fowler (2006) argues that in order to provide a platform for effective development planning, there is need to combine environmental considerations with the socio-political and economic perspectives.

To do this, all the major stakeholders (government, oil companies, local community residents, community-based organizations, and environmental groups) should be involved in all phases of project development, implementation and monitoring. Mathie and Cunningham (2003) contend that communities are weakened if they are not included in the stakeholder process and have to rely on outside institutions to intervene on their behalf to solve their problems. Outside institutions cannot do enough to strengthen local communities because of their vested interest in maintaining the dependency. To anticipate and deal with problems, such as oil spills, international conventions and national policies regarding spills and other kinds of adverse events should be made part of the agreement between the government, oil companies and the host communities. These agreements should include the acquisition of modern equipment and materials for oil spill (Faure & Hui, 2003). It is also important to develop mechanisms to see that agreements between oil companies and communities are adhered to and enforced.

Careful attention should be paid to monitoring programs. Such programs should be well defined and developed throughout the life of a project from the planning phases to decommissioning. Public disclosure should be a part of the process. Oil companies executing projects should be required to produce public documents evaluating their performance, forecasting and assessing effects on the environment and local communities, reporting on incidence of conflicts and violence, waste production and management, etc. Projects should be evaluated, audited and inspected by independent groups at regular intervals. Companies should develop their own internal inspection programs to ensure compliance with environmental standards, company policies, and the project environmental management plans. Special attention should be paid to discharges. An effluent discharge program should be designed to monitor and control the impact of operational discharges on the environment. This should include monitoring various points of discharge, the handling and disposal of oil- and water-based mud, as well as cuttings and methods of sampling during oil exploitation (Gardner, 2002).

An extensive public education program should be instituted to familiarize people with environmental issues related to oil and other extractive industries. This is particularly important in oil-producing communities. Programs should be developed to help local residents increase their knowledge about and awareness of the issues. Community-based organizations could be enlisted in identifying the needs of local residents and helping to address their concerns. These programs should also address issues related to health and safety. Nigeria needs stronger environmental protection laws and mechanisms to enforce them. Corporate social responsibility should be incorporated into efforts to protect people and the environment. This means that mechanisms should be put in place to help preserve the social and cultural fabric of host communities. It is also essential that project development should include the enhancement of the institutional infrastructure of oil-producing communities and the improvement in the quality of lives of local residents. Provisions should be made to include roads, water purification and delivery, electricity, sewage treatment, schools, hospitals, health care provision, libraries, computers, literacy education, community and recreational centers, job training and employment, living wage, housing, scholarships, sub-contracts (to help build or supply goods and services), multiplier businesses (such as shops and restaurants), compensation for land taken or resources damaged, etc. in the development of projects for the oil producing communities (Onibokun & Kumuyi, 1996).

An implication of the earlier discussion is that the people of Nigeria are not deriving maximum benefits from their oil resources. As a result, the Nigerian government and the oil companies have to be prepared to come to more equitable revenue-sharing agreements with oil-producing communities. This is one of the central demands of the community-based organizations and residents of oil-producing communities in general. These groups are also demanding increased local control of oil property, and transparency of government budgets (Zachary, 2006). Applying a political ecology approach to the analysis of environmental problems (i.e., analysis of the linkages and interactions of ecology and politics), we can see how the exploitation of natural resources, policymaking, corruption, and resource development strategies that minimizes local input and provides limited benefits to host communities leads to social stresses that result in conflicts (Homer-Dixon, 1999).

In conclusion, much has to be done to reduce environmental degradation and risk residents of oil-producing communities face in Nigeria. In addition, conflicts over oil production will continue to escalate, unless more attention is paid to the concerns of oil-producing communities. Consequently, there is an urgent need for the development of an effective policy framework that includes all the stakeholders in the management and control of oil resources.

REFERENCES

Adejuwon, J. (2006). *Food security, climate variability and climate change in Sub Saharan West Africa. A Final Report of Impacts and Adaptations to Climate Change* (AIACC), Project No. AF 23 Departments of Geography, Obafemi Awolowo University, Ile-Ife, Nigeria.

Aigbokhan, B. E. (2001). Resuscitating agricultural production. The Central Bank of Nigeria Occasional Papers, Resource Endowment, Growth and Macroeconomic Management in Nigeria. Available at http://www.cenbank.org/OUT/PUBLICATIONS/OCCASIO-NALPAPERS/RD/2001/OWE-01-6.PDF. Retrieved on June 4.

Amnesty International. (2005). Ten years on: Injustice and violence haunt the oil delta. *Amnesty International Report.* Available at http://web.amnesty.org/library/Index/ ENGAFR440222005

Amnesty International. (2006). Nigeria: Oil, poverty and violence. Available at http://www. amnesty.org/en/alfresco_asset/5170f914-a2b9-11dc-8d74-6f45f39984e5/afr440172006en.pdf

Bryant, R. L., & Brant, S. (2003). *Third world political ecology.* Oxford, UK: Routledge Taylor & Francis Group.

Business in Africa Online. (2007). Nigeria: Oil companies to hold firm despite unrest. Available at http://www.businessinafrica.net/new/west_africa/485671.htm

Daniel-Kalio, L. A., & Braide, S. A. (2002). The impact of accidental oil spill on cultivated and natural vegetation in a wetland area of Niger Delta, Nigeria. *Ambio: A Journal of Human Environment, 31*(5), 441–442.

Dicks, B. (1998). Environmental impacts of marine oil spills-effects, recovery and compensation. Available at http://www.itopf.com/environ.pdf

Energy Information Administration (EIA). (2006). Energy Information Administration Country Analysis Brief. Nigeria. Available at http://www.eia.doe.gov/emeu/cabs/ Nigeria/Background.html, http://www.eia.doe.gov/ipm/supply.html

Environmental Protection Agency (EPA). (2007). US Environmental Protection Agency, Introduction and Background to the Oil Pollution Prevention Regulation. Available at http://www.uscg.mil/d1/response/rrt/RCP_public.pdf

Environmental Rights Action/Friends of the Earth Nigeria (ERA/FOE). (2005). *Report on Gas Flaring in Nigeria: A Human Rights, Environmental and Economic Monstrosity.* Available at http://www.foei.org/en/publications/pdfs/gasnigeria.pdf

Faure, M., & Hui, W. (2003). The international regimes for the compensation of oil-pollution damage: Are they effective? *Review of European Community International Environmental Law, 12*(3), 242–253.

Federal Office of Statistics. (1999). *Poverty Profile of Nigeria: A Statistical Analysis of 1996/97 National Consumer Survey* (With reference to 1980, 1985 and 1992 surveys), Lagos, Nigeria.

Fowler, A. (2006). *What does sustainable development mean for NGDOs?* In the Virtuous Spiral. London, UK: EarthScan Publications Ltd.

Gardner, R. (2002). Overview and characteristics of some occupational exposures and health risk on offshore oil and gas installations. *Annals of Occupational Hygiene, 47*, 201–210.

Homer-Dixon, T. F. (1999). *Environment, scarcity, and violence.* Princeton, NJ: Princeton University Press.

Human Rights Watch. (2006). *The price of oil: Corporate responsibility and human rights violations in Nigeria's oil producing communities.* New York: *Human Rights Watch.*

Ibeanu, O. (2005). *Oiling the friction: Environmental conflict management in the Niger Delta, Nigeria.* Occasional Papers. Wilson Center, Washington, DC. Available at http://www. wilsoncentre.org/index.cfm?fuseaction = events.event_summary&event_id = 740129

Idemudia, U., & Ite, U. E. (2006). Corporate-community relations in Nigeria's oil industry: Challenges and imperatives. *Corporate Social Responsibility and Environmental Management Journal, 13*(4), 194–206.

Ikelegbe, A. (2001). Civil society, oil and conflict in the Niger Delta region of Nigeria: Ramifications of civil society for a regional resource struggle. *Journal of Modern African Studies*, *39*(3), 437–469.

International Crises Group. (2006). Fueling the Niger Delta crises. *Africa Report No.118*. Available at http://www.crisisgroup.org/library/documents/africa/west_africa/118_fuelling_the_niger_delta_crisis.pdf

Jerome, A. (2005). Managing oil rent for sustainable development and poverty reduction in Africa. UNU-WIDER Jubilee Conference. The Future of Development Economics. Available at http://www.wider.unu.edu/conference/conference-2005-3/conference-2005-3-papers/Jerome.pdf

Khan, S. (1994). *Nigeria: The political economy of oil*. London, UK: Oxford University Press.

Mathie, A., & Cunningham, G. (2003). Reflection on the transformation potentials of asset-based community development. University of Manchester Conference on Participation: From Tyranny to Transformation, February 27. Available at http://www.coady.stfx.ca/resources/publications/publications_presentations_driving.html

Nigerian Conservation Foundation Report. (2005). *Annual reports and accounts*. Lagos, Nigeria: Public AFFAIRS Unit.

Nigerian National Petroleum Corporation (NNPC). (2006). A Report on the Niger Delta Youths Stakeholders Workshop, NPC/AAPW, 45-64.

Nigerian National Petroleum Corporation (NNPC). (2008). Petroleum industry draft bill. Available at http://www.nnpcgroup.com/pib/petIndsBillDocs/PIBDraftBill2008.pdf

Nigerian National Petroleum Corporation (NNPC). (2009). Development of Nigeria's oil industry by Nigerian National Petroleum Corporation. Available at http://www.nnpcgroup.com/development

Nwokeji, G. U. (2007). The Nigerian national petroleum corporation and the development of the Nigerian oil and gas industry: History, strategies and current directions. Available at http://www.rice.edu/energy/publication.docs/NOCs/Paper/NNPC_Ugo.pdf

Obi, C. (2004). *The oil paradox*. Working Paper No. 73. Papers on Africa, University of Leipzig, Leipzig, Germany.

Okonta, I., & Douglas, O. (2001). *Where vultures feast: Shell, human rights and oil in the Niger Delta*. London, UK: Verso.

Omeje, K. C. (2006). *High stakes and stakeholders: Oil conflict and security in Nigeria*. Ashgate, London: Aldershot.

Onibokun, A. G., & Kumuyi, A. J. (1996). Urban poverty in Nigeria: Towards sustainable strategies for its alleviation. Centre for African Settlement Studies and Development (CASSAD) Monograph series No.4.

Osaghae, E. (1995). The Ogoni uprising oil politics minority agitation and the future of the Nigerian State. *African Affairs*, *94*, 325–344.

Parker, L., & Blodgett, J. (2007). Global climate change: Three policy perspectives. CRS Report for Congress. Available at http://fas.org/sgp/crs/misc/RL31519.pdf

Peet, R., & Watts, M. (1993). Development theory and environment in an age of market triumphalism. *Journal of Economic Geography*, *68*(3), 227–253.

Punch Newspapers. (2007). Oil spill site shocks Senate. Saturday, November 3. Available at http://www.eraction.org/index.php?option = com_content&task = view&id = 86&Itemid = 1

Rodriguez-Pose, A., & Vilalta-Buf, M. (2005). Education, migration and job satisfaction on returns of human capital in the EU. *Journal of Economic Geography*, *5*(5), 545–566.

Shell Sustainability Report. (2006). Available at http://www.shell.com/static/envirosc-en/ downloads/sustainability_report/shell_sustain_report_2006.pdf

United Nations Commission for Human Rights (UNCHR). (2005). Concluding observations of the Committee on the Elimination of Racial Discrimination. Nigeria, Committee on the Elimination of Racial Discrimination. Available at http://www.unhchr.ch/tbs/doc.nsf/ (Symbol)/CERD.C.NGA.CO.18.En?Opendocument

United Nations Development Program (UNDP). (2006). *Niger Delta Human Development Report*. Available at http://hdr.undp.org/en/reports/nationalreports/africa/nigeria/nigeria_ 2006_en.pdf, http://hdrstats.undp.org/countries/country_fact_sheets/cty_fs_NGA.html

U.S. Agency for International Development (USAID). (2006). *Nigeria Economic Performance Assessment*, USAID County Analytical Support (CAS) Publication Project. Available at http://pdf.usaid.gov/pdf_docs/PNADF350.pdf

Watts, M. (2004). *The sinister political life of community economies of violence and governable spaces in the Niger Delta, Nigeria*. Working Paper No.3. IIS, University of California, Berkeley, CA, USA.

World Bank. (2001). State and governance in Nigeria. Public Sector and Capacity Building Program, *Africa Region Report*, February 2. Available at (http://www.info.worldbank. org/etools/docs/library/5783/StateandGovernance Nigeria.htm).

World Bank. (2007). Nigeria at a glance. Available at http://devdata.worldbank.org/AAG/ nga_aag.pdf

Zachary, G. P. (2006). Nigeria: The next quagmire? *AlterNet*, 5March 14. Available at http:// www.alternet.org/story/33282/

Joseph Effiong is a senior research fellow at the Centre for Social Policy Research and Development in Uyo, Nigeria. He can be reached by email at cojosn@yahoo.com or by telephone at 234-802-787-6076.

PART V
SPATIAL ANALYSIS

BUILDING COMMUNITY CAPACITY? MAPPING THE SCOPE AND IMPACTS OF EPA'S ENVIRONMENTAL JUSTICE SMALL GRANTS PROGRAM

Shalini P. Vajjhala

ABSTRACT

Purpose – *State and national environmental justice (EJ) programs have expanded in recent years to address new risks and challenges. Several programs including the Environmental Protection Agency's (EPA) Environmental Justice Small Grants (EJSG) program have helped to facilitate this growth. Since 1994, more than 1,000 small grants have been awarded through the EJSG to support communities in developing solutions to local environmental and public health problems. This chapter evaluates the collective impact of these investments.*

Design/methodology/approach – *Using Geographic Information Systems (GIS) to map the locations of EJSG funds relative to data from the Toxics Release Inventory (TRI), this chapter addresses two main questions. First, are grants being awarded to the types of communities (low-income, minority areas facing major environmental hazards) intended to be served by the program? Second, have there been any*

Environment and Social Justice: An International Perspective
Research in Social Problems and Public Policy, Volume 18, 353–381
Copyright © 2010 by Emerald Group Publishing Limited
All rights of reproduction in any form reserved
ISSN: 0196-1152/doi:10.1108/S0196-1152(2010)0000018014

significant environmental changes in EJSG areas since the start of the program?

Findings – *Results of county-level spatial analysis reveal that EJ grants are only in part being awarded to minority or low-income counties facing higher than the national average TRI releases and that average toxic releases have increased significantly in EJSG counties in some EPA regions relative to non-EJSG counties.*

Originality/value – *These results and the novel application of mapping methods to tracking small grants allocations highlight the need for systematic EJ program evaluation and coordination.*

INTRODUCTION

Since the advent of the environmental justice (EJ) movement, numerous research studies have centered on understanding if and to what extent minority and low-income communities are disproportionately burdened with significant environmental hazards. In contrast, far less research attention has been given to assessing federal agency activities intended to mitigate inequitable impacts of environmental hazards on minority and low-income communities. Although more than 15 years have passed since the signing of Executive Order (EO) 12898 "Federal Actions to Address Environmental Justice in Minority Populations and Low-Income Populations" (EO 12898, 1994), which mandates federal agencies to address EJ in their policies and procedures, the programs associated with this mandate have not been systematically evaluated.

Unlike environmental regulations, which set specific performance criteria or standards enforceable by law, the EJ requirements established by EO 12898 are directed solely at federal agency procedures and programs. Despite this limited reach, the requirements set forth in EO 12898 are very broad, addressing both the process of making equitable decisions and their desired outcomes. As a result, most agency initiatives designed in response to this EO are also expansive, ranging from building community capacity, improving public awareness, and educating citizens about exposure to environment hazards to expanding public participation. The far-reaching goals and aims of both EO 12898 and related agency EJ programs make the impacts of this mandate difficult to assess and evaluate.

To bridge the growing gap between EJ research studies and state and federal EJ programs, this chapter uses spatial analysis techniques to evaluate one of the long-standing, relatively consistent sources of federal agency EJ program data: the U.S. Environmental Protection Agency's (EPA) Environmental Justice Small Grants (EJSG) database. Since the program's inception in 1994, more than 1,000 grants have been awarded to help communities develop solutions to local environmental and public health problems. Despite the program's long history and national scope, the collective impact of these investments has never been evaluated.

This chapter uses Geographic Information Systems (GIS) to plot the locations of grants made through the EJSG program and then compares the patterns of these investments to county-level toxic releases reported in the Toxics Release Inventory (TRI) to address two major research questions. First, are EJ small grants being awarded to the types of communities (low-income, minority areas facing major environmental hazards) intended to be served by the program? Second, have there been any significant environmental changes in the areas that have received EJ small grants since the start of the program in 1994? The goals of this analysis are to establish a systematic approach to EJ evaluation for the EJSG program specifically, to put forward a method for reviewing federal and state EJ mandates more generally, and to lay the groundwork for setting priorities for future EJ investments.

THE ROLE OF SPATIAL ANALYSES IN ENVIRONMENTAL JUSTICE RESEARCH

Early EJ analyses show significant disparities in the location of environmental hazards in primarily poor and minority communities compared to other communities with lower minority populations. Seminal works on this topic include U.S. General Accounting Office's (GAO) study of EPA's Region IV, which found that three of the four off-site hazardous waste landfills in EPA's Region IV were in African American communities although African Americans constituted a minority of the region's total population (GAO, 1983); a 1987 United Church of Christ report, which examined 415 operating commercial (off-site) hazardous waste facilities and found such facilities were more likely to be located in communities with significant minority populations (Commission for Racial Justice, 1987); and the book *Dumping in Dixie: Race, Class, and Environmental Quality* by Robert Bullard (1990).

As mapping and measurements tools have grown more sophisticated, EJ studies have also evolved to examine changes in the timing and locations of environmental hazards, risk exposure, and other more detailed measures of inequity, using finer-grained spatial data and more targeted evaluations of local populations. Studies by Mohai and Bryant (1992) and Mohai and Saha (2007) illustrate the evolution of national-level EJ assessments over time. Stretesky and Hogan (1998), Pastor, Sadd, and Morello-Frosch (2004), and Saha and Mohai (2005) all highlight different approaches to state-level analyses of the relationships between demographics and toxic hazards for Florida, California, and Michigan, respectively. Similarly, other recent studies include even finer-grained levels of analysis, such as Szasz and Meuser (2000) focused on Santa Clara County and Lejano and Iseki (2001) focused on the Los Angeles area. Finally, various studies apply different methods to evaluate specific EJ issues, including prioritization of Superfund sites (Anderton, Anderson, Oakes, & Fraser, 1997), environmental litigation and regulatory enforcement (Ringquist, 1998; Ringquist, 2001), and urban commercial property valuation (Ihlanfeldt & Taylor, 2004).

Evaluations of these and other key EJ studies illustrate the wide range of methods and results that have emerged over time. For example, Shapiro (2005) states, "The majority of early environmental justice studies indicate environmental inequities. The record is mixed, however, among the more methodologically-sophisticated studies" (Adeola, 1994; Anderton, Anderson, Oakes, & Fraser, 1994; Cutter, Holm, & Clark, 1996; GAO, 1995; Glickman & Hersh, 1995; Hamilton, 1995a, 1995b; Jenkins, Maguire, & Morgan, 2004; Lambert & Boerner, 1997; Mohai, 1995; Morgan & Shadbegian, 2003; Oakes, Anderton, & Anderson, 1996; Yandle & Burton, 1996). In contrast, in their overview of socioeconomic disparities in EJ research, Mohai and Saha (2006) find that a majority of studies show "statistically significant racial and socioeconomic disparities associated with hazardous sites."

Despite variations in the approaches to evaluate distinct EJ issues in the studies described in the preceding text, one common feature of these analyses, as emphasized by Bowen, Sallinga, Haynes, and Cyran (1995), Been (1995), Szasz and Meuser (1997), and Mohai and Saha (2006), is that they reveal the importance of spatial scale and point to significant differences in evidence of environmental injustice depending on the unit of analysis (e.g., county and census tract).[1] Moreover, despite advances in spatial analysis tools and technologies that allow evaluations of EJ issues at multiple scales, most studies focus on the sources of environmental injustice, and there is limited research applying EJ spatial analysis methods for evaluating proposed solutions, such as federal programs intended to address environmental injustice (Holifield, 2001).

This trend in EJ research toward increasingly detailed analyses and evaluations of specific environmental hazards has resulted in a divide between EJ research and government EJ initiatives and programs, which remain extremely broad in scope and intent. As Bowen (2002) points out, "If environmental managers and policy-makers do not recognize the high levels of empirical uncertainty surrounding the [environmental justice] issue, they are apt to attribute an empirically unwarranted level of concreteness to the empirical research findings, thus leading to poorly conceptualized and therefore potentially harmful policy and management decisions." Similarly, in his book *The Promise and Peril of Environmental Justice*, Foreman (1998) highlights key barriers to moving EJ from a federal agency mandate to a more broadly enforceable regulation. He identifies a lack of clear environmental priorities and a process for setting such priorities as some of the main obstacles to implementing and enforcing EJ standards.

The difficulties associated with setting EJ priorities and addressing scientific uncertainties are evident when considering the wide variety of approaches different agencies have taken to meet federal EJ requirements. Because federal agencies, ranging from EPA to the Department of Transportation, have focused on different aspects of EO 12898 relevant to their specific agencies' responsibilities and needs, systematically assessing and comparing agency EJ initiatives and their impacts require a scalable approach to program evaluation.

For this reason, this chapter focuses on the EPA EJSG program. By evaluating the EJSG program as a whole, it is possible to demonstrate how small-scale agency program data can be examined collectively to begin to address the question of whether or not disproportionately affected minority and low-income communities are receiving sufficient attention and resources through EJ initiatives at a national level.

The need for this type of comprehensive assessment is now critical. Despite the lack of evidence on the impacts or effectiveness of federal agency EJ programs, there is a renewed public and political interest in national EJ policies and programs (Little, 2007). Additionally, states have been moving forward with EJ rules and action plans of their own for addressing injustice. To date, 19 states have passed legislation or established regulations to promote EJ and 10 additional states have taken partial measures to address EJ-related issues (Bonorris, 2004; Robért, 2007).[2] As EJ policies directed at federal and state agencies have become increasingly widespread and far-reaching, the EJSG program has been held up as a model and is now being adopted by states like California to build community capacity in the face of new environmental risks and impacts.

Because this program is one of the most organized and outcome-focused approaches to mitigate local environmental injustice, it is critical to develop a clear system for defining and measuring success, before the program is further extended and applied to wider regions and new types of projects. To lay the groundwork for such an evaluation, this chapter examines whether the grants awarded to date have fulfilled the EPA's own selection criteria and assesses to what extent these grants correspond to broader patterns of changes in the distribution of environmental hazards. The following section provides a brief overview of the EJSG program.

THE EPA ENVIRONMENTAL JUSTICE
SMALL GRANTS PROGRAM

Following the founding of the National Environmental Justice Advisory Council (NEJAC) in 1993 and the passage of EO 12898 in 1994, EPA established the EJSG program and awarded its first round of small grants.[3] Since this time, funds have been disbursed to various organizations and projects, including studies and interventions on air quality, children's health, farm worker safety, hazardous waste disposal, pollution prevention, radon, and recycling, among others (EPA, 2001). Over the past 13 years, approximately $18 million have been awarded through the program as a whole; however, as Fig. 1 shows, funding for the program has steadily declined. The EJSG program started with a budget of $500,000 in the first year and then reached a peak of $3 million the following year. Overall, the program's funds have supported an average of 90 grants of approximately $17,000 each per year from 1994 to 2005 (EPA, 2006a).

For most of its first decade, the goals of the EJSG program remained broadly focused on "the use of collaborative problem-solving to address local environmental and/or public health issues" (EPA, 2006b). Under this broad mandate, the EPA Office of Environmental Justice defined several criteria for grant selection. These selection criteria include "geographic and socioeconomic balance, diversity of project recipients, and sustainability of benefits of projects after the grant is completed" in each EPA region where projects are proposed (EPA, 2001).

To maintain geographic balance, all EJSG applications are evaluated in the EPA region of the applicant organization, and program funds are allocated evenly across all 10 EPA regions.[4] All proposals are reviewed competitively in the region where the proposed projects are located, making

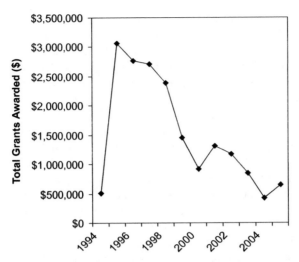

Fig. 1. Total EJSG Program Funds 1994–2005. Compiled from EPA (2005), EJSG Awarded. EPA Office of Compliance and Enforcement Database. *Source:* Available at http://www.epa.gov/compliance/environmentaljustice/grants/ej-smgrants.html. Retrieved on August 9, 2006.

the distribution of funds highly diffuse within the spatial domains of each EPA region. Additionally, EJSG evaluation criteria prioritize proposals that show community involvement in the proposal's development and implementation, ensuring to a degree that grantee organizations are proximate to the communities they intend to serve.

As outlined in the preceding text, the EJSG program selection criteria specifically prioritize diversity in geographic spread, organizational type, and project focus to support a wide range of relevant organizations and projects. However, this same goal of reaching a wide variety of groups and addressing a broad range of hazards also makes it is difficult to define, compare, or measure success even when comparing projects in the same areas or those projects addressing the same types of hazards or problems.

In an effort to periodically evaluate the grants program, the Office of Environmental Justice has issued two reports since 1994 on project best practices funded through the program (EPA, 2001). Additionally, the agency has created an online database with profiles of grantee organizations to disseminate program information (EPA, 2005). Despite the importance of both these measures, the result of these efforts is a focus on individual project successes that provides little sense of the impact and effectiveness of the EJSG program as a whole in reaching its target populations and supporting coordinated environmental improvements at a large scale.

As part of the most recent EJSG program revision and update in June 2006, EPA (2006b) has reoriented the program in an effort to better manage the outputs and outcomes of funded projects. This new focus is part of the agency's larger strategic plan, where evaluating effectiveness of programs and demonstrating the impact of funded projects is a priority. To this end, the EJSG program's structure and application requirements have become significantly more formal. The Office of Environmental Justice issued a new application guide with more stringent technical and eligibility requirements and raised the maximum award to $50,000 for a required period of 2 years.

The guidelines for eligibility still encompass the same types of organizations funded in previous years; however, the criteria are now stricter. In the past, eligible applicants included community-based grassroots organizations, churches, tribal governments, and other nonprofit organizations. Now organizations must demonstrate eligibility under the program by showing that they are local, small-scale, community-based nonprofit organizations that are not a part of any larger regional or national group. Furthermore, organizations are required to be physically located in the same communities as the affected population and the environmental or public health problem they are seeking to address, and, to the greatest extent possible, they must also include members from these same affected areas.

Although these new requirements appear to be intended to make the program more directed and easier to evaluate, it is unclear to what extent the existing requirements were effective at reaching target populations and problems. The following section illustrates how spatial analysis methods can be applied to evaluate the implementation of both past and newer EJSG grant selection criteria.

SPATIAL ANALYSIS METHODOLOGY AND ASSUMPTIONS

Because many EJ issues are defined as place-based, evaluating EJ programs lends itself to spatial analysis. Existing EJ research already draws heavily on GIS to map and analyze population distributions and exposures to environmental hazards. The contribution of this study is in its integrated analysis of a specific federal agency program, and intervention alongside the types of social–environmental relationships is captured in earlier EJ work. The focus here is on illustrating the geographic distribution of EJ grants relative to regional changes in the distribution of environmental hazards.[5] This type of spatial analysis allows for comparisons of minority populations, poverty rates, and changes in toxic environmental releases over time in counties funded by the EJSG relative to those counties not funded by the program.

By using Census data to map poverty rates, population distribution and TRI releases, this approach allows for national program evaluation with existing, publicly available county-level data. The framework used here follows three basic steps relevant for various EJ program assessments: compilation, coordination, and evaluation.

First, as part of EPA's documentation on the EJSG program, the Office of Environmental Justice releases a comprehensive listing of all grants awarded every year.[6] These listings provide information on grants, including geographic information such as the grantee organization's address, zip code, EPA region, and other project information. On the basis of a compiled database of all 1,080 grants awarded to date, the zip code of each grant awarded was used as a geographic identifier to plot each grant by its latitude and longitude coordinates.[7] Grants were then be summed by zip code, plotted based on zip code coordinates, and mapped as shown in Fig. 2.[8]

Second, using the U.S. Census Zip Code Tabulation Areas database, which matches each zip code to the best corresponding county, the EJ small grants were then assigned to counties to coordinate databases and allow for spatial comparison with Census Poverty and Minority Population Data and TRI data.[9] Poverty and race data were downloaded from the Census Small Area Income and Poverty Estimates (U.S. Census Bureau, 1993, 2004),[10] and TRI releases were downloaded from publicly available EPA TRI data summaries of total pounds of annual toxic releases by county (TRI, 1988–2004).[11]

Using the zip code as the unit of analysis and consolidating all EJ small grants awarded in the same zip codes, 497 zip codes have received one or more EJ small grants, averaging approximately $31,500 each, during the period from 1994 to 2005. Because in many cases zip codes are smaller than counties, aggregating the grant data to the county level yields fewer counties than zip codes with 346 counties receiving total grant funds averaging approximately $45,300 each to date.[12] To give an overview of the spatial relationships between EJSG counties and TRI data at a broad level, Fig. 2 illustrates the distribution of all EJ grants by zip code relative to the number of TRI release points by state.[13]

Third, analyzing and comparing differences in the distributions of minority populations, poverty rates, and TRI releases allow for consistent program evaluation. Because the initial criteria for EJSG awards (from 1994

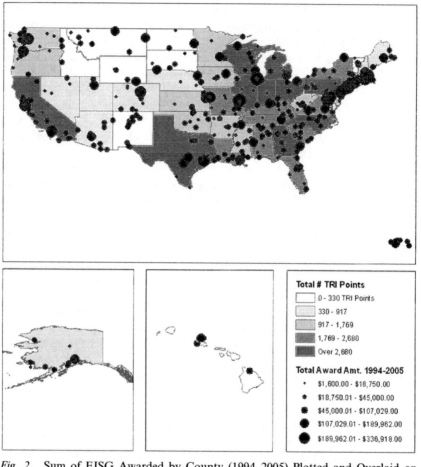

Fig. 2. Sum of EJSG Awarded by County (1994–2005) Plotted and Overlaid on Total TRI Release Points by State. Compiled from ESRI Geography Network GIS Server. EPA TRI Map Download. *Source:* http://www.geographynetwork.com. Retrieved on August 10, 2007.

to 2006) specifically prioritize minority and low-income communities at risk from environmental hazards, these data sources support analysis of how well the geographic distribution EPA's EJ small grants across all EPA regions correspond to the locations of target communities (counties) with large minority populations and high poverty rates and to what extent toxic releases have changed in these counties over time.

It is important to note here that this framework for analysis, while robust, contains several implicit assumptions based on the data being used, the scale (county level) of evaluation, and the method of aggregation. For example, it is assumed, based in part on EJSG program criteria, that organizations funded by the EJSG are in relatively proximity (within the same county) as the population and environmental hazards they are targeting to allow for county-level comparisons of funds disbursed and environmental and demographic characteristics. There are various more recent spatial analysis methodologies that involve address-matching and pinpointing of specific populations and hazards (Lejano & Iseki, 2001; Mohai & Saha, 2006, 2007; Pastor et al., 2004; Saha & Mohai, 2005; Stretesky & Hogan, 1998; Szasz & Meuser, 2000). Although Office of Environmental Justice documentation of EJSG awards includes some address information for grantee organizations, these addresses and finer-grained spatial data do not capture the wider area typically served by most EJ small grants. Therefore, this analysis focuses deliberately on zip code–level information to capture to the greatest extent possible both the specific location where grants were awarded and the general area of communities intended to be served.

Additionally, it is assumed that the TRI provides a useful estimate of environmental hazards at large. Because the TRI provides one of the few national-level databases on a wide range of pollutants and chemical contaminants, TRI data are used in a large number of EJ analyses, and their strengths and limitations are well documented in the literature (Been, 1995; Cutter et al., 1996; Morello-Frosch, Pastor, Porras, & Sadd, 2002; Pastor, Sadd, & Hipp, 2001). The most important limitation of these data for the purposes of this analysis is that even as one of the best-available nationally representative sources of information, the TRI still represents only a subset of potential environmental hazards faced by minority and low-income communities. Additionally, individual EJ small grants are awarded to address various issues, not all of which are directly related to specific environmental toxics hazards, making it difficult to "match" grants to standard TRI categories of toxic releases.

For example, EJ small grants have been disbursed to promote education and awareness about asthma. Although some of the air pollutants captured in the TRI are linked to asthma rates, there are many other possible contributors and causes of asthma, including indoor air pollution, that are not necessarily reflected here. As a result, at this level of evaluation, this analysis does not make any causal links between toxic releases and EJSG awards. Instead, the goal of this analysis is to identify patterns of EJ funding and investment and place these investments in the context of broader patterns of environmental change over time, using the TRI as a proxy to form the basis for more detailed program evaluation.

MAPPING PATTERNS OF EJSG FUNDING

On the basis of the data described in the preceding section, this section details the results of county-level analyses focused on the two main research questions outlined at the beginning of this chapter. These analyses highlight the differences between the percentages of minority populations, poverty rates, and average toxic releases in EJSG and non-EJSG counties using 1993 as a baseline year. The year before the start of the EJSG program is used as a baseline because it provides a big picture of the EJ "landscape" that motivated the distribution of the first several years of funds when the largest amounts and greatest numbers of EJ small grants were awarded. Additional analyses compare differences in EJSG and non-EJSG counties between two periods from 1988 to 1993, from when TRI data were first made available to the start of the EJSG in 1994 to the period from 1994 to 2004, after a decade of grants awarded. The following sections focus, respectively, on assessing, first, if and to what extent EJ grants were awarded to counties matching the program criteria of significant minority or low-income populations facing environmental hazards, and second, if and how the distribution of toxic releases has changed over time in EJSG counties relative to other counties.

DEMOGRAPHIC CHARACTERISTICS OF EJSG AND NON-EJSG COUNTIES

Using the county-level estimates of poverty, minority populations, and TRI releases, the first question this analysis seeks to answer is, Are EJ small grants being awarded to the low-income, minority, high environmental hazard communities intended to be targeted by the program? As Fig. 3 illustrates, taking all counties that have received EJ grants since the EJSG program's inception through 2004 and examining their demographic and environmental characteristics reveal that EJSG counties did, in fact, have higher poverty rates, larger minority populations, and also much higher total environmental releases in 1993 than those counties that did not receive grants at anytime during the period from 1994 to 2004.

Detailed analysis of grantmaking in EPA regions reveals a more complex story. From the regional analysis, it is less clear that EJ small grants are

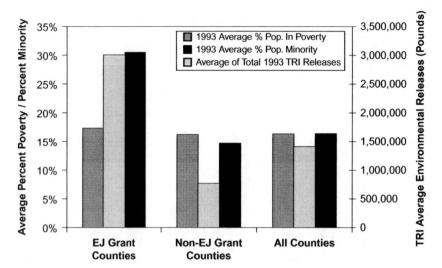

Fig. 3. Average Percent Poverty (U.S. Census Bureau, 1993), Average Percent Minority Population (U.S. Census Bureau, 1993), and 1993 Average of Total On-Site and Off-Site Toxic Releases (TRI, 1988–2004) at the County Level for all EJSG Counties (Where One or More Organizations Received EJ Small Grants between 1994 and 2005), Non-EJSG Counties (Those Counties without Any EJSG Recipient Organizations), and the Combined National Average (All Counties; EPA, 2005).

being awarded to communities that have both higher than average poor or minority populations and higher than average TRI releases in the same county. Taking the national averages of 1993 TRI releases, poverty rates, and percent minority populations by county, counties were assigned to one of four categories based on whether each county TRI, minority, and poverty averages were above or below the national averages. All counties were coded into one of four categories, as shown in Fig. 4, and 1993 TRI, minority, and poverty averages were calculated for each of these categories.[14]

Results of these comparisons reveal that the majority of EJ small grants have been awarded to counties with higher-than-average minority or poor populations relative to the national average and below-average TRI releases. If the program criteria were being applied to reach EJ communities with the highest poverty rates, minority populations, and toxic releases, one would expect to see the largest number of grants and the greatest proportion of funds awarded to above-average TRI and the above-average minority or poverty counties.

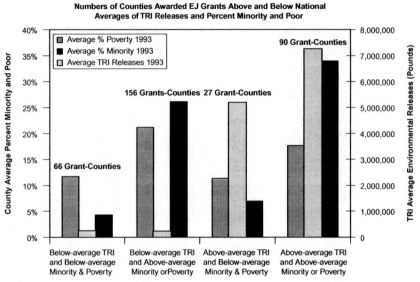

Fig. 4. Summary of Descriptive Statistics for all EJSG Counties Disaggregated by 1993 County Average Minority, Poverty, and TRI Releases Relative to the 1993 National Averages. EJSG Counties with Above-Average TRI Releases in 1993 *and* Above-Average Poverty Rates *or* Above-Average Percent Minority Population Received only 90 out of 339 Total Grants Awarded. These Results Show that the Majority of EJ Small Grants and Funds have been Awarded to Communities with Higher Minority and Poor Populations, But Not Higher TRI Releases.

Not only did fewer counties in this category receive funding, the total grant funds awarded to these counties, totaling approximately $6.2 million, were less than the total funding of $7.0 million awarded to the 156 EJSG counties in the below-average TRI and above-average minority or poverty category. The remaining funds were split between the last two categories with $1.6 million awarded to below-average TRI and below-average minority/poverty counties, and $720,000 to above-average TRI and below-average minority/poverty counties.

These results might appear counterintuitive to the results presented in Fig. 3, where EJSG counties have both much higher-than-average environmental releases and higher minority and poor population rates; however, the results are consistent. What Fig. 4 illustrates is that although there are fewer EJ small grants awarded to counties with above-average TRI releases, the average releases in pounds of chemicals in these counties are so much higher than other counties that it brings the average up across all EJSG counties.

Because EJ small grants are awarded at the EPA regional level, Table 1 further disaggregates these county-level data based on regional averages instead of a single national average to assess whether some regions are performing better than others at soliciting applications and supporting organizations in counties that are above the 1993 regional averages in both the TRI and the minority or poverty categories. As the table indicates, more than 50 percent of all counties receiving EJ grants in regions 2, 5, and 1 were above the regional averages for both TRI releases and minority or poverty rates. In contrast, regions 9 and 6, which include California and the Southwest among other states and territories, have the highest 1993 regional averages of percent minorities by county at 34 percent and 26 percent, respectively, but only 33 percent and 24 percent of the EJSG counties in these regions fall into the above-average TRI and above-average minority or poverty category.

Several possible explanations exist for why the EJ small grants awarded in the program's first decade have been distributed in this manner. First, it could be that there are far fewer grant applicants representing the "worst affected" counties with above-average TRI releases and above-average minority or poverty rates. Second, any highly localized environmental disparities could be masked at the county level, and different regional interpretations of the grant selection criteria could emphasize specific problems and priorities differently across EPA regions. Third, because funds are divided equally across EPA regions, this distribution constraint could leave regions with lower minority or poor populations or those with fewer large TRI releases no option but to award grants to organizations in counties that are below the national average in any category – poverty rates, minority populations, or TRI releases. Finally, regions with many counties above the national average on all three criteria might not have had sufficient funding to reach all qualified counties that applied for funding.

Overall, these results highlight the need to evaluate EJSG counties in a broader context and also to consider the potential for using demographic and environmental data to identify EJSG geographic priority areas or non-EJSG counties that meet the criteria for funding through the program but have not applied for or received grants. Together, the programmatic, demographic, and environmental databases used here illustrate how different types of data can be integrated to allow for improved program evaluation and future funding allocation.

Table 1.   Descriptive Statistics on EJSG Counties Sorted by Category into Above- and Below-Average TRI, Minority, and Poverty Rates Relative to EPA Regional Averages.

Distribution of EJSG Counties by EPA Region Based on Regional Average Minority, Poverty, and TRI Estimates

EPA region	Below-average TRI and below-average percent minority or poverty				Below-average TRI and above-average percent minority or poverty			
	Percent of EJ counties	Average percent minority, 1993	Average percent poverty, 1993	Average all TRI releases, 1993 (1000s of pounds)	Percent of EJ counties	Average percent minority, 1993	Average percent poverty, 1993	Average all TRI releases, 1993 (1000s of pounds)
1	17	4	9	266	22	5	14	136
2	0	5	4	203	27	14	13	178
3	9	6	11	237	41	20	18	187
4	18	9	15	273	38	32	25	220
5	9	2	10	289	27	5	15	255
6	19	13	16	329	52	39	25	260
7	14	1	11	56	49	9	18	87
8	11	3	11	98	67	17	18	142
9	17	15	10	130	50	41	18	212
10	11	6	11	128	61	24	16	130
National	14	6	12	234	44	23	20	207

TOXIC RELEASES IN EJSG
AND NON-EJSG COUNTIES

The second question this analysis seeks to answer is, Have there been any significant social or environmental changes over time in the counties that have received EJ small grants to date? This section of the chapter focuses on evaluating how the EJ landscape and distribution of environmental hazards has changed over time in EJSG and non-EJSG counties. Note that this comparison does not require or suggest a causal link between EJ small grants and changes in the TRI. It is not assumed that grants are awarded based on the locations of high TRI releases nor is it assumed that EJ small grants are of a sufficient size, scope, or duration to affect changes in the amounts of TRI chemicals released in EJSG counties. Instead, what this analysis is intended to illustrate is how time-series data can be used to understand the implications of changes in the locations of environmental hazards for past and future EJ funding.

Distribution of EJSG Counties by EPA Region Based on Regional Average Minority, Poverty, and TRI Estimates

Above-average TRI and below-average percent minority or poverty				Above-average TRI and above-average percent minority or poverty				National average		
Percent of EJ counties	Average percent minority, 1993	Average percent poverty, 1993	Average all TRI releases, 1993 (1000s of pounds)	Percent of EJ counties	Average percent minority, 1993	Average % poverty, 1993	Average all TRI releases, 1993 (1000s of pounds)	Average percent minority, 1993	Average percent poverty, 1993	Average all TRI releases, 1993 (1000s of pounds)
9	4	9	1,138	52	19	13	2,083	9	12	868
0	0	0	–	73	26	12	1,923	19	12	1,018
13	5	12	3,689	38	23	15	3,174	15	15	1,063
14	11	15	5,326	29	39	21	5,181	23	20	1,308
3	3	8	2,871	61	19	13	5,552	6	12	1,350
5	17	17	10,294	24	42	22	24,336	29	21	3,005
3	2	11	1,562	35	13	15	2,436	5	14	603
7	6	11	14,982	15	19	12	13,441	10	14	2,374
0	17	7	5,577	33	50	17	5,109	34	15	1,455
18	9	11	1,972	11	19	13	2,281	16	14	885
8	7	12	4,215	35	27	16	5,869	16	16	1,443

On the basis of county-level poverty and minority population data from the 2000 Census, neither average poverty rates nor proportions of minority populations have changed significantly in EJSG counties relative to non-EJSG counties since 1993 before the start of the EJSG program. In contrast, there have been major changes in TRI releases over the same period of time.[15] Looking at the core chemicals included in the earliest TRI reports, total environmental releases have declined over time; however, with the addition of several new chemicals and industries to the TRI, reported releases have increased overall (Natan & Miller, 1998). To take into account these reporting requirement changes, this analysis focuses solely on between-group comparisons of EJSG and non-EJSG counties and not on within-group analyses.

As a first test of how TRI releases have changed in EJSG and non-EJSG counties, averages of the total annual on-site and off-site TRI releases by county were separately calculated for both types of counties. Looking at two specific periods, pre-1994 (1988–1993) before the implementation of EO 12898 and the start of the EPA EJSG programs, and post-1994 (including the year 1994 through 2004) during which EJ small grants were disbursed, Fig. 5 shows that average TRI releases have increased significantly in EJSG counties compared to non-EJSG counties.[16] In absolute terms, this is to be expected because additional chemicals were included in reports filed between 1988 and 2004. But what is striking is that the change in average pounds released per county in non-EJSG counties is approximately 1 percent, whereas the increase in EJSG counties is approximately 16 percent over the pre-1994 average.

Although this increase in both types of counties is largely due to changes in reporting requirements, one would expect that the percent increase across EJSG and non-EJSG counties would be of similar magnitude unless the chemicals and industries added to the inventory were already disproportionately represented in EJSG counties. A second explanation for why TRI releases in EJSG counties have increased more than in non-EJSG counties is that the program is continually adding communities with chronically high levels of toxic releases to the set of grant recipients. Therefore, on average

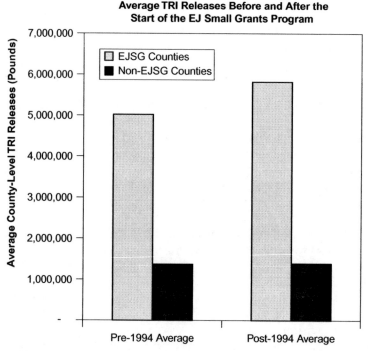

Fig. 5.   Change in Total Toxic Releases Before and After the EJSG Program (1994) in EJSG and Non-EJSG Counties.

across all EJ grant counties, if releases in preexisting EJSG counties are not decreasing in significant enough proportions to offset the higher releases in new counties added to the program, overall average toxic releases would show an increase.

To take this timing issue into account, average TRI releases were calculated for each county for all the years before the starting year in which each EJSG county was awarded its first grant and then for all years after the first grant. Comparing average toxic releases pre- and post-award for all EJSG counties reveals that average releases are very similar between the two periods with an average of 5.1 million pounds per county in the pre-grant period and 5.0 million pounds in the post-grant period. As the pre-grant period amount in EJSG counties is higher than the pre-1994 amount shown in Fig. 5, this suggests that counties with higher toxic releases were added in the more recent years of the program.

Looking in more detail at the distribution of TRI releases over time (Fig. 6) reveals that not only have total toxic releases (unadjusted for

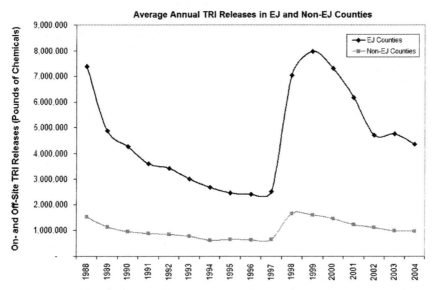

Fig. 6. Variations in County Average Annual TRI Releases (Pounds of Chemicals) in EJSG and Non-EJSG Counties. The Large Increase after 1997 is the Result of TRI Reporting Additions Where Seven New Industry Sectors Were Required to Report Beginning in 1998, Including Metal Mining, Coal Mining, Electric Utilities, Chemical Wholesale Distributors, Petroleum Bulk Storage/Terminals, Hazardous Waste Management Facilities, and Solvent-Recovery Facilities.

changes in reporting) increased in both EJSG and non-EJSG counties over time but also that counties with much higher average toxic releases were selected as EJSG counties later in the program, especially in 2004. Disaggregating the data even further shows that significant differences exist between EPA regions, and the largest post-1994 increases in both EJSG and non-EJSG counties occur primarily in EPA regions 8, 9, and 10, as shown in Fig. 7. Examining regional pre- and post-grant differences in TRI releases similarly reveals that EJSG counties in most regions have experienced decreases in average TRI releases after receiving awards; however, average releases have increased in regions 3, 8, 9, and 10 relative to the pre-grant period.

Several possible explanations exist for these differences between EJSG counties and non-EJSG counties and also for the regional disparities within EJSG counties, such as historical and geographic variations in the locations of manufacturing and industry. For this reason, it is important to emphasize that the EJ grants program is relatively recent and a very small program relative to larger environmental investments focused on site cleanup, monitoring, testing, enforcement, and other related activities. Additionally, the program's funding has been steadily dropping over the past decade as shown in Fig. 1. Therefore, the findings presented here are not intended to imply any causal connection between EJ grants awarded to date and either reductions or increases in TRI releases; however, they are intended to highlight the importance of assessing how EJ funds are being distributed relative to both long-standing and emerging hazards.

In response to the question outlined at the beginning of this section, these results highlight that environmental conditions (indicated by total TRI pounds of toxic releases) have, in fact, changed differently over time in EJ grant counties than in non-EJ grant counties. Because EJ grants are not focused on large-scale mitigation of environmental hazards, higher post-grant TRI releases in EJ grant counties in specific EPA regions do not mean that the EJSG program is not fulfilling its intended mission.

In fact, in areas where high toxic releases remain a problem after more than a decade, the types of immediate local outreach and education efforts funded by the EJSG are critical to help long-term residents avoid harmful exposures to the greatest extent possible until site cleanup can occur. In contrast, these results bring into question the long-term effectiveness of other larger federal environmental investments relative to EJ objectives if environmental conditions in at-risk low-income and minority communities remain degraded or deteriorating.

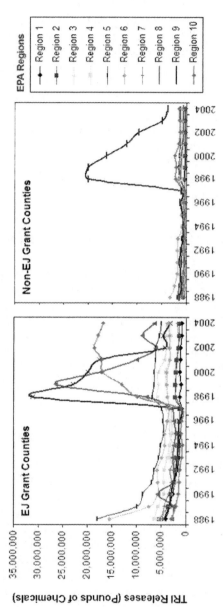

Fig. 7. Annual Average TRI Releases (Pounds of Chemicals) by EPA Region for All EJSG and Non-EJSG Counties.

Although the EJSG provides funds primarily for small-scale activities, this program is only one of many environmental funds, ranging from in size and scope from the slightly larger EPA Community for a Renewed Environment program to the significantly larger Superfund program. The framework for spatial analysis applied here could potentially be extended to evaluate investments occurring in parallel to the EJSG focused on mitigating significant hazards. This type of comparative assessment could provide a launching point for greater coordination and incremental EJ investment across various scales from local outreach, large site-level cleanups, regional monitoring and sampling, and national mitigation of new environmental hazards. The following sections summarize the main findings of this research and highlights additional opportunities for systematic EJ evaluation linking program objectives.

SUMMARY OF RESULTS AND LESSONS LEARNED

In answer to the two main research questions posed at the beginning of this chapter, the analyses here suggest that EJ small grants are only partly being awarded to the types of counties intended to be served by the program, and the majority of the program's funds to date have not been distributed to counties with both above-average TRI releases and above-average minority or low-income populations. Second, there have been significant environmental changes in the areas that have received grants since the start of the program, and some EPA regions show improvement or reductions in toxic releases in EJSG counties, whereas others show significant increases in total toxic releases over time.

The primary lesson from this study is that without a systematic approach for evaluating the distribution and impact of EJ grants, there is little basis for understanding regional variability, evaluating local impacts, or prioritizing new investments. As the spatial analytic methods used here demonstrate, some counties awarded EJSG funds now face significantly higher toxic releases and risks – even after more than a decade of federal EJ attention. Therefore, as the EPA moves forward with changes to the EJSG program it is important to simultaneously establish a system for identifying measurable program outcomes, such as changes in pollution, exposure, and community health indicators; increases in local public participation in EJ outreach efforts; leveraging of EJ funds by community organizations; that can be compared to larger social and environmental indicators. These program measures can then allow for more detailed analysis at multiple scales and for multiple outcomes, cross-agency comparisons, and broader EJ policy development.

Summarized below are several recommendations that the EPA Office of Environmental Justice could consider in its next evaluation of the EJSG program to support improved evaluation and coordination:

- Establish clearer criteria for grant selection both to better reach intended target populations and to allow for more systematic follow-up and evaluation.
- Reevaluate equal allocation of EJSG funds by EPA region to reflect regional differences in minority populations, poverty rates, and environmental hazards.
- Conduct 3–5 year evaluations of the geographic distribution of grants relative to larger social or environmental changes.
- Coordinate EJSG program with other larger awards for environmental assessment, monitoring, or site cleanup to identify new underserved areas/ populations.

Building on these recommendations, it is possible to extend the preliminary spatial analysis approach outlined here as a tool for both program evaluation and priority setting. Fig. 8 highlights one potential application of this approach for identifying future outreach opportunities and defining strategic funding priorities. By mapping the geographic distribution of TRI releases, minority populations, and poverty rates for each county relative to the national average and overlaying the locations of all EJ grant counties to date, it is possible to identify above-average TRI and above-average minority or poverty counties that have not yet received grants.

Using this analysis as a diagnostic tool can help to establish a baseline for defining EJSG priority areas or conducting targeted recruitment for grant applications in underrepresented counties or regions. In the long term, such analysis could further play a decision support role and assist in identifying patterns and trends in investments and environmental improvements or degradation to allow for the types of larger, more targeted, and more coordinated interventions recommended in the preceding text. Taken as a whole, this chapter provides a worked example of EJ program evaluation that can be adapted to support the implementation and evaluation of a wide variety of related EJ programs in the future.

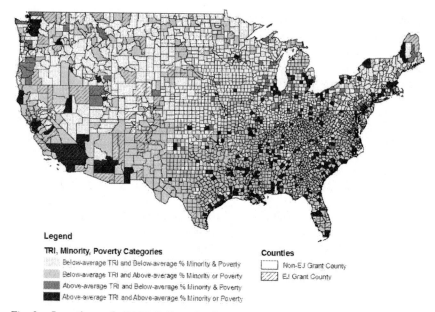

Fig. 8.   Locations of all EJSG Counties from 1994 to 2005 Relative to All Counties Mapped by Category of TRI and Minority Populations or Poverty Rates Relative to National Averages.

CONCLUSIONS

The approach to EJ program evaluation put forward here is especially important in the face of new threats and hazards to existing EJ communities. With new risks, such as climate change, facing growing numbers of newly vulnerable populations, effective and flexible local and national EJ rules and programs are vitally important. As the 2005 Gulf Coast hurricane season demonstrated, there is still significant variability in the exposure of minority and low-income populations to environmental risks and their long-term impacts (Bullard, Mohai, Saha, & Wright, 2007). To respond to these challenges, EPA needs to evaluate whether its current EJ requirements are being met and also to determine whether programs are reaching and meeting the needs of the at-risk areas and target populations they are intended to serve.

There are several key areas for future research that could help support this type of program development. For example, the approach outlined here could be applied to data on EJ small grant applications to determine whether and to what extent applications are being received from areas with the greatest minority or poverty rates and TRI releases. Similarly, improved data on the specific problems/issues being addressed by EJ small grants and other funds could allow for more detailed spatial analysis of the relationships between specific types of toxic releases (and other hazards), exposure risks, and grants on hazard mitigation versus general outreach and education. Using mapping and spatial analysis to support these assessments at various scales can lay the groundwork for communicating the results of different programs and coordinating interventions between communities and agencies at local, state, and national levels.

NOTES

1. Mixed results produced by variations in spatial scale are defined as a "modified areal unit problem" (MAUP). For general discussions on the MAUP and its implications, see Openshaw (1984) and Unwin (1996).

2. See also http://www.serconline.org/ej/stateactivity.html for a summary of state environmental justice action (Retrieved on December 27, 2007).

3. NEJAC evolved out of a 1990 conference organized at the University of Michigan. See Taylor (2000) for an overview of this history.

4. See http://www.epa.gov/epahome/locate2.htm for a map and full listing of all states and territories by EPA Region (Retrieved on August 9, 2006).

5. In this chapter, the term *minority* is used to refer to members of all nonwhite populations. The government defines minority populations as "individual(s) who are members of the following population groups: American Indian or Alaskan Native, Asian or Pacific Islander; Black, not of Hispanic Origin, or Hispanic." Low-income populations are identified using the Census Bureau statistical poverty thresholds.

6. Information on all grants awarded from 1994 to 2005 through the EJSG program to date are posted online through the EPA Office of Compliance and Enforcement website as individual PDF files. Online source: http://www.epa.gov/compliance/environmentaljustice/grants/ej-smgrants.html (Retrieved on August 9, 2006).

7. Approximately 130 grants are missing address and zip code information in the EPA online listings of awardees. As a result, the GIS maps and analyses here are based on 946 of the total 1,080 grants awarded.

8. Zip code latitude and longitude coordinates were downloaded from the U.S. Census Bureau (1990–2000) Gazetteer Files at http://www.census.gov/tiger/tms/gazetteer/zips.txt. Retrieved on August 9, 2006.

9. See http://www.census.gov/geo/ZCTA/zcta.html for more information on the Census Bureau's tabulation process for matching zip codes and counties.

10. Census.gov poverty database downloads: http://www.census.gov/did/www/saipe/data/statecounty/data/1993.html and http://www.census.gov/did/www/saipe/data/statecounty/data/2004.html. Retrieved on January 12, 2007.

11. Online source: TRI Explorer http://www.epa.gov/triexplorer/geography01. htm?year = 1993 and http://www.epa.gov/triexplorer/geography01.htm?year = 2004. Retrieved on January 10, 2007.

12. Of the total 346 counties analyzed here, 7 of these counties, located in U.S. territories, including Guam, American Samoa, and the U.S. Virgin Islands, have insufficient data on minority populations and poverty rates in these areas to allow for comparisons with the other counties in the dataset. Therefore, Table 1 and Figs. 3 and 4 that compare minority and poverty rates in EJ grant and non-EJ grant counties do not include any of the counties in these regions; however, all other results are based on the full dataset of 346 EJ grant counties.

13. It is important to note that this map is based on a count of the total number of facilities with toxic releases (TRI release points) and not on total environmental releases in pounds. All analyses from this point forward in the chapter use data on total TRI releases, referred to interchangeably as total releases or total pounds of toxic releases.

14. The categories defined for the purposes of this analysis include counties with either the percent minority or the percent poverty above the national average as being in the above-average minority or poverty category to take into account EJSG program criteria targeting minority or low-income populations.

15. It is important to note than when evaluating total pounds of releases across the period under consideration here, several chemicals have been added to the reporting criteria. Therefore, in absolute numbers, the 2004 releases are higher, because many more chemicals are being reported; however, comparing only those chemicals also included in the 1988 reports shows that releases declined steadily. These changes are summarized by EPA at http://www.epa.gov/triexplorer/year-sum.htm (Retrieved on January 18, 2007).

16. Results of two-tailed t-tests comparing pre-1994 TRI releases (millions of pounds) in EJSG counties ($\bar{x} = 5.02$) and non-EJSG counties ($\bar{x} = 1.37$) are significant at $p < 0.0001$, $t(337) = 5.38$. Between county post-1994 TRI releases (millions of pounds) in EJSG counties ($\bar{x} = 5.82$) and non-EJSG counties ($\bar{x} = 1.39$) are also significant at $p = 0.006$ [$t(326) = 2.77$]. Because of changes in TRI reporting requirements in the post-1994 period and variations in the number of years pre- and post-1994 that TRI releases were reported by different counties, this analysis focuses only on between-group (EJSG and non-EJSG counties) comparisons and does not include any county-level or within-group analysis of rates of change of TRI releases.

REFERENCES

Adeola, F. O. (1994). Environmental hazards, health, and racial inequity in hazardous waste distribution. *Environment and Behavior, 26*(1), 99–126.

Anderton, D. L., Anderson, A. B., Oakes, J. M., & Fraser, M. R. (1994). Environmental equity: The demographics of dumping. *Demography, 31*(2), 229–248.

Anderton, D. L., Anderson, A. B., Oakes, J. M., & Fraser, M. R. (1997). Environmental equity in superfund: Demographics of the discovery and prioritization of abandoned toxic sites. *Evaluation Review, 21*(1), 3–26.

Been, V. (1995). Analyzing evidence of environmental injustice. *Journal of Land Use and Environmental Law, 11*(1), 1–28.

Bonorris, S. (Ed.) (2004). *Environmental justice for all: A fifty-state survey of legislation, policies, and initiatives.* San Francisco: Public Law Research Institute at Hastings College of Law, University of California.

Bowen, W. (2002). An analytical review of environmental justice research: What do we really know? *Environmental Management, 29*(1), 3–15.

Bowen, W. M., Sallinga, M. J., Haynes, K. E., & Cyran, E. J. (1995). Toward environmental justice: Spatial equity in Ohio and Cleveland. *Annals of the Association of American Geographers, 85*(4), 641–663.

Bullard, R. (1990). *Dumping in Dixie: Race, class, and environmental quality.* Boulder, CO: Westview Press.

Bullard, R., Mohai, P., Saha, R., & Wright, B. (2007). *Toxic wastes and race at twenty 1987– 2007: Grassroots struggles to dismantle environmental racism in the United States.* New York: United Church of Christ.

Commission for Racial Justice. (1987). *Toxic wastes and race in the United States: A national report on the racial and socio-economic characteristics of communities with hazardous waste sites.* New York: United Church of Christ.

Cutter, S. L., Holm, D., & Clark, L. (1996). Role of geographic scale in monitoring environmental justice. *Risk Analysis, 16*(4), 517–526.

EPA. (2001). *Environmental justice small grants program emerging tools for local problem-solving* (2nd ed.). Washington, DC: U.S. Environmental Protection Agency.

EPA. (2005). EJ small grants awarded 1994–2005. EPA Office of Compliance and Enforcement. Available at http://www.epa.gov/compliance/environmentaljustice/grants/ej-smgrants. html. Retrieved on August 9, 2006.

EPA. (2006a). Environmental justice small grants program fact sheet. Available at http:// www.epa.gov/compliance/environmentaljustice/resources/publications/factsheets/fact-sheet-ej-small-grant-3-2010.pdf. Retrieved on January 18, 2007.

EPA. (2006b). Environmental justice small grants program application guidance, June 22, 2006. Available at http://www.epa.gov/compliance/environmentaljustice/resources/publications/ factsheets/fact-sheet-ej-cps-grants-6-13-06.pdf. Retrieved on January 5, 2007.

Executive Order 12898. (1994). *Federal Register, 59*(34).

Foreman, C. (1998). *The promise and peril of environmental justice.* Washington, DC: Brookings Institution Press.

GAO. (1983). *Siting of hazardous waste landfills and their correlation with racial and economic status of surrounding communities.* Washington, DC: U.S. General Accounting Office.

GAO. (1995). *Hazardous and non-hazardous waste: Demographics of people living near waste facilities.* Washington, DC: U.S. General Accounting Office.

Glickman, T., & Hersh, R. (1995). *Evaluating environmental equity: The impacts of industrial hazards on selected social groups in Allegheny County, Pennsylvania.* Discussion Paper no. 95-13. Resources for the Future, Washington, DC.

Hamilton, J. T. (1995a). Pollution as news: Media and stock market reactions to the toxics release inventory data. *Journal of Environmental Economics and Management, 28,* 98–113.

Hamilton, J. T. (1995b). Testing for environmental racism: Prejudice, profits, political power? *Journal of Policy Analysis and Management, 14*(1), 107–132.

Holifield, R. (2001). Defining environmental justice and environmental racism. *Urban Geography, 22*(1), 78–90.

Ihlanfeldt, K. R., & Taylor, L. O. (2004). Externality effects of small-scale hazardous waste sites: Evidence from urban commercial property markets. *Journal of Environmental Economics and Management, 47*(1), 117–139.

Jenkins, R. R., Maguire, K. B., & Morgan, C. L. (2004). Host community compensation and municipal solid waste landfills. *Land Economics, 80*(4), 513–528.

Lambert, T., & Boerner, C. (1997). Environmental inequity: Economic causes, economic solutions. *Yale Journal on Regulation, 14*(1), 195–234.

Lejano, R. P., & Iseki, H. (2001). Environmental justice: Spatial distribution of hazardous waste treatment storage and disposal facilities in Los Angeles. *Journal of Urban Planning and Development, 127*(2), 51–62.

Little, A. G. (2007). Not in whose backyard? *New York Times Magazine*, September 2. Available at http://www.nytimes.com/2007/09/02/magazine/02wwln-essay-t.html?ex = 1190001600&en = 30ce6c3c17d837d0&ei = 5070. Retrieved on September 4, 2007.

Mohai, P. (1995). The demographics of dumping revisited: Examining the impact of alternate methodologies in environmental justice research. *Virginia Environmental Law Journal, 13*(4), 615–653.

Mohai, P., & Bryant, B. (1992). Environmental racism: Reviewing the evidence. In: B. Bryant & P. Mohai (Eds), *Race and the incidence of environmental hazards: A time for discourse.* Boulder, CO: Westview Press.

Mohai, P., & Saha, R. (2006). Reassessing racial and socioeconomic disparities in environmental justice research. *Demography, 43*(2), 383–399.

Mohai, P., & Saha, R. (2007). Racial inequality in the distribution of hazardous waste: A national-level reassessment. *Social Problems, 54*(3), 343–370.

Morello-Frosch, R., Pastor, M., Porras, C., & Sadd, J. (2002). Environmental justice and regional inequality in Southern California: Implications for future research. *Environmental Health Perspectives, 110*(2), 149–154.

Morgan, C., & Shadbegian, R. (2003). *Environmental justice and emission trading: Evidence from the electric utility industry* (March). Washington, DC: EPA National Center of Environmental Economics.

Natan, T. E., & Miller, C. G. (1998). Are toxics release inventory reductions real? *Environmental Science and Technology, 32*(15), 368–374.

Oakes, J. M., Anderton, D. L., & Anderson, A. B. (1996). A longitudinal analysis of environmental equity in communities with hazardous waste facilities. *Social Science Research, 25*(2), 125–148.

Openshaw, S. (1984). *The modifiable areal unit problem.* Norwich, UK: Geo Books.

Pastor, M., Sadd, J., & Hipp, J. (2001). Which came first? Toxic facilities, minority move-in, and environmental justice. *Journal of Urban Affairs, 23*(1), 1–21.

Pastor, M., Sadd, J. L., & Morello-Frosch, R. (2004). Waiting to inhale: The demographics of toxic air release facilities in 21st-century California. *Social Science Quarterly, 85*(2), 420–440.

Ringquist, E. J. (1998). A question of justice: Equity in environmental litigation, 1974–1991. *The Journal of Politics, 60*(4), 1148–1165.

Ringquist, E. J. (2001). The need for sound judgment in analyzing U.S. Environmental Protection Agency enforcement actions. *Law & Society Review, 35*(3), 683–698.

Robért, P. A. (2007). The state of the states: progress in environmental justice law and policy? Paper presented at The State of Environmental Justice in America 2007 Conference, March 29–31, Washington, DC. Available at http://ejconference.net/images/Robert.pdf. Retrieved on September 20, 2009.

Saha, R., & Mohai, P. (2005). Historical context and hazardous waste facility siting: Understanding temporal patterns in Michigan. *Social Problems, 52*(4), 618–648.

Shapiro, M. D. (2005). Equity and information: Information regulation, environmental justice, and risks from toxic chemicals. *Journal of Policy Analysis and Management, 24*(2), 373–398.

Stretesky, P., & Hogan, M. J. (1998). Environmental justice: An analysis of superfund sites in Florida. *Social Problems, 45*(2), 268–287.

Szasz, A., & Meuser, M. (1997). Environmental inequalities: Literature review and proposals for new directions in research and theory. *Current Sociology, 45*(3), 99–120.

Szasz, A., & Meuser, M. (2000). Unintended, inexorable: The production of environmental inequalities in Santa Clara County, California. *American Behavioral Scientist, 43*(4), 602–632.

Taylor, D. E. (2000). The rise of the environmental justice paradigm: Injustice framing and the social construction of environmental discourses. *American Behavioral Scientist, 43*(4), 508–580.

TRI. (1988–2004). Toxics release inventory: Public data release. U.S. Environmental Protection Agency, Office of Pollution Prevention and Toxics. TRI Explorer. Available at http://www.epa.gov/triexplorer/. Retrieved on January 10, 2007.

Unwin, D. J. (1996). GIS, spatial analysis and spatial statistics. *Progress in Human Geography, 20*(4), 540–541.

U.S. Census Bureau. (1990–2000). United States Census Gazetteer Files. Available at http://www.census.gov/tiger/tms/gazetteer/zips.txt. Retrieved on August 9, 2006.

U.S. Census Bureau. (1993). Poverty database. Available at http://www.census.gov/housing/saipe/estmod93/est93ALL.dat. Retrieved on January 12, 2007.

U.S. Census Bureau. (2004). Poverty database. Available at http://www.census.gov/did/www/saipe/data/statecounty/data/2004.html. Retrieved on January 12, 2007.

Yandle, T., & Burton, D. (1996). Reexamining environmental justice: A statistical analysis of historical hazardous waste landfill siting patterns in metropolitan Texas. *Social Science Quarterly, 77*(3), 477–492.

Shalini P. Vajjhala is a Fellow at Resources for the Future. She can be reached by email at shalini@rff.org or by telephone at 202-328-5129.

PART VI
PERCEPTIONS, ATTITUDES
AND DIVERSITY

RACE, GENDER, AND FACULTY DIVERSITY IN ENVIRONMENTAL DISCIPLINES

Dorceta E. Taylor

ABSTRACT

Purpose – *The lack of diversity in environmental institutions has been a concern of environmental justice activists and scholars for several decades now. Although studies have been conducted on the level of diversity in environmental groups, environmental organizations, and student participation in environmental programs, little research has been conducted on faculty diversity in environmental departments. This chapter examines the status of minority faculty in university environmental programs in the United States.*

Design/methodology/approach – *The chapter examines results from a national survey of 2,407 faculty in several environmental disciplines.*

Findings – *The results were consistent with national studies of science and engineering (S&E) faculty that find that Hispanics, blacks, and Native Americans are underrepresented among the faculty in these units. The analysis also points to the fact that female faculty are underrepresented and are in a more vulnerable position than male faculty.*

Originality/value – *The examination of race and gender indicates that scholars should pay more attention to the interaction effects of these*

Environment and Social Justice: An International Perspective
Research in Social Problems and Public Policy, Volume 18, 385–407
Copyright © 2010 by Emerald Group Publishing Limited
All rights of reproduction in any form reserved
ISSN: 0196-1152/doi:10.1108/S0196-1152(2010)0000018015

variables to identify the different levels of vulnerability that female faculty in these disciplines face.

INTRODUCTION

One of the early concerns of the environmental justice movement was the lack of racial diversity in environmental institutions. As discussed in the introductory chapter, these concerns were expressed in the United Church of Christ (UCC, 1987) report, in other scholarly works of the period (Taylor, 1989, 1992), at the 1990 environmental justice conference held at the University of Michigan (Bryant & Mohai, 1992), and in a letter penned by grassroots environmental justice activists that was directed at the largest mainstream environmental organizations (Shabecoff, 1990). This inspired some researchers to conduct diversity studies during the 1990s. Two studies of the demographic characteristics of environmental organizations were published in 1992. Whereas Snow (1992) found the 248 staff of mainstream environmental organizations surveyed to be 79 percent male and over-whelmingly white, the Environmental Careers Organization (ECO, 1992) study found that 32 percent of the 63 mainstream environmental organizations studied had no minorities[1] on staff.

Adams and Moreno (1998) also conducted a study of environmental agencies around the same time. Their study of the demographic composition of the staff of state natural resources agencies in 1993 found that minorities constituted 8.4 percent of the 12,245 workers found in such departments in 16 southeastern states and the U.S. Virgin Islands. More recently, Stanton's (2002) diversity study found that 11.5 percent of the staff of 61 organizations in the Natural Resources Council of America was composed of minorities. My own 2005 study of the demographic characteristics of 243 environmental organizations found that minorities constituted 15.8 percent of the staff (Taylor, 2010).

I have also analyzed data on diversity in federal agencies. The analysis found that in 2006, there were 187,000 workers in five environmental agencies (Department of Agriculture, Department of Energy, Department of the Interior, the Environmental Protection Agency, and the Nuclear Regulatory Commission) plus one environmental unit of the Department of Commerce (National Oceanic and Atmospheric Administration). Females constituted 40.9 percent of this workforce and minorities 23.7 percent. However, when the gender and racial composition of only the land and resource management units[2] of the aforementioned agencies was analyzed, females constituted 36.4 percent of the staff. Minorities made up 15.6 percent of the staffs of said units (Partnership for Public Service, 2007). The percentage of minority staff in the land and resource management units is similar to the percentages found in my organizational study (the federal environmental agencies in my study consisted of the land and resource management units of the agencies).

Investigators have also conducted pipeline studies to find out about diversity in academic environmental programs. Valdez (1995) studied the enrollment of Hispanic students in wildlife and fisheries programs in 10 universities in 7 western states from 1982 to 1994 and found the programs enrolled low numbers of Hispanics and graduated less than five per year. Valdez's findings corroborate the results from earlier studies conducted by Hodgdon (1980, 1982) who found that minority students comprised between 2.2 percent and 5.1 percent of the wildlife, fisheries, and related programs studied in more than 70 colleges.[3] Hodgdon (1980) also found that female students comprised 24.8 percent of wildlife programs and 19.6 percent of fisheries programs. My study of 1,239 students in environmental programs[4] – conducted between 2003 and 2005 – found that 28.0 percent were minorities and 57.1 percent were female (Taylor, 2008, 2007).

Researchers have also examined diversity trends in science and engineering (S&E) programs (of which environmental programs are a subset). Studies show that the number of women enrolled in S&E disciplines has increased steadily for some time now. Females have earned 50 percent or more of the bachelor's degrees awarded since 2002. In 1983, females comprised 36 percent of the graduate students in S&E; they comprised 47 percent of the group in 2003. The percentage of underrepresented minority students enrolling in S&E fields has also increased. Underrepresented minorities comprised 6 percent of S&E students in 1983; in 2003, they constituted 11 percent. Over the same period, the percent of Asian students in S&E disciplines climbed to 7 percent (National Science Board, 2006; see also Babco & Jesse, 2005).

FACULTY DIVERSITY

Despite the interest in diversity in environmental institutions, researchers have paid little attention to faculty diversity in environmental programs. The data on faculty diversity comes from national studies of S&E fields. Data shows that women earned 45 percent of the doctorates awarded in

S&E in 2003 (National Science Board, 2006). National Science Foundation (NSF) data also shows that Asians earned 26 percent of the S&E doctorates awarded in 2003, whereas underrepresented minorities (blacks, Hispanics, and Native Americans) earned 9 percent of said degrees. A study found that of 280,000 S&E doctorate degree holders employed in 2003, 214,030 of those were faculty in academic institutions (Table 1). Of the 214,030 faculty, 19.4 percent were minorities. More specifically, 11.5 percent were Asian, 3.8 percent black, 3.2 percent Hispanic, 0.7 percent were Native American, and 0.2 percent were other. The study also found that blacks and Hispanic doctorate degree holders were more likely than other racial groups to work in educational settings. That is, 61.6 percent of blacks and 58.7 percent of Hispanics worked in educational settings. In comparison, 48.5 percent of whites, 48.6 percent of Native Americans, and 36.5 percent of Asians worked in academic settings. The study also noted that because the portion of S&E doctorates being awarded to minorities was increasing over time, minorities accounted for a higher percentage of the faculty who received their doctorates in 2000 or later than in earlier years. Consequently, of the faculty who received their doctorates after 1999, 16.6 percent were Asians, 6.8 percent were black, 4.4 percent were Hispanic, and 0.6 percent were Native Americans. Another way to look at this is to see what percentage of the faculty within each racial group got their degree after 1999. My analysis of the NSF data shows that 6.4 percent of the white faculty got their degrees since 1999. However, 10.2 percent of Asians, 12.9 percent of blacks, 9.8 percent of Hispanics, and 5.7 percent of Native Americans got their degrees after 1999 (National Science Foundation [NSF], 2004, 2006).

Some scholars have focused their attention on the status of women in the professoriate. Recent studies have found that lower percentages of women than those obtaining S&E doctorates enter the professoriate. The data also suggests that the more advanced the rank of faculty, the lower the percentage of women found in those ranks (Handelsman, 2005; National Science Foundation [NSF], 2007). NSF data shows that Asians earned 26 percent of S&E doctorates in 2003, whereas underrepresented minorities earned 9 percent of them (NSF, 2006). Research on the racial diversity of faculty has found very few minority faculty in top-ranked chemistry departments (Mervis, 2001; Beutel & Nelson, 2005, 2006). This raises the question – what is the status of minority faculty in college and university environmental departments?

This chapter will discuss data from my study of faculty in academic programs. The study examines the demographic characteristics of faculty specializing in environmental disciplines, related sciences, engineering, social

Table 1. Demographic Characteristics of Faculty with Science and Engineering Doctorates in 2003.

Demographic Characteristics	Total Sample		Whites		Asians		Blacks		Hispanics		Native Americans		Other	
	Number	%	Number	%	Number	%	Number	%	Number	%	Number	%	Number	%
All S&E doctoral degree holding faculty	214,030	100.0	172,390	100.0	24,630	100.0	8,140	100.0	6,930	100.0	1,570	100.0	360	100.0
Year of doctorate														
Pre-1970	19,510	9.1	17,070	9.9	1,470	6.0	310	3.8	440	6.3	180	11.5		
1970–1974	25,380	11.9	22,360	13.0	1,680	6.8	650	8.0	440	6.3	200	12.7		
1975–1979	24,730	11.6	21,430	12.4	1,830	7.4	950	11.7	360	5.2	160	10.2		
1980–1984	26,010	12.2	22,130	12.8	2,400	9.7	670	8.2	610	8.8	160	10.2		
1985–1989	30,010	14.0	23,650	13.7	3,660	14.9	1,280	15.7	1,140	16.5	280	17.8		
1990–1994	35,570	16.6	26,530	15.4	5,730	23.3	1,390	17.1	1,660	24.0	190	12.1		
1995–1999	37,400	17.5	28,200	16.4	5,370	21.8	1,850	22.7	1,610	23.2	310	19.7	70	19.4
2000 or later	15,420	7.2	11,020	6.4	2,510	10.2	1,050	12.9	680	9.8	90	5.7		
Rank														
Professor	94,550	44.2	79,800	46.3	8,670	35.2	2,590	31.8	2,530	36.5	820	52.2	140	38.9
Associate professor	58,430	27.3	47,200	27.4	6,400	26.0	2,520	31.0	1,980	28.6	280	17.8		
Assistant professor	53,250	24.9	39,270	22.8	8,540	34.7	2,690	33.0	2,180	31.5	430	27.4	150	41.7
Instructor	7,800	3.6	6,120	3.6	1,020	4.1	350	4.3	250	3.6				
Tenure status														
No tenure system at institution	7,500	3.5	5,860	3.4	950	3.9	400	4.9	260	3.8				
No tenure system for position	12,940	6.0	10,990	6.4	1,090	4.4	380	4.7	370	5.3	100	6.4		
Tenured	130,290	60.9	108,340	62.8	12,720	51.6	4,260	52.3	3,800	54.8	1,000	63.7	170	47.2
On tenure track but not tenured	43,510	20.3	32,180	18.7	6,690	27.2	2,400	29.5	1,750	25.3	390	24.8	90	25.0
Not on tenure track	19,790	9.2	15,010	8.7	3,180	12.9	700	8.6	760	11.0				

Table 1. (*Continued*)

Demographic Characteristics	Total Sample		Whites		Asians		Blacks		Hispanics		Native Americans		Other	
	Number	%	Number	%	Number	%	Number	%	Number	%	Number	%	Number	%
Faculty occupational field														
Computer and mathematical sciences	21,220	9.9	15,470	9.0	4,450	18.1	630	7.7	610	8.8				
Biological, agricultural, and other life sciences	46,280	21.6	37,530	21.8	5,510	22.4	1,230	15.1	1,550	22.4	380	24.2		
Physical and related sciences	27,140	12.7	22,820	13.2	2,730	11.1	490	6.0	840	12.1	200	12.7		
Social and related sciences	55,350	25.9	46,190	26.8	3,600	14.6	2,780	34.2	2,060	29.7	600	38.2	120	33.3
Engineering	19,940	9.3	13,950	8.1	4,380	17.8	820	10.1	660	9.5				
S&E-related field	21,260	9.9	17,440	10.1	2,260	9.2	890	10.9	470	6.8	170	10.8		
Non-S&E field	22,840	10.7	18,990	11.0	1,700	6.9	1,300	16.0	750	10.8	100	6.4		
Sex														
Female	60,730	28.4	48,650	28.2	5,830	23.7	3,220	39.6	2,490	35.9	450	28.7	100	27.8
Male	153,300	71.6	123,740	71.8	18,810	76.4	4,930	60.6	4,440	64.1	1,120	71.3	270	75.0

Source: Compiled from NSF (2006).
Note: Cells with counts of less than 50 are not reported.

sciences, and the humanities.[5] The chapter analyzes survey data collected from a national sample of 2,407 faculty. The data was collected between 2004 and 2005. The chapter examines the level of racial and gender diversity among the sample and in the departments they currently work in.

SAMPLE CHARACTERISTICS

The sample was predominantly white. The 2,074 white respondents constituted 86.2 percent of the sample. There were 89 Asians comprising 3.7 percent of the sample, the 62 Hispanics made up 2.6 percent, the 60 blacks constituted 2.5 percent, and the 24 Native Americans accounted for 1.0 percent of the sample. In addition, there were 29 other nonwhite (mixed-race or other minority) faculty that comprised 1.2 percent of the sample. Sixty-nine (2.9 percent) of the sample did not reveal their race. Overall, the 264 minority faculty comprised 11.0 percent of the sample. How does this compare to the larger S&E field? The percentage of minorities in my sample was lower than that found in the NSF data reported in Table 1 (NSF, 2006).

This sample was also predominantly male. The 1,489 males accounted for 61.9 percent of the sample. There were 833 females in the sample; they comprised 34.6 percent of the sample. Another 85 respondents accounting for 3.5 percent of the sample did not reveal their gender. My sample had a higher percentage of females than was found in the 2003 NSF faculty study. The NSF study reported that 28.4 percent of its sample was female (see Table 1).

Departments to which Respondents Belonged

Respondents were asked to say what departments they were in. For analytical purposes, they were grouped into 17 categories (Table 2). Faculty from the biological sciences comprised the largest portion of the sample; they accounted for 37.2 percent of it. Those in agricultural sciences departments comprised 11.4 percent of the sample followed by the 10.0 percent in earth and atmospheric sciences departments. Table 2 also summarizes the percentage of each racial group in the sample by the departments they were in. As the table indicates, less than 10 percent of the respondents who were in geography, general sciences, ecology, humanities/other, and ocean and marine sciences departments were ethnic minorities.

The distribution of nonwhite faculty across the disciplines was not uniform. As mentioned before, nonwhite faculty comprised 11.0 percent of

Table 2. Racial and Gender Characteristics of the Sample.

Department	Total Sample		Race					Gender		
	Total *n*	Total sample (%)	White	Total minority (%)	Under-represented minorities	Asian	Race unknown	Male	Female	Gender unknown
Total sample	2407	100.0	86.2	11.0	7.3	3.7	2.9	61.9	34.6	3.5
Environmental studies	138	5.7	83.3	11.6	5.8	5.8	5.1	56.6	41.3	2.2
Biological sciences	895	37.2	87.0	10.6	7.8	2.8	2.3	55.6	40.6	3.8
Natural resources	152	6.3	88.8	9.2	5.9	3.3	2.0	71.1	25.0	3.9
Environmental sciences	130	5.4	84.6	10.0	9.2	0.8	5.4	63.1	33.1	3.8
Agricultural sciences	274	11.4	84.3	14.6	10.9	3.6	1.1	72.3	24.5	3.3
Forestry	56	2.3	78.6	16.1	10.7	5.4	5.4	67.9	30.4	1.8
Geography	94	3.9	90.4	8.5	2.1	6.4	1.1	71.3	27.7	1.1
Earth and atmospheric sciences	240	10.0	88.8	9.2	5.4	4.2	2.1	67.5	30.0	2.5
Engineering	88	3.7	81.8	15.9	4.5	11.4	2.3	69.3	27.3	3.4
Ecology	46	1.9	91.2	8.7	6.5	2.2	0.0	56.5	43.5	0.0
Environmental design, landscape architecture, urban planning	46	1.9	82.6	17.4	13.0	4.3	0.0	69.6	30.4	0.0
Chemistry	55	2.3	89.1	7.3	5.5	1.8	3.6	65.5	34.5	0.0
Social sciences	39	1.6	82.1	17.9	10.3	7.7	0.0	59.0	35.9	5.1
Humanities/other	33	1.4	93.9	6.1	6.1	0.0	0.0	45.5	42.4	12.1
Science (general)	44	1.8	90.9	6.8	4.5	2.3	2.3	56.8	38.6	4.5
Ocean and marine sciences	26	1.1	96.2	3.8	0.0	3.8	0.0	46.2	53.8	0.0
Undisclosed	51	2.1	64.7	7.8	3.9	3.9	27.5	54.9	27.5	17.6

the sample. Of that amount, underrepresented minorities accounted for 7.3 percent of the sample, whereas Asians constituted 3.7 percent (Table 2). As numerous NSF studies indicate that Asians are represented at a higher rate than other racial or ethnic minorities in S&E fields (see, e.g., National Science Board, 2006), this analysis analyzes Asians separately from other minority groups when appropriate.

Nonwhite faculty constituted 11.6 percent of those in environmental studies departments. Underrepresented minorities and Asians each accounted for 5.8 percent of the respondents in environmental studies. All minority faculty accounted for 10.6 percent of those in biological sciences departments. Of that percentage, most (7.8 percent) were underrepresented minorities; Asians constituted only 2.8 percent of biological sciences faculty in the sample. Just over nine percent of the respondents who were in natural resources departments were nonwhites; underrepresented minorities comprised 5.9 percent of the sample, whereas Asians made up 3.3 percent. Ten percent of the respondents in environmental sciences departments were minorities. However, the vast majority of those (9.2 percent) were underrepresented minorities.

Of the respondents indicating they belonged to agricultural science departments, 14.5 percent were minorities. Underrepresented minorities accounted for 10.9 percent and Asians 3.6 percent of that amount. Nonwhites constituted 16.1 percent of the respondents reporting that they were in forestry departments. Of that amount, 10.7 percent were underrepresented minorities and 5.4 percent were Asians.

Only 8.5 percent of the respondents in geography departments were nonwhites. Of those, Asians (6.4 percent) were much more likely to be said departments than other minorities (2.1 percent). Like geography, less than 10 percent of the respondents in earth and atmospheric sciences departments were minorities. Of the faculty, 5.4 percent were underrepresented minorities and 4.2 percent were Asians. Almost 16 percent of the respondents in engineering department were nonwhites. Asians (11.4 percent) were far more likely than other minorities (4.5 percent) to be in engineering departments. On the contrary, underrepresented minorities constituted 6.5 and Asians 2.2 percent of ecology departments.

Much higher percentages of underrepresented minorities were found in environmental design/landscape architecture/urban planning departments than Asians. Of the 17.3 percent nonwhites in such departments, underrepresented minorities made up 13.4 percent. Only 7.3 percent of the respondents belonging to chemistry departments were nonwhites. Asians comprised 1.8 percent of the faculty in chemistry departments, whereas other minorities comprised 5.5 percent. The greatest percentage of ethnic and racial minority faculty (18 percent) were found in social science departments. Of the social science faculty, 10.3 percent were under-represented minorities, whereas 7.7 percent were Asians.

Only 6.1 percent of the faculty belonging to humanities/other departments were nonwhites; none of them were Asians. Nonwhite faculty also comprised 6.8 percent of those in general sciences departments. More specifically, underrepresented minorities made up 4.5 percent and Asians 2.3 percent of the respondents indicating they belonged to general sciences departments. The percentage of nonwhites reporting they belonged to ocean and marine sciences departments was lower than in any other department. No underrepresented minority respondent indicated they belonged to such departments, whereas 3.8 percent of Asians did.

Females in the sample accounted for a higher percentage of each department than racial minorities did. While no department exceeded 18.0 percent minority, the percentage of females identifying themselves as members of departments ranged from 24.5 percent in agricultural sciences to 53.8 percent in ocean and marine sciences (see Table 2). Female respondents also constituted 43.5 percent of those in ecology departments, 41.3 percent of those in environmental studies, and 40.6 percent of those in the biological sciences.

So, how did race and gender interact to influence the distribution of faculty in the various departments? Table 3 reports that overall white males constituted 54.2 percent of the sample, whereas white females comprised 29.7 percent. Asian males were about twice as likely to be in the sample than Asian females. Asian males constituted 2.3 percent of the sample, whereas Asian women comprised only 1.2 percent of the sample. There were similar percentages of black makes and females in the sample. Black makes made up 1.2 percent of the sample compared to black females comprising 1.3 percent. The percentage of blacks and Hispanics in the sample was somewhat similar. Hispanic males constituted 1.4 percent of the sample, whereas Hispanic females made up 1.0 percent of it. Native Americans constituted around 1.0 percent of the sample. Native American males comprised 0.6 percent of the sample, whereas Native American females made up 0.4 percent of it.

More specifically, over 60 percent of the respondents in earth and atmospheric sciences, agricultural sciences, natural resources, and geography departments were white males. That is, white males were about two to three times as likely as white females to indicate that they belonged to these departments. The percentage of white females indicating they belonged to

Table 3. The Interaction of Race and Gender in Departmental Characteristics.

Department	Total	White Male		White Female		Asian Male		Asian Female		Black Male		Black Female		Hispanic Male		Hispanic Female		Native American Male		Native American Female		Other Minority Male		Other Minority Female		Race and Gender Unknown	
	n	n	%	n	%	n	%	n	%	n	%	n	%	n	%	n	%	n	%	n	%	n	%	n	%	n	%
Total sample	2407	1304	54.2	714	29.7	55	2.3	29	1.2	29	1.2	31	1.3	34	1.4	25	1.0	14	0.6	10	0.4	20	0.8	9	0.4	133	5.5
Environmental studies	138	66	47.8	48	34.8	6	4.3	2	1.4	1	0.7	3	2.2	1	0.7	0	0.0	0	0.0	1	0.7	2	1.4	0	0.0	8	5.8
Biological sciences	895	447	49.9	306	34.2	12	1.3	11	1.2	4	0.4	18	2.0	16	1.8	15	1.7	2	0.2	4	0.4	6	0.7	4	0.4	50	5.6
Natural resources	152	96	63.2	34	22.4	3	2.0	1	0.7	4	2.6	1	0.7	0	0.0	0	0.0	1	0.7	0	0.0	2	1.3	1	0.7	9	5.9
Environmental sciences	130	73	56.2	34	26.2	1	0.8	0	0.0	2	1.5	2	1.5	0	0.0	3	2.3	2	1.5	2	1.5	0	0.0	0	0.0	11	8.5
Agricultural sciences	274	170	62.0	55	20.1	5	1.8	5	1.8	10	3.6	1	0.4	5	1.8	5	1.8	2	0.7	1	0.4	5	1.8	0	0.0	10	3.6
Forestry	56	28	50.0	15	26.8	3	5.4	0	0.0	2	3.6	0	0.0	1	1.8	0	0.0	2	3.6	0	0.0	0	0.0	1	1.8	4	7.1
Geography	94	60	63.8	24	25.5	4	4.3	2	2.1	2	2.1	0	0.0	0	0.0	0	0.0	0	0.0	0	0.0	0	0.0	0	0.0	2	2.1
Earth & atmospheric sciences	240	145	60.4	64	26.7	6	2.5	3	1.3	2	0.8	2	0.8	4	1.7	1	0.4	1	0.4	0	0.0	1	0.4	1	0.4	10	4.2
Engineering	88	49	55.7	23	26.1	8	9.1	1	1.1	0	0.0	0	0.0	1	1.1	0	0.0	3	3.4	0	0.0	0	0.0	0	0.0	3	3.4
Ecology	46	24	52.2	18	39.1	0	0.0	1	2.2	0	0.0	1	2.2	0	0.0	0	0.0	0	0.0	0	0.0	2	4.3	0	0.0	0	0.0
Environmental design, landscape architecture, urban planning	46	26	56.5	12	26.1	1	2.2	1	2.2	1	2.2	0	0.0	3	6.5	1	2.2	0	0.0	0	0.0	1	2.2	0	0.0	0	0.0
Chemistry	55	31	56.4	18	32.7	1	1.8	0	0.0	0	0.0	1	1.8	0	0.0	0	0.0	1	1.8	0	0.0	1	1.8	0	0.0	2	3.6
Social sciences	39	21	53.8	9	23.1	1	2.6	2	5.1	1	2.6	0	0.0	0	0.0	0	0.0	0	0.0	1	2.6	0	0.0	2	5.1	2	5.1
Humanities/other	33	14	42.4	13	39.4	0	0.0	0	0.0	0	0.0	1	3.0	1	3.0	0	0.0	0	0.0	0	0.0	0	0.0	0	0.0	4	12.1
Science (general)	44	23	52.3	15	34.1	1	2.3	0	0.0	0	0.0	1	2.3	1	2.3	0	0.0	0	0.0	0	0.0	0	0.0	0	0.0	3	6.8
Ocean & marine sciences	26	11	42.3	14	53.8	1	3.8	0	0.0	0	0.0	0	0.0	0	0.0	0	0.0	0	0.0	0	0.0	0	0.0	0	0.0	0	0.0
Discipline unknown	51	20	39.2	12	23.5	2	3.9	0	0.0	0	0.0	0	0.0	1	2.0	0	0.0	0	0.0	1	2.0	0	0.0	0	0.0	15	29.4

particular departments ranged from 20.1 percent in agricultural sciences to 53.8 percent in ocean and marine sciences.

The starkest gender differences were seen between Asian males and females. Asian males were eight times as likely as Asian females to be in ecology departments. They were three times more likely than Asian females to indicate they belonged to environmental studies and natural resources departments. Asian men were also twice as likely to belong to geography and earth and atmospheric sciences departments than Asian females. On the contrary, Asian females were twice as likely as Asian men to be in social science departments.

While ecology and social sciences were the only two departments in which Asian women outnumbered Asian males, more black female respondents indicated they belonged to biological science, ecology, social science, humanities/other, and general science departments than black males. The largest disparity between black males and females was in the biological sciences where the percentage of black females was about five times greater than that of black males. On the contrary, the percentage of black males in agricultural science was about 10 times greater than the percentage of black females belonging to that discipline.

Hispanic females were about three times as likely as Hispanic males to belong to environmental science departments. However, unlike other racial groups where males were more likely to be in agricultural sciences than females, equal percentage (1.8 percent) of Hispanic males and females indicated they belonged to agricultural science departments. No Native American respondent indicated they belonged to six departments – geography, ecology, environmental design/landscape architecture/urban planning, humanities/other, general sciences, and ocean and marine sciences.

TENURE STATUS OF RESPONDENTS

In addition to knowing which departments respondents belonged to, it is important to examine their rank and the way in which rank is related to race and gender. Having assessed the level of racial and gender diversity in each department, it is important to know how faculty are distributed in various faculty ranks. That is, how are factors such as race, gender, and age related to rank? To this end, study participants were asked to indicate their rank. The data showed that most of the respondents held tenured positions. In all, 92 (3.8 percent) of the respondents held endowed chairs, 913 (37.9 percent) were full professors, and 636 (26.4 percent) were associate professors. Among the untenured faculty, 504 (20.9 percent) were assistant professors, whereas 176 (7.3 percent) were in nontenure-track positions (Table 4). The nontenure-track positions include lecturers, research scientists, adjunct appointments, and so on. The remaining 86 respondents (3.6 percent) did not indicate their rank.

So, how did the rank of minority faculty compare to that of whites? And, how did the rank of female faculty compare to that of males? White males were more likely to hold faculty positions in the highest ranks than they were to hold untenured and nontenure-track positions. In comparison, higher percentages of white female faculty were in the untenured and nontenure-track ranks than in tenured positions. This same pattern held for minority males and female. Minority female faculty were more likely to hold tenure-track and nontenure-track positions than faculty positions of the highest ranks.

Hence, white males – who comprised 54.2 percent of the sample – also held 54.3 percent of the endowed chairs. White male faculty also held 67.5 percent of the full professorships. At the same time, they held only 40.7 percent of the assistant professorships and 38.1 percent of the nontenure-track positions. In contrast, white female – who comprised 29.7 percent of the sample – held 30.4 percent of the endowed chairs. However, white females held only 19.2 percent of the full professorships. They held 34.4 percent of the associate professorships, 40.5 percent of the assistant professorships, and 41.5 percent of the nontenure-track positions.

White males were about twice as likely as white females to hold an endowed chair; however, Asian males – who held three of the four endowed chairs – were three times more likely than Asian females to have an endowed chair. Both white and Asian males were about three times as likely to hold full professorships than white and Asian females respectively. Asian males deviated from the norm in one important way. Asian males were more likely than Asian females to hold nontenure-track positions; this is the reverse of the pattern seen for other males vis-à-vis this position. White, black, Hispanic, and Native American females were more likely than their male counterparts to hold nontenure-track positions.

Whereas four Asians held endowed chairs, only three other minorities held endowed chairs. No black females, Hispanics, or Native American females held endowed chairs; one black and two Native American males held endowed chairs. Furthermore, although black females comprise 1.3 percent of the sample, they held only 0.5 percent of the full professorships. However, black females also held 4.5 percent of the nontenure-track

Table 4. Race, Gender, and Tenure Status of Respondents.

Tenure Status	Total n	White Male		White Female		Asian Male		Asian Female		Black Male		Black Female		Hispanic Male		Hispanic Female		Native American Male		Native American Female		Other Minority Male		Other Minority Female		Race and Gender Unknown	
	n	n	%	n	%	n	%	n	%	n	%	n	%	n	%	n	%	n	%	n	%	n	%	n	%	n	%
Total sample	2407	1304	54.2	714	29.7	55	2.3	29	1.2	29	1.2	31	1.3	34	1.4	25	1.0	14	0.6	10	18.5	20	0.8	9	0.4	133	5.5
Endowed chair	92	50	54.3	28	30.4	3	3.3	1	1.1	1	1.1	0	0.0	0	0.0	0	0.0	2	2.2	0	0.0	1	1.1	0	0.0	6	6.5
Full professor	913	616	67.5	175	19.2	20	2.2	7	0.8	13	1.4	5	0.5	10	1.1	5	0.5	5	0.5	2	3.0	7	0.8	1	0.1	47	5.1
Associate professor	636	320	50.3	219	34.4	12	1.9	6	0.9	6	0.9	10	1.6	14	2.2	8	1.3	3	0.5	1	4.0	7	1.1	2	0.3	27	4.2
Assistant professor	504	205	40.7	204	40.5	16	3.2	14	2.8	5	1.0	8	1.6	9	1.8	8	1.6	3	0.6	1	2.5	4	0.8	4	0.8	23	4.6
Nontenure track	176	67	38.1	73	41.5	3	1.7	1	0.6	1	0.6	8	4.5	0	0.0	4	2.3	1	0.6	4	10.5	1	0.6	1	0.6	12	6.8
Undeclared	86	46	53.5	15	17.4	1	1.2	0	0.0	3	3.5	0	0.0	1	1.2	0	0.0	0	0.0	1	1.9	0	0.0	1	1.2	18	20.9

positions. Similarly, Hispanic females comprised only 1.0 percent of the sample; yet, they held only 0.5 percent of the full professorships. They were more concentrated in the untenured positions; they held 1.6 percent of the assistant professorships and 2.3 percent of the nontenure-track positions. Native American females – who comprised 0.4 percent of the sample – held 0.2 percent of the full professorships. Like Hispanic females, they held 2.3 percent of the nontenure-track positions.

Hence females tend to have greater representation in the lowest and most vulnerable faculty ranks. In general, they were more likely to hold untenured and nontenure-track positions than males. On the contrary, males held a higher percentage of the highest ranked positions – the endowed chairs and full professorships.

How is rank related to age, gender, and length of time since acquiring a doctorate? There was a significant relationship between the age of the respondent and their faculty rank. That is, older respondents had higher status appointments. Most of the endowed chairs and full professorships were held by respondents 50 years and older. Seventy-five percent of those holding endowed chairs and 78.7 percent of full professors were 50 years or older. On the contrary, only 7.0 percent of the assistant professors and 39.2 percent of the nontenure-track faculty were in this age category.

Gender and rank was also related as males tended to be older than females. For instance, 55.7 percent of the male respondents were 50 years or older but only 35.2 percent of females were in this age range. Race and age was also correlated. Racial and ethnic minorities tended to be younger than whites – 32.9 percent of nonwhites were 50 years and older compared to 49.9 percent of whites. In general, white male respondents were generally older than white female or nonwhite respondents. Hence, not only were white male respondents older than the rest of the sample, generally speaking, they also were more likely than other groups to have their doctorates the longest and have the most experience in their fields. Overwhelmingly, the respondents who had their doctorates the longest held the highest status positions like endowed chairs and full professorships.

The 2003 NSF faculty study revealed similar patterns in S&E faculty nationwide. Whites were more likely to be in tenured positions than untenured or nontenure-track positions. Generally speaking, lower percentages of minorities were in tenured positions than whites. Additional analysis is provided in Table 5. The table examines each faculty rank to see what portion is composed of minority faculty. As the table indicates, 84.8 percent of the full professors and 80.8 percent of the associate professors are white. Minorities comprise a larger portion of the untenured faculty – assistant

Table 5. Tenure Status of Faculty with Science and Engineering Doctorates in 2003.

Demographic Characteristics	Total Sample	Whites		Asians		Blacks		Hispanics		Native Americans		Other	
		Number	%	Number	%	Number	%	Number	%	Number	%	Number	%
All S&E doctoral degree holding faculty	214,030	172,390	80.5	24,630	11.5	8,140	3.8	6,930	3.2	1,570	0.7	360	0.2
Rank													
Professor	94,550	79,800	84.4	8,670	9.2	2,590	2.7	2,530	2.7	820	0.9	140	0.1
Associate professor	58,430	47,200	80.8	6,400	11.0	2,520	4.3	1,980	3.4	280	0.5		
Assistant professor	53,250	39,270	73.7	8,540	16.0	2,690	5.1	2,180	4.1	430	0.8	150	0.3
Instructor	7,800	6,120	78.5	1,020	13.1	350	4.5	250	3.2				
Tenure status													
No tenure system at institution	7,500	5,860	78.1	950	12.7	400	5.3	260	3.5				
No tenure system for position	12,940	10,990	84.9	1,090	8.4	380	2.9	370	2.9	100	0.8		
Tenured	130,290	108,340	83.2	12,720	9.8	4,260	3.3	3,800	2.9	1,000	0.8	170	0.1
On tenure track but not tenured	43,510	32,180	74.0	6,690	15.4	2,400	5.5	1,750	4.0	390	0.9	90	0.2
Not on tenure track	19,790	15,010	75.8	3,180	16.1	700	3.5	760	3.8				

Source: Compiled from NSF (2006).
Note: Cells with counts of less than 50 are not reported.

professors and lecturers. It should also be noted that among minority groups, Asians hold faculty positions in much higher percentages than under-represented minorities. Asians held 9.2 percent of the full professorships. In comparison, underrepresented minorities held less than 3 percent of these positions. Similarly 11.0 percent of the associate professorships were held by Asians compared to less than 5 percent of such positions held by underrepresented minorities. Asians were also more than three times as likely to hold tenure-track positions than other minorities. Whereas Asians held 16.0 percent of the assistant professor positions, only 5.1 percent of blacks, 4.1 percent of Hispanics, and 0.8 percent of Native Americans had assistant professorships (NSF, 2006).

DEMOGRAPHIC CHARACTERISTICS OF RESPONDENTS' OWN DEPARTMENTS

To put the discussion of my study's sample in perspective, respondents were asked to report on the demographic characteristics of their own depart-ments. In general, the departments to which the respondents belonged were predominantly white and leadership positions such as department head were most likely occupied by white male faculty members. Respondents listed the total number of white males, white females, minority males, and minority females in their department. These numbers were summed to provide a rough estimate[6] of the total numbers of faculty in each group. In all, the number of faculty respondents reported totaled 35,539. Of that number, the majority – 24,098 or 67.8 percent – were white males. The number of white females totaled 7,922 or 22.3 percent. The number of minority faculty reported by respondents comprised about 9.9 percent of the total. That is, the 2,429 nonwhite males made up 6.8 percent of the total, whereas the 1,090 minority females constituted 3.1 percent of the total.

White males were most numerous whereas minority females were the least likely to be found in these departments. The mean number of white male faculty in all departments was 11 (SD = 9.551). The mean for other groups was much lower. The mean number of white females was 3.78 (SD = 3.568). Much smaller numbers of minorities are on the faculty of these departments than either white males or females. The mean number of minority males was 1.39 (SD = 2.047) and the mean number of minority females was .67 (SD = 1.229). While respondents reported that their department had a many as 153 white males, none reported having more than 63 white females, 20 minority males, or 16 minority females in their unit.

Table 6. Respondents' Report of the Race and Gender of the Faculty in their Departments.

Number of Faculty in Department	White Males		White Females		Minority Males		Minority Females	
	Number	%	Number	%	Number	%	Number	%
None	9	0.4	114	4.7	669	27.8	949	39.4
One	78	3.2	354	14.7	535	22.2	467	19.4
Two to four	414	17.2	1021	42.4	426	17.7	190	7.9
Five to nine	731	30.4	514	21.4	93	3.9	16	0.7
Ten or more	959	39.8	102	4.2	19	0.8	5	0.2
Do not know	216	9.0	302	12.5	665	27.6	780	32.4

There were striking differences in the number of each type of faculty in the departments. Only 9 (or 0.4 percent) of the respondents reported being in departments with no white males on the faculty (Table 6). The vast majority of departments also had white female faculty too; only 4.7 percent did not. In contrast, 669 (27.8 percent) of the respondents reported being a department with no minority male faculty and 949 (or 39.4 percent) were in departments that had no minority females on the faculty. If minorities were on the faculty, the most likely scenario was that there were only one or a few. Whereas 70.2 percent of respondents reported being in department that had five or more white males and 25.6 percent reported being in departments with five or more white female faculty, only 4.7 percent were in departments that had this number of minority males and 0.9 percent had this number of minority female faculty.

DISCUSSION AND CONCLUDING REMARKS

There is an impressive body of research that focus on S&E faculty. However, studies that examine faculty diversity in environmental disciplines are not common. This is critical because the levels of diversity among environmental faculty appear to be so low. Understanding and enhancing diversity in all sectors of the environmental workforce is important because the environment has emerged as a major sector in society. Not only is the American environmental workforce large, the environmental movement is influential and environmental issues are dominating the social, economic, and political landscape. As issues like climate change, sustainability continue to dominate policies, life experiences, and decision making, questions arise – are academic institutions equipped to deal effectively with the environmental challenges ahead? Who comprises the academic environmental workforce? That is, who are our environmental educators and to what extent do they reflect the demographics, experiences, and views of general population? What should be the role of minorities in the future academic environmental workforce?

Research on S&E faculty usually focuses on race or gender. However, my study points to need to do more in-depth research on environmental disciplines. It also suggests that more attention should be paid to how race and gender interact to put minority female faculty in more vulnerable or tenuous positions in the academe.

My study supports the findings of earlier research indicating that females are underrepresented in the faculty ranks. It also supports earlier findings that indicate that females occupy the lowest faculty ranks in higher proportions than males (see, e.g., Handelsman, 2005; Stewart, Malley, & LaVaque-Mantay, 2007). However, data presented above from my study indicates that minority females are the least likely to be on the faculty of the disciplines studied, are often the sole nonwhite faculty in the departments, and are least likely to occupy faculty positions of the highest ranks. Although data such as those from NSF (2006) indicates that Asians are much more likely to hold faculty positions in S&E departments, analysis of my data shows that Asian women are not as likely as Asian men to be appointed to such positions or hold positions in the highest faculty ranks. My study suggests that Asian women are more similar to other underrepresented minorities than they are to Asian men in terms of the portion of them holding faculty positions and the type of positions they hold.

My study raises several questions – why are minority faculty present in such low percentages in the disciplines studied? Is this a function of lack of interest in the sciences on the part of minorities? Does it stem from ineffective recruitment or institutional structures that retard retention (in undergraduate and graduate science programs or while on the faculty)? Could the low percentages of minorities also be a reflection of problems with hiring or promotion? The data will be analyzed in future publications to see how these and other factors such as work load, opportunities to network and collaborate, leadership opportunities, and mentoring relate to the status of minority faculty in these disciplines.

This analysis also points to the need for environmental justice to focus more attention on institutional diversity and labor force dynamics. The larger issue of labor force dynamics is going to be critical in coming years.

In addition to working on environmental issues to improve quality of life in minority and low-income communities, environmental justice activists have to think in terms of jobs for people in such communities. If environmental organizations hire only a few minorities or if only a few minorities are able to get jobs in emerging green economy, then this will have significant implications for low-income and minority communities. The academic portion of this should not be ignored. Although one could argue that college-educated students and doctorate-holding minorities are elites who can hold their own in the job market, one has to see lack racial diversity in the disciplines studied in the larger context of lack of diversity in the larger green labor force.

Environmental justice activists are beginning to advocate more forcefully for job opportunities in low-income and minority communities. Some are at the forefront of efforts to open green collar jobs to minorities. Some groups such as Sustainable South Bronx and Green For All have made job creation a part of their agenda (Sustainable South Bronx, 2008; Green For All, 2008). Multicultural Environmental Leadership Development Initiative (MELDI, 2009) website has an extensive green jobs center. However, this effort cannot and should be concentrated solely on entry-level jobs. As institutional studies conducted by this author have shown (Taylor, 2008), minority environmental professional are more concentrated in lower status professional jobs than in top positions. By focusing on the entire spectrum of the green workforce, environmental justice advocates will be able to make more compelling arguments about the need for diversity both in terms of numbers of minorities hired and also in terms of promotions and rank.

NOTES

1. This chapter will make references to minorities and underrepresented minorities. In the context of this chapter, the term "minorities" refers to blacks, Latinos/Hispanics, Asians, Native Americans, and other nonwhites. The term "underrepresented minorities" is more specific – referring only to a subset of this group. It refers to blacks, Latinos/Hispanics, and Native Americans.

2. Bureau of Reclamation, Bureau of Land Management, Farm Service Agency, U.S. Forest Service, Natural Resource Conservation Service, Reclamation and Enforcement, National Park Service, Fish and Wildlife Service, National Oceanic and Atmospheric Administration, and the United States Geological Survey.

3. The related disciplines studied were conservation, environmental education, environmental biology, natural resources, outdoor recreation and parks, zoology, forestry, land and resource management, range science, and water resources management.

4. This included the following disciplinary fields: biological sciences, forestry, natural resources, agricultural sciences, geological sciences, geography, environmental sciences, environmental engineering, and social sciences.

5. The disciplinary specializations of respondents were categorized as follows: general biology, ecology, zoology, botany, microbiology, forestry, natural resources, chemistry, environmental sciences, agricultural sciences, geography, oceanography and marine sciences, physics, public health, engineering, social sciences, education, and humanities/other.

6. These figures should be treated as very rough estimates because some respondents did not provide a count of faculty in their units. In addition, there may be some double counting as more than one faculty from the same university completed surveys and jointly appointed faculty in interdisciplinary units may be counted in more than one place.

ACKNOWLEDGMENTS

Funding for this research was provided by the National Science Foundation.

REFERENCES

Adams, C. E., & Moreno, M. (1998). A comparative study of natural resource professionals in minority and majority groups in the southeastern United States. *Wildlife Society Bulletin, 26*(4), 971–981.

Babco, E. L., & Jesse, J. K. (2005). Employment in the life sciences: Mixed outlook. *BioScience, 55*(10), 879–886.

Beutel, A. M., & Nelson, D. J. (2005). Gender and race-ethnicity of faculty in top science and engineering research departments. *Journal of Women and Minorities in Science and Engineering, 11*, 389–403.

Beutel, A. M., & Nelson, D. J. (2006). Gender and race-ethnicity of faculty in top social science research departments. *The Social Science Journal, 43*, 111–125.

Bryant, B., & Mohai, P. (1992). *Race and the incidence of environmental hazards: A time for discourse.* Boulder, CO: Westview Press.

Environmental Careers Organization. (1992). *Beyond the green: Redefining and diversifying the environmental movement.* Boston, MA: Environmental Careers Organization.

Green For All. (2008). About us. Available at http://www.grenforall.org/. Accessed on June 15, 2008.

Handelsman, J., Cantor, N., Carnes, M., Denton, D., Fine, E., Grosz, B., Hinshaw, V., Marrett, C., Rosser, S., Shalala, D., & Sheridan, D. (2005). More women in science. *Science Magazine, 309*August 19, 1190–1191.

Hodgdon, H. E. (1980). Enrollment of women and ethnic minorities in wildlife curricula: 1977. *Wildlife Society Bulletin, 8*(2), 158–163.

Hodgdon, H. E. (1982). Wildlife enrollment of women and ethnic minorities in 1979. *Wildlife Society Bulletin, 10*(2), 175–180.

Mervis, J. (2001). New data in chemistry show 'zero' diversity. *Science Magazine, 292*May 18, 1291–1292.

Multicultural Environmental Leadership Development Initiative. (2009). Green jobs center. Available at http://www.meldi.snre.umich.edu

National Science Board. (2006). *Science and engineering indicators* (pp. 2-1–2-39). NSB 06-01. Arlington, VA: National Science Foundation, Division of Science Resources Statistics.

National Science Foundation. (2004). *Women, minorities, and persons with disabilities in science and engineering: 2004.* NSF 04-317. Arlington, VA: National Science Foundation.

National Science Foundation. (2006). *Academic institutions of minority faculty with S&E doctorates.* Arlington, VA: Science Resources Statistics.

National Science Foundation. (2007). Website with reports on campus diversity. Available at http://www.nsf.gov/funding/pgm_summ.jsp?pims_id = 5383. Accessed on April 10, 2007.

Partnership for Public Service. (2007). Best places to work in the Federal Government, American University, Institute for the Study of Public Policy Implementation, School of Public Affairs, Washington, DC. Available at http://www.bestplacestowork.org/BPTW/about. Accessed on November 26, 2007.

Shabecoff, P. (1990). Environmental groups told they are racists in hiring. *The New York Times,* February 1, p. A20.

Snow, D. (1992). *Inside the conservation movement: Meeting the leadership challenge.* Covelo, CA: Island Press.

Stanton, R. G. (2002). *Environmental stewardship for the 21st century: Opportunities and actions for improving cultural diversity in conservation organizations and programs.* Washington, DC: Natural Resources Council of America.

Stewart, A. J., Malley, J. E., & LaVaque-Mantay, D. (2007). *Transforming science and engineering.* Ann Arbor, MI: University of Michigan Press.

Sustainable South Bronx. (2008). About us. Available at http://www.ssbx.org/. Accessed on November 10, 2008.

Taylor, D. E. (1989). Blacks and the environment: Toward and explanation of the concern and action gap between blacks and whites. *Environment and Behavior, 21*(2), 175–205.

Taylor, D. E. (1992). Can the environment attract and maintain the support of minorities. In: B. Bryant & P. Mohai (Eds), *Race and the incidence of environmental hazards: A Time for Discourse* (pp. 28–54, 224–230). Boulder, CO: Westview Press.

Taylor, D. E. (2007). Employment preferences and salary expectations of students in science and engineering. *BioScience, 57*(2), 175–185.

Taylor, D. E. (2008). Diversity and the environment: Myth–making and the status of minorities in the field. *Research in Social Problems and Public Policy, 15,* 89–148.

Taylor, D. E. (2010). Green jobs and the potential to diversify the environmental workforce. *Journal of Land Resources and Environmental Law, 30*(2).

United Church of Christ. (1987). *Toxic waste and race in the United States.* New York: United Church of Christ.

Valdez, R. (1995). Hispanic undergraduates in wildlife and fishery sciences in the western United States. *Wildlife Society Bulletin, 23*(4), 574–578.

Dorceta E. Taylor is an associate professor at the University of Michigan's School of Natural Resources and Environment. She teaches courses in environmental history, environmental justice, tourism and climate change, and social movements. She is the director of the Multicultural Environmental Leadership Development Initiative (http://www.meldi.snre. umich.edu) and author of *The Environment and the People in American Cities, 1600s-1900s: Disorder, Inequality, and Social Change*. She can be reached by email at dorceta@umich.edu or by telephone at 734-763-5327.

WHY CAN'T THEY WORK TOGETHER? A FRAMEWORK FOR UNDERSTANDING CONFLICT AND COLLABORATION IN TWO ENVIRONMENTAL DISPUTES IN SOUTHEAST MICHIGAN

Sarah Lashley and Dorceta E. Taylor

ABSTRACT

Purpose – *This chapter analyzes two environmental conflicts in Southeast Michigan. It analyzes how activists in each community framed each conflict and what factors prevented the groups from collaborating.*

Design/methodology/approach – *This essay uses a multi-method approach. Researchers used participant observation, interviews, and archival information gleaned from government documents and newspapers.*

Findings – *Both community groups had a common opponent – a corporation that had closed its facilities in a predominantly black, low-income urban community and relocated it to a predominantly white, middle-class, rural community. Both communities had complaints about*

Environment and Social Justice: An International Perspective
Research in Social Problems and Public Policy, Volume 18, 409–449
Copyright © 2010 by Emerald Group Publishing Limited
All rights of reproduction in any form reserved
ISSN: 0196-1152/doi:10.1108/S0196-1152(2010)0000018016

*pollution, yet they did not collaborate with each other in their campaigns
against the corporation.*

Originality/value – *The essay blends two theoretical approaches – social
movement and conflict theories – to help in the assessment of how the
conflicts unfolded and why collaboration between activists in the two
communities did not occur. This is one of the first attempts to analyze
environmental justice conflicts from this perspective.*

INTRODUCTION

Today, environmental justice conflicts are not only widespread they take
many shapes and forms. In the U.S. environmental justice conflicts arise for
various reasons. Some of the most common types of conflicts involve
disagreements between activists and corporations. These disagreements
frequently involve the siting of facilities in communities that do not want to
host them, operation of facilities perceived as dangerous to host communities, emissions, disposal of hazardous wastes, occupational health and
safety, community relations, and the abandonment of facilities. Conflicts of
this sort are common in the state of Michigan, and they are often related to
abandoned or hazardous industrial sites. There are 65 sites on Superfund's
National Priorities List awaiting cleanup in Michigan. An additional two
sites have been proposed while 17 have been removed from the list
(Environmental Protection Agency [EPA], 2008a, 2008b). Brownfield sites
are more common. There are more than 450,000 brownfield sites nationwide. More than 2,000 of those are in Detroit and the surrounding areas of
Wayne County (EPA, 2007a, 2007b).

This chapter examines two environmental conflicts that arose in Southeast Michigan. The two communities involved are located 43 miles apart. In
the first, Riverbend, activists in the predominantly black Detroit neighborhood organized a campaign to get the Continental Aluminum Recycling
Company (Continental Aluminum) to clean up its abandoned facility. The
second conflict arose in predominantly white, semi-rural Lyon Township.
Activists in Lyon Township organized a campaign against Continental
Aluminum to reduce its emissions. These two cases are of interest because
they offer an opportunity to study collaborative processes. That is, what
opportunities existed for these two communities to collaborate and to what
extent did they? This is important since both communities had a "common
enemy" so to speak. Cases like these raise larger questions about

environmental justice conflicts – under what conditions can activists of different backgrounds collaborate and what conditions foster such actions? More specifically, this study explores how the two campaigns were organized. It also proposes a framework for analyzing conflicts such as these. It is by identifying the opportunities and barriers to collaboration that individuals and organizations can begin developing strategies to foster collaboration. The analysis relies on information gathered from interviews, archival research, and demographic data. It also draws on two theoretical perspectives – social movement and conflict management theories.

OVERVIEW OF THEORETICAL CONCEPTS

Conflicts and Collaboration

Susskind and Weinstein (1980) argue that as the number of environmental disputes increase, it seems like the capacity of our legal, political, and social institutions to deal with such disputes effectively has been diminished. They attribute this failing to a government that governs less as it responds to special interest groups more, leaving many conflicts to be settled in courtrooms. However, legal processes and battles are not ideal for all environmental disputes, including environmental justice disputes. Thus, much room exists for the exploration and implementation of alternative dispute resolution, including collaborative processes and coalition building.

The growing complexity of environmental issues and remedies requires cooperation and the creation of partnerships and coalitions between individuals, organizations, government officials, and agencies. These partnerships allow for the sharing of knowledge and resources necessary to successfully solve problems (Jakobsen, Hels, & McLaughlin, 2004). By establishing partnerships, building coalitions, and establishing collaborative processes, better informed and more effective decisions can be made through the utilization of shared perspectives, information, and experiences (Wondolleck & Yaffee, 2000). Despite the potential benefits of collaboration, barriers to its implementation may exist.

The effectiveness of collaboration is influenced by a host of factors. These factors may include organizational culture, lack of incentives, lack of shared vision, group and individual characterizations, mistrust, and a shortage of resources (Wondolleck & Yaffee, 2000). These and other factors are analyzed in this examination of the barriers to collaboration between Detroit's Riverbend community and Lyon Township.

Social Movement Theory

Framing
For the purposes of this study, framing is defined as the language that people use to identify the issues and stakeholders to a conflict. Two aspects of framing are of relevance. It is a subconscious reflection of how individuals, organizations, and communities perceive, understand, and interpret issues and events, including their own role in events. Framing is also a "means of structuring the understanding of an issue so as to incite action" (Gamson, 1997; Gray, 2003; Snow, Rochford, Worden, & Benford, 1986; Taylor, 2000). It is a mechanism for our minds to categorize and organize data to translate it in meaningful ways. This subconscious translation assists individuals in sorting and predicting the significance of new data, events, and experiences (Gray, 2003).

Although the earlier discussion refers to frames as a subconscious tool that affects how individuals perceive situations, frames may also be utilized to define issues and motivate action (Snow et al., 1986). This aspect of framing is not subconscious, but rather it is strategically designed to influence how others perceive and act in a given situation. Motivating individuals or groups to act is not easy. Hence collective action frames are a means of structuring the understanding of an issue to stimulate the audience to perceive the issue as one that requires action (Gamson, 1997).

A central feature of the framing process is the generation of diagnostic attributions; that is, the identification of problems and the imputation of blame or causality. Collective action frames are also emergent and action-oriented. That is, the ideas, beliefs, and norms are developed as activists identify grievances, conceive issues, and refine how they articulate their positions. The frames are action-oriented because there is a focus on recruiting individuals to movements who want to and who are able to do something about their grievances. Thus, the creation and utilization of collective action frames that can appeal and stimulate action is important. In the creation of such frames, activists should consider the target audience, the salient issues to be communicated, and the most effective strategies for conveying these issues (Taylor, 2000).

However, activists are not the only ones who frame an issue. Quite often, opponents or targets of action play a role in the framing. Opponents' interpretations of conflicts provide counterframes. In effect, social movement activists and their opponents frame and counterframe issues as conflicts or movements evolve (see Mottl, 1980; Marx, 1997 for more on countermovements and counter framing). In the case of environmental justice conflicts, corporations are quite adept in creating their own counterframes.

Resource Mobilization
Resource mobilization theorists posit that resources, opportunities, linkages between groups and outside support are significant factors in social movement formation and longevity. They contend that activists have to organize and aggregate the resources necessary to initiate and sustain social movements (McCarthy & Zald, 1977; Oberschall, 1973; Gamson, 1975; Tilly, 1977). In the study of American social movements involving minorities (like the civil rights, farm worker, and red power movements), theorists have found the greatest period of movement activism, organizing, and movement building coincides with an infusion of monetary resources and institutional support from outside the traditional base of support (Jenkins & Perrow, 1977; Nagel, 1996; McAdam, 1983; Haines, 1984).

Tactics and Strategies
Social movement theorists also argue that tactics are important to movement dynamics and maintaining momentum (Tarrow, 1994, 1993; Nagel, 1996; Jenkins & Perrow, 1977; McAdam, 1983; Koopmans, 1993; Whittier, 1997; Minkoff, 1997). Tactical interactions between movement activists and opponents are an essential component of movement dynamics. According to McAdam (1983) activists have to devise novel tactics constantly to keep opponents off balance to gain an edge.

METHODOLOGY

A multi-method approach was used in this study that involved collecting archival data conducting and interviews. The archival data were collected from newspaper articles printed in the *Detroit News, Detroit Free Press, South Lyon Herald,* and the *Oakland Press.* These were obtained through the Internet and public library holdings and were printed between 1998 and 2005. In addition, interviews were conducted with reporters from the aforementioned newspapers in 2004. The articles were used to help identify key participants in the conflicts as well as the salient issues in the controversy.

Semi-structured face-to-face hour-long interviews were conducted. Initial participants were identified through the examination of archival materials. Individuals who were quoted or listed as holding leadership positions were contacted and interviewed. Additional participants were identified through a snowball sampling technique wherein the first wave of interviewees was asked to identify other key participants in the conflicts. Thirteen interviews were conducted with community organizers, residents, and community officials. Seven of the interviews were with individuals familiar with the struggles in Lyon Township. Of the seven individuals, four were men and three were women. Four of the individuals were resident organizers, one was a resident and public representative of the township, one was a representative of the county, and one was an employee of a regional environmental organization. Six of the interviews were with individuals who were familiar with the struggles in Riverbend. Of the six individuals, three were women and three were men. Two interviewees were employees of the city, whereas four of the interviewees were local environmental organizers.

THE CONTINENTAL ALUMINUM
RECYCLING COMPANY

Two campaigns – one in Riverbend and one in Lyon Township – have been launched against Continental Aluminum. Continental Aluminum is a recycling plant that accepts one-inch square pieces of aluminum from automobiles, home appliances, and other scrap metals. The scraps are heated to 1,100 degrees Fahrenheit, the impurities are skimmed off and the remaining melted metal is poured into molds that form 25-pound ingots. Continental Aluminum's operation is important to Michigan's auto industry. Manufacturers such as Ford, General Motors, and other auto parts suppliers purchase and use ingots in the production of car transmissions and aluminum cones (Lee, 2002).

Secondary aluminum supplies such as those recycled at Continental Aluminum accounted for approximately one-third of the United States' total aluminum supply of 10.69 million metric tons in 2000. This represents a decrease of 6.6 percent from the previous year. Overall, the nation's total aluminum supply decreased by 4.1 percent between 1999 and 2000. Primary production of aluminum accounts for 34.3 percent of the total supply while imports account for 33.5 percent of the aluminum supply (Aluminum Association, 2004). The remaining 32.2 percent is supplied through secondary recycled recovery.

The processes used to recycle aluminum scraps are known to emit hydrogen fluoride, chlorine, hydrogen chloride, carbon monoxide, carbon dioxide, and compounds of manganese, nickel, lead, and chromium (EPA, 1995). As Table 1 shows these pollutants have been associated with a

Table 1. Pollutants Emitted During Aluminum Recycling.

Pollutants	Health Effects
Hydrogen chloride	Laryngitis, bronchitis, pulmonary edema, irritation to eyes, skin, and mucous membranes
Hydrogen fluoride	Laryngitis, bronchitis, pulmonary edema, irritation to eyes, skin, and mucous membranes
Chlorine	Irritation to upper respiratory tract, eyes, and lungs
Carbon monoxide	Fatigue, chest pains, impaired vision and coordination, headache, dizziness, confusion, and nausea

Sources: Environmental Protection Agency (1995) and Occupational Health and Safety Administration (2004).

number of illnesses and diseases. According to the Occupational Safety and Health Administration (OSHA), exposure to hydrogen chloride may result in laryngitis, bronchitis, and pulmonary edema as it is irritating and corrosive to the eyes, skin, and mucous membranes. Exposure to hydrogen fluoride results in the same conditions. According to the Environmental Protection Agency (EPA), chlorine also results in irritation of the eyes, lungs, and upper respiratory tract (Occupational Safety and Health Administration [OSHA], 2004).

Continental Aluminum is owned and operated by Metal Exchange Corporation. Metal Exchange Corporation is headquartered in St. Louis, Missouri, and operates offices, warehouses, and plants in nine states – Missouri, California, Nebraska, Kentucky, Alabama, North Carolina, Pennsylvania, New York, and Michigan. The multinational corporation that specializes in the import and export of commodities also operates in Canada, Mexico, Argentina, Brazil, Chile, Venezuela, China, Japan, and Taiwan (Metal Exchange Corporation, 2003).

Operating in Riverbend

Riverbend is located along West Jefferson Avenue in Detroit (Wayne County). Among its neighbors is the sprawling Daimler Chrysler plant. The community of Riverbend has a host of non-profit and community organizations. Continental Aluminum began its operations at 1610 Algonquin Road in Detroit in 1989. During its decade of operation at this site, Continental Aluminum amassed seven Wayne County citations for emissions violations, including citations for releases of air contaminants, visible smoke, and improper operations. Additionally, they were cited 12 times by the Detroit Fire Department for poor exhaust, improper storage of slag metal, and faulty sprinklers and fire systems. According to Fire Sergeant Daniel Cheney, "Continental Aluminum was notorious in our firehouse." In addition to the citations, a fire broke out at the facility in January 1992 that exposed four firefighters to ammonia gas (Pearce, 2000b). A *Detroit News* article described the scene as follows:

> Molten aluminum was improperly taken to a storage building before being adequately cooled. The hot metal was then placed over a buried line of natural gas. The threat of explosion from the natural gas line and an 'ammonia release reaction' from the metal led to the emergency alarm to firefighters ... Exposed firefighters were evacuated and emergency crews eventually maneuvered a front loader to scoop the metal away from the gas line. (Pearce, 2000b)

Lawsuits were also filed against the company. In a case decided in 1995, an employee – Stanislaw Golec – successfully sued the company after an accident at the plant resulted in him being severely burned in an explosion that splattered molten aluminum all over him. The trial records detail numerous safety violations at the plant (*Golec v. Metal Exchange Corporation*, 1995; see also *Metal Exchange Corporation v. J. W. Terrill*, 2005). Before ending its operations in Detroit, Continental Aluminum paid the Wayne County $50,000 in 1997 for repeated air pollution violations (*Recycling Today Magazine*, 2000; Associated Press, 2000b).

Although operations at this site ended in 1998 because of Continental Aluminum's desire for a larger and more modernized facility, evidence of its existence still remains. Its smokestacks are still intact, graffiti covers its decaying walls, and garbage litters its grounds. A site inspection completed by the City of Detroit on September 11, 2003, indicates that while the existence of solid or hazardous waste is unknown, it is expected based on the site condition (City of Detroit Department of Environmental Affairs, 2003). Although the site is not currently listed on the state's inventory of polluted former industrial sites, Wayne County officials believe that if testing is permitted by the owners that the site would qualify (Michigan Department of Environmental Quality [MDEQ], 2009; Pearce, 2000b; EPA, 2008a, 2008b).

Operating in Lyon Township

Lyon Township, founded in 1834 and officially chartered in 1979, sits in the southwest corner of Oakland County in southeastern Michigan. Its 32 square miles are bounded by Dixboro Road and Napier Road to the west and east, respectively, and by Pontiac Trail and Eight Mile Road to the north and south, respectively. The township incorporates all of New Hudson and portions of South Lyon, Wixom, Milford, and Northville. Lyon Township's 11,041 residents are served by the seven members of its Board of Trustees, including a supervisor, clerk, treasurer, and four trustees (Charter Township of Lyon, 2004; City-Data.com, 2009).

Following the closure of its Algonquin Road plant, Continental Aluminum Recycling opened a facility at 29201 Milford Road in New Hudson in 1998. Lyon Township is approximately 43 miles northwest of the Algonquin Street site. Continental Aluminum's move from Riverbend to Lyon Township was unanimously approved during a 1996 Lyon Township Planning Commission meeting. During testimony from Continental Aluminum's then president James Shanahan, it was asserted that the move was not motivated by pressure from any regulatory agency, but rather that, "The old building didn't quite suit our process any longer" (quote copied from Gearhart, 2000). The citations that Continental Aluminum received during its tenure in Riverbend were not disclosed.

The state of Michigan also aided the move of the Continental Aluminum Recycling Plant to Lyon Township as the company received a $5.5 million tax-exempt bond through the Industrial Development Revenue Bond Program (Pearce, 2000a; *Recycling Today Magazine*, 2000, 2001; Associated Press, 2000a). This program provides tax-exempt status to small manu-facturers that can demonstrate that their facility will provide additional jobs or overall benefit to Michigan (Citizens Research Council of Michigan, 2001). In hindsight, members of Lyon Township's planning commission agree that more thorough research on Continental Aluminum should have been done before approving the move.

Noise became an immediate concern of residents. As a result the township commissioned a study in 1999 that found that the noise emanating from Continental Aluminum's plant violated the township's noise ordinance. By 2003, two noise-related lawsuits had already been filed against the company (Charter Township of Lyon of Trustees, 2003b). Moreover, Continental Aluminum was cited for violations several times. Within the first two years of operation, Continental was cited five times by the Michigan Department of Environmental Quality (MDEQ) for violating emissions standards and operating permits. Specifically, these MDEQ citations include uncontrolled emissions of chlorine and hydrogen chloride as well as improperly installed and operated pollution-control equipment. State records indicate that inves-tigators were called to the plant 44 times during this period (Colling, 2000; Pearce, 2000b; *Recycling Today Magazine*, 2000; Associated Press, 2000a).

In March 2000, the MDEQ ordered Continental Aluminum to cease emitting high levels of chlorine and hydrogen chloride from its plant or face possible criminal charges. Two months later, the EPA put the company on its "significant violators list" of most watch polluters – a move that could have resulted in daily fines of $27,500 and criminal charges.[1] In August of the same year, Lyon Township issued citations to Continental Aluminum for 83 violations that carried a potential fine of $41,500. In the process of renewing their operating permit, MDEQ ordered Continental Aluminum raise its smokestack from 50 feet to 80 feet, pay a $30,000 fine for past pollution, reduce air emissions, and monitor their smokestack filters more closely (Associated Press, 2000a, 2000b; *Recycling Today Magazine*, 2000).

Complaints against the company continued, and in September 2000, 113 residents of Lyon Township and Detroit filed a class-action lawsuit against Continental Aluminum alleging that the company knowingly released chlorine, hydrogen chloride, and hydrogen fluoride into the air at both locations from which it operated. Plaintiffs also charged that they suffered heart and lung damage from the emissions. The suit also alleged that the company violated Wayne County's permits and that the company was "in complete disregard for the property rights, health and welfare of the residents" (quote copied from Associated Press, 2000a; *Recycling Today Magazine*, 2000). In March 2003, Wayne County Circuit Court Judge Isidore Torres denied the class action certification in the lawsuit against the company. In ruling against the plaintiffs, the judge argued that claims were "unsuitable" for class action treatment and were "neither legally compelling nor logically persuasive" (Halinski, 2003a). Despite the judge's ruling that the case could not proceed as a class-action suit, it remained in the court system and parties worked on a settlement. Plaintiffs were barred from speaking about the case or settlements (Lee, 2004; Charter Township of Lyon Board of Trustees, 2004a). However, in a 2003 Lyon Township Board of Trustees meeting, Continental Aluminum's former president Bill Altgilbers reported that the board had a list of things they wanted Continental Aluminum to do, including installing additional pollution-control devises that cost $700,000. However, at the last meeting, the attorneys dropped those demands and asked for $1,000,000 instead. Altgilbers – who claims the company was willing to comply with the list of plaintiffs' demands – took this to mean that "they [the plaintiffs] don't care about environmental improvements, they just want money" (Charter Township of Lyon Board of Trustees, 2003c; Altgilbers, 2003a).

Lyon Township residents continued to express concerns about emissions from the Continental Aluminum facility and in 2002 township officials and two environmental groups petitioned the Agency for Toxic Substances and Disease Registry (ATSDR) conduct an assessment to determine if emissions from the plant were having an impact on public health. Township residents were most concerned about exposure to aluminum, barium, beryllium, cadmium, chromium, copper, lead, manganese, selenium, and zinc. Working in collaboration with the Michigan Department of Community Health (MDCH), the ATSDR collected and assessed air samples over a three-month period in 2004 and the results released in 2005. The exposure investigation found that with the exception of beryllium, samples contained the remaining compounds. However, the concentrations of the compounds were well below screening levels[2] and were unlikely cause adverse health impacts (Table 2). The study also monitored the air for acidic aerosols such as hydrogen chloride and hydrogen fluoride. Such aerosols can cause eye, nose, and throat irritation. Monitoring did detect intermittent releases of acidic aerosols. The concentrations detected exceeded only long-term screening levels. Since the exposure was intermittent, the study determined that no adverse health impacts were expected. Residents were also concerned about odors. Consequently, the assessment investigated the release of volatile organic compounds (VOCs)[3] from the plant. The study found that though there were VOCs captured in samples, there was not a consistent source, and the concentrations were well below the screening levels. No further action was recommended at the site (Agency for Toxic Substances and Disease Registry, 2005, 2006).

Other problems continued to crop up in and around the Continental Aluminum facility. In 2002, the Department of Environmental Quality fined

Table 2. Airborne Metal Particulates Sampled in the Lyon Township Health Evaluation.

Chemicals	Highest Concentration Detected (mg/mg^3)	Lowest Screening Level (mg/mg^3)
Aluminum	0.00055	0.15
Barium	0.00011	0.5
Beryllium	Not detected	0.002
Cadmium	0.0000013	0.005
Chromium	0.0000055	0.000006
Copper	0.000047	100
Lead	0.000013	0.05
Manganese	0.000016	0.00004
Selenium	0.000012	0.2
Zinc	0.000064	10

Source: Compiled from Agency for Toxic Substances and Disease Registry (2006).

the company $86,995 for violations of hazardous waste management codes; they were also ordered to spend $5,400 on a supplemental environmental project (MDEQ, 2003). The following year a local resident walking on the bike path behind the plant noticed metal containers marked "Hazardous Waste" on the property. He referred the matter to the township's board of trustees for further investigation. When asked about the contents of the barrels, Bill Altgilbers stated that they contained the dust from the bag houses and that the storage pad for such materials was outside. When asked whether MDEQ required such materials to be stored inside or out, Mr. Altgilbers indicated that he did not know (Charter Township of Lyon Board of Trustees, 2003a). Fires also continue to plague Continental Aluminum after its move to Lyon Township. In 2002 a fire shut down operations for several weeks (Halinski, 2003b). The company was back in the news recently when an explosion inside a charge well[4] of one of the furnaces at the plant injured three people in April 2009 (Associated Press, 2009).

A FRAMEWORK FOR ANALYZING COLLABORATION

Residents of Lyon Township and Riverbend organized campaigns against Continental Aluminum. On the surface there seems to be much in common between Lyon Township and Riverbend activists and that collaboration between the two groups might further each community's cause. The question arises – why aren't activists collaborating? The following analysis helps us to understand why much collaboration did not occur. For the purposes of this study, we have developed a framework for identifying and analyzing factors that could foster or hinder collaboration. This framework is based on a synthesis of ideas from conflict management and social movement theories. Table 3 provides a summary of the main constructs analyzed and a comparison of how these played out in each community. This framework is specific to the two case studies analyzed here; however, it can be modified such that it can be used to analyze other conflicts of an environmental or non-environmental nature.

Issue Identification

Issue identification is an important element in the way activists perceive and define the issues they organize campaigns around. Opposition to

Table 3. Framework for Analyzing Conflict in the Lyon Township and Riverbend Campaigns.

Constructs	Movement Dynamics	Lyon Township	Riverbend
Issue identification	Year in which community opposition began	1998	1999
	Stage in the production cycle when opposition began	Facility was operating in township	Facility was already closed and abandoned
	Focus of the conflict	Current operating procedures	Remediation of an abandoned site
	Problems identified	Noise, pollution, odors, irritants	Pollution, unsecured site
	Blame attributed to	Continental Aluminum	Continental Aluminum
	Perception of issue	Continental Aluminum perceived as the source of problems	Continental Aluminum perceived as a symptom of pervasive problems affecting the community
	Scope of problem	Defined as a local issue, but parent company was also targeted	Defined as local issue
Goals	Setting and articulating objectives	Close facility or secure cleaner operations	Clean up site, develop site
Resource mobilization	Activists mobilized (human resources)	Township residents	Riverbend residents, Detroiters Working for Environmental Justice, Sierra Club, and National Wildlife Federation
	Institutions utilized	Township institutions, state and federal environmental agencies, courts, senator	Environmental Justice and mainstream environmental organizations, city government
	Technical expertise used	Technical experts consulted	None
Framing	Frames used and themes evoked	Residents' health, reduce emissions, property values, land ownership, community integrity	Community development, declining neighborhood, site remediation, brownfields
	Environmental justice frame used in the conflict	No	Yes
	Activists' definition of "community"	The township	Riverbend neighborhood, City of Detroit

Table 3. (*Continued*)

Constructs	Movement Dynamics	Lyon Township	Riverbend
	Who framed the discourse	Township residents	City-wide environmental justice organizers, Riverbend residents
	Efficacy of activists and leaders	Activists saw themselves as efficacious; efficacy of township officials sometimes questioned	Activists saw themselves as efficacious
	Corporate responsibility	Activists perceived Continental Aluminum as eroding the trust residents had in the company, residents felt betrayed by the company	Activists felt abandoned by Continental Aluminum, they felt the company did not engage them during he campaign
	Corporate counterframing	Continental Aluminum frames itself as a good neighbor; the company's publicity focus on its recycling activities, advanced technologies, awards, community support	There is no mention of Riverbend in the company's materials.
Tactical interactions	Targets of action	Activists targeted Continental Aluminum, Metal Exchange, township officials, state environmental agency, federal health agency	Activists targeted Continental Aluminum, city officials, other corporations
	Activists tactics and strategies	Organize protests, file lawsuit, circulate flyers, pressure township boards and commissions, push for environmental sampling and public health assessment, publicize in media, post lawn signs, send e-mails, circulate contact information of corporate executives	Produce video, publicize in media, pressure city council, file lawsuit
	Corporate tactics and strategies	Establish hotline for residents to contact company, conduct home visits, attend board of trustees meeting, conduct own noise study, sue the township, allow community members to tour facility	No action taken

Continental Aluminum's facility began in 1998 in Lyon Township and was rejuvenated in 1999 in Riverbend. Although the two communities organized campaigns that targeted the company, the campaigns focused on different stages of the production cycle. In Lyon Township, residents organized against a facility that was operating and was a key actor in township affairs. Campaigns against the company focused on hazardous emissions, operating permits and standards, monitoring the company's operations, air quality, soil contamination, noise, and odor. Residents knew what kinds of toxic compounds and contaminants the facilities emitted and sought to monitor and reduce them (Agency for Toxic Substances and Disease Registry, 2005, 2006; Lee, 2004).

In contrast, Riverbend activists were focused on the post-production end of the manufacturing cycle. Their campaigns centered on an abandoned facility and derelict property. Continental Aluminum is no longer a key actor in the neighborhood or city for that matter. Its importance is marked by its absence and lack of engagement with community activists and residents. Riverbend campaigns against the company highlighted soil contamination; dilapidated buildings; and an unsecured, dangerous facility. Unlike Lyon Township, Riverbend residents and activists are operating in an arena of the unknown. They do not know what's left on the Continental Aluminum site or what they are being exposed to (see Hattam, 2003 for a discussion of the site). Although Lyon Township residents can call in township, state and federal officials to respond to complaints when they see, smell, or hear something coming from Continental Aluminum's plant, Riverbend residents have no such luxury. During the MDCH/ATSDR's exposure study, for instance, sampling occurred where residents indicated they smelled obnoxious odors, felt the effects of VOCs, or saw smoke (Agency for Toxic Substances and Disease Registry, 2005, 2006).

In effect, Riverbend residents are battling a virtual phantom. As one resident stated, "Continental made our lives miserable ... It was hard to breathe around here ... We still don't know what the smoke did to our lungs, what they left in the building over there or in the soil" (copied from Pearce, 2000b). Riverbend residents cannot substantiate their complaints with visual evidence of smoke. Moreover, there are no odors to document or test. If chemicals are being released into the air and soil from Continental's facility – they do not know what these are so they do not know what they should be detecting. Although Riverbend activists monitor the abandoned facility, their focus is on the remediation of the site, not on any on-going operations.

Both communities identify pollution of the air and soil as the major problems they want to see alleviated. Riverbend residents want to see the abandoned facility secured, tested, and cleaned up. Lyon Township residents also identify foul odors, irritants, and noise as nuisances that should be abated. As Harold Grove, a one of the Lyon Township residents who filed suit against Continental Aluminum stated, "We still hear their noise through the night and smell their odors" (*Recycling Today Magazine*, 2000). Another resident, Claude Pfeffer, testified at a township Board of Trustees meeting attended by Continental Aluminum's president in 2003 that he used earplugs at home rated at 29 decibels and could still hear the droning noise. Arthur Booth, who lived about a mile-and-a-half from the plant, also testified that he did not want to let his children sleep with earplugs, so he turned on fans to drown out the noise. Dennis Ostach, who lived about half-a-mile from the facility, purchased triple-pane windows to block out the sound but could still hear the drone. Bob Schram whose house was 2.5 miles from the plant also attended the meeting to complain about the noise (Charter Township of Lyon Board of Trustees, 2003b). Steve Adams, a trustee, addressed the company's president as follows:

> Mr. Altgilbers has stood before this Board and stated he wants to be a good neighbor! Good neighbors, Mr. Altgilbers, do not keep their fellow neighbors up at night with noises that prevent them from sleeping ... if you and your parent company are sincere you will take care of the problem ... Our township showed that we want to be good neighbors by the great job our Fire Department and Firefighters did in limiting a fire that could have taken out your whole building. I don't care to debate the ambient sound levels as I have heard it, our citizens have heard it, and you have admitted you have heard it. The township in 1999 funded a study that indicated that you were over the acceptable sound levels. But good neighbors do not need studies. They take care of concerns that affect their neighbors. (Charter Township of Lyon Board of Trustees, 2003b)

Altgilbers responded by saying that Continental Aluminum was negotiating with an acoustic engineering firm to evaluate the noise coming from the plant. In March 2004, Altgilbers reported to a Board of Trustees meeting that Continental would use silencers at the plant. By August of that year, Harold Grove reported that noise had been greatly reduced. Residents also reported that the noise had decreased in the ATSDR health study (Charter Township of Lyon Board of Trustees, 2003b, 2004c, 2004d; Agency for Toxic Substances and Disease Registry, 2006).

Not only do social movement activists play the critical role of identify problems, they perform an equally important function of attributing blame or causality (Taylor, 2000). Both communities identified a common actor to whom they attributed blame – Continental Aluminum. Although Lyon Township officials voted on bringing Continental Aluminum to the community after deliberating at a meeting in 1996 and admitted later on that they could have done more background research on the company before approving the relocation, residents of the township do not blame the township's Planning Commission. In a similar vein, Riverbend activists place little or no blame on city and county officials who allowed Continental Aluminum to abandon the facility without remediating the site.

Although both communities imputed blame to Continental Aluminum, each had a different perception of the company's role in the problems they identified. Lyon Township residents saw Continental Aluminum as the sole source of the problems and put their attention squarely on the actions of the company. On the contrary, Riverbend activists saw Continental Aluminum as a symptom of more pervasive problems that the Riverbend neighborhood and the city of Detroit face. This perception is evidenced by the central role that the Continental Aluminum site plays in a short film created by the National Wildlife Federation on the eastside community. As the film opens, images of the abandoned Continental Aluminum facility fill the screen while a narrator speaks of the environmental ills that fill the community that is hoping for a renaissance. The narrator intones: "Detroit is still dealing with the unchecked environmental polluters who have left their mess for someone else to clean up. Local families are left with the burden of bringing up the next generation with the threat that the water they drink or the air that they breathe may be dangerous to themselves, their children, and their children's children" (National Wildlife Federation, 2000). Similar sentiments were expressed in interviews with community leaders and activists. One interviewee referred to Continental Aluminum as the "poster child" that characterizes the rest of Detroit. He indicated that Continental Aluminum was being used in publicity materials to demonstrate the problem of brownfields in the city of Detroit and to mobilize residents and city officials to resolve problems such as these. Hence, the distinction between seeing a company as the source of a community's problems versus as a symptom of larger problems is an important one that has significant implications for what activists focus and how they frame the issues.

Both Lyon Township and Riverbend activists defined their struggles as local in scope and kept the focus on local (or city-wide in the case of Riverbend) issues. However, Lyon Township residents targeted Continental Aluminum's parent company, Metal Exchange too. Activists circulated the contact information of company executive to residents and urged them to be in touch with the company; they even threatened to go to St. Louis to express their discontent. As Mr. Adams stated in a township board of trustees meeting in which he addressed Continental Aluminum's president,

To assist you, Mr. Altgilbers, in helping your Corporate Parent Company Executives understand what our citizens are going through, I have supplied our citizens with the address, telephone number, e-mail address and the name of Tom Akers, the Executive VP of the Metal Exchange Corp. Joe Shigley [Supervisor of the Board of Trustees] and I have already sent an e-mail to Mr. Akers and will probably be giving him daily updates. If this doesn't work, we will be going to the Chairman of the Board. The distance from our small community makes them indifferent to our problems and at night they go home to their Executive homes in St. Louis and sleep in peace with no hum/drone to contend with. (Charter Township of Lyon Board of Trustees, 2003b)

Clarity of Goals

Activists usually establish goals or benchmarks for campaigns such as the ones organized against Continental Aluminum in Riverbend and Lyon Township. Riverbend residents and activists had clear goals when it came to the question of what should be done with the facility they had organized their campaign around. They wanted to see the site cleaned up to make room for future development.

However, in the case of Lyon Township the goal of the campaign is somewhat unclear. Although some residents were calling for the facility to shut down, it seemed that some would be content with a reduction in emissions and safer operations. The desire to see the facility closed is reflected in statements from residents and township officials. As one Lyon Township resident asserted, "Continental fooled us once – by lying to us. Let's shut them down." A Lyon Township official underscored this point, "Continental has not improved and we'd like to see them move out" (Pearce, 2000b). Residents also posted yard signs reading, "Shut 'em down," "Just say 'no' to Continental Aluminum," and "If you can't comply, it is time to say bye-bye." A flyer for a March 30, 2000 meeting read as follows:

For over two years the plant has emitted large quantities of hydrogen fluoride, hydrogen chloride, and chlorides on the community, including a local Elementary school 1/2 mile from the plant. Neighbors have complained of various health impacts from burning eyes and blurred vision to various breathing disorders including asthma. Recent testing has shown that the plant may have been emitting up to 300% its permitted levels of Hydrogen Chloride into the community since it started operation. The plant has been cited several times for 901 violations and this week the DEQ cited them for violating their permit limits HCL and HF. Local residents have called for the DEQ/EPA to immediately shut the plant down and conduct a complete investigation of the plants emissions. (Doyle, 2000)

Although Lyon Township officials are sensitive and responsive to residents' concerns, they seem in no hurry to shut down Continental

Aluminum. Describing the township as one having a "fast growing industrial, research, and manufacturing base," it lists Continental Aluminum as its eleventh largest employer (Lyon Township, 2009). Continental Aluminum has revenues of $7.1 million and has 60 employees (ZoomInfo, 2009).

Mobilization of Resources

Both social movement and conflict management theorists identify the mobilization of resources as critical elements in movement building and conflict resolution. Social movement theorists argue that resources are critical to initiating and sustaining movements (McCarthy & Zald, 1977; Oberschall, 1973; Gamson, 1975; Tilly, 1977). Conflict management theorists argue that sharing knowledge and resources help in solving problems (Jakobsen et al., 2004) while Wondolleck and Yaffee (2000) argue that more effective decisions can be made through the sharing of information and perspectives.

Three aspects of resource mobilization are analyzed in this chapter – human resources, institutions, and technical expertise. In Lyon Township, residents concerned about the operations of Continental Aluminum emerged as activists who participated in the campaign against the company. They relied on their own ideas and energies to drive the campaign. Though they got help from the Ecology Center in Ann Arbor in petitioning the ATSDR to conduct a health assessment, residents controlled the campaign (Agency for Toxic Substances and Disease Registry, 2006). Township residents also acted as individuals or as a collective, depending on the activity. In one instance, a township resident whose son attended Dolsen Elementary that is located about a half-a-mile downwind of the Continental Aluminum plant battled with the South Lyon School Board about soil testing. The school board declined the MDCH's request to test the soil of the school[5] (Board of Education of South Lyon Community Schools, 2004; Lee, 2004).

The story is different in Riverbend. Although Riverbend residents are active in the campaign against Continental Aluminum, environmental justice organizers in the city of Detroit played a key role in bringing neighborhood residents' attention to the company, initiating, and sustaining the campaign. The campaign got started when an environmental justice organizer read about the conflict in Lyon Township in an article that made reference to the abandoned Riverbend facility. While residents of Riverbend certainly hold a stake in the conflict, the bulk of the organizing around

Continental Aluminum has been conducted by Detroit environmental justice organizations such as Detroiters Working for Environmental Justice and the Michigan Sierra Club's Environmental Justice organizer. These organizations have taken the responsibility for educating residents, gaining media attention, communicating with city officials, and, overall, overseeing the relationship between Continental Aluminum, residents, and the City of Detroit. As a result, the focus of the campaign is not always on the Riverbend neighborhood or on Continental Aluminum but on the larger framework of environmental justice in the city as a whole. Actions and events are coordinated and mediated through a network of neighborhood activists and the organizational and personal interests represented in the citywide environmental justice organizers.

In Lyon Township the mobilization occurs on a township level. This happens despite Continental Aluminum's attempts to situate itself as a New Hudson company. The company's website and press releases use the framing of the smaller geographic entity; however, township residents do not perceive the problems as ones that only the residents of New Hudson should concern themselves with (Continental Aluminum, 2009). The township is the community affected and the mobilization occurs in that wider geographic scale. In the Riverbend campaign the mobilization occurs at both the neighborhood and citywide level.

Activists in both communities drew on an array of community and outside institutions to tap into their resources throughout the campaigns. Although Lyon Township is relatively rural, residents used their township's institutions of governance extensively to file complaints against and exercise oversight over Continental Aluminum and to bring in additional state and federal resources. Within a few years of Continental Aluminum's move to the township, officials called in a state agency (MDCH) and a federal agency (ATSDR) to conduct a comprehensive health assessment. This is in addition to the use of the MDEQ to help in the permitting and monitoring of the plant. Township residents also used the courts to air their grievances and settle their disputes with the company. Residents have also benefited from the resources of environmental groups that have worked with them.

As mentioned earlier, Riverbend has a large number of community-based institutions. This provided a good base to build on. The campaign drew in resources from the city's environmental justice organizations in the form of community organizers. National mainstream environmental groups, namely the Sierra Club and the National Wildlife Federation, also provided resources. The Sierra Club's environmental justice organizer was quite involved in the campaign. Activists also got the city government involved – the city would like Continental Aluminum to relinquish the property to them so that clean-up and redevelopment can proceed. Residents have also used the courts – some participated in the class-action lawsuit that was filed against the company. Although the EPA listed Continental Aluminum on its watch list while the company operated in Riverbend, activists have not been able to bring in state and federal resources to conduct health assessment the way Lyon Township residents have.

Lyon Township residents have been able to get many more technical experts to listen to their claims than Riverbend residents. In Lyon Township, health and environmental experts from state and federal agencies have investigated residents' claims about air pollution, soil contamination, and health impacts. Riverbend residents have not gotten such attention from said experts. However, Riverbend residents were able to get a film crew to make a movie about the community while the stories of the people in Lyon Township have not been documented in this way. Both communities have worked with legal experts.

Framing

Master Frames

To be successful, social movement activists must be able to communicate grievances clearly and effectively. The process by which problems are understood, defined, and articulated is referred to as framing (Taylor, 2000; Gamson, 1997; Snow et al., 1986). Residents of Lyon Township and Riverbend used different frames to describe the problems they faced with Continental Aluminum. Noise, discussed earlier, was a master frame that fueled much of the early organizing in Lyon Township. Lyon Township activists also used community integrity as a master frame.[6] That is, they saw the conflict as a struggle to maintain their community's integrity. Community integrity included peace of mind and the rural ambiance. The township's website currently describes the area as a community of farms, horses, and large-lot development (Lyon Township, 2009). According to Lyon Township resident Bob Schram, he moved to Lyon Township for the rural atmosphere and fresh air. In complaining about the noise from Continental Aluminum he said, "Well the rural atmosphere is being taken care of real quick" (Charter Township of Lyon Board of Trustees, 2003a). Residents fear that Continental Aluminum is being operated in a way threatens the integrity of the community. It is interesting that residents do not object to the size or the look of the plant – these are not referenced in their campaigns.

Public health is another master frame used by Lyon Township activists. Residents claim that emissions from the plant are making them sick. They worry about safeguarding their health as well as the health of the children (future generations). This position was clearly articulated by one resident who attended a public hearing and whose daughter was born with a lung tumor. According to the resident, "I came up here not to publicize my daughter's condition but to stop it, so it doesn't happen again to another pregnant woman or to another baby or to another person. We have to stop this ... You are killing our community" (quote copied from Gibbons, 2001). A mother whose son attended Dolsen Elementary School said, "It seems like the school board thinks that we're trying to shut the school down. I'm not trying to shut it down. I just want to know that it's a safe place for my children to go" (copied from Lee, 2004). Joe Shigley, a Lyon Township trustee, wonders about the connection between health and Continental Aluminum. He said, "More of us seem to be having breathing problems", he said. "Shouldn't we wonder about the connection?" (quote copied from *Recycling Today Magazine*, 2000). Several people interviewed for this study complained of asthma, emphysema, nosebleeds, and other upper-respiratory conditions. Residents assert that these conditions did not arise until Continental Aluminum began operating in Lyon Township. Local residents also reported similar symptoms in the ATSDR health assessment (Agency for Toxic Substances and Disease Registry, 2006).[7]

Property values and land ownership were the other prominent frames used by Lyon Township residents. They argue that Continental Aluminum's actions are causing their property values to decline and that threatens their ability to own land. In Lyon Township, where the median home value was $211,700 in 2000 and where the median price of homes sold was $245,500 in 2007 and $233,000 in 2008 (U.S. Census Bureau, 2000; Lyon Township, 2009), a local resident recounted how he and his wife worked all their lives to buy a few acres in Lyon Township. He closed his story with, "We built our dream house and it is turning out to be a nightmare." Three years after Continental Aluminum began operating in the county, one resident expressed concern that her home could not be resold. She said, "Our property has been devalued. Who would want to buy our house now?" (quote copied from Pearce, 2001). South Lyon School Board President, Peggy Connelly, also highlighted the importance of property to community residents when she said, "I think they're afraid of hurting people's property values and the investment they have in their homes" (quote copied from

Lee, 2004). Hence, residents felt their property values were declining although the above data indicate that property values were increasing through 2007. The fiscal crisis of 2008–2009 resulted in nationwide declines in home prices.

Additional frames were evident in the campaign. These implicit frames include the growing pains from the encroachment of suburban sprawl and corporate accountability. These ideas emerged as residents spoke of the recent changes to their community. When asked how respondents would describe Lyon Township, all seven respondents interviewed answered that the formerly rural area is experiencing tremendous growth. Another minor or submerged frame that residents evoked was that of encroaching suburban sprawl. The concern was expressed at Board of Trustees meetings. The township went from 9,450 residents in 1990 to 13,927 in 2008. Moreover, 5,419 of those people live relatively close to the plant – that is, in the same zip code as Continental Aluminum (U.S. Census Bureau, 2008, 2000, 1990; see for example Charter Township of Lyon Board of Trustees, 2004b). The building that is needed to accommodate such growth concerned long-time residents.

Lyon Township residents did not use the environmental justice frame in their campaign. Although they identified grievances, said Continental Aluminum was harming them and sought justice for their community, activists did not see the campaign as an environmental justice one per se. This might be the case because the township had worked with Continental Aluminum to relocate them to New Hudson. Township officials supported the move. Although Continental Aluminum did not disclose all its violations and fines to township officials before it relocated, township officials and residents knew what kind of industrial facility was moving in. Moreover, the company's track record of violations and fines could have been found out with a phone call to Detroit. In the more typical environmental justice case, corporations follow the path of least resistance and target low-income and minority communities for siting their facilities. In some instance, residents have no knowledge that facilities have been approved or that zoning ordinances were changed to facilitate siting (see for example Blumberg & Gottlieb, 1989; Bailey, Faupel, & Gundlach, 1993; Cole & Foster, 2001).

Continental Aluminum's move to Lyon Township should be put in the larger context of what happened to Detroit in the past four decades. By the time Continental Aluminum pulled up stakes, the city had witnessed a hemorrhaging of people, jobs, and institutions. The beneficiaries were the suburbs and semi-rural townships such as Lyon. As the population moved away from the Detroit, commercial and industrial enterprises followed them. The vacant lots, hulking remains of industrial facilities, and the shuttered buildings that dot the Detroit landscape are part of the larger trend of disinvestment that the city experienced (Sugrue, 1996; Chandler, 1999).

Activists in the Riverbend campaign use the environmental justice master frame to articulate their grievances. This frame links environmental experiences and outcomes with race, class, gender, and other social factors. The conflict with Continental Aluminum is perceived as one of many examples of environmental inequalities residents of Riverbend and the wider city of Detroit experience. Activists note that in moving to its new, clean facilities in the fields of predominantly white, middle-class Lyon Township, the company failed to clean up the facility it shut down in the predominantly black, low-income inner city neighborhood. As Table 4 shows, in 2000 Lyon Township was 96.6 percent white with a median household income of $67,288. In contrast, Riverbend was 89.2 percent black[8] with a median household income of $25,020 (U.S. Census Bureau, 2000). The table also shows that in Detroit, Riverbend is one of the poorer neighborhoods of the city. The racialization of the discourse in Riverbend is reflected in one organizer's statement, "We cannot talk about Continental Aluminum without talking about environmental justice. We cannot talk about environmental justice without talking about environmental racism."

Community development was another master frame evoked in the Riverbend campaign. Activists saw a neighborhood in decline and wanted to revitalize it. The Riverbend neighborhood lost not only industry – it lost people too. The neighborhood went from 24,548 residents in 1990 to 19,224 residents in 2000. Home prices have nosedived in the neighborhood and Detroit. The median home value in Detroit was $63,600 in 2000. The median home value in Riverbend in 2000 was $47,000. In December 2008, the median price of homes sold in the city was $7,500 (U.S. Census Bureau, 2000, 1990; Jones, 2009; Mullins, 2009). It is not that Riverbend residents – and Detroiters in general – are not concerned about home prices; they are. However, home prices in the neighborhood and city has to be put in the larger context of how the housing stock has fared during the shift of population from the city to the suburbs. Between 1980 and 2000, Detroit lost 21 percent of its population. The city had a population of 1,203,339 in 1980. The population declined to 1,027,974 in 1990 and to 951,270 in 2000.[9] At the same time the population in the Detroit metropolitan area increased from 4,266,654 in 1990 to 4,456,428 in 2000. The outmigration is partly responsible for a housing market in which prices are artificially low for a city its size and location. Detroit is a waterfront city located on the Detroit River

Table 4. Demographic Characteristics of Lyon Township and Riverbend in 2000.

| Demographic Characteristics | United States | Michigan | Lyon Township | Jurisdictions Incorporated into Lyon Township (in full or in part) | | | | | Detroit | |
				New Hudson	South Lyon	Wixom	Milford	Northville	Detroit City	Riverbend
Total population	281,421,906	9,938,444	11,041	5,419	23,442	16,183	12,172	36,559	951,270	19,224
Race										
White	65.1	78.8	96.6	96.7	97.0	91.5	97.3	91.2	9.6	9.0
Black	12.3	14.2	0.4	0.3	0.3	2.2	0.4	3.0	81.6	89.2
Native American	0.9	0.6	0.4	0.4	0.3	0.5	0.3	0.3	0.3	0.2
Asian	3.6	1.8	0.6	0.3	0.7	2.5	0.5	3.5	1.0	0.4
Hispanic	12.5	3.3	1.5	1.8	1.3	2.9	1.2	1.6	5.0	0.9
Other	5.5	1.3	0.5	0.5	0.4	1.4	0.3	0.4	2.5	0.3
Housing occupancy										
Owner occupied	66.2	73.8	91.6	86.8	86.0	51.9	85.6	78.5	54.9	43.9
Renter occupied	33.8	26.2	8.4	13.2	14.0	48.1	14.4	21.5	45.1	56.1
Vacant housing units	9.0	10.6	4.4	4.2	4.5	3.6	3.2	3.9	10.3	16.3
Education										
High school graduate	56.0	61.6	63.7	65.3	56.0	57.8	60.2	45.1	58.6	54.7
Bachelor's degree or higher	24.4	21.8	26.0	24.7	24.4	33.5	31.2	47.7	11.0	9.0
Employed	63.9	64.6	75.2	78.6	68.5	79.2	71.7	65.1	56.3	56.7
Income										
Median household income	$41,994	$ 44,667	$67,288	$66,875	$67,463	$45,977	$64,009	$79,579	$29,526	$25,020
Per capita income	$21,587	$22,168	$27,414	$25,127	$29,688	$26,563	$28,258	$39,885	$14,717	$14,533
Families below poverty level	9.2	7.4	3.4	4.4	2.1	4.4	4.4	1.3	21.7	27.5
Individuals below poverty level	12.4	10.5	4.2	4.9	3.5	5.2	6.2	2.3	26.1	33.1
Median home value	$119,600	$115,600	$211,700	$192,600	$200,900	$195,000	$209,400	$267,400	$63,600	$47,100

Source: U.S. Census Bureau (2000).

across from Windsor, Canada. The Detroit River connects Lake St. Clair to Lake Erie. However, the prices benefit residents of the city who trade off lower home prices for higher rates of home ownership. A Brookings Institution study of the 23 Living Cities[10] found that 54.9 percent of households own their home in Detroit; this rate of homeownership is above average for the cities studied. Fifty-three percent of the blacks in the city own their own homes (Brookings Institution, 2003; U.S. Census Bureau, 2000, 1990, 1980). Communities such as Riverbend are close to the waterfront; hence revitalization of the neighborhood could be connected to the larger waterfront improvement projects underway in Detroit.

Detroit is putting a lot of effort into revitalizing its neighborhoods, and Riverbend activists do not want the community to be overlooked. Redevelopment is occurring because of Brownfield Redevelopment Authority, Southwest Detroit Contaminated Sites Task Force, and Empowerment Zone grants. Non-governmental organizations such as Detroiters Working for Environmental Justice, Sierra Club, and Southwest Detroit Environmental Vision are quite involved in these redevelopment processes too. Although Continental Aluminum still owns the property in Detroit's Eastside, city officials are actively trying to obtain the property so that it too may become the subject of urban redevelopment plans. Although Riverbend residents (and Detroiters as a whole) have seen their property values plummet, activists are not as concerned about individual property values as they are about creating a more vibrant and livable community. Their interests are vested in revitalizing Riverbend and similar neighborhoods through the re-use of defunct commercial and industrial properties.

Poverty and the health of residents were also minor frames used in Riverbend. It is on the minds of residents. Residents claim that when continental operated in the community, it was smoky and that made it difficult to breathe. They also worry about soil contamination (Pearce, 2000b).

Definition of Community, Control of the Discourse, and Efficacy
In both campaigns, activists expressed strong attachment to their communities and used the concept of community in their master frames. But, how was community defined? In Lyon Township, the community was defined as the residents and township officials of the jurisdiction. The definition is more complicated and fluid in Riverbend. Because some of the activists were from outside the neighborhood, "community" is sometimes defined as Riverbend itself while at other times it expands to encompass the entire city and beyond. This is the case because in Riverbend community is not

perceived only as people living within a bounded physical space; it also refers to an ideological affinity – i.e., a community of interests and concerns that extends beyond the boundaries of Riverbend.

The residents and officials of Lyon Township control how the campaign against Continental Aluminum is articulated. This is not the case in Riverbend. Because environmental justice activists identified the problem and initiated the Riverbend campaign, they have always had a strong influence on how the issues are framed. Neighborhood activists play a role in the social construction of the discourse so the frames that emerge from this campaign result from the interaction between neighborhood residents and citywide environmental justice activists.

Efficacy is of relevance here. Efficacy refers to the sense of empowerment individuals and groups feel; they perceive they have the ability to change things. Individual efficacy is the feeling an individual has that he or she can change things, whereas group efficacy refers to the belief that others in a group can change conditions (Taylor, 2000; Sharp, 1980; Eisinger, 1972; Verba & Nie, 1972). Activists in both communities perceived themselves as efficacious. However, in Lyon Township, there were times when residents questioned the ability and willingness of township officials to get Continental Aluminum to comply with their wishes (see for example Charter Township of Lyon Board of Trustees, 2003c).

Corporate Responsibility and Counterframing

Wondolleck and Yaffee (2000) identify trust as an important element of collaboration. Not only is it important in determining whether groups can work together, it is important in understanding the relationship between host communities and corporations. Residents of both communities consider trust is important in this relationship. They describe the trust that exists between themselves and Continental Aluminum in negative terms. In the case of Lyon Township, the trust that existed when the company first moved to town evaporated quickly. Residents and township officials describe their feelings in terms of betrayal. In Riverbend, the feeling is more akin to abandonment and lack of engagement. Activists in both communities have channeled these feelings into rhetoric that highlight the "us" against "them/they" dichotomy. The "us" refers to either activists from Lyon Township or Riverbend, whereas the "them" or "they" in both campaigns is Continental Aluminum (see Gamson, 1992, 1997). One Lyon Township resident put it succinctly, "They affected my quality of life. I couldn't even open the windows or sleep at night. As long as Continental causes problems for me, I will cause problems for them."

Continental Aluminum is very conscious of its image and has not allowed activists to be the sole actors in the conflict establishing a frame. The company, through its websites, press releases, and statements its president and spokespersons make, has created an effective counterframe to challenge the frames that emerge from Lyon Township. The company does not acknowledge Riverbend on its website. Continental Aluminum projects an image of a good neighbor, an award-winning "environmentally committed" company involved in recycling that employs the latest technologies at its facilities, and one that sponsors community events and is responsive to area residents. The company's home page opens with the following description:

> Continental Aluminum operates one of the most advanced secondary aluminum smelters in the United States. State-of-the-art equipment, ISO 9001 certification of our processes, and strict quality and environmental controls ... and a responsible corporate neighbor in our community .... As a responsible corporate neighbor, Continental Aluminum provides all the environmental benefits of aluminum recycling, from one of the country's most strictly monitored and controlled smelting facilities. (Continental Aluminum, 2009)

Sharing the home page is a message from the company's new president, J. David Rinehart, which reads as follows:

> I'm pleased to tell you that Continental Aluminum is working hard every day to lead the industry in environmental and safety performance. Recently, the Michigan Occupational Safety and Health Administration (MIOSHA) recognized Continental Aluminum for its outstanding safety record with its Bronze Award for Safety. We are continuing to strive for safety & health excellence for our employees and the recognition this may bring in terms of future safety awards ... To the employees of Continental Aluminum, being a good neighbor is simply not negotiable and Continental has made substantial investments to this end. We continue to spend time and money to reduce air emissions and noise ... at our plant, beyond regulatory standards. Continental Aluminum is also an active member of the community and is supportive in a number of local charities as well as civic causes, etc. (Rinehart, 2009)

The company also uses the findings of the technical experts community residents brought in to conduct the health assessment to its advantage. In response to the findings in the of the preliminary MDCH/ATSDR assessment the company issued a statement saying, "A public health consultation released by the Michigan Department of Community Health shows no determinative evidence that Continental Aluminum creates any health hazards to the community and that the company's plant is operating within the established health-based screening limits" (Halinski, 2003c). After the final report on the health assessment was released, former president Altgilbers (2005) said, "I am very pleased that the agencies of the state of Michigan and federal government conducted a comprehensive scientific study, thoroughly analyzed the results, and determined – very unambiguously – that Continental Aluminum is not a public health hazard to the community ... I commend the Michigan Department of Community Health and members of the community for conducting such a thorough investigation based on sound science that applied technical methods. I hope now that the community can come together and move forward."

Altgilbers also took the opportunity to cast residents of the township as misinformed. In a company newsletter circulated in 2003, Altgilbers, 2003b stated, "Since I have been president of Continental Aluminum, I have made it a priority to meet with local citizens. I am constantly surprised by the misinformation in the community." He followed up with this statement two months later, "Sometimes when someone makes a claim not based on facts over and over, people may believe it. I've heard and read claims that Continental Aluminum poses a threat to nearby Dolsen Elementary School. Scientific tests have proven this is untrue." Here again, the president was using the results of tests conducted at the behest of community residents by the South Lyon Community School to the advantage of Continental Aluminum (Altgilbers, 2003b). Altgilber's perception of community residents as being misinformed is consistent with that of his predecessor, Wayne Perry. When Perry was president of the company he stated that residents were confusing "occasional nuisances for actual hazards." Perry also stated that, "We have a very aggressive plan of attack for these problems. Every stack we have has been tested and we're legal. The odor that some residents talk about smells like money to me" (quote copied from Pearce, 2000b). The company's website makes no mention of studies such as the 1999 noise study that report results that are problematic for Continental Aluminum (see Charter Township of Lyon Board of Trustees, 2003b).

The Bronze Award[11] plaque for outstanding safety is displayed on the Continental Aluminum's home page, and the company moves quickly to put its spin on occupational and safety incidents likely to cause it negative publicity. For example, within hours of the fire that broke out at the plant in 2009, the company issued a press release thanking the county's fire and emergency medical crew and assuring the public that the fire was not caused by a gas leak (Halinski, 2009).

Tactics

At the same time activists and Continental Aluminum battle each other to gain the upper hand in the framing of the conflict; activists have to be strategic about what tactics they employ and who or what they target. Lyon Township activists focused on Continental Aluminum as the main target of action of their campaign, but they also targeted township officials as well as state and federal agencies to get them to respond to their complaints. They also employed various strategies during the campaign. Residents staged demonstrations outside of the plant and made staked signs bearing anti-Continental Aluminum slogans that they displayed in their yards. The signs had slogans such as, "They're killing us in our sleep and on weekends," "The quality of my life depends on wind direction." As mentioned earlier, some residents filed lawsuits against the company. Another tactic involved getting state and federal agencies to conduct studies and monitor the practices of the company.

Riverbend activists' main target of action is Continental Aluminum. However, activists also engaged city officials to get them to respond to the grievances and concerns being aired. Activists made a video portraying the company negatively. They have also used the media to publicize the issue. Some residents were party to the lawsuit against Continental Aluminum.

Continental Aluminum is involved in the tactical maneuverings too. The company uses tactics such as listening to residents' complaints, establishing a hotline answered by the company's president, attending township meetings and responding to questions, keeping a close eye on health assessments, while projecting a good neighbor and responsible corporate citizen image. Continental also manages to project an image of being the wronged party. They do this by highlighting the findings of the health assessment, their occupational safety award, the fact that a judge did not certify residents for a class-action lawsuit and that the court ruled in their favor when the company sued Lyon Township for the right to restore its building the way it wanted to after the 2002 fire at the plant (Halinski, 2003b).

Leverage and Concessions

In a case like this, who has leverage and what kind? Lyon Township has more leverage than Riverbend. This is the case because the factory is still operational in the township. As such township residents can apply pressure on the company to change its practices. For instance, in response to residents' complaints, Continental Aluminum established a complaint hotline in 2002. Calls to the hotline increased dramatically after a flyer with a township complaint form attached to it was circulated (Charter

Township of Lyon Board of Trustees, 2003b). Residents can also apply pressure on township, state, and federal agencies to see that each monitors the company. The township has leverage when it comes to overseeing the permits the company needs to operate, taxes, incentives, etc. Residents of Riverbend have very limited influence on the company and are not in a position to apply significant pressure to the company.

Continental Aluminum has leverage it can use against Lyon Township if necessary. As the eleventh largest employer in the township, it creates jobs the township needs. It also pays taxes and is an important part of the industrial infrastructure the township uses to drive its economy. Businesses such as Continental Aluminum create multiplier effects that are hard to ignore. That is, there are usually a host of related businesses that are dependent on companies such as Continental Aluminum. Continental Aluminum holds the trump card when it comes to Riverbend – the company can decide what to do with the Detroit property and when.

Residents of Lyon Township have been able to wring important concessions from Continental Aluminum. They were able to get the company to monitor and reduce its emissions, put on stack silencers, set up a hotline, establish open doors so that residents could tour the facility, and close the bag houses on some weekends to reduce noise.

Conflict Mediation and Corporate Community Relations

Thus far, the conflict between Continental Aluminum and the two communities have been mediated through the courts as well as other institutions. In the case of Lyon Township, not only have residents filed suit against the company, Continental Aluminum has sued the township over zoning regulations (Halinski, 2003b). Township boards and commissions as well as state and federal agencies have also functioned as mediators in the conflict. The Lyon Township Board of Trustees has also called on political elites such as State Senator Nancy Cassis to help mediate the conflict (Charter Township of Lyon Board of Trustees, 2003a, 2003b, 2003c). In Riverbend, the city council is helping to mediate the conflict between residents and the company. Riverbend residents have also used courts to negotiate the conflict.

Lyon Township residents, township officials, and Continental Aluminum have attempted to maintain cordial relations with each other. However, a lack of trust between the stakeholders makes the relationship challenging. Township officials and the company engage each other routinely over business matters; however, activists and the company tend to engage each other most frequently through protests, allegations, and monitoring of each other's behavior. Continental Aluminum's relationship with Riverbend is strained as Continental Aluminum has not acknowledged or engaged with residents or community leaders of Riverbend. Activists feel abandoned and ignored; consequently, they resort to videos casting the company as a villain. With no response from Continental Aluminum, the campaign in Riverbend has effectively ended while the campaign in Lyon Township has been drastically reduced. It remains to be seen whether the campaign in Lyon Township will reemerge or follow the fate of the Riverbend campaign.

DISCUSSION AND CONCLUSION

This brings us back to the question – given that these two communities were fighting a common corporate actor, why didn't activists from the two communities collaborate with each other? Collaboration can take various forms. There can be extensive collaboration that in cases such as this could take the form of joint campaigns. It could also be separate campaigns with jointly coordinated events or it could be information sharing or sharing of tactics and strategies.

In the two campaigns analyzed earlier, some see the problem as one of race, social distance and space. For instance, Rhonda Anderson, the environmental justice organizer for the Sierra Club, had this to say about the possibility of collaboration between the two communities, "Detroit communities are segregated and isolated, so there's little conversation across borders," says Anderson. "Solving environmental problems becomes even more complicated when you can't get people to speak to issues of race or poverty" (quote copied from Hattam, 2003). Although racial and class differences can prove challenging when collaboration is attempted, they are not insurmountable. Activists in the greater Los Angeles area overcame this hurdle in the LANCER conflict. In that struggle, low-income Hispanic and black women as well as middle-class white activists worked to oppose an incinerator (Blumberg & Gottlieb, 1989).

As Table 5 shows, race and class are not the only factors that could have limited or inhibited collaboration between the two sets of activists. Of the 31 factors examined, there were only two factors that were operationalized the same way both communities – the party to whom blame was attributed and how the scope of the problem was defined. There was some overlap for nine of the factors, but for 20 of them, there were no commonalities between the

Table 5.   Summary of the Commonalities in the Lyon
Township and Riverbend Conflicts.

Constructs	Movement Dynamics	Commonalities in the Two Cases
Issue identification	Year in which community opposition began	No
	Stage in the production cycle	No
	Focus of the conflict	No
	Problems identified	Some overlap
	Blame attributed to	Yes
	Perception of issue	No
	Scope of problem	Yes
Goal setting	Setting and articulating objectives	No
Resource mobilization	Activists mobilized (human resources)	No
	Institutions utilized	Some overlap
	Technical expertise used	No
Framing	Frames and themes evoked	Some overlap
	Environmental justice frame used	No
	Activists' definition of "community"	No
	Who framed the discourse	No
	Efficacy of activists and leaders	Some overlap
	Corporate responsibility	Some overlap
	Corporate counterframing	No
Tactical interactions	Targets of action	Some overlap
	Activists tactics and strategies	Some overlap
	Corporate tactics and strategies	No
Leverage	Points of community leverage	No
	Points of corporate leverage	No
Concessions	Corporate concessions	No
	Community concessions	No
Conflict mediation	Legal actions, the courts	Some overlap
	Other mechanisms	Some overlap
Corporate–community relations	Nature of community relationship with corporation	No
Demographics	Community characteristics	No
	Race	No
	Class	No
	Level of urbanization	No

two communities. Hence, on most dimensions of the conflicts, the activists on both sides perceived and framed the issues differently. They mobilized different resources and employed different strategies and tactics. Their points of leverage were different and they got different levels of concession from the company. This being the case, it would have been quite unlikely for the two groups to mount a joint campaign. However, some other limited form of collaboration – such as information sharing – was still possible but did not occur.

It is true that residents of Lyon Township and Detroit did participate in a class action suit against Continental Aluminum; however, this does not necessarily translate itself into collaboration for social movement activism. The attorney for the plaintiffs was a Southfield (suburban Detroit) lawyer. In cases such as these, clients initiate or are recruited to participate in the action. They may not necessarily meet with each other. The actions are coordinated through the attorney and are aimed at a legal settlement, not movement building. The secrecy that surrounds settlements may even stymie later activism.

Continental Aluminum played a role in inhibiting collaboration between the groups as well. The company treated the two groups of activists differently and in so doing created incentives for them to organize separately. Although the company negotiated with Lyon Township residents, listened to their complaints, visited their homes to respond to problems, accede to some of their demands, took steps to mitigate some of the problems, and support their community events, this type of relationship was not established with Riverbend. In cases such as these, it is unlikely that the activists and residents who are making some headway with a company such as Continental would risk losing their leverage and hard-fought victories by aligning with the group that the company is either ignoring or engaging in a limited way. On the other side of the coin, the group that is being ignored or paid little attention feels slighted. They are more likely to take issue with the company and focus their efforts on getting the company's attention rather than the attention of activists in another community.

In reality the activists in both communities had limited resources and deployed these as best they could to get results. The two cases point to the enormous challenges communities face in getting corporations to safeguard public health and to clean up their abandoned facilities. When the facilities are still operational, host communities such as Lyon Township stand a chance of forcing companies to comply with environmental regulations and operate safely. However, once facilities are abandoned, the task becomes much more difficult. As the Riverbend case demonstrates, even when the owner of the facility is known and is still operating nearby, companies can still get away with leaving their derelict property in whatever state they choose for years.

Currently, companies are given incentives for establishing themselves in new communities and, quite often, public health and safety are not given enough consideration. These cases highlight the need for cities and other jurisdiction to be tougher on both the front end and back end of their transactions with companies seeking to set up facilities in their communities. They need to do more research into companies before they establish themselves in host communities. Host communities can also establish parameters for decommissioning facilities when the company exits the community. States have a role to play too. The state of Michigan could have made clean up of the Riverbend site a condition of Continental Aluminum getting the incentive package to move to Lyon Township, but did not. These cases are not unique. The challenge that faces communities involved in environmental justice conflicts is to recognize how to work with others to maximize their potential.

NOTES

1. At any time there may be about 80 Michigan companies on the list. Companies have about 270 days to comply with regulations.

2. Screening levels are concentrations below which no adverse health effects are expected.

3. VOCs are chemicals that easily enter a vapor state and can cause odors.

4. A charge well is the area where scrap metal is fed into the furnace.

5. The board argued that since the ATSDR study found that concentrations of chemicals were below screening levels and that samples were taken at Dolsen, then soil testing was not necessary (Board of Education of South Lyon Community Schools, 2004). In 2004 two pre-teen children at the school tested positive for high levels of aluminum (Charter Township of Lyon Board of Trustees, 2004e).

6. For more on master frames and submerged frames see Taylor (2000).

7. When examined, the asthma hospitalization rate for New Hudson per 10,000 people from 1998 to 2001 was 3.6, 3.1, and 2.3. The asthma hospitalization for New Hudson, South Lyon, and Milford combined was also calculated and found to be 7.6 per 10,000 (Agency for Toxic Substances and Disease Registry, 2006).

8. Blacks comprise 81.6 percent of the city of Detroit in 2000.

9. Detroit was the sixth largest city in the country in 1980; it slipped to seventh in 1990 and fourteenth in 2000.

10. The living cities are: Atlanta, Baltimore, Boston, Chicago, Cleveland, Columbus, Dallas, Denver, Detroit, Indianapolis, Kansas City, Los Angeles, Miami,

Minneapolis/St. Paul, New York City, Newark, Oakland, Philadelphia, Phoenix, Portland (Oregon), San Antonia, Seattle, and Washington, D.C.

11. Continental Aluminum reduced its injury rate from 36 in 2002 to 4 in 2004 (Charter Township of Lyon Board of Trustees, 2005).

REFERENCES

Agency for Toxic Substances and Disease Registry. (2005). *Health consultation responsiveness public comment release. Continental Aluminum exposure investigation: Air monitoring results,* MDCH releases exposure investigation report on Continental Aluminum. Available at http://www.michigan.gov/documents/Continental_Aluminum_Exposure_ Investigation_Report_for_Public_Comment_116878_7.pdf. Retrieved on August 28, 2009.

Agency for Toxic Substances and Disease Registry. (2006). *Health consultation responsiveness summary. Continental Aluminum exposure investigation: Air monitoring results.* Available at http://www.michigan.gov/documents/ContinentalAluminumResponsivenessSummary_ 158848_7.pdf. Retrieved on August 28, 2009.

Altgilbers, B. (2003a). Continental is committed to environmental monitoring. *Continental's Corner.* September. Available at http://www.continentalaluminum.com/ca_news_ad_- sep1.pdf. Retrieved on August 30, 2009.

Altgilbers, B. (2003b). Tests show no problems at Dolsen Elementary School. *Continental's Corner.* November. Available at http://www.continentalaluminum.com/ca_news_ad_ nov1.pdf. Retrieved on August 30, 2009.

Altgilbers, B. (2005). Comprehensive investigation confirms Continental Aluminum poses no health risks. *Continental's Corner.* Available at http://www.continentalaluminum.com/ ATSDRfinding3.pdf. Retrieved on August 30, 2009.

Aluminum Association. (2004). Industry overview. Available at www.aluminum.org/template. cfm?Section = The_Industry. Retrieved on October 31, 2004.

Associated Press. (2000a). Civil lawsuit filed against recycling company. September 11. Available at http://www2.fluoridealert.org/Pollution/Specialty-Metal-Industries/Civil- lawsuit-filed-against-recycling-company. Retrieved on September 1, 2009.

Associated Press. (2000b). Recycling company added to EPA "Significant Violators List". May 10. Available at http://www2.fluoridealert.org/Pollution/Specialty-Metal-Industries/ Recycling-company-added-to-EPA-significant-violators-list. Retrieved on September 1, 2009.

Associated Press. (2009). 3 injured at aluminum plant explosion. April 17. Available at http:// www.clickondetroit.com/news/19204540/detail.html. Retrieved on September 1, 2009.

Bailey, C., Faupel, C., & Gundlach, J. (1993). Environmental politics in Alabama's Blackbelt. In: R. Bullard (Ed.), *Confronting environmental racism: Voices from the grassroots* (pp. 107–122). Boston: South End Press.

Blumberg, L., & Gottlieb, R. (1989). *War on waste: Can America win its battle with garbage.* Covelo, CA: Island Press.

Board of Education of South Lyon Community Schools. (2004). Minutes of the regular meeting, August 16. Available at http://www.southlyon.k12.mi.us/BM%208-16.pdf. Retrieved on August 29, 2009.

Brookings Institution. (2003). *Detroit in focus: A profile from Census 2000* (November 1). Washington, DC: Brookings Institution.

Chandler, M. O. (1999). Staying the course: Detroit's struggle to revitalize the inner city. In: W. D. Keating & N. Krumholz (Eds), *Rebuilding urban neighborhoods: Achievements, opportunities, and limits* (pp. 105–123). Thousand Oaks, CA: Sage Publications.

Charter Township of Lyon Board of Trustees. (2003a). Minutes, February 3. Available at www.lyontwp.org/uploaded/files/2003.02.03.bt.minutes.pdf. Retrieved on August 29, 2009.

Charter Township of Lyon Board of Trustees. (2003b). Minutes, April 7. Available at www.lyontwp.org/uploaded/files/2003.03.03.bt.minutes.pdf. Retrieved on September 1, 2009.

Charter Township of Lyon Board of Trustees. (2003c). Minutes, May 5. Available at www.lyontwp.org/uploaded/files/2003.03.03.bt.minutes.pdf. Retrieved on September 2, 2009.

Charter Township of Lyon Board of Trustees. (2004a). Minutes, February 2. Available at http://www.lyontwp.org/105.html. Retrieved on September 2, 2009.

Charter Township of Lyon Board of Trustees. (2004b). Minutes, June 7. Available at http://www.lyontwp.org/105.html. Retrieved on September 2, 2009.

Charter Township of Lyon Board of Trustees. (2004c). Minutes, March 1. Available at from http://www.lyontwp.org/105.html. Retrieved on September 2, 2009.

Charter Township of Lyon Board of Trustees. (2004d). Minutes, July 6. Available at http://www.lyontwp.org/105.html. Retrieved on September 2, 2009.

Charter Township of Lyon Board of Trustees. (2004e). Minutes, October 4. Available at http://www.lyontwp.org/105.html. Retrieved on September 2, 2009.

Charter Township of Lyon Board of Trustees. (2005). Minutes, May 2. Available at http://www.lyontwp.org/105.html. Retrieved on September 2, 2009.

Charter Township of Lyon. (2004). Our town. Available at http://www.lyontwp.org/links/links_frame.htm. Retrieved on November 28, 2004.

Citizens Research Council of Michigan. (2001). *Survey of economic development programs in Michigan.* Report 334. Available at http://www.crcmich.org/PUBLICAT/2000s/2001/rpt334.pdf. Retrieved on April 4, 2005.

City-Data.com. (2009). Lyon Township, Oakland County, Michigan. Available at http://www.city-data.com/township/Lyon-Oakland-MI.html. Retrieved on August 29, 2009.

City of Detroit Department of Environmental Affairs. (2003). *Site inspection worksheet.* Detroit, MI: Department of Environmental Affairs.

Cole, L. W., & Foster, S. R. (2001). *From the ground up: Environmental racism and the rise of the environmental justice movement.* New York: New York University Press.

Colling, J. (2000). Demonstration slated Saturday at Continental. *South Lyon Herald,* March 30.

Doyle, M. B. (2000). Protest Saturday to shut down Continental Aluminum. *Enviro-Mich,* March 30.

Eisinger, P. (1972). The pattern of citizen contacts with urban officials. In: H. Hahn (Ed.), *People and politics in urban society.* Beverly Hills, CA: Sage Publications.

Environmental Protection Agency. (1995). Compilation of air pollutant emission factors, AP-42. Available at www.epa.gov/ttn/chief/ap42. Retrieved on October 31, 2004.

Environmental Protection Agency. (2007a). *EPA awards brownfields grants to 16 Michigan communities and organizations.* Washington, DC: Environmental Protection Agency.

Environmental Protection Agency. (2007b). *Brownfields and land revitalization: About brownfields.* Washington, DC: Environmental Protection Agency.

Environmental Protection Agency. (2008a). NPL fact sheets for Michigan. Available at http://www.epa.gov/R5Super/npl/michigan/index.html. Retrieved on February 16, 2008.

Environmental Protection Agency. (2008b). National priorities list sites in Michigan. Available at http://www.epa.gov/superfund/sites/npl/mi.htm. Retrieved on February 16, 2008.

Gamson, W. (1975). *The strategy of social protest.* Homewood, IL: Dorsey Press.

Gamson, W. (1997). Constructing social protest. In: S. Buechler & K. Cylke (Eds), *Social movements: Perspectives and issues* (pp. 228–244). Mountain View, CA: Mayfield Publishing Company.

Gearhart, J. (2000). Smells like money: Oakland county residents raise a stink about Continental Aluminum. *From the Ground Up, 32*(2), 17–20.

Gibbons, A. (2001). Voters voice fears at hearing. *South Lyon Herald,* June 14.

Golec v. Metal Exchange Corporation. (1995). January 17, 208 Mich. App. 380; 528N.W.2d 756.

Gray, B. (2003). Framing of environmental disputes. In: R. J. Lewicki, B. Gray & M. Elliott (Eds), *Making sense of intractable environmental conflicts* (pp. 11–34). Washington, DC: Island Press.

Haines, H. H. (1984). Black radicalization and the funding of civil rights: 1957–1970. *Social Problems, 32*(1), 31–43.

Halinski, D. (2003a). Wayne County judge rejects class action against Continental Aluminum. Press release, March 12. Available at http://www.continentalaluminum.com/rel031203.html. Retrieved on August 28, 2009.

Halinski, D. (2003b). Oakland County judge rules that township acted unconstitutionally. Press release. March 5. Available at http://www.continentalaluminum.com/rel030503.html. Retrieved on August 28, 2009.

Halinski, D. (2003c). State finds no evidence of health hazards by Continental Aluminum. Press release. March 21. Available at http://www.continentalaluminum.com/rel032103.html. Retrieved on August 30, 2009.

Halinski, D. (2009). Continental Aluminum resumes operations: no gas leak involved in incident as company continues investigation. Press release. April 17. Available at http://www.continentalaluminum.com/ContinentalAluminumresponseF.pdf. Retrieved on August 30, 2009.

Hattam, J. (2003). Eco-equality. *Sierra, 88*(2), 51–52.

Jakobsen, C. H., Hels, T., & McLaughlin, W. J. (2004). Barriers and facilitators to integration among scientists in transdisciplinary landscape analysis: A cross-county comparison. *Forest Policy and Economics, 6,* 15–31.

Jenkins, J., & Perrow, C. (1977). Insurgency of the powerless: Farm worker movements (1946–1972). *American Sociological Review, 42*(2), 249–268.

Jones, T. (2009). Detroit's outlook falls along with home prices. *Chicago Tribune,* January 29.

Koopmans, R. (1993). The dynamics of protest waves: West Germany, 1965 to 1989. *American Sociological Review, 58*(5), 637–658.

Lee, A. (2002). Continental owned by Metal Exchange. *The Detroit News,* October 1.

Lee, A. (2004). Soil test demand at school blocked. *The Detroit News,* August 26.

Lyon Township. (2009). Lyon Township: a community you can live in! Available at http://www.oakgov.com/peds/assets/docs/community_profiles/LyonTwp.pdf. Retrieved on August 29, 2009.

Marx, G. T. (1997). External efforts to damage or facilitate social movements. In: S. Buechler & K. Cylke (Eds), *Social movements: Perspectives and issues* (pp. 360–384). Mountain View, CA: Mayfield Publishing Company.

McAdam, D. (1983). Tactical innovation and the pace of insurgency. *American Sociological Review, 48*(6), 735–754.

McCarthy, J. D., & Zald, M. (1977). Resource mobilization and social movements: A partial theory. *American Journal of Sociology, 82*(6), 1212–1241.

Michigan Department of Environmental Quality. (2003). Continental Aluminum. February 27. Available at www.deq.state.mi.us/documents/deq-whm-enf-hwp-53contalum.doc. Retrieved on September 1, 2009.

Metal Exchange Corporation. (2003). About us. Available at www.metalexchangecorp.com. Retrieved October 31, 2004.

Metal Exchange Corporation v. J. W. Terrill. (2005). October 18. 173S.W.3d 672; 2005 Mo. App.

Minkoff, D. (1997). The sequencing of social movements. *American Sociological Review, 62*(5), 779–799.

Mottl, T. L. (1980). The analysis of countermovements. *Social Problems, 27*(5), 620–634.

Mullins, L. (2009). Median home price in Detroit drops to $7,500. *U.S. News and World Report*, March 2.

Nagel, J. (1996). *American Indian ethnic renewal: Red power and the resurgence of identity and culture.* New York: Oxford University Press.

National Wildlife Federation. (2000). *Eastside story: The rebirth of an urban neighborhood.* Ann Arbor, MI: National Wildlife Federation.

Oberschall, A. (1973). *Social conflict and social movements.* Englewood Cliffs, NJ: Prentice-Hall.

Occupational Safety and Health Administration. (2004). Health guidelines. Available at from www.osha.gov/SLTC/healthguidelines/. Retrieved on October 31, 2004.

Pearce, J. (2001). Residents demand shutdown of foundry. *The Detroit News*, June 7.

Pearce, J. (2000a). Lawsuit targets Oakland polluter. *The Detroit News*, September 11.

Pearce, J. (2000b). Detroit polluter fouling suburbs. *The Detroit News*, February 18.

Rinehart, J. D. (2009). A message from the president. Available at http://www.continentala-luminum.com/home.html. Retrieved on August 30, 2009.

Recycling Today Magazine. (2000). Detroit-area recycler slapped with class-action lawsuit. *Recycling Today Magazine*, September 11.

Recycling Today Magazine. (2001). Complaints filed against foundry. *Recycling Today Magazine*, June 8.

Sharp, E. (1980). Citizen perceptions of channels for urban service advocacy. *Public Opinion Quarterly, 44*(3), 362–376.

Snow, D., Rochford, E. B., Worden, S., & Benford, R. (1986). Frame alignment processes, mircromobilization, and movement participation. *American Sociological Review, 51*(8), 464–481.

Susskind, L., & Weinstein, A. (1980). Towards a theory of environmental dispute resolution. *Boston College Environmental Affairs Law Review, 9*(2), 311–357.

Sugrue, T. (1996). *The origins of the urban crisis: Race and inequality in postwar Detroit.* Princeton, NJ: Princeton University Press.

Tarrow, S. (1993). Cycles of collective action: Between moments of madness and the repertoire of contention. *Social Science History, 17*(2), 281–308.

Tarrow, S. (1994). *Power in movement: Social movements, collective action and politics.* Cambridge: Cambridge University Press.

Taylor, D. (2000). The rise of the environmental justice paradigm. *American Behavioral Scientist, 43*(4), 508–579.

Tilly, C. (1977). Getting it together in Burgundy. *Theory and Society, 4*(4), 479–504.

U.S. Census Bureau. (1990). *Census of population and housing.* Washington, DC: Department of Commerce.

U.S. Census Bureau. (2000). *Census of population and housing.* Washington, DC: Department of Commerce.

U.S. Census Bureau. (2008). *Population estimates.* Washington, DC: Department of Commerce.

Verba, S., & Nie, N. (1972). *Participation in America: Political democracy and social equity.* New York: Harper and Row.

Whittier, N. (1997). Political generations, micro-cohorts, and the transformation of social movements. *American Sociological Review, 62*(5), 760–778.

Wondolleck, J. M., & Yaffee, S. (2000). *Making collaboration work.* Washington, DC: Island Press.

ZoomInfo. (2009). Continental Aluminum Corporation: summary. Available at http://www.zoominfo.com/Search/CompanyDetail.aspx?CompanyID = 29775233&cs = QFB xlWBrY. Retrieved on August 29, 2009.

Sarah Lashley is a Mellon post-doctoral fellow at Colby College. She can be reached by email at slashley@umich.edu

Dorceta E. Taylor is an associate professor at the University of Michigan's School of Natural Resources and Environment. She teaches courses in environmental history, environmental justice, tourism and climate change, and social movements. She is the director of the Multicultural Environmental Leadership Development Initiative (http://www.meldi.snre.umich. edu) and author of *The Environment and the People in American Cities, 1600s–1900s: Disorder, Inequality, and Social Change.* She can be reached by email at dorceta@umich.edu or by telephone at 734-763-5327.

CONTEXT AND SIGNIFICANCE OF STUDY

For more than 30 years environmentalists have leveraged various spiritual and religious traditions to advance environmental awareness, concern, behavior, and activism. In this quest, Islam has been largely ignored. This is due, in part, to Western misconceptions about Islam than the lack of an established Islamic value system regarding the environment. Scholars have analyzed the theological roots of Islamic environmental values (Ammar, 2000; Haq, 2001; Masri, 1992; Nasr, 2001; Tanner & Mitchell, 2002), but few discuss Muslim environmental activism. Although some researchers have studied the environmental policies of Muslim governments such as Saudi Arabia and Iran (Al-Gilani & Filor, 1997; Zekavat, 1997), and pro-environmental behavior in Egypt (Rice, 2006), grassroots Muslim approaches to environmental issues in pluralistic, secular states have been understudied. My research attempts to fill this void by providing an understanding of American Muslims' environmental behaviors.

Although this project received immense support from the Muslim community, I often encountered the following sentiment – "Muslims aren't environmentalists – we have other things to worry about." Many American Muslims believe they must focus on voicing their disapproval of policies such as the war in Iraq or the U.S. Patriot Act. Other Muslims believe their priority should be on building a pan-ethnic and cohesive Muslim community with a special emphasis on bridging the gap between African-American Muslims and Muslims of Middle Eastern or South Asian heritage. Still others feel Muslims should focus on transforming public misperceptions about Islam and its followers. With such issues taking primacy in inter-Muslim debate, few American Muslims feel an urgent calling to take on environmental issues.

The alarming increase of anti-Muslim sentiment since September 11, 2001 bombing of the World Trade Center highlights the need for Muslims to become more visible as social activists and philanthropists. Muslims who are active in these roles will provide a counterbalance to the Western image of Muslims as terrorists. By taking leadership roles on a variety of national and local issues, Muslims can provide input in policies that impact their communities.

When increasing Muslim support of various causes, it would be a mistake for Muslims to ignore environmental activism. Environmental organizations are taking a stand on a number of social policies that will have significant impacts on Muslims. For instance, the controversy in the Sierra Club about the group's position on immigration illustrates the important role environmental organizations play in national American politics. As anti-immigration advocates attempt to take control of the Sierra Club board (Pfeffer & Stycos, 2002), it is clear that the lack of minority participation in that organization impacts how the organization defines its priorities and policies. Muslim participation in such environmental organizations helps ensure that Islamic viewpoints are included in all policy debates.

ISLAM'S ENVIRONMENTAL ETHIC

American Muslim environmental activists can look to their religion to find ideological support for taking environmental action. The roots of an Islamic environmental ethic (as are the roots of all Islamic values and laws) are based in the Qur'an. Because verses of the Qur'an were revealed to the Prophet Muhammad in Arabic, Muslims consider this to be God's chosen language. Any Qur'anic translations inevitably change the meaning of God's message and are therefore illegitimate. Translations may give readers an idea of God's intended message, but should not be prevailed on to reveal the truth. For Muslims the Qur'an provides more than general moral guidelines: it offers concrete rules on all types of human behavior, including social, political, penal, and environmental actions. The Qur'an is divided into 114 chapters (*surahs*), which are subdivided into verses. Approximately 500 verses discuss nature and give instruction on how Muslims should handle environmental matters (Masri, 1992).

Other important sources of Islamic guidance are *sunnah, hadith, fiqh,* and *shari'ah*. The s*unnah* is the Prophet Muhammad's actions and the term *hadith* refers to the text that recorded the Prophet's life. After the Qur'an, the *sunnah* provide the most important source of guidance for Muslims. Combined, the Qur'an and *sunnah* serve as guides for Muslims to achieve a "comprehensive social order" (Haider, 1984). *Shari'ah* is the canonical laws of Islam based on the Qur'an and *sunnah*. A literal translation of *shari'ah* is "source of water," and it is regarded as "the source of life in that it contains both legal rules and ethical principles" (Izzi Deen, 1996). In Islam, *shari'ah* is a term that covers both governmental and moral laws: there is no separation between church and state in Islam. Muslims see no reason to enact separate civil laws when God has provided detailed laws that govern all aspects of human life.

Nature's Place in Islam

Nature's role within the Islamic paradigm can be found in the Qur'an's discussion of the three primary reasons for the creation of the universe.

The foremost reason is to represent God's power and goodness. One author notes, "nature has no *meaning* without reference to God: without Divine purpose it simply does not exist (Manzoor, 1984). Nature, as a symbol of God, is intended to guide humankind and also to test their faith and conduct. Creation's second purpose is to serve God. The universe's third purpose is to serve as a tool for humans to use in their quest to serve God. God provided humans with the earth as a test to see how well they make use of it.

Humankind's Role on Earth

According to Islam, humans are defined as those who are under obligation to God. God created Adam and Eve (equal halves) to act as his *khalifa*, or vicegerents, on earth (Haq, 2001). According to the Qur'an, humankind willingly accepted the role as God's vicegerents and be responsible for God's earth. It is only this heavy moral responsibility that places humans in a superior position over animals and plants: natural creatures are not accountable, as are humans, for their actions (Haq, 2001). God's nonhuman creations are inherently *muslim*, or those who have surrendered to God (Rahman, 1989). When looking at the relationship in this light, humans must treat all creation as part of the *ummah* – the global community of Muslims. Muslims have specific responsibilities to this group and the *shari'ah* sets boundaries on individualism and recognizes the rights of this larger community (Hope & Young, 2000). The Qur'an enjoins Muslims to work together as an *ummah*, as this is the only way to achieve the ideal Islamic social and political order (Rahman, 1989).

Although humanity carries a position of superiority, humans do not have the right to "subdue" or claim "dominion" over God's property (Haq, 2001). The Qur'an makes it clear that the earth is for the use of all creatures, not just humans (Timm, 1994). Humans must partake of the earth's bounty only the limits prescribed by Islam. Muslims are enjoined to "Enjoy the bounties of God's provisions but do not over-indulge" (Manzoor, 1984). One verse from the Qur'an states:

Eat of their fruit
In their season, but render
The dues that are proper
On the day that the harvest
Is gathered, But waste not
By excess: for Allah
Loveth not the wasters (An'am: 141) (Akhtar & Gul-e-Jannat, 1995)

Responsibility toward Animals and Natural Resources

Islam's environmental ethic is based on the concept that all relationships are established on justice (*'adl*) and equity (*ihsan*) (Izzi Deen, 1996). The Prophet Muhammad instructed, "Verily Alllah has prescribed equity (*ihsan*) in all things. Thus if you kill, kill well, and if you slaughter, slaughter well. Let each of you sharpen his blade and let him spare the suffering of the animal he slaughters" (Izzi Deen, 1996). The Qur'an states, "There is not an animal on earth, nor a flying creature flying on two wings, but they are peoples unto you (Surah 6:38)" (Izzi Deen, 1996). The Prophet Muhammad is also noted as saying, "For [charity shown to] each creature which has a wet heart there is a reward" (Izzi Deen, 1996).

Islam's respect for animal life is illustrated in it's injunction for Muslims to only eat *zabeeha* meat, or meat from animals who have been slaughtered according to Islamic guidelines. Muslims are required to slaughter their livestock by slitting the animal's throat in a "swift and merciful manner, saying, 'Bismillah Allah-u-Akbar;' 'In the name of God, God is Most Great.' This is in acknowledgment that the life of this creature if taken by God's permission to meet one's lawful need for food" (Halalpreneur, 2001).

Environmental and Social Justice

Islam's environmental ethic is closely tied to its emphasis on social justice. The Qur'an emphasizes social justice by prioritizing the dignity and rights of the elderly, disabled, orphaned, indigent, and hungry. The text exhorts Muslims to be fair in trading and against hoarding wealth (Haq, 2001). The Qur'an repeatedly emphasizes the equality of all people, regardless of sex, race, or status. Each human life must be valued equally and treated without discrimination. This sense of equality and compassion extends to the natural world. Nasr (2001) notes, "It is pleasing in the eyes of God not only to be kind to one's parents, but also to plant trees and treat animals gently and with kindness." As God's vicegerents, humans are obligated to treat all aspects of the world – both human and nonhuman – with respect and humility. Humans must promote peace, harmony, justice, and respect among all peoples (Akhtar & Gul-e-Jannat, 1995).

MUSLIM ENVIRONMENTALISM
IN THE UNITED STATES

Muslim environmentalism in the United States will be shaped by the various religious values discussed earlier as well as by Western environmental thought. Education on how the Qur'an, *sunnah, hadith,* and *shari'ah* support environmental action will be very important in giving a Muslim environmental movement religious legitimacy. These religious texts and edicts provide a spiritual and moral basis for environmental action. The historical and present-day environmental experiences from Muslim countries will also shape how Muslim Americans identify important environmental issues and also how they tackle them. As authors Hope and Young (2000) note, "It is impossible to consider the possibilities for a full-fledged Islamic environmental ethic without considering the political, economic, and historical aspects of Islam as a living community. This is true of all religions – but particularly true of Islam, which is seen as a way of life."

If the American Muslim community can agree on a unified environmental platform, and commit to its advancement, American Muslims could become environmental leaders for the Muslim world. Hope and Young (2000) take this one step further: "The potential is enormous. If the disparate forces of Islam, the worlds' fastest growing religion, were to get together and take off, it could become a leader in the ecospiritual movement."

RESEARCH ON PRO-ENVIRONMENTAL BEHAVIORS

We should understand the current state of research regarding environmental behaviors before exploring how Islamic environmental values are practiced in everyday life. Since there are few studies regarding Muslim environmentalism, this chapter examines the broader literature regarding environmental behaviors of the mainstream population in the United States and other Western countries. This chapter focuses specifically on pro-environmental behaviors (PEBs) and environmental activism. PEBs are actions that have beneficial consequences on the natural environment regardless of the intent (e.g., the individual may conduct the activity primarily to save money, conform to social norms, or benefit the environment). It is behavior that benefits the environment in the long run.

This study further defines pro-environmental behaviors as "private," home-based behaviors; and uses the term environmental activism to refer to "public," group-oriented behaviors and civic activities that promote community-wide environmental benefits. This chapter considers activities such as reuse, recycling,[1] and household energy conservation as fitting into the first category, whereas membership in environmental organizations and participation in community-wide activities fall in the second category. Similar categorizations have been used in previous studies (Hunter, Hatch, & Johnson, 2004; Mohai, 1992, Tindall, Davies, & Mauboulés, 2003; Zelezny, Chua, & Aldrich, 2000).

Religious Participation and Political Activism

Religious participation is viewed as a potential determinant of environmental behavior and activism. Mazumdar and Mazumdar (1999) note that "At the macro societal level, religion, particularly non-Western non-Christian religions, continues to dominate the lives of its believers both men and women." Religious participation reflects both the psychological factors of beliefs and attitudes as well as the social factors of community norms.

In this vein, a survey by the Henry J. Kaiser Family Foundation conducted in 2000 that showed 64 percent of voters agreed "protecting the environment is a moral issue involving beliefs about what is morally right or wrong" (Clayton & Opotow, 2003). Other research indicates people of different classes and backgrounds around the world share this view that morality and the environment are connected (Clayton & Opotow, 2003). Some branches of the environmental movement seek to build on this morality issue by making explicit connections between religion and environmental issues.

Throughout U.S. history, religious institutions played an important role in mobilizing political activism. Churches were instrumental in advancing the civil rights movement and have recently taken a highly visible role in promoting conservative politics. Religious institutions, like other societal rule-makers, partake in the socialization process that teaches individuals about each religious community's socially acceptable values, to learn the vocabulary to communicate these principles, and to prioritize them (Fransson & Gärling, 1999). Religious services provide attendees with political cues and messages, both from the religious leaders who may advocate or condemn certain issues and other members who discuss various issues among themselves (Schlozman, Burns, & Verba, 1994). This religious forum for discussion often places political issues in a moral light and encourages individuals to support the same policies as their religious institutions. Musick, Wilson, and Bynum (2000) note that the literature on social movements delineates the crucial role that social networks play in mobilizing activism. Religious communities provide their members with information and incentives to volunteer for those causes that are promoted by this institution. Religious institutions have also played important roles in the mainstream and environmental justice movements (Taylor, 2000).

Racial and Ethnic Differences

Since the 1980s, large numbers of racial and ethnic minorities have become involved in the environmental justice movement (Taylor, 2000). Although not studied much in relation to environmental activism, religious participation and its impact on social activism has been shown to differ by racial and ethnic groups. Church attendance is related to volunteering, for both African-Americans and whites, but the impact is stronger on African-Americans (Musick et al., 2000). African-American political activity is also correlated with regular church attendance (Arp & Boeckelman, 1997) and African-Americans are more likely than whites to develop civic skills at church. Studies also found that in regard to volunteering, African-Americans are more likely than whites to place great importance on the recommendations of a church, union, or other organization to which they belong (Musick et al., 2000).

Racial differences also impact the level and type of activism conducted within religious institutions. Musick et al.'s (2000) study found that African-American churches are more socially active than white churches and become involved in different types of social activism. White congregations were more likely to focus on youth recreation, anti-abortion campaigns, and refugee aid programs while African-American congregations are more likely to target civil rights issues, meal services, community development, and dissemination of public health information. African-Americans were more likely than whites to volunteer for their churches and for community-action groups, work-related organizations, and political groups. In contrast, whites were more likely to volunteer for issues regarding youth, education, the environment, and the arts.

Regarding environmental activism, Arp and Boeckelman's (1997) study found that African-American church members were more likely to be more environmentally active (e.g., advocating environmental issues to elected officials, mobilizing, and rallying around environmental problems) than non-members. For whites, church attendance had no impact on environmental activism. The researchers contend that this difference occurs because each group has different issues which are most salient to them.

There is some evidence to indicate that frequent church attendance may actually inhibit volunteering for secular causes, but more so for whites than for blacks (Musick et al., 2000).

Although researchers have extensively documented the church's integrative and mobilizing role in African-American communities, recent trends indicate that this is diminishing. Educated, middle-class blacks are leaving the church because it is no longer the only path to professional advancement whereas the urban poor are increasingly converting to Islam (Musick et al., 2000). As increasing numbers of African-Americans convert to Islam, they bring their previous church's norms of social activism to their mosques. As a result, African-American mosques are more socially active than mosques with predominantly immigrant members (Bagby, Perl, & Froehle, 2001).

Gender Differences

Differences in religious participation are not restricted to racial and ethnic differences; gender is also a significant factor. In the United States, women make up the majority of participants in Christian activities and institutions (Leonard, 2003). Women are also more likely to regularly attend religious service and more likely to donate time and money to religious-based activities (Musick et al., 2000, Schlozman et al., 1994).

In most societies, women's roles have been traditionally focused in the home while men's roles were centered in the public arena (Schlozman et al., 1994). In the United States, participation in voluntary organizations gave women more resources and support for volunteering than it provided for men (Musick et al., 2000). As a result, religious institutions may be the best path for activism for some women, including Muslims.

Yet Muslim women's roles in Islamic institutions are fraught with contention, especially in the United States (Goodstein, 2004). Muslim women have a difficult time obtaining leadership positions in their local mosques and often find themselves in secretarial or menial positions (Goodstein, 2004). Although Islamic law is generally interpreted in a way that prevents women from leading mixed-gender mosque and prayer activities (Mattson, 2005) the Islamic Society of North America (ISNA),[2] one of the oldest and largest national Muslim groups in the United States (ISNA, 2009), elected a woman as its first female president in 2006[3] and has set an important example for Muslim women's leadership in American Islamic organizations.

In sum, participation in religious institutions has been shown to be a factor in political activism, but more research needs to be done to clarify how this participation influences different types of environmental activism, especially for Muslim women. Furthermore, when considering religious participation and environmental activism, the impacts of gender and race/ethnicity seem to be important mediators and should be included as variables in future research.

STUDY DESIGN AND METHODOLOGY

To explore Muslim environmental behavior, I conducted a national survey of American Muslim women. The study focuses specifically on women because of their influence on the environmental activities conducted in their homes. Since women have a greater role in running their homes, their environmental attitudes and beliefs have an increased influence on how their households participate in environmentally friendly behaviors.

Specifically I wished to identify patterns related to Muslim women's PEBs, environmental activism, and outdoor activities. I also wanted to explore what influenced Muslim women's PEBs and environmental activism, and examine the relationships between religious belief, religious practice, and religious community and PEBs and environmental activism. To answer these questions, I conducted a web and email survey of a snowball sample of 331 Muslim women aged 18 and older. The survey was conducted from March through December of 2003.

DEMOGRAPHIC CHARACTERISTICS

The sample was divided into four ethnic groups. The 32 blacks/Latinos constituted 9.7 percent of the sample, the 73 Middle Easterners comprised 22.5 percent, the 168 South Asians made up 51.7 percent, and the 52 other Muslims constituted 16 percent of the sample. The sample was young; 45.1 percent (144) of the respondents were 18–24 years old, 47 percent (150) were 25–34 years of age, and 7.8 percent (25) were 35 years and older. The sample was also highly educated. Only 6.8 percent (22) had a high school diploma or less education; 26.5 percent (86) had some college, 36.4 percent

(118) had a bachelor's degree, and 30.2 percent (98) had a graduate or professional degree.

One hundred and thirty-three or 41 percent of the sample worked full or part-time, 158 or 48.8 percent were students, and 33 or 10.2 percent were not in the workforce (retired, unemployed, and home maker). Most of the respondents were suburban or rural – 202 or 62.2 percent lived in suburban/rural areas while 123 or 37.8 percent lived in the city. Most of the respondents were from the Midwest (primarily Southeast Michigan and Chicago) – 53.5 percent (174) were from this region. Forty-eight or 14.8 percent were from the Northeast, 80 or 24.6 percent were from the South whereas 23 or 7.1 percent were from the West. Most respondents were homeowners: 171 or 55 percent owned their homes whereas 140 or 45 percent were renters.

Ethnic Differences

As Table 1 shows, black/Latino Muslims were older than the remainder of the sample. They were more likely to be employed and far more likely to live in the city than other Muslims. Most (62.5 percent) were also from the Midwest. In contrast, Middle Eastern Muslims were the youngest group – half of them were in the 18–24 age group. Most (53.4 percent) were students. South Asians were the group most likely to live in the suburbs or rural areas – 69 percent of this group lived outside the city.

NEIGHBORHOOD CHARACTERISTICS

Neighborhood Problems

Respondents were asked to rate the seriousness of six environmental and social factors in the neighborhoods they live in. They rated these on a four-point Likert scale with 1 being a serious problem to 4 being not a problem at all. A means comparison analysis was conducted and the results are reported in Table 2. Generally speaking, respondents lived in neighborhoods where abandoned or boarded-up houses, foul odors, litter, vermin, and lack of trees were not seen as serious problems. All of these variables scored sample mean of 3.0 or greater – means ranged from 3.16 to 3.41. Crime was seen as a more serious problem; it had a mean of 2.86.

Table 1. Ethnic Differences between Muslim Women.

Demographic Characteristics	Total Sample		Black/Latino		Middle Eastern		South Asian		Other	
	Number	Percent	Number	Percent	Number	Percent	Number	Percent	Number	Percent
Age										
18–24 years old	142	44.8	9	30.0	36	50.0	76	46.1	21	42.0
25–34 years old	150	47.3	13	43.3	34	47.2	79	47.9	24	48.0
35 years and older	25	7.9	8	26.7	2	2.8	10	6.1	5	10.0
Educational attainment										
High school diploma or less	22	6.8	1	3.1	7	9.6	8	4.8	6	11.8
Some college	86	26.5	14	43.8	18	24.7	41	24.4	13	25.5
Bachelor's degree	118	36.4	10	31.2	24	32.9	63	37.5	21	41.2
Graduate or professional	98	30.2	7	21.9	24	32.9	56	33.3	11	21.6
Employment status										
Employed full or part time	133	41	17	53.1	25	34.2	72	43.1	19	36.5
Student	158	48.8	12	37.5	39	53.4	79	47.3	28	53.8
Not in workforce	33	10.2	3	9.4	9	12.3	16	9.6	5	9.6
Residence										
City	123	37.8	21	65.6	29	39.7	52	31.0	21	40.4
Suburbs/rural	202	62.2	11	34.4	44	60.3	116	69.0	31	59.6
Region										
Northeast	48	14.8	4	12.5	10	13.7	26	15.5	8	15.4
Midwest	174	53.5	20	62.5	37	50.7	88	52.4	29	55.8
South	80	24.6	7	21.9	18	24.7	44	26.2	11	21.2
West	23	7.1	1	3.1	8	11.0	10	6.0	4	7.7
Home ownership										
Homeowner	171	55.0	13	43.3	43	59.7	98	62.0	17	33.3
Renter	140	45.0	17	56.7	29	40.3	60	38.0	34	66.7

Table 2. Mean Scores Indicating the Seriousness of Problems in Neighborhoods in which Respondents Reside.

Demographic Characteristics	Crime	Abandoned Houses	Foul Odors	Litter	Vermin	Lack of Trees
Total sample mean	2.86	3.41	3.34	3.12	3.30	3.17
Ethnic background						
Black/Latino	2.22	2.84	3.10	2.66	3.23	3.12
Middle Eastern	2.79	3.30	3.33	3.11	3.32	3.11
South Asian	3.05	3.57	3.39	3.23	3.38	3.23
Other	2.69	3.40	3.33	3.02	3.02	3.02
Age						
18–24 years old	2.95	3.43	3.37	3.18	3.29	3.22
25–34 years old	2.88	3.45	3.38	3.14	3.33	3.11
35 years and older	2.44	3.24	3.17	2.84	3.21	3.28
Educational attainment						
High school diploma or less	2.52	3.17	2.91	2.57	2.78	3.00
Some college	2.80	3.36	3.31	3.00	3.24	3.10
Bachelor's degree	2.90	3.46	3.38	3.21	3.32	3.29
Graduate or professional	2.93	3.43	3.40	3.23	3.42	3.10
Employment status						
Employed full or part time	2.84	3.38	3.36	3.10	3.32	3.19
Student	2.84	3.40	3.28	3.10	3.25	3.10
Not in workforce	2.94	3.61	3.48	3.24	3.39	3.33
Residence						
City	2.61	3.15	3.07	2.89	3.13	2.93
Suburbs/rural	3.01	3.57	3.50	3.26	3.40	3.31
Region						
Northeast	3.06	3.47	3.40	3.28	3.31	3.25
Midwest	2.72	3.30	3.19	2.97	3.27	3.07
South	3.02	3.57	3.56	3.31	3.31	3.32
West	2.96	3.57	3.61	3.26	3.48	3.26
Home ownership						
Homeowner	2.94	3.48	3.46	3.15	3.35	3.27
Renter	2.73	3.29	3.15	3.02	3.19	3.01

However, there was significant variations in the sample as the demographic factors were analyzed. Table 2 also indicates that crime, the factor most likely to be a serious problem, was most often reported by black/Latino Muslims. The ethnic differences were very significant ($F = 7.349$, $p = .000$). Black/Latino Muslims were also significantly more likely than other ethnic groups to report living in neighborhoods were abandoned and boarded-up houses are a serious problem ($F = 7.182$, $p = .000$). The other significant interaction can be seen with black/Latino Muslims being more likely to report living in a neighborhood with litter ($F = 3.343$, $p = .020$). These results are not surprising since most black/ Latino Muslims live in cities. Age was significant in only one instance – the oldest respondents were more likely to report crime being a serious problem in their neighborhoods than other respondents ($F = 2.852$, $p = .059$). Educational attainment was significant in two instances. The least educated respondents – those with high school diploma or less were more likely than other respondents to report living in neighborhoods with litter ($F = 3.713$, $p = .012$) and vermin ($F = 3.237$, $p = .022$). Although there were no significant interactions involving employment status, there was a significant interaction between residence and all of the dependent variables. The interaction between residence and crime ($F = 12.575$), abandoned houses ($F = 18.758$), and foul odors ($F = 18.424$) was significant to the $p = .000$ level. It was significant to the $p = .001$ level for litter ($F = 11.228$) and lack of trees ($F = 12.300$) to the $p = .010$ level for vermin ($F = 6.666$). For all of the dependent variables, city residents were more likely than suburban/rural residents to report a serious problem with the factors examined.

There were significant interactions between region and four of the dependent variables. In all four cases, the Midwest standout as the region in which respondents were more likely to report a more serious problem with crime ($F = 2.721$, $p = .044$), abandoned or boarded-up houses ($F = 2.266$, $p = .081$), foul odors ($F = 4.177$, $p = .006$), and litter ($F = 3.001$, $p = .031$). There were significant interactions between homeownership and four of the dependent variables. Renters were more likely to report serious problems with crime ($F = 3.332$, $p = .069$), abandoned or boarded-up houses ($F = 3.756$, $p = .054$), foul odors ($F = 9.551$, $p = .002$), and lack of trees ($F = 5.345$, $p = .021$).

Neighborhood Quality

Respondents were also asked to rate five aspects of neighborhood quality on a six-point Likert scale with 1 being very poor and 5 being very good. Unsure was coded as 0. Table 3 shows the mean comparison for neighborhood quality. Overall, respondents felt their neighborhood quality was good – they gave a rating of 3.5 or higher on all factors related to

Table 3.   Means of Respondents' Rating of Neighborhood Quality.

Demographic Characteristics	General Environment	Air Quality	Water Quality	Neighborhood Upkeep	Parks, Playgrounds
Total sample mean	3.54	3.5	3.58	3.89	3.77
Ethnic background					
Black/Latino	3.10	3.09	3.31	3.50	3.19
Middle Eastern	3.48	3.44	3.49	3.81	3.68
South Asian	3.74	3.70	3.73	4.06	3.92
Other	3.21	3.24	3.38	3.73	3.77
Age					
18–24 years old	3.66	3.72	3.71	3.92	3.77
25–34 years old	3.50	3.40	3.51	3.91	3.83
35 years and older	3.21	3.04	3.32	3.72	3.60
Educational attainment					
High school diploma or less	3.09	3.22	3.57	3.43	3.57
Some college	3.53	3.57	3.53	3.77	3.48
Bachelor's degree	3.54	3.55	3.60	3.97	3.84
Graduate or professional	3.62	3.44	3.59	4.01	4.00
Employment status					
Employed full or part time	3.52	3.43	3.54	3.83	3.69
Student	3.58	3.61	3.68	3.93	3.80
Not in workforce	3.30	3.21	3.21	3.97	3.97
Residence					
City	3.27	3.21	3.40	3.56	3.44
Suburbs/rural	3.70	3.68	3.69	4.09	3.98
Region					
Northeast	3.51	3.72	3.50	3.85	3.85
Midwest	3.53	3.49	3.59	3.85	3.70
South	3.56	3.45	3.66	4.01	3.76
West	3.52	3.35	3.43	3.83	4.13
Home ownership					
Homeowner	3.75	3.66	3.77	4.07	3.84
Renter	3.26	3.28	3.33	3.66	3.67

neighborhood quality. However, there were significant differences in the sample worth noting.

Ethnicity was significant for all factors. Black/Latino Muslims had the lowest mean scores for all five factors. The significance levels were: general environmental quality ($F = 7.193$, $p = .000$), air quality ($F = 4.791$, $p = .003$), water quality ($F = 2.707$, $p = .045$), neighborhood upkeep ($F = 4.126$, $p = .007$), and quality of parks ($F = 4.283$, $p = .006$). Only the first two factors had significant interactions with age. The youngest respondents rated the general neighborhood quality the highest ($F = 2.846$, $p = .060$). The youngest respondents were also the ones who rated air quality in the neighborhoods they lived in the highest ($F = 6.581$, $p = .002$). There was a linear relationship between education and neighborhood upkeep. That is, the more educated the respondent, the more likely they were to indicate they lived in a neighborhood where upkeep was good ($F = 2.938$, $p = .033$). The most educated respondents were also most likely to report that the parks and playgrounds in their neighborhood were in good condition ($F = 3.974$, $p = .008$). Respondents who were not in the workforce rated their water ($F = 2.411$, $p = .091$) and air quality ($F = 2.863$, $p = .059$) much lower than other respondents.

The differences between city and suburban residents were significant to the $p = .000$ level for four of the five factors – general environmental quality ($F = 16.582$), air quality ($F = 15.676$), neighborhood upkeep ($F = 24.602$), and quality of parks ($F = 19.839$). The interaction with water quality was also significant ($F = 5.775$, $p = .017$). In all instances, respondents who lived in the city were more likely to rate these factors much lower than suburban/rural residents. There were no significant interactions between region and factors related to neighborhood quality. However, homeownership was significant in all but one case. Homeownership was significant to the $p = .000$ level for three factors – general environmental quality ($F = 22.070$), water quality ($F = 14.339$), and neighborhood upkeep ($F = 14.661$). It was also significant for air quality ($F = 10.572$, $p = .001$). In every case, renters were far more likely to rate the indicators of neighborhood quality lower than homeowners.

OUTDOOR ACTIVITIES

Given the neighborhoods respondents lived in and the way they felt about the quality of such neighborhoods, what kinds of outdoor activities did they participate in? Respondents were asked to say what kinds of outdoor recreational activities they participated in the year before being surveyed. The results in Table 4 indicate that American Muslim women generally participated in a range of outdoor activities, despite differing Islamic norms governing women's public dress and behaviors (Weiss, 1994).

Walking/hiking was the activity most frequently participated in – 93 percent of the respondents reported participating in this activity in the past year. There was little variation in the sample vis-à-vis this activity.

Table 4. Percent of Muslim Women Participating in Outdoor Activities.

Demographic Characteristics	Walking, Hiking	Spent Time Outdoors	Picnic	Jogging, Running	Attend Sports Event	Garden- ing	Swimm- ing	Badminton, Tennis	Team Sports	Yard Games	Bicycling, Mountain Bike	Roller Blading, Skating	Sailing, Boating	Golfing	Fishing, Hunting
Total sample percent	93.0	85.4	77.8	54.4	40.4	35.3	32.2	24.6	24.0	23.4	21.9	15.2	11.9	5.2	4.3
Ethnic background															
Black/Latino	93.8	87.5	56.2	40.6	40.6	18.8	28.1	9.4	15.6	15.6	25.0	12.5	6.2	3.1	0.0
Middle Eastern	90.3	84.7	80.6	54.2	44.4	40.3	30.6	26.4	31.9	20.8	13.9	20.8	12.5	4.2	1.4
South Asian	96.4	84.4	81.4	59.3	43.1	38.3	34.7	29.3	25.1	25.1	23.4	15.0	13.8	6.0	5.4
Other	90.4	90.4	76.9	48.1	26.9	32.7	28.8	15.4	13.5	26.9	25.0	9.6	9.6	5.8	7.7
Age															
18–24 years old	95.5	86.7	83.9	64.3	46.2	30.8	35.7	33.6	37.8	29.4	21.7	15.4	14.0	4.2	5.6
25–34 years old	92.5	87.2	75.2	53.0	36.9	36.9	31.5	19.5	12.8	19.5	22.8	16.1	11.4	6.0	4.0
35 years and older	90.6	80.0	56.0	12.0	28.0	56.0	20.0	8.0	12.0	16.0	16.0	4.0	8.0	8.0	0.0
Educational attainment															
High school/less	87.0	73.9	87.0	60.9	52.2	30.4	39.1	60.9	47.8	34.8	30.4	21.7	21.7	0.0	0.0
Some college	95.3	86.0	74.4	62.8	44.2	31.4	32.6	20.9	30.2	30.2	19.8	11.6	8.1	7.0	5.8
Bachelor's degree	93.2	89.8	83.1	50.8	37.3	32.2	30.5	20.3	23.3	22.0	16.1	14.4	12.7	6.8	6.8
Graduate/professional	93.9	83.7	73.5	50.0	37.8	44.9	32.7	25.5	17.3	17.3	28.6	17.3	11.2	3.1	1.0
Employment status															
Employed	95.5	86.5	71.4	52.6	39.1	39.1	33.8	20.3	20.3	20.3	21.8	16.5	12.0	4.5	3.0
Student	92.5	85.5	83.0	62.9	44.7	32.7	33.3	30.2	31.4	27.7	23.9	15.1	13.8	6.3	5.7
Not in workforce	90.6	84.4	81.2	18.8	25.0	37.5	18.8	15.6	0.0	12.5	12.5	6.2	3.1	3.1	3.1
Residence															
City	93.6	88.8	79.2	54.4	42.4	30.4	29.6	19.2	21.6	18.4	23.2	13.6	13.6	4.0	2.4
Suburbs/rural	93.5	84.1	77.6	54.7	39.3	38.8	33.8	28.4	25.4	26.9	21.4	15.9	10.9	6.0	5.5
Region															
Northeast	91.5	91.5	83.0	48.9	34.0	27.7	46.8	23.4	17.0	19.1	29.8	25.5	14.9	6.4	6.4
Midwest	92.2	83.9	73.9	55.6	42.2	35.0	26.7	24.4	26.1	22.2	23.9	14.4	11.1	3.9	4.4
South	93.7	83.5	81.0	53.2	38.0	39.2	34.2	26.6	22.8	29.1	15.2	10.1	10.1	2.5	3.8
West	100.0	91.3	87.0	60.9	47.8	39.1	39.1	21.7	26.1	21.7	13.0	17.4	17.4	21.7	0.0
Home ownership															
Homeowner	94.1	85.3	78.2	54.7	41.8	42.9	31.8	27.6	27.1	25.3	21.8	14.7	9.4	5.9	2.9
Renter	91.6	85.3	76.9	53.8	38.5	25.9	35.7	21.7	20.3	21.0	22.4	15.4	14.0	4.2	5.6

However, there were much more noticeable variations in the sample when other activities were examined. For instance, respondents with less than a college education were much less likely than other respondents to indicate that they spent time outdoors. Although 73.9 percent of respondents with less than a college education spent time outdoors, 83.7 to 86 percent of other respondents did.

Black/Latino Muslims and the oldest Muslims were much less likely to have attended a picnic than other respondents. Although 77.8 percent of the sample indicated they went to a picnic, only 56.2 percent of black/Latino Muslims and 56 percent of those 35 years and older did likewise. Respondents who were in the oldest age group and those not in the workforce were the least likely to report going jogging/running. Although 54.4 percent of the sample participated in this activity, only 12 percent of those 35 years and older and 18.8 percent of those not in the workforce participated in this activity.

Among the four ethnic groups, black/Latino Muslims had the lowest rate of participation in 9 of the 15 activities examined in the table. Age mattered also. The oldest respondents had the lowest rate of participation in all but two of the activities in the table. Although there was no clear pattern with educational attainment, there was a noticeable pattern with employment status. Respondents who were not in the workforce reported the lowest rate of participation in 14 of the 15 activities. Despite the differences in the neighborhoods that city residents and suburban/rural respondents reported earlier in the study, the differences in the rates of participation between city and suburban/urban residents was insignificant. The regional differences were also insignificant, so were the differences between those who rented versus those who owned their homes.

Table 5 examines how many activities respondents participated in and whether the differences were significant. In addition to the 15 activities listed in Table 4, respondents indicated whether they participated in other activities. In all, 3.3 percent indicated they participated in other activities. A composite score was created for all 16 activities and a means comparison analysis conducted. Scores ranged from 0 to 16. Overall, respondents participated in a mean of 5.54 activities in the year before being surveyed. Three demographic variables were significant – ethnicity, age, and employment status. As the table shows, black/Latino Muslims participated in fewer activities than other Muslims. The oldest respondents also participated in much fewer activities than younger respondents, and respondents who were not in the workforce participated in fewer activities than other respondents. How do these results compare to those of national studies? Although

Table 5. Means Comparison of Number of Outdoor Activities in which Muslim Women Participate.

Demographic Characteristics	Mean Number of Activities	d*f*	*F*	*p*
Total sample mean	5.52			
Ethnic background		3	3.309	.020
Black/Latino	4.56			
Middle Eastern	5.60			
South Asian	5.84			
Other	5.13			
Age		2	7.746	.001
18–24 years old	6.04			
25–34 years old	5.30			
35 years and older	4.28			
Educational attainment		3	1.546	.203
High school diploma or less	6.48			
Some college	5.66			
Bachelor's degree	5.39			
Graduate or professional	5.41			
Employment status		2	7.763	.001
Employed	5.43			
Student	5.90			
Not in workforce	4.16			
Residence		1	0.986	.321
City	5.38			
Suburbs/rural	5.65			
Region		3	0.561	.641
Northeast	5.66			
Midwest	5.44			
South	5.46			
West	6.09			
Home ownership		1	1.190	.276
Homeowner	5.66			
Renter	5.36			

78 percent of this survey's respondents stated that they went on a picnic at least once in the past year, only 55 percent of the participants in the National Survey of Recreation and the Environment (NSRE) did likewise (Cordell, Green, & Betz, 2002).

PRO-ENVIRONMENTAL BEHAVIORS

This study examined participation in nine PEBs. Respondents were asked to rate their participation in these environmental behaviors by ranking them on a five-point Likert scale with 1 being never and 5 being always. The results of a means comparison analysis are shown in Table 6. The table shows that the mean sample score for 6 of the items were 3.0 or higher. The three activities that the sample participated in least frequently were conserving gasoline (mean = 2.62), using organic products (mean = 2.68) and using eco-friendly products (mean = 2.82). The activities with the highest means were purchasing *zabeeha* meat (4.16) and conserving electricity (4.10).

Muslims categorized as other, had the highest means for seven of the nine PEBs. They had the highest means for turning down the thermostat; reusing items; conserving electricity, water, and gasoline; and using eco-friendly products as well as organic products. The oldest respondents were also the ones who had the highest mean scores for six of the nine PEBs. They were more likely to turn down the thermostat, reuse item, conserve electricity and water, and use eco-friendly and organic products. For six of the nine PEBs, respondents with less than a college degree had lower means than those with a college or advanced degree. This was the case for turning down the thermostat, conserving electricity and water, using eco-friendly and organic products, and purchasing *zabeeha* meat.

Respondents who were not in the workforce were the most likely to report turning down the thermostat, conserving electricity and water, using organic products, and purchasing *zabeeha* meat. Suburbanites/rural respondents were had higher mean scores for turning down the thermostat, reusing items, conserving water, recycling, and purchasing *zabeeha* meat.

A composite variable was created by summing the nine scores of each respondent's PEBs. That means that respondents could get a minimum score of 9 and a maximum of 45. Scores ranged from 16 to 42. Table 7 contains the result. As the table shows, three demographic factors had significant variations – ethnicity, educational attainment, and region. Muslims categorized as other participated in PEBs more frequently than other Muslims. Those with a graduate or professional degree participated in PEBs most frequently as did Muslims who lived in the West.

Zabeeha

More than three-fourths of all respondents (76.7 percent) stated that they buy *zabeeha* meat often or always. There was also a very strong relationship

Table 6. Means Comparison of Muslim Women's Participation in Private Pro-environmental Behaviors.

Demographic Characteristics	Turn Down Thermostat	Fix Broken Items-Reuse	Conserve Electricity	Conserve Water	Conserve Gasoline	Recycle	Using Eco-Products	Using Organic Products	Purchase Zabeeha Meat
Total sample mean	3.18	3.34	4.10	3.73	2.62	3.57	2.82	2.68	4.16
Ethnic background									
Black/Latino	3.13	3.38	4.19	3.47	2.63	2.91	2.78	3.28	4.19
Middle Eastern	3.07	3.37	4.05	3.77	2.51	3.53	2.64	2.70	3.63
South Asian	3.18	3.30	4.07	3.75	2.51	3.68	2.79	2.49	4.43
Other	3.39	3.52	4.21	3.83	3.06	3.67	3.19	2.94	4.12
Age									
18–24 years old	3.01	3.38	3.98	3.63	2.64	3.57	2.69	2.61	4.14
25–34 years old	3.22	3.32	4.19	3.77	2.60	3.59	2.89	2.76	4.23
35 years and older	3.96	3.36	4.44	4.12	2.48	3.44	3.12	2.88	4.12
Educational attainment									
High school/less	3.05	3.48	3.74	3.48	2.65	3.22	2.30	2.22	3.74
Some college	3.01	3.33	3.88	3.59	2.72	3.64	2.67	2.63	4.19
Bachelor's degree	3.33	3.27	4.29	3.80	2.46	3.49	2.90	2.77	4.34
Graduate/ professional	3.21	3.46	4.16	3.86	2.71	3.71	2.99	2.78	4.10
Employment status									
Employed	3.27	3.34	4.19	3.78	2.50	3.61	2.88	2.69	4.09
Student	3.03	3.39	4.00	3.66	2.78	3.59	2.80	2.65	4.20
Not in workforce	3.69	3.24	4.24	3.91	2.30	3.30	2.67	2.88	4.36

Table 6. (*Continued*)

Demographic Characteristics	Turn Down Thermostat	Fix Broken Items-Reuse	Conserve Electricity	Conserve Water	Conserve Gasoline	Recycle	Using Eco-Products	Using Organic Products	Purchase Zabeeha Meat
Residence									
City	2.97	3.28	4.12	3.67	2.82	3.34	2.90	2.75	4.13
Suburbs/rural	3.32	3.40	4.09	3.78	2.49	3.71	2.77	2.65	4.20
Region									
Northeast	3.40	3.44	4.15	3.65	2.75	3.81	2.79	2.71	3.94
Midwest	2.96	3.30	4.05	3.71	2.67	3.55	2.85	2.62	4.11
South	3.35	3.38	4.11	3.76	2.38	3.29	2.70	2.64	4.40
West	3.82	3.35	4.36	3.87	2.74	4.17	3.04	3.26	4.22
Home ownership									
Homeowner	3.26	3.43	4.06	3.78	2.39	3.70	2.76	2.56	4.24
Renter	3.12	3.27	4.18	3.67	2.94	3.40	2.90	2.83	4.04

Table 7. Means Composite Score for Private Pro-Environmental Behaviors between Muslim Women.

Demographic Characteristics	Mean Composite Score	df	F	p
Total sample mean	30.22			
Ethnic background		3	2.684	.047
Black/Latino	29.90			
Middle Eastern	29.27			
South Asian	30.24			
Other	31.86			
Age		2	2.275	.105
18–24 years old	29.73			
25–34 years old	30.55			
35 years and older	31.91			
Educational attainment		3	2.826	.039
High school diploma or less	27.91			
Some college	29.72			
Bachelor's degree	30.62			
Graduate or professional	30.96			
Employment status		2	0.092	.913
Employed	30.31			
Student	30.16			
Not in workforce	30.56			
Residence		1	0.829	.363
City	29.92			
Suburbs/rural	30.46			
Region		3	2.947	.033
Northeast	30.62			
Midwest	29.84			
South	30.00			
West	33.19			
Home ownership		1	0.053	.818
Homeowner	30.23			
Renter	30.37			

between ethnicity and purchase of *zabeeha* meat – 87.5 percent of black/Latino Muslims, 85.2 percent of South Asian, and 76.9 percent of other Muslims purchased *zabeeha* meat. In contrast, only 55.8 percent of Middle Eastern Muslims purchased this kind of meat. This difference is due to contrasting interpretations of the Islamic law that allows Muslims to eat meat slaughtered by Christians and Jews (see SoundVision 2007 for a more detailed discussion on this issue). Middle Eastern Muslims are more likely to follow the interpretation that livestock slaughtered by Christians (or other "People of the Book") may be eaten if the words "In the name of God" are simply recited before eating. In contrast, South Asians are more likely to take a stricter view in requiring all of the *zabeeha* requirements for slaughter have been completed.

Comparison with National Studies

When the results of this study were compared to surveys of general population, the results show that Muslim women follow the same trends as the general population. A 2007 Gallup Poll found that 89 percent of Americans reported that they engage in some level of recycling (Dunlap, 2007). This study found that 92.1 percent of respondents reported that they recycled. Tarrant and Green's study found that just over one-third of respondents recycled often; 59.6 percent of the respondents in this study recycled often or always. A survey of high school students found that 65 percent reported taking steps to conserve water frequently (Hamilton College, 2007). This compares to 61.4 percent of the respondents in this study taking steps to conserve water often or always. A Gallup Poll also found that 85 percent of respondents took steps to reduce energy use (Dunlap, 2007). This compares to 91.5 percent of this study's sample doing likewise.

Researchers have also examined green consumption patterns. One study found that 32 percent of Americans buy organic products occasionally (Gardyn, 2002). In comparison, 31.4 percent of the respondents in this study reported purchasing organic foods sometimes and 24.4 percent purchased organic foods often or always. Only 15.9 percent of the sample reported that they never purchased organic food. A Harris Poll conducted in 2007 found that 50 percent of all Americans purchased organic foods at least some of the time (Raw Food Life, 2007). Tarrant and Green's (1999) study found that just over one-third of respondents reported that they purchase environmentally friendly products often. Twenty-six percent of the respondents in this study bought environmentally friendly products always or often. Gallup's 2007 poll also found that 70 percent of Americans purchased products that are better for the environment at least once in the preceding 12 months (Dunlap, 2007). This compares to 89.9 percent of respondents in this study who reported purchasing and using these products.

PUBLIC ENVIRONMENTAL ACTION

The study also examined Muslim women's attitudes toward environmental regulation, institutional memberships, and willingness to work on environmental projects. Ninety-seven percent of the respondents indicated that they favored strong environmental laws. As Table 8 shows, 84.8 percent of the sample reported that they would be willing to work on environmental projects whereas 77.4 indicated a willingness to make monetary contributions to environmental causes. However, only 8.2 percent belonged to an environmental organization. The women were more likely to belong to a women's group – 22.6 percent belonged to such groups.

Age was a significant factor in whether or not the respondent belonged to an environmental organization. Although 4.9 percent of 18–24-year-olds and 7.3 percent of 25–34-year-olds belonged to environmental organizations, 28 percent of those 35 years and older belonged ($X^2 = 15.890$, $p = .000$). Educational attainment was also significant. Although 14 percent of respondents with a graduate or professional degree belonged to environmental organizations, 4–7 percent of the remaining respondents did ($X^2 = 6.572$, $p = .087$). Educational attainment was also significant in the likelihood that a respondent belonged to a women's group – those with a graduate or professional degree was much more likely to belong to a women's group ($X^2 = 12.643$, $p = .005$).

RELIGIOUS PARTICIPATION

Before delving into Muslim environmental activism, it is useful to assess respondents' understandings of Islam's environmental ethic. The survey asked respondents what Islam says about the environment. In their narrative responses, 57 percent stated that caring for the environment was a form of religious duty; 29.5 percent stated that Islam demands the preservation and/or protection of the environment, and 20.3 percent stated that Islam says to respect/honor the environment. These responses show that respondents already have a religious framework which would support an Islamically oriented environmental movement.

To understand the number of respondents affiliated with a religious community, the survey asked if respondents attended mosques regularly. Since congregational prayer is not required for women, Muslim females can fulfill their daily religious obligations without ever setting foot into a religious institution (Mattson, 2005). So although the question of mosque

Table 8. Public Environmental Action between Muslim Women.

Demographic Characteristics	Belong to Environmental Organization	Belong to Women's Groups	Willing to Work on Environmental Projects	Willing to Contribute Money to Environmental Causes
Total sample percent	8.2	22.6	84.8	77.4
Ethnic background				
Black/Latino	12.5	25.0	93.6	87.5
Middle Eastern	6.8	20.5	86.3	73.9
South Asian	7.1	25.9	81.6	75.6
Other	9.6	13.5	88.4	80.8
Age				
18–24 years old	4.9	22.2	84.7	76.3
25–34 years old	7.3	23.0	84.6	76.7
35 years and older	28.0	24.0	84.0	88.0
Educational attainment				
High school/less	4.3	26.1	91.3	69.6
Some college	7.0	19.8	85.9	72.1
Bachelor's degree	5.1	14.5	83.9	80.5
Graduate/professional	14.0	34.3	83.8	79.8
Employment status				
Employed	10.4	22.6	86.5	80.6
Student	6.9	23.4	83.6	76.7
Not in workforce	3.0	18.2	81.8	69.7
Residence				
City	11.9	24.0	88.8	75.2
Suburbs/rural	5.9	21.9	82.1	78.7
Region				
Northeast	0.0	20.8	79.2	70.9
Midwest	9.5	26.3	89.3	78.5
South	10.0	16.7	83.5	75.0
West	8.7	17.4	95.6	91.3
Home ownership				
Homeowner	7.0	21.8	83.6	81.9
Renter	9.0	22.4	87.5	71.3

attendance is not a perfect measure of religiosity, it provides evidence of ties to a religious institution that could impact decision-making. Over half (56.1 percent) of respondents attend a mosque regularly (Table 9). Even those who do not attend a mosque regularly have connections to religious

Table 9. Mosque Activism and Environmentalism between Muslim Women-Percent of Respondents.

Demographic Characteristics	Attend Mosque Regularly	Projects With Other Mosques	Projects With Other Religious Groups	Social Services	Neighborhood Clean-Up	Environmental Talks	Act on Community Environmental Problem	Participate in Environmental Campaign
Total sample percent	56.1	67.1	62.7	53.5	20.9	12.5	10.3	4.7
Ethnic background								
Black/Latino	65.6	71.0	54.8	61.3	26.7	6.9	10.0	3.3
Middle Eastern	54.2	63.0	63.0	52.1	30.1	13.7	15.1	8.2
South Asian	57.2	67.1	63.5	50.9	16.4	12.7	7.2	2.4
Other	48.1	68.0	64.0	58.0	18.4	12.2	14.3	6.1
Age								
18–24 years old	57.6	69.2	62.9	56.6	22.0	17.6	11.9	7.7
25–34 years old	53.7	66.2	64.2	51.4	21.1	6.8	8.2	1.4
35 years and older	64.0	66.7	62.5	50.0	13.0	13.0	8.7	0.0
Educational attainment								
High school/less	52.2	60.9	56.5	52.2	27.3	13.0	8.7	4.3
Some college	57.0	74.1	62.4	58.8	17.9	21.4	10.6	5.9
Bachelor's degree	55.6	63.2	61.5	50.4	22.6	9.6	9.6	4.3
Graduate/professional	57.1	67.3	64.9	53.1	19.4	7.2	11.3	3.1
Employment status								
Employed	50.0	63.2	60.9	51.1	19.1	11.5	9.9	2.3
Student	59.5	71.2	63.5	56.4	22.1	15.6	11.5	7.1
Not in workforce	63.6	60.6	63.6	45.5	18.2	0.0	3.0	0.0

Table 9. (*Continued*)

Demographic Characteristics	Attend Mosque Regularly	Projects With Other Mosques	Projects With Other Religious Groups	Social Services	Neighborhood Clean-Up	Environmental Talks	Act on Community Environmental Problem	Participate in Environmental Campaign
Residence								
City	53.2	67.5	57.4	50.4	23.3	10.9	13.3	5.0
Suburbs/rural	57.7	66.7	65.7	55.2	19.0	12.9	8.5	4.0
Region								
Northeast	58.3	57.4	53.2	42.6	8.7	4.3	2.1	2.1
Midwest	56.2	65.1	65.5	51.4	17.9	13.4	9.9	4.7
South	55.7	78.8	65.0	66.2	34.2	15.0	15.0	6.2
West	52.2	60.9	52.2	47.8	21.7	13.0	13.0	4.3
Home ownership								
Homeowner	62.0	70.8	69.0	55.0	19.6	17.1	9.4	5.9
Renter	48.9	61.4	54.0	50.7	23.0	7.2	12.4	3.6

institutions (all but 12 respondents answered the question asking the location of their mosque). A majority of respondents (60.9 percent) attend suburban or rural mosques while the others attend mosques in urban areas. Most respondents attend a mosque in the area where they live – 84.2 percent of suburbanites attend suburban mosques and 70.8 percent of urban dwellers attend urban mosques.

Black/Latino Muslims were more likely to attend mosque regularly than other respondents. The oldest respondents were more likely to attend mosque regularly than younger respondents. Study participants who were not in the workforce and suburban/rural residents were also the most likely to attend mosque regularly. More than half the respondents (67.1 percent) indicated that their mosques collaborated with other mosques, or non-Muslim religious groups (62.7 percent) on projects; 53.5 percent of the respondents said their mosques engaged in social services such as food pantries.

A relatively small percentage of respondents indicated that their mosques were involved in environmental activities – 20.9 percent indicated their mosques conducted neighborhood clean-ups, 12.5 percent sponsored environmental talks, 10.3 percent acted on an environmental problem in the community, and 4.7 percent participated in an environmental campaign. Though respondents in the Northeast were more likely than respondents in other regions to say they attended mosque regularly, they were the least likely to say their mosques collaborated with other mosques on projects, offered social services or sponsored environmental activities. Urban mosques were more likely to conduct neighborhood clean-ups, act on community environmental problems, and participate in environmental campaigns than suburban/rural mosques.

Perceptions of Muslim Activism

Respondents were asked to indicate how they perceived overall Muslim environmental and social activism. Most respondents believed their Muslim communities were generally inactive regarding environmental and social activities. In all, 41.4 percent of the respondents thought Muslims were active or very active in social issues. None thought that Muslims were very active in environmental affairs; however, 5.3 percent thought Muslims were active in environmental issues. This might signal that there is little or no pressure among Muslims to engage in these activities. Despite this perception of limited activism among Muslims, it should be noted that there are community groups such as the Arab Community Center for Economic and Social Services (ACCESS) in Dearborn, Michigan that have incorporated environmental justice activities as a significant part of their agenda (ACCESS, 2009).

CONCLUSION

The results of this survey show that Muslim women participate in a range of outdoor activities; however, there are important demographic differences to take into account. In particular, it seems that women who were not in the workforce participated in the lowest number of outdoor activities – this was much lower than the mean number of activities participated in by other respondents. American Muslim women also participated regularly in both private and public PEBs. Comparisons with national surveys show that American Muslim women conduct private PEBs at the same or higher levels as the general U.S. population. Though Muslim women were less likely to participate in some public PEBs (such as belonging to an environmental organization) than private PEBs, a high percentage indicated they would be willing to participate in other types of public PEBs such as working on environmental projects or making contributions to environmental causes. It should be noted that membership in an environmental organization measured actual participation while willingness to work on projects or contribute money measured potential participation. If actual participation in such activities were measured, the percentages might be lower. Nonetheless, these results could be interpreted as Muslim women having the potential to move beyond PEBs and become more involved in environmental activism.

Though the study found limited environmental activism occurring in the mosques, these religious institutions have the potential for bringing about increased activism in Muslim communities. Although Muslim women are engaging in environmental behaviors at least as frequently as other Americans, they believe that as a group, Muslims are not taking much action on environmental issues. This feeling is substantiated by the low percentage of respondents who report that their mosques participate in environmental activism. This points to the untapped potential for mosques to build on the religion's existing environmental ethic and develop an environmental agenda that incorporates the unique strengths of this multi-ethnic, multiracial community.

A solid foundation for an environmental ethic exists within the Islamic tradition. However, this environmental ethic has not been translated into much environmental activism in mosques in the U.S. Consequently, American Muslim women are left to pursue environmentalism through individual and secular outlets through which they are already participating in a range of environmental activities. These women's participation in outdoor recreational activities and their willingness to participate in public PEBs do not seem to be impacted by the more conservative Muslim traditions that restrict women's public behaviors.

A natural progression to increased environmental involvement can be facilitated through an activity that Muslims are already familiar with – the purchasing of *zabeeha* meat. By supporting the purchase of *zabeeha* meat from organic farmers, mosques can develop a link between individuals' environmental behaviors, religious behavior, and broader environmentalism. This can also grow into communal activism if the mosque creates a committee that advocates organic processes to those involved in the husbandry of animals. One example of such an effort is the Taqwa Eco-Halal program coordinated by Faith in Place, a multidenominational organization based in Chicago, Illinois (Faith in Place, 2009).

The growth of environmentalism within mosques will help Muslims "walk the talk" of the environmental ethic embedded within their religion. In addition, it will help develop Muslim leadership on issues that are gaining increased political attention throughout the world. This type of leadership will be critical in helping Westerners understand the depth of Islam while showing commitment to working with other groups to improve global health and wellbeing.

NOTES

1. Although recycling can also take place in the public sphere (as in throwing cans/bottles into recycling bins in public places), this study assumes that the largest quantities of materials are recycled from the home.

2. ISNA was founded in by North American Muslims to establish "an open, pluralistic platform for presenting Islam, supporting Muslim communities, developing educational, social and outreach programs" (ISNA, 2009).

3. Dr. Ingrid Mattson was elected as ISNA's President after serving as Vice President for 5 years (Duncan Black Macdonald Center, 2009).

REFERENCES

ACCESS. (2009). ACCESS Organizational Website. Available at www.accesscommunity.org/. Retrieved on October 19.

Akhtar, B. K., & Gul-e-Jannat. (1995). *The Holy Quran on environment*. Karachi, Pakistan: Royal Book Company.

Al-Gilani, A., & Filor, S. (1997). Policy and practice: Environmental policies in Saudi Arabia. *Journal of Environmental Planning and Management, 40*(6), 775–788.

Ammar, N. H. (2000). An Islamic response to the manifest ecological crisis: Issues of justice. In: H. Coward & D. C. Maguire (Eds), *Visions of a new earth: Religious perspectives on population, consumption, and ecology* (pp. 131–146). Albany, NY: State University of New York Press.

Arp, W., III., & Boeckelman, K. (1997). Religiosity: A source of black environmentalism and empowerment? *Journal of Black Studies, 28*(2), 255–267.

Bagby, I., Perl, P. M., & Froehle, B. T. (2001). *The mosque in America: A national report*. Washington, DC: Council on American-Islamic Relations.

Clayton, S., & Opotow, S. (2003). Introduction. In: C. Susan & O. Susan (Eds), *Identity and the natural environment* (pp. 1–24). Cambridge, MA: MIT Press.

Cordell, H. K., Green, G. T., & Betz, C. J. (2002). Recreation and the environment as cultural dimensions in contemporary American society. *Leisure Sciences, 24*(1), 13–41.

Duncan Black Macdonald Center. (2009). Faculty: Ingrid Mattson. Available at http:// macdonald.hartsem.edu/mattson.htm. Retrieved on October 18.

Dunlap, R. E. (2007). The state of environmentalism in the U.S. Gallup News Service website. Available at www.galluppoll.com/content/?ci = 27256. Retrieved on September 14.

Faith in Place (2009). Faith in Place Organizational Website. Available at http://www. faithinplace.org/. Retrieved on October 20.

Fransson, N., & Gärling, T. (1999). Environmental concern: Conceptual definitions, measurement methods, and research findings. *Journal of Environmental Psychology, 19*(4), 369–382.

Gardyn, R. (2002). The big O-organic food market continues to grow in the United States. Available at http://findarticles.com/p/articles/mi_m4021/is_2002_Oct_1/ai_92087422. Retrieved on September 15, 2007.

Goodstein, L. (2004). Muslim women seeking a place in the mosque. In: *The New York Times*, New York, 22, July. Available at www.masnet.org/articleinterest.asp?id = 1446. Retrieved on October 18, 2009.

Haider, G. S. (1984). Habitat and values in Islam: A conceptual formulation of an Islamic city. In: Z. Sardar (Ed.), *The touch of midas: Science, values and environment in Islam and the West* (pp. 170–209). Manchester, UK: Manchester University Press.

Halalpreneur, E. (2001). What is Zabiha? Available at www.ehalal.org/zabiha.html. Retrieved on October 14, 2007.

Hamilton College. (2007). *Hamilton college national youth polls: Climate change and environmental issues poll*. Available at www.hamilton.edu/news/polls/Climate/HCClimate ChangePoll.pdf. Retrived on September 13. Clinton, NY: Hamilton College.

Haq, N. S. (2001). Islam and ecology: Toward retrieval and reconstruction. *Daedalus, 130*(4), 141–177.

Hope, M., & Young, J. (2000). *Voices of hope in the struggle to save the planet* (pp. 153–189). New York: The Apex Press.

Hunter, L. M., Hatch, A., & Johnson, A. (2004). Cross-national gender variation in environmental behaviors. *Social Science Quarterly, 85*(3), 677–694.

ISNA. (2009). ISNA organizational website. Available at http://www.isna.net/ISNAHQ/pages/ About-Us.aspx. Retrieved on October 19, 2009.

Izzi Deen, M. Y. (1996). Islamic environmental ethics, law, and society. In: R. S. Gottlieb (Ed.), *This sacred earth. Religion, nature, environment* (pp. 164–173). New York: Routledge.

Leonard, K. I. (2003). *Muslims in the United States: The state of research.* New York: Russell Sage Foundation.

Manzoor, P. S. (1984). Environment and values: The Islamic perspective. In: Z. Sardar (Ed.), *The touch of midas: Science, values and environment in Islam and the West* (pp. 150–168). Manchester, UK: Manchester University Press.

Masri, A. B. A. (1992). Islam and ecology. In: F. Khalid & J. O'Brien (Eds), *Islam and ecology* (pp. 1–23). London, UK: Cassel Publishers Limited.

Mattson, I. (2005). *Can a woman be an Imam? Debating form and function in Muslim women's Leadership.* Available at http://macdonald.hartsem.edu/muslimwomensleadership.pdf. Retrieved on October 18, 2009. Hartford, CT: Hartford Seminary.

Mazumdar, S., & Mazumdar, S. (1999). 'Women's significant spaces': Religion, space, and community. *Journal of Environmental Psychology, 19*(2), 159–170.

Mohai, P. (1992). Men, women, and the environment: An examination of the gender gap in environmental concern and activism. *Society and Natural Resources, 5*(1), 1–19.

Musick, M. A., Wilson, J., & Bynum, W. B., Jr. (2000). Race and formal volunteering: The differential effects of class and religion. *Social Forces, 78*(4), 1539–1571.

Nasr, S. H. (2001). Islam and the environmental crisis. *Islamic Quarterly, 34*(4), 217–234.

Pfeffer, M. J., & Stycos, J. M. (2002). Immigrant environmental behaviors in New York City. *Social Science Quarterly, 83*(1), 64–81.

Rahman, F. (1989). Islam and health/medicine: A historical perspective. In: L. E. Sullivan (Ed.), *Healing and Restoring* (pp. 149–172). New York: Macmillan Publishing Company.

Raw Food Life. (2007). The Harris Poll #97: Large majorities see organic food as safer, better for the environment and healthier – but also more expensive. Available at http://www.rawfoodlife.com/Latest_Raw_Food_News/NY_Times_6_17_07/Harris_Poll_10_8_07_Synopsis/harris_poll/harris_poll.htm. Retrieved on September 15, 2007.

Rice, G. (2006). Pro-environmental behavior in Egypt: Is there a role for Islamic environmental ethics? *Journal of Business Ethics, 65*(4), 373–390.

Schlozman, K. L., Burns, N., & Verba, S. (1994). Gender and the pathways to participation: The role of resources. *Journal of Politics, 56*(4), 963–990.

SoundVision. (2007). Zabiha or Non Zabiha: Three scholars' opinions. Available at http://soundvision.com/Info/halalhealthy/maududi.asp. Retrieved on October 14, 2007.

Tanner, R., & Mitchell, C. (2002). *Religion and the environment.* New York: Palgrave Macmillan.

Tarrant, M. A., & Green, G. T. (1999). Outdoor recreation and the predictive validity of environmental attitudes. *Leisure Sciences, 2*(1), 17–30.

Taylor, D. (2000). The rise of the environmental justice paradigm: Injustice framing and the social construction of environmental discourses. *American Behavioral Scientist, 43*(4), 508–580.

Timm, R. E. (1994). The ecological fallout of Islamic creation theology. In: M. E. Tucker & J. A. Grim (Eds), *Worldviews and ecology: Religion, philosophy, and the environment* (pp. 83–95). Maryknoll, New York: Orbis Books.

Tindall, D. B., Davies, S., & Mauboulés, C. (2003). Activism and conservation behavior in an environmental movement: The contradictory effects of gender. *Society and Natural Resources, 16*(10), 909–932.

JUMANA VASI

Weiss, A. M. (1994). Challenges for Muslim women in a postmodern world. In: A. S. Ahmed & H. Donnan (Eds), *Islam, globalization and postmodernity* (pp. 127–140). London, UK: Routledge.

Zekavat, S. M. (1997). The state of the environment in Iran. *Journal of Developing Societies*, *13*(1), 49–72.

Zelezny, L. C., Chua, P., & Aldrich, C. (2000). Elaborating on gender differences in Environmentalism. *Journal of Social Issues, 56*, 443–457.

Jumana Vasi is an associate program officer at the Charles Stewart Mott Foundation. She can be reached by email at jzvasi@mott.org

CONCLUDING REMARKS

Environment and Social Justice: An International Perspective will make a significant contribution to the environmental justice literature. The volume presents the findings of some of the latest research in the field. Its international perspective allows the reader to consider the cases presented from both local and global perspectives.

The first chapter of the book traces the rise of the environmental justice movement in the United States. It also shows how the environmental justice discourse and research has spread to other parts of the world. As environmental justice ideas spread, they have been adapted to suit the local contexts in which they were being applied. Activists from around the world have found the environmental justice frame attractive and readily adaptable to their circumstances. This has resulted in the rapid spread of the movement globally. This has also resulted in the spread of environmental justice research as scholars from around the world have examined environmental justice issues over the past two decades.

Access to open space is a rising concern in the environmental justice movement. Taylor's chapter on Central Park and the changing funding models being used in American public parks is quite timely. As cities become more congested and polluted, urban residents need green space urgently. However, cities are cutting back on park funding in places where the demand for open space is greatest. The private funding of parks is being touted as a solution, but this approach raises questions about equity. There are also doubts that small, inner city parks can remain viable if they are required to raise funds for maintenance and upkeep through private financing. The story of the funding of American parks could have repercussions in other countries too. America has developed an urban park system that has been replicated in other parts of the world. If it is perceived that American cities have abdicated their role as funders and stewards of their urban parks, then other countries might consider withdrawing public funds from the development and maintenance of public parks. This would have dramatic effects in countries that already have inadequate urban park infrastructures.

The concern about space and livability in urban areas goes beyond parks. As Gin and Taylor's chapter indicate, low-income and minority

485

communities are struggling to prevent displacement that can arise from the gentrification of poor neighborhoods. Activists involved in these struggles want pleasant, livable, and affordable neighborhoods. Gin and Taylor examine the extent to which they can effectively organize their communities and communicate the goals of their movements to the media. Gin and Taylor's analysis identifies conditions under which activists can be very effective in getting their messages across to supporters and the media.

Khan's chapter tackles the question of poor people's access to safe and healthy food in London. This discussion is timely as the issue of food security has taken on urgency in postindustrial countries such as the United States and the United Kingdom. Food security is linked to the question of sustainability. As cities transform and the suburbs expand, some have become food deserts because supermarkets and grocery stores follow affluent customers who flee inner city neighborhoods. Ensuring that the poor have access to affordable, healthy food will be a problem that industrialized and developing countries have to confront and resolve in years to come.

Chitewere and Taylor argue that some urban residents respond to the degradation in cities and the lack of open space by establishing exurban ecovillages. The case study of an Upstate New York ecovillage examines the internal conflicts some activists face in establishing such enclaves. The authors also analyze how the notion of sustainable living that underpins the establishment of ecovillages is embedded in a culture of consumption – green consumption – that could undermine sustainability goals of such developments.

The two chapters in Part II of the book also focus on consumption. Unlike the middle-class residents of ecovillages, minorities and the poor are found to be most vulnerable to toxic fish consumption. Pallo and Barken's chapter examine food advisories and the way in which the Environmental Protection Agency and the Food and Drug Administration's policies influence exposure to toxins found in seafood. Nordenstam and Darkwa's chapter examine the consumption of fish caught in the Great Lakes. Their comparison of white and minority anglers indicate that anglers do not necessarily heed toxic fish advisories and exposure to toxins could be quite high.

While Nordenstam and Darkwa found a disconnect between Great Lakes anglers' awareness of toxic fish advisories and their behavior (eating fish caught in the lakes), loss of land was a theme explored in the two chapters in Part III. Bhardwaj examines how poor farmers in India are losing their farms at an alarming rate. The farmers respond to the loss of land and inability to pay for the cost of farming by committing suicides. She explores how the introduction of genetically modified seeds and government policies (such as lack of funding support) are exacerbating the problem. Freeman and Taylor's chapter also focus on land loss among black American farmers. They document the dramatic decline in the rate of land ownership among blacks and examine whether heritage tourism could be a mechanism to help generate income while helping in the preservation of black-owned farmlands.

Part IV of the book examines the impacts of oil and gas exploration on fence line communities. Baptiste and Nordenstam found that rural Trinidadians were aware of oil and gas exploration issues, expressed great concern for the environment, but had not mobilized to take action to protect the environment. The socioeconomic conditions of Trinidadian villagers whose communities are either oil-bearing or are producers of oil and gas were similar to those found by Effiong in his analysis of the oil and gas industry in Nigeria. The poverty endemic in communities that host multinational oil and gas operations has resulted in a high level of conflict and violence. Unlike Nigerians, Trinidadians have not resorted to wide-spread violence to reap a share of oil profits or get social services for their villages.

Vajhalla's chapter examines the way in which government policies in the United States influence the distribution of funds to poor environmental justice communities. Vajhalla analyzes the Environmental Protection Agency's small grants program to find out whether the most impoverished communities are the ones receiving the funds. She uses spatial analytic techniques to identify which communities had the greatest burdens of toxins combined with the highest levels of poverty. Although poor communities were being funded, the lion's share of the grants was not going to the most vulnerable ones.

Taylor's chapter on institutional diversity harkens back to a long-standing theme in environmental justice. It tackles the question – how diverse are American environmental institutions? The chapter focuses on faculty diversity academic environmental programs. Consistent with other studies either of the science and engineering fields or of the diversity in environmental organizations, Taylor's study found that minorities were underrepresented in the discipline, least likely to be in the highest status positions and most likely to be untenured or in nontenure-track positions. Females were also underrepresented in the academic disciplines studied. Diversity is receiving growing attention from scholars, policy-makers, and the media. It is becoming increasingly relevant as the environmental workforce grows in size, but also because dramatic demographic shifts are under way in the American workforce. As the mavericks who founded brash, new environmental organizations in the 1960s and 1970s age, a new generation of leaders will have to be trained to replace them. Furthermore, as the society focuses more on green technologies and green economies, projections are that the environmental sector will expand to meet the needs of the changing economy. This raises the question: will the environmental sector continue to shun minority workers? Moreover, how viable will this sector be if it does not recruit and recognize minority talent and incorporate them into the labor force?

The trends under way in the United States are likely to have a ripple effect to other industrialized countries. In Canada and Western European countries, environmental organizations formed decades ago are run by aging leaders. They too will face a turnover in the workforce as well as a transition to a green economy that will require large number of workers. Minorities have not been incorporated well into the environmental workforce of these countries either. Although ethnic minorities constitute a much smaller percentage of the population in these countries than in the United States, the questions about diversity are still pertinent.

Diversity is also important from a movement-building and policy-making perspective. If environmentalists and environmental workers are drawn only or primarily from the ranks of the white middle class in these countries, then how effective will they be in enlisting minorities and the poor to join in environmental initiatives? With the increased awareness and scrutiny (vis-à-vis diversity) that has accompanied the environmental movement over the past four decades, mainstream environmental activists lose legitimacy if they are perceived as not being sensitive to diversity issues, collaborating with minorities and the poor, and incorporating them into environmental activities.

Lashley and Taylor's chapter examines the environmental activism of two communities in Southeastern Michigan. It focuses on the factors that prevented the communities from collaborating with each other. One community was a poor, predominantly black neighborhood on the Detroit's Eastside, whereas the other was a middle-class, predominantly white suburban community in Lyon Township. The tensions around collaborating is a microcosm of some of the larger problems encountered when the question of diversity in the environmental movement arises. Lashley and Taylor present a framework for helping the reader to understand the factors that hindered collaboration. Collaboration may have been an effective strategy to utilize, because both communities were polluted by and fighting against the same corporation.

The inability to forge cross-class, cross-race ties is a problem that still plagues the mainstream environmental and environmental justice movements on a national level. Although there are many successful collaborations that can be readily identified, there is still reluctance to attempt collaborations because of the awkwardness that arise during the process of building those ties. This translates itself into labor force dynamics also. Organizations that have no or very few minorities or poor people working in them find it challenging to recruit and incorporate such folks into their workforce. In some cases when there is successful recruitment, retention is difficult because of the challenges that arise in navigating class, race, and cultural differences.

Vasi's chapter examines environmental perceptions, attitudes, and activism among Muslim women living in the United States. Like several of the preceding chapters, Vasi explored environmental attitudes and perceptions among nonwhites. An underlying theme of the volume is the question of whether minorities are active in environmental affairs, whether they are interested in environmental issues, and are concerned about it. While Lashley and Taylor focus on the actions of white and minority activists – most of whom were females – Vasi examines the attitudes and actions of Muslim females. As was found in other studies in this book such as Gin and Taylor's study of San Francisco Bay Area activists, Baptiste and Nordenstam's study of Trinidad, and Freeman and Taylor's study of black farmers' attempts to develop heritage tourism, minorities around the United States and in the rest of the world are interested in environmental issues, concerned about them, and are quite active in environmental affairs. This point cannot be overstated.

The studies contained in the volume point to some consistent patterns and trends. The environmental justice movement is a vibrant global movement that takes many shapes and forms in different countries. Research has always played a vital role in enhancing our understanding of the movement as well as shaping it. The studies included here point to areas of energetic organizing and effectiveness in some environmental justice communities and areas where much work needs to be done to help people bridge the gap between their awareness and concerns and activism.

This volume also highlights the need to help communities, such as those in Nigeria, develop nonviolent conflict resolution strategies to deal with multinational corporations and governments that are insensitive to the needs of resource-rich but economical-destitute communities on the periphery of their countries. It points to the need to pay more attention to the North–South dynamics that accompany the extraction of resources such as oil and gas from developing countries to fuel the appetites of citizens in wealthy, industrialized countries. The point should not be lost on the reader that the most impoverished communities discussed in this volume were communities producing enormous wealth for major corporations because of the valuable oil and gas reserves around them. However, such communities are still not able to reap enough economic benefits to have a decent standard of living or hold corporations accountable for environmental degradation.

As we look to the future, it is likely that conflicts between environmental justice activists and corporations will be common for some time to come. This is one area in which the entire environmental community could unite more effectively to ensure that corporations behave more responsibly, reduce their inputs and hazardous outputs, and treat minority and poor communities around the world with greater respect. It is clear that our focus cannot be trained on only what affects each of us individually or affects our local communities. Overconsumption connects all of us. The exploitation of the people and resources in small African and Trinidadian villages happens to fuel the appetite for energy in the West. It also happens because many people do not take the time to understand how processes and practices are connected. The barriers of race and class prevent most from looking across those lines to see how our life styles and behaviors are tied to each other.

The promise of environmental justice is that by focusing on the relationship between environment, social conditions, and justice, current and future generations of activists and scholars can bridge traditional divides and spearhead transformative environmental change.

Dorceta E. Taylor is an associate professor at the University of Michigan's School of Natural Resources and Environment. She teaches courses in environmental history, environmental justice, tourism and climate change, and social movements. She is the director of the Multicultural Environmental Leadership Development Initiative (http://www.meldi.snre.umich. edu) and author of *The Environment and the People in American Cities, 1600s–1900s: Disorder, Inequality, and Social Change.* She can be reached by email at dorceta@umich.edu or by telephone at 734-763-5327.

Dorceta E. Taylor
Editor